CAMBRIDGE LIBRARY

Books of enduring scholai

History

The books reissued in this series include accounts of historical events and movements by eye-witnesses and contemporaries, as well as landmark studies that assembled significant source materials or developed new historiographical methods. The series includes work in social, political and military history on a wide range of periods and regions, giving modern scholars ready access to influential publications of the past.

A History of Cyprus

Sir George Francis Hill (1867–1948), was perhaps best known as a numismatist, although his scholarly interests and accomplishments included a range of time periods and subjects. A classicist by training, Hill built his career at the British Museum's department of coins and medals. In his forty-three years there he produced volumes on coins of antiquity; Greek history and art; coins, heraldry, and iconography of medieval and Renaissance Italy; and treasure troves. In 1931 Hill became the Museum's director and principal librarian, the first archaeologist to hold this post. His four-volume *History of Cyprus* (1940–52) ranged from Cyprus's earliest years to the twentieth century, and became the standard text on the subject. It is a valuable resource for scholars of the country, of antiquity and of the Mediterranean world. Volume 1 describes the land of Cyprus before unravelling its history from the Stone Age to the Crusades.

Cambridge University Press has long been a pioneer in the reissuing of out-of-print titles from its own backlist, producing digital reprints of books that are still sought after by scholars and students but could not be reprinted economically using traditional technology. The Cambridge Library Collection extends this activity to a wider range of books which are still of importance to researchers and professionals, either for the source material they contain, or as landmarks in the history of their academic discipline.

Drawing from the world-renowned collections in the Cambridge University Library, and guided by the advice of experts in each subject area, Cambridge University Press is using state-of-the-art scanning machines in its own Printing House to capture the content of each book selected for inclusion. The files are processed to give a consistently clear, crisp image, and the books finished to the high quality standard for which the Press is recognised around the world. The latest print-on-demand technology ensures that the books will remain available indefinitely, and that orders for single or multiple copies can quickly be supplied.

The Cambridge Library Collection will bring back to life books of enduring scholarly value (including out-of-copyright works originally issued by other publishers) across a wide range of disciplines in the humanities and social sciences and in science and technology.

A History of Cyprus

VOLUME 1:
TO THE CONQUEST
BY RICHARD LION HEART

GEORGE HILL

CAMBRIDGE UNIVERSITY PRESS

Cambridge, New York, Melbourne, Madrid, Cape Town, Singapore, São Paolo, Delhi, Dubai, Tokyo

Published in the United States of America by Cambridge University Press, New York

www.cambridge.org
Information on this title: www.cambridge.org/9781108020626

© in this compilation Cambridge University Press 2010

This edition first published 1940
This digitally printed version 2010

ISBN 978-1-108-02062-6 Paperback

This book reproduces the text of the original edition. The content and language reflect the beliefs, practices and terminology of their time, and have not been updated.

Cambridge University Press wishes to make clear that the book, unless originally published by Cambridge, is not being republished by, in association or collaboration with, or with the endorsement or approval of, the original publisher or its successors in title.

A HISTORY OF CYPRUS

CAMBRIDGE
UNIVERSITY PRESS
LONDON: BENTLEY HOUSE
NEW YORK, TORONTO, BOMBAY
CALCUTTA, MADRAS: MACMILLAN
TOKYO: MARUZEN COMPANY LTD

All rights reserved

FRONTISPIECE

Swedish Cyprus Expedition

LIMESTONE HEAD FROM VOUNI

A HISTORY OF CYPRUS

BY

SIR GEORGE HILL,
K.C.B., F.B.A.

*

VOLUME I

To the Conquest by Richard Lion Heart

CAMBRIDGE
AT THE UNIVERSITY PRESS
1940

PRINTED IN GREAT BRITAIN

To

W. H. B. : C. J. P. C.
E. J. F. : C. R. P.
V. S.

CONTENTS

PREFACE

The interest which Cyprus has recently aroused in many quarters makes it needless to apologize for putting forth an account of its history. Prudence, perhaps, might have suggested waiting until the present activity in excavation and research should quiet down, and their results become more definite. On the other hand many, like the writer, must feel that some sort of guide through the maze of authorities is desirable: and it was the wish to clear up in his own mind the facts about a subject which has interested him for more than thirty years, that prompted him to undertake such a compilation. More than a compilation it does not pretend to be: yet, even so, it has proved to be a task more arduous and complex and even less within his capacity than he had expected; and it will perhaps be felt that he has done little more than indicate the many problems, without solving any of them.

The main difficulty has lain in the fact that Cyprus has had no continuous history of its own, except to some degree in the Lusignan period. What light we have on it is chiefly a pale and shifting reflection from the activities of the great powers which from age to age have found it necessary to deal with it on their way to some more important objective. Any picture of its fortunes must therefore be patchy and ill-composed, its lights and shadows forced and perhaps often misleading. For the same reason, to set its history in true perspective one would need a mastery of the history of all the peoples who came into contact with it, whether as colonists or as conquerors. Failing that qualification, unattainable in this age of specialization, its historian must be content to submit his sketch to the most competent specialists of his acquaintance, and adopt their corrections. This has been done throughout. No mere list of acknowledgements would indicate the degree of the author's indebtedness to those who, as will partly appear from the footnotes, have been consulted and have ungrudgingly helped at every turn. Such a list of names is therefore not given. But a general expression of gratitude to former colleagues in nearly every Department of the British Museum, to the officials of the Cyprus Department of Antiquities, and finally to those, to whose kind offices are owing the photographs from which the illustrations have been made, cannot be omitted here.

The present volume takes the history of the island down to its conquest by Richard Lion Heart. With that episode a new perspective opens, so that it seems a suitable point at which to pause.

A word may be permitted on the spelling of proper names and technical terms. After much consideration the attempt to attain consistency was abandoned in favour of the avoidance of pedantry. Generally speaking, Latin forms have been used, except for the shorter names of places and quite modern names to which every visitor to Cyprus is accustomed, such as Troodos. As to *k,* it has been kept occasionally, but the uncouth *kh* combination is usually avoided. Such inconsistencies, while they will not please many, will it is hoped offend fewer than uniformity would have done. In oriental names intelligibility to the ordinary reader, rather than accuracy and consistency, has been aimed at, and diacritical marks avoided as far as possible except in the footnotes.

The dedication records, for those who can interpret it, the writer's obligation to friends, by whose companionship and aid on two visits to the island, in 1934 and 1938, much that would otherwise have been difficult or tiresome was rendered easy and delightful.

GEORGE HILL

London, August 1939

ILLUSTRATIONS AND MAPS

PLATES

For permission to reproduce the photographs of Plates I*a*, II and XIII my thanks are due to the Director of Antiquities and the Curator of the Cyprus Museum. The Swedish Cyprus Expedition kindly provided the photographs for the Frontispiece and Plate III (lower portion), and allowed Plate III (upper portion) to be made from their publication. Major Vivian Seymer took special photographs for Plates I*b* and X. The blocks, the loan of which I owe to the Cyprus Monuments Committee, were made from Mr Cave's photographs for the Appeal issued by the Committee in 1934. That of the Salamis capital (Plate VII) was made for the British Museum *Catalogue of Sculpture*, Vol. II, 1900, Plate XXVII. For this and the casts of the coins on Plate V, as for the photographs on Plate XI, I have to thank the Trustees. Messrs Mangoian Brothers presented me with the beautiful view of Vouni on Plate VI.

MAPS

LISTS OF BOOKS

These two lists do not pretend to be systematic or complete. Many general histories and works of reference have been omitted, because the reader will have no difficulty in identifying them. The first list expands the abbreviations of titles most commonly used throughout the volume; the second enumerates those books which are commonly cited by the authors' names alone.

I

ABBREVIATIONS

B.C.H. *Bulletin de Correspondance Hellénique.* Athens and Paris, 1877– .

B.M.C. *British Museum Catalogue of Greek Coins.* By R. S. Poole and others. London, 1877– .

B.M. Inscr. *The Collection of Ancient Greek Inscriptions in the British Museum.* By C. T. Newton and others. 4 parts. London, 1874–1916.

B.M. Sc. *Catalogue of Sculpture in the Department of Greek and Roman Antiquities.* Vol. I, Part II. Cypriote and Etruscan. By F. N. Pryce. London, 1931.

B.M. Terr. *Catalogue of Terracottas.* By H. B. Walters. London, 1903.

B.M. Vases. *Catalogue of Greek and Etruscan Vases.* Vol. I, Part I. Prehistoric and Aegean Pottery. By E. J. Forsdyke. London, 1925. Vol. I, Part II. Cypriote, Italian and Etruscan Pottery. By H. B. Walters. London, 1912.

B.S.A. *Annual of the British School at Athens.* London, 1895–

C.A.H. *Cambridge Ancient History.* Cambridge, 1924–39.

C.C.M. *Catalogue of the Cyprus Museum.* By J. L. Myres and M. Ohnefalsch-Richter. Oxford, 1899.

C.I.G. Boeckh (A.), etc. *Corpus Inscriptionum Graecarum.* 4 vols. Berlin, 1828–77.

C.I.L. *Corpus Inscriptionum Latinarum.* Berlin, 1862– .

C.I.S. *Corpus Inscriptionum Semiticarum.* Paris, 1881– .

C.M.H. *Cambridge Medieval History.* 8 vols. Cambridge, 1922–36.

Excav. Cypr. British Museum. *Excavations in Cyprus.* By A. S. Murray, A. H. Smith and H. B. Walters. London, 1900.

Exc. Cypr. See List II, Cobham.

F.H.G. *Fragmenta Historicorum Graecorum.* Ed. C. et Th. Müller. 5 vols. Paris, 1878–85.

G.D.I. *Sammlung der griechischen Dialekt-Inschriften.* Ed. H. Collitz and others. I, pp. 1–80: "Die griechisch-kyprischen Inschriften in epichorischer Schrift", by W. Deecke. Göttingen, 1884.

H.C.C. Metropolitan Museum of New York. *Handbook of the Cesnola Collection.* By J. L. Myres. New York, 1914.

Hdb. *Handbook of Cyprus.* By R. Storrs and B. J. O'Brien. London, [1930].

H.L. See List II, Bouché-Leclercq.

I.G. *Inscriptiones Graecae.* Berlin, 1873– . Ed. II (Minor). Berlin, 1913– .

I.G.R.R. *Inscriptiones Graecae ad Res Romanas pertinentes.* Paris, 1906– .

I.L.N. *Illustrated London News.* Various dates from 1931– .

Jac. See List II, Jacoby.

J.H.S. *Journal of Hellenic Studies.* London, 1881– .

K.B.H. *Kypros, die Bibel und Homer.* By M. Ohnefalsch-Richter. Berlin, 1893. English edition, *Kypros, the Bible and Homer.* London, 1893. (References are to the former.)

K.K. See List II, Georgiades.

Κυπρ. χρον. Κυπριακὰ Χρονικά. Larnaka, 1923– .

L.B.W. *Voyage archéologique en Grèce et en Asie Mineure.* By P. Lebas and W. H. Waddington. Vol. III, Part I. Paris, 1870.

Miss. See List II, Schaeffer.

M.L. *H.* See List II, Mas Latrie.

O.C. See List II, Oberhummer.

O.K. See List II, Oberhummer.

O.G.I.S. W. Dittenberger. *Orientis Graeci Inscriptiones Selectae.* 2 vols. Leipzig, 1903–5.

P.G. J. P. Migne. *Patrologiae Cursus Completus....* Series Graeca. Paris, 1857–66.

P.I.R. *Prosopographia Imperii Romani.* Ed. Klebs and others. 3 vols. Berlin, 1897–8. Ed. II, by Groag and Stein. Berlin and Leipzig, 1933– .

P.L. J. P. Migne. *Patrologia Latina.* Paris, 1844–64.

R.D.A. Cyprus Department of Antiquities. *Annual Reports.* Nicosia, 1915, 1916, 1933– .

R.E. Pauly-Wissowa—Kroll—Mittelhaus. *Real-Encyclopädie der Classischen Altertums-Wissenschaft.* Stuttgart, 1894– .

Rec. Cr. Arm. *Recueil des Historiens des Croisades. Documents Arméniens.* 2 vols. Paris, 1869–1906.

Rec. Cr. Grecs. The same. *Historiens grecs.* 2 vols. Paris, 1875–81.

Rec. Cr. Occ. The same. *Historiens Occidentaux.* 5 vols. Paris, 1844–95.

Rec. Cr. Or. The same. *Historiens Orientaux.* 5 tomes. Paris, 1872–1906.

S.C.E. *Swedish Cyprus Expedition. Finds and Results of the Excavations in Cyprus*, 1927–31. By E. Gjerstad and others. Stockholm, Vols. I, II, 1934; Vol. III, 1937; Vol. IV to follow.

S.E.G. *Supplementum Epigraphicum Graecum.* Leyden, 1923– .

S.P.C. See List II, Gjerstad.

Syll. W. Dittenberger. *Sylloge Inscriptionum Graecarum.* Ed. II, 3 vols. Leipzig, 1898–1901; Ed. III, 4 vols. Leipzig, 1924.

II

AUTHORS

Amadi. *Chroniques d'Amadi et de Strambaldi.* Publ. par R. de Mas Latrie. Coll. des doc. inéd. sur l'hist. de France. Paris, 1891.

Bevan (E.). *History of Egypt under the Ptolemaic Dynasty.* London, 1927.

Bouché-Leclercq (A.). *Histoire des Lagides.* 4 vols. Paris, 1903–7. Cited as *H.L.*

Bustron (Florio). *Chronique de l'île de Chypre.* Publ. par R. de Mas Latrie. Coll. des doc. inéd. sur l'hist. de France. Paris, 1886.

Casson (S.). *Ancient Cyprus.* London, 1937.

Chapot (V.). "Les Romains et Cypre", in *Mélanges Cagnat.* Paris, 1912.

Cobham (C. D.). *Excerpta Cypria.* Cambridge, 1908.

Cohen (D.). *De magistratibus Aegyptiis externas Lagidarum Regni provincias administrantibus.* The Hague, [1912].

Cooke (G. A.) *Text-Book of North Semitic Inscriptions.* Oxford, 1903.

Dussaud (R.). *Les civilisations préhelléniques.* 2e éd. Paris, 1914.

Engel (W. H.). *Kypros.* 2 vols. Berlin, 1841.

Enlart (C.). *L'art gothique et la Renaissance en Chypre.* 2 vols. Paris, 1899.

Georgiades (K. P.). Ἡ Καταγωγὴ τῶν Κυπρίων. Leukosia, 1936. Cited as *K.K.*

Gjerstad (E.). *Studies on Prehistoric Cyprus.* Uppsala Universitets Årsskrift. Uppsala, 1926. Cited as *S.P.C.*

Gunnis (R.). *Historic Cyprus.* London, 1936.

Hackett (J.). *History of the Orthodox Church in Cyprus.* London, 1901.

Kyprianos. Ἱστορία χρονολογικὴ τῆς νήσου Κύπρου. Venice, 1788. [I have used the reprint, Leukosia, 1933, but given the original pagination.]

Lang (R. H.). *Cyprus.* London, 1878.

Lusignan (Père Estienne de). *Chorograffia et Breve Historia Universale dell' Isola de Cipro.* Bologna, 1573.

—— *Description de toute l'isle de Cypre.* Paris, 1580.

MACHAERAS (Leontios). *Recital concerning the Sweet Land of Cyprus, entitled Chronicle.* Tr. and ed. R. M. Dawkins. 2 vols. Oxford, 1932.

MAS LATRIE (L. de). *Histoire de l'Île de Chypre sous le règne de la Maison de Lusignan.* I. *Histoire* (to 1291). 1861. II, III. *Documents* (to 1670). 1852–5. Paris, 1852–61. Cited as M.L. *H.*

MENARDOS (S.). Τοπωνυμικὸν τῆς νήσου Κύπρου. In Ἀθηνᾶ, XVIII. Athens, 1906.

OBERHUMMER (E.). *Die Insel Cypern.* I. München, 1903. (No more published.) Cited as *O.C.*

—— *Kypros.* In Pauly-Wissowa, *Real-Encyclopädie,* XII. Stuttgart, 1924. Cited as *O.K.*

OTTO (W.) "Zur Geschichte der Zeit des 6. Ptolemäers", in *Abh. Bayer. Akad., Phil.-hist. Abt.,* N.F., Heft XI, 1934.

OTTO-BENGTSON. "Zur Geschichte des Niederganges des Ptolemäerreiches." By W. Otto and H. Bengtson. *Ibid.* Heft XVII, 1938.

PERISTIANES (H. K.). Γενικὴ Ἱστορία τῆς νήσου Κύπρου. Leukosia, 1910.

SAKELLARIOS (A. A.). Τὰ Κυπριακὰ ἤτοι γεωγραφία, ἱστορία καὶ γλῶσσα τῆς νήσου Κύπρου. 2 vols. Athens, 1890–1.

SATHAS (K. N.). Μεσαιωνικὴ Βιβλιοθήκη. II. Venice, 1873.

SCHAEFFER (C. F. A.). *Missions en Chypre,* 1932–1935. Paris, 1936. Cited as *Miss.*

SJÖQVIST (E.). "Die Kultgeschichte eines Cyprischen Temenos", in *Archiv für Religionswissenschaft,* XXX. 1933.

SOTIRIOU (G. A.). Τὰ Βυζαντινὰ Μνημεῖα τῆς Κύπρου. I. Athens, 1935. Cited as *Byz. Mn.*

SPYRIDAKIS (K.). *Euagoras I von Salamis.* Stuttgart, 1935.

STEWART (B.). *My Experiences of the Island of Cyprus.* London, 1906.

STRACK (M. E. D. L.). *Die Dynastie der Ptolemäer.* Berlin, 1897.

SVORONOS (J. N.). Τὰ Νομίσματα τῶν Πτολεμαίων. 4 vols. Athens, 1904–8.

UNGER (F.) and KOTSCHY (Th.). *Die Insel Cypern.* Vienna, 1865.

THE HISTORY OF CYPRUS

CHAPTER I

THE LAND

Soon after the British occupation of Cyprus in 1878, a German archaeologist wrote:

> He who would become and remain a great power in the East must hold Cyprus in his hand. That this is true, is proved by the history of the world during the last three and a half millennia, from the time of Thutmes III of Egypt to the days of Queen Victoria.[1]

Since he wrote, nothing has happened, on land, on the sea, or in the air, to lessen the force of his words. The historian is reminded of them at every turn, beginning with his realization of the geographical position of the island, which lies towards the N.E. angle of the eastern basin of the Mediterranean, between lat. 34° 34′ and 35° 42′ N. and long. 32° 16′ and 34° 36′ E. of Greenwich. Asia Minor and Syria can be seen from it with the naked eye, Beirut, Haifa, Port Said and Alexandria are within the sailor's or flier's easy reach.

The third largest island in the Mediterranean (being a good deal smaller than Sicily and Sardinia), it has an area, according to the official figures, of 3584 square miles. It is thus somewhat larger than the two English counties of Norfolk and Suffolk combined.[2] Its greatest length, from W.S.W. to E.N.E. (i.e. from Paphos harbour or C. Drepanum

---

[1] Gustav Hirschfeld, in the *Deutsche Rundschau*, XXIII, 1880, p. 270.

[2] Oberhummer, art. *Kypros* in Pauly-Wissowa, *Real-Encyclopädie*, XII, 1924, 62, makes it 9380 sq. km. (3622 sq. m.). (Norfolk and Suffolk measure about 3560 sq. m., but estimates vary according to the administrative areas included.) The basis of all modern maps is Kitchener's survey (1885). On the geography of Cyprus, in the widest sense, E. Oberhummer's *Die Insel Cypern*, I (no more was published), Munich, 1903, is the standard and indispensable work. I refer to it as *O.C.*, and to the article *Kypros*, which gives full references up to date, as *O.K.*

to C. St Andreas), is 138 miles; its greatest breadth, from N. to S. (i.e. from C. Kormakiti to C. Gata), 60 miles.

How and when did the island come to be there?[1]

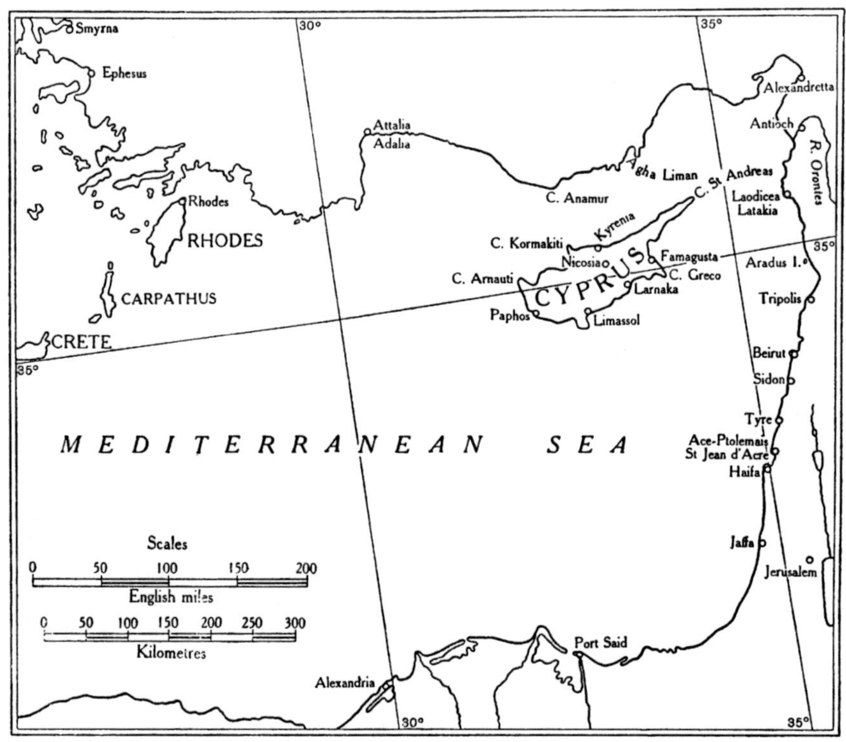

From the point of view of the geologist, it is not very ancient.[2] The oldest rocks, known as the Trypanian series, are attributed to the Cretaceous and early Eocene period. They probably underlie the whole

---

[1] Pliny (*N.H.* II, 90, 204) thought that Nature made islands by tearing them away from the mainland (cp. Est. de Lusignan, *Chorogr.* fo. 2; Kyprianos, p. 1). This guess, which has been naïvely regarded as based on some lost historical source (Georgiades, *K.K.* p. 1), was fantastically developed by medieval Arab writers (*O.C.* pp. 44, 53 f.; cp. p. 106).

[2] Passing over earlier accounts of the geology, we may mention the following: C. V. Bellamy and A. J. Jukes-Browne, *The Geology of Cyprus*, Plymouth, 1905; 2nd ed. [1927] (Crown Agents for the Colonies); Bellamy, *Geological Map of Cyprus*, 1905; F. R. C. Reed, *Geology of the British Empire*, 1921, pp. 15–20; C. G. Cullis and A. B. Edge, *Report on the Cupriferous Deposits of Cyprus*, 1922; Cullis, "Sketch of the Geology and Mineral Resources of Cyprus", in *Journ. R. Soc. Arts*, 1924, pp. 624–47; F. R. Cowper Reed, "Contributions to the Geology of Cyprus", in *Geol. Mag.* LXVI, 1929;

island, and appear as the backbone of the compact limestones and marbles of the Kerynia range along the north coast. Contrary to the old belief, these marbles are both various and admirable, and all the marbles used in the buildings of ancient Cyprus, with one exception, can be matched in the beds of the Kerynia range.[1] These limestones must have formed an ancient land surface during the greater part of the Eocene period, as a result of uplift. Then came a period of subsidence; and in the sea below which the land sank were deposited, first, the products of erosion—the Kythrean sandstones and shales, probably of Oligocene age, which lie disconformably on the Trypanian series, and line the flanks of the Kerynia range, running out along the Karpass peninsula. With the complete submergence of the land and the development of clearer water conditions, a series of chalky limestones and marls were deposited; these comprise the Idalian series, of Miocene age, which overlie the Kythrean in conformable sequence.[2] This Idalian series probably, at one time, covered the whole area of what is now the island. By the time these chalky deposits were being made, the water must have been of moderately great depth. But then followed, towards the end of the Miocene, a period[3] of earth-movement and igneous activity, during which there

---

LXVII, 1930; R. Storrs and B. J. O'Brien, *Handbook of Cyprus* [1930], pp. 234–59; J. R. Partington, *Origins and Development of Applied Chemistry*, 1935, pp. 356–69. The account in the text is based on Bellamy and Jukes-Browne, but has been thoroughly revised and largely rewritten with the kind assistance of Mr K. P. Oakley. The geologists do not mention any signs of active vulcanicity within recent times on the island itself, but Stewart (pp. 126 f.) speaks of a hot air vent and a hot spring on Pentadaktylos, phenomena generally associated with the last stage of a volcanic cycle.

[1] It is still held by archaeologists that "all Cypriote marble sculptures are probably made of imported marble" (Westholm, *Temples of Soli*, p. 125). Marble columns at A. Chrysostomos come from a local quarry. That Cyprus produced good marble was noticed long ago by A. Thevet (Cobham, *Exc. Cypr.* p. 179). "These marbles of the Kerynia range represent limestones which have become 'recrystallized' through the heat of igneous activity and earth-pressure" (Oakley).

[2] The gypsum of the Idalian series is a valuable economic product, used both for building stone and for plaster of Paris (Cullis, pp. 628 f.). The limestones furnish also abundant flints, still used for the primitive threshing implement or *dhoukani* (*ibid.* p. 630 and R. H. Lang, *Cyprus*, 1878, p. 214). It is incorrect, therefore, to say (J. L. Myres and H. Ohnefalsch-Richter, *Catalogue of the Cyprus Museum*, henceforward referred to as *C.C.M.*, p. 13) that Cyprus contains no flint. Umber (*terra d'ombra*) is another important Idalian product.

[3] Not necessarily the first in the history of the land; one, for instance, seems to have preceded the deposition of the Kythrean sandstones, which are partly composed of volcanic material (Cowper Reed, *Geol. Mag.* LXVI, p. 446).

was uplift and folding of the sediments, accompanied by the intrusion of dyke-rocks and the extrusion of basaltic lavas. Mountain ranges originated at this time; in the north the Kerynia range, which contains igneous intrusions here and there among the limestones and marbles already mentioned; in the south and west the great massif of Troödos, which is largely composed of intrusive and volcanic rocks. Cyprus must at this time have been part of Asia, the Kerynia range and Troödos, with the plain between them, being continuous with Mts Amanus and Casius and the Lower Orontes valley. During the later part of the Pliocene period the land sank again, but not so deep as before; the sea covered the plain, but the heights of Troödos and the Kerynia range appeared as islands. The best of the notably fine building stones of Cyprus are from the shelly limestones of the Pliocene and Pleistocene deposits.

A new movement of elevation, or fall in sea-level, at the beginning of Pleistocene times, brought Cyprus to the surface again. It seems probable that connexion with the mainland existed in the direction of the Gulf of Alexandretta. The vertebrates found in the cave-breccias of the island presumably made their way from the mainland by this connexion. From the high points of the mountains came floods which began the carving out of the deep valleys which form so picturesque a feature of the present landscape. The washings which they brought down, deposited on the lower levels (sometimes to a depth of seven metres), gave to portions of the central plain its present great fertility. A final subsidence relative to sea-level left the island within its present limits, more or less. It has been suggested, somewhat hazardously, that this subsidence, or some phase of it, is still celebrated by the annual Whitmonday festival of the Kataklysmos.[1] Raised beaches round the island testify to intermittent changes in sea-level since the main subsidence.

Such is the position and general lay-out of the land. Its geographical relation to the mainland (the advantages and disadvantages of which will become apparent as this history proceeds) may now be more precisely defined. The outstretched finger of the Karpass points significantly to Syria, with which the history which we are going to read has always been so intimately bound up. The north coast of the island is generally

---

[1] Bellamy and Jukes-Browne,[2] p. 56. The festival seems to be connected with the cult of Aphrodite. Ohnefalsch-Richter, *Kypros, die Bibel und Homer* (henceforward referred to as *K.B.H.*), p. 343; also M. H. Ohnefalsch-Richter, *Sitten und Gebräuche auf Cypern*, 1913, pp. 96 ff.

described as being forty miles from that of Cilicia (but that is between nearest points). Cilicia is indeed generally visible, and on clear days so are the summits of Taurus, some eighty miles away. From the extreme eastern point of the island to Syria it is less than seventy miles, and on clear days from certain heights, for instance, from Stavrovouni, Lebanon is discernible. With favouring winds the sailor can reach Syria in a day. On the other hand, Egypt is much farther off. From Larnaka to Port Said is more than 260 miles; so that relations with Egypt naturally did not begin so early as with Anatolia and Syria.[1]

The two mountain ranges already mentioned, with a broad plain between them, characterize the relief. Of the two ranges the northern, with its jagged outline, is particularly impressive. It runs, at a distance of some three miles from the shore, for about sixty miles, from above Lapithos on the west to Kantara Castle on the east, from which point it falls away along the Karpass peninsula. For want of a name of its own it is known as the Kerynia range. Its heights shelter the plain from the north, taking much of the moisture from the winds which blow from Anatolia. Its highest peak,[2] Kyparissovouno, above Larnaka tis Lapithou, measures 3357 ft.; but its most striking summit is "Five Fingers", Pentadaktylos (2430 ft.). The castles of St Hilarion, Buffavento and Kantara (Pl. XV) stand romantically on peaks of 2380, 3131 and 2068 ft. respectively. These sites, chosen doubtless for strategic reasons, command wide and wonderful views over the sea and in other directions. The chief pass from the plain to the sea through this range is on the modern road from Nicosia to Kerynia (1250 ft.); another road runs north from Leukoniko, over a low pass (850 ft.) under the western flank of Mt Olymbos, providing the quickest access to the north coast from Salamis and accounting for the many ancient settlements in the neighbourhood

---

[1] A number of actual distances, compared with ancient calculations, are given in *O.C.* pp. 95–6. Some of them differ slightly from the following (true to about ½ m.), which I owe to the kindness of the Curator of Maps of the Royal Geographical Society: C. Kormakiti to C. Anamur, 43 m.; Kerynia to Agha Liman, 75 m.; C. St Andreas to Mouth of Orontes, 83 m.; the same to Latakia, 76 m. (to Minat-al-Baidha about the same); Famagusta to Mouth of Orontes, 132 m.; Larnaka to Beirut, 127 m.; the same to Port Said, 264 m. These figures have been converted from the nautical mileage shown on the Admiralty Chart. See also Schaeffer, *Miss.* pp. 1 f., for distances between the island and the Syrian coast.

[2] These heights are taken from the Survey of 1932; they differ from those given in the latest edition of the *Handbook* (1930).

of Akanthou,[1] while the western end of the range is turned by the road from Nicosia through Myrtou to Lapithos.

It would be natural to identify the Mt Olymbos just mentioned with the Olympus, of which Strabo says: "the mountain ridge is called Olympus, and has a temple of Aphrodite Akraia, which women are not allowed to enter or see". But there is general agreement to place the ancient Mt Olympus at the extremity instead of at the root of the Karpass. Strabo's account of this part of the island is, however, by no means satisfactory.[2]

The narrow strip of land between the range and the sea is very fertile, and, with its romantic mountain background, this is perhaps the most attractive region in the island. Places such as Lapithos and Karavas have fine springs of fresh water. The finest of all the springs in the island, however, issues from the southern flank of Pentadaktylos, appearing at Kythrea. It now feeds a multitude of local mills; but its waters once, by means of an aqueduct, supplied the needs of Salamis, some twenty-three miles distant. The source from which this and other springs derive is probably local, depending on the rainfall in the Kerynian hills, although the theory that they come from the Anatolian mountains across the sea is not so absurd as some have supposed.[3]

The central plain, commonly but loosely called the Mesaria[4] or Mesarea, consisting mostly of sedimentary limestones, stretches for some

---

[1] Oberhummer in *Ztschr. d. Ges. f. Erdk.*, Berlin, XXVII, 1892, p. 449.

[2] The application of the name Olymbos to the peak above Akanthou may, as Hogarth says, not be old (*Devia Cypria*, p. 83, n. 2); on the other hand, so dignified a name as Olympus seems unsuitable to the hillock to which modern writers attach it. On the name Olympus in general, see E. Oberhummer in *Anz. Akad. Wiss. Wien*, LXXIV, 1937, pp. 92 ff.

[3] Sir Samuel Baker, for instance (*Cyprus as I saw it*, 1879, p. 76), scouts the idea (which is local tradition) as "simple nonsense". But it is seriously suggested by Unger, p. 70; cp. *O.C.* p. 227, who dissents. On the water supply, see C. Reid, *Report on the Water-Supply of the Island of Cyprus*, Foreign Office, 1908; R. Oakden, *Report on the Finances and Economic Resources of Cyprus*, Crown Agents, 1935, pp. 133 ff.; and C. Raeburn, Gov. of Cyprus *Progress Report for* 1937, *Water Supply in Cyprus*, Nicosia, 1938, where the reasons for supposing the source to be local are stated, the chief being the variation with the rainfall and the lack of mineralization, which would have been present had the water gone to a great depth on its way from the source.

[4] Commonly written Mesaoria, or the like, from the idea that it means the space between the mountains (so, e.g., Est. de Lusignan, *Descr.* fo. 7 v°). It has been suggested that the word is of Frankish origin (*massaria*), and has been extended from the cultivated estates to the plain as a whole (*O.K.* 64). This is disputed by Chatzidaki

sixty miles from Morphou Bay on the west to Famagusta Bay on the east. Remains of the harder rocks, which have mostly been eroded, form here and there striking "table-mountains", which were sometimes used for early settlements. The most notable of these are at Leondari Vouno, south-east of Nicosia, and C. Greco (Pedalium). The plain is now treeless (save for modern planting), but the soil, as already noted, is very fertile, producing in most seasons fine crops of grain.[1] The general aspect is arid, except in spring, when it is clad in the green of the young crops and a wonderful garment of flowers. But in old times (by which Eratosthenes, our informant, probably means the period of the earlier Greek settlers) the plains were so heavily wooded and covered with bush that agriculture was impossible. The growth was to some degree kept down by cutting timber, partly for smelting the copper and silver ore from the mines, partly for shipbuilding; but, this being of little avail, leave was given, to whoso wished and was able, to clear and keep the land as his own property free of taxation.

The two larger streams of the Mesarea, the Pedias (ancient Pediaeus) and the Yialias,[2] both rising in the eastern portion of the Troödos massif, flow, the former past Nicosia, the latter past Dali (Idalium), to the bay of Salamis. They have little water except in flood-time (and then too much). Another stream, with its many tributaries, drains the western part of the plain and flows into Morphou Bay. Its ancient name is uncertain; but it may have been Satrachus.[3]

Some short streams which, descending from Mt Troödos, water the southern strip of coastland, may be mentioned, e.g. the Kouris (ancient Lycus) issuing near Curium (Episkopi); and the Diarrhizos, which

---

(Ἀθηνᾶ, VI, 1894, pp. 3–64), who connects it with μεσάρις = μέσος. Strictly speaking it means only the eastern portion of the plain (*O.C.* pp. 160 f.).

[1] On the fruitfulness of Cyprus, and testimonies thereto from antiquity onwards, see *O.C.* pp. 270 ff. Cyprus, says Ammianus Marcellinus (XIV, 8. 14), was so rich in natural resources that without any external supplies it could build a ship and send it to sea fully equipped from truck to keelson. Not all the central plain is fertile; see *O.C.* p. 163.

[2] Yialias is said (*O.C.* p. 166) to derive its name from Idalium, and Mas Latrie (*M.L. H.* I, p. 60) actually gives an alternative modern name of the river as Idalia. But, if so, why did not Idalium become Yiali?

[3] Nonnus (*Dion.* XIII, 420) places the Satrachus near Paphos, in which case it must be the Diarrhizos (see next note). Ross (*Journey to Cyprus*, tr. C. D. Cobham, Nicosia, 1910, p. 71) identifies the Satrachus with the Dali river, but has not found many to follow him.

issues by Kouklia, the site of Old Paphos.[1] The Basilopotamos, Basileus, or Great River (Vasilopotamo, Vasilikos), issuing by Mari, is associated with the landing of St Helena. Some have identified it with the Tetios of Ptolemy, though that name is claimed also for the insignificant brook which flows past Arpera and Kiti.[2]

Mt Troödos (Trogodos in antiquity) and its foothills occupy the greater part of the southern and western portion of the island, the thousand feet contour on the south and west being seldom more than four miles from the coast. Its core of igneous rocks is surrounded by a girdle of tertiary limestones and marls. Its highest point, Chionistra,[3] measures 6403 ft., and was from antiquity a sanctuary; in the Middle Ages a chapel of St Michael stood there. On the heights the snow lies late into spring. At the place Troödos itself, at 5600 ft., there is now the summer station of the Government, and the mountain is rapidly becoming popular as a summer resort from Egypt and Palestine. It is tempting to identify Chionistra with Strabo's second Mt Olympus, "the breast-shaped", as is commonly done. But Stavrovouni, an isolated peak far to the east, though only 2258 ft. high, is so striking in its contour, that its claim to the name Olympus has been strongly urged.[4]

It is in the foothills of the Troödos range that copper, the most important product of the island, was mined in antiquity, especially along the coast district from Marium to Soli, and also on the north-east slope

---

[1] By some identified with the Bocaros, but on insufficient evidence. See M.R. James in *J.H.S.* IX, 1888, pp. 182–3. The reading *Bo-ka-ro-se* on the coins is not certain, nor is the attribution of the coins to Paphos: B.M.C. *Cyprus*, pp. lxiv f.

[2] *O.C.* p. 157.

[3] Kionia (4659 ft.), above the monastery Machaeras, is probably the ancient Aoïon: *O.C.* p. 154.

[4] Much confusion reigns about the two mountains Olympus. Cotovicus, for instance (*Itin. Hier.* 1619, Cobham, *Exc. Cypr.* p. 195), Est. de Lusignan (*Chorogr.* fo. 5, 5 v°) and Archbishop Constantius in 1776 (Κυπριὰς χαρίεσσα in Περιγραφὴ τῆς Μονῆς τοῦ Κύκκου, 1819, p. 135; tr. in Cobham, p. 312; Gunnis, *Historic Cyprus*, p. 447) mix up the two passages of Strabo, and confound the Olympus, which had the temple of Aphrodite Akraia, with that of Mt Troödos. Strabo's words about the latter, after speaking of Citium, are (XIV, 6. 3): "then (comes) the city of Amathus, and between (them) a small town called Palaea and a breast-shaped mountain Olympus; then Curias (a foreland) of peninsular shape". Thus Olympus from the sea would be seen between Citium and Amathus; and this points to Stavrovouni rather than to any peak of the main mass of Troödos. On the identification see also Menardos, Τοπωνυμικόν (Ἀθηνᾶ, XVIII, 1906), p. 325; Hackett, *Hist. of the Orthodox Church of Cyprus*, 1901, p. 440.

at Tamassus,[1] the Homeric Temese, now probably at Politiko. Near Marium (Polis tis Chrysochou), at Limni-Pelathousa, and near Leuka, at Skouriotissa and Mavrovouni, copper is being worked by modern enterprise.[2] Nearly all the modern copper-mining leases and prospecting permits are on the extreme edges of the igneous area.

In antiquity, long before the Roman period, indeed as early as the second millennium, copper was exported from this region, both in the form of ore and in ingots of more or less refined metal. Ore and scoriae of the same composition as those found at Skouriotissa have been found not only at Enkomi in Cyprus itself, but at Ras Shamra on the Syrian coast, in deposits of the fourteenth and thirteenth centuries.[3] And we shall see that copper, both unrefined and refined, was sent to Egypt from Asy, which may be Cyprus, in the time of Thutmose III.

There is some uncertainty about the extent to which iron was mined in Cyprus in antiquity, although ore in the form of pyrites occurs in considerable quantities in the rocks of Troödos.[4] Gold, which according

---

[1] In *Od.* I, 184, Athena, in the guise of Mentes, pretends to be voyaging ἐς Τεμέσην μετὰ χαλκόν, taking iron to exchange. But many maintain (most recently O. Davies in *B.S.A.* XXX, 1932, p. 81) that this is Temesa in Bruttium, and ancient writers were divided on the question. I think that the balance of evidence seems in favour of the Cypriote place. See *O.C.* p. 176, and Oberhummer's art. *Tamassos* in *R.E.* IV A, 1932, 2095; also Philipp, art. *Temesa, ibid.* V A, 1934, 495. Davies is concerned (though he fails) to prove that Cyprus copper was not mined until the very end of the Bronze Age; but Homer is not evidence for so early a date and need not count against his main thesis, even if the Temese of the *Odyssey* is in Cyprus. Myres (*Who were the Greeks?* p. 438) probably exaggerates the wealth of Cyprus in iron when he says that for Mentes to take iron to Cyprus was carrying coals to Newcastle, and therefore Temese cannot be Tamassus. See below, n. 4.

[2] Details in *Hdb.* pp. 251 ff. See also Cullis and Edge (above, p. 2, n. 2); T. A. Rickard, "A Journey to Cyprus", in *Univ. of California Chron.* XXXII, 1930, pp. 423 ff., and "Copper Mining in Cyprus", in *Bulletin* 306, March 1930, of Institution of Mining and Metallurgy; O. Davies, "Copper Mines of Cyprus", in *B.S.A.* XXX, 1932, pp. 74–85; Schaeffer, *Missions en Chypre* (henceforward referred to as *Miss.*), pp. 94–101.

[3] Schaeffer, *Miss.* pp. 95–101.

[4] Bellamy and Jukes-Browne,[2] p. 63; *O.C.* p. 184; *C.C.M.* p. 22 ("Cyprus has considerable masses of iron ore of fair quality, and there is evidence that they were discovered and worked as soon as the knowledge of the metal extended"). Georgiades (*K.K.* p. 13) reports an ancient iron-mine near Asproyia. A legend associated the Telchines, the first workers in iron and copper, with Cyprus, which they inhabited after leaving Crete on their way to Rhodes (Strabo, XIV, 2. 7, p. 654; Nicol. Damasc. fr. 116, *F.H.G.* III, p. 459; cp. Paus. IX, 19. 1). Engel, I, p. 198, thinks the route was the other way about. In any case, it is a long way round; and it is to be suspected that

to a fragment of Pseudo-Aristotle was found on Mt Boucasa in the Troödos range,[1] is once more being produced in the island in small but payable quantity. Silver, as we have already seen from Eratosthenes, was also anciently mined, and this may account for the large issues of silver coinage in the Ptolemaic age.[2]

Next in importance to copper now seems to be the short-fibred asbestos (Greek *amíantos*) which was mined in antiquity, and is now extensively worked at Amiandos, a few miles east of Troödos.

The trees of the highlands and foothills are most commonly the Aleppo pine and the black pine; the once famous cedars have almost disappeared.[3] In antiquity, Cyprus was one of the chief sources of shipbuilding timber in the eastern Mediterranean.[4] There are also cypresses and an evergreen oak endemic in the island (*Quercus alnifolia Cypria*). The all-useful carob is largely cultivated and its bean exported—this is indeed now the most important export crop. The stately eucalyptus trees were first planted since the British occupation; but the attempts at re-afforestation have had disappointing results,[5] mainly because of the

---

Cyprus has been dragged in, because it was assumed that the earliest metal-workers must have had a home in the island which was so early a source of copper. Cp., for the Dactyls, ch. v, p. 86, n. 2.

[1] Boucasa is conjecturally identified with the hill Phoukasa to the north of Troödos (Sykutris in Κυπρ. Χρον. I, 1923, p. 340). For traditions concerning ancient gold production in Cyprus, see Est. de Lusignan, *Chorogr.* fo. 14 v° (Tamassus), and 87; *O.C.* p. 183.

[2] In Hudūd al-'Ālam, *The Regions of the World*, tr. V. Minorsky, 1937, p. 59, Cyprus is described as having mines of silver, copper and plasma (*dahanj*). This work was compiled in 982/3.

[3] *O.C.* p. 44, quotes from Eutychius how Thomas, Patriarch of Jerusalem († about 821), took advantage of the absence of the Moslems to cut fifty cedars and have them brought to Jerusalem.

[4] The legend of Semiramis told that she had shipwrights from Phoenicia, Syria and Cyprus to build her river-ships (Diod. Sic. II, 16. 6). The invention of the *kerkouros* was attributed to Cyprus (Plin. *N.H.* VII, 209). But the references in Assyrian texts (*O.C.* pp. 6, 8) and in Ezekiel (xxvii, 6) seem to be to fine woods, not ship timber. However, in the latter passage, G. A. Cooke (*Crit. and Exeg. Comm. on the Book of Ezekiel*, p. 297) regards ivory as an intrusion, and translates "thy boards they fashioned of 'pines' from the isles of Kittim". The traditional rendering *box tree* is unsuitable here; box-wood might be inlaid with ivory for small ornamental articles, but if *ivory* goes out as an intrusion, there is no reason to keep the traditional *box-wood*, which could not be used for shipbuilding.

[5] On the forest problems, see A. H. Unwin in *Great Britain and the East*, Cyprus Supp. 4 Feb. 1937, pp. 12 f. Sir Arthur Evans informs me that recent enquiries throw

goats, which are more precious in the eyes of the Cypriote than any speculative advantage to be gained by the cultivation of timber. On the western and southern slopes of Mt Troödos olive,[1] vine and carob are cultivated to a greater extent and with more success than in other parts of the island.

The wine[2] of Cyprus, though not without reputation in antiquity, became really famous from the time of the Second Crusade. The best culture was on the estates of the Knights Hospitallers, especially on the Grand Commandery of Kolossi; hence the name Commanderia given to the finest quality, which is said to be made in exactly the same way as it was centuries ago in various places on the slopes of Troödos. When fine, it resembles Madeira, and indeed the Madeira vine itself is actually derived from Cypriote stock.

In the flat, low ground in the neighbourhood of Larnaka and Limassol, where once were lagoons, are found the great salt-lakes,[3] from the dried-up beds of which a large supply of salt is obtained. Famous in antiquity, the salt industry flourished greatly in the Frankish period, providing the main revenue of the island. It now supplies merely local needs. The Larnaka lake is, from this point of view, much the more important of the two.

The only harbour, properly speaking, in the island is at Famagusta, where a line of rocks and banks, with the help of moles, provides a modest shelter. This is mentioned by Strabo under the name of Arsinoe. The ancient harbour of Salamis, about four miles to the north, is now

---

doubt on his statement (*Palace of Minos*, II, 1928, p. 463, n. 1) that afforestation has increased the rainfall. The Cypriotes have, however, long attributed its increasing scarcity to deforestation. But in Italy the "boscofili" argued that the rainfall was increased by deforestation: D. Bocci, *Sulle condizioni igieniche...del Distretto di Famagusta* (Estr. dal Giornale del Genio Civile, Roma, 1881, p. 20). On the violence of the rain when it does fall, see B. Stewart, *My Experiences of the Island of Cyprus*, London, 1906, p. 26. As to goats, which are sometimes said to outnumber the human population, the number of registered animals was, in 1936, 266,480; in 1937, 211,033: *Annual Report* for 1937, p. 19.

[1] Olives of secular age at Dali: Baker, p. 45.

[2] F. Unger and Th. Kotschy, *Die Insel Cypern*, pp. 447 ff.; *O.C.* pp. 310 ff. In the time of Mas Latrie, *l'Île de Chypre*, 1879, p. 55, the best Commanderia was grown not at Kolossi, but in the Larnaka district.

[3] *Hdb.* pp. 276 ff. The Government monopoly now yields an annual revenue of about £32,000; in 1878 it was over £25,000 (Lang, *Cyprus*, p. 260). Less important salines are or were those near Famagusta (*O.C.* p. 111) and Nicosia (Lang, *loc. cit.*). Britain, in making the treaty with Turkey, undertook not to export Cypriote salt in competition with Turkish salines (Stewart, p. 175).

filled with sand. The estuary of the Pediaeus must, at the beginning of historical times, have extended far inland, almost, but probably not quite, as far as Enkomi.[1] But by 306 B.C. the entrance was narrow, and may not long after have become unfit for naval purposes.[2] Pseudo-Scylax, enumerating (probably towards the middle of the fourth century B.C.) the cities of the coast, mentions Greek Salamis (with a closed harbour safe in winter), Carpasia, Kerynia (Kyrenia), Lapethos of the Phoenicians, Soli (this too with a winter harbour)[3], Greek Marium, Amathus[4] ("its people are autochthonous"), and adds: "all these have harbours which are deserted". Paphos and Citium he does not even mention. The roads of Larnaka (which in antiquity had a closed harbour) and Limassol are safe for large vessels except in south-easterly gales. Other small harbours, as at Paphos and Kerynia, must have been much more freely used in the days of smaller shipping than they are now. Thus it has been observed that the harbours of Aphendrika, Ayios Philon (ancient Carpasia, of which the harbour is mentioned by Strabo), Exarchos, Machairiona, Gialousa and many more on the north coast must have served for trade with the opposite coast of Asia Minor, although generally speaking the roadsteads on the southern coast were much more convenient than the northern, which were exposed to the north wind.[5] Strabo also mentions the harbour at Soli and roadsteads or anchorages at Curium and Old Paphos, and a harbour, which must have been tiny, at Leucolla between Salamis and Pedalium.[6]

---

[1] Oberhummer (*O.C.* p. 124) thinks Enkomi may once have been actually on the sea. For the remains of the town, which existed as early as the eighteenth or seventeenth century at Enkomi, and was in the Mycenaean age the chief source from which Cypriote copper was exported to Syria, see Schaeffer, *Miss.* pp. 83–93. Probably the silting up of the estuary caused it to be superseded by Salamis, and the fall of its "opposite number", Ras Shamra, the increasing importance of iron instead of bronze, and the development of Citium by the Phoenicians, may have robbed it of its importance.

[2] Ten ships of Demetrius Poliorcetes sufficed to block the mouth (Plutarch, *Dem. Pol.* 16; Diod. Sic. xx, 50): W. H. Buckler in *J.H.S.* LV, 1935, p. 78, n. 40.

[3] When the harbour, the site of which is still traceable, became silted up, is uncertain, but it was before the fourth century after Christ (Westholm, *Temples of Soli*, p. 21).

[4] Kyprianos (p. 24) says that in his time (1788) remains of the harbour and its defensive works were still visible. The plan in *Excav. Cypr.* p. 88 marks a piece of wall on the shore, and from the acropolis the lines of the harbour-works are visible under water.

[5] A. Savorgnano, *Discrittione delle cose di Cipro*, tr. Luke, p. 15.

[6] Also landing-places (πρόσορμοι) at C. Zephyrium and Arsinoe between Old and New Paphos.

A feature of the shore, in the neighbourhood of Paphos, is the extraordinary production of foam, due to the disintegration of animal and vegetable marine organisms. There can be no doubt that this has a bearing on the myth of the birth of the Cyprian Goddess from the foam of the sea.[1]

Characteristic, too, of the coast in general, is the large number of striking headlands, which gave to the island one of its ornamental epithets, Cerastis, the "horned".[2]

It may be doubted whether the prevalent currents in the sea surrounding Cyprus were of much importance in regard to ancient trade relations. The great current which runs north along the Syrian coast, and turns west along the south coast of Asia Minor, has a branch which flows from C. St Andreas to C. Kiti, and may have facilitated the first stage of the Phoenician out voyages; and that which, coming from the west, divides and flows along the north and south coasts may have helped the Greek colonists on their outward way. But in neither case were they useful to the returning voyager.

The climate of Cyprus has had from antiquity an unenviable reputation for excessive heat, which is liable to inconvenience the conduct of anything, from war to excavations;[3] probably when it was more thickly wooded there was less drought than there is at present in summer. The thermometer at Nicosia has been known to reach 43·9° C. (111° F.),[4] exceeding the record for Cairo (42·7° C.). But the maximum temperature at Troödos, in the season July to September 1927, was only 26·6° C. (79·9° F.). As in most Mediterranean lands, there is a very dry summer and a rainy winter season, with its maximum in December. Upon the altar of Aphrodite at Paphos, according to ancient legend, rain never fell. Summer drought is still the chief handicap of the cultivator. Since 1881, modern methods of dealing with his other great enemy, the locust (more effective but less picturesque than those employed in olden days), have reduced the plague to manageable proportions.[5]

---

[1] Unger and Kotschy, pp. 543 ff.; *O.C.* pp. 108 ff.

[2] Xenagoras in Schol. to Lycophron, 447: Engel, I, p. 18, n. 17.

[3] Machaeras, §§ 655, 682. Martial's *infamem nimio calore Cyprum* (IX, 90. 9) is a commonplace.

[4] Stewart (p. 31) records a maximum shade-temperature of 115° F. at Nicosia, but this may not be official.

[5] On the locust plague see *Hdb.* pp. 179 ff., and, for the magical measures adopted against it, especially Dawkins on Machaeras, II, pp. 69 ff. The Turks, says Mariti in 1769 (*Viaggi*, I, p. 170), considering it a sin to resist the chastisements of God, prohibited the destruction of locusts.

In the course of this history we shall have much opportunity to test the theory of Hippocrates, that the character of a people is determined by the nature of their land, and the saying which Herodotus puts in the mouth of Cyrus, that "soft countries are wont to produce soft men; for it does not belong to the same land to grow admirable fruits and men who are good fighters".[1]

---

[1] Hippocr. Περὶ ἀέρων, 24; Herod. IX, 122.

CHAPTER II

THE STONE AGE

(*See Map at p.* 24)

In this[1] and the following chapter, in which such terms as Neolithic, Chalcolithic, Copper and Bronze Ages are employed, it is necessary to explain that they must not be taken in the precise and exclusive sense in which they used to be understood, as representing, that is to say, a regular chronological succession. Recent excavation has brought to light irregularity and overlap in these phases of culture. For instance, bronze has not yet been found in Babylonia in late Sumerian sites, although it was used for a time in the early Sumerian period. No copper has been found on such a site as the early settlement at Samarra, although the pottery there is partially, if not wholly, contemporary with that from Tell Halaf, which is associated with copper tools. Polished stone axes are commonly found in Syria associated with metal, and may be actually connected with metal types. We shall see that the "Neolithic" sites in Cyprus do not conform to a rigid typological scheme.

The existence of a Stone Age[2] in the island was unsuspected until quite recently, and only a few sites have been properly excavated. Nevertheless, more than thirty sites can, on the evidence of surface finds or trial excavations, be attributed to the Neolithic or Chalcolithic periods.[3] They are, for the most part, situated on low, but not flat,

---

[1] This chapter has had the advantage of criticism in draft by Prof. Sidney Smith, by whose kind assistance a number of defects have been removed.

[2] The human remains from burials earlier than the Bronze Age so far discovered are scanty and in damaged condition, and the professional craniologists have as yet hardly ventured to draw conclusions from them (see Guest in *R.D.A.* 1936, pp. 58–62). On the Stone Age in Cyprus generally, see Dikaios in *R.D.A. ibid.*, especially pp. 63–71, and in Κυπρ. Σπουδαί, II, pp. 237 ff.

[3] Of a Palaeolithic stage nothing has yet been found, though, in view of the close connexion of the island with Anatolia and Syria, it may well have existed: Schaeffer, *Miss.* pp. 2–4.—Although, in accordance with current usage, in this chapter such cultures as those of Khirokitia and Erimi are described as "Neolithic", it should be noted that many archaeologists hold that the forms of vessels show that they belong to a stage when the use of metal was becoming known. Comparison may be made with

ground, along the fringes of the hills, and, as a rule, not actually on the seashore: the hill country was little inhabited, and so was the great central plain, except where the rivers assured a supply of water.

Within the limits of Cypriote Stone Age culture, an attempt has been made to distinguish two stages, an early Neolithic (or even "pre-Neolithic") and a full Neolithic. The "pre-Neolithic", it is supposed, is represented by a settlement at Petra tou Limniti, an island off the north coast between the bays of Chrysochou and Morphou, about four miles west of Vouni;[1] the Neolithic, by the much more important settlement at Khirokitia (Pl. I *a*), thirty miles from Nicosia on the Limassol road, and not much more than four miles from the sea by the Maroni torrent.[2] At the former, a poor little place, the Swedes found irregularly circular hut-sites, on the lower levels, while those on the upper two levels were rectangular and divided into two rooms. No pottery was there, but implements of stone, flint, obsidian (a material not native to Cyprus) and bone, as well as rude stone idols. The absence of any pottery and the exclusive use of stone for vases proved, in their opinion, that the culture was "pre-Neolithic". But these people had already domesticated the ox, the sheep and the pig, and made implements out of their bones. Indeed, the very early attribution of this and other settlements is seriously disputed.[3] It is now generally believed that Petra, which the excavators called "pre-Neolithic", is Neolithic, like Khirokitia, as is shown by the presence of perfectly made polished stone axes, a stone vase with relief decoration, a dolerite idol which has a face and even indications of ears, and the like.[4] The absence of pottery may be accidental or at most indicate that the site is an archaic Neolithic one.

Palestine, for which the most recently suggested chronology for the periods preceding ± 3000 B.C. is as follows (G. E. Wright in *Bull. Amer. Sch. of Or. Research, Jerusalem and Bagdad*, April 1937, pp. 24–5): 5000 B.C.?—Neolithic, sub-Chalcolithic | 4000 B.C.? Lower and Middle Chalcolithic | ± 3400 B.C. Upper Chalcolithic | ± 3200– ± 3000 B.C. Early Bronze. First phase of "Alpha".

[1] *Swedish Cyprus Expedition. Finds and Results of the Excavations in Cyprus*, 1927–31. By E. Gjerstad and others. Vol. I, 1934, pp. 1 ff.

[2] Dikaios in *Comptes rendus de l'Acad. d. Inscr.* 18 Sept. 1936; *I.L.N.* 26 Dec. 1936; *Syria*, XVII, 1936, p. 361, n. 2; *Ztschr. f. Ethn.* LXVIII, 21 Sept. 1936, pp. 384–7; Megaw, *J.H.S.* LVI, pp. 157 f.; LVII, p. 142; Dikaios in *R.D.A.* 1936, pp. 82–7.

[3] Schaeffer in *Syria*, XVI, 1935, pp. 208 ff.; Ch. Picard in *Journ. des Savants*, 1935, p. 246; Schaeffer, *Miss.* p. 16.

[4] Dikaios also (*Syria*, XVII, p. 362, n. 1; *R.D.A.* 1936, p. 70) regards it as contemporaneous with Khirokitia (i), i.e. of the first stage of the Neolithic, with general use of stone vases.

PLATE I

Phot. Cyprus Museum

a

KHIROKITIA

Cyprus Museum   *b*   Phot. Seymer

BLACK STONE FROM KOUKLIA

At Khirokitia (Pl. I *a*) the use of stone vases was also general; only on the surface layer there have been found specimens of red polished pottery which, it is claimed, is the earliest yet found in Cyprus, and resembles sherds found in the lowest layers of the Neolithic settlement at Erimi. The houses were circular, with stone sub-structures, on which walls of mud-brick were erected; how they were roofed is not known; there is no trace of carbonized material, representing wattle and daub, but the suggestion that the roofs were corbelled domes of mud-brick seems very hazardous. Many flint and stone implements were found. There were also stone figurines of very rude style, and stone ornaments. But the chief interest of the site lay in a circular stone construction, too large for an ordinary dwelling, lying within an outer horseshoe-shaped stone enclosure. Within the inner circle were a number of burials, one under a square platform, and remains of animal bones and human skulls were found in the corridor between outer and inner enclosures, and in the latter, what appear to have been sacrificial tables, all suggesting that the whole place had a sacred character. A second campaign has discovered many more skeletons on another part of the site. Absolute chronology, is of course, not possible, but the excavator would date the settlement to the first half of the fourth millennium.

An intermediate stage between Khirokitia and Erimi is represented by a settlement at Sotira in the Limassol district, about five miles north-west of Erimi, which is characterized by large quantities of the same red pottery and some red-on-white pottery like that of Erimi. This settlement may belong to the middle of the fourth millennium.[1]

At Erimi, on the left bank of the Kouris, about a mile from Episkopi, and about the same distance from Kolossi, is the most important Neolithic site yet discovered in Cyprus.[2] Here were found a number of houses in superimposed layers; these houses showed a development from the simple circular type to a more elaborate one, still circular but with internal divisions. The earlier dwellings were constructed with posts in a circle, while the later, from the eighth layer upwards, had stone foundations, with central post supports for the roof, which may, as in many

[1] *I.L.N.* 26 Dec. 1936, p. 1174; *R.D.A.* 1936, pp. 63 f.

[2] Dikaios in *I.L.N.* 23 Dec. 1933, pp. 1034 ff.; *Antiquity*, VIII, 1934, pp. 86 f.; *I.L.N.* 19 Jan. 1935, pp. 97 f.; *J.H.S.* LV, 1935, pp. 170 f.; *Syria*, XVII, 1936, pp. 357 ff.; *R.D.A.* 1935 (Nicosia, 1936), pp. 6–10; *Ztschr. f. Ethn.* LXVIII, 21 Sept. 1936, pp. 381–4; *R.D.A.* 1936 (1938), pp. 1–81. A full account of the excavation is to appear in *Archaeologia*.

modern Cypriote village-houses, have been made of wattle and daub, and so have disappeared, but for traces, which have survived, of clay with impressions of brushwood. *Bothroi*, pits for storage or burial (one contained a skeleton), were sunk in the rock. The tenth or lowest level was on the bed-rock. But in an adjacent area, only partially excavated, still lower levels, down to a thirteenth, were reached. Outside the huts were small constructions which served as kitchens or workshops, though sometimes the hearth was in the house.

Burials were found both inside and outside the houses. But there is no trace here, as at Khirokitia, of rites in honour of the dead.

Implements and utensils of stone and flint and bone, ornaments in steatite, and primitive figurines in terracotta and stone, a copper tool (found at a depth of 2·40 m., i.e. above the fifth layer from the top) and copper needles (found in the cultivated earth) were associated with considerable remains of pottery. Of these the more important were red wares (including those with a red slip and red polished ware) and white wares (both plain and painted with, usually, geometric patterns). At first sight, in view of the predominance of the red polished ware in the Bronze Age, we should expect to find it prevailing in the upper levels at Erimi. But it is the white wares which, insignificant in proportion at the bottom, become predominant at the top, and exactly the converse happens with the red wares. The same development is shown at another Neolithic settlement at Ayios Epiktitos, about four miles east of Kerynia. The presence of the copper tool above mentioned indicates that when Erimi was abandoned, its culture had reached what is called the Chalcolithic Age; so much must be admitted even by those who reject the theory that Cyprus, like Palestine, was really in the Chalcolithic stage in the fourth millennium, though it cannot show copper implements. The resemblance between the red wares of the two ages represented at Erimi and at Vounous is, it is said, superficial, for the later wares show forms imitating leather vessels or gourds, such as are not represented in the Neolithic. So, it is argued, there must be a considerable gap between the latest Erimi culture and the beginnings of the "Early Cypriote", represented especially by the early stage of Vounous. This gap has been estimated at about four centuries (say 3000–2600 B.C.). That is one view; on the other hand, it is urged that the red polished ware of Erimi and other so-called Neolithic sites is technically (apart from the shapes) hardly to be distinguished from that of the Bronze Age: and accordingly it is maintained that the gap of four centuries above mentioned does not exist, and the end of the Erimi settlement, with its trace of bronze, or rather copper, must be brought down to something like the middle of the third millennium.[1] We shall return to this question in the next chapter. By the second half of the third millennium it would appear that Cyprus was in full possession of the art of working copper, for the Vounous cemetery of the Early Bronze Age has produced metal weapons of a type characteristic of, if not peculiar to, Cyprus.[2]

Similarly, the trend of opinion is now towards bringing down the antiquity of other settlements claimed as Neolithic. Such are Alonia ton Plakon (Lapithos), with semicircular huts, and Kythrea, with circular huts like those at Erimi. These show three kinds of pottery, the red polished, plain white and painted (red-on-white) wares. The first of these three tends to increase, showing the approach of the Bronze Age, when it was in general use.[3]

At Vounistiri, 1½ km. north-west of Phrenaros, in the Famagusta district, Gjerstad[4] found a house-floor (the walls had completely disappeared), which he dates to the Neolithic period. From the lay-out of the floor he concludes that it had an outer larger living-room and an inner sleeping-room (the "but and ben" type which is first found in the Eastern Mediterranean in the Stone Age at Magasa in Crete). This house used no pottery (possibly gourds instead), but the character of the flint-implements found shows that it was in the Neolithic Age. So far no other Neolithic settlement of this type has been found in Cyprus.

There is no trace, during either the Stone Age or the Bronze Age, of cremation of the dead. Circular pits (bothroi) sunk in the ground on the

---

[1] So Schaeffer, in *Syria*, *loc. cit.* and in *I.L.N.* 16 Feb. 1935, p. 246. More recent excavations at Vounous by Stewart have, however, produced pottery showing connexion with that of Erimi, which may perhaps narrow the supposed gap of 400 years.

[2] As Schaeffer points out (*Miss.* pp. 94–5) the investigations of Oliver Davies ("Copper Mines of Cyprus", in *B.S.A.* xxx, pp. 74–85) are inconclusive, and cannot be accepted unless they are confirmed by excavations, which have not yet been attempted, in the slack-heaps of the ancient mines.

[3] *S.C.E.* I, pp. 13 ff., 277 ff. At Kythrea, in one of the huts, was found a green steatite idol (6·4 cm. high) of a seated figure, without indications of features or sex (which had probably been shown in colour): Schaeffer, *Miss.* p. 9. Dikaios (*R.D.A.* 1936, p. 71) groups Lapithos and Kythrea with Erimi (ii) as Chalcolithic, about 3000.

[4] *Antiquaries Journal*, VI, 1926, pp. 54–8. Dikaios (*R.D.A.* 1936, p. 70) regards the remains as too vague in character to allow of definite attribution to any stage of Neolithic or Chalcolithic.

eastern site at Lapithos have been taken to indicate an agrarian funerary cult, but the association with the tombs is not clear.[1]

A ceramic problem of far-reaching significance is raised by the resemblance which has been noted between the Erimi pottery with patterns, usually geometrical, in red on a white or buff slip, on the one hand, and pottery characteristic of certain Chalcolithic sites in Thessaly. It does not yet appear how far there is correspondence also with pottery from a series of Peloponnesian sites from Corinth and Phlius to the neighbourhood of Tegea in Arcadia, and also from the Argive Heraeum.[2] On the other hand, there are connexions with primitive pottery from sites in North Syria or even farther east, and before attempting to draw conclusions as to trade relations with the Balkan peninsula at a very early period, we must wait for cumulation of evidence[3] and the discovery of links in the shape of similar wares in Asia Minor.

---

[1] *S.C.E.* I, pp. 14 ff. Ch. Picard (*Journ. des Savants*, 1935, p. 247) states that they adjoin the tombs, but this is hardly borne out by the plan.

[2] See Dikaios in *R.D.A.* 1936 (1938), pp. 41 ff. He considers that the resemblance of the Erimi wares to those of the Asiatic mainland is in ornamentation only, while closer affinity with the First Neolithic wares of Thessaly may be established both by ornamentation and quality of ware. The resemblance of the sherds from Kalavaso in Cyprus to the Thessalian ware was recognized by Forsdyke: B.M.C. *Vases*, I, i, 1925, nos. A 75. 1–6. For the distribution of the style in Peloponnese, see A. J. Evans in *J.H.S.* XLV, 1925, p. 262. More precise information, however, is required before it can be asserted that those particular varieties of Thessalian ware, the resemblance to which of Erimi ware has been noted, are actually represented in the south of Greece. I do not, for instance, see in the illustrations of the pottery from Gonia in Corinthia (C. W. Blegen, *Metr. Mus. Studies*, III, 1930), or of that from the Neolithic sites which preceded the Argive Heraeum (the same, *Prosymna*, pp. 24, 370 f.), any of the peculiar fringe pattern which is said to be common to Tsangli in Thessaly and Erimi in Cyprus. Ordinary lattice-decoration is distributed from Thessaly to Babylonia (Hall, *Civilization of Greece in the Bronze Age*, 1928, p. 21); the primitive types of ornament and fabric are apt to come into existence in different places owing to convergence of conditions, and not to direct contact.

[3] On the necessity for which, see Gjerstad, *S.P.C.* pp. 291 ff. In *Antike*, IX, 1933, p. 262, he observes that the nearest parallels to Cypriote Stone Age pottery are to be found in East Anatolia and Syria, and it would seem that the Stone Age culture of North Syria, East Anatolia and Cyprus had a common origin. Schaeffer (*Miss.* pp. 22–3) notes the resemblance between the Cypriote "aeneolithic" pottery and that found in the lower layers of level IV at Ras Shamra (of the fourth millennium; but see previous note). But he considers it at present impossible to establish connexion between the "aeneolithic" pottery of Cyprus and of Asia Minor. (Instead of the unpleasant hybrid "aeneolithic" I use "chalcolithic", except in quotations.) Early types of Syrian pottery have also been found at Hama and in the Amk plain, but the

Before leaving the Stone Age it is fitting to mention the existence of certain megalithic monuments for which a high antiquity has been claimed. The most famous are the two stone pillars which stand lonely near the coast by Old Paphos. These and similar objects, to the number of some fifty, in other places in the island are probably, as Guillemard and Hogarth long ago maintained, connected with the pressing of olives, and are not religious monuments. The supposed resemblance to the conical stones or baetyls of antiquity does not exist.[1]

On the other hand, there are two megalithic buildings: one now the chapel of the Panayia Phaneromeni at Larnaka;[2] the other at Salamis, known as the Prison of St Catherine.[3] But the latter certainly, and the former probably, are hardly earlier than Graeco-Roman times.

Most important is the monument revered by the Moslems as the tomb of Umm Haram in the Hala Sultan Tekke, situated in a delightful green shade on the western shore of the Salt Lake of Larnaka. It consists of three huge stones, one resting horizontally on the other two, which stand upright: a trilithon of regular type, now covered with draperies, and protected by its sanctity from closer examination by the infidel.[4]

---

brief reports as yet published make it advisable to suspend judgement on their relation to Cypriote ware.

[1] Ohnefalsch-Richter, *K.B.H.* Pl. XVIII; Dussaud, *Civ. Préhell.*[2] p. 349. Oberhummer continued to adhere to the cult-monument theory (see *O.K.* 82 f., where other references are given). These are not the only oil-presses to be consecrated; Myres, *C.C.M.* p. 14, n. 3, reminds us that megalithic Roman oil-presses in Tripoli were once taken for temples.

[2] L. Ross, *Arch. Ztg.* IX, 1851, p. 327, Pl. XXVIII; Ohnefalsch-Richter, *ibid.* XXXIX, 1881, p. 313, Pl. XVIII; Jeffery in *Archaeologia*, LXVI, 1915, p. 170; Oberhummer, *Kition* in *R.E.* XI, 1921, 544, with other references.

[3] First mentioned by the pilgrim Ludolf (1336–41, *M.L.H.* II. p. 214; Cobham, *Exc. Cypr.* p. 20). Illustrations in Unger-Kotschy, *Die Insel Cypern*, 1865, p. 534; Ohnefalsch-Richter in *J.H.S.* IV, 1883, pp. 111–16, Pls. 33, 34. The full investigation by Myres, *Archaeologia*, LXVI, 1915, pp. 179–94 (cp. Jeffery, *ibid.* pp. 171–4) was unknown to Oberhummer, *Salamis* in *R.E.* I A, 1920, 1841, where otherwise full references to earlier literature will be found.

[4] During the invasion of Cyprus by Muawiya in A.D. 647, 648 or 649, the lady Umm Haram, a relation of the prophet, died of a fall from her mule and was buried here. A legend resembling that of the House of Loreto attaches to the stones. Cobham in *Journ. R. Asiatic Soc.* 1897, pp. 81–101; *O.K.* 83; Gunnis, p. 120 (the date incorrect). See also M.L. *H.* I, p. 87, and below, chap. XII. Mariti (*Viaggi*, 1769, I, p. 179) says that until 1760 there was only a small Turkish oratory there, but that next year Ali Aga, the governor, built the mosque.

CHAPTER III

THE BRONZE AGE[1]

I. THE REMAINS

(*See Map at p.* 24)

More precise datings than are possible in the Neolithic period are attempted when we come to the Bronze Age. The scheme generally adopted is on the pattern of that which is accepted for Crete and the Greek mainland, but in accordance with what has been said in the preceding chapter, the beginning of the Bronze (Copper) Age is dated later by some 400 or 500 years.[2] We thus have:

	B.C.
Early Cypriote I	2600–2100
,, ,, II	
,, ,, III	
Middle ,, I	2100–1900
,, ,, II	1900–1750
,, ,, III	1750–1600

[1] This chapter, like the preceding, owes more to the generous help of Prof. Sidney Smith than can be adequately acknowledged. Many of his suggestions have been bodily incorporated. I am also indebted for many valuable criticisms to Mr R. D. Barnett, who read the first draft of the chapter.

[2] Gjerstad, *Studies on Prehistoric Cyprus* (*S.P.C.*), p. 335 (with 3000 B.C. as the beginning). Acknowledgment may be made here once for all to this, which is still the most systematic outline of the remains of Bronze Age Cyprus. Gjerstad's scheme corresponds roughly with the most recent scheme for Syria-Palestine (Early Bronze or, rather, Copper Age, 3000–2000; Middle Bronze, 2000–1550; Late Bronze, 1550–1100). See Schaeffer in *Syria*, XVI, 1935, p. 208. In what follows the term Bronze Age is used for the whole stretch from 2600 to 1000; the earlier phase, to about 2100 B.C., is more correctly described as the Copper Age, when the implements "owe their hardness to the presence of copper oxide, not of tin" (Myres, *H.C.C.* p. xxix). Analyses of a certain number of bronzes from Cyprus are given by Dussaud, *Civ. Préhell.*[2] pp. 252 ff. See also p. 27, n. 2. For the history of the pottery of Cyprus, after a beginning had been made by Sandwith, the foundations were scientifically laid by Myres and Ohnefalsch-Richter, *C.C.M.* A later classification by Gjerstad, Union Académique Internationale, *Classification des Céramiques ant.*, *Classification of Cypriote Pottery*, 1931. Still more recent, in general outlines, Schaeffer, *Miss.* 1936, pp. 108 ff.

Late Cypriote I } 1600–1400
" " II } 1400–1200[1]
" " III } 1200–1000

These dates must of course be taken with a considerable margin for possible error, since they are for the most part derived from contacts with systems which have been worked out in other regions, especially Egypt, Crete and the Greek mainland, and are themselves only approximate. For instance, views differ by a century about the end of the Late Helladic III period, some putting it about 1200, others about 1100.[2] On that date depends the beginning which we assign to Late Cypriote III, since that is the period in which imports into Cyprus from Greece practically ceased owing to the drying up of the source of supply.

With this warning another may be coupled, and that is that a certain lag may be observed in the development of Cyprus throughout its history.[3] We have already noticed this in connexion with the dating of the end of the Neolithic Age. It is a general rule that peoples who receive but do not originate do not begin to imitate foreign models until the supply of those models from the countries producing them falls off. When Mycenaean ware ceased to be imported into Cyprus, the island began to produce its own ware, the so-called "sub-Mycenaean". Motives which have disappeared elsewhere survive here, just as more than two thousand years later zigzag and dog-tooth mouldings survived in the architecture of Cyprus long after they had been given up in the lands of their origin. It may be that this tendency to survival is partly due to the fact that—so far as we know—the cultural development of Cyprus was never broken, as for instance was that of Crete, where the civilization was suddenly destroyed twice.[4] But this lack of historical disturbance can only have confirmed a conservatism which must have been inherent in the people.

The distribution of the population[5] in the Bronze Age seems to have differed somewhat from that in the Stone or Chalcolithic Age. In both

[1] J. F. Daniel (*Amer. Journ. Arch.* XLII, 1938, p. 269) is inclined to make L.C. II end in the third, and L.C. III begin in the last, quarter of the thirteenth century B.C.

[2] See Gjerstad, *S.P.C.* p. 330, n. 3.

[3] If, owing to its geographical position, it received Oriental impulses earlier than the Aegean (cp. V. Müller, *Frühe Plastik in Griechenland und Vorderasien*, p. 166), it was for the same reason behind the times in assimilating Greek impulses.

[4] Casson, p. 3. He assumes, however, as we have seen, a complete disruption between the Neolithic and Early Bronze Age.

[5] What has been said on the craniology of the Bronze and later Ages in Cyprus is so

periods sites were inhabited in the south coastal fringes, and on the slopes of the higher (western) part of the northern range. But in the Bronze Age none are marked in the extreme west where a number of sites had been inhabited earlier, while they are numerous in the Karpass, which is blank for the preceding period. Bronze Age sites are also much thicker in the area between the mountain ranges. The sites occupied were still, however, mostly on the flanks of the highlands, the highlands themselves being too much exposed, and the plains in many parts too thickly wooded, for primitive habitation.[1]

The strongest springs[2] are found on the flanks of the northern range, at the junction of the limestone and the overlying sandstones or marls. In their neighbourhood settlements may be looked for. The seaside would naturally also attract settlers, but more especially when overseas traffic increased.

The Bronze Age sites are usually on the sloping ground of a hill-side or on the top of a small plateau, the arable area below being reserved for agriculture. The population was mainly pastoral and agricultural. But the fortresses show that life was not always peaceful; although the use of the bow and arrow seems to have been little, if at all, known.[3]

---

inconclusive and based on so scanty materials that little more can be done here than refer to the two comparatively recent publications which I have noticed on the subject: L. H. Dudley Buxton, "Anthropology of Cyprus", in *Journ. R. Anthrop. Inst.* L, 1920, pp. 183–235 (unfinished) and C. M. Fürst, "Zur Kenntnis der Anthropologie der prähist. Bevölkerung der Insel Cypern", in *Lunds Univ. Årsskr.* N.F. 2, Bd. XXIX, Lund, 1933. Cp. also Myres, *Who were the Greeks?* 1930, pp. 59 f.; Georgiades, *K.K.* pp. 42–64. All that need be said here is that the craniological evidence, so far as it is intelligible, does not seem to contradict the archaeological, since it shows that while in the Bronze Age the Asiatic element predominates, and while the mesocranic skulls from Enkomi and A. Iakovos show analogies with those of Argolis, pointing to the settling of Greeks in those places as early as the fourteenth century (Georgiades, *K.K.* p. 54), in the Iron Age the long-skulled (Mediterranean?) race increases. There is also in the Bronze Age evidence of artificial deformation of the skull; one peculiar fashion of this is strongly represented at Enkomi and may have originated there. (The latest excavations at Khirokitia show that deformation was practised in the preceding period.) Earlier speculations on the primitive ethnology of the island are summarized by Dussaud, *Civ. Préhell.*[2] pp. 449 ff. Recent discoveries of the Neolithic culture of Cyprus, viewed in the light of excavations in Anatolia and northern Syria, render all these speculations futile.

[1] Gjerstad, *S.P.C.* p. 17.

[2] Unger und Kotschy, p. 69.

[3] Bronze arrow-heads of Mycenaean age from Enkomi: Murray, Smith and Walters, *Excavations in Cyprus*, p. 16, fig. 28; *C.C.M.* p. 184, no. 25. Dussaud (*Civ. Préhell.*[2] p. 266) thinks some bronze objects described as awls (*C.C.M.* p. 53, nos. 565–71) may be arrow-heads.

CYPRUS

○ Stone Age Sites
■ Bronze Age Sites
Contours

Scales

0 5 10 15 20 25
English Miles

0 5 10 15 20 25 30 35 40
Kilometres

Petra tou Limniti
Pomos
1000
Leuka
Yialia
Katydhata
Linou
2000
4000
3000
Peristerona
Meladhia
4619
Trimithousa
Philousa
Terra
3000
4000
6403
A. Anargyri
5000
2000
Kedhares
1000
Ktima
2000
1000
Kouklia
Sotira
Episkopi
Erimi
Curium
Asomato

Vasilia
Lapithos
Karavas
Kerynia
A. Epiktitos
Troulli
Melandryna
Bellapais
Aghirda
Vounous
Krini
Dikomo
Kephalovryso
Kythrea
Trypimeni
Psilatos
Milea
Marathovouno
A. Iak
Trikomo
Chrysiliou
Nicosia
A. Paraskevi
Leondari Vouno
Dhenia
Kokkini Trimithia
Paleometokhi
Meniko
Laksha
Yeri
Phoenichais
A. Sozomenos
Anayia
Nikolidhes
Potamia
Politiko
Pera
Dali
Alambra
Lymbia
Sinda
Enkom
Kalopsida
Pyla
Xylotymbo
Larnaka
Hala Sultan Tekke
Klavdia
Arpera
Dromolaksha
Kiti
Khirokitia
Alaminos
Kalavaso
Psemmatismeno
Maroni
Pyrgos
Moni
Mari
Pendaskino
Zarukas
1000
2000
3000
4000
4659
5098
2427
2430
3067
2374

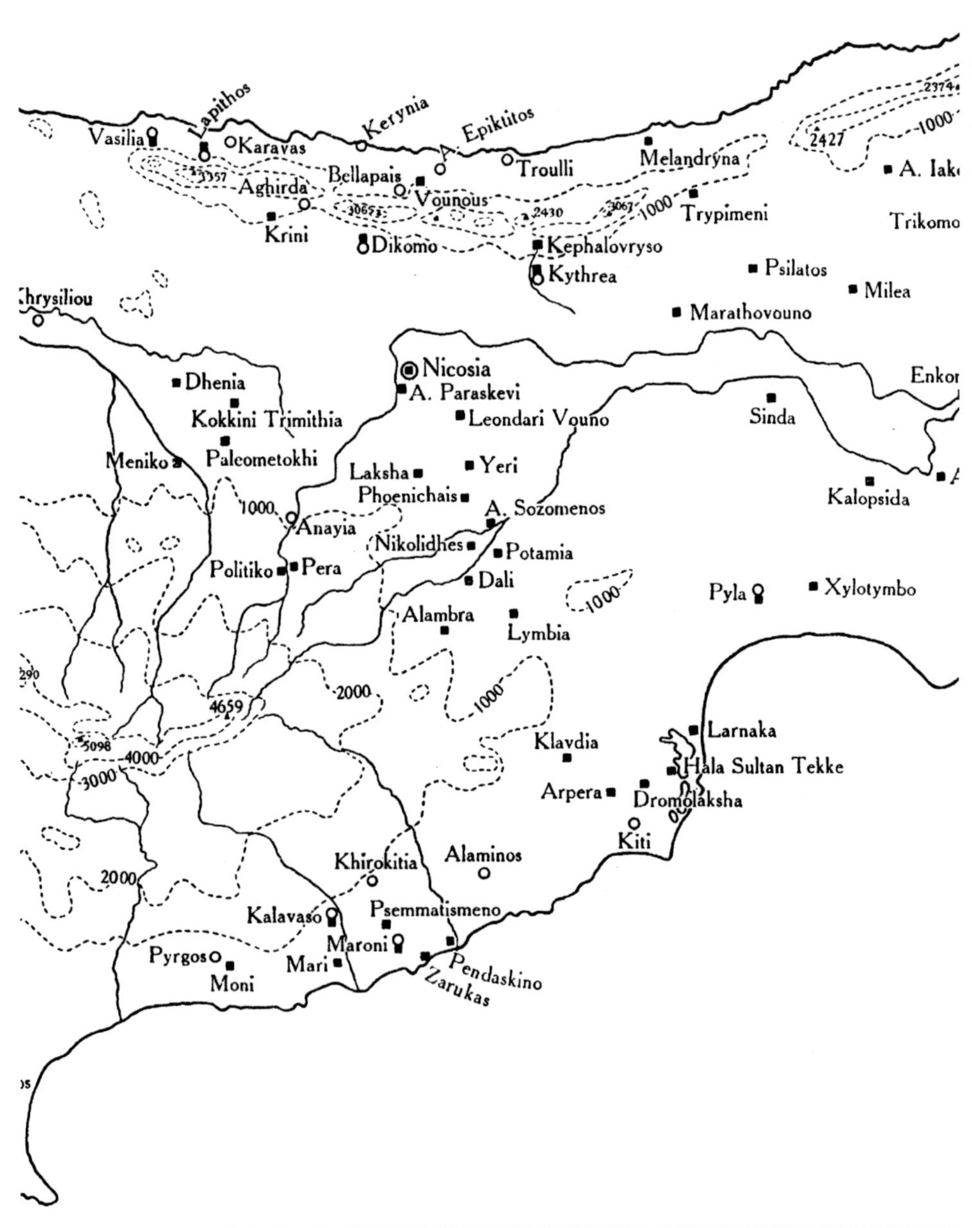
Vasilia
Lapithos
Karavas
Kerynia
A. Epiktitos
Troulli
Melandryna
Bellapais
Aghirda
Vounous
Krini
Dikomo
Trypimeni
Kephalovryso
Kythrea
Psilatos
Milea
Marathovouno
A. Iak
Trikomo
2427
1000
2430
1000
Nicosia
A. Paraskevi
Leondari Vouno
Dhenia
Kokkini Trimithia
Paleometokhi
Meniko
Laksha
Yeri
Phoenichais
A. Sozomenos
Anayia
1000
Nikolidhes
Potamia
Politiko
Pera
Dali
Alambra
Lymbia
Sinda
Enkor
Kalopsida
Pyla
Xylotymbo
1000
2000
1000
4659
4000
3000
2000
Klavdia
Larnaka
Hala Sultan Tekke
Arpera
Dromolaksha
Kiti
Khirokitia
Alaminos
Kalavaso
Psemmatismeno
Maroni
Pyrgos
Moni
Mari
Pendaskino
Zarukas

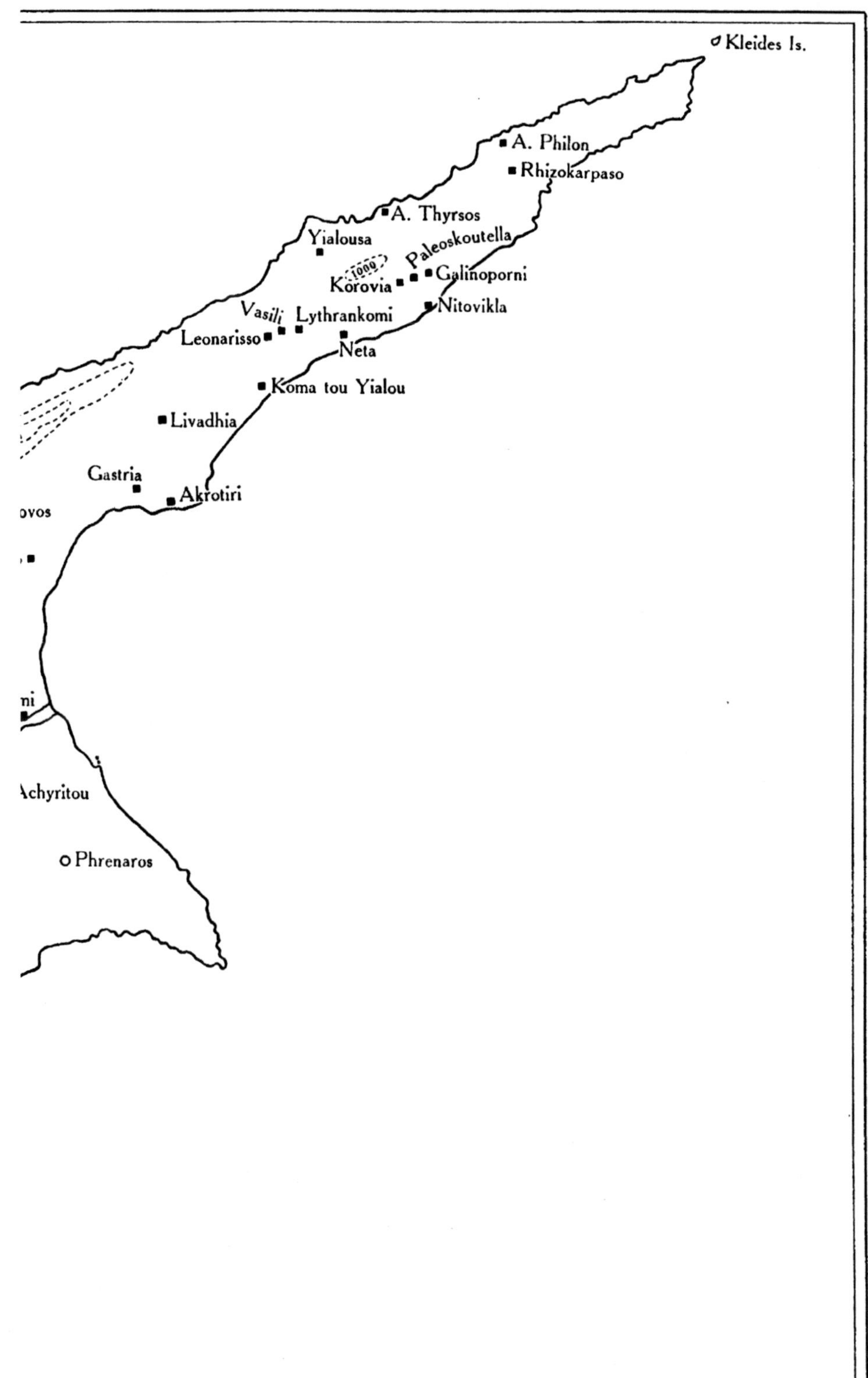

Kleides Is.
A. Philon
Rhizokarpaso
A. Thyrsos
Yialousa
Paleoskoutella
1000
Korovia
Galinoporni
Nitovikla
Vasili
Lythrankomi
Leonarisso
Neta
Koma tou Yialou
Livadhia
Gastria
Akrotiri
Achyritou
Phrenaros

The architecture of the Bronze Age, so far as can be judged from the few foundations remaining, shows an advance on the usually if not always circular constructions of the Neolithic men. The foundations of the walls were of small stones; the upper portions, now lost, are supposed to have been of sun-dried bricks, and plastered inside; the roof probably supported by beams and, as in some modern houses, covered with branches or clay-stiffened straw.[1] The plan is more or less rectangular; and there were larger houses containing a number of rooms. Something like a fortress, perhaps of more than one floor, has been excavated at Nikolidhes, north of Dali, and another noted 3 km. to the north-east; while in a third at Nitovikla in the Karpass an upper floor is also indicated.[2] At Idalium throughout the Late Cypriote III period the Western Acropolis was protected by a massive rampart of mud-brick on a stone foundation.[3]

The tombs[4] in which the dead were buried were of two main types, cavities sunk direct in the earth or rock, or chamber-tombs, caverns also sunk in earth or rock but entered not directly, but either through a small doorway from a vertical shaft, or else from a long inclined cutting or *dromos*, sometimes with roughly cut steps. The plan of the tombs sometimes approaches the rectangular, but is most usually round or oval. These chamber-tombs are again of three kinds: cave-tombs with a slightly curved or flat roof; *tholos*-tombs with a beehive-shaped roof; and built tombs, or cave-tombs which are lined with masonry. But the kinds, as enumerated, do not represent development in time, though

---

[1] The practice of building on a foundation and lower courses of stone, the rest being of sun-dried brick, and roofing with beams supporting reeds covered with clay, is noticed by Mariti (*Viaggi*, I, 1769, pp. 68 f.), who observes that such buildings resist earthquake shocks better than houses all of stone. Mud-brick on stone foundation was common in western Asia and is found sporadically both in time and place; as not only in Assyria, where stone can be obtained easily, but also in Babylonia, where it had to be dragged great distances. There is evidence of the use of mud-brick construction on the "Neolithic" site of Khirokitia.

[2] *S.C.E.* I, pp. 371 ff. Schaeffer in *Syria*, XVI, 1935, p. 210, thinks Nitovikla may represent a last stand of the natives against the Achaean invasion. The excavators, however, date it in the seventeenth–sixteenth centuries B.C., though a second occupation went on to the fifteenth century (Schaeffer, *Miss.* p. 63).

[3] *S.C.E.* II, p. 626.

[4] A very important cemetery has been explored at Vounous near Bellapais (Dikaios in *I.L.N.* 31 Oct. 1931, 5 Dec. 1931, 10 Dec. 1932; Schaeffer, *ibid.* 16 Feb. 1935 and *Miss.* pp. 30–48), with remarkable pottery illustrating the religion of the early Bronze Age people, of which later.

as might be expected the built tombs seem to belong to the latest period of the age. As to burial customs, there is no evidence of cremation; traces of fire which have been observed indicate burnt offerings. We shall return later to the nature of these offerings which were made to the dead.

In the first of the three main chronological divisions, Early, Middle and Late Cypriote, together with the continued use of stone axe-heads, mace-heads and corn-bruisers, and pottery (especially the red-polished ware), copper implements appear from the beginning, becoming more various and advanced in type as time goes on. The pottery is hand-made; in fact wheel-made native pottery is very rarely found until the end of the Bronze Age. Terracotta is also used for corn-bruisers and spindle-whorls, and, towards the end, for idols, when also the first jewellery appears in the shape of copper rings, beads of white paste, and even gold and silver ornaments.[1] The silver of Bronze Age Cyprus is usually, though not always,[2] largely alloyed with lead—presumably a natural alloy.

The relation of the pottery of the Copper Age to that of the preceding phase remains to be worked out. Before the discovery of the earlier sites described above, it was thought that the art of pottery was introduced in the Copper Age in a fully developed stage from the mainland. The reason for this view was that though it exactly resembled in its fabric the pottery of pre-dynastic Egypt, the shapes were closely imitated from gourds and skin-vessels, suggesting that hitherto the people had used not pottery but perishable containers.[3] Now, however, the discoveries at Erimi and elsewhere show the existence of plentiful pottery in the later Neolithic or at any rate Chalcolithic period, and that not only in the uppermost layers. There are, nevertheless, as already remarked (p. 18), differences between the Neolithic and Early Bronze Age wares; the former have painted patterns, the latter incised; the latter have shapes reminiscent of other objects than pottery, such as gourds, while the former have bases, and so on.[4] There were differences between the cul-

---

[1] The gold spirals from an Early Cypriote III tomb at Lapithos are claimed to be the earliest gold found in Cyprus. Gjerstad in *Antiquity*, II, 1928, pp. 189 f.; *S.C.E.* I, p. 148, nos. 29–31: no. 32 in the same tomb was a lump of iron.

[2] Gjerstad, *S.P.C.* pp. 248 f.

[3] Myres, *H.C.C.* p. xxviii. On the survival of gourd-shaped pottery in modern Cyprus, see Casson, pp. 4–5.

[4] Casson, pp. 32 f. So in western Asia the incised pattern is at first used in con-

tures, also; thus burial in or immediately near houses was superseded by burial in cemeteries. It is noticeable, too, that the "Stone Age" sites rarely continued to be inhabited into the "Bronze Age", so far as the evidence of excavations up to the present goes. If, then, there was not a gap in time between the two cultures, there must have been a displacement of population, or an invasion by a new people.

The metal implements and weapons[1] found at Vounous are not the work of an infant industry. That the industry was native, and that the objects were not imported, is thought probable owing to the prevalence of the characteristic Cypriote dagger-blade (or lance-head), with tang ending in a hook which was sometimes riveted through the handle. In this period, although unalloyed copper continued to be used for objects such as tweezers, weapons such as those described show a skilful alloy of copper with antimony and tin. If these weapons are of native manufacture, it must follow that, from whatever source the materials for the alloy may have been imported, the copper industry was well developed during the Early Cypriote period.[2]

Such foreign relations as may be conjectured[3]—and the conjectures must be chiefly based on resemblances in pottery—seem to have been mainly with Syria. Red-polished ware closely resembling the hemi-

---

junction with the earlier painted patterns; as painted decoration dies out, incised patterns come to be used alone, and then die out too. "But the difference is not that between Neolithic and early Bronze, but merely marks a stage in the increasing use of metal" (Sidney Smith).

[1] See especially Schaeffer, *Miss.* pp. 38–48 and in *Syria*, XIX, 1938, p. 219. Blades fastened with rivets were in use alongside with tanged blades, the former probably for knives, the latter for daggers and lances. The supposed occurrence of Cypriote daggers in European Bronze Age sites is a myth. For the method of attaching the tanged blade to the hilt, see G. B. Gardner in *Bull. de la Soc. Préhist. Française*, no. 12, 1937; *Vaabenhistoriske Aarbøger*, Copenhagen, II b, 1938, pp. 145–51.

[2] Copper was exported from Cyprus not only in the form of the well-known ingots, but also, when transport was easy (as to Syria), in the form of ore. Some pieces of ore found at Ras Shamra have been shown by analysis to be Cypriote (Schaeffer, *Miss.* pp. 98–100). But the date of these specimens is Late Bronze Age, fourteenth–thirteenth centuries; there is no proof here for the Early Cypriote periods. Antimony must have come from Anatolian or North Syrian sources (R. Campbell Thompson, *Dict. of Assyrian Chemistry*, p. 116).

[3] The chaos of speculation about the relations between Cyprus and other lands in the Bronze Age is well described by Gjerstad, *S.P.C.*, especially p. 298. The neat picture of the unified culture, with the Second City of Troy as its focus, which was supposed to exist all over Asia Minor, and to take in Cyprus, may be seen displayed in Ed.

spherical bowls common at Vounous has been found in level III at Ras Shamra immediately below the level which contained the monuments of

---

Meyer, *Gesch. d. Alt.*[2] 1909, I, ii, pp. 668 f. In general it seems most in accordance with the teaching of history to regard Cyprus as less a base or centre of radiation than a transmitter.—As to Mesopotamia, the evidence for an invasion of Cyprus by Sargon of Agade about 2650 B.C. is difficult to assess. The idea that KU(G).KI, the tin-land, to which Sargon claimed to have extended his empire (quoted from Sayce by Peake, *Bronze Age*, p. 41) was Cyprus might have been worth consideration had it produced tin. In any case the reading is disputed, and the meaning of the word uncertain (Albright in *Journ. Am. Or. Soc.* XLV, 1925, p. 236). Yet, as Sidney Smith observes, the text contains a tradition that a Sargon, probably he of Agade, did cross the Mediterranean to two different lands, one Kaptara, the other of uncertain reading (*Early Hist. of Assyria*, p. 89). The late Assyrian version of the Omens says that Sargon "crossed the *western* sea and in the third year in the west his hand subdued [all the lands]". His Chronicle, however, says "he crossed the *eastern* sea and in the eleventh year his hand subdued the western land to its uttermost limit". It would seem that a tradition, earlier than the fourteenth century B.C., is behind the "Sea of the West" (S. Smith, *op. cit.* p. 84); and Naram-Sin certainly got as far as the Syrian coast. There may then have been an expedition to Cyprus, but it is unlikely that it amounted to more than a raid. A cylinder attributed to Sargon, found in Cyprus (Ward, *Seal Cylinders of Western Asia*, no. 181) proves, as Myres remarks (*C.C.M.* p. 20), nothing as to the upward date of the connexion; such cylinders passed from hand to hand and could be worn as amulets ages after they were made (Dussaud, *Civ. Préhell.*[2] pp. 272 f.). For example, an impression of a pre-Kassite cylinder seal of the end of the third millennium B.C. has been found on a sherd of L.C. II black slip ware of the thirteenth century B.C. (J. F. Daniel in *Amer. Journ. Arch.* XLII, 1938, p. 266). Therefore, *pace* Demargne (in *Ann. Éc. des Hautes Etudes de Gand*, II, 1938, p. 49), the significance of such cylinders may be over-estimated. The cylinder-seal (Myres, *H.C.C.* no. 4300) with the name of "Mâr-Ishtar, son of Ilu-bani, servant of the god Naram-Sin" (who has been identified with the grandson of Sargon) is proved by its style and technique to be of Syro-Cappadocian workmanship and not much earlier than the First Dynasty of Babylon (see King, *Sumer and Akkad*, p. 343; Hall's dating to the seventh century, *Oldest Civil. of Greece*, p. 113, must be a slip). The gold-mounted seal from the Bronze Age deposit at Ayia Paraskevi may be definitely dated to the same period. A cylinder with the name of Bin-gali-Sharri, grandson of Sargon, is also said to have been found in Cyprus. Beyond such isolated cylinders (the presence of which in the island, we repeat, is in any case no proof of occupation) there is no trace of early Babylonian influence in Cyprus. Of the Enkomi cylinders (H. B. Walters, *Br. Mus. Catal. of Engr. Gems*, 1926, pp. 14 ff.), only two are purely Babylonian, of the First Dynasty; and the others, excepting a few rude native Cypriote ones, are Syro-Cappadocian and Hittite importations. See L. W. King, *op. cit.* pp. 343 f. The earliest cylinder of which the discovery is scientifically attested (in a Middle Cypriote tomb) is dated by Ward to about 2000 B.C. (Ward, *op. cit.* no. 1159; Dussaud, *op. cit.* pp. 273 f.). On the other hand, cylinders are not found in deposits later than about 1000 B.C. (Ward, *op. cit.* p. 346, citing Ohnefalsch-Richter). The terracotta figurines of the so-called nude nature-goddess, on which Meyer (*op. cit.*

the Twelfth Dynasty; it is therefore to be dated to the end of the third millennium. This ware was separated by barren strata, and then by thick layers of coarse pottery, from the lowest portion of level III, which goes back to the beginning of the third millennium. Hence this red-polished ware at Ras Shamra can hardly be earlier than about 2500, and ceased to be used before the beginning of the Twelfth Dynasty, about 2000 B.C. This is roughly the period assigned to the similar pottery of Vounous.[1] Egyptian beads also show that communications were being opened with Syria, for it was probably thence, and not directly from Egypt, that the current of trade came.[2] Conversely, Cypriote pottery of the same period has been found in Syria. Generally speaking, partly perhaps because there are better harbours on the east and south-east coasts of Cyprus than on the north, Cypriote trade, in antiquity as in the Middle Ages, tended to be attracted towards the Syrian coast rather than to Asia Minor.[3]

At the same time, contemporaneity, if not direct connexion, of Vounous with Troy II may be illustrated by a "face-urn" from one of the tombs at the former.[4]

A solitary instance of an imported vase alleged to be Cretan is recorded for this period.[5] It is attributed to the third Early Minoan period, and was found in a tomb at Lapithos by the American excavators. Like the Middle Minoan vases which were imported into Cyprus in the next age, it does not prove direct contact with Crete.

In the Middle Cypriote period (approximately 2100–1600 B.C.) we are in the full Bronze Age, that is to say bronze is predominant for im-

---

p. 474) lays stress, do not show Babylonian influence; what Eastern strain is observable seems to be mainly Syrian (*C.C.M.* p. 27; cp. *Who were the Greeks?* p. 226). These are not cult-figures, and prove only the wide diffusion of magic (Sidney Smith).

[1] Schaeffer, *Miss.* pp. 36–7.

[2] Gjerstad, *S.P.C.* p. 302 ("faïence beads"). He apparently here, and on p. 305 (see p. 30, n. 2), does not distinguish between paste and faïence.

[3] Cp. Schaeffer, *Miss.* pp. 114–15. H. Frankfort (R. Anthr. Inst., *Studies in Early Pottery*, II, 1927, pp. 78–84) notes that the new technique of the White Painted ware, which first appears in Cyprus towards the end of the Early Cypriote period, is strikingly like the painted wares which existed in early days in Syria and Palestine.

[4] Schaeffer, *Miss.* p. 38. He accepts Dussaud's date of 2400–1900 for Troy II.

[5] Casson, p. 207. The vase was found in 1931, and recently identified by Myres as Early Minoan III. It is in the Museum at Nicosia. It is at present, to say the least, doubtful that Cyprus was already comprised in the sphere of Cretan trade (as Schaeffer says, *Syria*, XIX, 1938, p. 250, n. 2).

plements. Stone implements are still, however, in use, often preserving styles derived from the previous period. Foreign wares are imported from Syria. Silver becomes commoner, and gold continues to appear. Paste or faïence beads in great numbers, spindle-whorls of steatite, and bone implements are other characteristics of this period.

The foreign relations which began in the preceding period are extended and become more lively. There is no sign of direct communication with the West. But it was a time of racial movements in the Near East, such as that which led to the establishment of the Hyksos in Egypt. It is probable that the island did not escape invasion; there are indications at Nitovikla and Paleoskoutella of such troubles.[1] Cypriote pottery was sent to Palestine, perhaps to Syria, and to Egypt (although it seems that Egyptian pottery did not find its way to Cyprus). In return, Syria and Palestine sent masses of their pottery, and Egypt its beads.[2] Whether contact with Egypt was direct, we cannot say. But it could have been made through Syria, with which Egypt had a great deal to do at the end of the Twelfth Dynasty.

In the Late Cypriote period (1600–1000 B.C.) the island evidently became very prosperous. There was not much change in the types of the bronze instruments in use, but towards the end the approach of the next age is heralded by the occasional intrusion of iron instruments. In stone, just as in the Middle Cypriote period, when Early Cypriote types were retained, so now the fashions of the preceding period survive; development is apt to be slower in stone than in the more plastic materials. The precious metals, especially gold, are found in quantities; gems appear for the first time; we have beads of cornelian and lapis lazuli. The middle of the period (about 1400–1200) was the richest, if the tombs of Enkomi are a fair guide, in the abundance of gold and silversmithery, faïence and glass vases, gems, cylinders, seals, vases of steatite and alabaster, which the excavations have revealed.

In the sixteenth and fifteenth centuries the relations with Syria are illustrated by a bichrome pottery, painted in red and dark brown or black on buff slip, best known from the Bronze Age cemetery of Milea, near Leukoniko, which seems to have been imported from Syria (or

---

[1] Cp. Schaeffer in *Syria*, XIX, 1938, p. 238. He suggests that the red-on-black ware so prevalent in Cyprus from the end of the eighteenth and in the seventeenth century was perhaps not of Cypriote origin, because it is found at places like Nitovikla and Paleoskoutella, which present features not familiar in Cyprus. For Paleoskoutella, see below, chap. IV, p. 63 f.

[2] Gjerstad, *S.P.C.* p. 305 ("paste beads").

made in Cyprus in imitation of the foreign ware).[1] But the relations with Syria, Palestine and Egypt reached their maximum frequency in the middle of the period. Ras Shamra (Ugarit),[2] or rather Minat-al-Baidha (the "White Harbour", Leukos Limen, of the *Stadiasmus*), is the first Syrian landfall after leaving C. St Andreas. At Ras Shamra, in the second half of the second millennium, there was intruded a veritable Aegean and more particularly Cypriote colony. The population of this colony were not Semites, like the natives of Ugarit themselves, but were strongly impregnated with the culture of Cyprus, the Aegean or Mycenae, even if they did not actually come thence. Their skulls are mostly of the "Mediterranean" type, such as are also found in Mycenaean tombs at Enkomi. Ras Shamra was destroyed late in the Mycenaean Age, first by the Sea-Raiders; it seems to have been unimportant or non-existent in the time of Tiglathpileser I (about 1100–1070).

Excavation and soundings at the mouth of the Orontes have yielded indications of a settlement earlier than the Iron Age, which may well have been comparable to Ras Shamra.[3] Sir Leonard Woolley's recent excavations at Atchana (the ancient Alalakh), farther up the Orontes, have shown, from the finds in the palace, that the milk-bowls, hitherto supposed to be peculiar to Cyprus, were also made on the mainland, in the late fifteenth–early fourteenth century, but which factory had the priority cannot yet be determined.[4]

---

[1] Schaeffer, *Miss.* pp. 50–58. Characteristic is the metope decoration with the "Union Jack" pattern. Recently Heurtley (in *Qu. Dept. of Ant. Pal.* VIII, 1938, pp. 21–37) makes out a case for these two-colour vases of zone and metope style, with bird and fish decoration, dated about 1600–1500, being the work of a Palestinian painter or painters. They are wheel-made, and Cyprus at this time did not use the wheel.

[2] See especially the various communications by C. F. A. Schaeffer and R. Dussaud in *Syria*, X, 1929, pp. 285 f., XII, 1931, pp. 65 f., XIV, 1933, pp. 101 f., XV, 1934, pp. 120 f., XVI, 1935, pp. 162 f., 208 f., XVII, 1936, pp. 108 f.; Dussaud, *Les découvertes de Ras-Shamra (Ugarit) et l'Ancien Testament*, 1937; Schaeffer, *The Cuneiform Texts of Ras Shamra-Ugarit* (Brit. Acad. Schweich Lectures, 1939), p. 19.

[3] L. Woolley in *Antiquaries Journal*, XVII, 1937, pp. 1 ff. If there was a Mycenaean settlement at al Mina, it has been washed away; but Sabouni, three miles up the river, goes back to the Mycenaean Age, though the nature of the site prevents it from repaying excavation. The statement of the French excavators that the mouth of the Orontes was not a safe anchorage in early times is not borne out by Woolley (see *J.H.S.* LVIII, 1938, p. 3).

[4] In *The Times*, 3 Sept. 1938, p. 12 (cp. *Ant. Journ.* XIX, 1939, p. 31), on the evidence of a single sherd found under the foundations of the oldest city-wall, Sir Leonard Woolley gives the mainland a priority of three centuries. On the "law of the single

A remarkable if confused echo of this connexion between Cyprus and the Syrian coast in the Mycenaean Age is preserved in the legend[1] that Casos son of Inachus (thus connecting Mt Casius with the Argolid) married Amyce, also called Cit(t)ia, the daughter of Salaminus, king of Cyprus, and with her there came to Syria men of Cyprus and dwelt on the acropolis. Casos had also allowed Cretans to settle on the acropolis. Descendants[2] of these Cretans and Cypriotes were transplanted by Seleucus to his foundation Antioch on the Orontes.[3]

But we may trace Cypriote commerce with regions farther east than Syria. It has been observed that among the fine ceramic ware with polychrome glaze, probably contemporary with the Eighteenth and Nineteenth Egyptian Dynasties, found at Ashur, there is some (as, for instance, a rhyton in the shape of a woman's head) from the same manufactory as that which has been found at Enkomi.[4]

Cypriote pottery also found its way to Egypt,[5] commonly in the form of small narrow-necked jugs (*bilbils*) for ointment; and the contact with

---

sherd", which seems to apply here, see Rhys Carpenter in *Amer. Journ. Arch.* XLII, 1938, p. 59.

[1] Pausanias Damasc. fr. 4, *F.H.G.* IV, p. 469b; Engel, *Kypros*, I, 1841, pp. 241 f.; Dussaud in *Syria*, X, 1929, pp. 301 f.; Evans, quoted by Woolley, *Ant. Journ.* XVII, pp. 13 f.; Dussaud, *Découvertes de Ras Shamra*, pp. 23 f.

[2] Not contemporary Cypriotes, as Chapot seems to think (*Mélanges Cagnat*, p. 61, n. 3).

[3] Amyce is thus the personification of the Am(u)k plain (Woolley, as above, p. 14), as it is called as early as the fourteenth century B.C. in the Amarna Letters. This neighbourhood has topographically a better founded claim than Ras Shamra to connexion with the legend quoted in the text.

[4] H. R. Hall in *C.A.H.* II, p. 430 note: "Did it come to Enkomi and to Ashur from a common source, perhaps in Cilicia or Northern Syria?" Cp. his *Civil. of Greece in the Bronze Age*, 1928, pp. 225–6 and art. in *J.H.S.* XLVIII, 1928, pp. 64–74; S. Smith, *Early Hist. of Assyria*, pp. 226, 332. The Enkomi rhyton is figured in *Excav. Cypr.* Pl. III; Dussaud, *Civ. Préhell.*[2] p. 246. Vases from the same factory have since been found in Palestine (*Pal. Qu.* IV, Pls. XXVII–XXIX, Tall Abu Hawām) and Ras Shamra (*Syria*, XIV, pp. 105–6, Pls. XI, XII). Marinatos (*Arch. Anzeiger*, XLIII, 1928, 534–54) takes all these faïence objects to be Assyrian; Casson (1937, p. 55) is quite satisfied of their Cypriote origin. In any case we have evidence of trade relations between Cyprus and Assyria, though not necessarily direct.

[5] Cypriote models were imitated in Egyptian paste and alabaster for re-export to the Aegean: Gjerstad, *S.P.C.* 323. Some pots from Kahun bear the same kind of marks painted under the foot, resembling signs of the Cypriote syllabary, as are found on the vases of Mycenaean style from Cyprus and Ras Shamra (Schaeffer, *Miss.* p. 79).

Egypt is further illustrated by the finds of Egyptian objects in tombs in Cyprus.[1] At Enkomi were found a scarab of Tiy, the queen of Amenhotep III, and a silver ring of his son Amenhotep IV Akhenaton, giving dates in the first third of the fourteenth century; a necklace of a type which is said not to occur more than a century after the latter king's time; and various other scarabs of the Eighteenth and Nineteenth Dynasties. The most recent scarabs found at Enkomi belong to the time of Ramses III (first quarter of the twelfth century). No Mycenaean pottery occurs in the tombs which contain these Ramesside scarabs. The Enkomi datings are confirmed by evidence from other places, such as Curium.

The relations between Cyprus and the West must also have been direct. Cypriote ware found its way to Thera and Melos and even to Athens and Peloponnese,[2] Late Helladic and Minoan pottery to Cyprus,[3] although the last may have come by a roundabout way, since no Cypriote vases seem to occur in Crete. The amount of pottery of the Late Helladic period which went to Cyprus or was made there in the middle of the Late Cypriote period was very great. By this time the copper mines were in full working and in exchange for its pottery the West was drawing on the island for its copper.[4] This then was the acme of prehistoric Cyprus; the island was a lively centre of Levantine exchange.

It is still a hotly disputed question how far the "Cypro-Mycenaean" wares of this period are rightly so-called, that is to say whether they were made by Cypriote potters under Mycenaean influence, or im-

---

[1] See D. Fimmen, *Kretisch-Mykenische Kultur*, Liepzig u. Berlin, 1921, pp. 177–80, for a summary and a useful determination of the amount of reliance that can be placed on scarabs. In this connexion it may be noted that the so-called Tell el-Yahudiye pottery, for which Junker has claimed a Nubian origin, and which would, if he were right, prove relations between Cyprus and Egypt at least as early as 1600 B.C., is probably of Asiatic origin, nor is it certain that it goes back as early as the Twelfth Dynasty; although Starkey thought he had found evidence in Palestine of its being late Twelfth Dynasty (Sidney Smith). See *Syria*, XVII, 1936, p. 144, note 4, and Schaeffer, *Miss.* p. 69, n. 1.

[2] Casson, p. 38.

[3] Forsdyke in *J.H.S.* XXXI, 1911, pp. 110 ff.; Gjerstad, *S.P.C.* pp. 209 f.

[4] A bronze foundry, with the workman's tools, was found at Enkomi in 1896 (*Excav. Cypr.* pp. 15 ff.; Dussaud, *Civ. Préhell.*[2] pp. 249 f.); many similar tools have been found at Ras Shamra (*Syria*, XII, 1931, p. 66). But the Enkomi foundry is evidently late in date and affords no evidence for the Early or even Middle Bronze Age.

ported.[1] There appears to be no doubt that the great mass of "chariot-vases" come from Cyprus and, next in quantity, from Syria. If not made in the island, and not imported direct from the West, were they made in the "Mycenaean" settlements in Syria, such as at Ras Shamra, or elsewhere? For a rival to Syria, as the stage by which Mycenaean culture and wares penetrated to Cyprus, has been proposed in Cilicia.[2] It must be admitted that the chain is weak. Archaeologically it depends on the fact that there has been found in Cilicia Late Helladic III ware and also, in much greater quantity, Hellado-Cilician ware, which the finder thinks was made in Cilicia by Mycenaeans, and not by Cilicians. That the Cilicians had an admixture of Greek Achaean blood would be indicated by the statement of Herodotus that they used to be called "Hypachaioi",[3] if we could be sure that the reading of his text is correct. There were also legends indicating a Mycenaean push into Cilicia: for instance, the wandering of Bellerophon as far as the Aleian plain, and the foundations of Mopsus and Amphilochus. To these we may add, as showing the connexion with Cyprus, the legends which made Cinyras a son of Sandocus, and attributed the origin of the divination from kids' entrails, practised by the Cinyradae, to the Cilician Tamiras.[4]

---

[1] The latest discussions in Schaeffer, *Miss.* pp. 75 ff., Georgiades, *K.K.* p. 315 and Casson, pp. 43 ff. See also Forsdyke in *Essays in Aegean Archaeology pres. to Sir A. Evans*, 1927, p. 29. He there publishes a Late Mycenaean pot from Maroni, of Aegean shape, but with an Asiatic motif of goats and trees (see H. Danthine, *Le palmier dattier et les arbres sacrés dans l'iconographie de l'Asie orientale ancienne*, Paris, 1937, p. 200 and Pl. 175, fig. 1038); yet the composition seems to be derived from a wall-painting. Schaeffer and Dussaud hold that the chariot-vases (of which many have been found at Enkomi) were made in Cyprus; Gjerstad and most others that they were imported into the island. If the former, the Cypriote workshops must have come into action towards the end of the fourteenth or the beginning of the thirteenth century. Many of the vases in question bear potters' marks resembling signs from the Cypriote syllabary (*Miss.* p. 119). But it must be remembered that syllabaries of this type were not confined to Cyprus.

[2] Gjerstad, "Cilician Studies", in *Rev. Archéologique*, III, 1934, pp. 155–203. In criticizing this theory, Casson (p. 118) has attributed what Hesiod says of Soli in Cilicia to Soli in Cyprus.

[3] Meaning that they had been half-Graecized by the post-Trojan colonies (E. O. Forrer in *Klio*, XXX, 1937, p. 137). But most scholars believe that the word is a Greek corruption of a native name. The various interpretations suggested are discussed by I. Levy in *Mélanges Émile Boisacq*, II, 1938, pp. 119–27. He himself corrects Ὑπαχαιοί to Ὑλαχαιοί, meaning 'Cilicians', connecting the word with *Ḫilaku* or *Ḫilakku* (in one instance *Ḫiliku*) of the Assyrian texts, and חלך or כלך of the fourth-century satrapal coins of Cilicia.

[4] Below, p. 75.

But even if another Ras Shamra is found in Cilicia, it will hardly prove that Cilicia was the source from which Cyprus was supplied with Mycenaean products. Geographical considerations favour the view that the stream of commerce flowed through the Cilician channel, depositing its wares on the coasts of Cyprus on the south and of Cilicia on the north, on its way to Syria.

It has been argued that, although the horse was known in Cyprus as early as about 2000, since bones of sacrificed horses have been found in a grave of that period, the use of horse-drawn chariots was first introduced by the "Mycenaean" colonists, because the chariot vases afford the earliest representation of such scenes.[1] The evidence is inadequate, and, indeed, if the vases were imported, they prove nothing of the sort. In any case, the horse doubtless came from Asia, where it was known before 2000 B.C.

Towards the end of the period we have been considering, the tide of prosperity began to ebb. An indication is the decreasing commonness of gold. In the following period, the last division of the Late Cypriote (L.C. III), that is about 1200 to 1000 B.C., the imports from the West dwindle away;[2] the Mycenaean vases which had once come so plentifully were no longer available, and but little of the wares which succeeded them in Greece, the Protogeometric, found its way to the island. The pottery required for daily use was supplied by a local fabric, known as sub-Mycenaean. This local manufacture may have begun before the fall of Mycenae, the Achaean migration eastwards, and the cessation of Mycenaean imports into the island; but naturally when such imports were no longer available, the local fabric, which had begun in imitation of the Mycenaean, became much more important. There was no violent break with the past.[3] At the same time the potters went on making

---

[1] Georgiades, *K.K.* p. 318.

[2] The cemetery at Enkomi continued in use until the eleventh century (indeed the ivories have been dated as late as 900–875: W. v. Bissing, *Röm. Mitt.* XLIII, 1928, pp. 56–9), but Mycenaean imports stopped in the twelfth. There is no Mycenaean pottery in the tombs which contained Ramesside scarabs. Schaeffer (*Miss.* pp. 80ff.) dates the latest Enkomi tombs between 1150 and 1100. The pottery is partly wheel-made. Changes in funeral customs and the appearance of the iron knife he attributes not to a normal development, but to the immigration of a new people, who, however, picked up certain elements of the Mycenaean tradition which had prevailed in their new home. Possibly, he suggests, they came from Ugarit after its fall (*Cuneiform Texts of Ras Shamra-Ugarit*, p. 29).

[3] Cp. T. Burton Brown, "Achaean Pottery", in Liverpool *Annals of Arch. and Anthr.* XXI, pp. 52 f.

ware of the old Cypriote types. Gradually the two styles affected each other and a fusion resulted, producing the Cypriote Geometric style.[1]

II. THE RECORDS

What is the import of such records as exist from Egyptian, Hittite or Mesopotamian sources of the period to which these archaeological data apply? How far was Cyprus under Egyptian or Hittite or Assyrian domination? We have already seen reason to regard the tradition of an invasion of Mediterranean islands by Sargon of Agade in the third millennium as insufficiently attested. But coming down to the fourteenth century and later we find evidence, on which theories of a confused and unsatisfactory character have been based, of relations between Egypt and the Hittite kingdom on the one hand and on the other two regions, Asy and Alashiya, which have by some been identified with Cyprus. In the documents, the rulers of these regions appear in the position of vassals to the Pharaohs or Hittite kings. There is much dispute about the meaning to be attached to the names Asy (formerly read Aseby) and Alashiya-Alasa.[2] Both, as we have said, have been identified with Cyprus; on the other hand, an attempt has been made to challenge this identification and to place both Asy and Alashiya in northern Syria or on the southern coast of Asia Minor, somewhere in the Cilician region.[3] At the risk of tedium, it seems necessary to state the arguments on both sides, even though the issue must remain uncertain.[4]

---

[1] J. F. Daniel in *Amer. Journ. Arch.* XLI, 1937, pp. 81 ff.

[2] Alasa or Arasa is the form used in the hieroglyphic records for the cuneiform Alashiya. But the material in official documents is extremely scanty, consisting only of three references, of which one is doubtful and another restored.

[3] As for instance by Carl Niebuhr (see next note) who finds the name surviving in the island of Eleoussa! (Strabo, XIV, 5. 6).

[4] The passages bearing on the question, from Egyptian or cuneiform sources, can most conveniently be consulted in O.C. pp. 3 f., 420 f.; G. A. Wainwright in *Klio*, XIV, 1915, pp. 32 f.; E. Forrer, s.v. *Alašija* in Ebeling und Meissner, *Reallexikon der Assyriologie*, I, 1932, pp. 67–8. A powerful attack on the identification of Asy and Alashiya-Alasa with Cyprus was delivered by Wainwright in *Klio*, *loc. cit.* pp. 1 ff.; this was, however, in many points rebutted by F. Schachermeyr in *Klio*, XVII, 1921, pp. 230 f., and the general opinion seems to be in favour of accepting the identification. Out of the mass of writing on the subject, other than that already cited, the following may be mentioned: G. Maspero, in *Rec. de Travaux*, X, 1887, pp. 209–10; W. Max Müller, *Asien und Europa*, 1893, pp. 261 f., 336, and *Ztschr. f. Assyriologie*, 1895–6, pp. 257 ff.; Carl Niebuhr, *Stud. u. Bemerk. z. Gesch. d. alten Orients*, I, 1894, pp. 97–102; H. R. Hall, *Oldest Civil. of Greece*, 1901, pp. 163, 321; Winckler in *Mitt. Deutsch.*

One or two preliminary statements may be made at the outset. In the first place, if neither Asy nor Alashiya is Cyprus, then this important island, which undoubtedly must have played a part in the history of the eastern Mediterranean in the second millennium, is unnamed in the documents, and that is hardly credible. Secondly, the point has been made that Asy and Alashiya cannot both be Cyprus because they are mentioned side by side, and the king of Alashiya speaks as if he were king of the whole land; but this argument has no weight, because Cyprus may well have been divided up under more than one ruler, then as later. This would also make it possible to believe that both Hittites and Egyptians could have been in control of Alashiya, each of a different part, at the same time. On the other hand, it is remarkable that Asy and Alashiya are never spoken of in the old records as "lands of the sea" or "lands across the sea", by which term, for lack of one more precise, both Egyptians and Babylonians described islands. To this it may per-

---

Orient. Gesellsch. XXXV, 1907, p. 41; W. Max Müller, *Egyptolog. Researches*, II, 1910, pp. 91–2; Hall in *Journ. Manchester Eg. and Or. Soc.* 1913, pp. 33 f.; Weber in Knudtzon, *Die El-Amarna Tafeln*, II, 1915, p. 1076; Smolenski in *Ann. du Serv. des Ant. de l'Égypte*, XV, 1915, pp. 59–60; Hrozný, *Die Sprache d. Hethiter*, 1917, p. 99; E. Forrer in *Mitt. Deutsch. Orient. Gesellsch.* LXI, 1921, p. 32; Sommer in *Ztschr. f. Assyr.* XXXIII, 1921, p. 95; Hall in *Anatolian Studies pres. to Ramsay*, 1923, p. 179; the same, *Anc. Hist. of the Near East*,[6] 1924, p. 243 and in *C.A.H.* II, 1924, p. 280; H. Gauthier, *Dict. des noms géogr. contenus dans les textes hiéroglyphiques*, I, 1925, pp. 40, 48, 96, VI, 1929, pp. 118 f. and index s.v. *Chypre*; *O.K.* 1924, 59, 86 f.; A. Götze, "Ḫattušiliš" in *Mitt. Vorderas.-Aeg. Gesellsch.* XXIX, 3, 1924, p. 25; E. Forrer, *Forschungen*, II, 1, 1926, p. 11; F. Bilabel, *Gesch. Vorderasiens u. Ägyptens*, 1927, p. 10, n. 5; S. Przeworski, "Grecs et Hittites" in *Eos*, XXX, 1927, pp. 432 ff.; Götze, "Madduwattaš" in *Mitt. Vorderas.-Aeg. Gesellsch.* XXXII, 1928, pp. 37–9 and 154 f.; E. Meyer, *Gesch. d. Alt.*[2] II, 1928, p. 139; H. Bossert in *Mitt. Altorient. Gesellsch.* IV, 1928–9, p. 278; Götze, "Neue Bruchstücke zum grossen Text des Ḫattušiliš", p. 19 (in *Mitt. Vorderas.-Aeg. Gesellsch.* XXXIV, Heft 2 = Hethitische Texte, V, 1930); F. Sommer, *Ahhijawa-Urkunden*, Munich, 1932, p. 337; E. Power in *Dict. de la Bible*, Supp. II, 1934, pp. 1 f.; Schachermeyr, "Hethiter u. Achäer", in *Mitt. Altorient. Gesellsch.* IX, Heft 1, 2, 1935; Brandenstein in *R.E.* Supp. VI, 1935, 212; S. Casson, *Anc. Cyprus*, 1937, pp. 110 ff.

I have not considered the suggested identification with Salamis of *Srmn*, of which King Nigmed of Ugarit was "Master" in the middle of the second millenium—an identification described by Schaeffer (*Cuneiform Texts of Ras Shamra-Ugarit*, p. 32) as open to criticism.

For continual kind help in the discussion which follows, I am indebted not only to Prof. Sidney Smith and to Mr Barnett, but to Mr Gadd and Mr Edwards of the British Museum, as well as to Prof. Glanville. None of them is of course in any way responsible for any opinion which I have myself expressed.

haps be replied that Cyprus was the nearest to Egypt of all these distant shores, and familiarly enough known to need no appellation of the kind. For the Assyrians, it was much more remote; so that when it is mentioned, from the eighth century onwards, in Assyrian records, its position in the midst of the sea is emphasized.

We must start the consideration of the problem, not with the early texts, but with a passage in the trilingual Decree of Canopus, dating from 238 B.C., with which may be connected a passage in another Ptolemaic text. In the Decree, *Kypros* in the Greek is equated with *Salmina* in the demotic (evidently the chief city being used for the whole island) and in the hieroglyphic with a word which used to be variously read,[1] but which is now generally agreed to be *Sbyna*, and to which is added the qualification "in the midst of the sea". It has been plausibly suggested that the hieroglyphic form has been assimilated to the demotic, by taking over the termination *-ina*. Detaching this, we have left the stem *sb*, which is the same word as was vocalized earlier as *Aseby* and later as *Asy*.[2]

---

[1] *O.C.* p. 2 gives the various readings: Nebīnai, Ibinai, Sibinai, Sebiani, Mesīnai, Masinai. Hall (*Oldest Civil. of Greece*, p. 163 n.) explained the word as a corruption of *Iantânai*, and connected it with . . . *ntânai*, which is found after a lacuna in an Eighteenth Dynasty document (Sethe, *Urkunden d. XVIII. Dyn.* III, 733 m), and so with *Iatnana*, which is the Assyrian name for Cyprus in the time of Sargon, Esarhaddon and Ashurbanipal. Unfortunately it is not even certain that . . . *ntânai* is a place-name (H. Gauthier, *Dict. des noms géogr.* I, p. 57 end).

[2] On this, which concerns an obscure point of Egyptian phonology, I must quote Professor Glanville's own words: "As to the reading of the old Asy, once Asebi. The element which causes all the doubt is the sign 𓊃 which appears in about half a dozen words only. It indicates certainly two things: (1) 's' in the stem, and (2) the idea of motion (for this reason, perhaps, suitable in the spelling of a foreign place-name). In both the two commonest words in which it is used, *sb* and *ms*, it is usually filled out with either the 'b' written after it or the 'm' written before it as the case may be. But in the case of *sb* the 'b' is frequently left out of the spelling, and in the case of *ms* 'b', which is of course not required, is frequently put in, indicating that the scribe concerned was most familiar with 𓊃 as having the value *sb*. There are, however, philological arguments which suggest that on occasions the sign 𓊃 by itself did not carry a 'b' with it, but was read *s* simply. Moreover, in three different meanings of the stem 𓊃 there is definite evidence that the same word tends to be written first with 𓊃 alone and later with the sign followed by 'b'. Whether this indicates a change of pronunciation or merely that in later times the scribes were not so familiar with this comparatively rare sign, and therefore needed the phonetic complement 'b' to help them to remember the sound of the whole sign, is uncertain. Nor does it affect your argument as far as I can see. If old 'Asy' did occur in Ptolemaic documents one would, on

The other document, which is of uncertain Ptolemaic date,[1] has "the island of Seb" and the accompanying text speaks of "Asiatic copper of the island of Iufrus" which it has been proposed to emend to "Ḳufrus".

There is thus much reason to assume that to the Ptolemaic scribes Asy or Aseby meant Cyprus. It is ingenious, but hardly convincing, to argue[2] that by Ptolemaic times Cyprus had become so famous for its copper that the scribes held that the name of a land, which in the Eighteenth Dynasty produced so much copper as Asy did, must in those ancient days have been the name of that land which they themselves knew as famous for copper, i.e. Cyprus.

The inscriptions of the time of Thutmose III (1501–1447) indicate that Asy was in a state of subjection or vassalage to Egypt. The author of the famous poetical panegyric on the Pharaoh[3] makes Amon say "I have come, causing thee to smite the western land; Keftiu and Asy are in terror. I have caused them to behold thy majesty as a young bull", etc. The Karnak Annals of the same Pharaoh[4] speak of horses and mares and chariots of gold and silver as taken in booty from the land, and the tribute received thence includes unrefined copper, ingots of refined copper (in one payment as much as 2040 *deben*), pigs or blocks of lead, blue stone, blue carbonate of copper,[5] and elephants' tusks.[6]

---

the foregoing analogy, expect it to be written with a 'b' in the spelling, whatever its original pronunciation.

"Everything therefore seems to favour your argument that:

(1) *Sbyna* has taken over its ending *ina* from *Salmina*;

(2) the stem *sb* with which you are then left is the same word as earlier whether this is to be vocalized *ỉsy* (Asy) or *ỉsby* (Aseby);

(3) which must therefore be Cyprus (or part thereof)."

To this we may add that it has been suggested (H. Gauthier, *op. cit.* I, 1925, pp. 77–8) that if the reading *Amasi* which has been proposed for the name also variously read *Asi*, *Isy*, *Asbi* be correct, it may represent *Amathus*.

[1] Brugsch, *Rec. de Mon.* IV (Dümichen, *Geogr. Inschr.* II), Pl. LXVI, no. 8. The emendation to Ḳufrus is suggested by W. Max Müller, *Asien u. Europa*, p. 336. Approved by H. Gauthier, *op. cit.* I, p. 40. "Asiatic" as a description of copper does not, it must be admitted, help the argument for Cyprus here; unless Cyprus is thought of as an island of Asia.

[2] Wainwright, p. 15.

[3] Poetical Stele of Thutmose III, Cairo Museum. Brugsch, *Gesch. Aegyptens*, p. 355; O.C. p. 3. Breasted, *Anc. Records of Egypt*, II, § 659; *History of Egypt*,[2] 1909, p. 319.

[4] Brugsch, *op. cit.* pp. 301, 317, 320, 322; Breasted, *Anc. Rec.* §§ 493, 511, 521; O.C. pp. 3, 421.

[5] O.C. pp. 178–9; Blümner in *R.E.* XI, 2240.

[6] A remarkable bronze cauldron stand in the British Museum, said to come from Curium, has been interpreted in a way which, if correct, would lend it some interest in

As to ivory, it is known that in the second millennium ivory was a very important article of commerce, and was brought, for instance, from Crete (if Keftiu be Crete) by envoys to Egypt.[1] The tribute of lead may seem more difficult to explain, for Cyprus did not, it would appear, produce lead (although the earliest silver ornaments are strongly alloyed with it, and it is also present as an impurity in copper and bronze implements of the Early Cypriote period), but the quantities mentioned are not large (five blocks in one payment, one in another), and the metal can hardly have had so small a value as we are accustomed to attach to it, or why should it have been worth sending as tribute?[2] We are therefore entitled to assume that the lead, like the ivory, sent as tribute from Asy, was not a natural product of the land, but a valuable import.

Asy is also mentioned a number of times in the Geographical Lists of the Nineteenth Dynasty, under Seti I (1313–1292) and Ramses II (1292–1225);[3] under the latter king Alashiya is also grouped with it.[4]

---

connexion with the bronze and ivory from Asy (Barnett in *Iraq*, 1935, p. 209; Casson, pp. 128–9; H. Danthine, *Le palmier dattier et les arbres sacrés dans l'iconogr. de l'Asie orient. anc.*, Paris, 1937, p. 205 and Pl. 184, fig. 1093 *a–d*). It has been described as Phoenician, but has certain Mycenaean elements. The worship of a stylized tree is represented in one of the four panels: a man plays a harp before it, in the others one man brings an offering of fish, another carries on his shoulder an object of the same shape as the copper ingots of Bronze Age Cyprus, but pounced with dots, and the fourth holds a cup and, curving over his shoulder, what has been described as two enormous napkins (Barnett) or two tusks (Casson). The fact that the supposed ingot is dotted supports the view of Barnett that it is really a wine-skin; as to the napkins, they may not be well represented, but as tusks the objects are no more convincing. The offering of wine and the carrying of a long napkin over the shoulder are common in representations of ancient Oriental ritual. Casson's interpretation must therefore be rejected in favour of Barnett's.

[1] Schachermeyr, 1921, p. 231.

[2] Wainwright observes that it is an uncommon metal in Egyptian inscriptions. He considers the amount large; but it is small compared with the copper. The metal was used as a medium of exchange in Cappadocia in the nineteenth century and in Assyria in the fourteenth–twelfth (Sidney Smith, *Earlier History of Assyria*, pp. 160, 323).

[3] Most conveniently in Wainwright, pp. 19, 33–4.

[4] List of foreign countries famous for their mines, on the part of the temple at Luxor built by Ramses II. See W. Max Müller, *Egyptolog. Researches*, II, pp. 91–2. He observes that the geographer begins the list of mines in Asia with the malachite mines of Sinai. He "does not know any other mountain with important mines in the whole land of Syria. We should expect at least the Lebanon mentioned. The list then proceeds to Cyprus, which it mentions twice (24). First the mountain of *'sy* (read *'A*[*la*]*sya*) brings 'silver and copper in millions, in endless masses, in hundred thou-

There is no doubt that (leaving Alashiya aside for the moment) the other places or regions mentioned in connexion with Asy in these lists are mostly (probably all, but some of them are unidentified) on the mainland towards the north. But these lists are a sort of *cento* from earlier sources, and the geographical collocations in them, even if they have historical value, must not be taken too seriously.[1] And, since Cyprus is the only island that lay in the sphere of military activity of the Pharaohs, the only island in the sea between Egypt, Syria-Palestine and Asia Minor, there is nothing to surprise us in finding it associated with places on the mainland, seeing that there is nothing else with which it could be associated. Manetho's statement[2] that Seti campaigned against Cyprus, Phoenicia, the Assyrians and the Medes, has been cited in this connexion, but his authority, on the face of it, is of trifling value, and can carry no more weight, at the best, than the Geographical Lists, from one of which it was very possibly derived. The whole context is unhistorical, and may be only a garbled version of Manetho.

An examination of the sites of ancient copper mines in Cyprus has led one investigator[3] to the conclusion that evidence of the mining of copper in prehistoric Cyprus, i.e. in the Bronze Age, is lacking. Unless Alashiya or Asy is Cyprus, he holds, copper mines were not important in that island in the fifteenth century. It must be confessed that, if he were right, one of the strongest supports of the orthodox view would be knocked away. However, evidence that the mines of Skouriotissa were worked in the Bronze Age is forthcoming in the settlement at Katydhata, which was occupied from the Early Bronze Age down to Hellenistic times.[4] Further, if the bronze weapons of a highly developed type already mentioned (p. 27) are of native manufacture—and that, though not proven, is probable—then there must have been copper-working in

---

sands'; then that of '*A-r*(*e*)-*sa* offers the very same things. Thus our scholar does not seem to have coupled the two varying orthographies of the same name out of mere ignorance, but wilfully, knowing that the two orthographic variants were identical. A wide difference between ancient and modern scientific methods!" The list then goes on to the mines in Hittite country. This comment is, as regards Cyprus, a good example of *petitio principii*. It is very unlikely that the kings Seti and Ramses II, to whose time the documents with which we are concerned belong, ever ruled Cyprus, but the names may be derived from earlier lists.

[1] Schachermeyr, 1921, p. 232. [2] Müller, *F.H.G.* II, p. 573.

[3] O. Davies, *The Copper Mines of Cyprus*, in *B.S.A.* XXX, 1932, pp. 74–85. His view has been accepted by few; the last to criticize it adversely is Casson, pp. 122–6.

[4] *Ann. Rep. of the Curator of Antiquities*, 1916, pp. 5 ff.; Casson, p. 126.

Cyprus in the Early Cypriote period. Much more, in the period 1400 to 1200 B.C., when the island was at the height of its prosperity, it must have possessed some product to attract foreign imports, and it is difficult to see what that can have been except copper.

The evidence against placing Asy in Cyprus may therefore, on balance, be taken as not in any sense conclusive. But there is no necessity to assume that it was coextensive with the whole island.

Let us now turn to Alashiya-Alasa.

In this question we have no starting-point such as that afforded for Asy by the Canopus Decree; but the claims which have been made for its identity with Cyprus are even more vigorous. The details we hear about it are much more lively, for we have the official correspondence of one of its kings with the king of Egypt, probably Amenhotep IV Akhenaton (1375–1358), and we are told the name of a queen in a picturesque narrative of the eleventh century.

In the correspondence preserved in the Tell el-Amarna tablets,[1] the king of Alashiya writes to the Pharaoh as "his brother". The terms they are on are friendly, but it is clear that the king of Alashiya is the subordinate. He uses the cuneiform script and the Babylonian tongue. This, and the fact that he acknowledges the Babylonian god of battle and death, Nergal,[2] have been considered arguments against the identification of Alashiya with Cyprus. But Babylonian and cuneiform are used, it is replied, as a *lingua franca* and as the Latin script would be used, let us say, by a Russian diplomat. We shall see that early in the eleventh century, at one place in Alashiya, it was difficult to find anyone who understood Egyptian. It must be admitted that, if Alashiya, which used cuneiform, is Cyprus, it is strange that the island has produced no cuneiform documents or seals of the period.

From what the king says, we learn that his country is raided yearly by Lukki (probably pirates from the Lycian-Pamphylian region),[3] who plunder his towns. Emissaries pass between Egypt and Alashiya: "see, my brother, with thine emissaries have I sent mine to thee to Egypt".

---

[1] J. A. Knudtzon, *Die El-Amarna Tafeln*, 1915, nos. 33–40; commentary by Weber, pp. 1076 ff. The Pharaoh to whom no. 33 is addressed had just succeeded to the throne.

[2] E. Schrader, *Die Keilinschriften u. das Alte Test.*3 1902–3, p. 414, suggests that this Nergal is not the Babylonian god but a corresponding native Cypriote god indicated by the ideogram for Nergal.

[3] On the Lukki, who may be the same people who were allied with the Hittites at Kadesh, *c.* 1290, see Smolenski in *Ann. du Serv.* xv, pp. 54 ff.

With one letter he sends 500 (talents?) of copper as a "present"; that it is too little is due to the plague with which Nergal has slain all his people, so that the copper cannot be produced. In return the king begs the Pharaoh to send him silver, and again silver, and oxen, and oil. There is also evidence for export of wood to Egypt. A citizen of Alashiya resident in Egypt has died, and the king begs for his property to be sent over to his son and widow. One of the Pharaoh's emissaries seems to have been detained no less than three years in Alashiya; the excuse given is that the hand of Nergal was on the land and the king's young wife died. Another letter shows that if the king begged for oil from Pharaoh, he could also send him oil in return for his anointing; so too he sends oxen, ivory and a certain valuable wood, but in return he also asks for ivory, and that in the same letter. Clearly then these were sent as presents of value, not merely as tribute.[1] He promises to double any gifts which might be sent by the king of Hatti (the Hittite capital) and the king of Shanhar (Mitanni), and warns the Pharaoh not to have dealings with them.

A last reference to Alashiya in this correspondence is the statement by Rib-Addi, governor of Byblus, to the Egyptian king, that in order to please the king he had made it possible for the official Amanmasha to go to Alashiya.[2] Which looks as if he had some control over the land, but may only mean that he sent Amanmasha there in one of his ships.

Attempts have been made to explain some of the names of people of Alashiya mentioned in one of the letters (no. 37)—Pashtumme, Etilluna, Kunêa, Ushbarra and Belram or Belsham—as Greek, but without success; nor do they seem to be Semitic, except the second and the last.[3]

Earlier mention of Alashiya than the Tell el-Amarna letters seems, however, to be made in records of the time of Thutmose III,[4] in con-

---

[1] So R. v. Lichtenberg, *Beiträge zur ältesten Gesch. v. Kypros*, 1906, pp. 6 ff.

[2] Knudtzon, *op. cit.*, no. 114^{52}: ša-al-šu šum-ma la-a (mâtu) a-la-ši-ia uš-ši-ir-ti-[š]u a-na mu-ḫi-ka, which has been variously interpreted as meaning that Amanmasha went "to" or "from (through)" Alashiya (*O.C.* p. 426; Hall, *Anc. Hist. of the Near East*, p. 243). Prof. Sidney Smith informs me that the literal translation is "ask him; verily indeed the land of Alashiya I have made free for him with respect to you". The use of *šumma la* to introduce an affirmative oath was not understood by earlier translators.

[3] Weber in Knudtzon, *Die El-Amarna-Tafeln*, II, 1915, p. 1083.

[4] Wainwright, p. 33, no. 5. His numbers 8 and 19 seem to have got into the wrong column.

nexion with towns in the neighbourhood of Aleppo and the Euphrates. The geographical collocations under Seti I and Ramses II are open to the same criticism as in the case of Asy. In papyri of the Nineteenth Dynasty we find mentioned Fidi liquid, Inbu liquid of Alasa along with liquids from the Hittite land and other places on the mainland; mares of Alasa in similar collocation; and oil of Iupa brought by the children of Alasa.[1] And under Ramses III (1198–1167), in an inscription of his eighth year dealing with his Northern War, it is mentioned with Kheta (the Hittites), Kode, Carchemish, and perhaps Arvad. It was visited without resistance by the fleet of the northern "Peoples of the Sea" in the great attack directed against Egypt and defeated by Ramses.[2] It is perhaps no coincidence that the old city at Enkomi, which had enjoyed so flourishing a culture in the Mycenaean Age, ceased to be inhabited, and may have been destroyed, about this time, to be succeeded by Salamis on another site, just as the population of Citium seems, at the end of the Third Late Cypriote period, to have moved to a new site round the acropolis of Bamboula.[3]

Early in the eleventh century, about 1085, when Hrihor, high-priest of Amon, was on the throne, he sent his emissary Wenamon to Phoenicia to obtain wood from Lebanon. Wenamon's report[4] tells us that he was in danger of being seized by pirates at Byblus, but escaped, and was driven by the wind to Alasa, where he was nearly slain by the people. He was, however, carried before the "queen of the city", Hathaba (Heteb), and managed to find someone who understood Egyptian. The papyrus breaks off with this incident, and how Wenamon

[1] Maspero, *Rec. de Travaux*, x, p. 210: Fidi is perhaps pitch.

[2] Breasted, *Anc. Records of Egypt*, iv, § 64; W. F. Edgerton and J. A. Wilson, *Hist. Records of Ramses III. The Texts in Medinet Habu*, vols. i, ii (Chicago Orient. Inst. 1936), p. 53. "Yeres" (Arasa, Alasa) is equated with Alashiya, "Yereth", on the other hand, may be Arzawa (Cilicia) and not Arvad.

[3] Schaeffer, *Miss.* p. 93; *S.C.E.* iii, p. 74; Burn, *Minoans, Philistines and Greeks*, p. 147. There is a type of "leaf-shaped" sword (Peake's Type D) which is found in the Aegean and Egypt; part of one sword "which has probably been influenced by this type, though the butt and tang are different" (Peake, *Bronze Age*, p. 96) was found in a tomb somewhere in Cyprus. This type is dated to about the time of the raid of the Peoples of the Sea by the cartouche of Seti II which is found on one specimen. To regard the specimen from Cyprus as a relic of the raid is surely incautious.

[4] The Golenischeff Papyrus in Maspero, *Rec. de Travaux*, xxi, 1879, pp. 74–102; Breasted, *Anc. Records of Egypt*, iv, 1906, §§ 557–91; *Hist. of Egypt*,[2] pp. 513 ff. The whole story in A. R. Burn, *Minoans, Philistines and Greeks*, pp. 173–81. The portions relating to Alasa in Hall, *Oldest Civil. of Greece*, p. 321 and *O.C.* p. 423.

got back to Egypt is not known. That the people of Alasa were great mariners[1] is indicated by Wenamon's threat to the queen: "as for the crew of the prince of Byblus, whom they (the men of Alasa) sought to kill, their lord will surely find ten crews of thine, and he will slay them, on his part".

But Egypt is not the only source of our information about Alashiya. It is frequently mentioned in Hittite documents.[2] It first appears in the Boghazköy inscriptions within the sphere of Hittite political influence towards the end of the fifteenth century. King Tudhaliyash III was assassinated about 1400, and his brothers were sent into exile in Alashiya,[3] which must therefore at the time of the murder have belonged to the Hittite kingdom. King Muwattallish, son of Murshilish (about 1307–1290), seems to have confirmed, perhaps extended, the Hittite rule in Alashiya.[4] His successor Hattushilish III (about 1290–1260) was able, like Murshilish, to banish his political adversaries to Alashiya.[5]

In the last days of the history of the kingdom as recorded in the Boghazköy texts in the time of Arnuwandash III, i.e. just before 1200, Alashiya is still considered to be a state subject to the Hittites. It appears that one Madduwattash,[6] a vassal of the Hittite king, grew so strong that he eventually ruled *de facto* over south-west Asia Minor, and ventured to attack Hittite territory, including Alashiya. The text is much muti-

---

[1] Cp. the remarks of Dussaud, *Découvertes de Ras Shamra*, p. 63, on the importance of Cypriote shipping in early times, and the possible derivation of the Phoenician therefrom.

[2] The state of our knowledge of this question down to 1927 has been set out by S. Przeworski, "Grecs et Hittites", in *Eos*, XXX, 1927, pp. 432 ff.

[3] E. Forrer, *Forschungen*, II, 1, 1926, p. 11. The pestilence which raged in the Hittite kingdom after the war with the Hurri (i.e. after 1346) was attributed to the vengeance of the gods for the murder of Tudhaliyash III, the grandfather of Murshilish, and the banishment of the great-uncles mentioned in the text.

[4] The evidence has unfortunately been presented in a very unsatisfactory form. E. Forrer (*Mitt. Deutsch. Orient. Gesellsch.* LXI, 1921, p. 32) says that Muwattallish, son of Murshilish, undertook an expedition into the "lower land" (Cilicia) and conquered also "the island Alašija". If the document really describes Alashiya as an island, the whole dispute is settled. But Forrer gives no quotation of the text, and it is strongly to be suspected that the qualification of Alashiya as an island is his own interpolation.

[5] A. Götze, "Ḫattušiliš" in *Mitt. Vorderas.-Aeg. Gesellsch.* XXIX, 3, 1924, p. 25 and "Neue Bruchstücke zum grossen Text des Ḫattušiliš", *ibid.* XXXIV, 2, 1930, p. 19.

[6] A. Götze, "Madduwattaš" in *M.V.A.G.* XXXII, 1928, pp. 37–9 and 154 f.; F. Sommer, *Ahhijawa-Urkunden*, München, 1932, p. 337. Götze notes that the sea is not mentioned in connexion with Alashiya in this document.

lated, and has been restored and translated in different ways. From its obscurity there seem to emerge the following facts. Madduwattash certainly, in company with Attarshiyash of Ahhiyawa[1] and the "man from Biggaya",[2] invaded Alashiya, and took prisoners. Madduwattash apologizes to Arnuwandash, saying that he had no official knowledge that Alashiya really belonged to the Hittite kingdom; however, as the king claims the return of his prisoners, he will send them back. It is clear from this that there was at this time no *de facto* possession of Alashiya by the Hittites, whatever had been the case earlier.

If Biggaya or Piggaya could be certainly equated with Sphekeia, one of the ancient names of Cyprus, we should not be much nearer a solution of the question. Attarshiyash makes a raid on Alashiya accompanied by "the man from Biggaya". Those who believe that Biggaya is Sphekeia may assume that an exile from that land helped Attarshiyash to attack Alashiya, which, if they equate Alashiya with Cyprus, must be a name for another part of the island. But it might equally well be a part of southern Asia Minor. Obviously the evidence is insufficient to force any conclusion.

Thus, although all this evidence seems to suggest a gradual extension of Hittite influence over Alashiya, from the fifteenth century, and then its waning under attacks from the West, possibly by the Achaeans, shortly before 1200, it does not prove more than that Alashiya lay to the south of the Hittite country. One passage in the texts has been held to prove that it was near Amurru, and bordered the sea.[3] Another mentions copper as brought from (the city of) Alashiya from the mountain Taggata.[4]

---

[1] Hittite scholars do not generally accept, and some fiercely dispute, the equation of Ahhiyawa with Achaea, which assumes that these Achaeans, settled perhaps in the region of Pamphylia, were members of the great Achaean empire of Mycenaean Greece (Nilsson, *Homer and Mycenae*, 1933, p. 104). See Sommer, *op. cit.*

[2] See ch. v, p. 82 n. 1.

[3] Sommer, *op. cit.* p. 257, giving a different interpretation from Götze, *Neue Bruchstücke zum grossen Text des Ḫattušiliš*, p. 19, ll. 28–9.

[4] Schachermeyr, 1921, p. 238. The same writer in his "Hethiter und Achäer", *Mitt. d. altorient. Gesellsch.* IX, Heft 1, 2, 1935, p. 69, considers the identity of Alashiya with Cyprus as completely proved. As regards the "city" of Alashiya, the use of the determinative for "city" before the name is in accordance with the Hittite custom of naming countries after their capitals; there may actually have been no city of this name (Przeworski, *loc. cit.*). E. Power's identification of Taggata with Troödos (*Biblica*, x, 1929, p. 158) may be mentioned here for what it is worth.

With regard to this evidence from Hittite sources, one admission must be made, by those who favour the identification of Alashiya with Cyprus, as against their view. If the identification is correct, and Cyprus, or even only the northern coast of Cyprus, was under Hittite sovereignty, how can we explain the lack of Hittite antiquities in the island?[1] Only one important Hittite object has been found there so far, a gold seal, with Hittite inscription, from Tamassus. And seals travel far, and prove no direct connexion with the land where they were first produced. No stress can be laid on the Hittite characteristics of such objects as the ivory draught-box from Enkomi, for that points with equal probability to Syria.[2]

To this the supporters of the equation may reply that relics of Hittite penetration anywhere outside the actual limits of the Hittite empire are very scarce, though this is not true of sites belonging to the period of Hittite domination. In any case the actual hold of the Hittites on Alashiya seems to have been even slighter than that of the Egyptians.

One of the tablets of Ras Shamra[3] (dating from the thirteenth century) gives a list of peoples in relation with Ugarit; among these is mentioned a man or a clan called *'lšy*, which according to one view is Cyprus, according to another, Alshe, at the sources of the Tigris.

Finally, to exhaust the references from Eastern sources which have been made to this question, there is the Bibilical *Elishah*, one of the "sons of Javan".[4] Kittim was his brother, and the association of that name with Citium, as we shall see, is difficult to deny. So that, if Elishah is Alashiya, and Alashiya Cyprus, two out of the four nations whom these sons represent are at home in the one island: a hard thing to believe. In another passage[5] "benches (or decks) of ivory inlaid in

---

[1] Casson, pp. 116 f.

[2] Cp. Myres, *H.C.C.* p. 133: "obvious points of similarity between early Cypriote sculpture and the Hittite monuments of Asia Minor and North Syria...may be due rather to collateral borrowing from the old Babylonian culture of North Syria than to direct influence of Hittite art on that of Cyprus". The obviousness of the similarity is disputable; see Lawrence in *J.H.S.* XLVI, 1926, pp. 163–70.

[3] No. 1929, 2, ll. 12, 21, 29. Dhorme, *Revue Bibl.* 1931, pp. 37 f.; Hrozný, *Archiv Orientální*, IV, 1932, pp. 169–78; Virolleaud, *Légende phénic. de Danel* (*Bibl. du Service des Ant. de Syrie*, XXII), pp. 36 ff.; Dussaud, *Découvertes de Ras Shamra*, p. 56 note. Dhorme and Hrozný support the interpretation Alashiya, Virolleaud Alshe.

[4] Gen. x. 4 = I Chron. i. 7. The latest to deny the equation is E. Power in *Dict. de la Bibl.* Supp. II, 1934, col. 20.

[5] Ezekiel xxvii. 6, 7. See, however, p. 10, n. 4.

boxwood, from the isles of Kittim" and "blue and purple (cloth) from the isles of Elishah" are mentioned side by side. We shall discuss the significance of Kittim in another connexion.

It has been urged, as a powerful confirmation of the equation with Cyprus, that in historic times the worship of an Apollo Alasiotes [1] (Phoenician *Reshef Alahiotas*) is proved by a bilingual dedication at Tamassus. This evidence cuts both ways. It can be taken as indicating that Alashiya was a Cypriote place. But it is equally strong, if not stronger, evidence that it was not the place where the dedication was set up. The addition of the ethnic is more necessary in the case of a god imported from abroad than when he is native. The dedication in another Cypriote bilingual inscription to Apollo "Amyklos" does not prove that there was a place called Amyclae in Cyprus, but points to the famous Laconian sanctuary.[2] Nevertheless, those who argue that we must look outside the island for the place from which this Apollo came, go, in their way, too far. It is sufficient, granting their premiss that he must be foreign to Tamassus, to say that he may come from a sanctuary in some other part of the island. Whether Alashiya was the name of the capital as well of the island itself[3] we can hardly begin to consider in the present state of our evidence.

Finally, as an argument in favour of the identification, it has been represented that places called "Alassos" and "Ailasyka" still exist in the island. By the former is probably meant Alassa, on the Limassol-Platres road; by the latter, Aglasyka, a little village in the Mesarea.[4] In any case, nothing is more misleading than such connexions between ancient and modern names.

---

[1] Before the Alashiya controversy began, it was suggested that this name of Apollo was to be connected with Ἀλήσιον and similar names in Peloponnese; also that Ptolemy's Ἀλαία or Ἐλαία might be more correct than Strabo's Παλαιά, and represent *Ἀλασία; and finally that Heleitas (see next note) might be only another way of writing the same epithet. (Euting and Deecke in *Sbr. k. Preuss. Akad.* 1887, pp. 115 ff.)

[2] There was a third Apollo, Heleitas, "*Apollo of Helos*, either Helos in Lacedaemon or a Cyprian city of the same name"; cp. G. A. Cooke, *North Semitic Inscr.* 1903, p. 89. Hesychius s.v. Ἐλεία gives it as a name of Hera in Cyprus and Artemis in Messene. Bechtel, *Gr. Dial.* I, p. 453. For various names of Zeus in Cyprus bearing a more or less near resemblance to the name in question, see Euting and Deecke, *op. cit.* p. 118.

[3] So Schachermeyr, arguing from the Boghazköy text which seems to mention a city of the name.

[4] Sykutris in Κυπρ. Χρον. I, 1923, p. 290. Alassa is, according to Menardos (Τοπων. p. 335), wrongly called Khalasa in Kitchener's map and in the Census Returns.

From this discussion, unfortunately, no complete certainty seems to emerge. Both Asy and Alashiya-Alasa have claims to be situated in Cyprus; and if those claims are denied, other difficulties arise, the chief being that already indicated, to wit that Cyprus, at a time when it is shown by archaeological evidence to be very prosperous and in close touch with Egypt and Syria-Phoenicia, remains unmentioned by the records. Both, on the other hand, but more especially Alashiya, have claims to location somewhere in North Syria, although it is impossible to accept the theory that the name Asy may survive in the modern name of the Orontes (Nahr el 'Asi), which the Greeks called Axios.[1]

The control which Egypt and other powers in antiquity, and indeed down to the period of the Roman Empire, exercised over Cyprus was in any case as a rule little more than a precarious suzerainty. In the days of the Eighteenth Dynasty, and particularly of Thutmose III, the control of Cyprus, as of Syria, Phoenicia and Palestine, was an essential part of Egyptian policy.[2] But the island can never have been securely held.

An inscription of the time of Ramses III, if its interpretation and historical value were beyond suspicion, would be of much interest for relations with Cyprus in his time. It is on the temple at Medinet Habu,[3] and has a long list of names, among which many Egyptologists have agreed to recognize cities in Cyprus and southern Asia Minor. Unfortunately, the identifications are uncertain, and even the readings which were originally accepted have not been confirmed.[4] In any case, if the identifications were correct, they would not prove more than a pretence on the part of Ramses to hold cities in the island, a claim which he

---

[1] Wainwright, p. 31. Neat, if true. But, writes Professor Sidney Smith, it will not do. '*Aṣi* with a *ṣad* is Axios; the Greeks frequently so rendered *ṣad* by ξ: but the Egyptians rendered it by ž or *d*, not *s*.

[2] M. Rostovtzeff, *Hist. of the Anc. World*, I,[2] 1930, p. 75. Breasted, *Hist. of Egypt*,[2] p. 518.

[3] Brugsch, *Gesch. Aeg.* 1877, p. 603. Cp. Hall, *Oldest Civil. of Greece*, p. 169 note.

[4] In a list of thirty-nine names, Brugsch finds possible Cypriote equivalents for nos. 7–12, 20 and 21. They are Salomaski (which he takes for Salamis), Kathian (Citium), Aimar (Marium), Sali (Soli), Ithal (Idalium), [M]aqnas (Acamas; but there was no city of that name); the two which are separated from the rest are Kerena or Kelena (Kerynia) and Kir... (Curium). Unfortunately, these readings are not to be trusted. The names in question are thus given by J. Simons, *Handbook for the Study of Egyptian Topographical Lists*, Leiden, 1937, pp. 164 f.: ś-r-ṃ-ś-k, k-t-y-n, ỉ-y-m-r, ś-r, ỉ-t-r, d-n-ś, k-r-n, k-y-r-w. The readings by Jirju, "Die Ägypt. Listen Paläst. u. Syr. Ortsnamen", in *Klio*, Beih. XXXVIII, 1937, p. 44, are somewhat different.

might have found it difficult to substantiate. There would, of course, be nothing to surprise us in the existence of the Greek-looking names for cities in Cyprus at this time. In the first place, there can be little doubt that the Greeks were already in great numbers settled in the island by the beginning of the twelfth century. But, setting that aside, the places where the Greeks settled may have had indigenous names which the Greeks assimilated to names, like Salamis, known in their old country.

So much for the relations between Cyprus and the neighbouring Mediterranean lands in the Bronze Age.

III. THE WRITING

What language the Cypriotes of the Bronze Age spoke is still an unsolved problem. But (setting aside the cuneiform which, if we accept Alashiya as Cyprus, was used for official correspondence with Egypt) we have some traces, tantalizing enough, of their writing. The earliest comes from Vounous, from the Early Bronze Age cemetery, in the form of an incised inscription in what are described[1] as "Early Bronze Age Cypriote characters", on the handle of a jug of red polished pottery. It is a linear script, "having no relation to the Cypro-Minoan script of the Late Bronze Age, imported into Cyprus from the Greek mainland". Affinity is traced with the "linear degenerations of hieroglyphic script found on documents in the Proto-dynastic tombs of Abydos"; but, since several of the signs are peculiar to Cyprus, it is thought that a new script may have been developed in Cyprus out of the borrowed signs. All this appears to be very speculative, especially in view of the early date, seeing that the Vounous tombs are supposed to be before 2100 B.C. At that time it is unlikely that there was direct contact with Egypt.[2]

---

[1] *I.L.N.* 10 Dec. 1932, p. 929, fig. 10. I owe a tracing of the inscription to the kindness of Mr Dikaios.

[2] The pot-marks of the Early Dynastic period, with which this inscription is compared (Petrie, *Royal Tombs*, I, Pls. XLIV ff., II, Pl. LV) are not likely to be linear degenerations of hieroglyphs, nor does it seem possible to associate the Vounous characters with them. The inscription may belong to some ephemeral attempt at an alphabetic script, of the kind of which there seem to have been several examples in Syria-Palestine before 1500 B.C. (Sidney Smith). It is hardly likely that the rock-inscription at Tokhni (Casson, pp. 96–7) belongs to the same category. It is asserted by some to be modern, on account of the raw appearance of the rock. It has certainly been "kept up to date"; but the suggestion of S. Menardos, in Λαογραφία, II, 1910, pp. 295 f. that it is a magical

Witness is also borne to the early use of writing in Cyprus by an inscribed cylinder from a Bronze Age tomb at Ayia Paraskevi,[1] which has early linear signs parallel to the script which existed in Crete "long before the days of the advanced scripts A and B".

What have been called "Cypro-Minoan"[2] or "Cypro-Mycenaean" characters, according as one favours direct relations with Crete or with Greece, were undoubtedly current in the Late Cypriote periods II and III, more especially in the latter. They are preserved on clay balls from Enkomi; on various other small objects; and especially, mostly in single painted signs, not in groups, on Bronze Age pottery.[3] A number show parallels with the advanced linear forms known from Crete. There are also some parallels with the much later Cypriote-Greek syllabary.[4]

---

inscription of medieval date, connected with the theft of the relic of the Cross from Tokhni in 1318, has much to be said for it.

[1] Evans, *Palace of Minos*, IV, p. 763. Dussaud, however (*Civ. Préhell.*[2] pp. 428 f.), maintains that the cylinder on which Evans bases this statement shows the same kind of writing as other objects of the Bronze Age. The cylinder is in the Ashmolean Museum (Sayce Coll.). Cp. W. H. Ward, *Seal Cylinders of Western Asia*, figs. 1164, 1165.

[2] Cp., for example, H. Jensen, *Die Schrift*, 2nd ed. [1935], p. 100 (following Evans, and ignoring recent evidence, such as is referred to below (p. 51, n. 4, p. 52, n. 4).

[3] Engraved gold ring from Maroni which may be later, since (as Dussaud remarks, *Civ. Préhell.*[2] p. 431, n. 2), it shows the later Cypriote syllabary; "Cypro-Minoan" cylinder in the Louvre; one in the Cesnola Collection; a sherd from a tomb in the Enkomi necropolis (Evans, *Palace of Minos*, IV, 1935, pp. 758 ff.). As to the last, see *Man*, 1934 (Feb.), nos. 26, 27 and Casson, p. 74, n. 1. It was found by Myres in 1913, but not at Achiropietos, as Sittig says (*Ztschr. f. vergl. Sprachf.* LII, 1924, p. 201), nor on the "Acropolis" of Enkomi, and it is a potsherd, not a piece of limestone (note from Prof. Myres). Attempts at reading these signs were made by Persson (see below, p. 52, n. 4), who pointed out that similar signs are found painted on Late Bronze Age Cypriote vases (Markides, *Ann. Report of Curator of Antiquities*, 1916, pp. 16 ff.).

Persson's latest collection of material and attempts at decipherment may be seen in *S.C.E.* III, pp. 601 ff. A few signs, incised on pottery from Curium, are given (with improbable interpretations) in *Amer Journ. Arch.* XLII, 1938, pp. 72 f.; XLIII, 1939, pp. 102 f. Over seventy signs have been collected and tabulated by Casson (pp. 72–107, and in *Iraq*, VI, 1939, pp. 39–44), whose scepticism about interpretations hitherto suggested is justified.

[4] On the relation of the Cypriote signs to the Minoan, see Sundwall in *Jahrb. Arch. Inst.* XXX, 1915, pp. 57 f. A. E. Cowley (in *Essays in Aeg. Arch. pres. to Sir A. Evans*, 1927, pp. 4 f.) attempted to read some Minoan words with the help of the Cypriote syllabary; and H. T. Bossert (*Altorient. Stud. Br. Meissner gewidm.* II, 1929, pp. 274–89) also read the Philistine name *Padi* in identical signs on a Cypriote seal from Salamis and a tablet from Cnossus (most unconvincing).

This Cypriote-Greek syllabary,[1] which is found in use later, from the sixth to the third century, has separate signs for the open syllables, in which no differentiation is made between hard, soft or aspirated consonants, and for the vowels. Reduplication of consonants is not expressed, and the nasal is suppressed when it precedes a consonant, to which it was probably assimilated.[2] Thus the word which the Greeks would write as "Euelthontos" appears in Cypriote as "E-u-we-le-to-to-se".

Such a syllabary, as many have observed, was evidently designed for some language other than Greek, since the Greek fits it so clumsily.

Until recently, there was reason to suppose that the Greeks had nothing of the kind as a vehicle for their language before they migrated from Greece itself. But examples of a mainland Greek version of the Minoan script have been accumulating, a number of which correspond to those found in Cyprus.[3] There is an important inscription found at Asine, dating from about 1200. It is written in characters showing many resemblances to the Cypriote, and an attempt has indeed been made to transliterate it into more or less intelligible Greek on those lines.[4] It is possible therefore that the Greeks in Peloponnese before their colonization of Cyprus had a syllabary similar to the proto-Cypriote; for there is no reason to assume that the Asine inscription was the earliest instance of its use, although it is the earliest so far discovered. In the present state of our information, it seems best to assume the existence in the Aegean and in the Eastern Mediterranean of a widely distributed syllabic script or scripts which served the various languages until the Phoenician alpha-

---

[1] History of its decipherment (begun by George Smith with the help of Samuel Birch in 1872) in *O.K.* p. 88. For the texts see especially Deecke in Collitz, *G.D.I.* I, 1884. Later references in *O.K. loc. cit.*; add Georgiades, *K.K.*, pp. 77 ff. The most recent account, somewhat perfunctory, and concerned chiefly with its relation to Minoan, in Otto's *Handbuch der Archäologie*, I (no date), pp. 155–8, by W. v. Bissing. The angular character of the Cypriote script has suggested that its chief use was originally for inscriptions cut in wood (Myres, *H.C.C.* p. 301; Casson, pp. 93 f.). This would explain the disappearance of examples which would fill the gap between the Bronze Age script and that of later times. The tombs of Tamassus (see chap. X) are evidence that there was a wooden architecture of which the record is only preserved in stone imitation as in Lycia, which has an equally, if not more, angular script.

[2] Clermont-Ganneau, *Rec. d'Arch. Or.* I, 1888, pp. 193–7.

[3] Evans, *Palace of Minos*, IV, ii, pp. 737 ff. Casson, p. 89.

[4] A. W. Persson in *Uppsala Univ. Årsskrift*, 1930, Progr. no. 3; the same in *Corolla Archaeologica*, 1932, pp. 208 ff. (where references are given to other discussions).

bet gave the basis for a more efficient system of writing. Crete provides the oldest forms; the Asine inscription, which is about contemporary with the clay inscriptions from Enkomi, shows forms intermediate between the old Cretan and the later Cypriote. But none of the attempts at reading or translating the inscriptions can be regarded as convincing.

If the Greek alphabet was based on the Semitic, the structure was consolidated with the assistance of the old syllabary, whether we call it Aegean or proto-Cypriote. For it was this syllabary which provided the material for the vowels which were lacking in the Semitic alphabet. It has been observed that "whoever adapted the Semitic alphabet to vocalic as well as consonantal notation chose precisely the five vowels used in the Cypriote syllabary, in spite of the fact that a Greek ear heard at least seven vowels in the language". Cyprus, as a meeting ground of Greek and Phoenician, may well have been the place where the Greeks made the adaptation.[1] It was a typically Greek stroke of invention, giving as it did to writing the same sort of flexibility and power of expression, and hence of development, as the Greek genius infused into the elements which, in the other arts, it borrowed from the East.

Whether, however, the Greeks brought a syllabary with them, or first learned it in Cyprus, there is no doubt that it was used in the island for a non-Greek language, for a few inscriptions in a strange tongue, written in the later Cypriote syllabary, have survived.[2] They are mostly connected with Amathus, though one was found at Abydos in Egypt. Thanks to a bilingual, it is demonstrable that the signs have the same value as when used for Greek. This language, which it is convenient to call Eteocyprian,[3] was used down to the fourth century B.C. In this

---

[1] See Rhys Carpenter in *Amer. Journ. Arch.* XLII, 1938, p. 67.

[2] *O.K.* pp. 89 f., with references to earlier publications (add Dussaud, *op. cit.* pp. 437 f., with Pl. IX). Sittig in *Ztschr. f. vergl. Sprachf.* 1924, pp. 194–202. Transliterations in J. Friedrich, *Kleinasiat. Sprachdenkmäler*, 1932, pp. 49 f.

[3] Bork, in his study of the subject (*Mitt. Altorient. Ges.* V, 1, 1930) calls it "the language of Alashiya". Speculations on this Eteocyprian language are numerous; see P. Kretschmer's review of Meister's publication in *Glotta*, V, 1914, p. 260; Sittig, *loc. cit.*, and the attempt by E. Power, in *Biblica*, X, 1929, pp. 129–69 (cp. the same author's art. *Chypre* in L. Pirot's Supp. to *Dict. de la Bible*, II, 1934), to translate the inscriptions as Accadian. I mention this last for completeness' sake, and refer, for a destructive criticism of it, to H. Pedersen, in *Orientalistische Literaturzeitung*, XXXIII, 1930, pp. 962–9. Pedersen admits the possibility of certain Semitic connexions, as in the equation of *ana* with "ego" (Sittig in *Ztschr. f. vergl. Sprachf.* LII, 1924, pp. 196 f.), and genitives in *i* (asatiri = Ἀσάνδρω). On the proper names in the bilingual, see

connexion, it has been observed, the statement of the geographer Pseudo-Scylax, about the middle of the fourth century, is of great significance;[1] he ends his list of cities in Cyprus with: "Amathus (the people are autochthonous)...there are also other barbarian cities in the interior." Theopompus also believed[2] that the Amathusians were the remains of the pre-Greek people of Cinyras, who was expelled by Agamemnon and the Greeks when they took Cyprus. Generally, the extreme antiquity of Amathus was recognized by ancient writers. But the language remains unidentified.[3]

Pedersen in *Mélanges Boisacq*, II, 1938, pp. 161 ff. Myres's guess (*Who were the Greeks?* p. 95), that the language was that of the "Minoan" colonists who came from the Aegean to Cyprus in the fourteenth century, is unlikely; it must belong to an older stratum. For Georgiades (*K.K.* p. 92) this language is the same as the pre-Hellenic language of mainland Greece.

[1] Müller, *Geogr. Gr. Min.* I, p. 77, Scylax, c. 103.

[2] Müller, *F.H.G.* I, p. 295, fr. 111; Jac. II B, p. 558, fr. 103; Oxf. 101.

[3] Egyptian connexion of the Amathusians and their language is not probable, and, as we have seen, the evidence of the Tell el-Yahudiye pottery does not help to establish it, as *O.K.* p. 90 supposes. The solution is most likely to come from Asia Minor, if at all.

CHAPTER IV

THE RELIGION OF EARLY CYPRUS

The early history of Cyprus is richly illustrated by the literary traditions regarding its religion, and by the remains of sanctuaries and cemeteries which have been revealed by excavation.

It seems, therefore, desirable to interrupt here the more or less chronological arrangement of this history, in order to describe the more significant elements in the primitive religion of the island.[1] Many of the minor cults must be ignored, and it will be necessary in some cases to pass beyond the limits of the Bronze Age into more historical times.

In literary tradition, the light is concentrated on the worship of the Paphian Aphrodite, and for the most part projected from the Phoenician angle. By basing our considerations on the archaeological evidence, we shall obtain a perspective not so clear, but perhaps less misleading.

The excavations at Khirokitia show that in the "Neolithic" Age, probably not later than 3000 B.C., something like a cult of the dead was practised, since what appear to be sacrificial tables, and remains of animal bones in carbonized layers, were found in a burial enclosure. On the other hand, the later settlement at Erimi has so far yielded no sign of a cult of the dead, who were buried in holes in the ground (in one case inside a house). There is no trace in Cyprus down to the end of the Bronze Age of cremation of the bodies.

The great trilithon of Hala Sultan Tekke, described in chapter II, is the only sepulchral monument of its kind in the island; the sacred use to which it is put prevents any investigation of its nature.

In the Bronze Age we find plentiful illustration of the custom of supplying the dead with material support for his life in the next world.

---

[1] I must here express my thanks to Prof. A. D. Nock of Harvard, who was good enough to read the first draft of this chapter, and make many very valuable suggestions. The most extensive collection of archaeological material relating to the religion of Cyprus is to be found in the 218 plates of Ohnefalsch-Richter's useful but ill-arranged *Kypros, die Bibel und Homer*. In his text he lays more stress on tree-worship than later writers are inclined to do. Much material has of course been excavated since his book appeared in 1893.

Terracotta models of scenes of daily life (ploughing, washing of clothes, bathing, dancing, sailing in boats, etc.) seemed to imply and served to ensure that life would go on in the next world as it had on earth.[1] The offerings which were buried with the dead included, as we have already seen, not only food but domestic animals, horse, camel and dog, which were killed and laid with their masters to serve them in the next world. Weapons and other implements were sometimes represented by pottery models.[2]

The most remarkable tomb furnishings of this period which have been found hitherto are those from the cemetery of Vounous near Bellapais.[3] The cemetery is dated by the explorer to the First Cypriote period, 3000–2100 B.C.; there are, however, reasons for taking away the first four or five hundred years.[4] The pottery, much of which must have had significance from the point of view of cultus, since its fantastic developments must have rendered it quite useless for practical purposes, includes composite vases of various kinds. One of these,[5] 32½ in. high, made up of seven elements, is worth describing in detail (Pl. II *a*). Three gourd-shaped bodies joined together form the base; fastened between, and as it were growing out of them, are three small one-handled ewers, one with three spouts, the others with two. The necks of the gourds run up into the base of the topmost element, which is a one-handled, three-spouted ewer of the same kind as the smaller ones on the base. All these vessels communicate with each other. The ornament consists of the usual rows of incised triangles. Another complicated vase takes the shape of a hollow ring standing on four legs, and supporting two bowls and two one-handled ewers, of which one is completed by its neck running up into a smaller gourd-shaped spouted vase, itself with one handle. This was doubtless a libation vessel, for liquid poured into the bowls ran

---

[1] Dussaud, *Civ. Préhell.*[2] pp. 400 ff. An amusing group in the Louvre reminds us of the Homeric custom by which women ministered to men in the bath. A very complete model of a ploughing-scene was found at Vounous (the farmer's whole family in the field, a woman dandling her baby, a donkey (?) followed by a boy, carrying their food, or seed for sowing; the plough, an affair of yoke, beam and handle and share, not much more primitive than that used in Cyprus to-day); see Dikaios in *I.L.N.* 10 Dec. 1932, p. 929; *Man*, 1933, no. 134, pp. 132–3.

[2] Dagger and its sheath, and a comb (?) in Schaeffer, *Miss.* pl. XXI.

[3] Dikaios in *I.L.N.* 31 Oct. 1931, 5 Dec. 1931 and 10 Dec. 1932. Schaeffer, *Miss.* pp. 29–48.

[4] Schaeffer, *Miss.* p. 36.

[5] *I.L.N.* 5 Dec. 1931, p. 893, fig. 7.

through the ring and out at vertical channels in the legs.[1] The decoration of these vessels is not confined to incised ornament, and among the subjects modelled in relief on the bodies of the vases, and sometimes in the round, standing on the edges, we find a man with his arm round the neck of a woman, a woman carrying a baby in its cradle,[2] a conventionalized human figure holding snakes, heads of oxen or bulls, suspended snakes, stags,[3] doves (sometimes drinking from a bowl) and an animal, perhaps a hind, suckling her young. One bowl has round its rim four models of what resemble horseshoes, with nail-holes complete; if these were rightly identified, they would indicate the use of horseshoes some two thousand years before they were known in the West, for there seems to be no evidence that Greek horses were shod before Roman times. But they seem to be merely ornaments.

In one type of ritual vase the base is formed of four bowls. On this rises a tall plank-like erection, pierced with three holes, one above the other. In one example a small jug crowns the top; but in another the top develops into a female figure holding a child in front of her. It seems natural to interpret this figure as the Mother-Goddess, although the possibility that the figures usually regarded as divine may often be merely votaries must constantly be borne in mind.

But the most remarkable object hitherto found at Vounous is a model in pottery of what the excavator explains as a snake-worship ceremony in a *temenos* (Pl. II *b*).[4] It is a round tray containing a number of figures; three are dancing, holding two snakes between them; there is a seated figure, larger than the rest; a kneeling figure, and others, including a woman, carrying a child. Bulls are shown in pens, and a person appears to be trying to climb over the wall into the enclosure. From all this the excavator deduces that the ceremony is in honour of a snake-deity, but associated with him are a mother-goddess and a bull-god. That there was a worship associating the bull and the snake is further indicated by the reliefs on a bowl which show bulls' heads with snakes hanging from

---

[1] *Ibid.* fig. 6. This and other ring-shaped vessels are comparable with the *kernoi*, if that is the right name for the ring-vases of Cretan and Mycenaean cults (Nilsson, *Minoan-Myc. Rel.* 1927, p. 117).

[2] Schaeffer, *Miss.* Pl. XIV.

[3] *Mouseion*, XXXIII–IV, 1936, p. 95.

[4] See besides *I.L.N.*, *loc. cit.*, *Proc. Int. Congr. of Prehist. and Protohist. Sci.*, London, 1932 [1934], pp. 183–5; *Arch. Anzeiger*, 1934, cols. 79–80. Evans and Myres consider the scene to be a domestic rather than a public ceremony (*Man*, 1932, p. 213); but of its religious significance there can hardly be any doubt.

them. If it is true that the dancing figures wear horns on their heads, then the pottery models of horns, found in the same tomb which yielded the bowl just mentioned, may have been worn by performers in a ritual dance. The same tomb contained a complete bull's skeleton, the animal evidently having been sacrificed; among its bones was a bowl decorated with two small birds (doves?) and a horned (bull's?) head.

Two objects of gypsum, 9 in. high, shaped like planks, with the lower portion broader than the upper, are idols reduced to their lowest terms. Probably details were originally shown in colour. They seem to preserve an archaic or hieratic form,[1] for the pottery shows that the makers could make something much more easily recognizable as a human figure, and so do the plank-shaped images in terracotta and marble, such as those found at Lapithos, which represent a mother holding a baby, a mother and a baby in bed, or a man and woman in bed.[2]

There can be no doubt that the Vounous evidence proves the existence at this early age, in the third millennium, of a worship of a bull-deity,[3] with whom are associated snakes, and of a fertility cult, the symbol of which is the dove, though whether the women holding babies represent a mother-goddess or merely votaries,[4] we cannot be certain; also, the notion that we have indications of a sort of *hieros gamos*, or of a mystery, or of the horns of consecration so common in Crete, must be regarded for the present as doubtful.

The interest, in any case, of these early illustrations of the religion of Cyprus, in connexion with the cults with which excavations in Crete have made us familiar, is patent. The dove-cult, it has been remarked,[5] which in Cyprus goes back to the Copper Age, was not Mesopotamian in origin, but taken over by the Semites from Syro-Anatolia. The at-

---

[1] For the type in terracotta (with a protuberance for the nose but otherwise decorated with incised lines to indicate dress and features), see Schaeffer, *Miss.* Pl. XX, and Dussaud, *Civ. Préhell.*[2] p. 366. Other varieties—sometimes intended to indicate mother and child—in Ohnefalsch-Richter, *K.B.H.* Pl. XXXVI. On the stone idols of Cyprus in general, see V. Müller, *Frühe Plastik in Griechenland u. Vorderasien*, 1929, pp. 27–8.

[2] Gjerstad in *Antiquity*, II, 1928, pp. 189 f.

[3] On the religious significance of the bull in Cyprus, cp. Dussaud, *Civ. Préhell.*[2] p. 395; but one can hardly agree with him that the oxen which the king of Alashiya asked for from the king of Egypt (El-Amarna letter no. 35) were wanted for religious purposes.

[4] Hogarth, in *Essays in Aegean Archaeology presented to Sir Arthur Evans*, 1927, pp. 55 ff., quoted by Sjöqvist in *Arch. f. Religionswiss.* XXX, 1933, p. 359, in connexion with the Vounous model.

[5] Evans, *Palace of Minos*, IV, pp. 406–7.

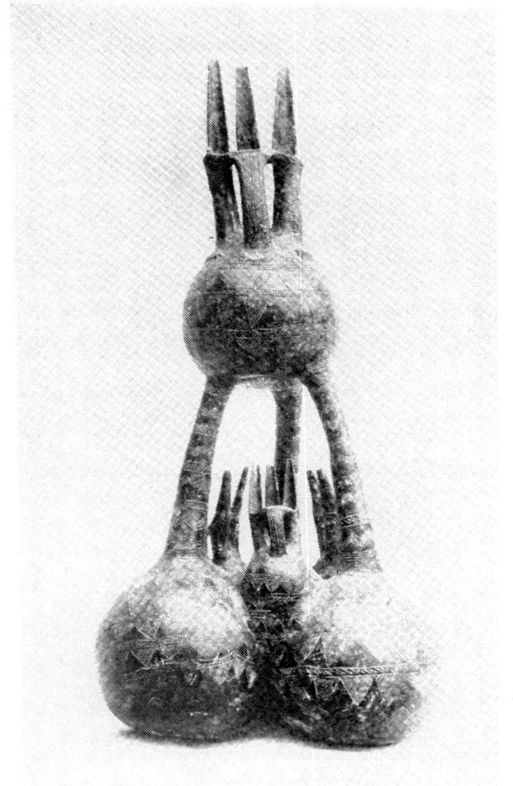

Cyprus Museum

a

b

BRONZE-AGE VASE AND MODEL FROM VOUNOUS

tempt to find Babylonian influence in Cypriote "Astarte" figures may be set aside.[1]

A sanctuary at Ayia Irini,[2] on the west of the Kormakiti peninsula, excavated by the Swedes in 1929–30, was founded in the last period of the Bronze Age (Late Cypriote III) and flourished until the last quarter of the Cypro-Archaic period II; it was then derelict for some four centuries, but there was a feeble revival in the first century B.C. For over a thousand years, then, the history of a Cypriote sanctuary is outlined by the work of the Swedish excavators.

Its greatest development was in the Iron Age, but it bears witness to the existence in the Bronze Age of some sort of cult of a bull-god, differing, however, in some respects from that revealed at Vounous.[3] A complicated system of houses surrounded on three sides a four-cornered open court. One of the houses, the sanctuary proper, contained a stone bench, which probably served for holding cult-objects and votive offerings, and a stone offering-table. Great *pithoi* served to collect the offerings. A small terracotta figure of a bull (not a bull-shaped vase such as is common in tombs of the Late Cypriote period) is paralleled by other terracotta figures of bulls, of which one, from Dali,[4] was found beside an offering-table in a house-chapel of Late Cypriote III, together with four larger terracotta bulls of painted ware. These figures were doubtless votive offerings. The actual sacrifices both at Ayia Irini and at Dali seem to have been vegetable; so that the bull does not take the place of an actual sacrificed bull. A large egg-shaped black stone, which was found beside a later altar in the same sanctuary at Ayia Irini, may, it is thought, have been the original fetish of the Bronze Age cult, which was preserved in the later stages of the sanctuary. It is suggested that, though the original seat of the "power" of the deity was in the aniconic stone, the deity was conceived[5] as a bull, and materialized in this terracotta votive statuette; the bull-god would be a

---

[1] Above, p. 28, note, at end. [2] *S.C.E.* II, pp. 642 ff.

[3] E. Sjöqvist, "Die Kultgeschichte eines Cyprischen Temenos" in *Arch. f. Religionswiss.* XXX, 1933, pp. 308 ff. What follows in the text is little more than a somewhat inadequate summary of Sjöqvist's exceedingly interesting interpretation of the cult-history. [4] On the Dali excavation see *S.C.E.* II, pp. 460 ff.

[5] Perhaps "conceived" is not the right word; as Prof. Nock observes, the theriomorphic stage may be merely a stage in modes of representation. All the time the deities may be thought of as human (so deities are shown in their epiphanies on Minoan-Mycenaean rings and gems), but the forms in which they appear may be bulls or snakes or birds or trees or even stones.

deity of harvest and fruitfulness, to whom the fruits of harvest would be sacrificed. At Dali olive-kernels were found on the offering-table. There seems to be no trace of the snake-attribute at Ayia Irini in the Bronze Age; for that we must wait until the Early Archaic phase of the sanctuary.

With the Iron Age came a great change; the original chapel and its surrounding rooms were carefully covered over with a layer of earth, and a temenos laid out over them, the sacred stone already mentioned being, however, preserved and set up again. In the new temenos there was a triangular altar built of small stones (remains of animal bones, with ashes and charcoal, lay upon it) as well as a large circular stone offering-table with saucer-shaped depressions, perhaps for libations. Many fragments of figures of bulls showed that the bull-worship of the previous period continued. But that blood-sacrifices were now offered is proved by the remains on the altar and by similar animal bones in a bothros within the temenos. A network covering, which is indicated on one of the bull-figures,[1] is paralleled from Crete, and explained as a ritual decoration; the bull to be sacrificed was clad in it. It is possible that in this phase of the development of the sanctuary, that is, early in the tenth century, we see the beginning of the change from the theriomorphic conception of the bull-god to a god of fruitfulness conceived in human form.[2] In the Early Archaic period, the sanctuary, which showed signs of decay towards the end of the Geometric period, took a new lease of life. The floor of the temenos was again carefully covered and levelled, as little damage as possible being done to the older remains. The more important votive offerings were collected and, together with new ones, placed beside a new altar, a monolith of *poros* stone. A bothros, sunk down to rock-level, was filled with ashes and Late Geometric sherds, representing the votives which it was not thought worth while to preserve. Another dump of damaged votives was made in a corner of the temenos. The sacrifices in the Early Archaic period, so far as can be judged from the remains, followed the old ritual, though no libation-table has been preserved. Among the votives, in addition to scarabs and seal-stones, we now find three kinds of terracotta figurines: bulls, monsters, and human figures. One group of bull-figures is distinguished by pairs of snakes which twine round their necks with the heads lying between the horns;[2] in one case the ceremonial network of the earlier

---

[1] *S.C.E.* II, Pl. CCXXIV, no. 2049. [2] Sjöqvist, p. 327.
[3] *S.C.E.* II, Pl. CCXXV, nos. 2027–8.

period is again indicated. The significance of the snake as an attribute of the gods of fertility and harvest, and the analogies provided by the Minoan cult, are here again called to our mind. The votive human figures of this period are of the simplest kind, some with one hand raised in adoration, others holding gifts. The monstrous figures are bull-centaurs, with human head, arms and body to the waist, attached to a four-footed bull's body; some are horned,[1] others not; some have snakes twining round them, or held in their hands; and, strangest of all, some are clearly hermaphroditic.[2] All these monsters hold up their hands in adoration. They are not therefore images of the deity himself, and it is suggested that they represent the spirits and daemons with which primitive man peoples nature; which he fears, but which are at the same time subordinated to the chief deity. And it seems to follow that if these servants of the deity are now conceived in a semi-anthropomorphic form, the deity himself must be fully anthropomorphized. This stage of religious development may then be dated, at least at Ayia Irini, at the end of the early archaic period, that is, in the second half of the seventh century. In the next period, the full Archaic, the temenos was somewhat enlarged, and the wall reconstructed; the old altar was taken over and provided (now or perhaps in the next period) with a mortar rim to keep off the wind, and an enclosure was erected which may, since its area shows two layers of humus, not otherwise forthcoming in the temenos, have contained sacred trees.[3] The remains of this period include the most remarkable collection of votive figures, mostly terracotta statuettes, which has ever rewarded an excavator (Pl. III); they were massed together, practically all *in situ*, in a semicircle about the altar; on the extreme wings, vases; in the inner circle, nearest to the altar, the smallest statuettes, models of chariots, equestrian figures and bulls; and then the other statues, arranged in order of size, so that the life-size figures stood on the outside edge.[4]

---

[1] Horned centaurs from other sites; *K.B.H.* pp. 250 f. One came from Amathus.

[2] Sjöqvist, p. 34, fig. 4; *S.C.E.* II, Pl. CCXXVII, no. 2044.

[3] This is the only sort of evidence of tree-worship on this site. It may be suspected that the tree-worship, to the elucidation of which Ohnefalsch-Richter devotes the greater part of his book, *K.B.H.*, was not native to Cyprus, but was a Phoenician importation. See n. 1, p. 63.

[4] Sjöqvist, p. 341, figs. 9, 10; *I.L.N.* 24 Sept. 1932, pp. 452–6; *Die Antike*, IX, 1933, Taf. 25; *S.C.E.* II, pp. 798 ff. They have now been set up more or less in the same position in the Cyprus Museum, *Report of the Department of Antiquities*, 1935, Pl. XIII, 3.

These votive figures represent the persons who dedicated them; the equestrian figures and the battle chariots, and the fact that some of the figures wear armour, show that the god to whom they were dedicated, if he was a fertility-god, was also a god of war.[1] Among some two thousand figures, there are only two of women. Was the shrine one of those to which women were not admitted? Figures of bulls and bull-centaurs appear, but in diminishing proportion; the hermaphroditic variety of the latter is not represented. The execution of the figures is exceedingly summary, except in regard to the heads (Pl. III), the body being often represented by little more than a cylinder; the head-dress is usually a conical helmet, probably meant to be of leather. But in one group of figures a band is worn, wound several times round the head; hair and beard are long, the long dress reaches to the feet, and the left hand may have held a sword or knife. These, it is supposed, may be priests. Two fragmentary figures show priests or votaries wearing bulls' masks on their heads, a ritual attire of which there are other examples from Cyprus,[2] as from many other places. Thus the bull-god of Ayia Irini is seen to have had appropriately his ceremonial dances or processions in which bull-masks were worn.

The sacred black stone—of nearly spherical shape, about 0·25 m. greatest diameter—which we have already mentioned, was apparently in use down to the late archaic period; marks of splitting by heat suggest that it may have actually stood on the altar near which it was found. It shows signs of having been anointed with oil or the like, according to a practice for which there are many parallels.[3]

Great numbers of scarabs, scaraboids, cylinders and seal-stones, were found in a layer along the north wall of the temenos, where it is supposed there was some sort of penthouse; together, with them, masses of fragments of bones and shells suggest that ritual meals may have been consumed in the temenos where the votaries deposited their gifts. Among all these remains, it is admitted that there is little trace of that tree-worship which is assumed to explain the enclosure described above, and the evidence for the existence in Cyprus of a combination of tree-

---

[1] Like Mars in early Rome. W. Warde Fowler, *Roman Festivals*, pp. 34 f., 48 f., etc.

[2] Myres, *H.C.C.* pp. 150–1, nos. 1029–30.

[3] Frazer, *Adonis, Attis and Osiris*,[3] I, 1914, p. 36. The ἐλαιοχρίστιον mentioned in an inscription from Paphos (B.M. no. 969) is the place where athletes oiled themselves in the gymnasium, and has nothing to do with the sacred stone (Dittenberger, *O.G.I.S.* II, 749) or any religious rite, as Zannetos quaintly conjectures (Ἱστορία, I, p. 399).

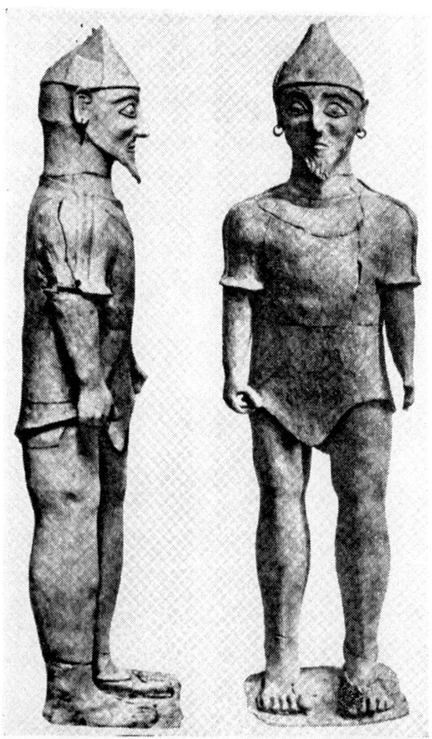

Swedish Cyprus Expedition

TERRACOTTAS FROM AYIA IRINI

worship with bull-worship, amply proven for Crete in an earlier age, has to be sought from representations on Cypriote cylinders and Graeco-Phoenician pottery,[1] although it is doubtful how far the tree in the latter cases is more than decorative.

The sanctuary which flourished so vigorously during the full Archaic period was destroyed by a flood. It was restored in the Late Archaic period, but gradually fell into decay, perhaps owing to the rivalry of another temple, remains of which, dating from the fifth century, exist across the ravine to the north. In Late Hellenistic times there was a revival; the fragments of votives from Late Archaic times were carefully collected and buried, and the surface again made up and levelled. The base of what was evidently an important statue, perhaps the cultus-figure itself, is the only significant find from this latest level.

The history of Ayia Irini throws so much light on the character of early Cypriote religion, that no excuse is necessary for the length of the summary which has been given. Would that the old excavators, who scrambled for antiques at Dali, Athienou ana elsewhere, had been interested in the history of the sites and possessed the modern technique of excavation. The results for the history of the religion, as of the art, of Cyprus would have been of even greater importance than those which have been gleaned, by the skill of the Swedish excavators, from the modest sanctuary of Ayia Irini.

Other Bronze Age burials furnish evidence of the cult of the dead. Thus at Paleoskoutella (near Nitovikla)[2] there are tumuli dating from

---

[1] Sjöqvist, pp. 349 f. Instances earlier than the Graeco-Phoenician age are scanty. See *K.B.H.* pp. 32 ff. and cp. Myres, *C.C.M.* pp. 24, 33. The sacred tree in Cyprus has recently been discussed by H. Danthine, *Le palmier dattier et les arbres sacrés dans l'iconographie de l'Asie orientale ancienne*, Paris, 1937, pp. 198–209. She concludes "il semble pourtant que l'originalité de Chypre se manifeste dans l'emploi, comme motif décoratif, du symbole sacré de l'Orient". A kind of tree-worship still survives in Cyprus; trees which are supposed to cure diseases are hung by devotees with rags of clothing or hair from their heads. The best known of these sacred trees is at A. Solomoni, New Paphos (*K.B.H.* Pl. XVIII). Such trees are commonly associated with holy wells. On this and analogous practices in Cyprus see *K.B.H.* pp. 120, 170; Magda Ohnefalsch-Richter, *Gr. Sitten u. Gebräuche auf Cypern*, 1913, pp. 39, 47; Gunnis, *Hist. Cyprus*, 1936, pp. 128, 144, 344; L. Ross, *Journey to Cyprus*, p. 36; O. M. Chapman, *Across Cyprus*, p. 76. But it is a world-wide custom, found in Patagonia, New Guinea, Central Africa, Palestine, India and the British Isles, and doubtless elsewhere.

[2] *S.C.E.* I, pp. 416 ff.; Picard, *Journ. des Savants*, 1935, p. 249. A pillar which stands in the chamber of the large tumulus, about opposite the entrance, has been explained as the symbol of the chthonic deity: Georgiades, *K.K.* pp. 211 f.

Middle Cypriote III, towards the end of the seventeenth century, which, though situated in a necropolis, contain no tombs, but appear from the internal arrangements (ledges, pits and cavities laid out on an intricate system) to have been cult places. These were abandoned before Late Cypriote times; the smaller tombs were emptied and their contents dumped in a large tumulus. It is suggested that this was done to make the resting-place of the dead safe from violation by the foreigners who were now beginning to invade the land. At Enkomi, in a tomb of Late Cypriote II[1], the dromos showed a layer of ash, which has been thought to indicate a ceremony of purification or sacrifice, carried out after the last burial had been made in the chamber itself; a skeleton which was found in the dromos has even been thought to belong to a slave sacrificed in this ceremony. But the evidence for human sacrifice seems as a rule to belong to a later date.

Thus the tombs at Kastros (Lapithos),[2] which yield such evidence, belong to the First Cypriote Geometric period (beginning about 1000 B.C.). Here were found skeletons buried in the dromoi; in one case, not only was the body buried outside the door of the tomb in the dromos, but fragments of bones were found below the stones of the door-packing, showing that the body was buried when the door was closed.

Of literary evidence for human sacrifices in Cyprus there is little. Most remarkable are two statements of Lactantius[3] and Porphyrius[4] concerning a ceremony at Salamis. The former attributes the introduction of the sacrifice of a man to Zeus to Teucer, the founder of the city. He gives no details of the rite, but Porphyrius says that the sacrifice used to take place in the month of Aphrodite,[5] and was first offered to Agraulus, the daughter of Cecrops and Agraulus; it lasted until the time of Diomede, to whom the sacrifice was then transferred (the temples of Athena and of Agraulus and Diomede were in the same enclosure). A pyre was piled up, the victim was led in by young men and ran three times round the altar, then the priest smote him with a spear in the throat, and he was thrown on the pyre and utterly consumed.

---

[1] *S.C.E.* I, pp. 467 ff.; tomb 11 (pp. 510 ff.).

[2] *S.C.E.* I, pp. 218 (tomb 412), 228 (417), 236 (420).

[3] *Divin. inst.* I, 21, 1.

[4] *De Abstin.* II, 54, 55. Repeated by Eusebius, *Praep. Evang.* IV, c. 16 and Cyril of Alexandria (Migne, *P.G.* 76, col. 697).

[5] In the Paphos calendar this month began on 23 September. Salamis had retained the Egyptian calendar long into the Imperial period.

This institution lasted down to a comparatively late date, possibly even to Roman times.[1] A sacrifice of an ox was substituted for it, and accepted by the god, says Porphyrius, as equivalent for the man. However deeply we may be shocked at the cruelty of this rite, to say that it savours rather of Oriental barbarity than of Greek humanity[2] is unreasonable, in the face of the overwhelming evidence for the survival of human sacrifice among the Greeks, even if we suppose that it originated in a pre-Hellenic stage. The information given by Lactantius and Porphyrius between them, and the connexion with Greek cults, point to the conclusion that the Salaminian rite was introduced by the Greek colonists. Zeus may have represented the primitive bull-deity, but there is no evidence that this particular rite was of primitive or specially Oriental origin.

A trace is preserved by Ovid,[3] in his account of the origin of the Cerastae, of the existence of a custom of sacrificing strangers to Jupiter

---

[1] Porphyrius has the puzzling statement that it was abolished by "Diphilus, king of Cyprus, who lived in the time of Seleucus the Theologian". Such a king is not otherwise recorded, nor do we know certainly who Seleucus Theologus was, or when he lived, though he may possibly be the Alexandrian grammarian who wrote 100 books about the gods, and was a contemporary of the Emperor Tiberius. Porphyrius may mean that this Seleucus mentioned Diphilus and the abolition of the rite as a contemporary event. On the other hand, it has been supposed that a definite date for the abolition of the rite is given by Lactantius, as taking place in the reign of the Emperor Hadrian. But Lactantius is probably drawing on a statement of Porphyrius (*de Abstin.* II, 56), which is: "that human sacrifices were stopped almost everywhere is stated by Pallas who made the best collection of material about the Mithraic mysteries in the reign of the Emperor Hadrian". It is fairly clear that the words ἐφ' Ἁδριανοῦ τοῦ αὐτοκράτορος give the date of Pallas the writer, not of the abolition of the rites; and so they are interpreted by Christ-Schmidt-Stählin, *Gesch. d. gr. Litt.* II, ii, 1924, p. 763. A king of Cyprus in the time of Hadrian there cannot have been, unless the title, which had been previously borne by the rulers of Salamis and Paphos as priests of Zeus and Aphrodite, was retained by them as a religious title after their royal dignity was abrogated. So the Ionian cities under the Empire preserved the title βασιλεὺς Ἰώνων for a functionary concerned specially, like the βασιλεύς at Athens, with the public cults. (Dittenberger, *O.G.I.S.* II, 489.) So Diphilus may, after all, have been contemporary with Tiberius or Hadrian, although, it is true, we should have expected some epigraphic evidence for the survival.

[2] Frazer, *Adonis, Attis and Osiris*,[3] I, p. 145.

[3] *Met.* X, 224, with the Narratio *ad loc.*, attributed to Lactantius Placidus, who says that the altar of Zeus adjoined that of Aphrodite. One explanation of the name Cerastia for Cyprus was that it was inhabited by horned men (Tzetzes in Lycophr. 447; *Etym. Magn.* s.v. Σφήκεια.)—Prof. Nock inclines to think that if an inference can

Hospes (Zeus Xenios) at Amathus. The custom gave offence to Aphrodite, who punished the offenders by turning them into bulls. The tale of the origin of the horned centaurs from the seed of Zeus in his pursuit of Aphrodite may be a fancy of Nonnus;[1] but this, and the story in Ovid, seem to reflect some dim memory of a rivalry and possibly a reconciliation between the two cults, the primitive of Aphrodite, the later of a god whose theriomorph was a bull, whether he were Dionysus or Zeus.

The Cypriotes, when they adopted from the Greeks the legend of Busiris, connected it with Cyprus; for it was a Cypriote priest, Thrasius or Phrasius, who went to Egypt and counselled Busiris to appease Zeus by instituting human sacrifice. As we know, Heracles, who was to be sacrificed as a stranger, turned the tables on Busiris. The story is hardly of primitive origin, but it was tacked on to Cypriote legend by means of Thrasius, who is described as either a relation or a priest of Pygmalion.[2] And it suggests the existence of the custom of human sacrifice in the native place of Thrasius.

Finally, something in the nature of human sacrifice seems to be indicated by Strabo,[3] who speaks (as though the custom had survived to his time) of a cliff to the west of Curium "from which they throw those who have laid hold of the altar of Apollo".

Thus nearly, if not quite, all the evidence concerning human sacrifice in Cyprus points to its having been introduced by the Greek colonists.

At Vounous and Ayia Irini and elsewhere we depend entirely on the archaeological evidence for the nature and history of the local cult. At Paphos, on the other hand, the evidence is almost entirely literary; the archaeological element is provided by one object only which may be of primitive date, and by coins and gems of the historical period.[4]

---

be based on the story in Ovid, it would be that Zeus was the primitive deity and Aphrodite the later comer; but I do not see that this follows. Incidentally, he remarks, the Ovid passage suggests that human sacrifice was *de facto* in desuetude; Diphilus may have abolished it *de jure*.

[1] *Dionysiaca*, v, 611–15; xxxii, 71–2. See *K.B.H.* pp. 255 f., where the story is connected with the terracotta figurines of horned centaurs. (One from Amathus, *K.B.H.* Pl. XLVII, 17.)

[2] The sources in Engel, *Kypros*, ii, pp. 90 f. According to one, Junius Philargyrius, it was Pygmalion himself who gave the advice to Busiris.

[3] xiv, 6. 3. This is possibly allied to the better-known custom at Leucas of annually throwing a criminal into the sea at the festival of Apollo (Strabo, x, 2. 9). It is interesting to find this god concerned in both cases.

[4] The actual temple has not yet been found or excavated; the site cleared by the

The legends[1] connected with Paphos are especially important because of the world-wide fame of the cult of Aphrodite, and also because of the connexion which they illustrate between Arcadia and Cyprus, in harmony with the undoubted connexion between the dialects of the two lands. Three or more strains are to be distinguished in the legends of the origin of the cult of the Paphian Aphrodite.[2] In one, the foundation of the temple of the goddess at Old Paphos is assigned to Agapenor, king of Tegea, who, on his return from Troy after the war, was diverted by storm to Cyprus. According to Pausanias[3], Agapenor was also at the same time the founder of (New) Paphos. Aphrodite had been worshipped at Golgi.[4] Strabo also makes New Paphos a foundation of Agapenor, but does not mention him in connexion with the shrine at

---

English in 1887, and supposed by them to be a temple on a Phoenician plan, is somewhere in the enceinte of the real temple, and has nothing Phoenician about it. Westholm, in *Acta Archaeologica*, IV, Copenhagen, 1933, p. 207.

[1] For these legends, and others of the Greek colonization of Cyprus in general, see Engel, *Kypros*, I, pp. 203–29; Busolt, *Gr. Gesch.* I,[2] 1893, pp. 318–21; R. Meister, *Gr. Dial.* II, pp. 126 ff.; *O.K.* p. 91. For Paphos especially, the admirable exposition by M. R. James in *J.H.S.* IX, 1888, pp. 175–92. These authorities make it unnecessary for me to give all detailed references to the ancient writers, and in the following discussion I do not pretend to deal exhaustively with the subject.

[2] In the Cypriote inscriptions Aphrodite is called simply "the lady" (*anassa*) or "the goddess"; in later inscriptions she is Παφία.

[3] VIII, 5. 2. Frazer's deliberate disregard (*Adonis, Attis and Osiris*,[3] I, p. 42 note) of the Agapenor legend is not justified in view of the connexion between Cyprus and Arcadia.

[4] Münter and (independently) Neubauer (*Comm. Philol. in hon. Th. Mommseni*, 1877, pp. 673–93) identify Golgi with Kouklia (Old Paphos), but the statement of Pausanias that, before the foundation of the temple at Paphos by Agapenor, Aphrodite was worshipped "at a place called Golgi" is surely rather against than for the identification. On the other hand, there is something to be said for the neighbourhood of Athienou, even though the dedications found in the temenos-site already excavated show that it was sacred to Apollo. Yorgos or Giorkos (στοὺς Γιόρκους), a spot near Athienou, where there are remains of an ancient city, and where there has never been a church of A. Giorgios to account for the name, may represent the ancient Golgi. Dedications to the goddess *Golgia* have been found at the neighbouring Dali (Collitz, *G.D.I.* I, 61; Hoffmann, *Gr. Dial.* I, p. 73, no. 136), at Arsos (between Athienou and Lysi), and at Akhna (between Famagusta and Larnaka), *S.E.G.* VI, nos. 830–3. None has been found in any other region, and these are all consistent with her shrine being at Athienou. On the identification, see Sakellarios, Κυπριακά, I, 1890, pp. 193 ff.; Menardos, Τοπωνυμικόν (Ἀθηνᾶ, XVIII, 1906, p. 321 and XXII, 1910, pp. 417 ff.); Peristianes, Γεν. Ἱστ. 1910, pp. 549 ff.; Oberhummer, art. *Golgoi* in *R.E.* VII, 1912, 1579 ff.

Old Paphos. The Arcadian connexion is further illustrated by the legend that Laodice, daughter of Agapenor (though another version makes Cinyras her father), dedicated a *peplos* in the temple of Athena Alea at Tegea, where she also founded a temple of Aphrodite Paphia.[1] Other links with Peloponnese are traceable in the Sicyonian origin of Golgos, the eponym of Golgi (where, as we have seen, there was a very early worship of Aphrodite), and the Corinthian origin of the rites of the Paphian priests.[2]

On the other hand, if we follow another line of legends, the foundation of the cult of Aphrodite was earlier than Agapenor's day. The priest-kings of Paphos traced their origin to Cinyras, the beautiful, the proverbially wealthy king of Paphos or of all Cyprus, who lived to a fabulous age, and whose grave was in the temple of Aphrodite, where also his successors were buried. One tradition made him the son of Amathusa, thus connecting him with another Cyprian seat of the worship of Aphrodite. He himself was dated during the time of the Trojan War; for it was he who, as the *Iliad* tells us, sent Agamemnon a notable cuirass[3] when he heard of the expedition against Troy; but he also played the bad joke of promising the Greek king a contingent of fifty ships, and sending only one, with models of the others, and of their crews, in clay. In return for which Agamemnon conquered Cyprus and drove Cinyras out of his kingdom.[4]

The legends which associate Cinyras with Apollo probably do not belong to the most primitive stratum. The name was connected with the word *kinyra* (the Hebrew *kinnôr*), a ten-stringed lyre,[5] and this con-

---

[1] Paus. VIII, 5. 3 and 53. 7. He quotes the inscription on the dedication as if he had seen it.

[2] Chr. Blinkenberg, "Le Temple de Paphos", in *Hist.-filol. Meddelelser* of the Kgl. Danske Videnskabernes Selskab, IX, 2, 1924, p. 31.

[3] The cuirass was of the "lobster" type, with strips of three metals (A. R. Burn, *Minoans, Philistines and Greeks*, p. 214). Westholm (*Acta Archaeol.* IX, 1938, p. 163) takes it for scale-armour, and describes fragments of splint-armour of the Iron Age from Amathus and Idalium.

[4] Schol. Hom. *Il.* XI, 20. Theopomp. fr. 111 M. (*F.H.G.* I, p. 295 = 103 Jac., 101 Oxf.) says that the Amathusians are the remains of οἱ μετὰ Κινύρου, who were expelled by the Greeks. I can find no other authority than this for Engel's assumption that there was an important priestly family of Cinyradae at Amathus as at Paphos (*Kypros*, I, pp. 170–3 and elsewhere).

[5] According to Engel (*Kypros*, II, pp. 109 ff.) Cinyras represents the music of the flute, not the lyre; hence the contest with Apollo, whose instrument is the latter. On

nexion is illustrated by the tale that Apollo defeated him in a musical contest, the penalty for defeat being death.[1] On the other hand, to Pindar he is the beloved of Apollo;[2] and he is also claimed as Apollo's own son.[3]

These Apolline legends have the appearance of either being inspired by the desire of the Greeks to fit Cinyras into their orthodox genealogy, or belonging to the Phoenician layer. They need not concern us in our consideration of the primitive cult of Aphrodite.

Still older than the tradition about Cinyras, if we are to trust Tacitus,[4] was that which attributed the foundation of the temple to Aërias; some also, he says, gave the name Aëria to the goddess herself. Aërias, he tells us, was the father of Amathus, who founded a temple of Aphrodite Amathusia. Here we have another link between Paphos and Amathus.[5]

Yet another body of tradition attributed a Phoenician origin to the cult of Aphrodite.[6] But this, though it goes back to Herodotus, is part of the general tradition which assigned to the Phoenicians much greater influence in the origin of Greek culture than our knowledge of Mediterranean archaeology permits us to accept.[7] We must, in fact, rule out of court all claims on behalf of a specifically Oriental (Babylonian, Syrian or Phoenician) origin for the Aphrodite cult, although parallel developments and later influence from such quarters may be freely admitted. All its features can be paralleled in Anatolia or in the Aegean. The earliest

---

the relation Cinyras-κινύρα, see Vlad Bănăţeanu in *Rev. des Études Indo-Européennes*, I, 1938, p. 132, who begs the question when he says that "ce Kinyras se trouve être roi de Chypre précisément à l'époque de l'influence des Phéniciens en Chypre".

[1] Schol. Hom. *Il.* XI, 20.

[2] *Pyth.* II, 15. The scholiast on Pindar explains the reference to the love of Apollo as meaning merely that he was a notable musician. But Pseudo-Clemens Romanus, *Hom.* V, 15, of course takes it in the worse sense.

[3] Schol. Pind. *loc. cit.* (his mother being Paphos; alternatively, he is the son of Eurymedon and a Paphian nymph); Schol. Theocr. I, 109. This phrase may also be taken in the same sense as Pindar's words, Engel, *Kypros*, II, p. 114.

[4] *Hist.* II, 3; *Ann.* III, 62.

[5] James (p. 176) quotes Alciati as reading *Uranium* for *Aëriam*, on the authority of a MS. This may reflect the epithet *Urania*, borne by the goddess; and possibly both names may be connected with the fact that her altar was in the open (Tümpel in *R.E.* I, 677).

[6] According to St Jerome, Phoenicians from Byblus founded Paphos in 540 after Abraham, i.e. in 1415 B.C. But it is improbable that there was any Phoenician settlement in Cyprus before the Iron Age.

[7] Chr. Blinkenberg, *Temple de Paphos*, pp. 33 f.

anthropomorphic representations of the mother-goddess in Cyprus are clothed; the nude goddess, with whom Babylonian representations have made us familiar, is a comparatively late development.[1] So, too, the name Adonis, though it became naturalized in Cyprus after the Phoenician penetration, towards the end of the Bronze Age or the beginning of the Iron Age, was only adopted in the place of earlier names for the gods of vegetation.[2] For the sacred doves of the Paphian goddess we do not need to seek a parallel or an origin in Phoenicia; their association in the Aegean with the Mother-Goddess and with a building of the same type as the temple at Paphos is proved by the gold bracteates of Mycenae.[3] The origin of the customs of ritual sacrifice of virginity and of religious prostitution[4] has, since antiquity, been referred to Babylonian and Syrian sources. But this is only one more instance of the Oriental mirage. We have no need to go further than Asia Minor for examples.[5] In Corinth and Eryx and Etruria these customs may have been of native growth, and there is no need to drag in the Phoenicians to account for them.[6]

---

[1] Dussaud, *Civ. Préhell.*[2] pp. 366 ff. On the influence of Cyprus and Phoenicia on the Aphrodite cult in the Aegean in the early archaic period, see Blinkenberg, *Knidia*, pp. 38 f., 206 f.

[2] Such as Pygmalion, Ao, Kirris, Gauas, some of which may belong to the primitive language of Cyprus. Dussaud, *Civ. Préhell.*[2] pp. 371, 389. The later legends make Adonis the son of Cinyras by his own daughter Myrrha, or by Metharme, daughter of Pygmalion. Out of the wild confusion of these and other tales (such as that which makes Cinyras the lover of Aphrodite) the anthropologists have picked material for spinning new theories (Frazer, *Adonis, Attis and Osiris*,[3] I, pp. 49 f.).

[3] Ohnefalsch-Richter, *K.B.H.* Pl. XXXVIII, 8–10 (for the dove-cult in general, see especially his pp. 278–88); Dussaud, *Civ. Préhell.*[2] p. 373; Blinkenberg, *Temple de Paphos*, pp. 17, 20.

[4] Herodotus, I, 199; other literary sources in Engel, II, pp. 136 ff.; James, pp. 184 f. and many other books. Religious prostitution, as Prof. Nock reminds me, takes two forms. In one, all women before marriage are obliged to sacrifice their virginity once to a stranger; in the other, as at Eryx, in Anatolia and at Corinth, there is a continual service. The former seems to have prevailed at Paphos. It may have originally had nothing to do with religion, but have arisen out of the primitive fear of the risk run by the man who first had intercourse with a virgin. But if it became attached to a cult, it is easy to see how the second, professional form would grow up. Cp. Nilsson, *Griech. Feste*, p. 367. Hostile Christian witnesses do not distinguish between the forms; both are equally prostitution for gain (e.g. Lactantius, *div. inst.* I, 17, 10: "Venus... auctor...mulieribus in Cypro fuit, uti vulg⟨at⟩o corpore quaestum facerent").

[5] Comana Pontica and Tralles; see Frazer, *Adonis, Attis and Osiris*,[3] I, pp. 36 ff.

[6] Still less in the case of Locri Epizephyrii (Justin, *Hist. Phil.* XXI, 3), as is done by

A reflection of the custom of religious prostitution at Paphos is perhaps to be found in the legend that three daughters of Cinyras by Metharme were driven by the vengeful wrath of Aphrodite[1] to give themselves to strangers, and ended their lives in Egypt.

At the annual festival of Aphrodite, men and women, from other cities as well as Paphos, walked by the road from New to Old Paphos (a distance of 60 *stadia*, or about 7½ miles).[2] At the mystery, the initiates received a lump of salt and a *phallos*, which they acknowledged by the payment of a coin to the goddess.[3] These symbols have been plausibly referred to the legend of the birth of Aphrodite from the sea.

But the most curious feature of the Aphrodite cult in Paphos was the aniconic representation of the godhead. Here again the endeavour has been made to find an origin in Phoenicia for the conical or meta-shaped object which stood for her, and which we see represented in the reproductions of the temple on ancient coins and gems.[4] But the cone of Paphos belongs to a class of primitive "symbols" which were widely distributed over Anatolia, and probably also over the Aegean and its western shores. In Crete, the pillar seems to have been more favoured, but there is no lack of evidence for sacred cones or *omphaloi*.[5] In Greece, in historical times, such old symbols had been replaced or doubled, at least in important sanctuaries, by statues; but at Delphi the omphalos remained as a record of the primitive fashion.[6] And it is interesting to

---

Hepding (*R.E.* VIII, 1467). If there was a primitive religious custom behind the promise of the Locrians (as from Athenaeus, XI, 516, it would appear there was) it was more likely to be of Sicel than of Phoenician origin.

[1] Apollod. *Bibl.* III, xiv, 3 (2). Had they, like the Propoetides of Amathus, to be mentioned later, denied her divinity?

[2] Strabo, XIV, 6. 3, p. 683.

[3] Clemens Alex. *Protrept.* I, p. 13 (Potter); Arnobius, *adv. Gentes*, V, 19; Jul. Firmicus Maternus, *de errore prof. rel.* c. x (passages given by James, p. 184).

[4] In 1904, in discussing the relation of this object with the pillar of the Minoan cult, I too accepted the Oriental origin (B.M.C. *Cyprus*, p. cxxxiii), as against Evans's theory that the original type was Mycenaean, but was modified by contamination with Oriental examples. Cf. Blinkenberg, *op. cit.* p. 14. I am still doubtful of the origin of the cone from the column, especially as the columns are invariably shown as tapering from above downwards.

[5] Evans, *Earlier Religion of Greece in the Light of Cretan Discoveries*, 1931, pp. 5 ff., esp. p. 12, fig. 3. Sjöqvist, in *Arch. f. Religionswiss.*, as above, p. 352, illustrates from a gold ring from Phaestus a baetyl of exactly the same shape as that found at Ayia Irini.

[6] Blinkenberg, *op. cit.* pp. 34 f.; Evans, *Earlier Religion of Greece*, p. 4.

find, on a signet-ring from the Vapheio tomb, a baetyl (standing at the foot of a sacred tree) which appears to have a double flat cap similar to that which finishes off the Paphian cone as represented on the coins.[1]

In Cyprus itself, the use of such primitive symbols in cultus was probably widely distributed. Besides the chief cone of Paphos, which may possibly actually survive to the present day in the large stone which was long *in situ* to the north-west of the site excavated by the British at Old Paphos, and is now in the Nicosia Museum (Pl. I *b*),[2] and the smaller cones found in the surroundings of the temple by the British excavators,[3] there was found at Ayia Irini, as we have already seen, a large egg-shaped black stone, probably from the earlier shrine. It was more or less *in situ* beside the later altar, having been, it is supposed, religiously preserved when the new temenos was constructed.[4] A conical obelisk of different type found at Athienou probably also served a similar purpose.[5] Across the water, in Pamphylia, the "simulacrum" of Artemis Pergaea, although, as depicted on the coins, it was provided with a head and disguised in a decorated sheath, was probably also a stone of more or less conical shape.[6] Most remarkable in this connexion is the conical object represented on certain coins of south-west Asia Minor, which the latest investigation assigns to some place on the Caro-Lycian border.[7] It may be only the fancy of the die-engraver that has developed out of the rude surface of the field of the coin, in the one case a pair of birds, in the other two bunches of grapes. But if the cone stands for Aphrodite or a

---

[1] Evans, *Earlier Religion of Greece*, p. 30, Fig. 12a. Dussaud, *Civ. Préhell.*[2] p. 413, takes the baetyl for a pithos in which the tree is planted.

[2] A. Westholm, "The Paphian Temple of Aphrodite" in *Acta Archaeologica*, IV, Copenhagen, 1933, p. 207; *Report of the Department of Antiquities*, 1935, p. 36. But this stone is black, whereas the only ancient author who mentions the colour of the cone of Aphrodite (Maximus Tyr. *Diss.* VIII, 8) says it was a white pyramid of unidentified material.

[3] *J.H.S.* IX, 1888, p. 180. These are all of white marble or limestone, which suggests that Maximus (see previous note) was right about the colour of the great cone.

[4] Sjöqvist, *Arch. f. Religionswiss.* XXX, 1933, pp. 317, 324; *S.C.E.* II, p. 702, no. 938 and Pl. CCXLIII, no. 5.

[5] Colonna-Ceccaldi, *Mon. ant. de Chypre, etc.* 1882, p. 44; Perrot et Chipiez, *Hist. de l'Art*, III, p. 273 (*Hist. of Art in Phoenicia, etc.* I, p. 284).

[6] B.M.C. *Lycia, etc.* Pl. XXIV. The goddess of Perga had the same title (*anassa*) as she of Paphos.

[7] B.M.C. *Lycaonia, etc.* Pl. XVI; Imhoof-Blumer, *Kleinasiatische Münzen*, II, 1902, p. 435; Robinson in *Num. Chron.* 1936, pp. 265 ff. Bossert in *Forschungen und Fortschritte*, XIV, 1938, pp. 338 f. regards this baetyl symbol as Hittite.

fertility-deity, it was natural that his fancy should turn in these two directions.

We have already noted the existence in the Bronze Age of a bull-deity, whose worship is illustrated at Ayia Irini and elsewhere. Of such bull-cults in the Aegean, especially in Minoan Crete, there is ample record. Our literary sources do not provide any evidence of such a god in connexion with the Paphian Aphrodite. Yet the bull is the regular type of the coins which are generally accepted as having been issued by the Paphian priest-kings in the fifth century.[2] It is true that on the earliest coins, of about 480 B.C., he is human-headed, and the inscription seems, though not quite certainly, to identify him with the river-god "Bocaros".[3] But from about 460 onwards he is an ordinary bull. The reverse type of these later coins is also regularly an eagle or an eagle's head. It may be suggested that the bull-god was identified with Zeus, and that in the Aphrodite of Paphos and the Zeus of Salamis[4] we have the descendants of the two primitive deities. At Paphos itself, Zeus appears unmistakably on a remarkable stater of about 385 B.C.,[5] and the figure on the reverse of the same coin is probably a Hellenized rendering of the Paphian Aphrodite.[6] Aphrodite and her dove or her rose[7] are the types of other Paphian coins of the fourth century. No trace of the snake-worship, of which the Bronze Age remains afford evidence, and

---

[1] See the section in *K.B.H.* pp. 250 ff. for horned deities in Cyprus in general.

[2] B.M.C. *Cyprus*, Pls. VII, VIII. The attribution to Paphos of the coins earlier than about 360 B.C. (when the types of Aphrodite and the dove begin) is conjectural. Those who prefer astrological explanations of coin types may remember that Cyprus was under the sign of Taurus, together with Parthia, Media, Persis, the Cyclades and the coast of Asia Minor.

[3] See above, ch. I, p. 8, n. 1. The bull is the personification of the river in two aspects, that of natural force (of which countries subject to alternate drought and storm have bitter experience when their torrents are in spate) and that of fertilizer. In both aspects, then, the affinity with Zeus is clear enough.

[4] The bull's-head capital from Salamis in the British Museum (here Pl. VII; see *J.H.S.* 1891, p. 133; *B.M.Sc.* II, 1900, Pl. XXVII) was, as Ohnefalsch-Richter has seen (*K.B.H.* p. 251), possibly from a cultus-pillar.

[5] B.M.C. *Cyprus*, Pl. VIII, 7. Whether he is Zeus Salaminius or a local Zeus Polieus of Paphos is uncertain, and for our purpose indifferent.

[6] Influenced, probably, by the Nemesis of Agoracritus. It is to be noted that she is dropping incense on a thymiaterion. The burning of incense at Paphos is mentioned as something special in *Od.* VIII, 363; *Hymn to Aphrod.* 58; cp. Vergil, *Aen.* I, 416, 417: "centumque Sabaeo ture calent arae".

[7] Engel, *Kypros*, II, pp. 192 f.

which was so closely associated with the Mother-Goddess in Crete, has as yet been found at Paphos. But it must be remembered, as we have already observed, that the actual site of the earliest temple has not yet been discovered.

Excavation of the actual site must be awaited before a definite reconstruction of the Paphian shrine can be attempted. But so much as follows seems to be probable, on the evidence of coins (Pl. V 8) and engraved gems:[1]

The temple lay-out consisted of a central shrine, containing the conical stone, with two wings.[2] In each of the latter was a column (the nature of the object that surmounted them is uncertain);[3] on the roof of each wing appears a bird, no doubt a sculptured dove. The central portion of the shrine had an upper storey, perhaps with windows, and the antae were terminated with what appear to be horns of consecration. Adjuncts, such as stars on either side of the cone, a star in a crescent above the top storey, or a garland hanging across the top, are seen in the representations, but are not of the essence of the construction.[4] The cone

---

[1] The articles of Blinkenberg and Westholm already referred to (together with the latter's further development of the subject in his *Temples of Soli*, pp. 158 ff.) have rendered previous discussions obsolete; but for illustrations of the material in coins and gems reference may still be made to B.M.C. *Cyprus*, pp. cxxvii–cxxxiv. *Pace* Blinkenberg (p. 19) the Mycenaean bracteates are not ignored in that work (p. cxxxi). Casson (p. 163, n. 1) has the idea, new if not true, that "this model of a shrine" (there were five) may be meant for the shrine of Paphos.

[2] The tripartite *liwan-type* of building, found later, e.g. in the fifth-century palace at Vouni, and characteristic of Anatolian domestic architecture. Gjerstad in *Corolla Archaeologica*, pp. 159 ff.

[3] They have been explained as mere capitals, or lamps, or doves. The Sardian coins which I have adduced as evidence for doves (p. cxxxii) dispense with the roofs to the side wings, and the birds which should be on the roofs have come down on to the columns. I have noticed the resemblance of these columns on the Sardian coins to Roman standards, but that they cannot be. It is true that at Hieropolis-Bambyce and Carrhae the standards of the legions quartered there are represented in the chapels where they were deposited, and at the former place the chapel is surmounted by the sacred dove of the Syrian Goddess (Strong and Garstang, *The Syrian Goddess*, p. 70; B.M.C. *Arabia, etc.*, pp. xcii f.). But there would be no legion at Sardes.

[4] The star and crescent indicate Phoenician influence, which need not be denied at a comparatively late date, and illustrate the epithet Urania which was borne by the Paphian goddess. For the connexion between Aphrodite Urania and Aphrodite ἐν Κήποις and the place Hierokepia (Yeroskipou) near Paphos, with a spring still known as the "Bath of Aphrodite" (*O.C.* p. 228), see Broneer in *Hesperia*, I, 1932, p. 53; Meritt, *ibid.* IV, 1935, p. 574.

itself was surmounted by a double flat cap.[1] In front of the shrine was a paved courtyard with a lattice fence, to which a gate with two wings gave access. The courtyard was semicircular.[2] The details of the objects in this courtyard are too obscure on the coins to allow of identification, though one may be a dove, and an altar would be expected.[3] Analogies to the general lay-out of the Paphian shrine, with its central portion flanked by two wings and its front court, have been found at Soli, where the first Aphrodite temple[4] dates from before 200 B.C. Although the connexion of this type of temple with Minoan Crete is clear, it appears that the type came to Cyprus by way of Anatolia or North Syria, direct connexion between Crete and Cyprus not being traceable.[5] This is quite in accordance with the other archaeological evidence. Nor is legend entirely silent on this point, for one of the many fathers attributed to Cinyras was Sandocus, a Syrian who migrated to Cilicia, married Pharnace, daughter of Megassares, king of Hyria (?), and founded Celenderis, on the Cilician coast.[6] Further, the art of divination from the entrails of kids, which was practised by the Cinyradae, had, according to a dim legend recorded by Tacitus, been originally brought to Paphos by the Cilician Tamiras. The priests[7] of the family of the Tamiradae had originally shared with the Cinyradae the service of the temple, but were ousted from it by the latter.

At Paphos[8] was shown the tomb of Aphrodite. Probably the cone

---

[1] Whether this is due to the influence of the sacred column with its capital must remain uncertain. See above, p. 72, for a parallel from Vapheio.

[2] It has been maintained that it must have been rectangular, and that the shape on the coins is due to the circular field. But, as I have observed (*op. cit.* p. cxxxiii), this is disproved by the coins of Drusus, on which the court could have been made rectangular as easily as semicircular.

[3] That the altar at Paphos was in the open we know, not merely from analogy (Westholm, *Acta Archaeologica,* IV, p. 218) but by the fact that the rain was said never to fall upon it. The altar of Aphrodite at Eryx was also in the open (Aelian, *N.A.* x, 50).

[4] Westholm, *Temples of Soli.* The goddess was here, in Roman times, identified with Cybele and called 'Αφροδίτη ὀρεία (p. 149; cp. *S.C.E.* III, p. 626). The name of the dedicator, T. Flavius Zeno, shows that the inscription is of Imperial times.

[5] Westholm, *Temples of Soli,* p. 166.

[6] Apollodorus, *Bibl.* III, 14, 3.

[7] Hesychius, the only other writer who mentions this family, describes them as priests in Cyprus.

[8] Pseudo-Clemens Romanus, *Hom.* v, 23: 'Αφροδίτης ἐν Κύπρῳ (θεωρεῖται τάφος). ['Αφροδίτης ὁ τάφος δείκνυται ἐν Πάφῳ is quoted by Engel, *Kypros,* II,

itself was regarded as her monument. We shall see that in her Ariadne hypostasis she had a tomb in Amathus.[1]

Reference has already been made (p. 73, n. 6) to the incense altar (called in Cyprus *kichētos*) or altars. No blood was shed upon the altars; nevertheless animals, though only of the male sex, were offered in sacrifice. Tacitus, to whom we owe these details, adds that kids were especially valued for the purpose of divination by entrails. And we know also that wild swine, and probably tame pigs, were sacrificed to her. The text of Johannes Lydus, on which we depend, is unfortunately not quite certain, but the most probable interpretation is that the priest, when sacrificing a pig, wore a fleece.[2] The assertion of Tacitus seems inconsistent with itself, and the view that small animals were slain in sacrifice seems to find some support in a small altar, suitable for small victims, which was found by the excavators.[3] Possibly the restriction to bloodless sacrifices applied only to the chief altar of the goddess. The connexion, if any, of these sacrifices with the ancient belief that sacrifices to the gods were invented by the Cypriotes[4] is obscure.

On the altar of Aphrodite rain never fell;[5] nor were flies ever seen about the doors of her temple.[6]

The immense importance of the Aphrodite cult, and the wealth of the temple, gave to the high-priest of the goddess at Paphos a position far beyond that involved in his merely religious functions; the priesthood

p. 75, n. 32, from a source to which he gives an impossible reference, and which I have been unable to trace.] *Vita S. Spyridonis*, ed. Delehaye, *Anal. Boll.* XXVI, p. 230: ἔνθα λέγει τὴν Ἀφροδίτην ἐν Πάφῳ τῆς Κύπρου ταφῆναι.

[1] On these tombs of gods, see Evans, *Earlier Religion of Greece*, p. 17.

[2] For other interpretations, cp. Nilsson, *Griech. Feste*, p. 368; for that favoured in the text, see Blinkenberg, *Temple de Paphos*, p. 23. Accordingly he takes κτίλος, the epithet which Pindar applies to Cinyras as priest of Aphrodite, in the Homeric sense of "ram". The wearing of shaggy skins, probably fleeces, by officiants at sacrifices is well attested, e.g. on the sarcophagus of Agia Triada (Dussaud, *Civ. Préhell.*[2] Pl. D; cp. Nilsson, *Minoan-Myc. Rel.* p. 134, on analogies from Egypt in the New Kingdom). The sacrifice of the wild swine is explained by Johannes Lydus by the Adonis legend; but for the sacrifice of pigs to Aphrodite in Paphos and elsewhere there is evidence from other writers (Antiphanes and Callimachus, in Athenaeus, III, 95f, 96a).

[3] James, p. 179. But, as already observed, they did not reach the temple itself.

[4] Nonnus ad Gregor. Nazianz. *in Iulianum* i, c. 70, Migne, *P.G.* 36, col. 1021.

[5] Tacitus, *Hist.* II, 3; Plin. *N.H.* II, 96, 210; James, p. 179.

[6] Andron Halic. fr. 16 (Müller, *F.H.G.* II, p. 352; Jacoby, *Fr. Gr. Hist.* I, p. 165, fr. 19, regarded as doubtful). The same was related of the temple of Hercules in the Forum Boarium at Rome (Plin. *N.H.* x, 29, 79).

became, in fact, a theocracy exerting its power over the whole island. Thus it was that when in 58 B.C. the Romans despoiled Ptolemy, king of Cyprus, of his kingdom, Cato offered him in exchange the high-priesthood of Paphos. It is true that Ptolemy preferred suicide, but the compensation was evidently not regarded as a mere insult. It has been observed that the temporal powers enjoyed by the archbishop of Cyprus under the Turkish rule bore some analogy to the old powers of the high-priest of Aphrodite.[1]

We may now turn to Amathus. It is clear from the records, historical[2] or legendary, that that city was of extreme antiquity, and even in historical times preserved the remains of an autochthonous population and their non-Greek tongue. It was also famous for a very ancient cult of Aphrodite. That it was of Phoenician origin we are entitled to deny, since it was only at a comparatively late date that the Phoenicians penetrated Cyprus. When they came they may have brought with them such cults as that of the Phoenician Heracles "Malika".[3] Their Adonis was also naturalized there in association with Aphrodite;[4] and Amathus was down to late times one of the centres of anti-Greek feeling, as its history shows. The site has unfortunately yielded nothing of early date, but the acropolis and city itself have not been excavated, the attention of explorers having been confined to the cemeteries.[5] But the British

---

1 L. Ross, *Journey to Cyprus*, tr. Cobham, p. 25.

2 Tacitus, *Ann.* III, 62; Ps. Scylax, 103; Stephanus Byz. *s.v.* I have dealt with the question of Phoenician elements at Amathus in *Mélanges Boisacq*, I, 1937, pp. 485 ff.

3 Hesychius, *s.v.* Μαλίκα.

4 Stephanus Byz. *s.v.* 'Αμαθοῦς.. The rites of Adonis here closely resembled those of Osiris, so that some identified the two. Paus. IX, 41, 2–5: the temple claimed to possess the necklace of Harmonia or Eriphyle, but Pausanias doubts whether it was the true one, which according to Homer was of gold, whereas that at Amathus was of green stones mounted in gold. Other shrines which claimed to have the necklace of Eriphyle were Delphi (Paus. VIII, 24, 10) and Delos (*I.G.* XI, 2, 161 B 42; Michel, *Recueil*, 833).

5 *Excav. Cypr.* pp. 89 ff. Two curious terracotta models of shrines containing cones (?), and marked by the Phoenician symbol of the sun surmounted by an inverted crescent, may be mentioned; *ibid.* p. 113, fig. 165, no. 1 (Walters, B.M. *Terr.* no. A 150); Ohnefalsch-Richter, *K.B.H.* Pl. CXCIX, 1, 2. The second, if Ohnefalsch-Richter's description is not fanciful, contains a veiled and mourning figure of Astarte exactly in the attitude of the goddess of Arca in Phoenicia known to us from Macrobius (*Sat.* i, 21. 5) and the coins of that place (B.M.C. *Phoenicia*, p. lxxii; Ronzevalle in *Mél. de l'Univ. St Joseph*, XV, 1930–1, pp. 141 ff.). L. P. di Cesnola rifled many tombs in the neighbourhood, but his statements about the source of his antiquities are, as

excavators acquired an inscription[1] which had been found on the site, recording a decree for the customary celebration of a sacrifice to Aphrodite, with the object of securing the fertility of the crops, and ordering the rendering to her temple of whatever was customarily due. The mover of the decree, a distinguished official, has the office of *hēgētor*, which we know from another source was the title of the priest who presided over the sacrifices to Aphrodite in Cyprus.[2]

Of peculiar interest is the version of the Ariadne legend preserved by Plutarch:[3]

But one Paeon, born in the city of Amathus, reciteth this clean after another sort, and contrary to all other: saying, that Theseus by tempest was driven [unto] the Isle of Cyprus, having with him Ariadne, which was great with child, and so sore sea sick, that she was not able to abide it. In so much as he was forced to put her on land, and himself afterwards returning aboard hoping to save his ship against the storm, was forthwith compelled to loose into the sea. The women of the country did courteously receive and entreat Ariadne: and to comfort her again (for she was marvellously out of heart, to see she was thus forsaken) they counterfeited letters, as if Theseus had written them to her. And when her groaning time was come, and she to be laid, they did their best by all possible means to save her: but she died notwithstanding in labour, and could never be delivered. So she was honourably buried by the Ladies of Cyprus. Theseus not long after returned thither again, who took her death marvellous heavily, and left money with the inhabitants of the country, to sacrifice unto her yearly: and for memory of her, he caused two little images to be molten, the one of copper, and the other of silver, which he dedicated unto her. This sacrifice is done the second day of September,[4] on which they do yet observe this ceremony: they do lay a

---

usual, not to be trusted. The famous silver patera which he stated to have been found there has, after being lost to sight for years, come to light in the British Museum (Myres in *J.H.S.* LIII, 1933, pp. 25–39); neither for it nor for the others of its class can a Phoenician origin be proven. See below, p. 101, n. 3.

[1] B.M. *Inscr.* IV, no. 975. Hesychius records that the sacrifice to Aphrodite at Amathus was called κάρπωσις. Since in Thera and Cos καρπόω is used of burnt-offering, the same sense has been assumed for κάρπωσις here (Bechtel, *Gr. Dial.* I, p. 449), but our inscription shows that it refers to the crops.

[2] Hesychius, *s.v.* Ἀγήτωρ. Cp. the dedication by the κοινὸν τῶν Κυπρίων in honour of Potamon τῶν ἐν Πάφωι γεγυμνασιαρχηκότων καὶ ἡγητορευκότων, Ditt. *O.G.I.S.* 164. The date of the decree is broken away, but it is ascribed to the early years of the Roman Empire.

[3] *Thes.* XX. I give North's translation more or less modernized.

[4] "Gorpiaios" is August, according to the Macedonian calendar, and October

young child [more correctly, young man] upon a bed, which pitifully crieth and lamenteth, as women travailing with child. They say also, that the Amathusians do yet call the grove where her tomb is set up, the wood of Venus Ariadne.

This remarkable story, in which one notes the indication of the custom of the couvade, offers many points for consideration; but those which concern us here are the connexion between Ariadne and Aphrodite through their quality of vegetation deities, and the possibility of a Minoan origin of the legend,[1] since Ariadne was particularly associated with Crete. On this latter point, however, it behoves us to be wary; for there are traces of the legend of Ariadne in other places, to wit, the Locrian Oenoe, Lemnos, Chios and Donusia, near Rhodes.[2] In these, though it may be the connexion with Dionysus that accounts for her occurrence, we may see indicated the possibility that Ariadne, like so much else that may be Cretan in origin, came to Cyprus, not directly, but by a roundabout way through the Aegean.

The story of the impersonation of the goddess in labour by a young man has been brought into connexion with another curious statement, which is due to the same writer, Paeon, and therefore probably concerns Amathus.[3] He says that the goddess took the shape of a man; and Macrobius[4] describes the statue of Venus in Cyprus as being bearded and having the male member, but clad in female dress and holding a sceptre. There was also a bearded Aphrodite in Pamphylia, which shows so many points of connexion with Cyprus. The bearing on this question

according to that of Seleucia. Paeon seems not to have used the Cypriote calendar; the use of the Macedonian or Seleucian suggests that he lived not earlier than the Ptolemaic period (Engel, *Kypros*, I, p. 11).

[1] Evans, *Earlier Religion of Greece*, p. 17. Nilsson, *Griech. Feste*, 1906, pp. 369 f., and *Minoan-Myc. Rel.* 1927, p. 454: the myth was invented to explain a cult-custom; the different versions of the Ariadne legend point to a cult in which her death was celebrated; the idea of the death of vegetation is applied to the goddess of fertility. This is preferable to the theory that the legend of Ariadne sprang from the chthonian character of Aphrodite (Farnell, *Greek Hero Cults*, 1921, p. 48).

[2] Wagner in *R.E.* II, 807.

[3] Hesychius, *s.v.* Ἀφρόδιτος. Catullus, 68, 51, calling the Amathusian Aphrodite *duplex*, confirms the attribution to Amathus.

[4] Sat. III, 8; *F.H.G.* I, p. 386. Reading *natura* for *statura* (*virili*) with Heinrich. On the exchange of clothes between male and female worshippers, see most recently Driver and Miles in *Iraq*, VI, 1939, p. 69. Other sources in Pauly-Wissowa, *R.E.* I, *s.v. Aphroditos*.

of the exchange of clothes between men and women at certain festivals cannot be discussed here. But it is not unreasonable, before leaving the subject of Amathus, with its legends of the origin of the horned centaurs from Zeus,[1] and of a hermaphroditic deity, to mention as possibly significant the terracotta figurines of hermaphroditic bull-centaurs which are among the most curious remains of the sanctuary of Ayia Irini.

The custom of religious prostitution seems to have prevailed at one time at Amathus as well as at Paphos.[2]

To sum up, the basic religion of primitive Cyprus seems to have been a fertility cult, the godhead being conceived in forms which are familiar to us throughout the Aegean and Asia Minor. In its primitive aniconic form it is a conical or ovoid stone. The theriomorphic expression of the religious idea is seen in the bull-god, with whom also are associated snakes and possibly sacred trees. The anthropomorphic phase finds expression in the shape, on the one hand, of the Mother-Goddess, who at Paphos and elsewhere becomes specialized as Aphrodite, and, on the other, of Zeus. The hermaphroditism, of which we have seen traces, expresses the idea that these two are complementary to each other.

Of the other deities worshipped in Cyprus, Apollo had the most widely disseminated cult;[3] some of the special appellations, such as

---

[1] The Zeus "Labranios", to whom dedications were found near Amathus (Cesnola, *Cyprus*, p. 285; Ohnefalsch-Richter, *K.B.H.* p. 21; Myres, *H.C.C.* nos. 1914–5), may have been imported from Caria (Zeus Labraundos) or Crete, but whether in prehistoric or historic times we cannot say. He may have been identified with Ba'al of Lebanon (see below, p. 107). Another local Zeus at Amathus in the third century B.C. was called Orompatas; his priest was an Aenianian (Sittig, *Hermes*, L, 1915, pp. 158 f.; Cook, *Zeus*, p. 869). The cult of Zeus Meilichios, to which a third-century inscription bears witness was, as Mitford says (*J.H.S.* LVII, 1937, p. 29), probably imported in Ptolemaic times.

[2] Herodotus, I, 199, after describing the practice in Babylon, says a similar custom prevailed in some places in Cyprus. The Propoetides of Amathus, according to Ovid (*Met.* X, 221, 238 ff.), were young women who denied the divinity of Aphrodite; under her wrath they were the first to prostitute themselves, and were turned by her into stone. The legend seems to have grown up in order to account for some group of statues. For another case of prostitution caused by the vengeance of Aphrodite, see above, p. 71.

[3] See especially *K.B.H.* Index, *s.v.* Apollo. Add, from Stephanus Byz., for Hylates, the three places Amamassus, Erystheia and Tembrus, none of which has been located (for the last, Sakellarios, I, p. 136, suggests Tempria near Soli). On Melanthios and Myrtates, see Peristianes, Γεν. Ἱστ. pp. 617 ff. Mageirios had a shrine at Pyla; but the

Alasiotas, Amphidexios, Amyklaios, Heleitas, Hylates, Mageirios, Melanthios (or Opaon Melanthios), Myrtates, have been or will be mentioned incidentally. But his worship does not seem to belong to the most primitive stratum, and was probably a Greek importation. So also doubtless was the cult of Hera.[1]

As very commonly happens in lands once Pagan and now Christian, a blurred memory of the ancient cult survives to modern times and is blended with Christian beliefs; so that in 1845 the priest at Pissouri thought it necessary to explain to Ludwig Ross, when the name of Aphrodite came up in conversation, that "now they do not call her Aphroditissa, now they call her Chrysopolitissa", and Aphrodite is but a name for the Blessed Virgin.[2]

---

restoration of his name in a scrap of inscription from Athienou (*Comm. in hon. Th. Mommseni*, p. 681) is extremely doubtful. For the phallic element in the cult of Opaon Melanthios, a fertility god, at Amargetti, see Herter in *R.E.* XIX, 1938, 1696.

[1] On the cult of Hera at Amathus, see *C.I.G.* 2643 (trees planted and dedicated to the gods in the neighbourhood of the Heraeum) and Perdrizet in *B.C.H.* XX, 1896, p. 351, on the *paranymphoi* who took part in the annual marriage of Zeus and Hera. A dedication to Hera from Dali, *B.C.H.* III, p. 166, n. 10.

[2] L. Ross, *Journey to Cyprus*, tr. Cobham, p. 86. But Mrs Chapman (*Across Cyprus*, p. 167) says that one of the names given to the Blessed Virgin Mary in Cyprus is still (1937) Panayia Aphroditissa.

CHAPTER V

THE GREEK COLONIZATION

The name by which the island became known to the Greeks and through them to the western world, *Kypros*, is of uncertain origin.[1] It is already used in Homer, first in the old episode in the eleventh *Iliad*, in connexion with the legend of Cinyras, and also in the *Odyssey*. Aphrodite is already *Kypris*, the Cyprian goddess. This is not direct evidence for an earlier period than the ninth century, but the name must have been in use earlier. It can have no connexion with the plant *kypros* (the Hebrew gopher, henna), which does not occur wild on the island.[2] Did the island give its name to or receive its name from the metal copper? Were it possible to see a connexion with the Sumerian word *zubar* for copper, the answer would be in favour of the second possibility.[3]

---

[1] The various literary and fancy names which the island acquired at the hands of the Greeks are discussed by Engel, *Kypros*, I, pp. 11 ff.; Sakellarios, I, pp. i ff. and *O.C.* pp. 88 f. Σφήκεια, it has recently been said, "must be identical" with a name mentioned in Hittite sources, *Biggaya* (Forrer in *Reallexikon*, s.v. *Alašija*; Brandenstein in *R.E.* Supp. VI, 212; but see Sommer, *Ahhijawa-Urkunden*, p. 342). Modern philological speculation seems to be in danger of returning to the eighteenth-century level. I. Chr. Tornarites, in Ἀρχεῖον Βυζαντινοῦ Δικαίου, I, Athens, 1930, pp. 24 ff., connects the name *Aeria* borne by Cyprus, as also King Aerias and Aphrodite Aeria, with *aes*, copper, which is philologically inacceptable.

[2] *O.C.* p. 91; *O.K.* p. 60. Nevertheless Georgiades (*K.K.* p. 3) still thinks this the most likely etymology.

[3] Brandenstein in *R.E.* Supp. VI, 212: Sumerian "*su-u-bar*, 'copper' (written UT. KA. BAR), which word was also by popular etymology transformed to *zabar*, 'shining stone'. In Elamite, also, for 'copper' we have the same stem (and no other word besides!), *čupar*. All these forms must be traced back to a common source with *cuprum*." It seems necessary to enquire how early the Elamite form occurs; a point on which Brandenstein says nothing. Scheil, *Délégation en Perse, Mémoires*, XI, 1911, p. 59 (I owe the reference to Mr Gadd), speaking of an Elamite text of the early to middle twelfth century, says that *saḫi*, the usual word for copper, alternates with the Babylonian *zubar* (*siparru*). Dr Campbell Thompson also refers me to the Elamite *zu-ba-ar* for the Assyrian *siparru* (*Délégation en Perse*, III, p. 79) and *zu-bar* (*ibid.* V, p. 10), both of the twelfth century. The name Κύπρος must have been in existence by that time, and there were immense quantities of copper in Elam. If the words are connected, why did the Assyrians later forget it and know only Yatnana as the name of Cyprus?

When did the Greek colonization of Cyprus begin? The literary tradition, with its tales of Agapenor and Agamemnon and Teucer, would place the movement after the fall of Troy, i.e. at the beginning of the twelfth century (the traditional date of the Trojan War being 1194–1184). This was the period in which the eastward movement of the "Peoples of the Sea", who had already attacked Egypt in the thirteenth century, towards the end of the reign of Ramses II,[1] culminated in the great raid down the coast of Palestine which was defeated by Ramses III when it had all but reached the borders of Egypt, about 1196. The agreement with the traditional Greek date for the fall of Troy may be only a coincidence. But in any case, the movement had begun long before the end of the thirteenth century. Like the conquest of parts of England by Jutes, Saxons and Danes, it began doubtless in raids, followed later by settlements, and two or three centuries is not too long to allow for the completion of the process. It was a process the converse of that expressed in the saying that "trade follows the flag". As we have seen, towards the end of the Middle Bronze Age, i.e. about 1600, Cyprus, although it was no longer isolated, but was in touch with Syria, had as yet no direct relation with Minoan or Helladic culture. Those direct relations with the Greek lands to the west began in Late Cypriote times, culminating in the middle of the period (about 1400–1200), at the same time as the "Mycenaean" civilization, of which the remains have been found in Syria, was at its zenith. Now the immense quantity of wares imported from the west which appears in Cyprus at this time, cannot have been without its accompanying settlers;[2] the Greek, though he may have begun as a raider, had a way, unlike the Phoenician, of actually making settlements at his points of commercial penetration; he was a colonist, not merely a trader. Imports from the west began to dwindle after about 1200. That meant that the sources of supply had begun to dry up. Cyprus had to begin to "do for itself". And so in the two centuries between 1200 and 1000 we find a new culture. At

---

[1] Egypt was then attacked by the Libyans in alliance with "Northerners coming from all lands". By their names they are (not always very persuasively) identified as Achaeans, Tyrrhenians (from Italy or Asia Minor), Lycians, Sardinians or Sardians, Sagalassians.

[2] It may be true that the appearance of a great mass of imported pottery and the absence of local imitations in Cyprus in the fourteenth century does not actually prove that there was Mycenaean settlement there; but neither does it prove that there was none: J. F. Daniel in *Amer. Journ. of Arch.* XLI, 1937, p. 83.

Ayia Irini, for instance, the old open temenos is superseded by a roofed house-chapel, as in Minoan and Mycenaean palaces. The pottery, with geometric designs in dark on light, combines in its shapes Mycenaean with Cypriote elements, the former predominating. The earliest Iron Age graves at Lapithos correspond to Mycenaean types, and differ from anything hitherto in use in Cyprus. This is the culture, we are assured, of the new Greek colonists.[1]

Such evidence as we have from the antiquities, therefore, points to the Greek movement into Cyprus having begun, at first unsystematically, about 1400, continuing later (possibly owing to the pressure of the Dorian invaders at home) in a more steady stream, definite settlements being established from about 1200. It is about 1400 that true Mycenaean pottery begins to find its way to the island in any quantity, although earlier imitations by native potters show that they knew it in sporadic importations.[2] Raids at an earlier period than the fourteenth century there had doubtless been; the north coast must always have been tempting to adventurers from Asia Minor from the time that such folk first began to trust themselves across the sea. Thanks to the easily defensible barrier of the Kerynia range, it is possible that these early, not very well organized, raids may not have penetrated far.[3] The fort of Nitovikla in the Karpass may represent a defence against such dangers; it dates from the seventeenth to the fifteenth century, having been once destroyed and rebuilt in the sixteenth. The evidence of the tumuli at the neighbouring Palaeoskoutella also points to fear of invaders about the same time. Possibly the movement of populations to which these early disturbances seem to point was connected with the Hyksos invasion from Asia Minor in the seventeenth century.

It was probably also to the north coast that the raids of the Lukki, be they Lycians or not, were directed in the second quarter of the fourteenth century, as recorded in the Tell el-Amarna letters—assuming that Alashiya was Cyprus.[4] And eventually, difficult as invasion by the north coast may have been, its vulnerable point was found in the Karpass. The

---

[1] Gjerstad in *Antike*, IX, 1933, pp. 263–7; cp. *Rev. Archéol.* 1934, pp. 155–203. He holds that the Mycenaean pottery of Cyprus in the thirteenth century came through Cilicia. Schaeffer, on the other hand, maintains (*Miss.* pp. 114–15) that the evidence from Cilicia is inadequate, and that the contact was more probably made through Syria. See above, p. 34.

[2] Schaeffer, *Miss.* pp. 73, 112.

[3] *Ibid.* pp. 114–15.

[4] Above, p. 42.

passage across the peninsula from north to south was short, and, once across, the road was open to the plain of Salamis and the Mesarea. It was in the Karpass that tradition placed the landing of the Greeks on the "Beach of the Achaeans". But this "Achaean" invasion was a movement which was due to the pressure exerted by the Dorians in the thirteenth century on the Achaeans in Peloponnese. The dialect[1] spoken by the Greeks survived in their old land in Arcadia; the close connexion between the Arcadian dialect and those of Pamphylia[2] and Cyprus serves as an indication of the route which the movement took. On this we may agree, whether we accept the identification as Achaeans of the Ahhiyawa of the Hittite documents, and their settlement in Pamphylia,[3] as proven or not. It has been suggested[4] that the geographical distribution of the Achaean (i.e. the Arcadian-Pamphylian-Cypriote) dialect must be explained, not by the immigration of Achaean tribes, who settled among an older population, but by an original geographically continuous disposition of the Achaeans, which was broken up by later immigration and emigration; Peloponnese, Pamphylia and Cyprus were inhabited before the Dorian invasion by Achaeans, who were able to maintain themselves only in the secluded interior of Peloponnese and in Cyprus. But the gap between Peloponnese and Pamphylia is so considerable that it seems preferable to assume eastward immigration of Achaeans from the former. And the lack in Cypriote of any of those Doric elements which are found in Arcadian indicates that the immigration must have taken place before the Dorian invasion.

From their Peloponnesian home the Achaean settlers introduced into Cyprus not merely a language—for which they used an ill-suited syllabary which they either brought with them[5] or found in the island, the Phoenicians not having yet arrived with their convenient alphabet —but names of places and institutions and cults. So, landing at the

---

[1] There is a notable resemblance of Cypriote to the vocabulary of Homer's Achaeans. With Arcadian, Cypriote was once part of a more united language, and this language may have provided some of Homer's vocabulary: C. M. Bowra, *Tradition and Design in the Iliad*, 1930, p. 143, and in *J.H.S.* LIV, 1934, pp. 54 f.; M. P. Nilsson, *Homer and Mycenae*, 1933, p. 175.

[2] It is not surprising that the Pamphylian contained some Doric elements; but the grouping with Arcadian and Cypriote is not thereby affected: E. Meyer, *Gesch. d. Alt.*[2] II, i, 1928, p. 548.

[3] Both doubted, e.g. by Christensen, *Iranier*, 1933, p. 196, and others; see above, ch. III, p. 46. Christensen seems to put the eastward drive of the Greeks too late.

[4] Nilsson, *Minoan-Myc. Rel.* 1927, p. 29. [5] See above, p. 52.

"Beach of the Achaeans" on the north coast of the Karpass, they made their way to the plain where—finding possibly a native name which had a somewhat similar sound—they gave to their settlement the name of Salamis.[1] The hero Telamonian Teucer was its founder (his tomb was shown there) and the ancestor of its dynasty of priest-kings.[2] At Olba in Cilicia, similarly, there remained down to Roman times a family of priest-kings, and a cult of Zeus, going back to a foundation by Ajax, son of Teucer.[3] The colonists brought with them to Cyprus priests or

---

[1] See above, p. 64.

[2] The people of Gergis in the Troad claimed to be descended from the Teucrians (Herod. v, 122). In Salamis, where the king's spies or "kolakes" were furnished by two families, called "Gerginoi" and "Promalanges", the former claimed to be connected with the Gergithians of the Troad, being descended from the prisoners whom Teucer brought with him to colonize Cyprus. One of them, it was said, returned from Cyprus to visit the land of his forefathers and there, with some Mysians whom he collected, founded a city which was called first Gergina, and then Gergitha. Some of the members of this expedition split off and settled in Cyme (Athen. vi, 256 b, c). Whether there is any historical substratum to this legend, in the form of an actual colonization of Cyprus from the Troad, or of Cyme from Cyprus, and whether the story has not been invented to account for similarity of names, may be doubted. But see Engel, *Kypros*, I, pp. 239–40. Engel seems to me in general gravely to over-estimate the value of the evidence for a Phrygian element in early Cypriote culture (I, pp. 186 ff.). He builds chiefly on the following rather flimsy foundation. (*a*) Servius, ad *Aen.* 3, 111, derives the name of the Corybantes from a copper-bearing mountain called *Korion* in Cyprus. (There was a place of the same name in Crete (Steph. Byz.); possibly there is confusion between the two islands. See also *O.C.* p. 177 note for other explanations.) The Cypriotes, according to Cratinus the Younger (Athen. iv, 177 a), used the Phrygian flute, and had a dance called *prylis*, which according to Aristotle (fr. 476, Schol. Pind. *Pyth.* II, 125) was the same as the *Pyrrhike*. (It is significant that the Berlin editors alter the MS. Κυπρίοις in this fragment to Κρησί. But H. L. Lorimer, in *Class. Quarterly*, XXXII, 1938, pp. 129–32, shows that Κυπρίοις is right; cp. Schol. T. on Ψ 130.) This flute and dance are characteristic of the Corybantes, who are in origin the priests of Cybele, the Phrygian Mother-Goddess. (*b*) There was a legend (Pollux, *Onom.* II, 95) of a son of Mestor in Cyprus being suckled by a goat (like the Zeus-child in Crete). This was at a place called *Alkathou kome*, but Engel goes beyond the evidence in calling him Alcathoüs and seeing a connexion with Phrygia in that name (A. son of Pelops). (*c*) There were Idaean Dactyls in Cyprus; two of them, Kelmis and Damnameneus, first discovered iron in that island (Euseb. *Praep. Evang.* x, 6. 5, *P.G.* XXI, 792; Clem. Alex. *Strom.* I, 16, 75, 4). (But they were also the first discoverers of copper, and so legend, as in the case of the Telchines, was persuaded to connect them with Cyprus.) All these very vague and doubtful indications do not warrant the assumption of Phrygian settlements in Cyprus, contrasting as they do with the comparatively precise stories about Greek colonization.

[3] The dynasty lasted down to the time of Augustus; Ajax son of Teucer was high-

seers who were known as *Achaiomanteis*.[1] At Idalium[2] there has been found proof of the worship of a god whom the Greeks equated with the Amyclaean Apollo, but the Phoenician settlers with their Reshef Mikal or Reshef of Mukl.[3] But the Greeks landed also farther west than the Karpass, for tradition attributed the foundation of Lapethos (Lapithos) to Laconians under Praxanor. But the Greek colonists here were, temporarily at least, afterwards ousted or held under by a Phoenician element, of which there are traces as late as Ptolemaic times.

Of Kerynia (Kyrenia, as it is generally but less correctly called), in contrast to the great part which it played in the Middle Ages, very little is known from antiquity; but the name seems to bring it into connexion with the Achaean colonists.[4] Two dedications to the Paphian goddess in the Cypriote script have been found there;[5] but no special connexion with Paphos can be deduced therefrom.

---

priest of Zeus at Olba and toparch of Cennatis and Lalassis, from A.D. 10/11 to 14/15 or later, when the power and dignities were transferred to M. Antonius Polemon. B.M.C. *Lycaonia, etc.*, pp. lii ff.—H. A. Ormerod, *Piracy in the Ancient World*, 1924, p. 88, suggests that the Thekel (*T'-k-k'-r'*) of the Sea-raiders, sometimes identified with the Teucrids of Cyprus, may be those of Cilicia.

[1] Hesychius. *s.v.* "Achaiomanteis, who hold the priesthood of the gods in Cyprus". The fact that in the fifth century a Cypriote, Zoes son of Timonax, calls himself "Achaios" (Hoffmann, *Gr. Dial.* I, p. 90, no. 190) cannot, as has been supposed, have reference to a primitive Achaean settlement; it merely means that he came from Achaea.

[2] The Greeks invented for Idalium a Greek founder Chalcanor (Steph. Byz.) whose name, it has been suggested, may be explained by the existence of copper-mines not far off, at Tamassus (Oberhummer in *R.E.* IX, 868).

[3] *C.I.S.* I, 89 (bilingual of Idalion, where the Cypriote reads τῶ 'Απόλωνι τῶ 'Αμυκλοῖ); G. A. Cooke, *North Semitic Inscr.* p. 76; Greek dedication 'Απόλλωνι 'Αμυκλαίωι (Colonna-Ceccaldi, *Monum. ant. de Chypre*, p. 197). The origin from Amyclae is commonly assumed, but it has also been maintained that the Phoenician name was primary; in any case, if the Greeks connected the Phoenician god with the god of Amyclae, that is enough to show that they were thinking of their original home. Most probably there was at Idalium a local god, with a name (not necessarily Phoenician) which reminded the Greeks of Amyclae. Cp. Myres, *H.C.C.* p. 127; S. A. Cook, *Rel. of Anc. Pal. in the light of Arch.* 1930, p. 129.

[4] Bechtel, *Gr. Dial.* I, p. 454. On the various guesses at the foundation of Kerynia, including the absurd attribution to Cyrus, see Peristianes, 'Ιστ. pp. 8 f. Cepheus is mentioned by Philostephanus (Tzetz. ad Lyc. 586) as having brought colonists from Achaea.

[5] A. P. di Cesnola, *Salaminia*, pp. 84–6; Collitz, *G.D.I.* I, p. 16, nos. 15, 16. Cesnola also illustrates a fragment which appears to bear Phoenician numerals, but as no details of the discovery are given, and the fragment is less than 3 in. long, Phoenician settlement in this spot cannot be inferred.

The name Lacedaemon was given to some place of uncertain position in the interior of the island. Certain cults of Apollo which may have been Greek importations or adoptions are recorded, the more important at Curium (which, since it is on the south coast, will concern us later), but also at places easily accessible when once Salamis and the Mesarea had been reached; thus there was Apollo Heleitas (Phoenician Reshef Eliyath, or some such form) at Tamassus;[1] Apollo Mageirios at Pyla (about eight miles north of Larnaka).[2] Asine, the site of which is unknown,[3] suggests a connexion with Argolis; it may possibly have been founded by the band of Dryopes who, legend said, fled from Cythnos to Cyprus when their king Phylas was conquered by Heracles. For Asine in Argolis owed its foundation to Dryopes.[4] If Dmetor of the house of Iasos, ruler of Cyprus, into whose hands Odysseus was given by his Egyptian captors, according to the tale he told Antinous (*Od.* XVII, 443), was a mere invention of his, yet the choice the poet made of a king of Argive descent is significant.

The westernmost promontory of Cyprus, Acamas, was said to be named from the son of Theseus, and Acamas and the Athenian Phalerus are given by Strabo[5] as the founders of Soli, whereas Plutarch[6] attributes the foundation of Aepeia (supposed to have been the predecessor of Soli) to Demophon, brother of Acamas. The city of Chytri, again, according to Xenagoras[7] in his book on Islands, was founded by

---

[1] Hoffmann, *Gr. Dial.* I, p. 75, no. 140; Cooke, *North Sem. Inscr.* p. 89.

[2] Collitz, *G.D.I.* I, no. 120; Hoffmann, *Gr. Dial.* I, p. 65, nos. 128, 129. Myres, *H.C.C.* pp. 127, 307, regards the epithet as a Greek shot at Melqarth, which seems improbable. S. Besques ("L'Apollon Mageirios de Chypre" in *Rev. Archéol.*, VI Sér., t. VIII, 1936, pp. 3 ff.) shows that the *Mageiroi* connected with the cult were important functionaries.

[3] The church of Panayia tes Asinou, above Nikitari on the stream of the same name, is suggested by Oberhummer. Cp. Menardos, Τοπωνυμικόν ('Αθηνᾶ, XVIII, 1906, p. 320). Another guess is that of Sakellarios (I, p. 202), who suggests Asha (Famagusta distr.). I do not know what is the reason of Skalieres ('Η Κύπρος, p. 12) for identifying Asine with Kalokhorio near Larnaka.

[4] Herod. VII, 90 (Cythnians in Cyprus); Diodorus, IV, 37, 2; Engel, *Kypros*, I, p. 224. Beloch (*Gr. Gesch.* I, ii,[2] p. 106) has a different but not very plausible explanation of the Dryopes in Cyprus.

[5] Strabo, XIV, 6. 3.

[6] Plut. *Sol.* 26. Oberhummer in *Ztschr. d. Ges. f. Erdk.*, Berlin, XXV, 1890, pp. 219 f., identified Aepeia with Vouni, the fine site, on a bluff four miles west of Soli, which has been excavated by the Swedes.

[7] Müller, *F.H.G.* IV, p. 527, fr. 10; Jacoby, *Fr. Gr. Hist.* II B, p. 1009, fr. 27.

Chytrus the son of Aledrus or Alexander, the son of Acamas. This group of foundations, therefore, represents the special Athenian contribution to the colonization of Cyprus, although, as we have seen, the cults of Salamis point to close connexion of that city also with Athens.[1] The story of the change of name from Aepeia to Soli, in honour of Solon, who suggested the move from Aepeia, is doubtless an aetiological invention.[2]

So much for the colonies on the northern coast, and in the plain and foothills which could be easily reached from it. But the Greeks, the stream of their movement being, so to speak, split by the westernmost point of the island at the promontory of Acamas, also passed along the south coast, where, as we have seen, the settlement associated by legend with Agapenor was made at Paphos. Farther eastward the city of Curium claimed to have been founded from Argos,[3] and to Argos also points the local cult of a god called Perseutas.[4] Curium also had an Apollo Hylates[5] (god of the woodlands), and an Apollo Lakeutes, an unexplained epithet. How far these are Greek importations, how far adoptions, it is not possible to say.

Was the kingship among the Greek importations?[6] As we see it in the fifth and fourth centuries, it is a pure despotism, except perhaps at Idalium. At Paphos especially, but also probably elsewhere, it was combined with, nay, rooted in, the high-priesthood. In the Homeric kingship there was nothing despotic, nothing in the professional sense

---

[1] Engel (*Kypros* I, p. 216) sees the colonization by the Salaminians under Teucer and the Athenians under Acamas as a joint undertaking.

[2] It is interesting to note that Soli in Cilicia had also a tradition connecting it with Athens and Solon: B.M.C. *Lycaonia, etc.* p. lxxi, n. 4. Cp. Lobel in *Bodleian Quarterly Record*, IV, 1924, p. 96, quoting *Pap. Oxy.* IV, 680.

[3] Herodotus, V, 113. But for "Argos", with its temple of Apollo Erithios, where Aphrodite found the body of Adonis, we must read "Arsos". Menardos in *J.H.S.* XXVIII, 1908, pp. 134 ff.

[4] Collitz, *G.D.I.* I, no. 45; L. P. di Cesnola, *Cyprus*, p. 425; Myres, *H.C.C.* p. 306, no. 1850; Bechtel, *Gr. Dial.* I, p. 453.

[5] The grove of Apollo at Curium was an inviolable refuge for deer (Aelian, *N.A.* XI, 7). Hylates was also worshipped at Drimou in the west of the island, between Polis tis Chrysochou and New Paphos: *K.B.H.* p. 21; Collitz, *G.D.I.* I, nos. 27, 28, 31, 32; Hoffmann, *Gr. Dial.* I, p. 53 f., nos. 94, 95, 98, 99.

[6] The question is asked by Casson, p. 67, who answers yes. He describes three sceptres, as well as other regalia. The sceptres are not earlier than the Late Bronze Age. The fine gold and enamelled one from Curium (p. 156) is of the seventh or sixth century.

sacerdotal. It may be that Achaean importations, such as the Teucrid dynasty, were grafted on to the original royal stock, which must have existed in Cyprus as in Anatolia and Syria-Palestine.

That among the arts which the Greeks brought with them to Cyprus that of poetry, and especially epic, should be included, is only to be expected; but the development of which we have evidence in the epic called the *Cypria* can hardly be earlier than the seventh century, if so early. Legend, it is true, provided a prophet-bard earlier than Homer, in Euclous. Among the prophecies later invented for him by Cypriote patriotism was one which made Cyprus the birthplace of Homer[1]—a claim which found little acceptance outside of the island. A second attempt to connect Homer with Cyprus took shape in the legend that he gave his daughter Arsiphone to the Cypriote Stasinus in marriage, and being a poor man gave as her dowry an epic poem, the *Cypria*.[2] The attribution of this poem to Homer was often questioned in antiquity, but not always on grounds that would appeal to modern critics. Thus Herodotus denies his authorship merely because of an apparent discrepancy with the *Iliad* in the account of the return of Paris to Troy. Modern criticism has recognized that the whole conception and outlook of the *Cypria* are different from those of the *Iliad* or *Odyssey*. The epitome and fragments, which are all that remain, show that the poem was compiled as a kind of introduction to the *Iliad*. Its contents are, at least in part, as old as those of the *Iliad*.[3] It was an historical epic, with no inner unity; its contents were much less simple, more various than those of either the *Iliad* or *Odyssey*. Aristotle[4] remarked that, while those epics would each provide material for one tragedy or two at the most, many could be drawn from the *Cypria*. It began with the determination of Zeus to deliver the earth of its too heavy burden of mankind, which had lost its fear of the gods; the means of destruction was to

---

[1] Paus. x, 24. 3. He is also said to have predicted the Persian invasion, *ibid.* x, 14. 6. See most recently Spyridakis in Διαλέξεις περὶ τῆς Κυπριακῆς ποιήσεως, Paphos, 1938, pp. 7–9.

[2] Besides the first substantial study of the *Cypria* in F. G. Welcker, *Der epische Cyclus*, 1835, 2nd ed. 1865–82, see the accounts in Engel, *loc. cit.*; Rzach in *R.E.* XI, 1922, 2379–2395; Christ-Schmidt-Stählin, *Gesch. d. gr. Lit.* I, i, 1929, pp. 208 f. and Spyridakis in Διαλέξεις περὶ τῆς Κυπριακῆς ποιήσεως, Paphos, 1938, pp. 10–14. The section from the *Chrestomathia* of Proclus most conveniently in T. W. Allen, *Homeri Opera*, V, 1912, pp. 102–5.

[3] Wilamowitz-Moellendorff, *Kleine Schriften*, V, 2, p. 124.

[4] *Poet.* c. 23, 1459 b.

be the slaughter of the Trojan War. There followed a long series of episodes, such as the wooing and marriage of Thetis; the dispute of the goddesses and the Judgement of Paris; the birth of Helen, begotten on Nemesis by Zeus in the shape of a swan; the rape of Helen; the rape by the Dioscuri of Hilaeira and Phoebe, daughters of Apollo (in other versions, of Leucippus); the quarrel with the Apharetidae; the death of Castor at the hands of Idas, of Lynceus by the spear of Pollux and of Idas by the lightning of Zeus; the journey[1] of Menelaus to stir up the Greeks to revenge, with the episode of the feigned madness of Odysseus; the first gathering in Aulis; the first abortive expedition and destruction of Teuthrania by the Greeks under the delusion that it was Troy; the battle on the Caïcus, where Telephus and Patroclus were wounded; Achilles at Scyros; the second gathering at Aulis; the expedition delayed by storms owing to the wrath of Artemis offended by Agamemnon; the invention of the game of draughts by Palamedes; Artemis appeased by the sacrifice of Iphigeneia; the landing at Troy and death of Protesilaus; the slaying of Cycnus by Achilles; the romantic episode of the desire of Achilles to see Helen and its gratification by Aphrodite and Thetis, in consequence of which Achilles restrains the Greeks from returning home; the sacking of Lyrnesus and Pedasus; the death of Troïlus; the allocation of Briseis to Achilles and Chryseis to Agamemnon; the sale by Patroclus of Lycaon to Lemnos; the death of Palamedes at the hands of Odysseus and Diomede, and the wrath of Achilles at the death of his friend, causing him to stand aside from the Greeks; and finally a list of the allies of Troy. The stage was thus set for the beginning of the *Iliad.* It will be observed what admirable material the episodes provided for treatment by later poets, especially Pindar, and in works of plastic and graphic art, from the throne of the Amyclaean Apollo by Bathycles and the chest of Cypselus onwards.[2] It is clear that the epic was immensely popular.

If a certain non-Homeric sophistication is discernible in the teleological tone of the introduction, in traces of ethical allegory (as in making Helen the daughter of Nemesis), and other features, the language and style, so far as the few remains allow us to judge, also point to a post-Homeric date. Nor, if the authorship is denied to Homer, can much be said in favour of Stasinus, except that most of the later Greek writers who

[1] In a digression here Nestor related a number of tragic stories, of Epopeus, Oedipus, the madness of Heracles, Theseus and Ariadne. They have nothing to do with the action of the epic (Wilamowitz-Moellendorff, *Kleine Schriften*, v, 2, p. 74).

[2] The illustrations of each episode are fully enumerated by Rzach, *loc. cit.*

ventured at all on an attribution seemed inclined to assign the poem to him, and indeed he is more definitely connected with the *Cypria* than any other poet with any other part of the Cycle.[1] Nothing is known of him except what we have already told of his legendary connexion with Homer;[2] but the name is Cypriote in character,[3] and since there is nothing in the matter of the epic which specially connects it with Cyprus,[4] authorship by a Cypriote might be, as indeed it was, regarded as accounting for the name it bears. It must be admitted that the idea of naming an epic after its author (still more so, after its author's birthplace) is feeble; all the other parts of the Cycle were named from their subject-matter.[5]

What part, if any, the *Cypria* played in the literary life of the Cypriotes it is impossible to say. It has been conjectured that rhapsodes recited it at the festival of the Aphrodisia at Salamis;[6] but for this there is no

---

[1] U. v. Wilamowitz-Moellendorff, *Die Ilias u. Homer*, p. 428, no. 2.

[2] The story that Homer could not afford to give any other dowry to his daughter than the poem is as old as Pindar (Aelian, *V.H.* IX, 15; but Stasinus is not mentioned in this passage).

[3] The number of Cypriote names beginning with "Stas-" is exceptionally large.

[4] Engel (I, p. 623) introduces into the argument of the *Cypria* the visit to Cyprus of Palamedes, who persuades Cinyras to help the Greeks (see p. 68); but of this there is nothing in the epitome of Proclus. Nor, so far as we know, did the epic contain anything about a visit to Cyprus of Paris, who was said to have taken his son Pleisthenes there (Schol. Eur. *Androm.* 880); also to have taken ships thence on a piratical expedition to Sidon (Dictys Cret. I, 5).

[5] The desire to explain the name *Cypria* may have led to the invention of a suitably named author, as seen in the alternative in Athenaeus, VIII, 334 b: εἴτε Κύπριός τίς ἐστιν ἢ Στασῖνος ἢ ὅστις δήποτε χαίρει ὀνομαζόμενος. There is a corrupt passage in XV, 682 e: ὁ μὲν τὰ Κύπρια Ἔπη πεποιηκὼς Ἡγησίας ἢ Στασῖνος· Δημοδάμας γὰρ ὁ Ἁλικαρνασσεὺς ἢ Μιλήσιος ἐν τῷ περὶ Ἁλικαρνασσοῦ Κύπρια Ἁλικαρνασσέως δ' αὐτὰ εἶναί φησι ποιήματα. Here it has been proposed by Hecker, omitting δ', to read Κυπρία (gen. of Κυπρίας); or, with Wilamowitz-Moellendorff (*Hom. Untersuch.* p. 337) we may emend to Κυπρίου, inserting ἢ Κύπριος after Στασῖνος. This harmonizes the two passages of Athenaeus and makes sense of γάρ. But *Kyprios* as a personal name seems to be confined to slaves or artisans; and the name Κυπρίας seems to be unprecedented.

[6] Engel, I, pp. 672 f. The evidence is the tenth Homeric Hymn: "Hail goddess, guardian of well-built Salamis and sea-girt Cyprus; grant me a lovely song." The sixth Hymn describes the birth of Aphrodite from the sea at Cyprus, and how the Horae, having attired her, introduced her to the company of the gods. These Hymns were doubtless recited at contests (VI, 19 f.) as proëms to longer works and, if so, why not composed in Cyprus for festivals of the goddess? (Christ-Schmid-Stählin, *Gesch. d. gr. Lit.* I, i, 1929, p. 241.) Spyridakis lays stress on the fact that fragments of a hymn to

positive evidence whatever. The fact remains that both the authorship of the poem and its connexion with Cyprus are mysteries never likely to be solved.[1]

The question how far the Cypriote nation was Greek naturally arises out of the foregoing pages. It is partly answered for us by the expressed opinion of an Athenian poet on the nature of the Cypriote. To him, it would seem, the Cypriote type was something strikingly foreign. That is the essential meaning of a curious passage in the *Suppliant Women* of Aeschylus.[2] The Argive king, enumerating alien racial types which the women suggest to him much sooner than the Argives they claim to be, says: "Similar to you, too, is the Cypriote stamp, which has been impressed in female forms by male artificers." In the enumeration the Cypriote women are placed between Egyptians and Indians. The use of terms proper to plastic art might seem to suggest that the poet had some actual work of Cypriote art in mind; but there is little doubt that he was

---

Aphrodite have actually been found in Cyprus (*S.C.E.* III, pp. 627 ff.: in iambic senarii, from the temple of Aphrodite at Soli). He goes further. Comparing the attiring of the goddess in the sixth Hymn with that of Helen in the *Cypria* (Allen, p. 119), he considers that the two passages point to a dependence of one poet on the other, or a common local origin. I fail to see any resemblance in conception or in details.

[1] It is not necessary to do more than mention Engel's suggestion that Stasinus was of Dorian origin (I, p. 605) and that the chief elements of the story of the epic are Laconian (p. 663); that does not make it any easier to explain the connexion with Cyprus. The same applies to the remark of v. Wilamowitz-Moellendorff that, Hegesias (or Hegesinus) being an Ionic name, the Salamis to which he belonged may have been the Attic and not the Cypriote (*Die Ilias u. Homer*, 1916, p. 428, n. 2).

[2] Aeschylus, *Supp.* 288–9: Κύπριος χαρακτὴρ τ' ἐν γυναικείοις τύποις εἰκὼς πέπληκται τεκτόνων πρὸς ἀρσένων. The operative words χαρακτήρ, τύποις, πέπληκται all curiously suggest a work of art, more especially a coin. But Cypriote coins as early as Aeschylus afford no material for supposing that he was thinking of coin types. The antithesis γυναικείοις—ἀρσένων seems meaningless, unless we accept the view expressed in Mazon's translation: "le type chypriote que, comme dans un moule, frappent les mâles au sein des femmes, résemble également au vôtre", or else explain the γυναικεῖοι τύποι as the daughters of the "male artificers" (though in that case the antithesis loses something of its point). Aeschylus is not thinking of works of art, but using a rather violent metaphor, drawn from the art of coinage, for the production of human forms by the ordinary process of generation. If we accept this, we have no need to puzzle ourselves with the question how Aeschylus could have seen a Cypriote statue, or to suggest that one of the Athenians who sailed for Cyprus with Aristeides after Mycale had brought back with him some souvenir of Cypriote art.

merely using these terms metaphorically. His words do not express his opinion of Cypriote sculpture. The passage has exercised the ingenuity of emendators; but all agree in leaving the general sense that the Suppliants make the king think of some alien non-Greek type. Obviously, in the face of such a fact, attempts which have been made, and will doubtless continue to be made, to prove that the Cypriotes were pure Greeks, must be futile.

CHAPTER VI

PHOENICIANS, ASSYRIANS AND EGYPTIANS

The first two or three centuries of the Iron Age are the darkest period in Cypriote history. The origin of the typical Iron Age style of Cypriote pottery is obscure, whether it was a local invention (if so, from what did it arise?), or due to a movement of population from Asia Minor, which also affected Syria and Palestine. The evidence for close contact with Syria, as shown by the "Cypriote" black-on-red pottery from al Mina, Sueidia, at the mouth of the Orontes, is said to culminate about 700. On the other hand, evidence from Palestine points to about a century earlier for the peak; in fact "Cypriote" Iron Age pottery seems to occur in Palestine earlier than it does in Cyprus. The historian must be content to leave untouched the question as to which was the originating region, until the archaeologist has provided him with more dated evidence.[1]

The trade relations with the West, which must have been lively from the seventh century at least, are illustrated by the spread of Cypriote terracotta figurines and stone statuettes, which were imported largely by such places as Rhodes and Cnidus. The "pudica" type of female figurine was evidently especially popular; and it may have been to such a little idol that Herostratus of Naucratis successfully prayed, when his ship was in danger (p. 110). The Aphrodite cult generally in the Aegean was profoundly influenced by Cyprus in the early archaic period.[2]

---

[1] For al Mina, see Woolley in *J.H.S.* LVIII, 1938, pp. 16 f., where will be found interesting suggestions about the origin of the "Cypriote" Iron Age style. It is, however, disputable whether, as he states, the iron used in Cyprus must have come from Asia Minor (see ch. I, p. 9, n. 4). The evidence from Palestine, Miss Kenyon informs me, is difficult to square with that from Syria; the date for the maximum proportion of "Cypriote" ware on Palestine sites is nearer 800 than 700; and there are "Cypriote" juglets in groups from Tell Fara which it is difficult to date later than the tenth century, and local imitations are common in the tenth–eighth centuries, whereas some Cyprus archaeologists date this ware as beginning about 850; they admit, however, that black-on-red ware does occur earlier, but suggest that it may be imported.

[2] See above, p. 70, n. 1.

So far as the Syrian market was concerned, however, Rhodes had by the middle of the seventh century begun to oust the Cypriote merchants. While Assyria was strong, it would communicate with its possession Cyprus through the ports of Syria and Phoenicia. The gradual breaking up of the Assyrian Empire in the last third of the seventh century would weaken this link and open the field to Egypt. Egyptian influence, which had hitherto passed chiefly through Phoenicia, now penetrated direct to the island, and, in the sixth century, crystallized into actual political domination.

We may now consider what our records say of the relations between Cyprus and Phoenicia, Assyria and Egypt, in that order. Nothing of the kind bearing on contacts with Asia Minor or northern Syria in this period has come down to us.

I. THE PHOENICIANS

Before we attempt to define the part played by the Phoenicians in the history of Cyprus, it will be convenient to establish the meaning of the name by which the island was known to the Hebrews, since it is closely involved with the name of the chief Phoenician settlement.

The Old Testament name[1] for Cyprus was *Kittim*. This is to be distinguished from *Chittim*, which means the Hittites. The name is a plural, and in the Septuagint, when it is not merely transliterated, is rendered as such.[2] How far back the use of the name may go, that is to say, what tradition is enshrined in the references which have come down to us in a late literary form not earlier than the eighth century, we cannot tell. We have already mentioned the identical references in Genesis and I Chronicles; the latter was certainly written after the time of the Captivity, probably in the fifth century. In the prophecy of Balaam,[3] Balak is warned that "ships shall come from the coast of Kittim, and they shall afflict Asshur, and shall afflict Eber, and he also shall come to destruction". Isaiah, in the second half of the eighth century, has two references. In the former (xxiii, 1), prophesying of what shall befall Tyre, he says: "Howl, ye ships of Tarshish; for it is laid waste, so that there is no house, no entering in: from the land of Kittim it is revealed

[1] See the admirable exposition in O.C. pp. 15 ff.

[2] Κήτιοι, Κίτιοι, Κιτιεῖς, γῆ Κιτιαίων, νῆσοι (τῶν) Χετιείμ, κ.τ.λ.

[3] Numbers xxiv, 24.

to them." In the latter (xxiii, 12): "Thou shalt no more rejoice, O thou oppressed virgin daughter of Sidon; arise, pass over to Kittim; even there shalt thou have no rest"—a passage which has been neatly referred to the flight of Lulî, king of the Sidonians, from the invasion of Sennacherib in 701. Later (about 630) the prophet Jeremiah (ii, 10) tells Israel to "pass over to the isles of Kittim, and see" (whether they have been false to their gods). Ezekiel, as we have already seen,[1] speaks of wood from the isles of Kittim. In all these passages modern commentators agree to recognize Cyprus. Later the reference is carried farther west, and the Vulgate is not wrong in rendering the Kittim of Daniel xi, 30 as the Romans, while in the First Book of Maccabees (i, 1 and viii, 5) it is quite certain that the Macedonians are meant. It is these latter equivalences that account for the Vulgate rendering of the passage in Ezekiel as "the isles of Italy", which is obviously wrong. But, since in that and in all earlier passages there is nothing specifically equating Kittim with Cyprus, it must be admitted that in some cases at least the earlier Hebrew writers, and not merely the later, may have been vague about the locality, and included in the connotation of the term any land farther westwards. However, the existence in Cyprus of the Phoenician foundation (Kition, Citium) was enough for later writers, from Josephus onwards, who traced a connexion between the city and the Hebrew name. The passage of Josephus[2] shows that he knew both the narrow and the wider interpretation of the name:

> but Chethimos had the island Chethima (this is now called Kypros); and from it all the islands and the more part of the places by the sea are named Chethim by the Hebrews; and the evidence for my statement is one of the cities in Kypros which availed to retain the appellation; for it is called Kitios by those who put the name into Greek, and even so it did not lose touch with the name of Chethimos.

---

[1] Ch. 1, p. 10, n. 4.

[2] *Ant. Iud.* 1, 6, 1. Cp. St Jerome on the passage of Jeremiah: "the isles of Cethim, which we must take to mean those of either Italy or the western parts, from the fact that the island of Cyprus, in which a city is called by this name, is near to the land of Judaea"—which is strange logic. Also Epiphanius, *Panarion Haeres.* xxx, § 25, 9 on the same passage: παντὶ δὲ δῆλον ὅτι Κίτιον ἡ Κυπρίων νῆσος καλεῖται, Κίτιοι γὰρ Κύπριοι καὶ ʽΡόδιοι. The last two words are a riddle; but the alternative reading Rodanim for Dodanim in Gen. x, 4 ("the sons of Javan; Elishah, and Tarshish, Kittim, and Dodanim") suggests an explanation. Both here and in I Chron. i, 7 the Septuagint has ʽΡόδιοι.

The status of the Phoenician people, to whom it was formerly the fashion to attribute so many of the elements which went to make up Greek culture, has of late years been considerably diminished. One or two gallant attempts have been made to recover an independent position for them in art,[1] but the fact remains that their place is still undefined, and for the most part they are regarded as mere carriers of other people's goods. Yet that they had technical ability of a high order it is impossible for anyone to deny who studies their epigraphy; so elegant a writing as is seen in some of their inscriptions cannot have belonged to a people wholly without taste. Unfortunately, in Cyprus, which was the first stage in the westward tend of their influence, they seem to have met with a Greek or a native strain which was not sufficiently strong to absorb them. No real synthesis was ever effected; although the people, in the regions where they met, may have become bilingual, and borne at the same time Greek and Phoenician names (like Praxidemus-Baalsillem of Lapethos), and the cults may have become hopelessly contaminated. It is probable, however, that the actual Phoenician population in Cyprus was less numerous than one might conjecture from the undoubted influence of Phoenician craftsmanship on the art of the island. From a few settlements on the coast, their handiwork would find its way everywhere, and be eagerly accepted and copied locally. Since their work lacks a determinate character, it becomes impossible to distinguish between what is imported ready-made from Phoenicia, and what is made in Cyprus, and in the latter case whether by Phoenician craftsmen or by Cypriotes. The very term Graeco-Phoenician is a confession of the extent of our ignorance.

If there was any communication between Cyprus and Phoenicia before the last phase of the Bronze Age, it was so slight that it can count for nothing in the historical development of the island. When the Phoenicians came they settled at one or two spots on the coast which already had a "Mycenaean" history. The most important was the

---

[1] Notably by F. Poulsen, *Der Orient und die frühgriechische Kunst*, 1912. R. D. Barnett, in his study of the Nimrud ivories (*Iraq*, II, 1935, pp. 179–210), seems to put the position fairly: "their achievement lay in the sphere of uniting the various artistic forms or devices of their Near Eastern neighbours for the benefit of their own constructive ideas.... Unhappily, they failed largely to create from their ingredients a real synthesis...." And in Cyprus "it is very probable that here, as elsewhere, they had no original art of their own, but borrowed from Cypriote—eventually from Mykenaean—sources, just as they borrowed from Assyria and Egypt": Myres, *C.C.M.* p. 22.

Sidonian[1] foundation of Citium, which became and remained until the fourth century the strongest Phoenician post in the island. But a "Mycenaean" necropolis in the immediate neighbourhood shows that the Phoenicians were not the first comers. The acropolis began to be inhabited at the end of Late Cypriote III and the beginning of the Cypriote Geometric age.[2] A sanctuary of Heracles stood there from the seventh century; but, strangely enough, no definitely Phoenician objects, other than the well-known late inscriptions, have been found. The earliest sculptures show rather Egyptian influence, though this may have come through Phoenicia, being modified in the course of transmission.[3]

In historical times, the Phoenician occupation (as indicated by the provenance of inscriptions in that language, for the most part not earlier than the fourth century) reached out into the interior, northwards and westwards. Slight evidence of a Phoenician element is forthcoming in Athienou,[4] where one such inscription has been found; the site is with some likelihood identified with Golgi, but the Phoenician origin of that name, which has been suggested, is exceedingly doubtful. Phoenician occupation is more evident at Idalium (Dali), which was conquered by Citium in the middle of the fifth century. A couple of inscriptions from Tamassus prove the existence of Phoenicians there in the fourth century, when for a time at least it belonged to the kings of Citium. From Chytri, from the precinct of the temple of the Paphian Aphrodite, comes an inscription about some king (the word *melek* being the only word of which the reading is certain).[5] There is also the far outlier of the Phoenicians at Lapethos in the fourth century and in Ptolemaic times, and probably as early as the fifth century. In the same century there were also Phoenicians at Marium.[6]

---

[1] Coins of Sidon of the second century B.C. proclaim her as metropolis of Carthage, Hippo Diarrhytus, Citium and Tyre. (B.M.C. *Phoenicia*, pp. cvi f.) The claim may be exaggerated, but there is no need to dispute it as far as concerns Citium.

[2] *S.C.E.* III, p. 74.

[3] Gjerstad in *Die Antike*, 1933, p. 272; Goethert in *Arch. Anzeiger*, 1934, 105–6. See below, ch. x.

[4] *C.I.S.* I, 96. On Golgi see above, p. 67, n. 4.

[5] Peristianes, Γεν. Ἱστ. pp. 929–35.

[6] The presence of Phoenicians at this spot in the north is certainly surprising. Strabo is the authority for the Laconian foundation; and the fact that Greek names compounded with Prax- seem to be characteristic of the place may be significant: besides the founder Praxanor we have king Praxippus, deposed by Ptolemy in 313/12 and, also in Ptolemaic times, Praxidemus son of Sesmai (Baalsillem was his Phoenician name)

All this evidence is quite late, and proves little more than that the Phoenicians, who favoured Persia, extended their sway in Cyprus at the time of the Persian domination.[1]

Next to Citium, Amathus is usually considered as having the strongest Phoenician character.[2] The site has so far produced no Phoenician inscriptions, and the "many indications of its Phoenician origin and sympathies"[3] which have been recognized must be considerably discounted, although there may have been direct control in the eighth century.[4] In still later times, as in the revolt of Onesilus and the struggle between Euagoras I and Persia, it cannot have been due to a Phoenician element that Amathus showed its sympathy with the Great King; for

---

who made a bilingual dedication to Athena Soteira ('Anath in the Phoenician) and was probably identical with Praxidemus, high-priest of Poseidon "Narnakios", known from a Greek inscription (Le Bas-Waddington, 2779). This Poseidon was probably Melqarth, who as "my lord Melqarth in Narnaka" was worshipped there and is mentioned in Phoenician inscriptions of early Ptolemaic date, or even in the fourth century. Osiris, Ashtart and the "god of Byblus" also had temples at Lapethos in these days. The source of these inscriptions is not Lapithos itself, but Larnaka tis Lapithou, which is separated from Lapithos by the highest point of the Kyrenia range. The modern name Larnaka is doubtless a corruption (suggested by the well-known port) of the original Narnaka. Lapithos itself has so far yielded no Phoenician inscriptions; but to it with tolerable certainty are attributed coins of the fifth century with Phoenician legends and heads of Aphrodite and Athena; they name a king Sidqmelek; a coin of the Praxippus above-mentioned has also been identified. Under the Ptolemies the governors of the district continued to be Phoenicians. It is this strong Phoenician element which justifies Alexander of Ephesus and Pseudo-Scylax in calling Lapethos Phoenician, but it does not disprove a Greek origin. For the authorities, see B.M.C. *Cyprus*, p. liii and Oberhummer, art. *Lapethos* in *R.E.* XII, 763 ff. There are also slight traces of Phoenicians at Marium, in the extreme north-west, where Phoenician letters are found on fifth-century coins: *Num. Chron.* 1932, p. 210. Beloch, *Gr. Gesch.* I, i,[2] p. 223 n. must therefore be corrected.

[1] E. Meyer, *Gesch. d. Alt.*[2] II, i, 1928, p. 554: the Phoenicians did not reach the interior until the middle of the fifth century.

[2] Perdrizet (*Bull. Corr. Hellén.* XX, 1896, p. 353) points out, and Peristianes (Γεν. Ἱστ. p. 255) also exposes, the error. See also my article "Amathus" in *Mélanges É. Boisacq, Annuaire de l'Inst. de Philol. et d'Hist. Or.*, Bruxelles, V, 1937, pp. 485–91. Amathus is still occasionally described as Phoenician, e.g. in *Pal. Quarterly*, VI, 1937, where, pp. 129 ff., it is suggested that certain kinds of ware, found there, as at 'Atlīt and other places in the north of Palestine, are Phoenician. But a few imported Phoenician objects in tombs of the seventh or sixth century do not prove Phoenician origin for a place much older. On the Eteocyprian inscriptions of Amathus, see ch. III, p. 53.

[3] Murray, Smith and Walters, *Excav. Cypr.* p. 89.

[4] If Amathus was Kartihadast (see below, p. 107).

Onesilus had no trouble with Phoenician Citium; while later Euagoras found Greek Soli as hostile as Citium and Amathus. The fact that even down to the fourth century the Eteocyprian population and language survived there shows that the Phoenician layer must have been very superficial. The worship of Heracles Malika at Amathus is generally regarded as of Phoenician origin, Malika representing Melqarth; but there is something to be said for the view that it is to be traced to Assyria, just as Assyrian influence may be seen in the colossus of Amathus.[1] The famous silver bowl,[2] said by L. P. di Cesnola to have been found in a tomb at Amathus, is one of a class of which, though it is generally labelled Phoenician, the origin is quite uncertain.[3]

In the circumstances, we shall do best to admit that the extent of the Phoenician settlement in Cyprus, outside of Citium, cannot be determined at present on archaeological evidence. Nor do the records give us much help.

Even of Citium, the one undoubted early settlement, there is no early mention in the records to which any certainty attaches. The identification with "Kathian" in the inscription of Ramses III at Medinet Habu is very doubtful.[4] The name Kittim, as we have seen, is used in the Old Testament rather for Cyprus as a whole than for Citium.[5] As to the

---

[1] Dussaud in *Mon. Piot*, XXI, 1913, p. 7. Malika, he holds, is not a deformation of Melqarth, but the Aramaic for *melek*, king; and at the time when the colossus was erected, Aramaic was the current language of Assyria. Still, the channel through which this influence passed may have been Syria. See, however, p. 330.

[2] This did not, as is commonly supposed, pass with the Cesnola Collection to New York, but was at some time acquired by John Ruskin, and is now in the British Museum: Myres, *J.H.S.* LIII, 1933, pp. 25 ff.

[3] These bowls, which are widely distributed over the Mediterranean (three have been discovered in Italian tombs which are dated to about 670 B.C.), have a very mixed Oriental repertory of design. Myres, the last to pronounce on the Amathus bowl, dates it probably to the beginning of the reign of Psammetichus I, but does not decide whether it was made in a Phoenician city, or in the interior, or in a Cyprus workshop. (Dümmler, in *Arch. Jahrb.* II, 1887, p. 93, thought that most of the silver paterae belonged to the time of Amasis, while the bronze ones were older.) The bronze bowls of Mouti Sinoas, to be mentioned below, are to be dated to the second half of the eighth century. But most of these objects seem to belong to the next century and, if so, are later than the period of Phoenician domination. For the bowls, see most conveniently F. Poulsen, *Der Orient u. d. frühgriechische Kunst*, 1912, pp. 20–37 (who maintains a Phoenician origin); Dussaud, *Civ. Préhell.*[2] 1914, pp. 307–16 (where earlier references will be found). Most recently, Casson, pp. 132–5.

[4] Above, p. 49, n. 4.

[5] Above, p. 97.

identification with Kartihadast in the eighth-century dedications from Mouti Sinoas and in the prisms of Esarhaddon of 673/2, we shall see that the claim of Citium to the name cannot be substantiated.

However, of the Phoenician rule in a limited part of Cyprus, the dedication on the bowls from Mouti Sinoas by the "servant of Hiram king of the Sidonians" is sufficient evidence in the eighth century. This Hiram is not the friend of David and Solomon, but a younger Hiram, who is recorded as king of Tyre, and paying tribute in 738 to Tiglath-pileser III.[1]

It has been asserted that the friend of David and Solomon was sovereign of Citium; that it had rebelled against him and been re-conquered; and it is suggested that if this reconquest led to the destruction of the old city and the foundation of a new one, we should have the explanation of the name Kartihadast given to the latter. But the assertion is baseless.[2]

There is better authority for a revolt of Citium in the reign of Elulaeus, king of Tyre, who had to send an expedition to reduce it to obedience. But whether this Elulaeus was identical with the Lulî whom Sennacherib drove out of Sidon in 701, to take refuge and die in Citium, is uncertain.[3]

Similar to the style of the lettering in the Mouti Sinoas bronzes is the

---

[1] The difficulty that he is called king of Tyre in the Assyrian record and king of the Sidonians in the Phoenician dedication is explained by Cooke, *North Sem. Inscr.* p. 54. "Sidonians" is a general term for Phoenicians used by the people themselves, by the Assyrians, by the Hebrews and by the Greeks. Further, as no king of Sidon is mentioned in the list of kings paying tribute in 738, it is to be supposed that Hiram II was king of both cities.

[2] The suggestion is due to Schrader (*Keilinschr. u. das Alte Test.*[3] 1902–3, p. 128). It seems to be based on Josephus, c. *Ap.* I, 119; *Ant.* 8, 146. What Josephus (or rather his authority, Menander of Ephesus) says, however, is that Hiram made an expedition against the *Itykaioi*, so Gutschmid for the vv.ll. Τιτύοις, Τιτυαίοις, Ηυκαίοις, that is, the people of Utica. Gutschmid's emendation seems more probable than that which is necessary for Schrader's view.

[3] Menander (ap. Joseph. *Ant.* 9, 283 f.) says that Elulaeus king of Tyre was besieged (apparently by Shalmaneser IV, 727–722) for five years, unsuccessfully, although Sidon, Arca, Palaetyrus and other cities fell away from him. Also that he reigned thirty-six years. If he succeeded the Hiram who was reigning in 738 soon after that year, his reign would come down approximately to 701, when Lulî, king of Sidon, was expelled by Sennacherib. The identity of the two is generally assumed, although Honigman (*R.E.* II A, 2218) prefers to distinguish them. If Tyre lost all its territory, this would explain the expansion of that of Sidon under Lulî.

inscription incised on a red bucchero jug in the Cesnola Collection.[1] These wares range from the beginning of the Iron Age (at the earliest about 1200 B.C.) down to the eighth or seventh century. There is no reason, so far as the inscription is concerned, to regard it as earlier than the eighth.[2]

Thus we have no direct or indirect evidence of the presence of Phoenicians in Cyprus before the eighth century. And, indeed, that century is the period of the greatest Phoenician activity. The penetration of Cyprus may have begun earlier, but hardly before 1000. It certainly cannot be put back as early as the eleventh century.[3]

The historical value of the list of "thalassocracies" preserved by Eusebius is so doubtful, that it seems unprofitable for the purpose of this history to discuss the question of the Cypriote thalassocracy. Widely differing dates have been proposed.[4] The period beginning with the

---

[1] Myres, *H.C.C.* no. 479, pp. 59 and 521. Casson (p. 132) thinks the vase may fall into the period 1000–800. But as vases which are prized sufficiently to be inscribed with the owner's name may be treasured for a long time after they are made and before the inscription is cut on them, it is by the form of the letters, rather than the ware, that we must date the inscription.

[2] Judging from the comparative table in Ullman's article (*Amer. Journ. Arch.* XXXVIII, 1934, p. 364) the style of this inscription comes nearest to no. 13 (the Ba'al Lebanon bowls). At the earliest it cannot be pushed back before the Gezer Calendar (no. 6), which is dated about 900.

[3] Rhys Carpenter in *Amer. Journ. Arch.* 1933, p. 18. He points out that, had there been a great Phoenician sea-trade and thalassocracy at the close of the second millennium, it must have left some trace on Cyprus. When Wenamon came to Cyprus, about 1070 (or 1085, see above, p. 44), the island was not Phoenician. Ullman (*loc. cit.*) has hardly met Rhys Carpenter's point about Cyprus, whatever we may think of his criticism of the theory of the date of the origin of the alphabet.

[4] See, for example, the discussion by Myres and Fotheringham in *J.H.S.* XXVI, 1906, pp. 84–130; XXVII, 1907, pp. 75–89, 123–30; and A. R. Burn, *Minoans, Philistines and Greeks*, 1930, pp. 56ff. Winckler (*Der alte Orient*, VII, 2, 1905, p. 22), since in the list the Cypriotes follow the Phrygians, makes the Cypriote period begin when Midas (Mita) submitted to Sargon after the expulsion of Merodach-Baladan from Babylon (710); Midas having been sovereign of the sea-states, Sargon transferred the thalassocracy to his new subjects. Myres, on the other hand, proposes 709 B.C. (the date of the embassy to Sargon) as the end of the thalassocracy beginning in 742 or 741; the war of Tiglath-pileser III with the federated Aramaean states ended in 741 (or 740; H. R. Hall, *Anc. Hist. of the Near East*[8] (ed. Gadd), p. 462) with the submission of Phoenicia, and this would be the opportunity for an anti-Phoenician faction in Cyprus to assert itself. Fotheringham, widely differing, would date the thalassocracy of Cyprus in the thirty-two years beginning in 868.

crushing of the Syrian and Phoenician power by Tiglathpileser III in 741 or 740 certainly has its attraction as removing the natural rivals of the Cypriotes on the sea.

II. THE ASSYRIANS

Cyprus appears in the Assyrian records[1] under the name of Yatnana, Yad(a)nana, or Atnana. In the "Display Inscription" of Sargon (724–705) at Khorsabad we read: "I cut down all my foes from Yatnana which is in the sea of the setting sun." In the same inscription, and in the stele, erected at Citium about 707 B.C. and now in Berlin (Pl. IV),[2] he boasts that:

seven kings of Ya', a district of Yatnana, whose district abodes are situated a seven days' journey [an exaggeration intended to emphasize the importance of the conqueror] in the sea of the setting sun, and the name of whose land, since the far-off days of the moon-god's time, not one of the kings, my fathers who (ruled) Assyria and Babylonia, had heard, (these kings) heard from afar, in the midst of the sea, of the deeds which I was performing in Chaldaea and the Hittite land, their hearts were rent, (fear fell) upon them, gold, silver, (furniture) of maple (?) and box-wood, of the workmanship of their land, they brought before me (in Babylon), and they kissed my feet.

---

[1] The passages collected in *O.C.* pp. 5–15. See D. D. Luckenbill, *Ancient Records of Assyria*, II, 1927, §§ 54, 70, 80, 82, 92, 96–9, 102, 186, 188, 309, 319, 326, 690, 709. For his theory of the origin and meaning of the name, see "Jadanan and Javan", in *Ztschr. f. Assyr.* XXVIII, pp. 92–9.

[2] E. Schrader, *Die Sargonstele in Berlin*, *Abh. Berl. Akad.* 1881. The connexion with Sargon was discovered by Rawlinson in 1850 (*Athenaeum*, 1850, nr. 1166, p. 235). The stone was found in 1845 in the ruins of ancient Citium, and reported by L. Ross. The Turkish Government thought of buying it, but drew back at the price of "3000 Spanish dollars" (E. Schrader, *Keilinschriften und Geschichtsforschung*, 1878, pp. 244 ff.). The British Museum also offered too small a price (£20). Eventually it was purchased by the Prussian Consul for "700 francs", and sent to Berlin in 1846 (C. J. Gadd, *Stones of Assyria*, 1936, p. 214). There is no authority for statements which were current in England that it was found at Dali, and that it was R. H. Lang who sent it to Berlin (e.g. Baker, *Cyprus as I saw it*, p. 54). There is no reason to doubt that the stele was originally set up at or near Citium, although not necessarily on the actual spot where it was found. The material has been identified as gabbro, which occurs in the island (Bellamy and Jukes-Browne, *Geology of Cyprus*,[2] p. 33). The passage (Luckenbill, § 188) recording the erection of the stele "at the base (?) of a mountain ravine...of (Y)atnan" is the sole precise proof that Yatnana is Cyprus or in Cyprus.

Connected with these and similar passages are the mentions of the Yamani. "I drew", says Sargon, "the Yamanean from out the sea of the setting sun like a fish...I subdued seven kings of the land of Ya'", etc.; or again, "who caught the Yamaneans out of the midst of the sea like fish..., who subjugated seven kings of Ya', a province of Yatnana, which is located a seven days' journey in the midst of the sea". In the Annals of Sargon[1] it is recorded that the "Hittites" placed Ya-ad-na or Iatna on the throne of Ashdod in place of Sargon's protégé. Here, for Ya-ad-na, a variant text reads Ya-ma-ni.

Sennacherib (705–681), in his bull-inscription from Nineveh, written after his sixth campaign, says: "In my third campaign I went against the Hittite land. Lulî, king of Sidon,—my terrifying splendour overcame him and from Tyre he fled to Yadnana in the midst of the sea, and died." After his sixth campaign Sennacherib employed "Tyrian, Sidonian and Yamanai[2] sailors, captives of his hand", to work on the Tigris.

Of great importance is Esarhaddon's prism-inscription, written in 673/2, of the rebuilding of the Royal Palace at Nineveh:[3]

> I summoned the kings of the Hittite land and those across the river.... Ekistura, king of Edi'al, Pilâgura, king of Kitrusi, Kîsu, king of Sillûa, Itûandar, king of Pappa, Erêsu, king of Sillu, Damasu, king of Kurî, Atmesu king of Tamesu, Damûsi, king of Kartihadasti, Unasagusu, king of Lidir, Busussu, king of Nurê,—ten kings of the land of Yatnana, of the midst of the sea... I gave them their orders and great beams.

The three groups of twenty-two kings enumerated by Esarhaddon are described as "kings of Hatti, the seashore, and the middle of the sea", the second comprising Palestine-Phoenicia.

Finally, we have, in the alabaster tablet of Esarhaddon from Ashur,[4] "the kings of the midst of the sea, all of them, from Yadanana (which is)

---

[1] Luckenbill, II, § 30.

[2] Luckenbill's note (§ 319): "Text Iadnanai, but stone seems to have Iamanai. The two are, however, synonymous."

[3] R. Campbell Thompson, *The Prisms of Esarhaddon and Ashurbanipal found at Nineveh*, 1927–8 (1931), p. 25, ll. 63–72; a duplicate of the prism published by Scheil, *Le prisme d'Assaraddon*, 1914. "Across the river" (*Ebir narî*) is Transpotamia, all the lands west of Euphrates. Cyprus was included, with Palestine and Syria, the Phoenician coast-plain, Ammon, Moab and Edom, under the three collective names Amurrû, Ebir nâri and Ḫathi (M. Streck, *Assurbanipal*, 1916, I, p. ccclx; III, p. 782); this grouping was perpetuated under Persian rule in the Fifth Satrapy.

[4] Luckenbill, § 710: (mat) Ia-da-na-na (mat) Ia-man.

Yaman, as far as Nusisi, submitted at my feet". Without concerning ourselves with the identification of Nusisi (which has been explained as Cnossus, or as a miswriting or misreading of Tarshish),[1] we note the precise identification of Yadanana with Yaman. It appears that there is no philological objection to the equation of Yaman with Yavan; both forms would not be used indifferently in the same dialect, but might correspond to each other in different dialects. And Yavan (Javan) means Ionians.

Out of all this has been evolved the theory that the name of the Danaans (the Egyptian Denyen)[2] is a component part of Yadanan, for which Yamani appears to be an equivalent. It is suggested that Yad(a)nana is the cuneiform rendering of "the isles of the Danaans". The word for "isle" is the same in Hebrew (אִי) and Egyptian (*iw*); but the Assyrians had no name for it. "Isles of the Denyen" was probably the name by which both Syrians and Egyptians referred to Cyprus and other lands occupied by the Danaans in the twelfth and following centuries. But it is supposed that, not recognizing the word "isles", the Assyrians took over the combination as a single word. Homeric scholars have recognized that in the *Odyssey* the name *Danaoi* has an archaic tinge; it is used of the older heroes of the days of the Trojan War. This fits in accurately with the fact that they are active in the time of Ramses III (1198–1167 B.C.). By the time of Sargon they had disappeared, and the Greeks who had taken their place were known as Ionians (Yavan to the Hebrews). So Esarhaddon's scribe, having apparently some historical knowledge, to prevent misunderstanding, is thought to have put the current name Yaman in apposition with Yadnana.

This ingenious theory does not confine Yatnana to Cyprus, but makes it include all the Greek lands with which the Assyrians came into contact. Cyprus, however, as the nearest and best known, was the island *par excellence*. The phrase "seven kings of Ya', a district of Yadnana" remains obscure. Is Yadnana here Cyprus, or the whole of the Danaan lands? If the latter, is Ya' Cyprus? These questions must remain unanswered.

---

[1] Meyer, *Gesch. d. Alt.*[2] III (ed. Stier), p. 79, n. 3: "Tarsisi—the only occurrence of this name among the Assyrians—misread Nusisi by the editor."

[2] The identification of the Denyen of the Egyptians with the Danai appears to be very generally accepted. The only mention of this name in Egyptian records belongs to the time of Ramses III.

Berlin Museum

STELE OF SARGON FROM LARNAKA

To return to the prism of Esarhaddon and its names of ten kings and kingdoms of Yatnana:[1] Edi'al is supposed to be Idalium, Kitrusi Chytri, Sillûa Salamis (a very doubtful equation!),[2] Pappa Paphos, Sillu Soli, Kurî Curium, Tamesu Tamassus, Lidir Ledrae, while for Nure no equivalent has been suggested. Most of these equations are generally accepted. Pilâgura may be Pylagoras,[3] Itûandar is certainly Eteander,[4] Damasu suggests Damasus; for the rest of the personal names it is better to refrain from conjecture. The list of places, if we accept the identification with Salamis, includes all the most important cities of Cyprus except Citium and Amathus. One of these may be concealed under the name Kartihadast (New City). Which is it?

Kartihadast is also mentioned in the Phoenician inscriptions on a remarkable little group of bronze bowls said to have been found in Cyprus at a spot on the hill Mouti Sinoas, about twelve miles north-east of Limassol and seven miles north of Amathus.[5] By the style of the writing these bowls are dated to the eighth century. They bear inscriptions to the effect that "...governor of Kartihadast, servant of Hiram, king of the Sidonians, gave this to Ba'al of Lebanon, his lord, of choicest bronze" (or possibly, "first-fruits of bronze"). Sinoas is in the region of the copper mines. If we ask why bowls dedicated to Ba'al of Lebanon were found in Cyprus, the answer is that some local Zeus (possibly "Labranios", of whom there was a cult not far away, at Phasoulla) was identified with the Syrian god.[6]

Now in view of the comparative nearness of the place, where these dedications are reputed to have been found, to Amathus and Limassol, and its considerable distance from Citium (fully twenty-eight miles as

---

[1] See the discussion in *O.C.* pp. 12 ff. In the readings of the names I have followed Luckenbill. Olmstead (*Hist. of Assyria*, 1923, p. 369) is perhaps better ignored on this subject. The reading Upridišša (which would suggest Aphrodisium) instead of Nurê cannot be maintained (see *O.C.* p. 14).

[2] Campbell Thompson makes *Si-il-lu-'-u-a* Soli, and does not interpret *Si-il-li*.

[3] Though this is not a personal name, but an official title.

[4] Two gold bracelets which Cesnola alleged to have been found at Curium bear in Cypriote script the name of *Eteandros*, king of Paphos (Collitz, *G.D.I.* I, nos. 46, 47; Myres, *H.C.C.* p. 392), but they can hardly be earlier than the sixth century. The two kings are, however, still regarded as one and the same by Meyer, *Gesch. d. Alt.*[2] III (ed. Stier), p. 91.

[5] *C.I.S.* I, 5; Ohnefalsch-Richter, *K.B.H.* p. 21, no. 47; Lidzbarski, *Handbuch der nordsem. Epigraphik*, p. 176; Cooke, *North Sem. Inscr.* no. 11; Rhys Carpenter in *Amer. Journ. Arch.* 1933, p. 12.

[6] So Ohnefalsch-Richter, *K.B.H.* p. 21.

the crow flies), it is tempting to make the suggestion that the "New City" may, after all, be Amathus. The title might have been given to it at the time of the Phoenician settlement.[1]

But if Kartihadast is Amathus, why is Citium omitted from the list of cities? It has been answered that it was at the time once more directly subject to the Phoenician king.[2]

If Kartihadast is retained for Citium, there is still the possibility of identifying Amathus with "Nurê". The name Amathus—which resembles city-names in Syria—may have been given by the Phoenicians to the place which the autochthones earlier called Nurê. But this is a mere guess.

A mysterious statement by Herodotus,[3] that some of the inhabitants of Cyprus came from Aethiopia, has been explained as referring to the "Asiatic Aethiopians", i.e. Assyrians, and indicating Assyrians who settled in Cyprus in the period just considered. The explanation is not plausible; neither can we suppose that Esarhaddon or Ashurbanipal, during their brief possession of Egypt, transferred Aethiopians, in the usual sense of the term, to Cyprus. We shall see that the reference may be to a settlement which took place under the Persian domination.

III. THE EGYPTIANS

With the break-up of the Assyrian Empire, which began in the last third of the seventh century, and culminated in the fall of Nineveh to the Medes and Babylonians in 612,[4] an end was put to the period of Assyrian rule in Cyprus. Henceforward the great power which dominates the situation, until the rise of Persia, is Egypt.

---

[1] The name Neapolis under which Limassol (Lemesos) became known at a date not yet determined might tempt us to identify it with Kartihadast. The anchorage, so much better than that of Amathus, would attract the Phoenicians. Unfortunately, the site seems to have preserved practically nothing of great antiquity, except one Graeco-Phoenician tomb (from which came a Protocorinthian vase, *C.C.M.* no. 1501). This shows that the site was inhabited in the seventh century. But had it been an important Phoenician settlement we should have expected more.

[2] Meyer, *Gesch. d. Alt.*[2] III (ed. Stier), p. 91: "Citium is never mentioned in the lists of Esarhaddon and Assurbanipal, because it now again belonged to the Tyrians." Sennacherib, after laying siege to Tyre in 701, made peace after five years; Tyre paid tribute again and got back some of its territory (*ibid.* p. 54 and II, 2, p. 127).

[3] Herod. VII, 90.

[4] Not, as formerly supposed, in 606: C. J. Gadd, *The Fall of Nineveh*, 1923. A shadow of the Assyrian Empire survived for a few years in Harran.

The literary records of the brief century of Egyptian domination are scanty. If we are to believe Diodorus,[1] Hophra (who reigned from 588 to 569, and whom the Greeks knew as Apries) made an expedition with a strong fleet and army against Cyprus and Phoenicia, defeated their combined forces in a great sea-fight, and returned with much spoil to Egypt. His successor Ahmose II (Amasis, 569–525) reduced the cities of Cyprus[2] and made many noteworthy dedications in its temples.[3] Herodotus,[4] who tells of dedications by Amasis at Cyrene, Lindos and Samos, mentions none in Cyprus, although he says that Amasis was the first of men to take Cyprus and subject it to tribute. This last statement, although it may seem to a certain degree inconsistent with what we know of Cyprus under the Assyrian Empire, indicates at least that the Egyptian domination was more firmly established than the Assyrian. And this is all that the literary authorities tell us of Cyprus under Egyptian sway. But, so far as regards Amasis, it is borne out by the archaeological evidence. Amasis, as we know from Herodotus, included among the gifts which he sent to Greek shrines portraits of himself: a painting to Cyrene, statues in stone to Lindos, in wood to Samos—where they still were in the days of the historian. And among the Cypriote statues and statuettes and heads which have been preserved, there are some of Egyptian type (though in native style), sometimes actually wearing the Egyptian royal head-dress, which may in some cases be actual portraits of Amasis, or of his son Psammetichus III.[5] Probably some portraits by Egyptian sculptors were imported; if so, they have not been preserved.[6]

It was in the reign of Amasis that the first Greek settlement was established at Naucratis by the Milesians. It is possibly to this time that we must refer the pretty story told by Polycharmus of Naucratis about his fellow-townsman Herostratus, a much-travelled merchant, who bought at Paphos a statuette of Aphrodite, a span high, of an archaic

---

[1] Diod. I, 68. I.

[2] How early in his reign we do not know. Some put it as late as after the fall of Babylon in 539 (though, as we shall see, Cyprus probably fell away from Egypt to Persia even before that date); but Hall (*C.A.H.* III, 1925, p. 306) suggests an early date, about 560, since the strong influence of Saite models on Cypriote art points to a comparatively long occupation.

[3] Diod. I, 68. 6.

[4] Herod. II, 182.

[5] Myres, *H.C.C.* no. 1363; Pryce, *B.M. Sc.* I, ii, nos. 10–15.

[6] See below, ch. x.

style of art. He was carrying it home when his ship was caught in a storm. In their distress the passengers addressed their prayers to the image of the goddess. Immediately the ship was filled with green myrtle boughs and a sweet savour. When it came safely to land, Herostratus lost no time in offering sacrifice to Aphrodite and dedicating the figure in her temple.[1]

[1] Athen. XV, pp. 675 f.; *F.H.G.* IV, p. 480. Polycharmus gives a date equivalent to 688/5 B.C., long before there was any regular Greek settlement there, although it is true that there were Greek shrines as early as the seventh century (Kees in *R.E.* XVI, 1959; cp. Blinkenberg, *Knidia*, p. 40). Note that the figure was of an archaic style of art, as a warning against dating strata by single dedications found in them. On the probable type of the statuette and the influence of Cyprus on the Aphrodite cult in the Aegean, see Blinkenberg, *op. cit.* pp. 38–42; cp. pp. 206 f.

CHAPTER VII[1]

FROM CYRUS TO ALEXANDER

I. TO THE DEATH OF CIMON

The Egyptian hold over Cyprus broke before the advance of the Persian Empire. The menace may have been felt as early as the fall of Croesus in Sardes in 546. Before the expedition of Cyrus against Babylon in 538 the Cypriotes voluntarily placed their forces at his disposal.[2] In acknowledgment of this support the Cypriotes, like the Cilicians and Paphlagonians, who had acted likewise, were not put under satraps sent out from the capital, but were allowed to retain their own rulers.[3] Cyprus became the western seaward limit of the Persian Empire.[4]

It is to the period of Persian rule that we may most probably refer the settlement in Cyprus of Aethiopians.[5] Cambyses made an expedition against the land of Cush, which was afterwards subject to Persia; for the Cushites are mentioned as subjects of Darius, and the Aethiopians are recorded by Herodotus as doing military service in the campaign of Xerxes.[6] Thus it is by no means impossible that Aethiopians should have been settled in Cyprus in the sixth or early fifth century.

---

1 The draft of this and the two following chapters was kindly read by Mr W. W. Tarn. To his careful criticisms and suggestions they owe much that is very inadequately acknowledged in the following notes.

2 While Herodotus (III, 19) is not explicit as to the date of their going over to the Persian side (he might even be taken to mean that this did not happen until Cambyses was preparing to attack Egypt in 525), Xenophon, if he is to be trusted at all in such matters, leaves no doubt that the Cypriotes had assisted Cyrus in his campaign against the Carians (*Cyrop.* VII, iv. 1) and willingly joined the expedition against Babylon (*Cyrop.* VIII, 6. 8: ὅτι ἑκόντες ἐδόκουν συστρατεῦσαι ἐπὶ Βαβυλῶνα).

3 Xen. *Cyrop.* VII, 4. 2; VIII, 6. 8.

4 Xen. *Cyrop.* I, 1. 4; VIII, 6. 21; 8. 1. The boast of Cambyses that he was a better man than his father, because he had added "Egypt and the Sea" to his dominions (Herod. III, 34), is probably but an idle story, and cannot be pressed.

5 Herod. VII, 90.

6 Herod. III, 17–25; Diod. III, 3 (the campaign of Cambyses); Herod. III, 97 and the Naksh-i-Rustam inscription, F. H. Weissbach, *Die Keilinschr. der Achämeniden*, 1911, pp. 88–9 (subject to Darius); E. Herzfeld, *Archäol. Mitt. aus Iran*, VIII, 2, 1936, p. 61 (list of subjects of Xerxes); Herod. VII, 69 f. (serving under Xerxes).

Though the island formed part of the Persian Empire, it enjoyed a kind of undefined independence. The royal status of the rulers of its cities was respected; later, when Euagoras I was negotiating for peace, it was as a king (subordinate it is true to the Great King) that he insisted on being recognized. When in the sixth century the Cypriote rulers begin to issue money, never does the figure of the Great King appear on it, as it does elsewhere,[1] and there is nothing in the types or symbols of the coins, Oriental though some may be in origin, which can be taken as proving a political relation to the Empire. It is a purely autonomous coinage, and such an institution is one of the prerogatives of sovereignty. Gold was not issued by any Cypriote king before Euagoras I, but that means little, because the issue of gold by Greeks before the last years of the fifth century was almost unheard of.

In the new organization, Cyprus was included with other regions "across the river",[2] such as Phoenicia and Syria-Palestine, in the Fifth Satrapy, thus perpetuating the arrangement which had prevailed under the last Assyrian kings. From Herodotus we know[3] that this Fifth Satrapy, including with Cyprus all Phoenicia and Syria-Palestine (stretching from Posidium to Egypt, excluding, however, a portion of Arabia), paid a tribute of 350 talents; the separate assessment of Cyprus he unfortunately does not state.

Cyprus now comes more clearly within the Greek horizon; the historian begins to look at it rather from the West than from the East. The institution of coinage, which had been familiar in western Asia Minor and the Aegean for centuries, was adopted during the reign of Euelthon of Salamis, who struck in his own name the first silver money in the island. He used a standard practically indistinguishable from (though, if anything, slightly heavier than) that which was eventually employed for the imperial Persian coinage.[4] That coinage was probably instituted

---

[1] Spyridakis, *Euagoras I*, p. 98. His interpretation of the significance of symbols such as the *ankh* (p. 70) cannot, however, be accepted.

[2] See above, p. 105, n. 3. Meyer, *Gesch. d. Alt.*[2] III, 1915, pp. 136–7.

[3] Herod. III, 91. O. Leuze, *Die Satrapieneinteilung in Syrien u. im Zweistromlande von 520–320*, 1935, p. 264, thinks that Cyprus was attached by Darius to the Syrian rather than to the Cilician Satrapy in order to avoid putting too much power into the hands of the native rulers of Cilicia to whom the latter satrapy was assigned. But he was probably only continuing an earlier arrangement.

[4] The normal weight of the Persian silver shekel is 5·6 gm. The heaviest known Cypriote coin is of 11·56 gm., which would thus outweigh two normal shekels, and

by Darius I; but the weight system to which it conformed may have been in use among the Persians before the introduction of coinage. Presumably the tribute received from the various provinces would be reduced to terms of this standard, in whatever form or denominations it was originally received. The use of the Persian standard for coinage in a Persian province, though not a necessity,[1] would thus be convenient. It seems reasonable to suppose, therefore, that Euelthon adopted the standard because he had come under Persian suzerainty; so that we may date the introduction of coinage at Salamis about 538. It precedes by a century more or less the introduction of coinage in Phoenicia.[2]

The history of Cyprus from now onwards, for centuries, is mainly the history of Salamis. Records of the other cities during the period of Persian rule are very scanty. Ten kingdoms in all were in existence in Cyprus in the middle of the fourth century,[3] the greatest being Salamis; the others were Paphos, Soli, Curium, Citium, Lapethos, Kerynia (?),[4] Marium, Amathus and Tamassus. Idalium, which had fallen to Citium about a century before, had ceased to exist as an independent kingdom. Probably these ten were the ruling states at the time when Cyprus became part of the Persian Empire. After Salamis, the most important

is only just under twice the weight of the heaviest known shekel (5·88 gm.): Hill, B.M.C. *Cyprus*, p. xxii and *Arabia, etc.* p. cxxii.

[1] The standard was in use in Phoenicia, for Aradus, when it began to issue money towards the end of the fifth century, adopted it; although it was not necessary to do so, seeing that other cities in Phoenicia had already begun to strike on the Phoenician standard. The large sums involved in tribute payments would of course be checked by weight, not counted in coins.

[2] Four staters and two fragments of staters of Salamis were among a late sixth-century find of Greek coins (the rest being mostly Thraco-Macedonian) of which 39 pieces with five lumps of melted silver were discovered at Ras Shamra. The hoard was in process of being melted down when it was buried, and must have originally comprised at least 154 pieces. Schaeffer in *Syria*, XVIII, 1937, pp. 152–4; full publication in *Mélanges Syriens off. à R. Dussaud*, I, 1939, pp. 461–85. The general aspect of the hoard is exactly similar to that of hoards from Egypt, which were likewise intended for the melting-pot.

[3] Diod. (XVI, 42. 4) estimates nine in 351.

[4] Kerynia was certainly under an independent ruler in 315. There is no evidence that Golgi was an independent state in the period that concerns us. Pasicyprus, king of Tamassus, sold his kingdom about the middle of the fourth century to the king of Citium (Duris, fr. 12, *F.H.G.* II, p. 472; Jac. II A, p. 139, fr. 4). See below, p. 150, n. 2.

was Citium. Its coinage begins towards the end of the sixth century, or soon after 500.[1] The sequence of its kings from Baalmelek I (about 479–449) down to Pumiathon (361–312) is more certain, thanks to local inscriptions and coins dated by regnal years, than anything else in the Cypriote chronology of this age.[2] Paphos must also have been important, although it appears but rarely in the records and the numismatic evidence is very inconclusive; it may be that its Cinyrad priest-kings were more concerned with the cult affairs of the chief religious centre in Cyprus than with politics, although there was a Paphian contingent (which did not distinguish itself) in the fleet of Xerxes. As to Idalium, we shall see that the sequence of its kings from about 480 to the middle of the century is fairly well fixed. Amathus appears at the time of the revolt of Onesilus as his powerful and bitter enemy. Soli, on the other hand, and Curium fought on the Greek side, although the king of the latter place, Stasanor, went over to the enemy at the battle of Salamis. The other cities mentioned above were evidently of very minor importance. What little we know of the inner constitution of these small kingdoms indicates that, with one exception, they were pure despotisms, all the power being concentrated in the hands of the king and his police.[3] Our information is not earlier than the fourth century, but the conditions had probably remained unchanged throughout the period before Alexander the Great. Beside the king were the members of his family, the men called *anaktes*, the women *anassai*, meaning no more probably than "princes" and "princesses".[4] It is true that Aristotle's pupil Clearchus of Soli, in his account of the institution of the *kolakes* or "flatterers", describes the *anaktes* as a kind of magistrates, an Areopagus,

---

[1] It cannot have begun much earlier, seeing that there were only a few staters of the earlier types in the Larnaka hoard, which was buried at latest shortly after 480. See Robinson, *Num. Chron.* 1935, p. 190; Newell in *Num. Notes and Monographs*, no. 82, 1938, pp. 14 ff. The latter interprets the Phoenician letters on the earliest inscribed coins as *m(elek) k(ittim)*.

[2] B.M.C. *Cyprus*, pp. xxix-xli. The sequence of Phoenician rulers was interrupted for one year, as we shall see, by Demonicus (388/7).

[3] Engel, *Kypros*, I, pp. 473 ff.; Spyridakis, *Euag. I*, pp. 101 f.

[4] Isocr. *Euag.* 72; Aristotle, fr. 483 (from his Cyprian Politeia) = Harpocr. and Suidas *s.v.* ἄνακτες καὶ ἄνασσαι· οἱ μὲν υἱοὶ τοῦ βασιλέως καὶ οἱ ἀδελφοὶ καλοῦνται ἄνακτες, αἱ δὲ ἀδελφαὶ καὶ γυναῖκες ἄνασσαι. The title *anax* is borne in a Cypriote inscription (Collitz, I, no. 18; Hoffmann, I, p. 47, no. 69) by Stasias, son of Stasicrates, king of Soli in the latter part of the fourth century. The word seems also to occur in one of the Eteocyprian inscriptions from Amathus (Dussaud, *Civ. Préhell.*[2] p. 438).

controlling a highly organized police-system.[1] The *kolakes*, he says, are part of the apparatus of tyranny, of ancient origin, employed by all the kings in Cyprus; they are of good birth, and no one, except those at the very head of affairs, knows them by sight or how many they are. In Salamis, which provides the model followed at other courts, they are divided into two families, the *Gerginoi* and the *Promalanges*. The former act as spies, mingling with the people in workshops and market-places, listening to what is said and reporting daily to the *anaktes*. The Promalanges act as investigators, making further inquiry when it seems desirable; thanks to an extremely subtle technique of disguise and manner they are able to pass unrecognized and penetrate the secrets of all suspect persons. These instruments of tyranny were evidently a highly organized form of the tools which were used in other courts, as for instance by Hiero I of Syracuse. If Isocrates is to be believed, Euagoras I was an exception to the rule, judging men not by what he heard but of his own knowledge.[2]

Idalium, however, if a recent interpretation of a famous inscription and of the coins is, as it seems to be, justified, enjoyed in the fifth century a constitution differing from what is known of other cities in Cyprus. The king and the *polis* seem to have been associated on more or less equal terms, indicating a considerable democratic element. This peculiarity may have been due to Athenian influence.[3]

We return to the history of Salamis. As to Euelthon himself, the few references in the historians[4] show in the first place that he was on the throne when, about 530, Pheretime of Cyrene, mother of Arcesilas III, fled to Cyprus and vainly appealed to him for help to restore her son. His great-grandson Gorgos[5] was reigning at the time of the Ionian

---

[1] Fr. 25, *F.H.G.* II, p. 310 (Athen. VI, 255f–256a); cp. fr. 26 (Athen. VI, 258a). Eustathius, *Sch. Il.* 13. 582, describes the *anaktes* as a distinguished order of persons (τάγμα ἔνδοξον). Spyridakis thinks (p. 102) that to these *anaktes* belong also the δυναστεύοντες, a term used by Isocrates (*Euag.* 26) in describing Abdemon; but it seems to be used in quite a general sense of the people who held power; Diodorus (XIV, 98. 1) describes Abdemon himself as δυναστεύοντα τῆς πόλεως, and that after he was on the throne.

[2] Isocr. *Euag.* 42.

[3] Spyridakis in Κυπριακαὶ Σπουδαί, I, 1937, pp. 61 ff.

[4] Herod. IV, 162; V, 104; Polyaenus, VIII, 47.

[5] According to Herodotus (V, 104) Gorgos was son of Chersis, son of Siromos, son of Euelthon. In VII, 98 Herodotus mentions among those who took part in the expedition of 480 Matten the son of Siromos of Tyre as well as Gorgos the son of Chersis of Cyprus. It has been suggested that Herodotus has intruded the name of the Tyrian

Revolt. Gorgos was expelled in 499/8, restored after the death of his brother Onesilus in 498, and took part in the expedition of 480.[1] The date of Euelthon's accession is unknown, and 560, which is usually accepted, is a mere guess. That he was the most powerful, if not the supreme, ruler of the island is indicated by his plentiful coinage,[2] on some issues of which, indeed, he seems to claim sovereignty over the whole of the Cypriotes. The obverse type of all his coins, as of those of his successors down to the time of Euagoras I, is a ram or a ram's head.[3] But when a reverse type is used, it is the *ankh*-symbol, which is borrowed from Egypt, presumably as indicating his royal status. And within the ring of the *ankh* is the Cypriote sign *Ku*[4]—so that the design proclaims him king of Cyprus (Pl. V 2). The only other fact recorded of Euelthon is that he dedicated to Apollo at Delphi a notable incense-altar, which, Herodotus tells us, stood in the Treasury of the Corinthians. It has not survived.

Siromos (Hiram, Χειράμ, as the Septuagint writes the name) into the genealogy, and that Chersis was the son, not the grandson, of Euelthon; it is thought that there is not time for three successions between Euelthon, who was reigning about 530, and Gorgos in 499. The difficulty may be met by assuming that Euelthon died a very old man; his son and grandson may have reigned but a few years each; and a Phoenician wife might account for his son being called by a Phoenician name. Cp. Busolt, *Gr. Gesch.* II,[2] p. 545, n. 6. There are coins apparently struck by the successors of Euelthon which are distinguished by signs which may be interpreted as representing Ḥiram (Χι), Chersis (Χε) and Gorgos (Γο-ρυ), and these would accord with the sequence given by Herodotus (B.M.C. *Cyprus*, p. xc). For a silver diobol which appears to bear the name of King Chersis in full, see Newell in *Amer. Journ. Num.* XLVIII, 1914 (1915), p. 68.

[1] Herod. V, 115; VII, 98.

[2] B.M.C. *Cyprus*, pp. lxxxv ff. The classification is largely conjectural, and it is not certain that the coins with types on both sides are necessarily all later than those with a flat reverse. See Robinson in *Num. Chron.* 1935, p. 185.

[3] This type is explained by Spyridakis (p. 93), as alluding to Persia, which, according to the oldest astrological geography, was under the sign of the Ram. But so was Egypt (Gundel in *R.E.* XI, 1879 and 1881); and it is little likely that Euelthon would combine allusions to Egypt (in the *ankh*, see below) and Persia on the same coin. Both his types were therefore probably Egyptian in origin. This is not incompatible with the view expressed above, that he adopted the Persian standard for his coinage because he had become a vassal of Persia; for types may be adopted for cultural reasons, while commercial or political interests dictate monetary standards.

[4] This is also used by his successors, down to Gorgos, if the classification of the coins which I have adopted is correct. I have assumed that his successors went on issuing coins in his name, but with signs of identification, as already mentioned (above, p. 115, n. 5, at end).

British Museum

COINS RELATING TO CYPRUS

We know practically nothing of the politics of Salamis and other Cypriote cities at this period. But there must have been a considerable anti-Persian faction in at least some of them. One of the strongholds of this sentiment, which was doubtless partly democratic, and therefore opposed to the power that upheld the local tyrants, but also partly just racial, was Soli. Its friendship with Athens is illustrated by the story, the main truth of which cannot be doubted, of a visit paid by Solon to its king,[1] Cypranor (or perhaps Philocyprus), when, it is said, the Athenian sage persuaded the king to remove his city from its inconvenient situation on the bluff of Aepeia to the site on the plain which it thenceforward occupied. (This latter part of the story, however, cannot be true, if Aepeia is rightly identified as Vouni (Pl. VI); for the palace at that place is not older than about 500 B.C.) According to Herodotus, the king Aristocyprus, who was killed fighting against the Persians at Salamis in 498/7, was the son of Philocyprus.

In the light of these relations between Soli and mainland Greece, it seems to be no mere coincidence that among the types of Cypriote coins issued in the years round the Ionian Revolt—in which Eretria and Athens were the only cities of the Greek mainland to take a part—are two, the gorgoneion and the cuttle-fish, which may be due to the in-

---

[1] The *Vita Arati* (ed. I. T. Buhle, II, 1801, p. 430), which professes to quote Solon, calls the king who took Solon's advice and named Soli after him, Cypranor. Plutarch (*Solon*, 26) calls him Philocyprus. Herodotus (v, 113), who knows of Solon's friendship with and praise of the king, as a model ruler, but does not mention the removal from Aepeia, also calls him Philocyprus. Engel (*Kypros*, I, p. 255 note), assuming the truth of the record that Solon paid more than one visit to Soli (he is said to have died on his second visit), suggests that Cypranor was on the throne at the time of the first and Philocyprus at that of the second visit. This eases the chronological difficulty caused by Herodotus's description of Aristocyprus, who was killed at Salamis in 498/7, as the son of Philocyprus. But the biography of Solon is so much entangled with legend that it is perhaps futile to attempt an even approximate chronology. Lobel (*Bodleian Quarterly Record*, IV, 1924, p. 96) supposes that "it seems more than ever probable that the whole story of the visit is constructed upon some ambiguous reference in the poems". That indeed we have in the *Vita Arati*; and the name of the place (or places, for both the Cilician and the Cypriote cities claimed the honour) would give a good start to the legend. But it seems too circumstantial to be wholly myth. Sykutris (in *Philologus*, LXXXIII, 1928, pp. 439–43, and Κυπρ. Γράμματα, II, 1936, pp. 209–11) discusses the whole question; the story that the place was refounded and named after Solon is, as he says, doubtless a myth; but there is no reason to doubt that Solon visited Cyprus, though the third and last distich of the fragment of the elegy is a forgery.

fluence of Athens and Eretria, and that there is some reason for the attribution of these coins to Soli.[1]

The outbreak of the Ionian Revolt[2] and, later, the news of the burning of Sardes—which must have been wrongly interpreted in many quarters as a great Greek achievement—the appearance of the Ionian fleet off Caria and the adhesion of the Carians to the cause, gave the anti-Persian party in Cyprus its opportunity. Gorgos was at the time on the throne of Salamis; his younger brother Onesilus tried to persuade him to revolt, had indeed been urging this step on him frequently for some time, even before the Ionian Revolt began. But it was in vain; and Onesilus decided to take the matter into his own hands. He seized the opportunity of his brother having gone out of the city to shut the gates against him. Gorgos fled to the Persians; and Onesilus mounted his throne and persuaded all the Cypriotes, except those of Amathus, even the Phoenicians in Citium, to join in the revolt against Persia. The refusal of Amathus has been explained by the alleged strength of the Phoenician element in its population; it would be easier to accept such a reason if Citium, where the Phoenician element certainly was considerable, had also remained loyal to Persia.

Onesilus proceeded to lay siege to Amathus. Before he could take it, however, he received the intelligence that a fleet carrying a large Persian force under the command of Artybius was expected in Cyprus. He sent envoys begging for help from the Ionians, who lost little time in arriving with a strong fleet. About the same time the Persians, who had been carried over from Cilicia to the Karpass, marched on Salamis, while the fleet was taken by its Phoenician crews round the extreme point of the peninsula (the Kleides) and lay off Salamis. The Cypriote kings offered the captains of the Ionian navy the choice of meeting the Phoenicians on the sea, or exchanging places with the Cypriotes and fighting on land; the Ionians, saying that they had been sent to keep the sea, and not to

---

[1] See, especially for the cuttle-fish type, Robinson on the Larnaka hoard, *Num. Chron.* 1935, p. 187. The hoard was apparently buried shortly after 480, when the Greeks were again attacking the Persians. Robinson also notes (p. 188) that the Athena-head of the Athenian tetradrachms of about 500 is imitated at Lapethos, "though, in view of the wide use of Athenian currency, the fact of its imitation need not be so significant".

[2] The Cypriote Revolt began in winter 499/8 and lasted until the reduction of Soli towards the end of winter 498/7: Busolt, *Gr. Gesch.* II,[2] pp. 545–7. Herodotus (v, 104, 108–15) is the only ancient authority.

Phot. Mangoian Bros.

VOUNI

Petra tou Limniti in the distance to right.

hand over their ships to the Cypriotes, chose the former course. The Persians having meanwhile arrived on the plain of Salamis, the Cypriote kings arrayed the pick of the Salaminians and the Solians against the Persians, and the other Cypriotes against the remainder of the invading troops, among whom was a force from Amathus. Onesilus volunteered personally to oppose Artybius, his Carian shield-bearer undertaking to deal with the Persian general's horse, which was trained to fight with its feet, rearing up against its opponent. In the ensuing conflicts, the Ionians were victorious on the sea, the Samians especially distinguishing themselves.[1] On land, Artybius fell, the Carian having slashed off his horse's feet. Nevertheless, the battle went against the Cypriotes; for Stasanor, the king of Curium, who commanded a large force, betrayed his side; and the Salaminian war-chariots—for this antiquated arm was still in use in Cyprus—followed his example. In the rout which ensued, fell Onesilus[2] and Aristocyprus, king of Soli. The Ionian fleet, learning of the disaster to their allies, sailed away home. The Salaminians opened their gates to Gorgos; the other Cypriote cities were gradually reduced, only Soli holding out for five months, when the Persians took it by mining the fortifications. Since the earliest palace and fortifications on the hill of Vouni date from about this time, it seems probable that it was fortified by the Persians in order to overawe the philhellene Soli. There is reason to suppose also that Marium, that strongly Hellenic city, now received a ruler, possibly a Phoenician, of Persian sympathies, for Cimon was obliged to reduce it as one of the first operations of his expedition some fifty years later.[3] The Cypriotes, after a year of freedom, were again "enslaved to Persia".

Accordingly Cyprus had to join in the expedition of Xerxes against Greece in 490. The Cypriotes provided a hundred and fifty ships.[4] It is

---

[1] The Phoenician fleet seems to have been put out of action for at least three years: *C.A.H.* IV, p. 223.

[2] Herodotus says that the Amathusians sent his head to be hung up over their gates. Bees hived in it, and the oracle, consulted, told the people to bury it and sacrifice to him annually as a hero, which they continued to do to the historian's day.

[3] Marium and Vouni: *S.C.E.* III, pp. 287–8. Phoenician inscriptions on coins of Marium, see above, ch. VI, p. 100, note.

[4] Herod. VII, 90. He adds a note that their kings wore on their heads the *mitra* (which must be the head-dress which the Persian kings are represented wearing, a kind of turban swathed round the head), but the others the *kitaris* (our texts read κιθῶνας, which is obviously wrong; Pollux, *Onom.* X, 163, evidently read κιτάρις in his MS.). Otherwise they were clad as the Greeks. As to the form of the *kitaris* there is much

possible that the Cilician and Cypriote contingents were combined in one force of about two hundred ships.[1] It seems impossible to disentangle the part played by the Cypriotes from the story of the fleet in general, as recorded by Herodotus.[2] Of the Cypriote commanders, he names[3] Gorgos the son of Chersis, the king of Salamis who had been restored to his throne after the crushing of the Revolt, and Timonax the son of Timagoras, of whom nothing else is known; also, in another place, Penthylus son of Demonoüs, in command of the Paphian contingent of twelve ships. The Cypriote fleet played but a poor part in the expedition, and Herodotus may have been right (though after the fact) in making Artemisia tell the Great King that the Cypriotes, like his other supposed allies the Egyptians, Cilicians and Pamphylians, were "no good".[4] The Paphian commander lost eleven of his ships in the storm off Sepias, and sailing in the remaining one, along with the other fourteen survivors of that disaster under the command of Sandōces, into the arms of the Greeks off Artemisium, was taken prisoner. Philaon, a younger brother of Gorgos, was also captured in the first engagement off Artemisium. Thirty ships, of which many may have been Cypriote, were taken by the Greeks in that battle.[5] There cannot have been many of the Cypriote contingent left to fight at Salamis.[6]

---

obscurity; the Greeks used it of the Persian tiara (Pollux, VII, 58: ἣν καὶ κυρβασίαν καὶ κίδαριν καὶ πῖλον καλοῦσιν). Probably here it means the cap with lappets worn by Persian satraps (see O. M. Dalton, *Treasure of the Oxus*,[2] 1926, pp. xxviii ff.). By "the others" Herodotus can hardly mean all the rest of the fleet, but probably only the officers.—It is doubtful whether the Cypriotes contributed to the land forces of the expedition in any numbers; for in the statement in Suidas (*s.v.* Ξέρξης) that the Cypriotes with the Egyptians and Phoenicians formed a large portion (very many myriads) of the land-forces, something has evidently fallen out between μυριάδας and τῶν Αἰγυπτίων or Αἰγύπτου.

[1] So J. A. R. Munro in *C.A.H.* IV, p. 274. Herodotus, however (VII, 91), gives the Cilician contribution as 100, and names their commander Syennesis, son of Oromedon (VII, 98). Diodorus (XI, 3. 7), who agrees with Herodotus about the Cypriotes, makes it eighty ships. After the disaster off Sepias, the fifteen surviving ships, some at least of which besides that of Penthylus may have been Cypriote, were under the command of Sandōces, who, though satrap of Cyme and called by Herodotus a Persian, was probably, to judge by his name, a Cilician.

[2] See the detailed studies by Tarn, *J.H.S.* XXVIII, 1908, pp. 202 ff. and Munro, *C.A.H.* IV, pp. 284 ff.

[3] Herod. VII, 98. [4] Herod. VIII, 68, 100. [5] Herod. VIII, 11.

[6] Diodorus (XI, 19) says it was the Phoenician and Cypriote ships that first broke at Salamis. Xerxes afterwards put to death the Phoenician commanders whom he con-

After the victory at Mycale, the Greeks turned their attention to Cyprus, the securing of which it was hoped might mean the immobilization of the Phoenician fleet. In the spring of 478 the allied fleet under Pausanias set sail: twenty Peloponnesian triremes, with thirty Athenian under the command of Aristeides, and a number of other ships of the allies.[1] Cimon also probably sailed with Aristeides. The task of winning over Cyprus seems to have given little trouble; the greater part of the island was reduced, the cities which were still in the hands of Persian garrisons being set free. Then the allied fleet sailed for the Hellespont.

The Persians, however, soon regained command, if only for a brief space, of the seas round Cyprus. That was essential, if they were again to push forward towards the Aegean.[2] At the time of Cimon's double defeat of the Persians on land and sea at the mouth of the Eurymedon in 468,[3] the Phoenician or Cypriote[4] squadron of eighty ships, whose support the enemy were expecting, was based on Cyprus. They had moved forward to some point on the Cilician coast when he took them by surprise and wiped them out.[5]

---

sidered most at fault, and threatened the rest with suitable penalties. Engel (*Kypros*, I, p. 273) infers from this that Cyprus was disaffected; it may well have been, though one can hardly read so much between the lines as he does. G. K. Skalieres, Ἡ Κύπρος, Athens, 1935, p. [4], says that the Cypriote ships, leaving the Persian ranks, ὑποβοηθοῦσι τὴν νίκην τῶν ὁμοφύλων. So might a Cypriote then have explained the incident.

[1] Thucydides, I, 94. Diodorus (XI, 44. 2) gives the number of the Peloponnesian ships as fifty, but does not mention the allies, so he perhaps includes their contingents in the fifty. On the date, see Busolt, *Gr. Gesch.* III, i, p. 64, n. 4. Diodorus and Justin (II, XV, 16) mention Aristeides as in command of the Athenians; Plutarch (*Arist.* 23, cf. *Cim.* 6) gives Cimon as his colleague or second-in-command.

[2] Beloch, *Gr. Gesch.* II,[2] i, p. 67.

[3] On the chronology, Busolt, *op. cit.* III, i, p. 143, n. 1.

[4] Phoenician, according to Plutarch (*Cim.* 13), Cypriote, according to Polyaenus (I, 34).

[5] This engagement could not have taken place off Cyprus, as Engel supposes (emending Ὕδρῳ in Plut. *Cim.* 13 to Κύπρῳ). Syedra (*Sedra*) on the Cilician coast is the most probable emendation. The account given by Diodorus (XI, 60, 6; cp. Suidas *s.v.* Κίμων) appears to invert the order of things, making Cimon sail first to Cyprus, where with 250 ships he defeated the enemy's 340, and then to the Eurymedon (61) where he used the stratagem of manning captured enemy ships with his own men in enemy clothes (so too Frontinus, *Strat.* ii, 9. 10). This stratagem is placed by Polyaenus (I, 34) in the engagement (which he locates off Cyprus) after the Eurymedon; the enemy forces here are described as Cypriote. Diodorus (or his source) seems to have made hopeless confusion of the story. If Syedra is the right location, Polyaenus may be ex-

This crushing defeat, however much it may have relieved Persian pressure farther West, seems to have had little effect on conditions in Cyprus. In 459–8 the Athenians and allies were again fighting in the island[1] and in Phoenicia, with a force of 200 ships under Charitimides.[2] But the Athenians, enticed by the alluring prospect of detaching Egypt (which was then in revolt from Persia under Inarōs), withdrew from Cyprus and sailed on the adventure which ended with the destruction of nearly their whole force. The island was left unprotected; and when the Persians organized their great expedition for the suppression of Inarōs, it was in Cyprus, Cilicia and Phoenicia that they built and fitted out the fleet of 300 triremes[3] which sailed for Egypt about the spring of 456,[4] while a great land-army marched by the Syrian and Phoenician coast. The Athenian expedition ended in disaster in the summer of 454, when the force capitulated in Prosopitis and was allowed to return home—a mere remnant—by Libya and Cyrene.[5]

Cimon had been removed from the field of Athenian politics by his ostracism in 461. Although he returned from exile after the battle of Tanagra in 457, he seems to have taken no great part in affairs, until in 450/49 he negotiated a five years' truce with Sparta, which allowed the Athenians once more, under his leadership, to resume activities against

cused for placing the engagement off Cyprus, for which the defeated enemy would naturally make, and the nearest point of which (C. Kormakiti) is less than ninety miles from Sedra. Of the well-known eight-line epigram (F. W. Hiller v. Gärtringen, *Hist. Gr. Epigr.* no. 49) only the first four lines belong to the Eurymedon. This epigram is sometimes falsely attributed to Simonides, and is associated by Diodorus (XI, 62. 3) with the Eurymedon. In the version in the *Anth. Pal.* (VII, 296) it commemorates the capture of 100 Phoenician ships in Cyprus (whereas Ael. Aristides, ii, p. 209 Dind. refers it to the Eurymedon, and so reads ἐν γαίῃ Μήδων instead of ἐν Κύπρῳ). See below, p. 124, n. 2.

[1] Tod, *Greek Historical Inscriptions*, no. 26: list of the members of the Erechtheid tribe who fell in action "in Cyprus, in Egypt, in Phoenicia, in Halieis, in Aegina, at Megara". Nothing more is known of any happenings in Phoenicia at this time. Thucydides (I, 104. 2) says merely that the Athenians and allies with 200 ships were in Cyprus when they were called to Egypt to assist Inarōs in his revolt against Persia. The number is confirmed by Isocrates, *de Pace*, 86 and Diodorus, XI, 74. 3. (The number forty in Ctesias, *Pers.* 29, *Ecl.* 32 is evidently an error.)

[2] Busolt, *Gr. Gesch.* III, i, p. 306, n. 2, emends the Charitimides of Ctesias to Charmantides, because the former name "does not occur in Attica". He has forgotten Aristophanes, *Eccl.* 293.

[3] Ctes. 33 (who gives the name of the fleet-commander as Oriscus); Diod. XI, 75. 2; 77. 1.

[4] For the chronology, Busolt, III, i, p. 328, n. 3.

[5] Thuc. I, 110. 1, with Ctes. 34 and Diod. XI, 77. 4, 5.

Persia, with the object of wiping out the disgrace of the disaster in the Delta. The Egyptian Amyrtaeus, it is true, who had supported Inarōs, had never been conquered, and was still holding out in the Delta marshes. When therefore a fleet of two hundred Athenian and allied ships sailed for Cyprus[1] under the command of Cimon and Anaxicrates, sixty of them were detached to the aid of Amyrtaeus. But this time—doubtless thanks to Cimon's clear-sightedness—the allies did not make the mistake of leaving Cyprus at the mercy of the enemy. How far Cimon was supported by the Greek cities in the island, we do not know. But he had to deal not only with Citium, but with Marium and Salamis; the last was held by a considerable Persian garrison. Marium it would appear that he took, and the restoration of a philhellene ruler there and at Vouni may well have been the result.[2]

But Citium and Salamis resisted, and before they could be reduced, Cimon died, either of disease or from a wound. It is likely that he fell a victim to a pestilence which attacked the besiegers.[3] His death was, perhaps by his own instructions, concealed from both allies and enemy

---

[1] Thuc. I, 112. 2–4. Details are added by Diod. XII, 3. 4; Plut. *Cim.* 18, 19. Others in Hill, *Sources for Greek History*, III, 153–8.

[2] The authority for the capture of Marium is Diod. XII, 3. 3: Κίτιον μὲν καὶ Μάριον ἐξεπολιόρκησε (where Μάριον is an emendation of the MS. Μαλόν or Μᾶλον. Possibly there was an alternative form of the name with λ; see B.M.C. *Cyprus*, p. lv, n. 1). But, since it is fairly certain that Cimon did not take Citium, we cannot presume too much on the last word. However, it is improbable that he would divide his forces too much, and we are probably right therefore in assuming that he disposed of Marium before attempting to deal with Salamis and Citium. Marium (afterwards Arsinoe) is at or near Polis tis Chrysochou, on the north-west coast, and not at Mari between Amathus and Citium. (*S.C.E.* II, pp. 181 f.)—As to Vouni, the first palace, built in a non-Hellenic style about the time of the Ionic Revolt, possibly by a medophil ruler installed there after the reduction of Soli (see above, p. 119), was succeeded about the middle of the century by a building more Hellenic in style; about which time also a temple of Athena was built. It is suggested that this was the work of a new king of Marium, who succeeded the medophil rulers there and also took over Soli. Two kings of Marium of the second half of the fifth century are known from their coins, Stasioecus and Timocharis. Their palace at Vouni lasted until the early years of the next century, when it was destroyed, not to be rebuilt; Soli, which shows signs of revival at the time, may have destroyed it: *S.C.E.* III, pp. 110, 287–8.

[3] Both Thucydides and Pseudo-Aristodemus (*F.H.G.* V, p. 15, xiii) give λιμός (famine) as the reason for the collapse of the expedition, but λοιμός (plague) is a practically certain emendation (cp. Beloch, *Gr. Gesch.* II,[2] i, p. 177 note). Thucydides mentions the death of Cimon (without its cause) first, and then the famine or plague. Aristodemus puts them the other way round. That Cimon died of disease is stated by

for thirty days;[1] by his own orders, too, the siege was raised and the fleet sailed away. When it came off Salamis, where presumably it would put in to take off the land-forces which had been besieging the city, a double engagement took place; but though the Phoenicians and Cilicians were defeated both at sea and on shore, the general in command, Anaxicrates, was killed, and there was evidently no possibility of holding the island. So the allied fleet sailed for home. The detachment from Egypt followed its example.[2] Cimon's remains were interred at Citium, or carried home to the family tomb outside the Melitid Gate at Athens.[3]

Diodorus (after Ephorus) and Cornelius Nepos (after Theopompus); Plutarch gives both alternatives. That he died during the course of the siege of Citium is stated by Plutarch, who, though he says Cimon was engaged in acquiring the cities in Cyprus (the emendation ἐν Κύπρῳ for ἐν κύκλῳ is certain), never says that he captured Citium; and though Pseudo-Aristodemus, Suidas and Nepos (*oppugnando* is an emendation; the text is *in oppido Citio*) say that he died in Citium, it cannot be assumed that the city had been captured.

[1] Phanodemus, the Atthidographer (*F.H.G.* I, p. 369, fr. 18) quoted by Plutarch, *Cim.* 19.

[2] Diodorus (Ephorus) puts the defeat of the enemy by sea and land before the death of Cimon, and makes the sea-fight take place off Cyprus (the allies capturing 100 ships with their crews), after which the allies chase the enemy to the coast of Phoenicia, disembark and defeat them on land, Anaxicrates falling in the fight, and then sail back to Cyprus. In all this fabric probably the only sound pieces are the name of the general and the capture of the hundred ships. For it is to this fight that the second half of the poem, which Diodorus (XI, 62. 3) and Aelius Aristides (ii, p. 209 Dind.) associate with the Eurymedon, probably refers. Diodorus seems, as Domaszewski has pointed out, to have run two epigrams of two distichs each into one of four; of these the first refers to the Eurymedon, the second to the battle of Salamis in Cyprus. Both were probably inscribed somewhere in the "stoa of the Hermae" in the Agora at Athens. See Domaszewski in *Sbr. Heidelb. Akad., phil.-hist. Kl.* v, 1914, pp. 16 ff.; L. Weber in *Philologus*, LXXIV, 1917, pp. 248 ff.; Wade-Gery in *J.H.S.* LIII, 1933, pp. 82 ff.; and most recently E. Loewy, "Zur Datierung attischer Inschriften", in *Sbr. Akad. Wien, phil.-hist. Kl.* CCXVI, 1937, pp. 26 ff.—There is no need to search for reasons to explain why the Athenian fleet sailed home by Salamis, instead of taking the shortest route along the southern coast, other than that given above. There is no reason, either, to dismiss the siege of Salamis as a mere tale; it was a sensible plan for Cimon to leave a force to hold the enemy in Salamis while he attacked Citium.—Isocrates (*de Pace*, 86) and Aelian (*V.H.* v, 10) put the Athenian losses in ships at 150. We know that of the 200 which started, sixty had gone to Egypt; but if, as Thucydides says, the Athenians were victorious off Salamis, the fleet cannot have been a complete loss. But it looks as if the victory was a Pyrrhic one, and the capture of 100 of the enemy's ships must have counted for much as a consolation.

[3] Plutarch (*Cim.* 19) adduces the monuments "unto this day called Cimonian" as evidence that Cimon's remains were brought back to Athens. But he also says that

Thus in 449/8 ended the Athenian championship of Hellenic interests in Cyprus against Persia. The oligarchic party, at whose head Thucydides son of Melesias took the place of Cimon, were no match for Pericles, who saw that Athens had enough to do to hold her own against Sparta.[1]

II. TO THE DEATH OF EUAGORAS I

Supported no longer by help from the homeland, Cyprus fell immediately and completely under the Persian yoke. Citium was now at the height of its power, having either some time before the latest Athenian expedition, or shortly after its failure, extended its rule over Idalium, and destroyed the temple of Athena, the religious symbol of Idalian independence.[2]

In Salamis, in which, as we have seen, the Persian party had probably held out, the Teucrid dynasty was displaced. A Phoenician exile, who had come there and attained a position of influence under the reigning king,[3] threw him out and seized the throne, eventually bringing the whole island under the power of the Persian king.[4] If we may believe Isocrates, the reaction against all things Greek, which must have begun

---

there was a tomb of Cimon at Citium, the people of that city having been commanded by the god to pay honour to him; and it is possible that at Athens he was commemorated by a cenotaph only. This story of the worship of Cimon at Citium recalls that told by Herodotus (v, 114) of the head of Onesilus (above, p. 119, n. 2).—When Pausanias (I, 29. 13) says that the remains of those who sailed with Cimon to Cyprus were buried in the Cerameicus, he must be referring to this, and not to an earlier, expedition.

[1] The statement attributed to Stesimbrotus by Plutarch (*Per.* 26) that, during the revolt of Samos, Pericles started on an expedition to Cyprus, is rightly regarded by Plutarch himself as not to be believed. Doubtless, when Pericles sailed for the open sea to meet the Phoenician fleet which was coming to the relief of Samos, some such rumour got about; but it is quite incredible: Busolt, *Gr. Gesch.* III, i, p. 11, n. 3, p. 548 note.

[2] See Note at the end of this chapter.

[3] Isocr. *Euag.* 19–20. Busolt (*op. cit.* III, i, p. 344) has confused this Phoenician with the later Abdemon.

[4] The coins attributed to Salamis between Gorgos and Euagoras present several very difficult problems, which are discussed at length in B.M.C. *Cyprus*, pp. xcii–c. The names of kings Nicodamus, Lacharidas and Euanthes seem to be fully attested. It is possible that coins of Salaminian types may have been issued in some other place by the Teucrids in exile. Euanthes appears to call himself βα. Κυ. (Χυ, Γυ), possibly king of Chytri, hardly of all Cyprus. There are no coins which can be attributed to the Phoenician usurpers until we come to Abdemon. If the city was really reduced to such a state as Isocrates describes, this is not surprising.

after the Egyptian disaster, was greatly encouraged.[1] Those rulers were considered the most admirable who raged most furiously against the Greeks.[2] Greeks were not admitted to the city, the arts and commerce decayed (the harbour of Salamis even seems to have fallen out of use).[3] The picture is, however, probably overdrawn, and it is not possible to maintain that it is reflected in Cypriote art of the time.[4] The evidence of imported works of art which have been found in Cyprus, but not in datable deposits, is difficult to balance. It is interesting to note that, as we shall see in a later chapter, two of the finest works of Greek sculpture from Cyprus can be dated by their style to the second quarter of the fifth century. But were they imported at the time when they were made, or later—even as late as the time of Euagoras?

The Phoenician exile was succeeded in Salamis by his descendants, during whose tenure of power Euagoras, a member of the Teucrid family, was born.[5] The fact that his family was not expelled from Salamis proves either that the rule of the Phoenicians was not so brutal as Isocrates would have us suppose, or that the rulers were so comfortably seated that they thought they could afford to despise the Teucrid representatives. If the latter, they were soon to find out their mistake.

---

[1] As Isocrates puts it (*Euag.* 20) τὴν πόλιν ἐξεβαρβάρωσε. It must be remembered that for Isocrates Euagoras is the pattern of all that is good and Hellenic, and that the shadows on the Persian side are consequently painted very black.

[2] Isocr. *Euag.* 49.

[3] *Ibid.* 47.

[4] Busolt, *Gr. Gesch.* III, i, p. 344, n. 2, says that there was a withdrawal of Greek influence. He bases this statement on the analysis by P. Hermann (*Das Gräberfeld von Marion*, 1888, pp. 24 ff.) of the contents of the fifth-century tombs of Marium. What Hermann says is that in the older graves, down to about 450, there are no Attic imports; Cyprus was almost totally cut off from Greece, owing to the continuous state of war with Persia; the passing successes of Pausanias and Cimon had no lasting effect. In the second half of the century the importation of Attic wares is resumed, though in less quantity than in the sixth century. The reason is that there is a state of peace, a tacit recognition of the hold of Persia on the island. So that commercial communication is possible. The evidence of Marium thus shows a revival of Attic imports just after the failure of Cimon's expedition. See chapter X, p. 219.

[5] K. Spyridakis (*Euagoras I von Salamis*, Stuttgart, 1935, p. 43) conjectures about 435. The careful monograph of Spyridakis contains all the material for forming a judgment on the character and career of Euagoras; but the much shorter article of Swoboda in *R.E.* VI, 1907, 820–8 is better balanced. As to the three orations of Isocrates which are a chief source for the history of the reign, there is a convenient edition by E. S. Forster, *Isocrates Cyprian Orations*, Oxford 1912, and a careful analysis of the *Euagoras* in particular has been published by J. Sykutris in *Hermes*, LXII, 1927, pp. 24–53.

They were not even safe from their fellow-countrymen. About 415[1] another adventurer, named Abdēmon, apparently a Tyrian, but supported from Citium, murdered the occupant of the throne of Salamis and seated himself on it. The place became unhealthy for Euagoras, at this time a youth of about twenty, and possibly already engaged in plans for upsetting the usurper. He fled in good time to Soli in Cilicia, where he immediately began to gather round him a small band of absolutely trusty followers—perhaps no more than fifty.[2] It is possible that there were Athenian volunteers among them.[3] When his plans were ripe, in 411,[4] he returned with his little band to Cyprus, and, without attempting to establish himself in a strong place of any kind, and gather round him more sympathizers, at once the very same night attacked his objective. Forcing an entrance at a postern gate, he captured the palace from the much larger force of its defenders, while the citizens played the part of spectators.[5]

Thus, taking due vengeance on his enemies, he restored the Teucrid dynasty and seated himself upon the throne of his ancestors.[6] He proceeded to strengthen the fortifications of Salamis, build a fleet, acquire

---

[1] Spyridakis, *Euag. I*, p. 43; Isocr. *Euag.* 26. Diodorus (xiv, 98) calls him Ἀβδήμονα τὸν Τύριον; Theopompus (fr. 111 M. = 103 Jac., 101 Oxf.), Ἀβδύμονα or Αὐδύμονα τὸν Κιτιέα. There is no reason whatever for supposing him to have been king of Citium, as Beloch lightly assumed (*Gr. Gesch.* III,[2] i, p. 37, n. 2, and ii, p. 99; also Meyer, *Gesch. d. Alt.* v,[3] p. 199). Although he may have been a Tyrian, his attempt on Salamis may well have been based on Citium. Some small coins with the Phoenician letters ʽ*Ab* are on good grounds assigned to his short reign in Salamis.

[2] Isocr. *Euag.* 28.

[3] Aristophanes, *Thesm.* 446 f. (the speaker's husband fell in Cyprus). The play was produced in 411: Spyridakis, p. 45. Whether Athens publicly supported Euagoras is more doubtful.

[4] Rather than 412, and certainly before 410, because the supply of corn and bronze for which Andocides claims credit (II, 11), and which seems to have come from Cyprus, arrived while the Athenian fleet was at Samos. Spyridakis, p. 44.

[5] So Isocrates, *Euag.* 30–32. There seems no reason to distrust these details; he had sympathizers among the citizens, as Swoboda observes (τοῖς φίλοις ἐβοήθησεν), but we may well suppose that they would not interfere while the result was in doubt. Theopompus, fr. 111 M. (= 103 Jac., 101 Oxf.); Diod. xiv, 98. 1.

[6] As Beloch shows (*Gr. Gesch.* III,[2] ii, p. 98), there is no reason to doubt (with Meyer, *Gesch. d. Alt.* v,[3] p. 199) that he belonged to the Teucrid family, though possibly he was not in the direct line, since, in that case, his father would hardly have been allowed to remain in Salamis during the Phoenician usurpation. What Pausanias (II, 29. 4) means by saying that the Teucrid kings continued to rule the Cypriotes down to Euagoras, it is difficult to say.

land, and generally make himself respected and feared by those who had despised him.[1] Whether formally recognized by the Great King[2] or not, he suffered at first no interference from that quarter. Cyprus was once more open to the Greeks of the homeland; adventurers of all kinds, respectable or dubious, found their way thither.[3] One of the latter was the orator Andocides. Expelled from Athens after the affair of the mutilation of the Hermae, he betook himself to Cyprus. This was in 415 or 414, before the return of Euagoras, and he seems to have gone to Citium, where, if his enemies are to be believed,[4] he was imprisoned by the king (Baalmelek II) on a charge of treachery, and barely escaped mutilation and death. Later he returned to the island, this time to Salamis.[5] He himself claimed[6] that he assisted the Athenian fleet with supplies of grain and bronze (which most probably came from Cyprus) while the fleet was at Samos, thus contributing to the victory of Cynossema (Sept. 411); and another large shipment of grain from Cyprus about four years later was also, he asserts, made possible by him.[7] Euagoras, however, found it necessary to imprison him for some offence, but he was again set free. According to his own account[8] he was in possession of a large and valuable estate in Cyprus, which had been given to him, for what services he does not reveal.[9]

But there must have been many others of character less suspect than Andocides who, obliged by the vicissitudes of home politics to leave their own cities, sought refuge with Euagoras.[10] The king's public relations with Athens were official and friendly, for about 410 Athens bestowed upon him honours which are recorded in a long but unfor-

---

1 Isocr. *Euag.* 47.

2 Darius II was succeeded by Artaxerxes II Mnemon in 405.

3 Spyridakis, *Euag. I*, p. 113.

4 [Lysias], *in And.* 26, 27.

5 *Ibid.* 28.

6 *De reditu suo*, 11, 12. The date of this oration is about 407.

7 *De red. suo*, 20, 21.

8 *De myst.* 4.

9 Though the nasty story in Plut. *X Orat. Vit.* p. 834 E, F may give an indication, and show at the same time why he got into trouble with Euagoras. [Lysias] *in And.* 28 merely says that ἀδικήσας εἵρχθη. Spyridakis (p. 107) thinks that both at Citium and at Salamis there may have been some sharp practice in connexion with deals in copper or grain.

10 Isocr. *Euag.* 51; he (like Theopompus, fr. 117 M. = 105 Jac., 103 Oxf., and Nepos, *Chabr.* 3) names only Conon, who after the defeat of Aegospotami (405) escaped to Cyprus with eight ships (Xen. *Hellen.* II, 1, 29).

tunately fragmentary inscription.[1] From other sources[2] we know that he was granted Athenian citizenship; it would seem that the inscription records arrangements for the regulation of disputes between citizens of Athens and Salamis, and perhaps actual alliance between the two states. A tantalizing reference to Tissaphernes (who was satrap of Sardes from 412 to 407) suggests that Euagoras may have been engaged in negotiations with him on behalf of the Athenian side, possibly when Tissaphernes was at Aspendus in 411.[3]

The picture drawn by Isocrates of the decay into which Salamis fell during the Phoenician usurpation may be exaggerated, but that Euagoras found plenty to reconstruct cannot be doubted. Unfortunately, the traces of the Greek city are for the most part overlaid with Roman and later constructions, or with sand, though there are indications of the line of walls which may date from his time. The harbour at the mouth of the Pediaeus to the south of the city is lost in swamp land.[4]

We have few details of the growth of the domination of Euagoras over the rest of Cyprus. No reliance can be placed on the fact that he is called "King of the Cypriotes" by this or that writer at any time.[5] We are told of a struggle with Anaxagoras "King of the Cypriotes", with whom Ctesias endeavoured to bring him to terms.[6] A king Agyris, possibly identical with Anaxagoras, is also mentioned as an ally of Persia, of whose removal Euagoras was accused by the rival cities when they appealed to the Great King.[7]

---

[1] *I.G.* I, 64, with restorations by Wilhelm in *Ath. Mitt.* XXXIX, 1914, pp. 290 f.; *I.G.* I,[2] 113; Spyridakis, *Euag. I*, pp. 46 ff. Dated 410 by Ed. Meyer, *Gesch. d. Alt.* IV,[2] p. 619; possibly as late as Jan. 409 (Spyridakis, p. 50).

[2] Isocr. *Euag.* 54 and the Letter of Philip (Dem. XII, 10). The inscription doubtless contained this fact, and ll. 7–8 are so restored.

[3] Thuc. VIII, 87; Spyridakis, p. 49.

[4] Oberhummer in *R.E.* I A, 2, 1839. The narrow stretch of sea between the shore and the Salaminian Islands was also used for the purposes of a port, as is clear from the battle of Salamis in 306.

[5] As by Pseudo-Lysias, VI, 28, speaking of a time as early as 399: Spyridakis, p. 51, n. 1.

[6] Ctesias, *Pers.* 29, *Ecl.* 63. That Anaxagoras may have been king of Soli is a conjecture of Engel (I, p. 297). The work of Ctesias ended with the year 398/7; so that the differences with the Great King, and the death of Anaxagoras, happened earlier than that year.

[7] Diod. XIV, 98. 2. The explanation of Agyris as a mistake for Anaxagoras (C. Müller, *Ctesiae...Fragmenta*, p. 77) is plausible, since shortly before Diodorus (XV, 95, 7) was writing of the Sicilian Agyris.

The Great King, it has already been remarked, had shown at first no active objection to the re-establishment of the Greek dynasty in Salamis; so long as Euagoras paid the regular contribution to the tax due from the Fifth Satrapy he may have been content. But when these contributions began to fall off, and as Euagoras gradually increased his power at the expense of other Cypriote rulers, King Artaxerxes could not fail to become uneasy.[1] The Athenian policy under the leadership of Conon was directed to establish friendly relations with Persia, as against Sparta; and it appears that Euagoras fell in with this scheme. Although he did not, as Conon proposed,[2] go in person to Artaxerxes, he began paying the tribute again, and creating by presents in suitable quarters a favourable atmosphere in the Persian court. The intermediary in all these negotiations, which began about 399,[3] was the physician and historian, Ctesias of Cnidus. The satrap Pharnabazus also played an active part.[4] The correspondence ended in Pharnabazus arriving in Cyprus with 500 talents and orders to raise a fleet of a hundred ships, which Euagoras exerted himself greatly to provide;[5] Conon was appointed to the command. Athens meanwhile despatched arms and crews which apparently reached Conon,[6] who, however, before the full complement was ready, probably early in 396,[7] sailed with forty ships to Caunus. The further course of events, which culminated in 394 in the decisive victory of Cnidus, and the end of the Spartan domination of the sea, does not directly concern this history. But one incident may be recorded. Reduced to serious financial straits, the pay of the forces being held back by the satraps[8] and many months in arrear, Conon, in the autumn of 398, went to Sardes to beg for funds from Pharnabazus and Tithraustes. The sum which he extracted from them was quite inadequate, and on his return to Caunus he had to face a dangerous mutiny of the Cypriote

---

[1] Ctesias, *Pers.* 29, *Ecl.* 63; Plutarch, *Artox.* 21.

[2] Engel (I, p. 298) takes Κόνωνος πρὸς Εὐαγόραν λόγος ὑπὲρ τοῦ πρὸς βασιλέα ἀναβῆναι to mean that Conon proposed that he himself should take the journey. Either interpretation seems possible.

[3] On the chronology, Swoboda in *R.E.* XI, 1322 f.

[4] Diod. XIV, 39; Justin, VI, i, 4–9; Orosius, III, i, 7.

[5] Isocr. *Euag.* 56; Pausan. I, 3, 2. Xenophon, *Hell.* III, 4, 1, shows that the Spartans received a report from Phoenicia that no less than 300 ships were in preparation.

[6] *Hellen. Oxyrh.* II, 1.

[7] Philochorus apud Didym. *de Demosthene* (Foucart, *Mémoires de l'Acad. des Inscr.* XXXVIII, i, 1909, p. 163): in the archonship of Suniades (397/6).

[8] Justin, VI, ii, 11.

mercenaries. These were a land-force, which Euagoras must have allowed Conon to enlist in addition to the men of the fleet. They mutinied on the suspicion that their own arrears were not to be paid, but only those of the rowers and *epibatai*. As their leader they chose a man whose name is not given (but he came from Carpasia in Cyprus). Conon's coolness and determination quelled the disturbance, although at one time it seemed as if the Cypriotes would sail away home.[1] A personal journey to the Persian court at Babylon provided him with ample funds.

After the victory at Cnidus,[2] grateful Athens once again acknowledged the help of Euagoras. Bronze statues of both Conon and the king were erected before the Stoa Basileios, near the image of Zeus the Liberator or Saviour.[3] Other details are mentioned in a scrap of an inscription that has been preserved; it records the award of very high honours to Euagoras (according to the now generally accepted reading and restorations, an olive-wreath, proclamation at the Dionysia, and invitation to the king and his descendants to a front seat at festivals).[4]

Of another scheme of Conon's for strengthening the opposition to Sparta, we know only that he sent his friend Aristophanes son of Nicophemus with Eunomus to Sicily to negotiate for a marriage alliance between the houses of Dionysius, tyrant of Syracuse, and Euagoras. The mission, however, had small success; we are not even certain that it was due thereto that Dionysius refrained from sending, as he had intended, naval reinforcements to the Lacedaemonians; and the marriage proposal came to nothing.[5]

Conon, who had continued in command of the Persian fleet, was not long to enjoy his triumph. At Sardes, where he had gone in 392 to

---

[1] The description of the mutiny in *Hellen. Oxyrh.* xv is vivid, in spite of the mutilations of the text. The restorations which make the mutineers actually return to Salamis cannot be accepted; as Ed. Meyer (*Theopomps Hellenika*, pp. 76–7) shows, the mutineers sailed not to Cyprus but to Rhodes, where they intended to seize the acropolis.

[2] There is no evidence for the suggestion that Euagoras was present at the battle, although it is not impossible: Spyridakis, p. 52.

[3] Pausan. I, iii, 2 (Zeus Eleutherios); Isocr. *Euag.* 57 (Zeus Soter); Demosthenes, XX, *Lept.* 70 (bronze statue of Conon). For other honours to Conon, see Swoboda in *R.E.* XI, 1331.

[4] *I.G.* II, 10b, p. 397=II,[2] 20; corrected by Wilhelm in *Ath. Mitt.* XXXIX, p. 291. In the small portion preserved there is no mention of a statue. Conon's name also survives in the fragment.

[5] Lysias, 19, *de bon. Arist.* 19, 20; Swoboda in *R.E.* XI, 1332.

counteract the schemes of the Spartan Antalcidas, he was imprisoned by the satrap Tiribazus, on the charge of betraying the Persian cause. He seems to have escaped to Cyprus, where he fell ill and died.[1]

Meanwhile, the activity of Euagoras was steadily directed towards making himself master of all Cyprus. By force of arms or by persuasion he, by 391, brought almost the whole island into subjection, but met with resistance from three cities: Citium, Amathus and Soli—this last city now, after a century's subjection to the king who ruled in Vouni, showing signs of revival, and perhaps succeeding, in the course of the subsequent fighting, in destroying the fortress which had held it down so long.[2] These three cities appealed to Artaxerxes, alleging that Euagoras had murdered one of the kings who was a friend of Persia;[3] this king may have been the Anaxagoras with whom Ctesias had a few years before been endeavouring to reconcile Euagoras. Artaxerxes[4] decided that the danger demanded an effort and an expenditure of more than 15,000 talents.[5] He gave instructions to Autophradates, satrap of Sardes, and Hecatomnōs, dynast of Caria, to equip army and fleet for the succour of his Cypriote allies, who had offered to help in recovering the island for the Persian dominion, although evidently they were hardly in a position to give effective assistance. But Artaxerxes was not well served by his officers, and it is doubtful whether any force actually crossed to the island.[6] Nevertheless, the threat moved Euagoras to look for help outside. First he sent an urgent appeal to Athens, which was, it is true, not able to render much help; but it managed to get together ten triremes. The envoys themselves were ill-equipped with

---

[1] Corn. Nep. *Conon*, 5, 3–4; Diod. xv, 43, 5; Lysias, 19, *de bon. Arist.* 39–41. See Swoboda in *R.E.* xi, 1333. Lysias says he made his will during his illness. Others maintained that he did not escape, but was taken to Persia and executed. His remains seem later to have been taken to Athens and buried in the Outer Cerameicus (Pausan. i, 29, 15).

[2] Diod. xiv, 98, 2, 3; Ephorus, fr. 134, (*F.H.G.* i, p. 271) where for 'Ωτιεῖς the emendation Κιτιεῖς is certain, bringing the passage into *verbatim* agreement with Diodorus. Georgiades (*K.K.* p. 15) finds commercial reasons for the resistance of especially these three cities. For Soli and Vouni, see *S.C.E.* iii, pp. 287 f.

[3] See above p. 129, n. 6.

[4] On the weakness of Persia at this time, see Spyridakis, pp. 54 f.

[5] Isocr. *Euag.* 60.

[6] Diod. xiv, 98. 4 says that Hecatomnos took a large force there; but we hear nothing more of it. But what we do hear further of Hecatomnos, and that from Diodorus himself (xv, 2. 3; cp. Isocr. *Paneg.* 162), is that he secretly aided Euagoras with money.

funds for fitting out the ships, hiring peltasts and buying arms. But private generosity came to the rescue; Conon's friend Aristophanes, whose father was then resident in Salamis, gave largely out of his own fortune, and begged and borrowed more from his friends.[1] The little fleet sailed under the command of Philocrates, son of Ephialtes (390), but got no farther than Rhodes, where the Spartan Teleutias, who was in command of twenty-seven ships, captured all the ten.[2] As Xenophon remarks, the situation was topsy-turvy; the Athenians, who were friendly to Artaxerxes, were sending help to his enemy Euagoras; and the Lacedaemonians, the enemies of Artaxerxes, destroyed the ships which were sailing to fight against him. Aristophanes himself was sent as ambassador to Euagoras, but apparently not on one of these unlucky ships. He was to come to an unhappy end a year or two later.

The other direction in which Euagoras sought support was Egypt.[3] King Acoris, son of Nepherites I, sent him a considerable force. From an allusion in the *Plutus* of Aristophanes, which was performed in 388, we learn that Athens also was in alliance with Egypt; there was thus a triple combination against Persia. Athens renewed its efforts. Thrasybulus was doubtless on his way to Cyprus with a fleet, when he was assassinated at Aspendus. In the spring of 387 another fleet of ten ships with 800 peltasts was sent out under Chabrias.[4] Landing on Aegina with this force, supported by more ships and hoplites from Athens, he disposed of the Spartan Gorgōpas, who had been giving much trouble to the Athenians, and was then able to sail unmolested on his way to Cyprus. There with his help Euagoras was able to subdue almost the whole island[5] and installed as king in Citium Demonicus, son of Hipponicus, to whom the first oration attributed to Isocrates is addressed.[6]

---

[1] Lysias, 19, *de bon. Arist.* 21–3, 43.

[2] Xen. *Hell.* IV, viii, 24.

[3] Theopomp. fr. 111 M (=103 Jac., 101 Oxf.); Diod. XV, 2. 3; Aristoph. *Plutus*, 178. Among the allies whom Acoris enlisted against Persia were, according to Theopompus, Barca and the Pisidians; the latter were especially valuable as making difficulties for the Persian government in Asia Minor. Spyridakis (*Euag. I*, p. 59) assumes direct alliance between Euagoras and the Pisidians; of this there seems to be no evidence.

[4] Xen. *Hell.* V, i, 10–13; Dem. XX, *Lept.* 76.

[5] Dem. *loc. cit.*; Corn. Nep. XII, 2, 2; Diod. XIV, 110. 5.

[6] Babelon has shown that a king Demonicus struck coins at Citium (*Perses Achéménides*, pp. cxxxi f.); the Attic influence betrayed by the coins (they actually reproduce the Athena Promachos of Pheidias) fits in well with the circumstances. There is a gap

As to Soli, we have no information; but it has been thought that the burning and desertion of the Palace of Vouni, which can be dated early in the fourth century, may indicate conquest by Euagoras; unless, indeed, it was the Solians themselves who destroyed Vouni, which is supposed to have been at that time under a philhellene ruler.[1] The third outstandingly hostile city, Amathus, may also have been reduced by Euagoras, but the fact cannot be established on the evidence of an allusion to the sending of corn to Athens by one of its kings, by name Rhoecus.[2]

It is possible that Euagoras marked his conquest of some places in Cyprus by issuing coins thence; but there is no certainty on this point.[3]

It was probably during the presence of Chabrias in Cyprus that Aristophanes and his father Nicophemus were put to death. For what reason, we can only conjecture, but it must have been connected with

---

in the fifth year of the series of dated coins of Melekiathon, king of Citium; and this gap is filled by the coinage of Demonicus. Hill, *Hist. Gr. Coins*, pp. 67 f. Newell in *Num. Notes and Monographs*, no. 82, 1938, pp. 18 ff. Melekiathon evidently recovered his city next year. Meyer (*Gesch. d. Alt.* v,3 p. 200) and Münscher (*R.E.* IX, 2196) groundlessly reject Babelon's brilliant combination. If Citium "successfully resisted" Euagoras, as Beloch says (*Gr. Gesch.* III, ii,[2] p. 228), this was later; the passage of Diodorus (xv, 3. 4) on which he relies refers to the time of the sea-fight off Citium. A son (...ippos) of this Demonicus seems later to have become king of Lapethos, judging from a Phoenician inscription of Larnaka tis Lapithou, which Honeyman dates about 345–315 (*Le Muséon*, LI, 1938, pp. 285–98). It is possible that this king's name was Praxippus, and that he was the grandfather of the Praxippus who was deposed in 312.

[1] Gjerstad in *Syria*, 1931, pp. 58 ff.; Spyridakis, *Euag. I*, p. 58.

[2] Eratosthenes, in book IX of his Amathusian history (Hesych. Ῥοίκου κριθοπομπία, Suidas Ῥύκου κριθοπομπία), says that "this king, who had been made a prisoner, and then returned home, sent barley to Athens". Engel (*Kypros*, I, p. 303) suggests that this incident fits the circumstances of the conquest of the cities by Euagoras; Rhoecus may have sent the barley in return for his release being effected by Athenian agency. It is true that, as Judeich remarks (*Kleinas. Stud.* p. 123, n. 1), Athens was hard put to it for grain when Antalcidas held up the exports from the Black Sea. But the affair of Rhoecus might also be connected with the expedition of Phocion in 351; coins bearing the initial syllable Po, and conjecturally attributed to Amathus, are to be dated about that time (B.M.C. *Cyprus*, p. xxiv).

[3] (*a*) Coins of the series conjecturally attributed to Amathus, distinguished by the Greek letter E: B.M.C. *Cyprus*, p. xxvii (iii); (*b*) gold coins of Euagoras distinguished by the Cypriote sign for Ko (Γo, Xo), which have been attributed to Golgi: *ibid.* p. xlvii.—There is even a possibility that Aristophanes issued certain coins, which bear the signs for the beginning of his name (*A.ri*) and the royal title, and have types showing Athenian influence (B.M.C. *Cyprus*, pp. xliii f.). But this is no more than a possibility.

the change in Athenian policy which was marked by the Peace of Antalcidas (before the middle of 386).[1]

The Peace, to which Athens, worn out by the skilful diplomacy and strategy of Antalcidas, was forced to agree, recognized the claim of the Great King that all the cities of Asia, and the islands Clazomenae and Cyprus, should be subject to him, while all the other Greek cities, small and great, should be autonomous, except Lemnos, Imbros and Scyros, which should as of old belong to the Athenians.[2] Euagoras was not a party to the Peace; but he lost the direct support of the Athenians, who, however, did not at first consider that they were bound to renounce their alliance with Egypt. Accordingly they withdrew Chabrias from Cyprus and allowed him to join Acoris, although it was not long before a Persian protest at Athens put an end to his services in Egypt.[3]

Euagoras was now left with only one open ally outside Cyprus; but owing to the preoccupation of Persia with its Greek enemies[4] up till now he had been able without opposition, nay actually with secret assistance from Hecatomnos, to put himself in what might seem an

---

[1] Lysias, 19, *de bon. Arist.* 7. The two were put to death without trial (therefore by military law). Beloch (*Gr. Gesch.* III, i,[2] p. 141) assumes that, in view of their close connexion with Euagoras, this can only have happened when Athens had broken with the latter. "Evidently Nicophemus and Aristophanes had then tried to persuade the Athenian army in Cyprus to mutiny and stand by Euagoras." Their property was confiscated; the speech of Lysias was delivered at the end of 387 or 386. Meyer, on the other hand (*Gesch. d. Alt.* v,[3] p. 265), considers that the two were condemned at Athens and the sentence forwarded to Cyprus, without giving them the opportunity of defending themselves.—Besides the speech of Lysias just cited, he delivered another on the confiscation of the property of Aristophanes, of which all that survives is a sentence (Harpocration *s.v.* Χύτροι) which states that one Demaratus was found guilty of betraying the city of Chytri—evidently an event in the same context, rather than at the beginning of the war, as, following Engel, Judeich believes (*Kleinas. Stud.* p. 118 n.).

[2] Xenophon, *Hell.* v, i, 31. Less precise: Diod. XIV, 110. 3; Justin, VI, 6. 1. Glotz-Roussel-Cohen, *Hist. Grecque*, IV, i, p. 4, gives Persia "the islands from Clazomenae to Cyprus", for which there is no warrant. Nolte, *Die histor.-polit. Voraussetzungen des Königsfrieden von* 386 *v. Chr.* 1923 (Frankf. a.M. Diss.), pp. 7 f. explains the inclusion of Clazomenae by the fact that it had important possessions on the mainland. The reason for the choice of Cyprus was of course obvious.

[3] Diod. XV, 29. 2, 3 says that Chabrias accepted the commission from Acoris without the authority of the Athenians; he was recalled by them on the protest of Pharnabazus. This is reported by Diodorus under 377/6, but must have taken place earlier, not later than 380; in 379 Chabrias was strategos in Athens. Lenschau (in *R.E.* XIX, 1938, 1847) dates his recall to the time of the earlier attack by Persia on Egypt, 388–386 (according to his chronology).

[4] Diod. XIV, 110. 5.

almost unassailable position. At one time in the course of the next few years[1] he even obtained possession of Tyre and some other cities of Phoenicia; he had a fleet of ninety triremes (of which twenty were Tyrian, and seventy Cypriote); his own land-army numbered six thousand,[2] those of his allies many more, while his abundant funds enabled him to hire a large force of mercenaries. From various sources, hostile or suspect to the Persian government, he received reinforcements.[3]

To deal with the danger from Cyprus and Egypt at the same time was beyond the capacity of Artaxerxes. He decided to attack Egypt first, and despatched thither the satraps Pharnabazus and Tithraustes and the governor of Syria, Abrocomas. The war, however, lasted for three years,[4] ending in complete failure for the Persians. Meanwhile, in Cyprus, Euagoras unhindered went from strength to strength. It was probably at this time[5] that he attacked the Phoenician coast-cities, gaining possession notably of Tyre, and detached Cilicia from the Persian allegiance.[6]

The preparation of the Persian attack on Cyprus was entrusted to

---

[1] Diod. xv, 2. 4.

[2] Isocrates (*Paneg.* 141) gives him only 3000 peltasts: the fewer his men, the greater his glory (Swoboda in *R.E.* vi, 823). Or the lower figure may belong to the time after Euagoras had been defeated at Citium and was shut up in Salamis (Spyridakis, p. 65, n. 1).

[3] Diod. *loc. cit.* Who was the "king of the barbarians" who supported him we do not know; Ἀράβων has been suggested instead of βαρβάρων, which would point to some ruler of the Hauran or Nabataea. Sievers emended to Βαρκαίων, which is at first sight attractive, since we know from Theopompus (fr. 111 M. = 103 Jac., 101 Oxf.) that Acoris was in alliance with Barca. But it is fairly clear from the coinage that at this time there was no king of Barca, which was a republic (Robinson, B.M.C. *Cyrenaica*, pp. 98–105). Isocrates, in his *Panegyricus* (161), dating 380, when the war was coming to an end, describes the parlous condition of the Great King: "have not Egypt and Cyprus revolted from him, Phoenicia and Cyprus been ruined by the war, and Tyre, his great pride, been captured by his enemies? Of the cities in Cilicia most are held by those who are with us, while the others can easily be taken; as to Lycia, no Persian was ever master of it." A slight exaggeration!

[4] Isocr. *Paneg.* 140. This war is usually dated to 385–383; for the arguments in favour of an earlier date (388–386), see Lenschau in *R.E.* xix, 1847.

[5] Rather than before the Peace of Antalcidas, as Swoboda (*R.E.* vi, 823) has it; Diodorus, it is true (xv, 2. 4) mentions the seizure of Phoenician cities in 386, but his chronology of all these events is very confused. Action against Phoenicia would not have been easy for Euagoras except when the Persian forces were entangled in Egypt.

[6] Isocr. *Paneg.* 161, *Euag.* 62.

Orontes and Tiribazus, the former being in command of the land-army, the latter of the fleet, in association with Glōs,[1] son of Tamos, a veteran from the army of Cyrus the Younger. Cilicia and Phoenicia, the usual sources for Persian naval recruitment, being unavailable, the preparations were made in Greek ports of western Asia Minor (Phocaea and Cyme), and Greek mercenaries must also have been enlisted in numbers from these parts.[2] The necessary first move was against Cilicia, which had to be secured as a base of operations. The organization of the expedition here is illustrated by coins issued in the name of Tiribazus from the Cilician mints of Issus, Mallus, Soli and Tarsus.[3] From Cilicia the fleet carried the army over to Cyprus.

Euagoras made a gallant resistance. A fleet of privateers harassed the enemy, driving off, sinking or capturing the ships which were carrying provisions from the base to the island. The invaders soon began to suffer privations, and a dangerous mutiny of the mercenaries broke out, in which some of the officers were killed. It was with difficulty quelled by the generals with the help of Glōs. After this incident the whole Persian fleet was despatched to Cilicia to bring provisions, which were thenceforward abundant.[4] Euagoras, for his part, drew sufficient supplies of grain, money and other equipment from Acoris. He was also able to obtain from the same source fifty ships, and, himself fitting out another sixty, raised the number of his navy to two hundred in all. Some time was given to severe training of this new fleet.[5] When the moment came to strike, Euagoras advanced with a portion of his land-army along the coast,[6] apparently towards Citium, and fought a successful engagement with a portion of the enemy's forces. Encouraged by this success, he made a surprise attack by sea on the Persian fleet,[7] which was coasting

---

[1] Diod. xv, 3. 2; Polyaen. VII, 20.

[2] Isocr. *Paneg.* 135, 153; Polyaen. VII, 20. Diodorus (xv, 2. 1, 2) gives a doubtless excessive estimate of the land-forces as 300,000, with cavalry, of the fleet as over 300 sail. See Spyridakis, *Euag. I,* p. 61, n. 1.

[3] B.M.C. *Lycaonia, etc.*, pp. cxxvii, cxxii, lxxiii, lxxviii; Imhoof-Blumer, *Kleinas. Münzen*, p. 450; Head, *Hist. Num.*[2] p. 722. These mints very possibly continued in operation to the end of the war. The literary authorities say nothing of the reduction of Cilicia, but the sheer necessity of the case, and the establishment of the mints, prove it.

[4] Diod. xv, 3, 1–3; Spyridakis, p. 62.

[5] Diod. xv, 3. 3, 4.

[6] Diod. xv, 4. 2.

[7] Diod. xv, 3. 4–6. The date must be 381. On the chronology, see Spyridakis, p. 63, n. 1. Polybius (XII, 25 f, 2) praises the accuracy with which Ephorus described the sea-fight off Citium.

along to Citium. At first, taking the enemy in disorder, he sank or captured a number of ships. Glōs, however, and the other captains rallied, and after a severe struggle turned the fortune of the battle. The Salaminians lost many ships and were put to flight.[1] It was a serious disaster. The Persians concentrated both land- and sea-forces at Citium, and then advanced to lay siege both by land and by sea to Salamis, where Euagoras had been forced to shut himself up. Tiribazus, leaving Orontes in charge, crossed to Cilicia, and travelled thence to the Persian court, to announce the good news of the victory; he was to come back with 2000 talents for the prosecution of the war.[2]

While Tiribazus was absent it would seem that the siege of Salamis slackened somewhat. Euagoras put his son Pnytagoras[3] in charge of all the affairs of Cyprus, and slipped away by night with ten ships to seek help from the Egyptian king; who, however, doubtless discouraged by the reversal of his ally's fortunes, received him without enthusiasm, and sent him back with a disappointingly small supply of money.[4] Euagoras found the siege being energetically pressed. Tiribazus had returned, and Orontes, who might have been easier to deal with, was no longer in charge.[5] Euagoras in his extremity was compelled to approach Tiribazus, who agreed to support his proposals for peace, if he would give up all the cities of Cyprus, remaining king of Salamis alone, paying a fixed annual tribute to the Great King and obeying him "as a slave his master". Euagoras assented to all these humiliating conditions except the last; he would stand to the Persian only in the relation of a king to his suzerain. To give up the rest of Cyprus, to begin again to pay the tribute, may have meant no more than the restoration of the old order; but Euagoras had enjoyed freedom from Persian domination on the one hand, and on the other the sweets of rule over less powerful cities, Greek or Phoenician. What exactly the last condition meant, beyond the mere point of honour, we cannot say. But one circumstance seems to suggest that it was a condition imposed by Tiribazus more on his own authority than on definite instructions from his master. This is the fact that this

---

[1] Cp. Isocr. *Paneg.* 141; Theopompus, fr. 111 M.

[2] Diod. xv, 4. 2.

[3] Diod. xv, 4. 3. The MS. has Πυθαγόραν, which was corrected by Wesseling, from Isocr. *Euag.* 62.

[4] Diod. xv, 8. 1 speaks of him as Acoris, who, however, had probably been succeeded by Nectanebo (Theopompus, *loc. cit.*). See Beloch, *Gr. Gesch.* III, ii,[2] pp. 122, 124.

[5] Diod. xv, 8. 2.

point of honour, which would have been so welcome to Isocrates as the panegyrist of Euagoras, is not mentioned by the orator.[1] It may be therefore that Tiribazus, who had, as there is reason to suspect, reasons for wrecking the negotiations, interpolated a condition which he knew Euagoras would reject, but that it was not in the official terms, and so did not come to the hearing of Isocrates.

Evidently Tiribazus was guilty of some underhand dealing, which is described as a sinister design against Euagoras.[2] If so, he met his master. Euagoras began to work on Orontes—who was doubtless quite ready to plot against the man who had pushed him aside—and with his help successfully undermined the position of Tiribazus. A despatch[3] went secretly from Orontes to Artaxerxes accusing Tiribazus of not taking Salamis though he was able to do so, of receiving envoys from Euagoras, of treating privately with Sparta, and the like. Artaxerxes, persuaded, with that readiness which seems characteristic of such rulers, that the charges were true, sent orders to Orontes to arrest Tiribazus, and send him in chains up to Susa. This was done,[4] and Tiribazus now disappears from the scene of this history. His fall made Glōs, who had married his daughter,[5] look to his own security. Deciding to revolt, he entered into an alliance with the king of Egypt, hoping to take over the fleet, whose devotion he had secured by favours to the officers. Advances which he made to Sparta were also eagerly welcomed. But before he was ready to take the decisive step, he was assassinated.[6]

Euagoras,[7] encouraged by the disappearance of his most active opponents, continued to hold out in Salamis. Once more he sought for

---

[1] As acutely observed by Grote, who adds: "his silence causes great surprise—not without some suspicion of the truth of the story".

[2] Theopompus, *loc. cit.* Εὐαγόρᾳ ἐπεβούλευσεν. Diod. xv, 8. 3 merely says that Tiribazus refused the conditions of Euagoras.

[3] Diod. xv, 8. 3–5.

[4] Theopompus, *loc. cit.* "Euagoras slandered Tiribazus to the King and with Orontes arrested him." This probably only means that Euagoras was the instigator of the plot. Polyaenus (VII, 14. 1) tells how Tiribazus, invited by Orontes for an interview, fell into a pit which was prepared for him. Plutarch (*de superst.* 168 E) relates that he resisted at first, but when told that he was being arrested by the king's orders threw away his sword and held out his hands for the fetters.

[5] Diod. xv, 9. 3–5. The king of Egypt at this time was no longer Acoris, as Diodorus calls him, but Nectanebo.

[6] Diod. xv, 18. 1.

[7] Diod. xv, 9. 1, 2.

help from Greece, but this time from Sparta.[1] It was in vain. Meanwhile in the enemy's camp Orontes had difficulties with the soldiers who, resenting the fall of Tiribazus, were in a mutinous temper and unwilling to press the siege. In his nervousness, he entered into a treaty with Euagoras, offering the same terms as Euagoras himself had been willing to accept from Tiribazus. Thus peace was at last concluded, Euagoras retaining the throne of Salamis, paying a fixed tribute, and being subject to Artaxerxes "as king to king". And so the war, which had lasted ten years,[2] came to an end in 380 or 379. It was no disgrace for Euagoras. For the Great King it was customary not to come to terms with revolting subjects until they were in safe custody.[3] From this fate Euagoras had escaped. But his plans for the sovereignty of all Cyprus were shattered, and the remaining six years of his life present an anticlimax. At the end, the state was bankrupt.[4]

The history of the last years of Euagoras is a tangle of conflicting evidence, concerning an unsavoury court scandal, the only importance of which is that it shows that the culture, which his panegyrist Isocrates paints in such rosy colours, was alloyed with less desirable qualities. According to the account which seems to be most plausible, an abortive plot was laid against him by one Nicocreon, with whose daughter both Euagoras and his son Pnytagoras were, unknown to each other, carrying on an intrigue. Nicocreon, when his plot was discovered, fled; but both the princes were assassinated by the Eleian Thrasydaeus, a eunuch, who had acted as pandar in this affair.[5]

---

[1] Isocr. *Paneg.* 135. Theopompus, *loc. cit.*, relates this after the fall of Tiribazus; though the order of the events as enumerated in the summary cannot be trusted, this seems a more likely time than the earlier date to which Spyridakis (*Euag. I*, p. 64) assigns it. On the other hand, the journey of Euagoras to Egypt, which Theopompus mentions after the appeal to Sparta, probably belongs to the early days of the siege (above, p. 138).

[2] Isocr. *Euag.* 64; Diod. *loc. cit.* The chronology has been much disputed, but the most generally accepted view is that given above. To fix the dates of all the various events, within the ten years, seems impossible with the evidence at our command. That evidence is conveniently marshalled by Beloch, *Gr. Gesch.* III, ii,[2] pp. 226–9; Swoboda in *R.E.* VI, 825–6; Spyridakis, p. 63. See, for a later dating, Lenschau in *R.E.* XIX, 1847. For Tiribazus, see H. Schaefer in *R.E.* VI A, 1434 ff.

[3] Isocr. *Euag.* 63.

[4] Isocr. 3, *Nicocl.* 31.

[5] Theopompus, *loc. cit.* Grote (Pt. II, ch. 76), accepting in the main the version of Theopompus, supposes that Thrasydaeus was left by Nicocreon in charge of his daughter; and that he used her as a decoy, tempting the king and his son to a secret

The death of Euagoras, according to the only authority who attempts to date it, fell in the year 374/3;[1] he had reigned about thirty-seven years. He was at his death an old man, but not so old as to suffer from the infirmities naturally associated with age.[2]

"Thus perished", says Grote, "a Greek of pre-eminent vigour and intelligence, remarkably free from the vices usual in Grecian despots, and forming a strong contrast in this respect with his contemporary Dionysius, whose military energy is so deeply stained by crime and violence." The verdict may still be accepted; for the scandals which have been mentioned in connexion with Andocides and Thrasydaeus, though bad enough, are, so to speak, common form in the history of absolute rule throughout the ages, and would hardly derogate from the claim, made by his panegyrist,[3] that he was worthy to rule not only over Salamis but over all Asia. It is necessary, moreover, if it is the historian's business to label his characters, that he should avoid that uncritical pro-Hellenism which sets down the virtues of Euagoras as "Greek", and his vices as "Oriental".

It would be easy to draw a picture of the economic and cultural conditions in the reign of Euagoras, but it would rest mainly on conjecture[4] or on vague statements, such as that of Isocrates, that Euagoras was re-

---

assignation, and so assassinating them. A pretty reconstruction, but perhaps rather more than the text will bear. Diodorus (xv, 47. 8) says that Euagoras was assassinated by the eunuch Nicocles, who then seized the throne. There is no practical doubt that Nicocles, the son of Euagoras, and the friend of Isocrates, succeeded his father; but that he murdered him, and that he was a eunuch, is a confusion on the part of Diodorus which may be disregarded. Aristotle (*Pol.* 1311 b, 4 ff.) gives the murder of Euagoras as an instance of vengeance taken by a eunuch, διὰ γὰρ τὸ τὴν γυναῖκα παρελέσθαι τὸν υἱὸν αὐτοῦ ἀπέκτεινεν ὡς ὑβρισμένος. Beloch (*Gr. Gesch.* III, ii,[2] p. 100), who seems to assume that eunuchs cannot have wives (which is by no means certain), maintains that the woman must have been Euagoras's son's wife; and that she was seduced by Euagoras (the Greek meaning "because of Euagoras's robbing his own son of his wife"). From Theopompus it appears that the woman was the daughter of Nicocreon. On this interpretation the eunuch was of the household of Nicocreon, in charge of her, and took the outrage as personal to himself. But it does not appear why he killed Pnytagoras also. There may be allusions to this tragedy in the generalities of Isocrates about the dangers run by tyrants (2, *ad Nicocl.* 5; 3, *Nicocl.* 36, 41: see Judeich, *Kleinas. Stud.* p. 132, n. 1).

[1] Diod. xv, 47. 8. This is generally accepted (see Beloch, *Gr. Gesch.* III, ii,[2] p. 99).

[2] Isocr. *Euag.* 71. If he was born about 435, he would have been about sixty.

[3] Isocr. *loc. cit.*

[4] It has been ably attempted by Spyridakis, *Euag. I,* pp. 104–16.

sponsible for the stream of men of letters, music and the arts that flowed to the court of Salamis.[1] Whether among these bearers of culture was Isocrates himself is unfortunately uncertain, in spite of his intimate connexion with Nicocles, the second son and successor of Euagoras; we know nothing of how much time, if any, he spent in the island.[2] His *Busiris* was a counterblast to the *Apology of Busiris*, a production of the sophist Polycrates, who was one of the crowd who went to Cyprus; Isocrates naturally was unwilling to allow a third-rate sophist to make an impression on the perhaps not too critical circles at the court of Salamis.[3] It seems that Nicocles was actually at some time a pupil of Isocrates;[4] he may have been sent by his father to school at Athens.

Apart from literary evidence, however, one class of monuments fortunately survives from the time of Euagoras which shows the effect of his Hellenizing policy, and that is his coinage.[5] This consists of gold and silver. The issue of gold has been considered significant as a challenge to the privileges of the Great King, to whom was reserved the right of coining in this metal. But the reason for the issue lay probably in military necessity,[6] and the date is more likely to have been during the ten years' war than as early as 406. The silver consists chiefly of staters and thirds of staters on the Persic standard; the latter were conveniently near in weight to the drachms of the Rhodian standard.[7] The rising Greek influence is seen in the fact that for the first time in Cyprus the Greek alphabet appears on the coins, though only in a tentative way;

---

1 Isocr. *Euag.* 50.

2 Engel, *Kypros*, I, pp. 331 f., believes that it was considerable. An anecdote in [Plut.] *X Orat. Vit.* 838 F makes him a guest of Nicocreon. Münscher, in *R.E.* IX, 2189, doubts whether he was ever there at all.

3 Münscher in *R.E.* IX, 2178.

4 On the evidence of Isocr. *Euag.* 78; Περὶ ἀντιδόσεως, 30, 40, cp. 67; Cicero, *de oratore*, II, 94.

5 B.M.C. *Cyprus*, pp. ci–ciii, 56–58; Spyridakis, *Euag. I*, pp. 68–95. The supposed bronze coins (Spyridakis, nos. 71–3) are probably the cores of once plated coins; this is certainly true of no. 73. The gold coins which Spyridakis would remove from Nicocles to his father really belong to the former (*J.H.S.* LVII, p. 98). Generally, the attempt of Spyridakis at a chronological classification of the issues seems to be unsuccessful.

6 Hill, *Hist. Gr. Coins*, p. 77, n. 1. The payment of mercenaries at the time was one gold daric a month, so that the quarter-daric (the largest denomination struck by Euagoras) would have been useful.

7 The Rhodian standard was actually adopted for the silver coinage by Euagoras II and his successors.

it is not until the reign of Euagoras II that it entirely ousts the Cypriote syllabary at Salamis.[1] The types used by Euagoras show a remarkable variety, compared with the uniformity of the longer series of other mints such as Amathus (?), Citium and Paphos, and of Salamis itself under his predecessors. There is little trace of the Oriental tradition, and the head of the bearded Heracles (Pl. V 3), and still more the figure of the young Heracles seated on a rock and holding a horn, strike quite a new, Hellenic note. Heracles is indeed the dominant figure of the coinage, and is chosen as such because he is the national Greek hero,[2] perhaps, indeed, as a direct challenge to the Heracles-Melqarth who figures even more prominently on the coinage of Citium.

III. TO ALEXANDER THE GREAT

The eldest son of Euagoras, Pnytagoras, had died with him. The next in succession was Nicocles,[3] who has indeed been suspected of not being

---

[1] At other mints: at Amathus(?) it is found only on a stater of Rhodian standard which may have been issued there in 391 by Euagoras (above, p. 134, n. 3); at Citium it occurs during the brief reign of Demonicus in 388/7 (above, p. 133, n. 6); at Marium not until Stasioecus II (before 315–312); at Paphos sometime before 360 B.C. (in B.M.C. *Cyprus*, p. 44, the head-line for no. 47 should be "*circa* 400–360 B.C."); at Soli on the coins of Pasicrates, about 331 B.C. The latest occurrence of the Cypriote syllabary on coins is under Menelaus at Salamis (312–306; B.M.C. *Cyprus*, p. cxiii).

[2] Spyridakis, *Euag. I*, p. 93.

[3] Isocr. 3, *Nicocl.* 42; 9, *Euag.* 1. It is convenient here, at the risk of later repetition, to deal with the genealogy and sequence of the remaining kings of Salamis, as most ingeniously reconstructed by Beloch, *Gr. Gesch.* III, ii,[2] pp. 99–101. The name of the wife of Euagoras, Leto, is known to us (Lucian, *pro imagin.* 27); by her, possibly also by others, he had a number of children. (Isocrates speaks of his combination of εὐπαιδία and πολυπαιδία: *Euag.* 72). The Pnytagoras who was placed in charge of affairs when Euagoras went to Egypt (above, p. 138) must have been his eldest son; he it was whom Thrasydaeus assassinated. Since Nicocles succeeded in 374/3, he must have been the second son. The statement in Diodorus (XV, 47. 8) that he was the eunuch who assassinated Euagoras and Pnytagoras is evidently a mere blunder. He died a violent death some time before the year 354/3, when Isocrates (Περὶ ἀντιδόσεως, 67) mentions him as having been king some time ago (τῷ κατ' ἐκεῖνον τὸν χρόνον βασιλεῖ). His successor was Euagoras II, very possibly a brother, since he claimed the throne as πατρῴα ἀρχή (Diod. XVI, 46. 2; for the phrase, cp. Xen. *Anab.* I, 7. 6). But he is generally taken for a son of Nicocles: so Judeich, *Kleinas. Stud.* p. 133, Beloch formerly, and Swoboda in *R.E.* VI, 1907, 827. He had but a short reign, and was expelled, probably at the time of the revolt of 351, since he is first mentioned when we hear that he was put in charge, with Phocion, of the expedition which Idrieus despatched to Cyprus; he is described then as having been king ἐν τοῖς ἐπάνω χρόνοις (Diod. XVI, 42. 7). Such a

unconcerned in the murder of his father. The suspicion, however, rests only on the statement of Diodorus, who says that the throne was seized by "the eunuch Nicocles" who had murdered Euagoras.[1] However this may be, Nicocles staged a magnificent funeral;[2] though it does not appear to be a fact that, as is commonly assumed, he ordered from the most famous orator of the day the eulogy which is the chief, if biased, source for our knowledge of the murdered king. Nicocles came to the throne a fairly young man, at an age when most men would be liable to commit indiscretions. If we could believe the speech which Isocrates wrote for him, he was a model of justice, mildness and restraint, and devoted himself to calming the opposition to his succession which evidently existed, redressing grievances, and restoring the shattered finances of the state.[3] But the three Cyprian orations of Isocrates must, of course, not be taken as straightforward historical documents. The circumstances

---

phrase is appropriate if the despatch of the expedition is to be dated, as Beloch makes out (*Gr. Gesch.* III, ii,[2] p. 287), as late as 345 or 344. Euagoras on his expulsion was followed by Pnytagoras, whom Beloch supposes to have been the son of the earlier prince of the same name; he would thus be a grandson of Euagoras I. His son Nicocreon was reigning by 331 (Plut. *Alex.* 29), and died in 311/10 (*Marmor Parium* in Jacoby, *Fr. Gr. Hist.* II, p. 1004, B. 17), being driven to suicide. Diodorus (XX, 21, under 310/9) and Polyaenus (VIII, 48), who tell the story of his death, call him Nicocles and Diodorus makes him king of Paphos, which probably did have at least two kings called Nicocles (B.M.C. *Cyprus*, p. lxiii). The contents-table to Diod. XX (δ′), however, gets half-way to the truth with "Nicocreon king of the Paphians". An inscription on the base of a statue erected to Nicrocreon at Argos (*I.G.* IV, 583) speaks of his father as being of the race of Aeacus. The name Nicocreon would have come to him from his great-grandfather.

The possibility that King Pnytagoras was the son, not of Pnytagoras, but of another son of Euagoras I, must not be excluded (Beloch, *ibid.* p. 101).

[1] From Isocrates (9, *Euag.* 1 f.; 3, *Nicocl.* 13, 28, etc.) it would appear that he was not merely the legitimate successor, but that there was nothing irregular about the manner of his succession: ταύτην ἔχω τὴν ἀρχὴν οὐ παρανόμως οὐδ' ἀλλοτρίαν ἀλλ' ὁσίως καὶ δικαίως, κ.τ.λ. Of course this is merely his own statement; he could have said no less in his situation.

[2] Isocr. *Euag.* 1: choric dances, music and gymnastic contests, horse-races and regattas.

[3] Isocr. 3, *Nicocl.* 31 f., 45. The straitened condition of the finances of Nicocles is illustrated by the smallness of his coinage. It consists only of rare gold and bronze coins. The absence of silver is significant (B.M.C. *Cyprus*, p. civ). The attempt of Spyridakis, *Euag. I*, p. 86, to attribute some of this gold to Euagoras I must be rejected without hesitation (see *J.H.S.* LVII, p. 98). The gold is of the nature of money of necessity (see above, p. 142) rather than of regular coinage.

of their origin are not precisely determined.[1] The *Euagoras* doubtless came very soon after the death of its subject; that it was ordered by Nicocles there is nothing to prove, and indeed he was not the sort of man to suggest the invention of what was practically a new literary mode. The *ad Nicoclem* is commonly supposed to have preceded the *Euagoras*, and the arguments for placing it a little later are not convincing. The last of the three orations is the speech to the king's subjects, which Isocrates puts into the king's own mouth. It may almost be read as an exercise in irony; the virtues which are therein extolled, and the advice given to his subjects, may be interpreted by their contraries, so far as the actuality is concerned. This reverse of the medal is shown to us by two almost contemporary historians,[2] who describe Nicocles as deliberately vying with Strato, king of Sidon, in the wildest excesses of luxury and debauchery. It has, however, been plausibly suggested that the real ground of his association with Strato lay in a common opposition to Persia, which would account at the same time for the interest which Isocrates took in him.[3] Contemporary gossip would ignore this, while fastening on scandals, for which there was doubtless ample evidence.

Nicocles and Strato alike met with a violent end; Nicocles as a prisoner,[4] probably, like Strato, about the end of the 'sixties, in connexion with the great Revolt of the Satraps.

An anecdote which illustrates the atmosphere of the tyrant's court, with its collection of travelling *virtuosi*, is told of the Athenian harpist Stratonicus, a notorious jester, who was forced by the king to take poison for having been too free in making fun of the young princes.[5]

---

[1] Sykutris in *Hermes*, LXII, 1927, pp. 24–53. Nicocles is said to have paid Isocrates twenty talents ὑπὲρ τοῦ πρὸς αὐτὸν γραφέντος λόγου: [Plut.] *X Oratorum Vitae*, 838 A.

[2] Theopompus, fr. 126 M. (=114 Jac., 111 Oxf.) and Anaximenes of Lampsacus (Jacoby, II A, p. 123, fr. 18), from Athen. XII, 531 a–d and Aelian, *V.H.* VII, 2. Very different, says Theopompus in effect, from the home-life of the Phaeacians as described by Homer.—I have been unable to find the authority for the statement in Glotz-Cohen (*Hist. Gr.* III, 1936, p. 479) that Nicocles built himself a palace at Salamis, which contained many precious objects, unless it is the reference in the passage of Theopompus to the παρασκευαὶ τῶν οἰκιῶν.

[3] H. Schaefer in *R.E.* XVII, 350.

[4] Maximus Tyr. *Diss.* XX, 2.

[5] Athen. VIII, 46. 352 d. The king is here called "Nicocles king of the Cyprians". No definite authority is given for the anecdote; whereas there is another circumstantial story for which the authority is the New Comedy writer Machon (Athen. VIII, 41,

The successor of Nicocles was Euagoras II, probably a younger son of Euagoras I.[1] When we first hear of him he had already lost his throne; it is likely that he was expelled by the anti-Persian party when in 351 Cyprus, following the example of Phoenicia and Egypt, revolted from Persia.[2] His place was taken by Pnytagoras.[3] Artaxerxes III Ochus (who had succeeded his father Mnemon in 359/8) was already sufficiently occupied with Egypt and Phoenicia; therefore, just as his father had done when attacking Euagoras I, he based the expedition on a western satrapy, charging the dynast of Caria, Idrieus, with the suppression of the revolt in the island. On the former occasion, Athens may have deserted the king of Salamis, but did not actively assist his enemies; on this, it was an Athenian, Phocion, who was enlisted by Idrieus to command the forty ships and eight thousand mercenaries. Associated with him was the exiled Euagoras.[4] But Idrieus seems to have been as unsatisfactory a servant to the Great King as his father Hecatomnos had been. It is possible that the expedition did not start until 345 or 344.[5]

At first all seemed to go well for Euagoras.[6] The island at this time numbered nine kings ruling each over his own city, under which were ranged smaller towns; all these kings, inspired by the example of

---

349 e, f): Stratonicus uttered a coarse jibe at the expense of Axiothea, wife of Nicocreon of Salamis, and was punished by drowning. But the other persons mentioned as contemporary with Stratonicus seem to place him in the first half of the fourth century rather than the second (Maas in *R.E.* IV A, 326 f.).—A confusion between this Nicocles and another, made by Judeich (*Kleinas. Stud.* p. 133), may be corrected here. The Nicocles whose name has been read in association with that of Timocharis would be a king of Paphos, not of Salamis; but, as a matter of fact, the reading cannot be verified (B.M.C. *Cyprus*, pp. lxxiv f.).

[1] See above, p. 143, n. 3. On his reign there is an essay by Spyridakis in Κυπρ. Γράμματα, II, 1936, pp. 412–22.

[2] Diod. XVI, 40. 5.

[3] Diod. XVI, 46. 1 (Πρωταγόρας the MSS.; cp. the mistake Πυθαγόρας for the elder Pnytagoras in XV, 4. 3).

[4] Diod. XVI, 42. 7.

[5] It is generally regarded as having been despatched in the spring of 350. So Judeich (p. 171, n. 1), who argues that Phocion must have been in Cyprus before the beginning of 349, when (p. 135) he was in command of the Athenians in Euboea. Beloch, however (III, ii,[2] p. 287) argues for the later date. At the time when Isocrates wrote his *Philippus* (and that was in 346) Phoenicia and Cyprus had been in revolt for some time (102), but Idrieus had not yet sent any force to Cyprus, for Isocrates (103) was in the hope that he might side with Philip against Persia. The expedition under Phocion and Euagoras must then have been delayed until some time after 346; but Phocion was back in Athens at the beginning of 343/2.

[6] Diod. XVI, 42. 3 ff.; 46. 1 ff. The nine kingdoms were (Beloch, *Gr. Gesch.* IV, ii,[2] p. 331) Salamis, Citium, Amathus, Paphos, Marium, Soli, Lapethos, Kerynia, Curium.

Phoenicia, had thrown off their allegiance to Persia. The invading force, immediately on its arrival, was directed against the chief of these cities, Salamis;[1] lines were drawn round it, a fortified camp constructed, and the place was invested both by land and sea. The island had long enjoyed peace and prosperity, and the invading army, being in possession of the open country, collected much booty. The news of these spoils attracted numbers of volunteers from Syria and Cilicia, so that finally the forces under Euagoras and Phocion had doubled in number. The other cities were quickly reduced to submission,[2] but Salamis held out under Pnytagoras. Finally, just as Tiribazus had been discredited with his master by the defender of Salamis (p. 139), so now Euagoras was successfully slandered to Artaxerxes, who accordingly lent his assistance to Pnytagoras. Euagoras, despairing of securing his restoration, retired from his undertaking; but he so far made good his defence against the accusations which had been brought against him that he was placed in possession of another and more important kingdom on the mainland, apparently Sidon. Pnytagoras, having voluntarily submitted to Artaxerxes, was left to rule over Salamis in peace. Euagoras, however, governed his new possessions so ill that he was obliged to flee; returning to Cyprus he was arrested and put to death.[3]

---

[1] Diod. XVI, 42. 8, 9.

[2] Diod. XVI, 46. 1. Judeich suggests (p. 135) that Phocion may have returned home at this stage.

[3] Diod. XV, 46. 3. Three classes of coins have to be considered in connexion with Euagoras II (B.M.C. *Cyprus*, pp. cv ff.). Of those bearing his name and probably struck in Cyprus during the ten years or so before his expulsion in 351 there is a fairly large series of gold, silver and bronze, on which the inscriptions (but for an occasional Cypriote sign) are in Greek. The gold bears on one side a head of Aphrodite in a mural crown; on the other the remarkable type of an eagle standing on the back of a lion which is devouring its prey, and accompanied by a star—a design apparently of solar significance. The larger of these gold coins are staters of Attic weight, the first gold coins of such a denomination to be struck in Cyprus. The silver is of the Rhodian standard. A second group of coins, silver of Rhodian standard, and bronze, bear Phoenician letters which have been explained as the initials of Euagoras (עע), and are of Phoenician workmanship. The provenance of these coins points to Caria and Ionia; a hoard found at Calymna contained also coins of Maussollus, Idrieus and Pixodarus. It is tempting to suppose that they may have been made for Euagoras while Idrieus was preparing his expedition. But, so far as is known, none have been found in Cyprus. A third group, with the same Phoenician letters, belongs to the series of regal coins of Sidon, and shows, from the numerals the coins bear, that the reign of the king who issued them extended into three years. The exceedingly attractive suggestion has accordingly been made that the kingdom with which Euagoras was invested was Sidon;

With the submission of Pnytagoras, the forces of Cyprus were once more at the service of Persia, and its highly trained navy, with that of the Phoenicians, was sufficiently formidable for Alexander the Great, with his small fleet, to refuse the risk of an engagement, which Parmenion advised him to take at Miletus.[1] The Cypriotes and Phoenicians had already in use the most important innovation that sea-fighting was to see until the invention of cannon. This was the true quinquereme, rowing five men to an oar, whereas the experimental quinqueremes which Athens was trying were enlarged quadriremes with five grouped oars each rowed by one man.

Since Alexander appears to have dispersed the greater part of his own fleet,[2] it was fortunate for him that, after Issus, Pnytagoras and the other Cypriote kings transferred their allegiance from Persia, and sailed into Sidon with a hundred and twenty ships.[3] The siege of Tyre was not proceeding very successfully. Alexander had undertaken it because he realized that he could not march in pursuit of Darius, leaving behind him Tyre unsubdued; he saw that the capture of Tyre would bring over to him not only the whole of Phoenicia but also Cyprus, which would either submit of itself, or be easily reduced.[4] This last problem was, however, solved for him by the Cypriotes themselves. When they joined him, he collected the Phoenician and Cypriote fleet from Sidon

---

the years during which he enjoyed it would then probably have been 344/3–342/1. The attribution, which is due to Babelon (*Perses Achéménides*, pp. clxxxiv f.), has been disputed, for the second and third classes alike, but remains in general acceptance. See B.M.C. *Cyprus*, as above, and *Phoenicia*, pp. xcvi f. As regards chronology, it must be remembered that the first and the last years which are represented by numbers on the coins need not be complete years; Euagoras's tenure of Sidon may therefore have been very short. It cannot have lasted after the year 342/1, since his successor, Strato II, issued coins with dates at least as high as 10, and his reign ended with the arrival of Alexander in Phoenicia immediately after Issus (Nov. 333).

[1] Arrian, *Anab.* I, 18. 7. The evidence for the new system of construction in Tarn (*Hellenistic Military and Naval Developments*, 1930, pp. 129–32).

[2] Diod. XVII, 22. 5.

[3] Arrian, *Anab.* II, 20. 3.

[4] Arrian, *Anab.* II, 17. Alexander, quite apart from native Cypriote opposition, may well have feared to leave Cyprus at his back. After the battle of Issus, the Greeks who had deserted his side for the Persian, notably Amyntas son of Antiochus, Thymondas son of Mentor, Aristomedes of Pherae and Bianor the Acarnanian (Berve, *Alexanderreich*, II, nos. 58, 380, 128 and 214), retired with some 3000 men in good order to Tripolis, and thence shipped across to Cyprus. But they did not remain there, but passed on to Egypt, where Amyntas was killed by the natives. Arrian, *Anab.* II, 13. 2, 3; Diod. XVII, 48. 1–5; Curtius, IV, 1. 27.

and sailed for Tyre. Pnytagoras with Craterus was in command of the left or landward wing, and the other Cypriotes were ranged with Alexander on the right.[1] The accession of the Cypriote and Phoenician fleets came as a surprise to the Tyrians, who decided to refuse battle at sea.[2] Alexander was now able to invest Tyre by sea, at least partially, the Cypriote ships under the nauarch Andromachus blocking the mouth of the northern harbour, the Phoenician ships being similarly disposed before the southern.[3] Cypriote and Phoenician engineers, under the command of Alexander's chief military engineer, Diades,[4] set up their engines of war on the mole, on the horse-transports which had come from Sidon, and on the slower triremes.[5] The Cypriote blockading fleet, however, met with disaster when the Tyrians, screening the mouth of the harbour with sails, manned a small detachment of thirteen ships with their best fighting men and made a sally at midday, which took the Cypriotes entirely by surprise. The quinquereme of King Pnytagoras was sunk at the first shock, so also those commanded by Androcles of Amathus and Pasicrates of Curium,[6] while the other ships were driven ashore and broken up. Alexander sailed round from the southern side

---

[1] Arrian, *Anab.* II, 20. 6; Curtius, IV, 3. 11.

[2] The Tyrians had only eighty triremes. Diod. XVII, 41. 1.

[3] Arrian, *Anab.* II, 20. 10. On this Andromachus, Berve, *Alexanderreich*, II, p. 39, no. 77.

[4] Diades is so described in a papyrus of the second century B.C. as in charge of the engines of war at the siege of Tyre. Diels, *Antike Technik*,3 1924, p. 30, n. 1. See Berve, *Alexanderreich*, II, p. 142, no. 267.

[5] Arrian, *Anab.* II, 21. 1.

[6] The text is Θουριέως; Doerner's emendation Κουριέως is generally accepted. Since Arrian calls Pnytagoras βασιλεύς, but omits that title in the case of Androcles and Pasicrates, it may be that these two were not actually kings of their respective cities at this time. Of this Pasicrates we hear no more; but Androcles is mentioned by Arrian (*Diad.* fr. 24, 6, Roos, II, p. 280) as one of those who made alliance with Ptolemy in 321. The phrasing is curious: "learning that of the kings in Cyprus Nicocreon the Salaminian and those who combined with him, Pasicrates the Solian and Nicocles the Paphian, this man and Androcles the Amathusian", etc.—as if Androcles was not quite of the same standing as the others. Again in 315 Diodorus (XIX, 62. 6) mentions but does not name an 'Αμαθουσίων δυνάστης, whereas the rulers of Salamis and Marium in the same passage are called βασιλεῖς. But in a Delian inventory of about 313 (*I.G.* XI, 2, 135) he appears as 'Ανδροκλῆς 'Αμαθουσίων βασιλεύς, having dedicated a gold crown in the temple of Apollo. Possibly he did not actually succeed to the throne until after 315. Peristianes, however ('Ιστ. p. 276, n. 1), points out that in the passage of Arrian the title βασιλεύς may be understood with Androcles and Pasicrates, and not expressed, to avoid pleonasm.

to the rescue, and the Tyrians escaped back into their harbour with some loss.[1] We hear no more of the Cypriote ships. But Pnytagoras was rewarded for his services by Alexander, who in dismissing him gave him, among other gifts, Tamassus in Cyprus,[2] for which he asked. The acquisition of Tamassus, with its copper-mines, must have been most valuable to Salamis, which had no sources of mineral wealth in its own territory. Other of the Cypriote kings who had helped in the siege were also suitably rewarded.[3]

The only other facts known about Pnytagoras concern his relations with Delos, which engraved on an offering made by him a decree of proxenia in his honour, and where he also dedicated golden crowns.[4]

On his return from Egypt in spring 331, Alexander celebrated his success by magnificent sacrifices and processions and choric and tragic performances. In these the Cypriote kings, especially Nicocreon of Salamis and Pasicrates of Soli, vied with each other as choregoi, the Athenian tragic actor Athenodorus, provided by Pasicrates, being victorious.[5] From the fact that Nicrocreon is described as king, we may

---

[1] Arrian, *Anab.* II, 21. 8, 9; 22. 1–5.

[2] Duris, fr. 12 M. (*F.H.G.* II, p. 472; Jacoby, *Fr. Gr. Hist.* II A, p. 139, fr. 4), from Athen. IV, p. 167 c, d. This land had previously belonged to King Pasicyprus, who, having exhausted his treasury by prodigality, sold it for fifty talents to Pumiathon (Πυμάτωνι the text) of Citium, and retired to spend his old age in Amathus. Since Pumiathon, in an inscription of his twenty-first year (probably 342/1), is called king of Tamassus as well as Citium and Idalium (*C.I.S.* I, 10; Cooke, *N. Sem. Inscr.* p. 55, no. 12), and no longer held the first place in his thirty-seventh year (326/5; *C.I.S.* I, 11; Cooke, no. 13) it follows that the place of which Pasicyprus was king, which he sold to Pumiathon, and which was doubtless taken away from Pumiathon by Alexander, was Tamassus (see Cooke, p. 56). Why Pumiathon lost it, we do not know; but it is possible that Citium was slower than other Cypriote powers to come over to Alexander's side. Plutarch (*Alex.* 32) informs us that a sword, remarkable for its temper and light weight, which Alexander carried, was a present to him from the King of Citium, who can be no other than Pumiathon.

[3] Curtius, IV, 8. 14.

[4] Homolle in *Mon. grecs publ. par l'assoc. pour l'encour. des études grecs*, 1878, p. 49: ἔχον προξενίαν Πνυταγόραι βασιλεῖ Σαλαμινίωι. Cp. *B.C.H.* VI, 155; Durrbach-Roussel, *Inscrr. de Délos*, no. 1409 Ba, col. II, 114. The royal title is not added after the name of the Pnytagoras who dedicated gold crowns, Ditt. *Syll.*[2] 588, l. 15, and *I.G.* XI, 161 B (Michel, *Recueil*, 833), 88, cp. Durrbach-Roussel, *Inscrr. de Délos*, no. 1429 A, col. I, 8; but he is probably the king.

[5] Plut. *Alex.* 29. Perhaps Plutarch's use of βασιλεύς must not be stressed; he knew that Nicocreon was king later. But if Pnytagoras had still been at Tyre, he would have taken part in these celebrations.—Pasicrates of Soli: it has been guessed that the name

assume that Pnytagoras had not only left Phoenicia, but had either renounced the throne of Salamis, or was dead.

Before moving against Darius, Alexander despatched the naval commander Amphoterus, brother of Craterus, with a fleet to deal with the opposition which Sparta was organizing in Peloponnese. To this fleet the Cypriotes and Phoenicians contributed a contingent of a hundred sail.[1]

Alexander took with him a following of distinguished Cypriotes. Two men of Soli, Nicocles, son of King Pasicrates, and Stasanor, were among them.[2] Hiero of Soli, also, was sent to circumnavigate the Arabian peninsula, and got as far as the mouth of the Persian Gulf.[3] For the Indus expedition of Nearchus, Alexander employed Cypriote rowers and shipwrights as well as Phoenician and Egyptian, and among the trierarchs in command were this Nicocles and Nithaphon, son of Pnytagoras of Salamis.[4]

The end of Nicocreon's reign belongs to the next chapter. At Citium, Pumiathon, as we have seen, fell into disgrace. In his thirtieth year (probably 333/2) he made a large issue of the gold coins which form his only currency; probably the object of this issue was the payment of the expenses of the siege of Tyre. From his thirtieth to his fortieth year (323/2) he issued no coins, but then resumed the privilege; from which

should be Stasicrates, since the existence of a king of Soli of that name, son of Stasias, in the latter part of the fourth century, is proved by inscriptions (*G.D.I.* I, 17, 18). But the form Pasicrates is vouched for by Arrian, *Ind.* 18. 8, in another connexion. The identification of Pasicrates of Soli with the Pasicrates of Curium whose ship was sunk at the siege of Tyre is also without foundation. See B.M.C. *Cyprus*, p. cxvi.

[1] Arrian, *Anab.* III, 6. 3.

[2] Arrian, *Ind.* 18. 8; Strabo, XIV, 6, 3, p. 683; Diod. XVIII, 3. 3. Alexander made Stasanor governor of Areia and Drangiane in 329, and later, in 321, he also received Bactria and Sogdiane. Stasander of Cyprus, who is supposed to have become satrap of Areia and Drangiane in 321, was not necessarily the same man (Beloch, *Gr. Gesch.* IV, ii,[2] p. 315); he may well have been a brother. (Tarn compares Nicanor and Nicander, sons of Nicon, *O.G.I.S.* 21, and Callicratides and Callistratus, sons of Callicrates, *G.D.I.* II, 2801.) Stasanor has been conjectured to be a member of the royal house of Soli, perhaps a brother of Pasicrates (Schiff in *R.E.* VI, 1139).

[3] Arrian, *Anab.* VII, 20. 7, 8. But it is not certain from which Soli, Cyprian or Cilician, he came. Berve, *Alexanderreich*, II, p. 183, no. 382.

[4] Arrian, *Ind.* 18. 8. The name is strange, and not otherwise recorded; accordingly it is very generally supposed (see the appar. crit. of Eberhard, *ad loc.*) that it is a corruption of Nicocreon, and that that king actually went with Alexander. On the principle *difficilior lectio potior* it is surely better to suppose that Nithaphon was a brother of Nicocreon. Had the trierarch been reigning king of so important a place as Salamis—in itself an unlikely supposition—Arrian would surely have mentioned his title.

we may conclude that at the death of Alexander he recovered his power, or some of it.[1] He survived, as we shall see, until 312, when he was put to death by Ptolemy.

How far Alexander interfered with the other kingdoms of Cyprus we do not know. A story that he deposed the reigning king of Paphos, for injustice and wickedness, and substituted for him one Alynomus, a poor man, and a relic of the race of the Cinyradae, which was dying out[2]—this story is a duplicate of one which is told of Abdalonymus of Sidon,[3] and both are probably mythical.

The only administrative change of which we have record is that Cyprus was made to play its part in the huge system of the Alexandrine coinage.[4] The independent issues of the regal mints became very scarce after Alexander's arrival in that region, although after his death, as we have seen, Pumiathon of Citium began again to issue his own gold. The chief mints put into action for Alexander's imperial coinage were Salamis and Citium, which were probably both working by 332; Paphos was also employed, though to a less degree. The activity of these mints was, of course, affected by the vicissitudes of the island after the death of Alexander, which will be described in the next chapter.[5]

Although the surviving evidence is scanty, there is no doubt that commercial relations between Greece, particularly Athens, and Cyprus, were very active during the fourth century. In 333/2 the Citian merchant community in Peiraeus was sufficiently large to demand and receive permission to found a temple to Aphrodite. Some dedications by Citians may be as early as the fifth century, and the terracotta statuettes

---

[1] Tarn (in *C.A.H.* VI, p. 432) says "the Cyprian kings were free allies (of Alexander) who coined gold, the token of independence". But the evidence of the coins seems rather to indicate that Alexander suppressed the independent gold coinage, using the mints to strike his own gold staters.

[2] Plutarch, *de Alex. Magni fort. aut virt.* II, 8, p. 340 D.

[3] Curtius, IV, 1. 19; cp. Diod. XVII, 46. 6 "Tyre"). Traces of the decaying Cinyradae are preserved in such titles as ἀρχὸς τῶν Κινυραδῶν, Κινύραρ[χος], which we find in late inscriptions at Paphos (L.B.W. 2798; *J.H.S.* IX, 1888, p. 249, no. 101). These were doubtless officials connected with the cult of the goddess, like the μαντιάρχης (L.B.W. 2795; *J.H.S.* IX, 1888, p. 234, no. 27).

[4] E. T. Newell in *Num. Chron.* 1915, pp. 294–322.

[5] Salamis and Citium began to strike gold and silver of Alexander's types in 332. There was also a less extensive coinage of silver from Paphos from about 330, and possibly from Marium. The few Alexandrine bronze coins produced by Salamis and Paphos were probably for local circulation.

from the Salt Lake site have been thought (though this is doubtful) to indicate intercourse with Athens from that time onwards. There is also evidence of the presence of a Salaminian community in Peiraeus, perhaps with its own cultus-union.[1] The corn-trade doubtless flourished throughout the fourth century in spite of difficulties. The Heracleides, son of Charicleides of Salamis, who, when bringing corn to Athens in 330/29 was caught by Dionysius, tyrant of Heracleia in Bithynia, and robbed of his sails, may have been of the Cyprian Salamis, but the circumstances show that he was on the Pontic voyage.[2]

NOTE

THE BRONZE TABLET OF IDALIUM

The famous bronze tablet of Idalium (*G.D.I.* I, no. 60; Cauer, *Delectus*,[2] 1883, pp. 303 ff.; Meister, *Gr. Dial.* II, pp. 150 ff.; Hoffmann, *Gr. Dial.* I, no. 135) has been referred to the period of the Ionian Revolt (498); so Meyer, *Gesch. d. Alt.* III, 1901, p. 305; Oberhummer, art. *Idalion* in *R.E.* IX, 868; Gjerstad in *S.C.E.* II, 1935, p. 625. This early dating seems to me less likely than one in the middle of the fifth century. The tablet is reported to have been found by treasure-diggers on the top plateau of the western acropolis of Idalium (*S.C.E.* II, p. 462). Reports of provenance of this kind are notoriously untrustworthy; but the Swedish excavators are inclined to accept this one. They are also convinced, on the evidence of the pottery, that this acropolis was deserted not later than 470. Now the tablet refers to a siege by the "Medes and Citians", during which the physician Onasilus, son of Onasicyprus, and his brothers had been compelled to tend the wounded without fee, and records the payment to them of an indemnity by the king Stasicyprus and the city. The fact that the king Stasicyprus was still reigning when the tablet was inscribed shows that the siege was unsuccessful. The Swedish excavators, trusting the report of the finding of the tablet, and concluding that it must be earlier than 470, since the acropolis was, they hold, deserted then, observe that the Revolt of 499/8 is the only known historical event with which the circumstances

---

[1] See E. Schürer, *Gesch. des jüdischen Volkes*, III,3 pp. 60 f., for Citians and Salaminians in Athens or Peiraeus. The decree of 333/2, Ditt. *Syll.*3 280. Of about the same time is a dedication to Aphrodite Urania by Aristoclea of Citium, *I.G.* II,[2] 4636. Dedications by Hellomenes of Cyprian Salamis, *I.G.* II, 3, 3295; Charita, daughter of Euboulus of Cyprian Salamis, wife of Epigenes son of Berenicides, *I.G.* III, 2, 2188. Cp. Köhler in *Ath. Mitt.* IV, 1879, p. 266. On the Larnaka statuettes, see below, ch. X, p. 223.

[2] Ditt. *Syll.*3 304; Rostovtzeff in *C.A.H.* VIII, p. 575.

described in the tablet can be connected. If this is correct, it follows that there must have been a king Stasicyprus reigning before that date. But it may not be conclusive, for we know very little of the history of Cyprus between the Revolt and Cimon's last expedition, except the temporary recovery of the island from the Persians after Mycale, in 478, and the fighting there in 459/8. There may have been plenty of occasions for an attack on Idalium by Citium, after 499/8, and before the one which finally succeeded, when Azbaal, son of Baalmelek I, conquered the place, as is inferred from the well-known dedicatory inscription from Idalium, dated in the third year of Baalmelek (II), king of Citium and Idalium, son of Azbaal, king of Citium and Idalium, son of Baalmelek (I), king of Citium. Azbaal and his successors continued to rule over Idalium until the general suppression of the kingdoms of Cyprus. When precisely Azbaal took it, we do not know. The Swedish excavators associate the desertion of the western acropolis with this conquest, and therefore date it to 470. That means that Azbaal was already king of Citium by 470. (Hitherto numismatists have assigned him to about 445–425.) And here we must consider the evidence of the coins.

The Larnaka hoard, published by Dikaios and Robinson, was buried very shortly after 480 (*Num. Chron.* 1935, p. 190; cp. Newell in Numism. Notes and Monographs, no. 82, 1937, p. 14). It contained no coins of Baalmelek I, although it was buried on the site of his own city. There is, it is true, often a time-lag to be allowed for in hoards (the latest coin in a hoard being possibly many years earlier than the actual date of deposit); but this cannot be lightly assumed in the case of local coinage. We may therefore take it that Baalmelek I did not begin to reign until after 480. This confirms the traditional date, *c.* 479, assigned to him. Unfortunately, we do not know how long he reigned. Unless he was succeeded by Azbaal after a very short reign, it is clear that the capture of Idalium cannot have taken place very soon after 480.

What, however, do the coins of Idalium tell us? They form a closely knit series, beginning shortly before 500, to judge from their style, and going down to the fall of the city. If that, as the Swedish excavators believe, took place about 470, we have but thirty years for the following series:

a. Uninscribed; incuse reverse.
b. King O.na.sa...; incuse reverse.
c. King Ki....; lotus reverse.
d. King Ka.ra...; lotus reverse.
e. King Sa....; lotus reverse.

Of these, three classes, *a*, *b* and *c*, were represented in the Larnaka hoard, which was buried about 480—some 10 coins of *a* or *b*, 17 of *b*, and 9 of *c*.

But of *c* only the first issue is represented in the hoard, not the later issues which seem to give a second syllable (*vo*), of the king's name. So Ki... evidently reigned some time after 480. It is to be noted that as blanks for these latest issues he used coins of Baalmelek I. If the date 499/8 is correct for the unsuccessful siege in the reign of Stasicyprus, his coins, if he struck any, must belong to series *a*. We should thus have the following sequence:

Before and after 499/8	Stasicyprus
Before 480	O.na.sa...
Before and after 480	Ki....
Between 480 and 470	Ka.ra and Sa...

That would be five kings in one generation with two reigns and a bit of a third crowded into the last decade; which is, to say the least, a record for which there are few parallels. The alternative is to identify the Stasicyprus of the tablet with the Sa... of series *e*, and to extend the period of Idalium's independence and coinage to about 450–445 (there is no need, as I once thought, B.M.C. *Cyprus*, p. lii, to bring it down later), dating its fall to after the failure of Cimon's expedition. If we accept the evidence of the pottery for the desertion of the western acropolis about 470 rather than twenty years later, this involves the assumption that the kings of Idalium continued to rule on the eastern acropolis, and that the tablet was not, after all, found where it was said to have been. There is also the possibility, if one may venture to suggest it, that the dating of the pottery may be out by some twenty years. It may be due to the prejudice of a numismatist, but I am inclined to accept this last assumption in preference to the supposition that the Larnaka hoard was "closed" some ten or twenty years before it was buried.—Most recently, the date of the tablet has been discussed by Spyridakis (in Κυπριακαὶ Σπουδαί, I, 1937, pp. 73 ff.). He gives the impression that he would have been glad, in accordance with his recognition of Athenian influence on the Idalian constitution, to give the lowest possible date as 456, the year of the failure of the Athenian expedition to Egypt, but being unwilling to dispute the "archaeological" evidence, he is forced to regard it as not later than 470.

The Idalium tablet is dated in the year of the eponymous magistrate Philocyprus son of Onasagoras. Robinson suggests that this Onasagoras may have been the king Onasa... of the series *b*; but it would suit the date we assign to the tablet if he were a later owner of the same name, especially as he is not given the royal title. Since the kings of Citium held Idalium from Azbaal to Pumiathon, the theory which brings the tablet down to the fourth century (Larfeld, *Syll. Inscr. Boeot.* 1883, p. xxx; Cauer, *Delectus*,[2] p. 306; Judeich, *Kleinas. Stud.* p. 125, n. 1; cp. Zannetos, Ἱστορία, I, p. 287; Beloch, *Gr. Gesch.* I, ii,[2] p. 107) must be rejected.

CHAPTER VIII

THE SUCCESSORS

The history of Cyprus for a generation after the death of Alexander is perhaps even more obscure than in the preceding period. The island was of course, owing to its geographical position and economic[1] importance as a source of ship-timber and copper, involved in the scramble for power between the Successors. Strategically it was of the utmost significance to the powers concerned. It may be true that Ptolemy I aimed at securing Syria as a base from which he could attack Cyprus;[2] it was equally true that the possession of Cyprus was essential to any Mediterranean power which wished to attack Syria.

In 321 Ptolemy I succeeded in securing the alliance of four of the Cypriote kings. Nicocreon of Salamis, Nicocles of Paphos, Pasicrates of Soli and Androcles of Amathus combined with him in the coalition against Perdiccas. They brought together a fleet of nearly 200 sail, and also laid siege to another city, perhaps Marium, which under its ruler remained loyal to the party of the Macedonian royal house. Perdiccas learned the news of this unfavourable turn in the situation in Cyprus when he reached Cilicia on his way to Egypt. He did not himself go aside to deal with it, but despatched a force of 800 foot and 500 horsemen under Aristonous of Pella, one of Alexander's body-guard, to succour the beleaguered city. The warships and transports which formed part of this expedition were commanded by the nauarch Sosigenes of Rhodes,[3] the foot by Medius of Larisa, the horse by Amyntas.[4] It is

---

[1] The mint of Salamis continued to issue coins of the imperial Alexandrine series; but from 320 to 317 they bore the name of Philip (Arrhidaeus), and after Philip's death that of Alexander (IV): Newell, *Num. Chron.* 1915 (see above, p. 152, n. 4). For Citium see below, p. 158, n. 3.

[2] Appian, *Syr.* 52: ἐπιχείρημα κατὰ Κύπρου.

[3] Cp. Polyaen. IV, 6. 9.

[4] All the above details are given by the precious fragment of the History of the Diadochi (τὰ μετ' Ἀλέξανδρον) by Arrian (ed. Roos, II, pp. 280 f.). As to the besieged city, one would be glad to be certain that, as everyone seems to assume, it was Marium. But this rests on an editorial conjecture. For where Reitzenstein restores Μαριέων, the MS. has κασιέων, and where he restores Μάριον the MS. has καριαν or ιαρεαν or ιαριων. —For Medius see Berve, *Alexanderreich*, II, no. 521; for Amyntas, *ibid.* no. 56.

indicative of the scrappiness of our information about these years that we know nothing of the result of these extensive preparations. Antigonus the One-eyed, who was now allied with Antipater and Craterus, must have passed from Asia Minor into the island, for it was thence that he came in autumn 321 to the meeting of the generals at Triparadeisus, at which the rearrangement of the satrapies was made after the death of Perdiccas.[1] It would appear that the fighting went on into 320, Cleitus having been sent to Cyprus by Antipater to deal with the remains of the expedition of Perdiccas. But later, when preparing for the new war which broke out in 318, Eumenes, who continued faithful to the royal house, was able to recruit for his army in Cyprus as well as in Pisidia,

---

[1] Arrian, *Diad.* I. 30 (ed. Roos, II, p. 264). Many assume that the operations of Antigonus are referred to in the inscription *C.I.A.* II, 331 (Roberts and Gardner, *Gr. Epigr.* II, no. 55; *I.G.* II,[2] I. 682; Dittenberger, *Syll.*3 409; Dinsmoor, *Archons of Athens*, p. 70), and also in the decree of Nasos (*I.G.* XII, 2. 645; Michel, *Recueil*, 363; Ditt. *O.G.I.S.* 4). The former records honours conferred on Phaedrus son of Thymochares; it states that Thymochares, having been elected strategos, sailed in the fleet which the Athenian people sent with [some twenty letters deliberately erased] to Asia and took part in the war in Cyprus, and captured Hagnon of Teos and the ships under him; immediately afterwards it goes on to mention the achievements of Thymochares in the year 315/4. Droysen conjectured that the erased name was that of Antigonus and that the war in Cyprus was that of 321/20 against the fleet of Perdiccas. This view is very commonly accepted; Beloch, *Gr. Gesch.* IV, i,[2] p. 89, n. 3, has no doubt of it; and Ferguson, *Hellenistic Athens*, p. 21, n. 3, somewhat cavalierly dismisses the alternative dating, which he attributes to Dittenberger (who however is following Klueber). This alternative view (which is accepted by Bouché-Leclercq, *H.L.* I, p. 25, no. 1; cp. Fiehn in *R.E.* VI A, 715) is that the war was that of 316/5, when there was fighting at sea for Cyprus between Antigonus on the one hand and Seleucus and Ptolemy on the other; Klueber supposed the erased words to be τεῖ τῶν Μακεδόνων δυνάμει (cp. Ditt. *Syll.*3 409: τῶι τῶν Μακεδόνων στόλωι) or ταῖς Κασσάνδρου ναυσίν. A slight argument in favour of the later date is the fact that the admiral of Perdiccas in the war of 321 was not Hagnon of Teos but Sosigenes of Rhodes. Hagnon, whose only other title to fame is that he wore silver studs in his shoes (Plut. *Alex.* 40), may be the man whose name appears as issuing magistrate on a Teian coin of the period 394–300 (B.M.C. *Ionia*, p. 312, nos. 24, 25). As to the Nasos decree in honour of one Thersippus, it relates first that he obtained from Antipater a lightening of the contribution of Nasos to the war, at a time, evidently, when Philip Arrhidaeus and Alexander IV were in the keeping of Antipater, which was not the case until after the death of Perdiccas; next it says that he also dealt with Cleitus in the matter of the expedition to Cyprus, and reduced a large sum to a small one. If the chronology is exact, this Cyprus expedition cannot be that of 321, but must belong to 320; other facts known about Cleitus practically limit it to this year (Ditt. *O.G.I.S.* 4, n. 6, and Münzer in *R.E.* XI, 667).

Lycia, Cilicia, Coelesyria and Phoenicia.[1] Possibly, with the death of Antipater in 319, the pressure on Cyprus from his side had been relaxed, although we might expect it to be increased from the side of Ptolemy.

The execution of Eumenes by Antigonus (winter 317/6) left the latter in the strongest position of all the claimants to the succession of Alexander. The field was set for a struggle between him and Ptolemy for the possession of Cyprus. He exerted himself to detach it from Ptolemy, who, as we have seen, had the support—which there is no reason to suppose that he had lost since 321—of at least four of the leading states. Agesilaus, the envoy of Antigonus, returned with the information[2] that Nicocreon and the most powerful of the other kings had made an alliance with Ptolemy, but that he himself had brought the kings of Citium,[3] Lapethos, Marium and Kerynia[4] on to the side of Antigonus.

---

[1] Diod. XVIII, 61. 4.

[2] Diod. XIX, 57. 4; 59. 1 (315). Agesilaus is made to speak as if the alliance with Ptolemy were recent (πεποίηνται συμμαχίαν), but this need not be taken literally.

[3] Pumiathon of Citium, who as we have seen (above, p. 152) seems to have recovered some of his power after the death of Alexander, began to strike his independent regal gold coinage again in 323/2 and continued to do so until his forty-seventh year (316/5). Newell also assigns gold and silver coins of Alexandrine types to Citium in two series, one dating "about 332–320", the other "after about 320". The mint would be used for the Alexandrine imperial coins, whether it was Ptolemy or Antigonus who was in control; but one or other of them might have stopped the regal issues, and perhaps Antigonus did this when Agesilaus "brought over" Citium to his side. As Newell observes (*Coinages of Demetrius Poliorcetes*, 1927, p. 15), Antigonus was a stickler for the proprieties and "allowed only coins of the pure Alexander type to be issued in his dominions". That would explain why Pumiathon had to stop his own gold in 316/5, though he continued on the throne three or four years longer; and the chronology adopted for his coinage in B.M.C. *Cyprus*, pp. xl f. is confirmed.

[4] The first three kings were respectively Pumiathon (see preceding note), Praxippus (who was deposed by Ptolemy in 313/2) and Stasioecus II (see below, p. 159, n. 3). As to Kerynia, Engel (*Kypros*, I, p. 365) conjectures that the king about this time was Themison, the Cypriote king to whom Aristotle dedicated his "Protrepticus" (Stobaeus, *Flor.* 95. 21). The chief reason for this conjecture is that we know the names of the kings of all Cypriote states except Kerynia about this time. The date of the "Protrepticus" is not known; but it is generally placed about the middle of the century, being earlier than the death of Plato in 347 (W. Jäger, *Aristotle*, tr. Robinson, p. 54). From its hortatory nature we may suppose it would be addressed to Themison at his accession, so that he must have reigned from about 350 to 316. Engel's further conjecture that this Themison was the nauarch who served under Antigonus at Tyre will not stand; in the first place the nauarch was probably a Samian (Diod. XX, 50. 4); and secondly, the way in which Diodorus mentions his arriving with his fleet from the Hellespont just about the time of the capture of Kerynia by Seleucus (XIX, 62. 6, 7)

Ptolemy immediately sent a first detachment of 3000 men, following it up by a much larger force, of 10,000 men under the Athenian Myrmidon, and 100 ships under Polycleitus, the whole expedition being under the command of his own brother Menelaus.[1] In Cyprus they found Seleucus, son of Antiochus, the future founder of the Seleucid dynasty. He had come with his fleet from the Aegean, where he had made an abortive attempt on Erythrae. At a council of war it was decided to detach Polycleitus with fifty ships to carry on the war in Peloponnese, and to send Myrmidon with his mercenaries to Caria to support Cassander, while Seleucus and Menelaus were to remain in Cyprus and, with the support of Nicocreon and the other allies, to deal with the cities that had fallen away to Antigonus. It may have been in the fighting that ensued at sea that an Athenian squadron under Thymochares captured Hagnon of Teos and his ships.[2] On land, the force of Seleucus took Kerynia and Lapethos by siege; Stasioecus,[3] king of Marium, was brought over, and the "dynast" of the Amathusians was forced to give hostages. Citium, however, refused to be persuaded, and siege was laid to it by the whole force.[4] It must have been reduced sooner or later, but continued restive under Ptolemy's yoke. In 312 in fact Ptolemy had to deal sternly with certain of the kings who were trying to shake off his rule. Pumiathon of Citium, whom he found in correspondence with Antigonus, he put to death, and the temple of Heracles-Melqarth, the religious focus of its life as a Phoenician city, was destroyed;[5] Praxippus, king of Lapethos, and the "dynast" of

---

makes the identification impossible. Another conjecture of Engel (*Kypros*, I, p. 363, n. 38), constructing a king Gordias of Chytri out of two detached scraps of the work of Alexander Polyhistor (ap. Steph. Byz. *s.v.* Χυτροί; *F.H.G.* III, p. 236, fr. 94), has too flimsy a basis to be worth considering.

[1] The acquisition of Cyprus by Ptolemy appears to be commemorated on an issue of coins with the symbol of a ship's *aphlaston* in the field, indicating "a naval victory or at least naval supremacy", which Mrs Baldwin Brett (*Trans. Int. Num. Congr.*, London, 1938, p. 26) dates about 310. A date a year or two earlier would suit the historical conditions better.

[2] See above, p. 157, n. 1.

[3] Stasioecus II. His fairly extensive and varied coinage in all three metals indicates that he must have reigned for some time before he was deposed, as we shall see, in 312 (B.M.C. *Cyprus*, pp. lx–lxii).

[4] Diod. XIX. 62. 6.

[5] A new era was initiated for Citium, beginning in 311: *C.I.S.* I, 93; Cooke, *N. Sem. Inscr.* no. 27 (thirty-first year of Ptolemy Philadelphus equated with the fifty-seventh year of Citium); F. M. Abel in *Rev. Bibl.* XLVII, 1938, p. 200. Beloch, *Gr. Gesch.* IV

Kerynia, being under suspicion of disaffection, were arrested; and Stasioecus of Marium was also punished, in what way is not certain; but from the fact that his city was razed to the ground and the inhabitants transferred to Paphos, it is probable that he suffered the extreme penalty. The confiscated cities, with the revenues of the expelled rulers, were handed over to Nicocreon of Salamis, who was made strategos of Cyprus, although Menelaus evidently also retained that title and its relevant powers. It was possibly this division of authority which led to the subsequent trouble.[1] Having made this settlement, Ptolemy sailed on a raid to northern Syria and Cilicia, and returned with much booty to Cyprus.[2]

But these arrangements lasted but a short time and collapsed in a notable tragedy. Nicocreon was reported to Ptolemy as being in secret communication with Antigonus, with a view to forming an alliance. Determined to make an example which would show other Cypriote rulers that such disaffection could not go unpunished, Ptolemy sent to Cyprus two of his "friends", Argaeus and Callicrates, with orders to kill Nicocreon. Taking a detachment of soldiers from Menelaus the strategos, they surrounded the king's house, informed him of Ptolemy's decision, and ordered him to commit suicide. After an attempt which he made at being heard in his own defence had received no attention, he killed himself. When his queen Axiothea heard of her husband's fate, she first killed her own unmarried daughters, to save them from falling into the hands of any enemy, and then persuaded the wives of the brothers of Nicocreon to choose death with herself (for Ptolemy

---

i,[2] p. 138, n. 2, I suppose by an inadvertence, refers this to Paphos, instead of Citium, and regards it as a proof that the kingdom of Paphos was suppressed at the same time as that of Salamis. Bouché-Leclercq objects to the dating of the crisis in Cyprus so late that it conflicts with the chronology of Diodorus, who relates it before the battle of Gaza (*H.L.* I, p. 48, n. 1); but the chronology of Diodorus cannot be trusted. On the destruction of the temple of Melqarth on the acropolis of Citium, see *S.C.E.* III, pp. 74–5.

[1] Evidently Nicocreon was regarded as "satrap" of Cyprus; a marginal note to the word στρατηγόν in the Paris MS. 1665 (R) of Diodorus (XIX, 79. 5) glosses it as σατράπην; and Diogenes Laertius (IX, 10. 58–9) makes Anaxarchus allude to him as "a certain satrap". But Menelaus had command of the army (Diod. XX, 21. 1).

[2] Diod. XIX, 79. 4–6. The passage referring to Stasioecus is corrupt, and something has fallen out between συνέλαβε and Στασιοίκου τοῦ Μαλιέως, which is the reading of R (Paris) and X (Venice, Marciana), while F (Laurentian) has Στασίοικον τὸν τοῦ Μαλιέως, and Rhodomannus corrects to καὶ Στασίοικον τὸν τῶν Μαριέων. Fischer suspects a larger lacuna. For the λ in the name of Marium, see above, p. 123, n. 2.

had issued no orders about the women, and indeed had given permission for them to go in safety). The palace thus suddenly became a shambles; and the brothers of Nicocreon closed its gates, set fire to the building and slew themselves. Thus ended in a holocaust Nicocreon and all the royal house of Salamis.[1]

---

[1] The story is well told by Diodorus (XX, 21), but of Nicocles of Paphos; Polyaenus (VIII, 48) tells the same story with variations: Axiothea is wife of "Nicocles king of the Cyprians"; Nicocles hanged himself and his brothers killed themselves; Axiothea, emulating the dead, called together their sisters, mothers and wives, and persuaded them all to die worthily of their race. So they closed the doors of the women's apartments and went up on to the roof. In the sight of the crowd that had collected round the palace, the women first slew their children whom they bore in their arms; then, setting fire to the roofs, some of them fell upon their swords, while others threw themselves into the flames. Axiothea, the protagonist in this scene of horror, when she saw the corpses of all the women who had died so nobly lying around her, stabbed herself and leapt into the flames, that not even her dead body should fall into the hands of her enemies. It is very generally, though by no means universally, agreed, however, that both Diodorus and Polyaenus are wrong, and that this happened to the house of Salamis. The *Marmor Parium* (ed. Jac. II B, p. 1004 B 17) has: ἀφ' οὗ [Ν]ικοκρέων ἐτελεύτησεν καὶ Πτολεμαῖος κυριεύει τῆς νήσου, ἔτη ΔΔΔΔΠΙΙ ἄρχοντος 'Αθήνησιν Σι[μωνί]δου, i.e. 311/10 (Diodorus has the story under the year of the next archon, Hieromnemon). In the table of contents to Diodorus (δ') the king is described as "Nicocreon king of the Paphians". From an anecdote about the Athenian harpist Stratonicus in a New Comedy poet of the third century, Machon (Athen. VIII, 349 e), we learn that Stratonicus was put to death at the instance of Axiothea "the wife of Nicocreon". This supports the attribution of the tragedy to Salamis. Niese (*Gesch. d. gr. u. mak. Staaten*, I, p. 306, n. 2), who accepts the attribution to Nicocles and Paphos, argues that reliance cannot be placed on the anecdote in Machon, and notes that Athenaeus tells another story of the death of the same Stratonicus, and this time it is connected with "Nicocles king of the Cyprians". Tarn considers the Alexandrine coins with the name of Nicocles in small letters in the hair of the lion's scalp (below, p. 164) to be very near proof that the episode belongs to the history of Paphos; and that, if it is correct to say that Ptolemy, when he took the royal title, meant that he was king not merely of Egypt but of Alexander's realm, then it is certain that Nicocles, in putting his name on the Alexandrine coinage, was guilty of treason to Ptolemy as representing Alexander. But these coins probably date from before 320, and must have become known to Ptolemy; had they been regarded as effectively treasonable, he would not have treated Paphos with favour, as he did later in 312. On the whole the evidence is in favour of Salamis, although there is still room for some doubt in the matter. The *Marmor Parium* does not settle it absolutely; for the deaths of Nicocles and Nicocreon may have nearly coincided in date. But Engel (*Kypros*, I, p. 368, n. 41) makes the excellent point that, if Nicocreon of Salamis is not the subject of this episode, it is extraordinary that we hear nothing more of him after this time. See also Bouché-Leclercq, *H.L.* I, p. 58, n. 1.

Nicocreon's relations with Greece are illustrated by two dedications. To Delphi he sent, with a couplet dedicating it to Apollo, a head of a stag with four antlers which he had taken in the chase.[1] On the other hand the Argives, in gratitude for a gift of bronze which he had sent to be used for prizes in the athletic contests at the Heraea, erected to him a statue, of which the inscribed base survives.[2] The epigram is interesting as asserting the descent of the king's family from Aeacus and their recognition of Argos in Peloponnese as their mother city. The name of Nicocreon also occurs a number of times, but without any title or ethnic, in the temple-inventories of Delos, where we find mention of a stelé with an inscription concerning the proxenia of Nicocreon, and of gold wreaths dedicated by him.[3] The probability that this Nicocreon is the king of Salamis is increased by the fact that the proxenia and dedications of Pnytagoras are also recorded in the inventories.

As early as the time of Nicocreon interest in the cult of Sarapis, which Ptolemy established in Egypt, began to be shown in Cyprus, possibly owing to Ptolemy's own propaganda. For we know that Nicocreon made enquiry of the god concerning his nature and received an oracular response, describing the deity as having the heavens for his head, the sea for his belly, the earth for his feet, his ears in the aether, and the sun for his eyes.[4]

Of the internal history of the court of Nicocreon we know no more than the gossip-mongers tell us. The story of Anaxarchus of Abdera is famous. This Democritean philosopher, being asked by Alexander the Great at a banquet what he thought of the entertainment, said, with an allusion to Nicocreon, that it lacked only one thing, and that was the head of a certain satrap. Nicocreon nursed his injury, and when Anaxarchus later, being forced to land in Cyprus against his will, fell into his power, the king ordered him to be brayed in a mortar with an iron pestle. Anaxarchus taunted him, saying "bray the shell[5] of

---

[1] Aelian, *N.A.* XI, 40; *Anthol. App.* I, 95.

[2] Hicks, *Hist. Gr. Inscr.*[1] no. 136; Michel, *Recueil*, 1265; Hiller v. Gärtringen, *Hist. Gr. Epigr.* no. 78; *I.G.* IV, 583; *Anthol. App.* I, 96. The chief prize at the Heraea was a bronze shield.

[3] *I.G.* XI, 2. 199 B 87 (στήλην χαλκῆν Νικοκρέοντος προξενίαν) and 161 B (= Michel, *Recueil*, 833) 54, 90 (gold crowns). See Homolle, *Archives de l'Intendance sacrée*, p. 38. 2; *B.C.H.* VI, p. 156, XV, p. 136.

[4] Macrob. *Sat.* I, 20. 16 f. Roeder, in *R.E.* I A, 2405, dates this enquiry about 312; all we can say is that it must have been before the fall of Nicocreon.

[5] The word used is θύλακον, bag. Diog. Laert. IX, 10. 58–9; Plut. *de virt. mor.* 10,

Anaxarchus, himself you cannot bray". When Nicocreon ordered his tongue to be cut out he spat it in the tyrant's face.

Less unpleasant is the anecdote of Dorion the flute-player.[1] When at dinner with the king he had praised a goblet, and the king said, "If you like, the same artist shall make you another like it", he replied "Let him make it for you, but do you give me this one".

A banquet in Nicocreon's palace was the occasion of another anecdote, of which the philosopher Menedemus of Eretria is the hero.[2] The king invited him and his friend Asclepiades, together with the other philosophers at his court, to a banquet which he was accustomed to give once a month. On this occasion Menedemus, with that outspokenness which he shared with most Greek philosophers of whom anecdotes have come down to us, protested that if entertainments offered to such people were a good thing they ought to be given daily; if not, then this one was superfluous. The king replied that he happened to be able to spare time on that day to listen to philosophers. Menedemus insisted that philosophers should be heard at every time, and he and Asclepiades would have paid the penalty of his boldness with their lives had not a flute-player got them out of the way.

The love-story of Arkeophron son of Minnyridas and Arsinoe daughter of Nicocreon[3] has evidently been worked up into a novel, and need only be mentioned here because of the detail that Nicocreon's reason for rejecting the lover's suit was that he was of Phoenician birth. It is only one of many touches which illustrate the antipathy between Greek and Phoenician which endured to a late date in Cyprus.

The anecdotists, especially Athenaeus, are full of stories which illustrate the abandoned luxury of Cypriote court life.[4] They are hardly worth repeating here; though perhaps they make it easy to see why the

---

p. 449 F; Val. Max. III. 3, ext. 4; Const. Porph. *de Thematibus*, I, 15. Cicero, *de nat. deor.* III, 82, says that he was torn to pieces (*excarnificatus*). It is interesting to find Ammianus Marcellinus (XIV, 9. 6) attaching this story to the Stoic Zeno. But the biting and spitting out of the tongue is part of the common stock of hagiography; see H. Delehaye, *The Legends of the Saints* (tr. Crawford, 1907), p. 35; *Légendes hagiographiques*, 1927, p. 34.

[1] Athen. VIII, 18. 337 e (from Lynceus of Samos).

[2] Diog. Laert. II, 17. 129 f.

[3] Antoninus Liberalis, 39. The story has analogies, of which the best-known is that of Iphis and Anaxarete (Ovid, *Met.* XIV, 698–760).

[4] The curious about such things may find them collected in Engel, *Kypros*, I, pp. 489 ff.

people, the moral fibre of whose rulers was weakened in this way, constantly fell a victim to whichever of its neighbours happened for the time to be the strongest.

After the fall of the Teucrid dynasty, Menelaus ruled over Salamis, and doubtless over all the other kingdoms which had been transferred to Nicocreon a few years before. A rare and small gold coinage was issued by him; the larger denomination (one-third stater) bears the Cypriote sign *ba*, showing that he was regarded as king.[1]

Paphos, which under the Ptolemies was gradually to supersede Salamis as the most important city of Cyprus, was in 321, as we have seen, ruled over by Nicocles, who then joined the coalition against Perdiccas. This Nicocles was the son of Timarchus.[2] He remained faithful to Ptolemy, and when in 312 Marium was razed to the ground, its inhabitants were transferred to Paphos. As we have seen, it was probably not he, but Nicocreon of Salamis, upon whom disaster came in 310.

Two points of unusual interest are to be noted with regard to the coinage of Nicocles. On one series of Alexandrine tetradrachms, dating from before about 320, which were struck at Paphos, his name is found on the obverse, engraved in microscopic characters among the hairs of the lion's scalp worn by Heracles; it seems a furtive kind of assertion of independence (Pl. V 4). Another remarkable coin has a head of Aphrodite wearing a *polos* surrounded by a circle of battlements, in her rôle of city-goddess. This may possibly[3] commemorate the fortification of the city, although it was nothing new in Cyprus; for we see on the

---

[1] B.M.C. *Cyprus*, pp. cxiii f. I doubt the attribution to Menelaus of the bronze coin described by Gjerstad, *S.C.E.* II, p. 566, n. 1392.

[2] Timarchus had two rows of teeth. According to Aristotle, fr. 484, ap. Poll. II, 95 he was the father, according to Pliny, *N.H.* XI, 63. 167, the son of Nicocles; perhaps the names alternated in more than two generations. (Pollux confuses this Nicocles with the son of Euagoras.) Nicocles is probably the "king of Paphos, priest of the Anassa, son of king Timarchus" known from Cypriote inscriptions (Hoffmann, I, p. 56, nos. 101, 102, cp. no. 105; Sittig, *Ztschr. f. vergl. Sprachf.* LII, 1924, p. 199; Mitford in *Buckler Anatolian Studies*, pp. 197 f.), and it must be he who is recorded in a couplet on a marble altar found at Paphos, which says that he fortified the city. See B.M.C. *Cyprus*, pp. lxiii f., and for his coins pp. lxxvii ff., and Newell in *Num. Chron.* 1919, pp. 64 f. Newell's attribution of a series of Alexandrine coins to Paphos was brilliantly confirmed by Endicott's discovery of the name ΝΙΚΟΚΛΕΟΥΣ engraved on a group of them. The inscription is too minute to be visible in our reproduction.

[3] As suggested by M. R. James, *J.H.S.* IX, p. 187.

coins of Euagoras II and his successors a goddess, who can hardly be any but Aphrodite, wearing a battlemented crown. On the reverse of the coin of Nicocles, which is inscribed "Paphian (coin) of Nicocles", is a figure of Apollo seated on the omphalos, which is an anticipation of the type which became famous under the Seleucid kings.

It might be supposed that all the other kingdoms of Cyprus, in addition to Salamis and Paphos, would come to an end at the same time; certainly that must have been true of all those which had been incorporated with Salamis.[1] But Soli seems to have been in an exceptional position. How long Pasicrates continued to reign after we last hear of him in 321, we do not know. His son Nicocles, as we have seen, accompanied Alexander to India. Eunostus, who is later found on the throne, may have been an elder brother of Nicocles, and the immediate successor of Pasicrates. Ptolemy, in reward for the fidelity of the house of Soli, married Eunostus to Eirene, his own daughter by the famous Athenian hetaira, Thaïs.[2]

There was a brief pause in the struggle between Ptolemy and his rival when peace was made late in 309, to last until Antigonus, his son Demetrius having freed Athens from the yoke of Demetrius of Phalerum, was ready to attack Ptolemy again. It may have been that he was only anticipating an expected breach of the peace by Ptolemy, who cannot have viewed without concern the successes of Demetrius in Greece.[3]

---

[1] Const. Porph. *de Thematibus*, I, 15 (after saying that Cyprus had formerly been ruled by many and divers kings) adds κατελύθη δὲ ἡ τοιαύτη βασιλεία ὑπὸ τῶν Μακεδόνων τούτεστι τῶν Πτολεμαίων.

[2] Athen. XIII, 576 e: Eunostus king of Soli is mentioned by Eustathius, p. 1332, 4 on *Il.* 23. 826. For the coins attributed, on very good grounds, to Eunostus, see Mrs Baldwin Brett, *Trans. Int. Num. Congr.* London, 1938, pp. 26 f. The silver tetradrachm of Alexandrine types is of Attic weight, and therefore earlier than the adoption of the Rhodian standard about 310. The presumption based on Athenaeus (Beloch, *Gr. Gesch.* IV, ii,[2] p. 332) that Ptolemy cannot have had children by Thaïs until after Alexander's death is refuted by the facts that of his two sons by her one, Leontiscus, was presumably of fighting age by the time of the battle of Salamis, when he fell into the hands of Demetrius, while the other, Lagos, won a chariot race at the Lycaea, probably in 308/7 (Ditt. *Syll.*3 314 B 8 f.; Tarn in *C.A.H.* VI, p. 424, n. 1). Tarn observes that none of the Alexander historians gives any hint that Thaïs at Persepolis was Alexander's mistress, and it is not even certain that Ptolemy ever married her. In view of these facts the notion that Eirene cannot have been married to Eunostus before 307 is to be rejected; and this squares with the evidence of the coins.

[3] Beloch, *Gr. Gesch.* IV, i,[2] p. 152. For the campaign, see Diod. XX, 46. 5–53. 1 (under 307/6); Plut. *Demetr.* 15, 16; Polyaen. IV, 7. 7 (the sea-fight only). The date is

Demetrius sailed from Athens in the spring of 306 with a contingent of thirty Athenian quadriremes added to his fleet. Failing to induce the Rhodians to join in the war against Ptolemy, he coasted on to Cilicia, and, collecting ships and men there, took them across to Cyprus—15,000 foot and 400 horse; of fast triremes he had more than 110 (to these probably we must add the thirty Athenian quadriremes),[1] of heavier warships fifty-three, and transports in sufficient numbers. Landing on the coast of the Karpass, he hauled his ships on shore and made them secure in an entrenched camp. He then stormed the towns of Urania[2] and Carpasia, and leaving his ships under a sufficient guard marched on Salamis.

---

given by *Marmor Parium* (ed. Jac. II B, p. 1004, 21: ἀφ' οὗ Δημήτριος Μουνυχίαν κατέσκαψεν καὶ Κύπρον ἔλαβεν... [ἔτη Δ] ΔΔΔ!!!, ἄρχοντος 'Αθήνησιν 'Αναξικράτους (307/6). The account of Diodorus, though not entirely free from rhetoric, is, as Beloch says (*ibid.* p. 154, n. 1) the best description of a sea-fight of those days that has come down to us. I make no apology for reproducing it in nearly all its detail. Nevertheless, as Tarn points out, it is unlikely that Demetrius had catapults on his ships. At the siege of Rhodes he had to put his catapults on round ships or on two quinqueremes lashed together; and the quinqueremes of his day would have been hampered by a catapult and most certainly would not have given a steady platform for shooting. Has Diodorus amplified the account of Hieronymus in the light of the practice of his own day?—The victory of Demetrius is mentioned briefly by Appian, *Syr.* 54, and Justin, XV, 2. 6–9; the latter records the release of Leontiscus and Menelaus.—An allusion to the victory is in the fragment of Alexis, the Middle Comedy writer (fr. 111 K., Athen. VI, 254 a), where a triple toast is given for Antigonus's victory, for the young Demetrius, and for Phila Aphrodite.—It has been suggested by Engel (*Kypros*, I, pp. 382 f.) that the actual locality of the battle was not off Salamis itself, but off Leucolla, a harbour placed by Strabo (XIV, 6. 3) between Pedalium and another harbour, Arsinoe, which is south of Salamis (i.e. probably Famagusta; Sakellarios, I, p. 186, identifies Leucolla with the harbour of Kōnnos). This is based on the passage of Moschion in Athenaeus (V, 209 e), which mentions the "sacred trireme of Antigonus, with which he defeated the generals of Ptolemy off Leucolla τῆς Κῴας". Here Engel accepts the conjecture Κύπρου for Κῴας. But this Antigonus is Gonatas, and the victory that of Cos. See Tarn in *J.H.S.* XXX, pp. 212 f.

[1] This makes altogether 193 ships, which is near enough to the 190 given by Plutarch; Polyaenus gives the total number as 170 only (but he probably omits the ten used to block the harbour). Diodorus does not mention the thirty Athenian quadriremes until he comes to the actual battle (XX, 50. 3).

[2] Niese (*Gesch. d. gr. u. mak. Staaten*, I, p. 318, n. 4) accepts Wesseling's conjecture Κερυνίαν, on the ground that there is no such place as Urania in Cyprus (a rash assumption); but Demetrius, having landed on the shore of the Karpass, and having Salamis as his objective, would hardly have diverged so far to the west as Kerynia. On the possible site of Urania at Aphendrika, see Hogarth, *Devia Cypria*, p. 85, and Peri-

Meanwhile Menelaus had collected troops from the garrisons in other parts of the island, and was waiting in Salamis; but when the enemy had approached to within four or five miles he went out with 12,000 foot and about 800 horse. After a short engagement he was routed and driven into the city, nearly 3000 men being taken prisoner and about 1000 killed. Demetrius at first distributed the prisoners among his own ranks; but finding them deserting to Menelaus for the sake of their possessions which had been left in Egypt,[1] he recognized that they could not lightly be made to change their allegiance,[2] and shipped them off to Antigonus in Syria. Menelaus, collecting his arms and engines of war in Salamis, put the walls in condition to stand the siege which he saw Demetrius intended, and sent to Ptolemy for help. Meanwhile Demetrius employed all the arts which won him the name of the "Besieger of Cities", constructing rams, tortoises, catapults and the like, and especially the so-called "City-taker", a tower on wheels, 45 cubits square and 90 cubits high, of nine stages carrying stone-throwers and arrow-catapults, the heavier engines being on the lower, the lighter on the upper stages.[3] The machine had a crew of more than 200 men. His various engines did much damage to the walls, although the besieged retaliated with contrivances of their own; and at last, when the capture of the city seemed imminent, they succeeded in setting fire to the machines of the besieger, which were all destroyed, with many of their crews. Nevertheless Demetrius persevered in the siege, trusting to time for success.

Meanwhile Ptolemy, on receiving news of the defeat of Menelaus, sailed from Egypt with considerable land and sea forces. Reaching Paphos, where he was reinforced by ships from the cities loyal to him, he coasted to Citium. His fleet numbered 140[4] warships, quinqueremes and quadriremes, with more than 200 transports for his army of no

---

stianes, Γεν. Ἱστ. pp. 533 ff. The latter strongly supports Hogarth's identification as against that proposed by Schröder and Ohnefalsch-Richter, and accepted by Oberhummer (*Ztschr. d. Ges. f. Erdkunde*, XXVII, 1892, p. 451, n. 3), with Rhani (cp. Kyprianos, p. 36, Γεράνι).

[1] On this point see G. T. Griffith, *The Mercenaries of the Hellenistic World*, p. 133.

[2] The mercenaries of the time, like those who served under the condottieri of the Renaissance, could usually be induced to transfer their services to the conqueror: W. W. Tarn, *Hellenistic Civilisation*,[2] p. 57.

[3] The biggest engines threw stones weighing as much as three talents (say 180 lb. av.).

[4] Plutarch gives 150.

less than 10,000 men. By land he sent orders[1] to Menelaus to despatch to him, if possible, the sixty ships which he had at Salamis, hoping with the 200 vessels thus at his command to win an easy victory. Demetrius, guessing his intention, left part of his force to contain the besieged, and put to sea with all his ships, carrying the best of his troops and fitted with stone-throwers and arrow-catapults. Sailing round the city from the north,[2] he lay at anchor at the mouth of the harbour out of range, thus preventing communication between Menelaus and Ptolemy. When the approach of the latter's formidable armada was signalled, he left his nauarch Antisthenes with ten ships to prevent Menelaus from issuing from the harbour, and sent his cavalry along the shore, in order, should there be any mishap, to rescue those who might swim to land. Himself, he sailed to meet the enemy, in command of 108 ships[3] in all, including those which were manned from the cities which he had captured. His heaviest vessels were heptereis (seven men to an oar), but most of the fleet were quinqueremes. On his left, or seaward, wing were seven Phoenician heptereis, and the thirty Athenian quadriremes, under the command of the nauarch Medius; these were supported in the rear by ten hexereis and as many quinqueremes. In his centre he placed his smallest ships under Themison of Samos and Marsyas of Pella.[4] The right wing was under Hegesippus of Halicarnassus and Pleistias of Cos, the chief navigating officer of the whole fleet.

Ptolemy had hoped at first to arrive and enter Salamis at night, but found himself at daybreak close to the enemy, who were ready for

[1] It may have been at this stage that the "threats and high talk" took place between Demetrius and Ptolemy, as Plutarch relates. Niese, *op. cit.* p. 319.

[2] Diod. xx, 49. 5: περιέπλευσε τὴν πόλιν. From this it follows that his fleet was lying off the shore, doubtless in the sheltered waters between the Salaminian Islands and the east walls of the city; the entrance of the harbour to which he moved was to the south of the city, at the mouth of the river Pediaeus.—Polyaenus gives a completely different account of the preliminaries of the sea-fight: Demetrius, having sailed round the promontory above Salamis, lay hidden under a cliff which formed a harbour; Ptolemy was about to disembark his troops on an open beach, and was just anchoring, when the ships of Demetrius appeared and attacked him; the fight was short and sharp, and Ptolemy was put to flight at once. One doubts whether any of this is to be accepted, save possibly the statement that Ptolemy was surprised.

[3] It has been suggested that 108 is a mistake for 180. But Demetrius was evidently outnumbered by Ptolemy's 140, which is described as a formidable number.

[4] Marsyas was not only a man of war, but the author of an important history of Macedon and a special work on Alexander the Great. Laqueur in *R.E.* xiv, 1995–1998.

battle. Signalling to his transports to follow at a distance in the rear, he took command of his left wing, with his heaviest ships. The whole fleet on either side joined in the customary prayers to the gods which the *keleustai* offered up. At a distance of about a third of a mile from the enemy Demetrius hoisted the agreed battle signal, a gilt shield, and, Ptolemy doing likewise, battle was joined, at first with arrows, stones and javelins; then at close quarters, the ships either driving alongside, sweeping away each other's oars, or charging prow to prow, or ramming the enemy amidships and boarding him. In the mellay, in which, as happens in sea-fights, victory does not necessarily fall to the better individual, but is often a matter of chance, Demetrius especially distinguished himself, fighting from the prow of his hepteres, killing many with his own hand with javelin or spear, while of the three men who covered him with their shields one fell to a spear-thrust and the two others were badly wounded. At last under the pressure of Demetrius (whose heptereis probably held the enemy in front, while the fast quadriremes attacked his right flank)[1] Ptolemy's right wing broke and fled, with the ships of the centre next to it; on the other hand Ptolemy, having with him his heaviest ships and the pick of his men, easily routed the ships opposed to him, sinking some, and capturing others with their crews. But turning back from this success, in the hope of easily dealing with the rest of the enemy, he saw that his right wing and centre were broken and about to fly, and that the ships of Demetrius were bearing down on him in force; and giving up the contest he ran for Citium.[2] Demetrius sent Neon and Bourichus[3] with troopships to pursue the enemy and pick up those who had fallen into the sea. He himself decked his ships with the *akrostolia* of the enemy and taking the captured ships in tow sailed for his own harbour at Salamis. During this engagement, Menelaus had manned his sixty ships and sent them out under the command of Menoetius to the help of Ptolemy; these, with the help of the troops in the city, forced the ten ships of Demetrius to retire from the narrow mouth of the harbour and run to where the land army was encamped; but Menoetius, finding himself too late to be of use, turned back to Salamis. In this battle Demetrius captured more than 100 transports, containing some 8000 men; of warships he took with their

[1] This explanation of the way in which Ptolemy's right was outflanked is due to Tarn.

[2] With eight ships only, all he saved, according to Plutarch.

[3] Bourichus is also known, from Athen. VI, 253 a, as a "kolax" of Demetrius.

crews forty[1] and destroyed some eighty, which were towed back in a waterlogged state to the camp by the city. Of his own ships twenty were destroyed.

Among the prisoners who fell into the hands of Demetrius, besides Menelaus, was Leontiscus, a son of Ptolemy. These two, with the friends of Menelaus, he sent back to Ptolemy, loaded with gifts, an act of chivalry by which he repaid the similar treatment which Ptolemy had accorded to him after the battle of Gaza. But the notorious courtesan Lamia, who was among the non-fighting complement ("servants, friends and women") in Ptolemy's fleet, he did not release; she, though no longer young, won his affections so completely that hereafter he seemed to love no other woman.

Ptolemy, giving up the struggle for Cyprus, sailed for Egypt. Demetrius took possession of all the cities in the island, enrolling their garrisons, to the number of 16,000 foot and some 600 horse, in his own army.[2] It was on the receipt of the news of this victory that Antigonus assumed the diadem and called himself "king", granting the same title to Demetrius, an example which Ptolemy,[3] despite his defeat, and the other Successors, Seleucus, Lysimachus and Cassander, were not slow to follow. Although the unity of the empire of Alexander was still a form, and these men claimed to be not kings of the territories over which they ruled, but successors to the heritage as a whole (Seleucus certainly never gave up hope of it), the assumption of the title none the less marks the break-up of the empire in fact, by emphasizing the irreconcilable aims of the claimants.

---

[1] Seventy, according to Plutarch.

[2] Plutarch (*Demetr.* 16) says that Menelaus, in handing over Salamis and his ships to Demetrius, gave up 1200 horse and 12,000 foot; but in c. 17 Aristodemus announces to Antigonus the capture of 16,800 prisoners. Plutarch also says that Demetrius behaved with magnanimity, burying the enemy's dead and letting the prisoners go free, and presenting 1200 panoplies to the Athenians.

[3] It has been thought that Ptolemy may have been called "king" in Egypt as early as the time of the death of Alexander IV, and also that the title was given him in Cyprus about the same time. (Bouché-Leclercq, *H.L.* 1, p. 72, n. 1.) The ground for this latter view is that in a bilingual inscription of Larnaka tis Lapithou (*C.I.S.* 1, 95; Cooke, *N. Sem. Inscr.* no. 28) he is called βασιλεύς in the Greek and *adon melakim* in the Phoenician, and this inscription, which is a dedication to Athena Soteira Nike, is dated by the editors about 312, presumably because it was then that Ptolemy put an end to the dynasty of Lapethos. It is, however, much more likely that the victory alluded to was that of 294 when Ptolemy finally secured Cyprus.

For some twelve years Antigonus and Demetrius, and after Ipsus Demetrius alone, ruled undisputed over Cyprus, thanks to their naval supremacy. It was their chief source of supply for the munitions of war.[1] Even the disaster of Ipsus did not shake the hold of Demetrius on the island. His mother Stratonice, who was in Cilicia at the time, was taken by him, with all his treasure, to Salamis.[2]

It would seem that Ptolemy must have acknowledged the right of Demetrius to Cyprus when about 299 or 298 he promised his daughter Ptolemais to Demetrius as wife,[3] and Demetrius for his part sent his brother-in-law Pyrrhus to Ptolemy as hostage.[4] When Demetrius lost on the Attic coast (295) a great part of the fleet with which he had sailed to attack Lachares in Athens, it was to Cyprus that he sent for more ships[5] while he occupied himself with the conquest of Peloponnese. But the troops and ships which he needed for these purposes meant that Cyprus was left defenceless, and this was the opportunity of Ptolemy. In fact Demetrius saw himself attacked on every side; Lysimachus seized his possessions in western Asia Minor and Seleucus invaded Cilicia. He decided to leave Cyprus to its fate, and all but Salamis surrendered, apparently without a blow, to Ptolemy (294).[6] Salamis, in which Stratonice, the aged mother of Demetrius, and his children were shut up, held out for some time. When at last it yielded, Ptolemy set them free, bestowing gifts and honours on them with the generosity which marked the relations of these two men.[7]

---

[1] For instance, the two iron cuirasses which were sent from Cyprus to Demetrius at the siege of Rhodes: Plut. *Demetr.* 21.

[2] Diod. *Exc.* XXI, 1. 4: Δημήτριος σὺν τῇ μητρὶ αὐτοῦ Στρατονίκῃ διατριβούσῃ περὶ Κιλικίαν σὺν τοῖς χρήμασι πᾶσιν ἔπλευσεν εἰς Σαλαμῖνα τῆς Κύπρου διὰ τὸ κατέχεσθαι ὑπὸ Δημητρίου. Plutarch, however (*Demetr.* 30), says that he fled to Ephesus after the battle. By the χρήματα Diodorus can hardly mean anything but the treasure of Kyinda; yet from Plut. *Demetr.* 32 it would seem that later (about 299) there were still 1200 talents there, which Demetrius took away to Syria when he went to meet Seleucus and give him his daughter Stratonice.

[3] Plut. *Demetr.* 32; Engel, *Kypros*, I, p. 387. But the marriage did not take place for some years (about 287: Beloch, *Gr. Gesch.* IV, i,[2] p. 235).

[4] Plut. *Pyrrh.* 4.

[5] Plut. *Demetr.* 33.

[6] "Ptolemy placed the aphlaston as symbol on later bronze coins of Cyprus after his reconquest in 295." Mrs Baldwin Brett, *Trans. Int. Num. Congr.*, London, 1938, p. 26, n. 2. Cf. above, p. 159, n. 1.

[7] Plut. *Demetr.* 35, 38. Engel (I, p. 388) and others attribute the defence of Salamis to Phila, and say that it was she who, with the children of Demetrius, was restored to him by Ptolemy. But the passages of Plutarch evidently refer to Stratonice (e.g. τῶν

The capture of Cyprus by Demetrius was marked by the suppression of all mints except that of Salamis.[1] Here for some years he continued to issue coins of the imperial Alexandrine types and inscriptions. It was not, apparently, until Antigonus was dead that he ventured on the innovation of a new coinage, in his own name, the splendid types of which commemorate the victory of six years earlier (Pl. V 5). On the obverse of the silver tetradrachm is a figure of Victory, holding a trumpet and a ship's *stylis*, alighting on the prow of a warship (one of the defeated enemy's ships, for the *stolos* is damaged); on the reverse is Poseidon brandishing a trident, with the inscription "of Demetrius the King".

τέκνων καὶ τῆς μητρός). Phila was probably in Greece at the time.—Engel suggests that it is to this siege that belongs the stratagem described by Polyaenus (v, 20): one Menecrates, when his troops were thrown back from the walls of Salamis, and fled to their ships, signalled to the steersmen to retire and hide behind a headland, so that the troops, though again repulsed, when they saw that they had no escape by sea, attacked a third time in desperation and took the city. Whether this Menecrates is identical with the man who attempted to murder Arsinoe, the widow of Lysimachus, after the latter's death (Polyaen. VIII, 57) is quite uncertain; and the identification with the officer of Perseus (Engel, I, p. 408, n. 24) is equally dubious.

[1] Newell, *Coinages of Demetrius Poliorcetes*, 1927. Most writers on Greek sculpture now deny that the "Victory of Samothrace", which so strongly resembles the type of the coins of Demetrius, is as early as his time, and agree that it dates from some fifty years later. Newell (pp. 32–3) discusses the question, and adduces some arguments in favour of the old view.

CHAPTER IX[1]

THE PTOLEMIES

Cyprus under the Ptolemies continued to be exploited by the ruling power, and more efficiently than had been its lot hitherto. For with the suppression of the petty kingdoms, or their reduction to mere shadows, all their resources flowed into the treasury of Egypt except in so far as, when the island was under separate rule, they may have been wholly or partially absorbed by the Ptolemy who reigned as king in Cyprus. There is no need to enumerate again the manifold products which made the island so valuable a source of supply. Its corn was always—at least when it was not itself the victim of drought—available for less fortunate states; just as during the famine years 330–326 in Greece Athens was helped by private traders in Cyprus[2] as well as Phoenicia, so Euergetes I was able to buy corn in Cyprus, as well as in Phoenicia and Syria and elsewhere, when Egypt was suffering from drought.[3] The mines were still worked effectively, if the silver from which the vast Cyprus coinage of the period was struck came from the island; although the epigraphic evidence from the copper-mining districts (Soli and Tamassus) so active in earlier times, indicates by its scantiness that they were no longer flourishing. The shipbuilding industry was as important as ever; it was apparently in Cyprus that Philadelphus built two of his largest

---

[1] Mr T. B. Mitford, whose acquaintance with the Greek and Roman epigraphy of Cyprus is equalled only by his generosity in placing his knowledge at the disposal of others, very kindly read this chapter in draft and proof. He has allowed me to anticipate freely much that will eventually appear in his forthcoming *Studies in the Epigraphy of Hellenistic Cyprus*. Innumerable corrections and additions have been made in consequence; some of them are acknowledged separately, but a general expression of my indebtedness is due here. The important contribution of W. Otto and H. Bengtson, "Zur Geschichte des Niederganges des Ptolemäerreiches" reached me after this chapter was in print; I have therefore been unable to make as much use of it as I should have wished, or to give reasons for differing from it.

[2] In 330/29 Heracleides, son of Charicleides of Salamis, was bringing corn to Athens when he was caught by the Heracleotes and robbed of his sails. See above, p. 153.

[3] The Canopus decree, 239/8 (Dittenberger, *O.G.I.S.* no. 56, l. 17). The demotic version uses *Salmina* for Cyprus, showing (unless it is due merely to conservatism) that Salamis was still the chief city, although it came later to be overshadowed by Paphos.

ships, a *triakonteres* and an *eikoseres*; his naval architect was Pyrgoteles son of Zoes, of whom the king thought so highly that he erected a statue to him at Paphos, of which the inscribed basis has survived.[1] Possibly it was abundance of timber in the Paphos district that caused the transference of the capital thither; for its harbour was dangerous and strategically less well situated than that of Arsinoe-Famagusta, the successor of Salamis. A probably inaccurate idea of the amount of the revenues, in the last days of the Ptolemaic rule, has been gathered from the fact that Ptolemy, king of Cyprus, when he killed himself in 58 B.C., left a treasure which brought at auction nearly 7000 talents, which he had accumulated during his reign from 80 to 58 B.C., so that his average annual accumulation must have been about 350 talents. It is true that comparisons with modern values, or even with figures from other ancient sources, are apt to mislead, because it is impossible to obtain exact equivalents in modern terms, and because different authorities do not always mean the same thing by the denomination "talent".[2] It may be observed that Diodorus Siculus, when he visited Egypt about 60 B.C., noted that the annual revenue of the king from Egypt was over 6000 talents, whereas Cicero put it at 12,500 talents. And the bribe with which Auletes secured the support of Julius Caesar was 6000 talents. Untrustworthy as these figures may be, they at least suggest that the fortune of Ptolemy was not unduly large. It must be remembered, however, that his estate was disposed of at a forced sale; even though Cato did his best to run up the bids, the real value must have been much greater.[3]

Nevertheless, in spite of the bleeding of the country, it is probable

---

[1] *O.G.I.S.* 39; cp. Athen. v, 203 d. Mitford observes that the inscription does not actually say that Pyrgoteles built the ships at Paphos or that he was a Cypriot. Still it is difficult otherwise to explain why his statue was put up at Paphos. Tarn (*Hellenistic Military and Naval Developments*, 1930, pp. 136 f.) gives the only plausible explanation of the *eikoseres* and *triakonteres* as ships with a system of oars grouped in pairs and in threes respectively, each oar being rowed by ten men.

[2] See Bevan, *The Ptolemaic Dynasty*, p. 352, n. 1. On private fortunes in the Hellenistic Age, see Tarn, *Hellenistic Civilization*,[2] p. 103.

[3] Plut. *Cato Minor*, 38. Beloch, *Gr. Gesch.* IV, i,[2] p. 339. Assuming that the talents were Attic silver talents of 6000 drachmae, and that the drachma represents about 9*d.*, the sum fetched by the treasure would be equivalent to more than one and a half millions sterling.—Cyprus must have been much richer under earlier kings; for the fact that not a single inscription of this Ptolemy's time is forthcoming indicates that it must have been in great poverty (Mitford).

that the lot of the inhabitants was less miserable than it must have been during the preceding centuries when it was continually ravaged by the armies of invaders or of the rival native kings. The Ptolemaic rule, with occasional intermissions, meant comparative peace.

Cyprus was organized as a military command, the governor-general having the title of *strategos* of the island.[1] To his functions (which were probably to a great extent civil as well as military)[2] were added, from the time of Epiphanes (203–181), that of high-priest, *archiereus*; and under and after Euergetes II (146–116) also that of admiral, *nauarchos*. By this time, the policy of the Ptolemies was no longer active enough in the Cyclades and the Mediterranean generally for the nauarch to be so important an officer as he had been in the previous century, so that it was now convenient to place the naval command in the hands of the military commander of Cyprus.[3] The strategos, except when the island was a kingdom by itself, was directly responsible to the king in Egypt; if occasionally the title *autokrator* was added to him,[4] it was presumably because owing to some crisis it was necessary to fortify his position,[5] but it is not likely that his responsibility to the king was lessened. The post was one of the greatest distinction, for it was the most important of all the commands in the Mediterranean. All the strategoi who are mentioned belonged to the highest rank in the Egyptian court, the "kinsmen" of the king, and a king's son was actually among them.[6] A vice-strategos is mentioned in a late Ptolemaic inscription.[7]

---

[1] στρατηγὸς τῆς νήσου (in inscriptions from outside Cyprus στρατηγὸς τῶν κατὰ Κύπρον); when the qualifying words are omitted it is usually if not always because the context makes it certain that the governor-general is meant. ὁ ἐπὶ Κύπρου στρατηγός is an informal appellation in an Attic decree, where exactitude in the title is not to be expected (*O.G.I.S.* 117). The indispensable work on the strategoi and other officials in Cyprus is D. Cohen, *de magistratibus Aegyptiis externas Lagidarum Regni provincias administrantibus*, The Hague, [1912]. Cp. also J. Lesquier, *Les institutions militaires de l'Égypte sous les Lagides*, Paris, 1911, and Bilabel in *R.E.* IV A, 244–6. Municipal strategoi are not to be confused with these governors-general; Heragoras son of Noumenius in a well-known inscription of Larnaka tis Lapithou is an instance. See below, p. 180, n. 1; 187, n. 1.

[2] Cohen, pp. 20–6.

[3] Lesquier, p. 74. Tarn, in *J.H.S.* XXXI, 1911, p. 258; the Egyptians withdrew from the Aegean in 146.

[4] *O.G.I.S.* 140 and 156; *J.H.S.* LVII, 1937, p. 37. These are all in the reign of Euergetes II.

[5] Dittenberger on *O.G.I.S.* 147, n. 7.

[6] *O.G.I.S.* 143. The identification is not certain. See L. Pareti in *Atti Acad. Torino*, XLIII, 1907–8, p. 511, n. 1. He is probably Soter II, (p. 199).

[7] Ἀντιστράτηγος τῆς νήσου: Potamon son of Aegyptus, *O.G.I.S.* 165; dedication at

Under the strategos, as a sort of adjutant-general or quartermaster-general, was the *grammateus* of the forces.[1] The separate regiments must have had their own commanders—usually known as *hegemones*, or, in the case of cavalry, *hipparchai*;[2] but changes in the organization must have been made from time to time and seem to be reflected in the nomenclature of both officers and troops.[3]

The garrisons in the towns of importance were under commandants, at first called *phrourarchoi*.[4] It appears that at some date after the time

---

Paphos by τὸ κο[ινὸν τὸ Κυπρί]ω[ν]. He was also ἐπὶ τῶν μετάλλων and gymnasiarch and *hegetor*, and an official τῶν περὶ τὸν Διόνυσον καὶ θεοὺς Εὐεργέτας τεχνιτῶν. In view of the last detail, Cohen's doubt (pp. 35 f.) as to the Ptolemaic date is unintelligible. There is nothing incredible in the supposition that a local man of distinction should have been made vice-strategos in an emergency.

[1] ὁ γραμματεὺς τῶν δυνάμεων, *O.G.I.S.* 154; Θεόδωρ]ος τῶν πρώτων φίλων καὶ ἐπὶ Σαλαμῖνος καὶ ἐπὶ τῆς κατὰ τὴν νῆσον γραμματείας τῶν πεζικῶν καὶ ἱππικῶν δυνάμεων, *O.G.I.S.* 155; πρὸς τῆι γραμματείαι τ[ῶν δυνάμεων], Mitford in *Arch. f. Pap.* XIII, p. 26. The separate regiments presumably had their own *grammateis*, subordinate to the *grammateus*-general. The theory that these *grammateis* were associated in a *koinon* is now satisfactorily exploded by Seyrig's restoration of *O.G.I.S.* 161, where we must read τὸ κοι[νὸν τῶν ἐν τῶι κατὰ] Κύπρον γραμμα[τείωι περὶ τὸν Διόνυσον] τεχνιτῶν, on the basis of the inscription, *J.H.S.* IX, 1888, p. 247, no. 94, which has [ἐν τ]ῶι κατὰ Κύπρον γραμματείωι περὶ τόν.... This *grammateion* of the Dionysiac artists had nothing to do with the *grammateia* κατὰ τὴν νῆσον (which was a branch of the military administration), but was probably merely the seat of the association. *B.C.H.* LI, 1927, pp. 144–7.

[2] Praxagoras son of Sosianax, a Cretan, was ἡγεμὼν ἐπ' ἀνδρῶν: inscription in the British Museum, attributed by Strack (*Dyn. der Ptolemäer*, no. 8) to Soter I, but according to Mitford of the second century and probably of Philometor. Under (according to Mitford) Philopator, Melancomas the Aetolian, son of Philodamus, was ἐπὶ τῆς πόλεως ἡγεμὼν καὶ ἱππάρχης ἐπ' ἀνδρῶν καὶ ἱερεὺς θεῶν Εὐεργετῶν (*O.G.I.S.* 134); Cohen, p. 43, shows, against Dittenberger, that ἡγεμών is not to be separated from ἐπὶ τῆς πόλεως, and is therefore not equal to ἡγεμὼν ἐπ' ἀνδρῶν. In *O.G.I.S.* 108 the editors restore Δίκτυ[ν, τὸν στρατηγὸν τῶν ἐν Κύπρωι τασσομένων] Κρητῶ[ν where ἡγεμόνα τῶν ἐν τῆι νήσωι τασσ. Κρ. is to be preferred; for there is no evidence that the officers commanding these regiments were called strategoi; and in *O.G.I.S.* 153, in honour of a strategos of the island, where the restoration τὸ κο[ινὸν τῶν ὑπ' αὑτὸν] τασσομένων Κρητῶν is given, τῶν ἐν τῆι νήσωι should be read. Similarly, in Strack, p. 252, no. 99, from Salamis, for τὸν γενόμενον ἐπὶ τῆς πόλεω[ς στρατηγόν ?] read [ς, ἀρετῆς ἕνεκεν καὶ εὐνοίας ἧς]. All these fairly obvious corrections have already been made by Cohen, p. 2, n. 5, and Mitford.

[3] E.g. the changes noted by Mitford, *Arch. f. Pap.* XIII, p. 21, n. 1.

[4] Poseidippus, phrourarch in Citium in time of Soter I or Euergetes I (Strack, no. 3; *O.G.I.S.* 20); another, a native of Aegium, name and city lost, of third century (Mitford in *Arch. f. Pap.* XIII, p. 19, no. 7); but *not* the supposed Onesagoras(?) son of

of Euergetes I the title of this officer was changed to "officer commanding the city".[1] The change seems to indicate some widening of functions; one may best render the title by "prefect".

Scattered information is provided by the inscriptions about other military officers, such as the *architekton*, and the semi-military *archikynegos*.[2]

The office of *epistates*, at any rate in Cyprus, must not be confused with that of the prefect mentioned above. It was something much more important, as is clear from the fact that, when Crocos enjoyed it, it was mentioned before his office of strategos.[3] It is impossible, with the information at our disposal, to be certain of the significance of the term in Cyprus; but elsewhere it seems to have meant a sort of High Commissioner, with full authority to execute the orders of the sovereign power, and there seems to be no reason why it should not have meant the same here, for it is borne by a man who is also entitled *strategos autokrator*.

Of the extent of the formidable army of mercenaries stationed in Cyprus[4] we can gather some idea from the fact that Soter II as king in

---

Stesagoras in Arsinoe (?), in time of Euergetes I (Strack, no. 47; P. M. Meyer, *Heerwesen der Griechen u. der Römer in Aegypten*, Leipzig, 1900, p. 19; Mitford, *loc. cit.* and p. 29, shows that φρουραρχοῦντος must be rejected in favour of γυμνασιαρχοῦντος).

[1] Cohen, pp. 42 f. ὁ ἐπὶ τῆς πόλεως is found as early as *c.* 193 (Mitford, *Arch. f. Pap.* XIII, p. 23 note). Such officers are found among Delphian *thearodokoi*, representing the cities of their command (Robert in *Journ. de Philol.* 1939, pp. 194 f.) It is probable that the original title was ὁ ἐπὶ τῆς πόλεως ἡγεμών; after Philopator to Euergetes II it is ὁ ἐπὶ τῆς πόλεως; thereafter the office was perhaps discontinued.

[2] 'Αρχιτέκτων: chief military engineer. See W. H. Buckler in *J.H.S.* LV, 1935, pp. 75–8: a decree from Old Paphos ordering the celebration of the day of one of these officers by the Corps of the Artillerists (ἀφέται).—See also above for a naval *architekton* (p. 174), and Sakellarios, I, p. 94, no. 43, for a Paphian dedication by four brothers and οἱ ὑπ' αὐτῶν τεταγμένοι κατὰ τὴν νῆσον ἀρχιτέκτονες.—'Αρχικύνηγος, Captain of the Royal Hunt (a title of the strategos): *O.G.I.S.* 143; Lesquier, p. 353. On the κυνηγοί of the Ptolemies, see Roussel in *Rev. Ét. Gr.* XLIII, 1930, pp. 361 f.; G. T. Griffith, *The Mercenaries of the Hellenistic World*, p. 126, n. 2. For other military officers see Mitford, *Mnemosyne*, 1938, p. 109 and *J.H.S.* LVII, p. 33, no. 7.

[3] *J.H.S.* IX, 1888, p. 247, no. 92; Mitford in *J.H.S.* LVII, 1937, p. 37. On the *epistates* elsewhere see Cohen, pp. 80 ff.

[4] αἱ δυνάμε[ις αἱ ἐν Κύπρωι τεταγ]μέναι (*J.H.S.* LVII, 1937, p. 29); or simply αἱ δυνάμεις (*O.G.I.S.* 154); πεζικαὶ καὶ ἱππικαὶ δυνάμεις (*O.G.I.S.* 155); αἱ ἐν] Κύπρωι τεταγμέναι πεζ[ικαὶ] καὶ ναυτικα[ὶ δυνάμεις, *Actes du Ve Congrès de Pap.* 1937, p. 299; αἱ ἐν Κύπρωι τασσόμεναι πεζικαὶ δυνάμεις (Strack, nos. 96 and 168). In Strack, no. 112, for τῶν ἐν τῆι νήσωι τασσομένων δυνάμ[εων the reading of the last word is not borne out by the stone (Mitford).

Cyprus had a force of 30,000 foot and horse at the siege of Ptolemais in 104.[1] It seems from Euergetes II Physcon to Alexander I to have been divided into what we may call regiments according (nominally at least) to the nationalities of the men; these divisions are revealed to us by the dedications made by them, usually through their unions or *koina*,[2] to the strategoi and other distinguished persons. Thus we have a dedication by the "Achaeans in military service in Cyprus and the other Greeks" to the strategos Seleucus son of Bithys (although, since this dedication was at Olympia, the terms may be unusual),[3] and others by the *koina* of the Cilicians, Cretans, Ionians, Lycians, Thracians, Ceians, and perhaps Aenianes. Men who did not belong to any of these nations might be attached as supernumeraries.[4] It is not certain that there was a general union of all the army.[5] There is no likelihood that the "union of the Cyprians" was military rather than civil in character.[6]

The mines of Cyprus being one of the sources of revenue, their finance must have been under the control of the chief financial officer. An inscription on the basis of a statue put up at Paphos to Potamon son of Aegyptus, who was *antistrategos* in the reign of Soter II, shows that he was also chief administrator of the mines.[7] It is, however, going beyond the evidence to infer from this solitary record that the administration of the mines was part of the regular functions of the strategos; in fact the special mention of it here suggests that it was not.

A Phoenician inscription from Larnaka tis Lapithou,[8] of which the date is 275 B.C.,[9] makes known to us one Yathan-ba'al, governor of the

---

[1] Josephus, *Ant. Iud.* XIII, 12. 3, p. 333; Meyer, p. 93, n. 342.

[2] See Meyer, pp. 92–4. These *koina* seem to be mentioned only from 144 to 107 (Mitford in *Mnemosyne*, 1938, p. 115 note).

[3] *O.G.I.S.* 151.

[4] E.g. τὸ κοινὸν τῶν ἐν Κύπρωι τασσομένων Θραικῶν καὶ τῶν συμπολιτευομένων, *O.G.I.S.* 143 and n. 6; cp. the ἀναφερόμενοι ἐν ταῖς [τάξεσι ?] of the Ceians (Mitford).

[5] In *O.G.I.S.* 159 (Strack, no. 129), τὸ κοινὸν τῶν κατὰ τὴν νῆσον (*immo* ἐν τῆι νήσωι) τ]ασσομένων..., an ethnic is to be supplied at the end. As to Strack, no. 112 (τὸ κοινὸν τῶν ἐν τῆι νήσ]ωι τασσομένων δυνά[μεων]); see above, p. 177, n. 4.

[6] M. San Nicolò, *Aegyptisches Vereinswesen*, I, 1913, p. 199, n. 3. Dittenberger (*O.G.I.S.* 164 and 165) assumes that it was. It does not occur before Soter II Lathyrus.

[7] *O.G.I.S.* 165 (above, p. 175, n. 7): ἐπὶ τῶν μετάλλων. The inscription is discussed by Mitford in *Proceedings of the Congr. of Epigraphy*, 1938, where it is suggested that Potamon was left by Soter II in Cyprus in 89.

[8] Ph. Berger, *Rev. d'Assyriologie*, III, 1894, pp. 69–88; Clermont-Ganneau, *Études d'Archéologie orientale*, II, 1897, § 21; Cooke, *N. Sem. Inscr.* no. 29; Oberhummer in *R.E.* XII, 764.

[9] It is dated "in the 11th year of the lord of kings, Ptolemy son of the lord of kings,

district, son of Ger-'ashtart, governor of the district; also the priest to the lord of kings, 'Abd-'ashtart, son of Ger'ashtart, governor of the district. The administration of Lapethos and its district was thus evidently, under the early Ptolemies, left in the hands of an important local Phoenician family. But from the scanty evidence we cannot assume that like conditions prevailed everywhere; at first, at least, there must have been many variations in the organization.

Of the internal constitution of the cities we know practically nothing. But at least the forms of liberty were preserved, as we may see from the fact that Paphos, for instance, had its own *boule* and *demos* and city-secretary.[1] But to suppose that there was any sort of republican independence, because such institutions were tolerated, or because the "city made dedications, or Carpasiote victors in the Panathenaic Games were

---

Ptolemy, which is the 33rd year of the people of Lapethos". If Ptolemy II Philadelphus is meant, the year is 275; if Ptolemy VI Philometor, it is 171; if Ptolemy IX Alexander, it is 107; and the era of Lapethos begins accordingly in 307, 203 or 139. [Incidentally, Oberhummer, *loc. cit.*, makes a curious mistake, putting the era ten years too late, while correcting Berger for rightly putting it ten years earlier.] Prof. A. M. Honeyman, having examined the stone in the Louvre, finds no authority for Clermont-Ganneau's restoration of the name of Cleopatra, so that the second possibility may be ruled out. As to the third, Oberhummer questions the survival of Phoenician so late as the second century, but Cyprus is full of surprising survivals. Phoenician survived in Byblus and Tyre into the Christian Era (Tarn, *Hellenistic Civilization*,[2] p. 139). Nevertheless the year 275 must be the correct year, since "the two wives" (i.e. Arsinoe I and Arsinoe II) are mentioned (Honeyman's new reading).

[1] A. H. M. Jones, *Cities of the Eastern Roman Provinces*, p. 488, n. 10. A dedication by two Carpasiotes at Delos, Durrbach-Roussel, *Inscrr. de Délos*, no. 1403 Bb 83/4. Carpasiote victors in Panathenaic Games, early in the second century: *I.G.* II, 966, 967 (II,[2] 2314, 2313). Onesander (*O.G.I.S.* 172: γραμματέα τῆς Παφίων πόλεως); Callippus (*O.G.I.S.* 166: δὶς γραμματεύσαντα τῆς βουλῆς καὶ τοῦ δήμου καὶ ἠρχευκότα τῆς πόλεως κ.τ.λ. 'Αρχεύειν, as Dittenberger shows, *ad loc.*, was some office connected with the city religion; Paphos, as we have already noted, also had its ἡγήτορες, officials of the Aphrodite cultus (above, p. 78, n. 2). The *boule* is also found at Chvtri (*J.H.S.* 1937, p. 33). Mitford notes that otherwise it has not yet been found mentioned until the reign of Soter II in Cyprus, or just before; *demos* is somewhat earlier (probably Philometor: *B.M. Inscr.* 975). Dedications by the city as such, cited by Jones, *loc. cit.* Paphos: *O G.I.S.* 84 (*J.H.S.* 1937, p. 31), 163, 166, 172; Salamis: 108, 156; Curium: 152; Chytri: 160. To these add: Arsinoe: *O.G.I.S.* 155; Amathus: Strack, no. 171; Citium: *B.C.H.* XX, p. 336, no. 1; Lapethos: *Arch. f. Pap.* XIII, p. 23, no. 11. At Citium an official called suffete or judge is mentioned, but whether his office was that connoted by the word elsewhere is uncertain (*C.I.S.* I, 47; Cooke, *N. Sem. Inscr.* no. 17). Nor is it by any means certain that חשב in *C.I.S.* I, 74 means a quaestor.

registered as "Carpasiotes from Cyprus", is to go beyond the evidence. There were city-strategoi, and, as in other Hellenistic cities, education was under the charge of a gymnasiarch.[1]

The organization of the mints of Cyprus was a matter of some importance.[2] We have seen that they were used for the issues of the imperial "Alexander" coinage; that Menelaus, Ptolemy's brother, had struck coins at Salamis during his short reign frcm 312 to 306, and that there are also rare issues in all three metals probably struck by Ptolemy's son-in-law Eunostus at Soli, before 306.[3] Soter probably struck a few unimportant bronze coins for local purposes in Cyprus before he lost it to Demetrius, but there is no evidence of any issues of gold or silver on his own account. Yet it is interesting to observe that before he finally settled on the Phoenician standard of weight for his Egyptian coinage, he used, as a transition from the Attic standard, the Rhodian, which, considering the importance of his commerce with Rhodes, he may have borrowed thence, but which had already been in use in Cyprus, at Salamis, since the time of Euagoras II.[4] It is only the more significant of the later issues that can be mentioned here. Under Philadelphus, after the deification of Arsinoe II (which dated from before her death in July 269), the mint-marks of Cypriote mints (Paphos, Salamis, Citium and perhaps a fourth mint) are first seen on the heavy gold coinage issued with her portrait and in her name. These memorial coins were struck through several reigns; at the three mints already mentioned as late as the time of Euergetes II. Of the other series of Philadelphus,

---

[1] City-strategoi at Paphos, Citium and Larnaka tis Lapithou: Mitford in *Mnemosyne*, 1938, p. 110. At Amathus, *B.M. Inscr.* 975. On the gymnasium at Chytri see Mitford in *J.H.S.* LVII, 1937, pp. 33 f.

[2] On the Ptolemaic coinage, the work of Svoronos, Τὰ Νομίσματα τοῦ Κράτους τῶν Πτολεμαίων, Vols. I–III, 1904, and Vol. IV (with German translation of Vol. I), 1908, has superseded all its predecessors. A searching review of it, always to be consulted, was given by K. Regling in *Ztschr. f. Numism.* XXV, 1906, pp. 344–99. A clear account is rendered by G. Macdonald in Head, *Historia Numorum*,[2] 1911.

[3] Above, p. 165, n. 2. Svoronos's attribution (*op. cit.* I, col. οβ′) of the gold coin with eagle on lion, generally accepted as an issue of Euagoras II (above, p. 147, n. 3), to a king of Soli in the period 310–305 must be rejected.

[4] Bouché-Leclercq, *H.L.* III, p. 274, is wrong in saying that it was the Phoenician system which he borrowed from Cyprus. It is interesting to note that the transition from the Attic to the Rhodian standard was made with the coins issued by Ptolemy about 310, on which he commemorated his conquest of Cyprus (Mrs Baldwin Brett, *Trans. Int. Num. Congr.* London, 1938, p. 26).

some may have been struck in Cyprus from 269 to 261, although the attributions are conjectural. Euergetes I (246–221) issued bronze coins with a cultus-figure of Aphrodite on the reverse, which may be from a mint in Cyprus, although they have also been attributed to Rhodes; and under Philopator (221–205) there is a class of gold coins with the portrait of Queen Arsinoe III which may have been issued in Cyprus. Under Philopator, also, it is probable that there began a series of silver coins with the bust of the king as Dionysus (Pl. V, 7); it was continued over several reigns.[1] Epiphanes (205–180) begins a great series of issues, chiefly of silver, from the mints of Paphos, Salamis, Citium and Amathus. A small undated group of silver tetradrachms must belong to the period 203–197, for they bear the first two letters of the name of the faithful strategos Polycrates. The history of the coinage of the mints of Cyprus henceforward becomes extremely complicated and difficult, and the attributions to various kings are often too uncertain to be used as historical evidence. After a time, under Euergetes II, what had been originally the mint-mark of Paphos came to be placed, for some reason, on coins issued from Alexandria, even when Paphos was no longer in Ptolemaic possession, making confusion worse confounded. Paphos, it has been suggested, had so much monopolized the production of the silver coinage that when that coinage was struck elsewhere its mint-mark was slavishly copied.[2] But in Cyprus almost certainly was minted a rare bronze coin of Cleopatra VII, on which her bust appears as Aphrodite with the baby Ptolemy Caesar in her arms.

The coinage, as a royal prerogative, was undoubtedly under the control of the strategos, and Polycrates, as already remarked, put his mark on the pieces issued during the period of his stewardship; his example was followed by some of his successors.

It was inevitable that the religious institutions of Cyprus should be profoundly affected by its connexion with Ptolemaic Egypt.[3] An

---

[1] Poole suggests (B.M.C. *Ptolemies*, p. li) that it was issued by the strategos as γραμματεὺς τῶν περὶ τὸν Διόνυσον τεχνιτῶν; he cannot have held that office, but the connexion with the artists is not unlikely.

[2] J. G. Milne in *Journ. Eg. Arch.* xv, 1929, pp. 152 f. The Alexandrian mint began to pirate the mark of Paphos in the thirtieth year of Euergetes II (140). The Alexandrian issues can be distinguished from the Paphian by their poorer though individual style: E. T. Newell, *Two Recent Egyptian Hoards* (Numismatic Notes and Monographs, no. 33, New York, 1927), pp. 20 ff.

[3] Bouché-Leclercq, *H.L.* III, p. 67.

illustration is seen in Nicocreon's enquiry about Sarapis.[1] That the dynastic cult should soon have been officially established there goes without saying, but how far, if at all, it was officially associated with those of local deities we cannot discern.[2] The references in the inscriptions to it are not too scanty. 'Abd-'ashtart (son of Ger-'ashtart, governor of the district of Lapethos) was eponymous priest of "the lord of kings, Ptolemy";[3] and at Idalium in 254 a dedication is dated by the year in which Amath-osir was *kanephoros* of Arsinoe Philadelphus.[4] At Citium, probably under Philopator, the Aetolian Melancomas son of Philodamus was priest of the Gods Euergetai.[5] Onesander of Paphos[6] was priest for life of Soter II Lathyrus and of the Ptolemaeion which he himself founded at Paphos. Artemo, the daughter of the strategos Seleucus, was, if the record is rightly restored,[7] priestess of Cleopatra III. Helenus, strategos during the reign of Alexander I in Cyprus, was priest for

---

[1] Above, p. 162. Dedications to Sarapis are, however, not early or frequent in Cyprus (one to him jointly with Euergetes I and Berenice, *O.G.I.S.* 63). There was a temple of Osiris at Lapethos in the time of King [Prax]ippus (?), who may have been grandfather of the king deposed in 312, or indeed, as Mitford thinks, that king himself. Prof. Honeyman dates the inscription which mentions him between 345 and 315. See above, ch. VI, p. 100. This same inscription names also the Phoenician deities Melqarth, Astarte, and the god of Byblus (presumably Adonis). This indicates that the Egyptian cult came not direct from Egypt, but through Phoenicia. The same may be said of the evidence of the personal name 'Abd-osir, which is found as the name of a Phoenician at Citium perhaps as early as 375 (*C.I.S.* I, 13). The worship of Isis at Soli, judging from the date assigned to the temples, began about the middle of the first century B.C. (Westholm, *Temples of Soli*, p. 147); but Mitford inclines to a much earlier date, even third century, for a number of the inscriptions; on the early use of cursive lettering, cf. *Arch. f. Pap.* XIII, p. 16 note.

[2] Collective dedications, like that at Chytri to the Gods Philometores Ptolemy and Cleopatra and Hermes and Heracles and the Council of Chytri (*J.H.S.* LVII, 1937, p. 33, where others similar are mentioned) do not prove a joint cult.

[3] Cooke, *N. Sem. Inscr.* no. 29 (inscription of Larnaka tis Lapithou of 275 B.C.), see above, p. 178, n. 9.

[4] *C.I.S.* I, 93; Cooke, *N. Sem. Inscr.* no. 27.

[5] *O.G.I.S.* 134.

[6] *O.G.I.S.* 172 and Mitford, *Arch. f. Pap.* XIII, p. 37, no. 18. He afterwards became librarian at Alexandria, but nothing is known of his attainments as a scholar, and Bouché-Leclercq (*H.L.* II, p. 115) thinks that the king chose him rather for his attainments as a courtier. Let us hope that he was a good administrator.

[7] *O.G.I.S.* 159: ἱέρειαν βασιλίσσης] Κλεοπάτρας θεᾶ[ς. καὶ ἱερέως is equally possible epigraphically, but we do not meet the priesthood in any of the inscriptions to Seleucus himself (Mitford).

life of the same Cleopatra.[1] Nowhere is there evidence that the head of the dynastic cult was a high-priest in Cyprus, any more than in Egypt itself. And this is one of the strongest arguments against the acceptance of the theory formerly prevalent that the strategos of the island, as archiereus,[2] an office which he filled from the time of Epiphanes, was high-priest merely of the dynastic cult, and not rather of all the cults of the island also;[3] in fact his title "high-priest of the island" or "high-priest of the temples throughout the island" has to be interpreted in its natural sense; and an inscription recently published gives to this sense specific expression.[4]

It is to be supposed that the addition of the high-priesthood to the functions of the strategos under Epiphanes (perhaps by Polycrates) meant that the revenues of the exceedingly rich temples of the island were made to contribute to the royal exchequer to a greater degree than before.[5]

Before this assumption of the high-priesthood of the island by the governor, was any office of the same general extent in existence in the island? It is very doubtful. Early in the third century at Lapethos a resolution was passed by "Praxidemus the high-priest and the priests of Poseidon Narnakios" in honour of their benefactor Noumenius son of Noumenius.[6] This probably only means that Praxidemus was head of the college of priests at that particular shrine. An inscription from Paphos has been restored on the assumption that a strategos was at the

---

[1] *J.H.S.* LVII, 1937, p. 36.

[2] 'Αρχιερεὺς τῶν κατὰ Κύπρον *scil.* ἱερῶν, ἀ. τῶν κατὰ τὴν νῆσον ἱερῶν (L.B.W. no. 2787), ἀ. τῶν κατὰ τὴν νῆσον or ἀ. τῆς νήσου: Mitford in *Arch. f. Pap.* XIII, p. 25. In the inscription, *J.H.S.* IX, 1888, p. 229, no. 11 (Strack, no. 112), the restoration ἱερέα τῆ[ς νήσου is probably wrong (Mitford).

[3] Bouché-Leclercq, *H.L.* III, p. 67, observed that there is no proof that the governor of the island was, as archiereus, the priest of the dynastic cult. Cohen's destruction of the theory that he was (pp. 26–32) is so complete that it is unnecessary to discuss the question again here.

[4] *Arch. f. Pap.* XIII, p. 25, no. 12.

[5] Dittenberger, *O.G.I.S.* 230, n. 2, thought that the idea of the combination of the high-priesthood with the governorship was borrowed by Epiphanes from Syria, when in 193/2 he married Cleopatra, the daughter of Antiochus III. But Mitford observes (*Mnemosyne*, 1938, pp. 118–19) that the inscriptions *J.H.S.* IX, nos. 32 and 107 prove the existence of the title before the marriage, and probably in the last years of the third century. He thinks it was Polycrates who made the innovation.

[6] L.B.W. no. 2779. A better text in Cesnola, *Cyprus*, p. 420. On Noumenius see Mitford, *Arch. f. Pap.* XIII, p. 16.

same time high-priest of the temples of Aphrodite throughout the island—which is certainly wrong; although there is evidence in Hellenistic times for a single priest of Aphrodite for all Cyprus.[1] Not until Roman times do we find a "high-priestess of the temples of Demeter throughout Cyprus".[2] It is by no means certain that the Romans here merely perpetuated a pre-existing system.

It was only to be expected that from the time of the deification of Arsinoe Philadelphus, the cult of the goddess, who was frequently identified with Aphrodite,[3] should have a vogue in Cyprus. We have already seen that her memorial series of coins was issued during many reigns from the chief mints, and that there was a worship of her at Idalium with an eponymous *kanephoros* as early as 254. This city, as one of the centres of the cult of Aphrodite, appropriately had an Arsinoeion.[4] There must have been shrines in her honour at the city of Marium, which was re-named after her, and at the harbours or anchorages which were similarly called, one (at Ammochostus) on the east coast between Salamis and Leucolla, the other on the south-west coast between Old and New Paphos; in fact, at the latter, Strabo mentions a temple and a sacred grove, although without naming the deity to whom they were dedicated.[5] Stone plaques and other objects (including an altar and an amphora), inscribed simply with the name of Arsinoe Philadelphus in the genitive, occur all over the islands of the Ptolemaic dominions (there is also one from Egypt), and of these at least nine have been

---

[1] *J.H.S.* IX, 1888, p. 251, no. 108. For Charinus, priest of Aphrodite for all Cyprus, see *B.M. Inscr.* 975 (about mid second century, and not Roman, as the editor supposed (Mitford)).

[2] L.B.W. no. 2801.

[3] E.g. the shrine dedicated to Arsinoe Cypris or Zephyritis by Callicrates on the promontory Zephyrium near Alexandria (Poseidippus ap. Athen. VII, 318d; Callim. *Epigr.* VI).

[4] *Rev. Arch.* XXVII, 1874, p. 90, no. 2.

[5] Strabo, XIV, 682, 683. In the latter passage Arsinoe comes next to the promontory and anchorage of Zephyria, which is perhaps no mere coincidence with the association at Alexandria (see preceding note). On the possible site see Hogarth, *Devia Cypria*, p. 42. Est. de Lusignan (*Chorogr.* f. 10 v°), followed by Kyprianos (p. 20), places it at Evdhimou, which, being four leagues east of Kouklia, is impossible if Strabo is right. Lusignan (*loc. cit.*) and Kyprianos (p. 46) place a fourth Arsinoe at Arsos (now in the Limassol district); the latter regards this as the place to which the Greek bishops of Paphos were banished. This is accepted by Hogarth (p. 4); but we know that they went to the Arsinoe at Polis tis Chrysochou (Marium). For Lusignan's Arsinoe at Leuka there seems to be no foundation.

found in Cyprus. The variety of the objects on which they occur shows, however, that the theory that they were boundary marks indicating that the land was the property, not of the queen during her lifetime, but of the goddess, is untenable. They are presumably dedications.[1] The *apomoira*, the tax of one-sixth on the produce of vineyards and gardens which Philadelphus established in Egypt for the benefit of the cult of Arsinoe in 265/4, was, we may assume, levied in Cyprus also.[2] A priest of Arsinoe is found as late as the second century.[3]

The dynastic cult was the religious focus of the Union or *Koinon* of Cyprus, of which we do not hear until the time of Soter II;[4] indeed, it is probable that this Union of the Cypriotes had little meaning except as an institution for the worship of the royal house. This cult helps to explain the existence of the innumerable minor unions which were characteristic of this age,[5] although the inscriptions from Cyprus relating to these *koina* seem as a rule to record compliments to the governors and their relations, and never directly to the royal house. There was also a guild of Basilistai, which in Cyprus, as elsewhere, must have been concerned with the dynastic cult.[6] A similar religious function was exercised by the union of the Dionysiac artists, for we find the divine Euergetai combined with the god Dionysus as the objects of worship by the union.[7]

Such was the organization which was gradually developed in the province which Ptolemy I Soter finally secured in 294, and which was to remain in Ptolemaic hands, whether as part of the Egyptian kingdom or as a kingdom by itself, for some two centuries and a half. It was undoubtedly a most valuable possession, and it is only an accident of historical record—which is naturally concerned with disturbances rather than peace—that we seldom hear of it except when it is the scene of

[1] *S.C.E.* III, p. 621. See Mitford in *Arch. f. Pap.* XIII, pp. 30 f.

[2] Cohen, pp. 69–74.

[3] Mitford, *ibid.* p. 28.

[4] Dittenberger, *O.G.I.S.* 164, 165 (time of Soter II).

[5] Bouché-Leclercq, *H.L.* III, pp. 173 f. M. San Nicolò, *Aegyptisches Vereinswesen*, I, 1913, p. 199; Kornemann in *R.E.* Supp. IV, 916–18.

[6] Peristianes, Γεν. Ἱστ. p. 945, no. 34; *J.H.S.* IX, p. 255, no. 124. At Thera, *I.G. XII Ins.* III, 443. Ziebarth in *R.E.* Supp. I, 244.

[7] Dittenberger, *O.G.I.S.* 161 (*S.E.G.* VI, 816), 163, 164, 166 (οἱ περὶ τὸν Διόνυσον καὶ θεοὺς Εὐεργέτας τεχνῖται); also Strack, no. 121; *B.C.H.* II, p. 145 (*S.E.G.* VI, 813). Cp. for the collocation of the θεοὶ Ἀδελφοί with Dionysus, Ptolemais (*O.G.I.S.* 50, 51). Poland in *R.E.* V A, 2512.

trouble. For the rest of Soter's reign its history is a blank; and in that of his successor Philadelphus we hear only that it was on the accusation of stirring up trouble in Cyprus that, shortly after the marriage of Philadelphus to Arsinoe II in 277, a half-brother of the king, a son of Soter by Eurydice, was put to death.[1] We do not know his name, but it has been conjectured that he was Meleager, who had been king of Macedon for a couple of months, until he was deposed in 279.

Philadelphus, however, left his mark on the island in the foundations, or re-foundations, which he made in the name of Arsinoe. Of the three which have already been mentioned, Marium-Arsinoe flourished down to the Middle Ages. The little place on the south coast is not heard of again. But that on the east coast can hardly have been anywhere but at Ammochostus, which was to become famous as Famagusta. In view of the gradual silting-up of the harbour of Salamis, this site, with the makings of the only considerable harbour in Cyprus, was shrewdly chosen. But it was slow in superseding Salamis; meanwhile Paphos grew in importance and by the first half of the second century had become the military and naval capital.[2]

Cyprus was, it is conjectured, the base of the Ptolemaic fleet which took part in an episode of the Third Syrian War which broke out immediately after the death of Antiochus II (246). The governor of Cyprus, whoever he was, came to the support of Berenice, the daughter of Ptolemy II, against Laodice, the widow of Antiochus. It has been suggested that the governor, whose report has survived in an obscure and mutilated papyrus, may, since he calls Berenice "sister", have been Lysimachus, the younger brother of Euergetes I, who had just succeeded to the throne. Although the governor captured Seleucia, and was triumphantly received in Antioch, the expedition was a failure, and Berenice and her son were murdered by Laodice's party.[3]

It is not until the time of Philopator (221–205) that inscriptions recording honours (usually in the form of statues) to the governors and other high officials become frequent. From the time of Menelaus on-

---

[1] Pausanias, I, 7. 1; Niese, *Gesch. d. gr. u. mak. Staaten.* II, p. 99, n. 2; Bouché-Leclercq, *H.L.* I, p. 166.

[2] Buckler in *J.H.S.* LV, p. 78; Mitford in *Mnemosyne*, 1938, p. 110.

[3] Mahaffy, *Petrie Pap.* II, 1893, no. 45; Köhler in *Sitzb. Akad. Berlin*, 1894, pp. 445 f.; Bevan, *House of Seleucus*, I, 1902, pp. 185–6; Bouché-Leclercq, *H.L.* I, 1903, pp. 249–51; Wilcken, *Chrestomathie*, 1912, no. 1; Roos, in *Mnemosyne*, LI, 1923, pp. 277 ff.; Tarn in *C.A.H.* VII, 1928, p. 716.

wards, we have no certain record[1] of any strategos of the island until the reign of Philopator, when Pelops, son of Pelops, is known to us from two inscriptions in honour of his wife Myrsine, daughter of Hyperbassas. Since they mention Philopator and his wife Arsinoe, "father-loving gods", they are later than Philopator's marriage (end of 217) and earlier than the birth of his son (9 Oct. 209). A dedication to Philopator by Pelops, who does not however call himself strategos, is also extant; and we know from Polybius that in 203 he was sent by the regent Agathocles on an embassy to Antiochus the Great.[2] It is probable that his successor in the governorship in this year was Polycrates, the son of Mnasiades, an Argive in origin, of whom more is known, and that for the most part favourable. He was in office during the minority of Epiphanes, who ascended the throne as a child in 203. In autumn 197 Polycrates resigned his office, being succeeded by Ptolemaeus, a Megalopolitan. In critical and difficult times Polycrates not only preserved the island for the child king, but amassed a considerable sum of money, which in due time he faithfully handed over.[3]

The troubled state of international affairs is illustrated by the fact that during Polycrates's last year of office Antiochus the Great of Syria, while

---

[1] Cohen (p. 6 note) is certainly right in excluding Heragoras son of Noumenius of Lapethos, who is mentioned simply as strategos (L.B.W. no. 2780). His date would seem to be about the middle of the third century. For further evidence on Heragoras see Mitford in *Arch. f. Pap.* XIII, pp. 16 f.

[2] Mitford in *J.H.S.* LVII, 1937, p. 31 (inscription of Famagusta, enabling him to restore correctly the similar Paphos inscription, *J.H.S.* IX, 1888, p. 252, no. 112, from which Strack (no. 65) raised the ghost strategos "Basileides"; cp. *O.G.I.S.* 84). The dedication by Pelops, *O.G.I.S.* 75. The embassy, Polyb. XV, 25. 10 (13 Büttner-Wobst). For the elder Pelops, son of Alexander, an officer of Philadelphus, see Wilhelm in *Anz. Akad. Wien*, LVII, 1920, p. 53; *S.E.G.* I, 364.

[3] Polyb. XVIII, 55. 6. The letters Πο on silver tetradrachms of Epiphanes (Pl. V, 6) mark them as issued by his authority (Svoronos, *op. cit.* nos. 1302–5). Regling, it is true, *op. cit.* p. 376, considers the attribution to Polycrates, and even to Ptolemy V and Cyprus, to be weak, while accepting Svoronos's other attributions to strategoi on the strength of their initials.—The basis of a statue of the young Epiphanes erected by him at Paphos: *O.G.I.S.* 93. In the Nicosia Museum is the basis of a statue of his son Polycrates erected by the city of Lapethos, giving his rank as a "principal friend", but not mentioning any office: Peristianes, Γεν. Ἱστ. pp. 943 f., corrected by Mitford, *Mnemosyne*, 1938, p. 118. For the career of Polycrates and his descendants see Mitford, *ibid.* pp. 116 ff.; the inscription, *ibid.* p. 104, Mitford now restores differently as a dedication to Polycrates, his children and his forefathers. On Ptolemaeus the Megalopolitan, his daughter Eirene and grandson Andromachus, see *Arch. f. Pap.* XIII, pp. 27 f.

all the time professing friendship to Egypt, had formed a plan to seize Cyprus. He had long had his eye on this tempting object; it had been, with other Egyptian possessions in Asia Minor and in southern Syria, his share in the division of spoils which he arranged with Philip V in 202,[1] when in the infancy of Epiphanes the possessions of Egypt seemed an easy prey. But when it came to the point, his crews were disaffected, and on his way from Ephesus he was detained by a mutiny off the mouth of the Eurymedon. This quelled, he was caught by a storm off the Saros, and lost nearly the whole of his ships and men; with the few that survived he limped back to Seleucia.[2]

With the reign of the sixth Ptolemy, Philometor, who succeeded Epiphanes as a child in 180, we enter upon what is perhaps the most difficult period of the history of Ptolemaic Cyprus.[3]

The attack on the island delivered by Antiochus IV Epiphanes of Syria in 168 was more effective than that of his predecessor. He had posed as the champion of Philometor against his younger brother Euergetes II (Physcon). But when the two brothers were reconciled, and Philometor had been readmitted to Alexandria to reign as joint king with Physcon, he threw off the veil, sent a fleet to Cyprus[4] and marched for the second time on Egypt. From the envoys of Philometor, who met him at Rhinocoloura, he demanded the cession of Cyprus as well as Pelusium.

In Cyprus the governor, Ptolemaeus called Macron, deserted the cause of Philometor and went over to Antiochus.[5] There was neverthe-

---

[1] See, however, Magie in *Journ. Rom. Stud.* XXIX, 1939, pp. 32 ff.

[2] Livy, XXXIII, 41; Appian, *Syr.* 4.

[3] On this reign, see especially W. Otto, "Zur Gesch. der Zeit des 6. Ptolemäers" in *Abh. Bayer. Akad., Phil.-hist. Abt.*, N.F. Heft XI, 1934. For the date of the death of Epiphanes, see *ibid.* p. 134.

[4] Livy, XLV, 11.

[5] II Macc. x. 13. He got the reputation of being doubly a traitor; because having been entrusted with Cyprus by Philometor he abandoned it and withdrew himself to Antiochus Epiphanes; μήτ' εὐγενῆ τὴν ἐξουσίαν ἔχων ὑπ' ἀθυμίας (the Vulgate has: *etiam ab eo recessisset*) φαρμακεύσας ἑαυτὸν ἐξέλιπε τὸν βίον. It is commonly supposed that this is the strategos of whom a fragment of Polybius (XXVII, 12 (13 B.W.)) says under the year 172 that he was nowise Egyptian (in character) but a sensible and business-like man; for, having taken over the island while the king (*scil.* Philometor) was still an infant, he carefully husbanded the finances, giving up nothing to anybody, although he was frequently asked to do so by the king's treasurers and was bitterly criticized for his closeness; but when the king came of age, he put together and despatched a considerable sum of money, so that both Ptolemy and his court were well pleased with his previous economy and closeness. Ptolemaeus, in other words, de-

less some resistance to the invader; but Ptolemy's forces were defeated both on sea and on land,[1] and the island thrown into utter disorder. But Rome, since the latter years of the third century, had begun to make its weight felt in the affairs of Egypt. Now it intervened, and its envoys, having at an interview which is related in every history-book frightened Antiochus into evacuating Egypt, sailed to Cyprus to see that his fleet was withdrawn.[2]

---

fended his charge against the attempts of the regents Eulaeus and Lenaeus to bleed the island for their own purposes (Otto, p. 25). Otto (p. 78, n. 4) doubts whether there was direct betrayal by Macron, in view of his earlier and later behaviour. It may be noted that the passage of Polybius has curious echoes of his account of Polycrates, who became governor of the island while Epiphanes was an infant, and saved up the revenues, to hand them over when the right time came. Engel (*Kypros*, I, p. 405) has noticed this suspicious circumstance. But it is difficult to assume a duplication in the record, although the fragment is only preserved by Suidas.—In an inscription from Old Paphos (*J.H.S.* IX, 1888, pp. 233 f., no. 24; Strack, no. 84; *O.G.I.S.* 105), in honour of Philometor (the son of king Ptolemy and queen Cleopatra, Gods Manifest), set up by a strategos and archiereus, an Alexandrian citizen, the name of the man is erased. He may have been Macron. The mention of the parents has suggested to the editors a date in Philometor's infancy and before his marriage with his sister (thus 181–172); but this is not a necessary inference, cp. e.g. Mitford, *Mnemosyne*, 1938, p. 112. The erasure may have taken place after Macron's desertion, or, as Dittenberger suggests, in 146, when Physcon took vengeance on his dead brother's friends and followers. This, we shall see, was the time when the names of persons who had honoured Eupator were similarly erased.—Macron appears to be the Ptolemaeus mentioned in *O.G.I.S.* 117, and, according to Mitford, may also be the strategos of the inscriptions *J.H.S.* XII, p. 181, no. 16 and *B.M. Inscr.* II, no. 388, if the latter concerns a strategos at all.

It is necessary, in view of a misunderstanding by Engel and others, to point out here that the officers of the Seleucid kings who are mentioned in II Maccabees as ἐπὶ Κυπρίων (iv. 29) or Κυπριάρχης (xii. 2) have nothing to do with the strategia of Cyprus, as Engel supposes (*Kypros*, I, p. 406—where Sostratus should be Crates—and p. 408), but were probably commanders of Cypriote mercenaries. Mitford suggests that Nicanor, in the latter passage, may be the mercenary captain of *S.E.G.* VI, 824 (date, late Epiphanes or early Philometor).

[1] Polyb. XXIX, 11 (27 B.W.), 10; Livy, XLV, 12. Engel (*Kypros*, I, p. 408, n. 24) suggests this campaign as an alternative for an earlier one (above, p. 172 n.), as the occasion on which Menecrates employed a stratagem to encourage his men in an attack on Salamis.—From an inscription, supposed, from the style of the lettering, to belong to about 200–170 (Ditt. *Syll.*3 622), it appears that Eraton, a Cretan of Axos, went on a campaign to Cyprus, settled, married, had children and died there. It is conjectured that the campaign mentioned was some thirty years before the cutting of the inscription. There is however no record of any war in Cyprus which would suit such a date. May a later date be assigned to the inscription, and the war be that of 168?

[2] Livy, XLV, 12. The discomfiture of Antiochus is mentioned in Dan. xi. 30; but

For some five years after the expulsion of Antiochus from Egypt and Cyprus, Philometor reigned jointly with his younger brother, afterwards Euergetes II (Physcon).[1] But when the inevitable breach came, towards the end of 164, Philometor had to fly from Alexandria. Roman representatives, five years before, had intervened dramatically to save Egypt from Antiochus; it was to Rome now that Philometor turned, travelling thither in person, and in the humblest guise, to throw himself on the mercy of the Senate.[2] The real intention of the Senate, when it came to a decision, if it was ever expressed, is not recorded; and it has been denied that the policy of dividing up the Egyptian kingdom was already in its mind.[3] Philometor returned, not to Alexandria, but to Cyprus; Roman envoys proceeded (though they did not leave Rome until late in spring 163, and then went first to Syria) with orders to do their best to reconcile the two brothers.[4] But it was the Alexandrians themselves, provoked by the cruel excesses of Physcon, who revolted and deposed him, and recalled Philometor (July 163).[5] The restored king showed moderation, due perhaps not only to his generosity and good sense, but also to the restraining influence of the Roman envoys. Physcon became independent king in Cyrene; Philometor retained Egypt and Cyprus. The arrangement was confirmed by a solemn treaty,[6] which, however, Physcon took the earliest opportunity of repudiating. He protested that he had been unfairly treated, and claimed Cyprus; even so, his share would be the smaller. He went in person to Rome to plead his cause; Philometor, on the other hand, was represented by envoys.[7] The Roman Senate's only aim was to keep Egypt

---

here "Kittim" means Western powers (see above, p. 97). What was once thought to be a monument of the short occupation by Antiochus survives in a silver tetradrachm of the usual types of the Seleucid kings, with a mint-mark which has been identified with Salamis. But the same mark is also found on Seleucid coins of Antiochus III, Seleucus IV and Demetrius I, who can never have issued money in Cyprus. B.M.C. *Seleucid Kings*, p. 111, no. 4a; E. Babelon, *Rois de Syrie*, pp. clxxx f.

[1] Porphyr. Tyr. fr. 7. 2. (*F.H.G.* III, p. 721; Jac. *Fr. Gr. Hist.* II B, 260, pp. 1199–1200.)

[2] Diod. XXXI, 18. The Archias who is mentioned as accompanying Philometor may be the future governor of Cyprus.

[3] Otto, p. 92, n. 5.

[4] Livy, *Epit.* 46; Polyb. XXXI, 12 (2 B.W.), 14. The orders to proceed to Egypt were sent after them.

[5] Diod. XXXI, 17e.

[6] Polyb. XXXI, 18 (10 B.W.), 5; Livy, *Epit.* 47 (post-dated about 158).

[7] Neolaidas and Andromachus. As to the latter, see Mitford, *Actes du Ve Congrès de Papyrologie*, 1937, p. 292, and *Arch. f. Pap.* XIII, pp. 27 f.

enfeebled, and its sympathies, if as is likely it knew by this time of Physcon's offer to bequeath his kingdom to Rome, were wholly inclined to him. It threw over Philometor.[1] T. Torquatus and Gn. Merula, Senatorial legates, were despatched with instructions to establish Physcon in Cyprus and bring about an agreement between the brothers, but without resorting to arms.[2] Physcon, indeed, was for invading Cyprus at the head of a mercenary force, but was dissuaded by the legates, and betook himself to Cyrene. Merula accompanied him, while Torquatus undertook negotiations with Philometor. But Philometor declined to budge an inch, and meanwhile the brutalities of Physcon in his kingdom all but cost him his throne. Merula and Torquatus, baffled, returned to Rome; there was another debate, both kings being represented by envoys, and the Senate, smarting under the snub administered by Philometor, again hurled a *senatus consultum* at his head; his envoy Menyllus was told to leave Italy at once and denounce the alliance between his master and Rome.[3] Philometor was unmoved, though Physcon began to recruit for an attack on Cyprus. It is highly probable that the envoys who were sent to convey the decision of the Senate to Physcon carried secret instructions encouraging him to take action against Philometor.[4]

But some years were to pass before he was able to carry out his plan. Meanwhile he was not the only king who coveted the possession of the island. Demetrius I Soter of Syria corrupted the governor,[5] Archias, with a promise of 500 talents and other favours. But the plot was discovered; and Archias, brought to trial, hanged himself (155).

It was probably in the next year (154) that the irrepressible Physcon staged another appearance before the Roman Senate, and that body, whether deceived or not by the scars of wounds which the king displayed as having been inflicted by assassins hired by his brother,[6] lent

---

[1] For interesting speculations as to the reasons for this change of policy, and its connexion with Physcon's bequest of his kingdom to Rome, see Otto, pp. 97, 109.

[2] Polyb. XXXI, 18 (10 B.W.).

[3] Polyb. XXXII, 1 (XXXI, 20 B.W.); Diod. XXXI, 23; Otto, p. 111.

[4] Otto, p. 112.

[5] Polyb. XXXIII, 3 (5 B.W.). Otto dates this episode 158/7 (p. 112, n. 4). That Archias was strategos is shown by an inscription from Old Paphos (*J.H.S.* IX, p. 232, no. 21, Mitford in *Mnemosyne*, 1938, pp. 115 f.) which records a dedication to him by the army.

[6] Drumann-Groebe, *Gesch. Roms*,[2] V, p. 138. Otto, p. 113, believes in the reality of the attempt, on the ground of the assertion in the Cyrene inscription to that effect,

itself once more to his designs. Philometor's advocates were dismissed, without being heard; no less than five legates, each with his own quinquereme, escorted Physcon, with orders to establish him on the throne of Cyprus, and letters went to all Rome's allies to say that they were free to assist his restoration.[1] But nothing more is heard of the Roman interference, and the allies did not take Physcon seriously. Indeed, the Cretan League actively supported Philometor.[2] Physcon landed in Cyprus, only to find himself soon surrounded in Lapethos by the superior forces of his brother, to whom he was forced to give himself up. Philometor's combination of prudence and magnanimity was even now not exhausted; he set his brother free, made a new treaty with him, acknowledging him as king in Cyrene in return for an annual tribute of corn, and promised him in marriage one of two daughters named Cleopatra.[3]

After this the Romans had the decency to give Physcon no more support against his brother. They were moved partly, perhaps, by the

---

and the scars which he exhibited. The evidence seems to me inadequate, at least so far as Philometor's guilt is concerned.

[1] Polyb. XXXIII, 5 (11 B.W.).

[2] Two inscriptions from Delos relate to this help from Crete (Bevan, *Ptol. Dynasty*, pp. 301–2). (1) *O.G.I.S.* 116; Holleaux, *Arch. f. Pap.* VI, 1920, pp. 10–11: Decree honouring Ptolemy, the "pious and god-fearing and gentlest of men", with a gold crown and two bronze statues, one in Crete and one in Delos, in order to show that those who fought with him in Cyprus remember the favours granted to their cities, etc. The peace which Philometor made with his brother is also mentioned. (2) Holleaux, *ibid.* p. 9: Dedication by the Cretan *koinon* in honour of Aglaus, son of Theocles, of Cos, who was in great favour with Ptolemy the Elder, fought in his campaign in Cyprus, and was *proxenos* of the Cretans in Alexandria, and so of service to the Cretan troops which were sent to fight as allies of Ptolemy by the Cretan *koinon.*—A commander of the Cretan mercenaries in Cyprus, Dictys, was honoured by the city of Salamis (*O.G.I.S.* 108; but Mitford restores this as belonging to the reign of Euergetes II); cp. also the dedication by Citium to Hagias son of Damothetus, the Cretan, archisomatophylax and ἐπὶ τῆς πόλεως (*O.G.I.S.* 113).

[3] Polyb. XL, 12 (XXXIX, 7 B.W.); Diod. XXXI, 33. Polybius attributes Philometor's behaviour to his magnanimity; Diodorus also mentions his fear of Rome, and the Cretan decree, *O.G.I.S.* 116 (see previous note), betrays this in its phase προαιρούμενος ἐν οἷς μάλιστα χαρίζεσθαι καὶ Ῥωμαίοις.—The chronology of these events is very uncertain. See Holleaux in *Arch. f. Pap.* VI, 1920, p. 17. Niese (*Gesch. d. gr. u. mak. Staaten*, III, p. 211) places the expedition of Physcon and his capture at Lapethos about 158/7, before the affair of Archias and the appeal to Rome. The order given in the text is that adopted by, among others, Bouché-Leclercq, Bevan and Otto, and follows the sequence of the fragments of Polybius. The latter tells the incident of Lapethos out of its chronological order, in connexion with the death of Philometor, as an example of his gentleness.

oration which Cato the Censor delivered in the Senate in praise of Philometor, "the excellent and most beneficent king";[1] although even his attitude to the question might have been without effect had not Rome had her hands sufficiently full elsewhere. In the eight years to the death of Philometor fell the wars with the Celtiberians, Andriscus, the Achaean League and Carthage.

It may be that all the opinions which are recorded about the character of Philometor should be taken with a certain amount of reserve, being inspired by political or personal feeling or subservience.[2] With all deductions, however, there is no doubt that Philometor shows well against the grim background of his time. Had he, for instance, when he had his brother in his power, behaved in the usual manner of the Ptolemies, one of the few passages in relief of the deplorable history of that family would have been erased.

Somewhat doubtful reasoning about the evidence has connected with the history of Cyprus the brief reign of Eupator, son of Philometor and Cleopatra II, who is assumed to have been made "viceroy" or even king of the island. The papyri show that he was associated as king with his father as early as April 152, but that probably he was no longer so associated in January 150, and in July of that year he was dead. It has been suggested that he was made king of Cyprus in order to strengthen the government, in view of the threat of attacks from the side of Physcon, such as had actually taken place in 154; also that this separation of Cyprus from Egypt was in accordance with Roman policy, and it was to Philometor's advantage to conciliate Rome, especially on the eve of his intervention in Syria on the side of Alexander Balas. Unfortunately the evidence for the presence of Eupator in Cyprus is not entirely convincing.[3]

---

[1] Drumann-Groebe, *Gesch. Roms*,[2] v, p. 138.

[2] Otto, p. 94, n. 3.

[3] For the evidence of the papyri, see H. Gauthier, *Le livre des rois d'Egypte*, IV, 1916, pp. 335 ff. On p. 297, n. 1, however, the same author seems to accept the evidence of the coin, to be mentioned later, as showing that the 1st year of Eupator corresponded with the 36th of Philometor. For the inscriptions in honour of the "god Eupator", one of which proves that he was son of Philometor and Cleopatra II, see *O.G.I.S.* 125, 126, 127. L. Pareti, "Ricerche sui Tolemei Eupatore e Neo Filopatore", in *Atti Acad. Torino*, XLIII, 1907–8, 497–519, speaks of the three inscriptions (which he puts at 153/2–151/0) as if they proved Eupator to be then in Cyprus—which of course they do not; although it may be admitted as remarkable that the three statues to Eupator as king were all erected in Cyprus, while none are yet known from Egypt. In all three the

But, whatever may have been the object of the scheme, whether Eupator was made king of Cyprus or not, it came to nothing owing to the breakdown, for some unknown reason, of the joint kingship, and the early death of the young man. But it was to be revived after a short delay. A coin of Paphos with a double date, equating the first year of a newly associated king with the thirty-sixth of Philometor, shows that in that year (146/5) Philometor must have placed another son on the throne beside himself. This was doubtless on the eve of his departure on his fatal expedition to Syria, this time against and not on the side of Alexander Balas. It was this son, who is now generally admitted to be Neos Philopator,[1] whom Physcon, if we could believe the tale, removed in so revolting a fashion from his path on the very day of his marriage with Philometor's widow. But it is only necessary to mention this episode here in order to emphasize the fact that it had nothing directly to do with Cyprus.[2]

---

name of the dedicator has been erased; it is generally assumed that this was done after the accession of Physcon, in submission to his policy of damning the memory of Philometor and all connected with him.—As regards Eupator, Otto (pp. 119 ff.) has an extremely ingenious argument. The evidence of the papyri is that Eupator received his cult-name in 153–2; in April 152 we find him associated on the throne with his father; in Jan. 150 he is no longer so associated; but he did not die until later, for an epigram of Antipater of Sidon (*Anth. Pal.* VII, 241), which (as Cichorius in *Rhein. Mus.* LXIII, 1908, p. 213, and R. Laqueur, in *Hermes*, XLIV, 1909, pp. 146–50, have between them shown) seems to relate to him, makes his death coincide with a total eclipse of the moon visible in Egypt; which points to 3 July or 28 Dec. 150. The three inscriptions therefore belong to the period 153/2–150. Because they mention Eupator alone, and not his father, Otto argues that when they were cut Eupator was no longer joint-king but sole king, and therefore his father was no longer ruler of Cyprus. It follows that Eupator, some time after April 152, ceased to be joint-king over the whole Egyptian kingdom, and became independent ruler (King) of Cyprus, Philometor having renounced Cyprus in his favour. Incidentally (p. 122), it is suggested that it was M. Aemilius Lepidus who installed Eupator as king in 152, and that this is the subject of a well-known Roman coin (Hill, *Hist. Rom. Coins*, pp. 51 ff.). The use by Antipater of ἄναξ, which was of old the title of the princes of Cyprus (above, p. 114), designates Eupator as ruler of the island. There are two weak points in this argument. In the first place, as Dittenberger remarks in connexion with the basis of a statue of Epiphanes (*O.G.I.S.* 93), the statues of joint-rulers might be put up separately, and the inscription would refer to each one separately. Secondly, no argument can be based on the use, which Cichorius stresses, of such a word as ἄναξ in a poetical context such as this: δὴ γὰρ ἄνακτας τοίους οὐκ 'Αίδας, Ζεὺς δ' ἐς Ὄλυμπον ἄγει.

[1] See especially L. Pareti, *loc. cit.*

[2] The first year of Neos Philopator would be reckoned from his accession, June

The most attractive, if not the ablest, of the Ptolemies was succeeded by the most unpleasant, Euergetes II, Physcon ("Pot-belly") or *Kakergetes*, as his unfortunate subjects nicknamed him.[1] In the persecution which raged for a time at his accession, many of the scholars who were the ornament of the Alexandrian Museum, if they escaped with their lives, fled to other lands.[2] Among them seems to have been the famous Homeric critic, Aristarchus of Samothrace, head of the library and teacher of Physcon himself and of Eupator; he left Alexandria to die in Cyprus.[3] The rule of Physcon in Cyprus was not popular, to judge by the fewness of dedications to him; in Alexandria during the

145, to 5 Epag. next, i.e. 27 Sept. 145 (Mitford). As to the coin of Paphos (B.M.C. *Ptolemies*, p. lxvii, Pl. XXXII, 9; Svoronos, no. 1509; Regling, p. 381, who refutes an absurd notion of Svoronos), it is necessary to emphasize three facts. First, like all the coins of the Paphian mint at this time, it is an issue of the regal Ptolemaic coinage; it bears no evidence of having been issued by anyone as king in Cyprus, or as "viceroy", though it does prove that a new king came to the throne in that year. (Incidentally, the non-existence of any coins of a second year suggests that this new king did not survive his first.) Second, the equation cannot be between the 36th year of Philometor and the 1st of his successor (i.e. Physcon); such dating would be admissible in, say, a private papyrus or epitaph, but not on a coin; for a coin is issued in the name of a reigning king, who does not mention his predecessor, though, if he is a co-regent, he naturally mentions the year of his colleague. The equation then can only mean that the two kings concerned were reigning at the same time. Third, it is really to Philometor's and not to Physcon's 36th year that the coin belongs; Svoronos preferred the latter date, but Newell has proved, by the evidence of a hoard, that the earlier is correct (*Two Recent Egyptian Hoards*, in Numism. Notes and Monographs, no. 33, 1927, pp. 24 f.). Bouché-Leclercq's doubt whether the A on this coin is really a regnal date is baseless (*H.L.* II, p. 81, n. 1). Otto (p. 128, n. 4) discusses the possibility of the double date on the coin referring not to an associated king but to the conquest of Syria, but, as I think rightly, rejects it.—There is one Cypriote monument which may belong to the short interval between the death of Philometor and the murder of Neos Philopator, and that is an inscription in which Demetrius II pays honour to his father-in-law Philometor (*S.E.G.* VI, 809). Since Demetrius (if Wilcken's hesitating restoration is right; and Mitford's reading of the stone supports it) calls himself Nicator, this inscription must be after the death of Philometor, as Otto (p. 130) points out, and obviously it cannot have been put up during the reign of Physcon, unless the island continued to hold out against him; as Mitford suggests it may have done, pointing to the Larnaka Amnesty (see below) as giving the end of the opposition.

[1] Philometor's death probably took place in Aug. 145 (Otto, p. 129 note).

[2] Andron Alexandrinus, *Chron.* fr. 1 (*F.H.G.* II, p. 352, from Athen. IV, 184 b. c). If, as seems to be the case, an amnesty was declared at the end of 145 or beginning of 144 (Mitford in *Actes du Ve Congrès de Papyrologie*, 1937, pp. 291–9; Otto-Bengtson, p. 27 note), the persecution did not last long.

[3] Athen. II, 71 b; Suidas, 3892, *s.v.* Ἀρίσταρχος.

first period of his reign, even if the accounts are exaggerated, he seems to have been responsible for a succession of horrors. Revolt finally came to a head in Alexandria in 131/0, and Physcon took refuge in Cyprus. With him went his niece-wife, Cleopatra III (the daughter of Philometor and Cleopatra II, Physcon's sister, whom he married after the death of Philometor), his son by Cleopatra II, called Memphites (as a hostage), and probably his children by Cleopatra III.[1] In Cyprus he collected a mercenary army for war against Cleopatra II and his country. Fearing that the Alexandrians might invite his eldest son, who was living in Cyrene, to mount the throne, he sent for him and put him to death.[2] The Alexandrian mob thereupon broke up Physcon's portrait-statues. Suspecting his sister of having inspired their destruction, he killed their son, Memphites, a lad of fourteen, and sent his head, hands, and feet to her as a birthday present. The birthday feast was turned into mourning, and the remains of the prince exhibited to the populace, as an earnest of what they might expect of their king. Such is the story handed down;[3] it is generally agreed that some at least of it is true; the close agreement of all the accounts in details, taken by some to indicate a legendary origin, may equally well point to its being based on fact.[4]

Alexandria, however, was not all Egypt, and Physcon, for whom the greater part of the country stood, was able to return from Cyprus in 129, Cleopatra II retiring to Syria for some five years, when she was again reconciled to the king. The period which elapsed between his return from Cyprus to his death in 116 was marked by no atrocities; on the other hand, there is evidence of much able administration and reform, which suggests that the horrible picture of his earlier days may have been coloured too darkly, although such inconsistency between a king's personal character and his public policy is common enough. In Cyprus there is no sign of any disturbance.

Of the strategoi of this reign recorded by inscriptions, one, whose

---

1 Livy, *Epit.* LIX; Justin, XXXVIII, 8, 11.

2 Justin, *loc. cit.* 12. For *a Cyrenis* Strack (p. 201, n. 33) proposes to read *ex Eirene*, Euergetes's concubine. Otto-Bengtson, p. 59 n., identify the son fetched from Cyrene with Memphites, and admit only one murder.

3 Diod. XXXIV–XXXV, 14; Justin, *loc. cit.* 12–15; Livy, *loc. cit.*; Val. Max. IX, 2, ext. 5; Orosius, V, 10. 7.

4 Bevan, *Ptol. Dyn.* pp. 323–4, has some judicious remarks on the attitude which the historian should take to this problem.

name is lost, dates in the period from the end of 144 or beginning of 143 to September 142.[1] Of the others, all, except one, held the position of high admiral (*nauarchos*) as well as that of strategos and high-priest. In the case of one of them, Crocos, the naval rank comes first. It was evidently an innovation. The title *autokrator* is also added to strategos. One of the three inscriptions concerning him, according to a plausible restoration, can be dated to the first part of 142. Between the naval and military titles here there is room for another, for which the editor suggests *epistates*, which Crocos holds in another inscription. In one from Delos he is given an additional, probably purely honorific, title, after *autokrator*, to wit, if the word is rightly restored, "supreme".

It has been reasonably conjectured that Crocos was made high admiral, probably in the latter part of 143 or early in 142, because Cyprus, owing to the loss of the Ptolemaic footing in the Aegean, now became the headquarters of the Egyptian fleet; the high command in the island therefore became naval as well as military.[2]

Crocos seems to have been succeeded by Seleucus son of Bithys,[3]

---

[1] So Mitford. In the inscription, *J.H.S.* IX, p. 228, no. 11, Cleopatra the sister is mentioned and probably her son or her children. This fixes the date between late 144 (before which Memphites cannot have been born) and Sept. 142, when Cleopatra III first appears as queen and wife.

[2] The date of his first inscription (=*J.H.S.* LVII, pp. 36–7, no. 11) Mitford fixes to the first part of 142 (restoring τὴν ἀδελφήν after Κλεοπάτραν) because the children of Cleopatra II are still recognized as Physcon's heirs. The Delos inscription (which mentions both queens: *O.G.I.S.* 140) must be after Physcon's second marriage. In this, ὑπέρ[τατον], the usually accepted restoration, reinforces *autokrator*, and is perhaps unofficial and colourless; in a Delian decree exactitude in titles of outsiders need not be expected. (Mitford however suggests ὑπέρμαχος, the king's "champion", comparing *O.G.I.S.* 147, where instead of the amusing current restorations he reads τ]οῦ συγγενοῦς καὶ ὑπερμάχου). The third inscription is *J.H.S.* IX, 1888, p. 247, no. 92, which Mitford restores thus: ναύαρχον]| καὶ ἐπιστάτην καὶ [ἀρχιερέα τῶν κατὰ τὴν νῆσον?]| καὶ στρατηγὸ[ν αὐτοκράτορα, κ.τ.λ. Mitford thinks, it is true, that both *epistates* and *hyper*... belong to the earlier history of the nauarchia, and were soon discontinued in Cyprus. Possibly, however, *epistates* means the highest *civil* administrative office in the island, to which a man might be specially appointed in a time of crisis; see above, p. 177.

[3] Stähelin in *R.E.* II A, i, 1247, no. 13. To the dedications add now that from Lebena in Crete, inscribed by Cretan mercenaries who had served in Cyprus (L. Robert in *Rev. de Philol.* 1939, pp. 153 f.). Mitford observes that the inscription *C.I.G.* 2625 (*O.G.I.S.* 154), on the evidence of which Seleucus was supposed to have been secretary of the forces before becoming strategos, is wrongly restored and has nothing to do with Seleucus.

who was a citizen both of Alexandria and Rhodes,[1] the latter being probably his birthplace. He was already a person of importance in 157, when Delphi gave him the honour of proxeny. His governorship of Cyprus began in 141 or 140; when it ended we do not know, but he was succeeded by his son Theodorus.[2]

This Theodorus, during his father's tenure of the strategia, was already of the rank of the "principal friends", prefect of Salamis and head of the secretariat of the infantry and cavalry forces. When he succeeded his father in the strategia, it was to hold it (if not at once, yet soon after) with the enhanced powers and title of autokrator. Since this points to a crisis in the affairs of the island, the years 129–8 when Physcon had regained possession of Alexandria, but not yet of the whole of Egypt, have been suggested as suitable. It is further conjectured that Theodorus retained office until about 124, when Cleopatra II was reconciled with her brother, and that, in connexion with this reconciliation, the governorship of the island was given to a prince, who is supposed subsequently to have taken or been given the royal title. For the successor of Theodorus in the strategia was probably the man whose initial *Ph*... occurs on a series of bronze coins issued in Cyprus.[3] The important appearance of these coins has prompted the thought that they were issued by a strategos who was a prince, and that he called himself king in 121/120, issuing in Cyprus also silver coins which have been supposed to bear the double dating year 50 (of Physcon) and year 1 (of himself).[4]

---

[1] Multiple citizenship (though probably it was not effective for more than one city at a time) was common in this age: Tarn, *Hellenistic Civil.*[2] pp. 79–80. It has been suggested that Seleucus gave up his Alexandrian citizenship because Physcon disliked the aristocracy of that city.

[2] Seleucus is strategos, nauarchos and archiereus in *O.G.I.S.* 152, which mentions both queens, but no children. That would mean that the sons of Cleopatra II were disinherited, the sons of Cleopatra III not yet born. Crocos was still in office after the marriage to the latter queen (see p. 197, n. 2); so Seleucus cannot have succeeded him before 141. Besides the two inscriptions added to the record of Seleucus by Mitford, reference may be made to *O.G.I.S.* 151 (Olympia), 153 (Knodhara), 159 (New Paphos: his daughter Artemo, priestess of Cleopatra III), 160 (Chytri: Olympias, daughter of Artemo; the rank of Seleucus is given as τῶν πρώτων φίλων, probably by an error of drafting).

[3] Svoronos, p. 265, nos. 1640–47.

[4] B.M.C. *Ptolemies*, p. 96, no. 99; Svoronos, no. 1526 (Paphos); no. 1613 (Citium); no. 1565 (Salamis). The letter A on the first two corresponds to a monogram on the third, and is therefore presumably not a date. Bouché-Leclercq, *H.L.* II, p. 81, n. 1; Svoronos, IV, cols. 313 f.; Otto-Bengtson, pp. 118 f.

Unfortunately that interpretation of the coins cannot be sustained, so that the assumption of a co-regency in 121/120 loses much of its basis; although a strategos (his name is not preserved) who was Master of the Royal Hunt but not nauarchos, and would therefore seem to have served under a prince, would fit the situation.[1]

Finally, among the strategoi of this reign, we have one who is named Ptolemy, son of the king, strategos and nauarchos and archiereus and archikynegos. This is probably the future Soter II Lathyrus, who, we shall see, was in Cyprus when his father died (28 June 116).[2]

The importance of the office of strategos autokrator, held by Crocos and Theodorus, is illustrated by the fact that they both, like the strategos whose name began with *Ph*, left their marks on the coinage. For two series of issues of Physcon bear in the field the initials of names beginning with *K* and *The*.[3]

It is further possible that the strengthening of the position of the strategoi in Cyprus about this time may be connected with the growth of piracy, which, especially in the hands of the Cilicians, had begun to flourish exceedingly with the decline of the Rhodian sea-power from about the middle of the second century. Although the general name for the pirates was Cilicians, that was only because the coast of Cilicia Tracheia was their original and most important haunt; but their example was followed in Syria, Cyprus, Pamphylia and Pontus, and almost all the coasts of the eastern Mediterranean. It is not possible to be certain how far the rulers of these regions connived at the practice.[4]

The successor of Physcon,[5] his elder son by Cleopatra III, Philo-

---

[1] *J.H.S.* IX, p. 225, no. 1. (So Mitford.)

[2] *O.G.I.S.* 143; Otto-Bengtson, p. 117, n. 2. They hold that it was in accordance with the express policy and written testament of Euergetes that an independent kingdom should be set up in Cyprus to accommodate the son who was not to be king in Egypt. In other words, the Empire was to be deliberately split up. This would be going much farther than the admittedly natural policy of sending princes to Cyprus with some sort of command. In any case this particular plan was eventually frustrated.

[3] Svoronos, nos. 1648–50 and 1651–2; Regling, pp. 384–5. The coins which Svoronos would connect with Seleucus (nos. 1412–14) are unimportant in appearance. As Seleucus was not autokrator, he may not have signed the coinage. The earlier instance of Polycrates shows, it is true, that a strategos could sign the coinage without possessing the office of autokrator; but that office, so far as our evidence goes, did not exist in his time.

[4] Appian, *Bell. Mithr.* 92–5; Kroll in *R.E.* II A, 1, 1039 f.

[5] On the date of the death of Physcon (28 June 116) see Otto-Bengtson, p. 113.

metor II Soter II, nicknamed Lathyrus, had for some reason encountered the hatred of his mother, who hoped to secure the succession for her younger son, Alexander. But she did not succeed in persuading the Alexandrian populace to her view; Lathyrus was recalled from Cyprus and it was Alexander's turn to retire thither (second half of 116). Nominally, he went as strategos; his mother's object, it was thought, was to hold him *in terrorem* over Lathyrus.[1] From 114/3, however, he counted himself as king, for in future reckoning his first regnal year is equated with the fourth of Lathyrus.[2]

To Alexander as king in Cyprus a letter was addressed by his cousin Antiochus VIII Grypus, in September 109, announcing that Seleucia in Pieria had been made a free city, as a reward for its fidelity to Antiochus and his father Demetrius II.[3]

The queen-mother ruled Lathyrus with a high hand. He had married, and was devoted to, his sister Cleopatra IV; her his mother compelled him to divorce before she allowed him to become king; he was forced to take as his wife his younger sister Cleopatra Selene.[4] The divorced Cleopatra made her way to Cyprus, where she raised an army which was doubtless intended for an invasion of Egypt, but which she eventually carried with her to Syria—a useful dowry for her when she became the wife of Antiochus IX.[5]

Before many years were over, however, the queen-mother, becoming tired of Lathyrus, who was perhaps showing too many signs of independence, staged an imaginary attempt on her life (108/7). Lathyrus had to fly from the threatened vengeance of the gullible mob, and betook himself to Cyprus, while Alexander was called to the throne on which

---

[1] The authority for these facts and suppositions is Pausanias, I, 9. 1, 2. Frazer, *ad loc.*, has confused this Ptolemy with Philometor I.

[2] Porphyr. Tyr. fr. 7. 3 (*F.H.G.* III, p. 721; Jac. 2 B 260, p. 1200); Otto, p. 120, n. 8. Otto-Bengtson's theory (pp. 162 f.) that Alexander was only strategos until 110, when he became king in Egypt, involves an arbitrary interpretation of the admitted certainty that he reckoned his regnal years from 114/3.

[3] *O.G.I.S.* 257; C. B. Welles, *Royal Correspondence in the Hellenistic Period*, New Haven, 1934, pp. 288 ff. The letter has also been attributed to Antiochus IX Cyzicenus, but the evidence seems rather in favour of Grypus.

[4] Justin, XXXIX, 3. 2.

[5] Justin, XXXIX, 3. 2, 3. Otto-Bengtson's conjecture (p. 147) that she was already in Cyprus, having been left there by Soter II to hold the island when he was called to the throne in 116, seems improbable. On the army recruited in Cyprus, see Bouché-Leclercq, II, p. 93, n. 1.

his mother had originally designed to place him.[1] The game of Box and Cox was fairly in progress.

The question has been raised whether, in this division of the Ptolemaic government of Egypt and Cyprus between two hands, we have a real division of the empire, or an arrangement of the two parts of the empire under one crown.[2] The question is perhaps academic, but it can be answered. Those who ruled in Cyprus, such as Physcon (when he had fled from Egypt, 131–129), Lathyrus, Alexander I, and "Ptolemy King of Cyprus", had their own coinage and own regnal dating. But, as regards the coinage, it must be observed that the types are not altered. Since the coinage is the most public expression of royal prerogative, we may take it that the claim of a ruler to the whole kingdom, confined though he may have been *de facto* to Cyprus, was never really relinquished. We shall therefore represent the Ptolemaic attitude towards the question fairly if we speak of these rulers as kings "*in* Cyprus" and not, at any rate not before the one who ascended the throne in 80 B.C., as kings "of Cyprus".[3] Even with this last ruler, the situation seems not to have been fairly faced, and the right of the Romans, when they took over the island in 58 B.C., was evidently not acknowledged in Alexandria, since the loss of Cyprus seems to have been the signal for the outbreak which drove Auletes out of his kingdom in 58.[4]

The last name in the list of recorded strategoi of Cyprus, until we come to the closing days of the Ptolemaic dynasty, is that of Helenus, son of Apollonius, who is commemorated in four inscriptions from Paphos and Salamis, and in a papyrus of 107/6. When Alexander went to Cyprus as strategos in 116, Helenus accompanied him; and when Alexander proclaimed himself king (between Sept. 114 and Sept. 113), he was promoted to be strategos and archiereus, but not nauarchos. For the nauarchia being the supreme naval command in the Mediterranean was, while there were kings both in Egypt and in Cyprus, retained in

---

[1] Paus. I, 9. 2; Justin, XXXIX, 4. 1; Porphyr. Tyr. *loc. cit.* (the Greek text gives the date, 10th year of Soter, 108/7); Bouché-Leclercq, *H.L.* II, p. 94, n. 2; Otto-Bengtson, pp. 178 f. Alexander may actually have been at Pelusium at the time (so Porphyrius); otherwise Lathyrus could hardly have ventured to Cyprus. Mitford thinks that he did not establish himself in Western Cyprus, but perhaps only in Salamis, and that is why the inscriptions of the strategos Helenus were defaced at Salamis but not at Paphos.

[2] Strack, pp. 64 f.

[3] So the consuls, according to the law preserved in the inscription at Delphi (below, p. 203), were instructed to write "to the king reigning in Cyprus", etc.

[4] Bouché-Leclercq, *H.L.* II, p. 142.

Alexandria, so that Alexander could not appoint Helenus to that post until he returned to Egypt (Oct. 107). The career of Helenus doubtless came to an end in 106/5 when Lathyrus re-established himself in Cyprus.[1] From that time onwards Lathyrus seems to have assumed the functions of strategos himself, for no strategoi are recorded during his reign. An *antistrategos*, Potamon son of Aegyptus, on the other hand, may have been appointed by him.[2]

Cleopatra, however, was ill content that Lathyrus should stay in Cyprus, except as her prisoner or a corpse; she gave instructions that he should be taken alive or dead, and the general in command, who allowed him to escape alive, paid for failure with his own life. We are assured (but may hesitate to believe) that it was not because the forces of Lathyrus were weaker, but because he hesitated to make war against his mother, that he retired,[3] apparently to Syria. Thence, however, he soon returned; for not only was he supported by those who had gone into exile with him, but of the remaining generals to whom Cleopatra entrusted the command of her troops, encouraged by the example which she had made of one of them, all (except two, the Jews Chelkias and Ananias, sons of Onias) promptly deserted to him.[4] He was established in the island by the end of 106 or beginning of 105.

He was evidently secure in his position, for he was able in 104, upon the invitation of the people of Ptolemais Ace, which was besieged by Alexander Jannaeus,[5] to embark on a futile adventure in Syria, whither

---

[1] *O.G.I.S.* 148; *J.H.S.* IX, 1888, p. 251, no. 109; LVII, 1937, p. 36; and Mitford, in his forthcoming *Studies*. The papyrus, as restored, describes Helenus as priest for life of Queen Cleopatra (III) Thea Aphrodite Euergetis, kinsman of the king, strategos, archiereus of the island and γραμματεὺς τοῦ ναυτικοῦ τῶν κατὰ τὴν βασιλήαν (P. Brux. E. 7155, *Chronique d'Égypte*, XXV, 1938, pp. 139 ff. For Apollodorus as the father's name Apollonius should be read, as Dr Bell informs me.) According to Otto-Bengtson (pp. 12, n. 6, and 220) the Helenus of the inscriptions held office early in the reign, and the Helenus of the papyrus was a different man; their arguments to this effect are unconvincing.

[2] So Mitford dates, *O.G.I.S.* 165.

[3] Justin, XXXIX, 4. 1–2.

[4] Strabo, fr. 3 (*F.H.G.* III, p. 491), ap. Joseph. *Ant. Iud.* XIII, 10. 4 (285–7). Strabo says that Lathyrus was joined at once by the majority, both those who returned from exile with him (some MSS. add ἡμῖν after συγκατελθόντες, which suggests that he was quoting Lathyrus himself or one of his adherents) and those sent afterwards by Cleopatra. He uses μετεβάλλοντο loosely, for those who went into exile with him never deserted him.

[5] Joseph. *Ant. Iud.* XIII, 12. 2 (328). Mitford (*Arch. f. Pap.* XIII, p. 35) connects the

he took a force of some 30,000 men to support Antiochus Cyzicenus, while his mother took the side of Grypus and the Jewish king. It all came to nothing (Lathyrus made an abortive attack on Egypt), and about 102 Lathyrus and Cleopatra were back in Cyprus and Egypt respectively.[1] Cleopatra now disappeared from the scene, to die in the autumn of 101, and a reconciliation was reached between Alexandria and Cyprus, Alexander marrying his niece Cleopatra Berenice, the daughter of Lathyrus.

Lathyrus thus remained in peaceful possession of Cyprus. The Romans regarded him as an ally or at least as a friend. The pirates in the Eastern Mediterranean were giving trouble once more, and one of the provisions of a law passed some time immediately after 100 B.C. was that the consul first to be appointed to deal with the pirates was to address letters to (among others) "the king reigning in Cyprus and the king reigning in Alexandria and Egypt and the king reigning in Cyrene and the kings reigning in Syria, all friends and allies of the Romans, pointing out that it is right for them to take care that no pirates should make any place under their rule a base for their fleets or be harboured by the inhabitants". The action taken by these rulers may have been ineffective, but their formal attitude was doubtless correct.[2]

In 95 Lathyrus interfered in the affairs of Syria once more, lending Demetrius Eucaerus, a son of Grypus, troops to enable him to set up as king in Damascus.[3] But he made no attempt to return to Egypt, until the opportunity came in 88, with the death of Alexander, who, after having been expelled from Alexandria by the populace according to the usual routine, sought refuge in Cyprus but lost his life there in battle with the Alexandrian admiral Chaereas.[4]

Larnaka altar, with its dedication to Zeus Soter and Athena Nikephoros, with this episode. Otto-Bengtson (p. 223) place it earlier, soon after 107/6.

[1] Joseph. *Ant. Iud.* XIII, 13. 3 (358).

[2] The provisions of this Law, in a Greek translation, are preserved in the Delphian inscription on the pedestal of Paullus Aemilius, E. Cuq in *C.R. Acad. Inscr.* 1923, pp. 129–50; *S.E.G.* I, 1923, p. 33, no. 161; III, 1929, p. 78, no. 378. Ormerod (*Piracy in the Ancient World*, 1924, pp. 242–7) and others have shown that this law is not the *Lex Gabinia* of 67 B.C., but must date between 100 and 96 B.C.

[3] Joseph. *Ant. Iud.* XIII, 13. 4 (370).

[4] Porphyr. Tyr. *loc. cit.*; Syncellus, p. 550 Bonn (a blundered copy from Porphyrius). From Porphyrius's word μεταπηδήσας it would appear that he actually reached Cyprus, and was not caught at sea. It does not, however, follow that Chaereas was strategos in Cyprus.

As a matter of course, Lathyrus was recalled to Alexandria,[1] and for eight years Cyprus was united to Egypt. We hear nothing of the island during this space, except that Sulla's lieutenant, L. Licinius Lucullus, visited it in 86 B.C. in his somewhat unsuccessful search for ships.[2] He had collected some from the Phoenician coast-cities; but on reaching Cyprus he was informed that the enemy were lying in wait for him. He therefore drew his ships ashore, and made enquiries in the various cities giving the impression that he intended to pass the winter there, but took a favourable opportunity to slip away to Rhodes.

Lathyrus died early in 80 B.C., leaving his daughter Berenice, the widow of Alexander I, whom he had associated with himself on the throne, its sole occupant. Alexander II, the son of Alexander I, was the only remaining legitimate representative of the house of Ptolemy, except Cleopatra Selene in Syria and her two sons. He was in Rome, whither he had been taken by Sulla. He was now sent back to marry Berenice and reign in Egypt. Within three weeks he had murdered her and been murdered in his turn by the mob. It was afterwards alleged at Rome that he left a will, in which, following the fashion of Hellenistic rulers, he bequeathed his kingdom (which would include Cyprus) to the Roman people. If there ever was such a will, it must have been extracted from him by Sulla while he was in Rome.[3]

To find a successor, the Alexandrians, without troubling themselves to consult the Roman Senate, turned to the illegitimate issue of Lathyrus. It may, however, have been in deference to the known dislike of Rome for a united Ptolemaic Empire that they now severed Cyprus definitely from Egypt. Of the two sons of Lathyrus by a concubine, they chose one, who became known as the Bastard or New Dionysus or Flute-player (Auletes), to reign in Egypt, while to his brother they gave the throne of Cyprus. This "Ptolemy King of Cyprus"—he was singular in having no nickname, perhaps because he lacked character—was to reign in the island until 58 B.C.[4]

---

[1] From the restoration of the inscription *J.H.S.* XII, p. 183, no. 20 (Strack, no. 137) proposed by Mitford, it appears that the troops left behind in Cyprus by Lathyrus dedicated statues to him, his wife Cleopatra Selene (who, it was hoped, after being three times married in Syria, might yet return to share her first husband's throne), and their daughter Berenice, the name of whose husband, Alexander, has been erased.

[2] Plut. *Lucullus*, 3; Appian, *Bell. Mithr.* 56.

[3] Bouché-Leclercq, *H.L.* II, pp. 118–19. Otto-Bengtson (p. 192) believe the will to have been not wholly forged.

[4] Trog. *Prol.* xl (omitting Alexander II).

It is not known whence the Alexandrians extracted this couple. A fragment of a speech by Cicero has been conjectured to mean that when Alexander II was killed, the future king of Cyprus was a boy in Syria.[1] From another source—Appian—comes a statement that Mithradates the Great of Pontus had betrothed two of his daughters, Mithradatis and Nyssa, to the kings of Egypt and Cyprus.[2] Though this is only mentioned in connexion with their death in 63 B.C., the betrothal must have taken place some time before, possibly at the time of the accession of the two kings, and as an element in the anti-Roman policy of Mithradates. But how he came into touch with these young men, and why it was from Syria that one of them at least came, is matter for speculation.[3] The betrothal, in the case of Auletes at least, came to nothing, for he was already married to Cleopatra Tryphaena by January 79 B.C.

There is no record of what action Rome took with regard to Cyprus; but it was many years before, in 59, Auletes, by the expenditure of much treasure in bribes and by humiliating himself in a way that earned him the contempt alike of his subjects and of those who took his money (and were naturally not averse to the continuation of so profitable a source of income), at last obtained the recognition of Rome, through Julius Caesar and Pompey. Their joint honorarium was 6000 talents. In this treaty, which recognized Auletes as king in Alexandria, ally and friend of the Roman people, Cyprus was ignored. Auletes has been blamed for betraying Cyprus; but since the Alexandrians had taken it upon themselves to give it an independent ruler, the blame must be shared with them. It is true that the king of Cyprus probably still looked upon himself as having a claim to the whole kingdom; at least he did not attempt to mark the complete independence of his island by any change in the types of his coinage.

To the Romans, however, these academic questions mattered little,[4] and when the time was ripe, they took Cyprus without consulting

---

[1] Cicero, *de rege Alexandrino*: "Quum ille Rex sit interfectus, hunc puerum in Syria fuisse." But who is *ille* and who is *hic* in this sentence is uncertain.

[2] Appian, *Bell. Mithr.* 111. These were the two girls who drank the poison which failed to have any effect on their father. At the time they were ἔτι κόραι, being brought up in their father's house. There is a difficulty about the interpretation of the passage; see Bevan, *Ptol. Dynasty*, p. 345, n. 3.

[3] As to which, see Bevan, *Ptol. Dynasty*, pp. 344 f.

[4] They at any rate took them less seriously than Strack, who observes (*Dyn. der Ptolemäer*, p. 65) that they annexed Cyprus without beginning a quarrel with Auletes about it.

Auletes or the Alexandrians. In 58 B.C., Caesar's henchman, the tribune P. Clodius Pulcher,[1] carried a law to reduce Cyprus to the condition of a province and confiscate the royal treasure, and Cato was appointed *quaestor pro praetore* to carry the transfer through.[2] On the part of Clodius it was a master-stroke of humour as well as policy thus to secure immense funds for his party, to get rid for the time, under cover of a professedly honourable mission, of the most obstinate of his opponents, and the man whose conscience must have been most revolted by his task, and to revenge himself for an old injury. For it was said that when Clodius was captured by Cilician pirates and appealed to the king of Cyprus to ransom him, he met with a refusal to pay more than two talents; a sum which even the pirates despised and returned, letting their prisoner go free without ransom.[3]

Avarice was, indeed, one of the charges trumped up against the unfortunate king, who was said to be grasping and ungrateful to his benefactors, a slave to his riches, and indeed despicable for every kind of moral vice. The charge of secret understanding with the pirates is hardly borne out by the episode of the ransom refused to Clodius, and is, indeed, mentioned by only one obscure commentator on Cicero.[4]

Indeed, the abuse lavished on the king of Cyprus has the air of being inspired by the desire to justify the robbery of his kingdom from a man whose worst fault was perhaps indolence. Had he been an active enemy of Rome, Cicero, even while glad of a stick with which to beat Clodius, could hardly have described him[5] as always the ally, always the friend

---

[1] The discreditable story of the annexation of Cyprus is in all the histories: Engel, *Kypros*, I, pp. 435 ff.; Drumann-Groebe, *Gesch. Roms*,[2] II, 1902, pp. 224–7; etc., etc. Recently, in G. Walter, *Brutus*, Paris, 1938, pp. 27 ff.

[2] Livy, *Epit.* CIV: "lege lata de redigenda in provinciae formam Cypro, et publicanda pecunia regia, M. Catoni administratio eius rei mandata est." Vell. Paterc. II, 45; cp. 38.

[3] Strabo, XIV, 6. 6, p. 684; Cassius Dio, XXXVIII, 30; Appian, *Bell. Civ.* II, 23. Chapot suggests (*Mélanges Cagnat*, p. 65), I know not on what authority, that the pirates only released Clodius on the approach of Pompey.

[4] *Schol. Bobiensia* ad Cic. *pro Sestio*, 57 (ed. Stangl, II, p. 133): "ferente autem rogationem Clodio publicatum fuerat eius regnum, quod diceretur ab eo piratas adiuvari." On the other hand, in the *pro Flacco*, XIII, 30: "Cyprum per Ptolemaeum regem nihil audere" apparently means, as Engel says (*Kypros*, I, p. 438, n. 47), that the king repressed the pirates who made Cyprus their base.

[5] *Pro Sestio*, XXVII, 59. In XXVI, 57, however, Cicero admits that he was not formally an ally. To Ammianus Marcell. XIV, 8. 15 he is "rex foederatus nobis et socius", and the motive for the annexation "aerarii nostri angustiae". Cp. Florus, III, 9: "sed

of Rome, a man whom to the knowledge of the Senate or of the Roman commanders no breath of serious suspicion had ever touched. There is no doubt that Cyprus was seized by Rome, not for any fault of the king's, but for the sake of his wealth, so welcome an accession to an empty treasury; and, allowing everything for Cicero's hatred of Clodius, it is impossible not to endorse the terms[1] in which he scarifies the author of the measure, and the disgrace which he brought upon the name of the Romans.

Cato, much against his will, departed on his mission.[2] In order to keep him absent as long as possible, Clodius imposed upon him as a first task the restoration of certain exiles to Byzantium. His status was that of quaestor[3] with praetorian imperium. Nevertheless, no government ship carried him; his suite included no military officer, but only two clerks, one of whom was a thorough-going criminal, the other a client of Clodius. Doubtless Clodius hoped that the king would make some show of resistance; if so, he was disappointed.[4] Cato perhaps himself expected that there would be trouble, and, having no force with him, prudently sent his friend Canidius Crassus[5] on before him to Cyprus to try and persuade the king to yield gracefully, offering him in the name of the Roman people a position in which he would lack neither wealth nor honour, that is to say the priesthood of the Paphian Aphrodite. He awaited Ptolemy's answer at Rhodes. When the news came, it was that

---

divitiarum tanta erat fama, nec falso, ut victor gentium populus, et donare regna consuetus, P. Clodio tribuno duce, socii vivique regis confiscationem mandaverit... quae res latius aerarium P.R. quam ullus triumphus implevit." Also Sextus Rufus Festus (ed. Foerster, 1874), c. 13: "...rex foederatus...penuria aerarii Romani...ita ius eius insulae avarius magis quam iustius sumus adsecuti."

[1] *Pro Sestio*, XXVI, 57; XXVII, 59. Cp. *De domo sua*, VIII, 20: "qui cum lege nefaria Ptolemaeum, Regem Cypri, fratrem Regis Alexandrini, eodem iure regnantem, caussa incognita, publicasses, populumque R. scelere obligasses: cum in eius regnum, bona, fortunas, patrocinium huius imperii immisisses, cuius cum patre, avo, maioribus societas nobis et amicitia fuisset: huius pecuniae deportandae, et si quis suum defenderet, bello gerendo M. Catonem praefecisti." On the reading *patrocinium* of the MSS. in preference to the *latrocinium* of the editors, see Otto-Bengtson, p. 193, n. 3.

[2] Plut. *Cato min.* 34–36; V. Chapot, "Les Romains et Cypre" in *Mélanges Cagnat*, 1912, pp. 66 ff.

[3] Vell. Paterc. II, 45; Aurel. Victor, *de vir. ill.* 80. 2.

[4] Chapot (*Mélanges Cagnat*, p. 67) regards this meagre retinue as an indication that no resistance was expected. The view expressed in the text seems to me more probable.

[5] The coins which Canidius was supposed to have issued in Cyprus were really issued in Cyrene. Robinson, B.M.C. *Cyrenaica*, p. ccvi.

the king had preferred death by poison to accepting the offer—a lucky thing, says Plutarch, for Cato—and that he had left a great treasure.[1] Doubting whether Canidius, in the circumstances, would be proof against temptation, Cato sent his nephew M. Brutus to supervise him, and himself went first to Byzantium, where he reconciled the exiles with the party in possession. When he eventually reached Cyprus,[2] he decided to realize in cash the immense mass of royal plate, furniture, precious stones and purple stuffs. With meticulous care, omitting no detail from his accounts, trusting no one of the officials or attendants at the sale, not even his own friends, personally appealing to the buyers to enhance their bids, he acted with a conscientiousness which was rare among Roman magistrates of his day, but which also shows how Roman *gravitas* can be not inconsistent with loss of dignity. Incidentally he gave offence to some of his friends by refusing to trust them. The sale realized something under 7000 talents.[3] To convey it in safety to Rome was a difficulty. He ordered to be made a number of cases, each to contain two talents and five hundred drachmae; to each of these was fastened a cord attached to a cork buoy which, if the ship was wrecked, would mark the spot. The treasure nearly all arrived in safety in the year 56, but an ironical fate saw to it that the two books containing, presumably in duplicate, all the details of his stewardship were both lost on the way. One of them he had entrusted to his freedman Philargyrus, who, putting out of Cenchreae, was lost with his ship. The other he carried himself as far as Corfù, where it also disappeared; he had camped in the market-place of Corcyra, where, the night being cold, the sailors lit fires, with the result that his tent was burned. The mouths of his enemies were stopped by the king's treasurers, whom he had brought with him (among them Nicias, for whose faithful stewardship Cato ob-

---

[1] Valerius Maximus (IX, 4, ext.), a hostile writer, says that he at first loaded into ships the great wealth which he had collected with miserly care, and which he saw was to be his undoing, and went out to sea, intending to scuttle the ships and drown himself with his treasure, and so deprive his enemies of their plunder; but could not bring himself to sink his gold and silver. Valerius, whose sense of humour seems crude, finds this ridiculous. Appian (*Bell. Civ.* II, 23) says that the king threw his treasure into the sea, which is certainly incorrect.

[2] Cassius Dio (XXXIX, 22. 3) says, somewhat innocently perhaps (so Chapot), that the Cypriotes received him gladly, expecting to become friends and allies of the Romans instead of slaves.

[3] For what follows see especially Plut. *Cato Minor*, 38, 39; also Cassius Dio, XXXIX, 22, 23. For the sum (which Chapot, p. 67, n. 2, seems to question) see above, p. 174.

tained his freedom from the Senate); but the loss of these books, which he had intended to serve as an example to others in charge of similar commissions, was a great disappointment to him. On arrival in the Tiber, Cato found everything prepared for something like a triumph, all the officials and all the populace crowding the river banks; but he rowed on in the royal galley to the docks, where he delivered the treasure, at which the crowd gaped the more. The Senate voted him an extraordinary praetorship and the scarlet-bordered toga, honours which he refused. The money went to finance the Civil War. It would perhaps, as Seneca said, have been better if Cato had been swallowed up by the sea with all the treasure.[1]

The detailed account of these proceedings has seemed worth reproduction, chiefly from Plutarch, with little abbreviation as a picture of the squalid background against which stands out the slightly stupid figure of the one man in whom something of the ancient Roman tradition survived. What Cato was really proud of, we are told,[2] was that no one was able to find fault with the way in which he had conducted the confiscation of the royal treasure and of the slaves of the royal household—prouder than of any gallant deed of war, since in that corrupt age it was rarer to find a man able to despise money than one who could conquer an enemy.

The slaves passed into the service of the state (though Nicias, as we have seen, was freed). It was the wish of Clodius that they should be called Clodii, but this, as well as a counter-proposal to call them Porcii, Cato was successful in preventing, and they were called Cyprii.[3]

We may note, as characteristic of both men, that a coolness arose between Cato and Cicero when (to the glee of their enemies) the orator later questioned the legality of Cato's mission, on the ground that the election of Clodius as tribune had been unconstitutional.[4] The fact that Cato executed the commission was enough, in his own opinion, to justify it.[5]

The annexation of Cyprus, it has been well observed,[6] was but the last stage in the encirclement of Egypt, following logically on the acquisition of Cilicia, Cyrene and Syria. Later, in 56, Cicero could write to Lentulus Spinther: "there is no *senatus consultum* which prevents

1 *Ad Marciam de Cons.* xx, 6.

2 Cassius Dio, xxxix, 22. 4.

3 Cassius Dio, xxxix, 23. 2.

4 Plut. *Cato Minor* 40.

5 Drumann-Groebe, *Gesch. Roms*,[2] v, p. 179.

6 Chapot, in *Mélanges Cagnat*, p. 66.

your having the right to restore Auletes to Alexandria; you, who hold Cilicia and Cyprus in your hand, can consider well what you are able effectively to undertake."[1]

Cyprus, then, became a Roman province. Its history as such will be described in the next chapter. But for a brief space it was to return to Ptolemaic rule, being treated as a valuable chattel by whichever of the leaders in the Civil War happened to be in a position to command it. After Pharsalus, Pompey, on the hapless voyage which was to end in the tragedy on the Egyptian shore, seems to have put in at Paphos,[2] where he must have learned of the conditions in Egypt which were to prove fatal to him. At this date the island was still a Roman province. But Julius Caesar, either before or after the riot which preceded the "Alexandrine War", is said to have restored it to the Egyptian crown, as an appanage to be enjoyed by the two younger children of Auletes, Arsinoe and the younger Ptolemy.[3] Still it was Cleopatra who drew the revenues, and issued coins for the island, on which she is represented holding in her arms the infant Ptolemy Caesar, her child by Julius Caesar.[4] Her strategos there at the time of the battle of Philippi was Serapion. To him C. Cassius Longinus, the tyrannicide, appealed for help, whereas Cleopatra's sympathies were naturally on the side of Dolabella. Whether willingly or no, Serapion, who had no instructions from Cleopatra, yielded to Cassius and sent him all the ships at his dis-

---

[1] Cicero, *ad fam.* I, 7. 4–5 (Tyrrell and Purser, 114).

[2] Orosius, VI, 15. 28. Valerius Maximus (I, 5. 6) says that he asked the name of a fine building which he noticed on the shore at Paphos, and was told that it was "Kakobasileia", which he accepted as a bad omen.

[3] Cassius Dio, XLII, 35. 5; Bouché-Leclercq, II, p. 193. As is well-known, Arsinoe, whom, with both the Ptolemies and Cleopatra, Caesar had with him, escaped with the help of the eunuch Ganymedes from his custody to the investing army, where she may actually have been proclaimed queen (Cassius Dio, XLII, 39. 1), and at any rate behaved as such. There seems to be no evidence that, as Engel states (*Kypros*, I, p. 456), Ganymedes took her to Cyprus. When the siege was over she fell into Caesar's hands and was sent to Rome, to figure in his triumph in 46 and eventually, in 41, to be murdered at Ephesus by the orders of Mark Antony at the request of Cleopatra. As to the younger Ptolemy, after the disappearance of his brother in Caesar's final crushing of the Alexandrine army, he was as a matter of course married to Cleopatra. He died in 45/4 B.C. Neither Arsinoe nor this younger Ptolemy really concerns the history of Cyprus. Engel's statement (*Kypros*, I, p. 456) that Julius Caesar let Herod the Great have half the revenue from the mines is a strange slip; it was Augustus who made this arrangement in 12 B.C. (see below, p. 238).

[4] B.M.C *Ptolemies*, Pl. XXX. 6; Svoronos, no. 1874.

posal. After the defeat of the Republicans he fled to Tyre, where Mark Antony, at the request of Cleopatra, had him put to death,[1] and appointed Demetrius, a freedman of Caesar, in his place.[2]

The possession of Cyprus with Egypt was confirmed by Mark Antony to Cleopatra in 36[3] when he left her for his disastrous Parthian expedition, and again on his return in 34 from his more successful Armenian campaign, when Ptolemy Caesar was associated with her. With her death in 30 B.C., and the murder of the boy, the island came finally into the hands of Rome.

---

[1] Appian, *Bell. Civ.* IV, 61. Cassius went to Cyprus in person, and wrote thence to Cicero on 13 June 43 B.C. from Krommyou Akra: Cicero, *ad fam.* XII, 13 (T. and P. 901).

[2] Cassius Dio, XLVIII, 40. 6.

[3] Plut. *Anton.* 36, 54; Cassius Dio, XLIX, 32. 5; 41. 2; Drumann-Groebe, *Gesch. Roms*,[2] I, 1899, p. 330.

CHAPTER X

THE ARTS IN PRE-ROMAN CYPRUS

The history which we have attempted so far to set forth has been an affair chiefly of drum and trumpet, punctuated with personal anecdotes of the petty courts of Cyprus. Of the intellectual or spiritual life of the island, so far as it is revealed in literature, we know practically nothing, and indeed it is impossible to say whether its literature had any special character of its own. The gallant attempt by Engel[1] to scrape together the information available about the cultural history of the Cypriotes results—apart from his analysis of the *Cypria*—in little more than a list of names of second- or third-rate authors. Judging from its contents, the epic of the *Cypria* had little to do with Cyprus, even if its author was a Cypriote. That there was early lyric poetry in the courts of Cyprus is suggested by an allusion in Pindar's *Second Pythian* to songs in praise of Cinyras. Cleon of Curium wrote a poem called *Argonautica*, from which Apollonius Rhodius, in his epic on the same theme, was accused of borrowing; whether he was identical with the elegiac poet Cleon is not certain. The island produced no tragic writer,[2] and only recorded one writer of comedies or burlesques, Sopater of Paphos, and he appears to have lived, at least for a time, in Alexandria.[3] Choral and theatrical performances of course played their part in Cypriote life, especially at Salamis, whither artists flocked from the time of Euagoras I. Kings of Salamis and Soli furnished choruses at Alexander's competitions at Tyre, and inscriptions of Ptolemaic date frequently mention the guilds of Dionysiac artists. From Graeco-Roman times all the larger cities must have had their theatres, though only Curium, Soli and New

---

[1] *Kypros*, I, pp. 594–716. See also Sakellarios, Κυπρ. I, pp. 776 ff. As this goes to the printer, I receive the Διαλέξεις περὶ τῆς Κυπριακῆς ποιήσεως of the "Kinyras" Society (Paphos, 1938), with a useful study of ancient Cypriote poetry by K. Spyridakis (pp. 1–24). On the *Cypria*, see above, ch. V, pp. 90–2.

[2] The tragic writer Dionysius, mentioned along with Criton, a kitharode, and a satyric poet whose name is lost, in a fragmentary decree of the college of Dionysiac artists (*B.C.H.* LI, pp. 144–7; *S.E.G.* VI, 813), will hardly be counted against the statement in the text.

[3] Körte in *R.E.* III A, 1, 1001–2. As late as the seventies of the third century.

Paphos have so far revealed theirs. But the significance of all this for literary history is negligible. Of historians, the best known is the Peripatetic, Clearchus of Soli, a pupil of Aristotle; and what is preserved of his is chiefly interesting for the light it throws on court-life in the fourth century. It is not history of a high standard.

There is, however, one figure outstanding from this mediocre level, and that is the philosopher Zeno of Citium, the founder of the Stoic school, and one of the most distinguished names in the history of philosophy.[1] Whether the Phoenician blood which was in him must take any credit for his greatness, it is impossible to say; but, as in the case of Thales of Miletus, to whom Herodotus gives a Phoenician origin, it may be that a mixture of blood was favourable, as it so often is, to the birth of genius. But Zeno's work was not done in Cyprus, and his life, or the part of it that counted, was passed in Athens. He is supposed to have died about 264. It is one of the ironies of history that the island proverbially notorious for luxury should have produced the founder of the Stoic philosophy. A less famous Cypriote name in philosophy was Eudemus, a Platonist and friend of Aristotle, who dedicated to him the "Eudemus, or concerning the Soul". He died in 354, killed in a battle of Dion's supporters against Callippus at Syracuse.[2] It seems that the better philosophers did not find the air of their native land congenial.

The bearing on Cypriote history of the remains of architecture, sculpture, metal-work or pottery has been noticed incidentally in the preceding chapters; and in a general history so much is all that can as a rule wisely be attempted. But a slight general sketch may be permitted.[3]

---

[1] For a recent study of Zeno see Spyridakis in Διαλέξεις περὶ τῶν κορυφαίων Κυπρίων φιλοσόφων καὶ πεζογράφων (pp. 1–26), Paphos, 1937.

[2] Cicero, *de Div.* I, 53; *R.E.* VI, 895.

[3] In compiling this chapter I have profited by many valuable criticisms and suggestions from Prof. Bernard Ashmole. On Cypriote art, especially sculpture, before the Roman period, the following special works may be consulted:

L. P. di Cesnola. *Descriptive Atlas of the Cesnola Collection of Cypriote Antiquities*, Vol. I, Sculpture. Boston, Mass., 1885.

G. Perrot and C. Chipiez. *History of Art in Phoenicia and its Dependencies.* 2 vols. London, 1885.

J. L. Myres and M. Ohnefalsch-Richter. *Catalogue of the Cyprus Museum.* Oxford, 1899.

A. de Ridder. Collection de Clercq, Tome V. *Les antiquités chypriotes.* Paris, 1908.

W. Déonna. *Les Apollons archaïques*, esp. pp. 301–6. Paris, 1909.

J. L. Myres. Metropolitan Museum of Art. *Handbook of the Cesnola Collection.* New York, 1914.

It is unfortunate that so little is left of the architecture before the Byzantine period; little more, indeed, than the plans of a few buildings. They tell us that the Cypriotes used, both in sacred and in secular buildings from the Bronze Age, with survivals (as in the Temple of Paphos) down to Roman times, the tripartite *liwan* type of building (a middle room opening on a court, with a smaller room on each side of it)—a type which is also found especially in Anatolia (whence it seems to have been carried by the Etruscans to Italy) and in northern Syria.

In spite of the influence exerted in some of the minor arts of Cyprus, especially pottery, by Mycenaean art, it is remarkable that Mycenaean architecture did not affect the island. The typical Mycenaean built *tholos*-tomb, for instance, is not found there;[1] burials of Mycenaean character are made in tombs of Cypriote style.[2] The Cypriotes, so far as we know, were satisfied with the architectural methods of their neighbours; why alter them, especially when the soft limestone made the excavation of tombs in the living rock such a simple matter?

The first palace at Vouni, dating no earlier than about 500, is the Cypriote expression of the *liwan* type of house mentioned above. It is not until about a century later that, in the second palace, the Greek idea of the megaron penetrates.[3] It has been observed, as an example of

---

C. Picard. *La Sculpture antique*, pp. 214–19. Paris, 1923.

A. W. Lawrence. "The Primitive Sculpture of Cyprus", in *Journal of Hellenic Studies*, XLVI, 1926, pp. 163–70.

V. Müller. *Frühe Plastik in Griechenland und Vorderasien*, pp. 148–66. Augsburg, 1929.

F. N. Pryce. *British Museum Catalogue of Sculpture*, vol. I, part II, Cypriote and Etruscan. London, 1931.

E. Gjerstad. "Die schwedischen Ausgrabungen auf Cypern", in *Die Antike*, IX, 1933, pp. 261 ff.

E. Gjerstad and others. *The Swedish Cyprus Expedition*, Vols. I, II, III. Stockholm, 1934–7. Vol. IV to follow.

A. Westholm. *The Temples of Soli*. Stockholm, 1936.

E. Gjerstad in *Archäologischer Anzeiger*, 1936, cols. 561–86 (Cypriote sculpture to about 500).

S. Casson. *Ancient Cyprus, its Art and Archaeology*. London, 1937.

[1] Casson, p. 61, quoting Schachermeyr, *Hethiter u. Achäer*, pp. 98 ff. (or rather 103).

[2] But modifications due to Mycenaean models do appear in the Transitional and Early Geometric periods, as Daniel has noticed. (*Amer. Journ. Arch.* XLI, 1937, p. 57.) Cp. Schaeffer, *Cuneiform Texts of Ras Shamra-Ugarit* (1939), p. 29.

[3] Gjerstad, in *Corolla Archaeologica*, 1932, pp. 145–71; Westholm, *Temples of Soli*, 1936, pp. 153 ff.

PLATE VII

British Museum

CAPITAL FROM SALAMIS

Cypriote survival-obstinacy, that the mud-bricks of which the walls of the palace are constructed in part are of the same thin tile-shape, and almost of the same dimensions, as the modern Cypriote mud-brick, which is quite different from that used in Greek lands.[1]

Other palaces, as at Salamis and Paphos, may have resembled that at Vouni, but were probably on a more magnificent scale, corresponding to the luxurious habits of the kings. No trace of them, so far as excavations have yet told us, remains. And, in general, architectural remains of the pre-Roman period are too scanty to allow of a critical estimate of its quality.

One architectural feature, however, must not be ignored. The column-capital, in ancient architecture, is the test of style. For in it the architect can go sadly astray, when he allows the exuberance of his fancy to obscure the constructive element. The Greeks took the lotus-capital, which was originally conceived as a flowering or decoration at the top of the shaft, and refined it down, so that it gave a real transition to the architrave, and visibly transmitted to the shaft the pressure of what it supported. Other styles, such as the Persian, sometimes show less constructive sense than an intelligent child with a box of bricks.

The Cypriote volute-capitals, of which a few examples survive in position, as on the half-columns flanking the entrances to tombs at Tamassus,[2] are ultimately of Egyptian origin, but the fact that they are common in Phoenicia-Palestine indicates that the Cypriotes borrowed them from the mainland, and not *vice versa*, and that what is Egyptian in them, as in so many other products of Cypriote art, came through Phoenicia.[3] The earliest in Cyprus may be dated to the sixth century. They fail to express the true function of the capital.

---

[1] Casson, pp. 5 f.

[2] The architecture of these tombs shows the imitation in stone of wooden construction, which suggests that much of the architecture which has disappeared was of the latter material. Lycia presents the same phenomenon.

[3] These capitals are of the type which, from its occurrence later in Aeolis, has been given the conventional name "Aeolic"; it is also frequently called "proto-Ionic". Examples dated to the tenth century have been found at Megiddo (G. Schumacher, *Tell-el-Mutesellim*, I A, 1908, p. 118, and H. G. May in *I.L.N.* 26 May 1934, p. 836). These were probably used in the same way as at Tamassus, on door-jambs; but from Megiddo also comes a pottery model of a shrine in which they are used at the corners of the building (*ibid.* p. 837). Examples said to have been found at Samaria seem to be as yet unpublished. For Cypriote examples in the Louvre, etc. see Perrot and Chipiez, *op. cit.* I, pp. 118 f.; *K.B.H.* Taff. XXVI, LVIII, LIX, cp. CLXIII. The Phoenician

In the well-known bull's head capital from the agora of Salamis (Pl. VII)[1] the volutes of the Ionic capital have been developed into the foreparts of bulls by the architect's fancy—not necessarily under Persian influence—and he has made an attempt at expressing the function of the capital, by inserting between them a caryatid figure which supports the weight of the abacus on its head and upraised arms. This capital has much more constructive character than those from Dali and Athienou. One may imagine the architects of Euagoras I attempting in this way to improve on Oriental fashions.

It is, as we have said, unfair to attempt an estimate of Cypriote architecture with the meagre material at our command. With sculpture, the case is different. Thanks to the facility with which the Cypriotes worked in stone and clay, we possess a great mass of material, at first on a small scale, afterwards, from the end of the seventh century, in large statues, from which an estimate of the quality of Cypriote sculpture can be formed. From the beginning, the influence of the neighbouring mainland, the Syro-Anatolian region, is dominant in the creation of the art of the Early Iron Age.[2] The "snow-man" technique (in which the separate parts are first modelled separately and then kneaded and stuck together) is not an independent discovery of Cyprus, but is adopted from the mainland, and mainland types are reproduced in a native style; modifications are shown only in details of decoration and the like. The Phoenicians, as we have seen, acted as carriers rather than as creators, bringing to Cyprus the inventions of other races. The century of Assyrian domination left little mark on Cypriote art; the connexion of the island with the mainland had for long been so close that the

---

disk under an inverted crescent is to be noted. On the palmette element, see H. Danthine, *Le palmier dattier et les arbres sacrés dans l'iconographie de l'Asie orientale ancienne*, Paris, 1937, pp. 208–9. The use of the capital or its pattern as a decorative element is frequent (e.g. Nimrud ivories, *Iraq*, II, Pl. XXIII, 2 and 4; and the Amathus sarcophagus).

[1] A. H. Smith, *B.M. Sc.*, II, 1900, no. 1510, Pl. XXVII. Fourth century B.C., probably.

[2] V. Müller, *op. cit.* p. 165. Gjerstad (in *Die Antike*, IX, 1933, p. 270) explains the stylistic likeness between the North Syrian and the oldest Cypriote plastic art by community of race. On the general character of Cypriote sculpture, Déonna (*Les statues de terre-cuite en Grèce*, p. 37) suggests that the character of softness, which is found in the works in stone, may be due to the great development of clay plastic, as seen in the terracottas. Many processes borrowed from clay technique are recognizable in Cypriote stone sculpture.

a

ropolitan Museum, New York

b

SARCOPHAGI OF AMATHUS AND GOLGI

Assyrian occupation could not make a clearly-cut impression on the art of the island-subjects of Sargon, Sennacherib and Esarhaddon. It has been shown that what there is of Oriental influence, in certain sculptures which are supposed to be Assyrian in style, flows rather from the neighbouring Syrian region.[1] The finds at Arsos and Leukoniko show that the oldest votive statues, at the former place in Egyptizing dress, and at the latter of the so-called Assyrian type, with long foldless drapery and mantle and pointed helmet, are followed immediately in each place by types showing Ionic Greek influence; and the two styles must therefore be more or less contemporary, and cannot be earlier than the beginning of the seventh century.[2] Egyptian influence is traceable in figurines as early as the seventh century, but it probably came not direct but through Phoenicia. For direct influence, there is no material evidence before the time of Amasis, and that is limited in extent. By early in the sixth century there was in Cyprus a flourishing art of statuary, as is illustrated by the votive figures from Ayia Irini, which begin about 600. But it is not there that the Egyptizing style is seen. It is found on temple-sites of south-eastern Cyprus.[3] Cyprus at this time is divided into two provinces in the domain of art; the distinction is not confined to sculpture, but extends to metal-work and ceramics. Now the province in which the Egyptizing style is found corresponds to the area most affected, according to the records, by Phoenician colonization, although, as we have seen, even in Phoenician strongholds like Citium no purely Phoenician art took root. What the Phoenicians did bring there was the Egyptizing element; and what resulted was a characteristic Cypriote art which had taken in certain Egyptian elements in the form which had been given to them by the Phoenicians. The Egyptian conquest may have outwardly favoured the development of the Egypto-Phoenician style (as we have seen, Egyptian royal portraits may have been imported, though none have been found in excavations), but this would probably have come about had there been no Egyptian conquest at all.

Perhaps the best illustration of the last flowering of Orientalizing Cypriote art, before Greek influence became predominant, is to be

---

[1] A. W. Lawrence, *op. cit.*; V. Müller, as above. The colossus from Amathus may show strong Assyrian influence (Dussaud in *Mon. Piot*, XXI, 1913, p. 7), but there is no reason to suppose that the channel was not Syria.

[2] Goethert in *Arch. Anz.* 1934, col. 99.

[3] See for what follows especially Gjerstad, *loc. cit.* pp. 271 f.

found in the famous sarcophagus from Amathus (Pl. VIII *a*),[1] with its elaborate mixture of Oriental motives and ill-regulated ornament. Of these ornaments, some are obviously of Greek derivation, others as obviously come from Egypt, whether directly or through Phoenicia; in both cases the execution is gross and unintelligent. The Golgi sarcophagus (Pl. VIII *b*) shows these exuberances pruned away, and the inspiration is much more definitely Greek, received, however, through painting rather than sculpture. This sarcophagus shows how the Cypriotes by the beginning of the fifth century had developed a characteristic style in which the Greek influence completely dominates the Egyptian.[2] And Cypriote it remains, even though, after the turn of the century, a Persian flavour may occasionally be discerned. A colossal statue at New York of an effeminate priest of Aphrodite, holding a dove, represents Cypriote sculpture at its most impressive, though not at its most attractive (Pl. IX).[3]

By the beginning of the fifth century, however, these Oriental forces fade before a mightier from the West, and an Ionic Greek style becomes dominant,[4] prevailing even in the province which we have described as subject to Egypto-Phoenician influence. In the early years of the century this Graeco-Cypriote style gives us perhaps the most attractive examples of the sculptor's art from the island. The *kore* from Vouni and the smiling head from a limestone statue from the same place (Frontispiece)[5] have something of the grace of the Greek works which inspired them, something of the charm of French Gothic. Nevertheless, it is only necessary to put them beside such works to see their weakness.

---

[1] Myres, *Ant. Denkm.* III, Taff. 1–4 and *H.C.C.* no. 1365. Myres dates it *c.* 550–500, which seems more probable than Casson's first quarter of the fifth century (p. 203). The Golgi sarcophagus (Myres, *Ant. Denkm.* III, Taff. 5, 6 and *H.C.C.* no. 1364) is, as Picard says (p. 216), later (so Myres, about 500–450).

[2] Myres (*H.C.C. loc. cit.*) surely exaggerates when he finds only the slightest hint of provincialism in the Golgi sarcophagus, and holds that it, "if made in Cyprus at all, must have been carved by an artist trained in one of the greatest schools of the Aegean". Probably the nearest he ever got to the Aegean would have been Lycia.

[3] Myres, *H.C.C.* no. 1351. The effeminate type has inspired the unhappy idea that the figure represents the bearded Aphrodite who was worshipped in Cyprus (above, p. 79).

[4] Gjerstad's theory (p. 273) that the Persian conquest, embracing the Ionian coast as well as Cyprus, brought the two districts closer together, seems to me far-fetched. Relations were lively enough without that compelling force.

[5] Published by Gjerstad, *op. cit.* Taff. 28, 29; also *S.C.E.* III, Pls. LI and XLVIII.

Metropolitan Museum, New York

PRIEST OF APHRODITE

The head just mentioned is the lineal ancestress of the fourth-century head from Potamia to which we shall come later. And degeneration begins to set in, so that, at the time when Athens was producing its greatest masterpieces, Cyprus had declined to a lifeless and stereotyped formulary.

It may seem at first sight inconsistent with the development of native sculpture in the fifth century—beginning on a fairly high level, and declining rapidly after the middle of the century—that the evidence of such a site as the necropolis of Marium[1] shows no imports of Attic pottery in the older graves down to about 450, after which the imports are resumed, though in less quantity than in the sixth century. But the taste for fine Greek vases does not necessarily carry with it a talent for sculpture on a large scale. And, in any case, the relations with Athens, which had been lively in the early years of the fourth century under Euagoras I, were broken off after his death, and never resumed.

It is inherent in the nature of sculpture, more than of other arts, that only the very best, or that which gives promise of developing into the best, is tolerable, except as a curiosity or an illustration of history. Cypriote sculpture never shows such promise of development; but it is so far interesting as it affords an accurate reflection of the character of the people who produced it. It is significant that the good marbles and the hard limestone which the island possesses were ignored by the local artists until Ptolemaic times, when the sculptors fell into line, to the best of their ability, with the Alexandrian style.[2] Up till then the Cypriotes contented themselves with the soft limestone, which by its structure favours a flatness of treatment.[3] This physical feature is only an expression in plastic form of a lack of mental keenness, of a natural indolence. A race with more mental activity would have been able to make more of its contacts with neighbouring races, coming from lands enjoying

---

[1] P. Hermann, *Das Gräberfeld von Marion*, 1888, pp. 24 f. In sculpture the fully developed fourth-century style follows without a break on the severe archaic (or the Cypriote form developed therefrom). See above, p. 126.

[2] Westholm, *Temples of Soli*, pp. 186 f. But it is pointed out that probably even at this time the marble sculptures at Soli were not made in the island, but imported. On the development of Hellenistic sculpture in Cyprus see the same book, pp. 188 ff. The date, second century B.C., given by Goethert (in *Arch. Anz.* 1934, col. 80) to the fine Pentelic marble sarcophagus at Bellapais is of course a misprint for second century after Christ.

[3] Myres, *H.C.C.* p. 130.

the most lively culture of their time, even though it only knew them as invaders whose sole aim was to exploit the resources of the island.

It is not, therefore, very likely that the cutting off of Cyprus from Greek influence during the greater part of the fifth century, and even more so after the reign of Euagoras I, was responsible for the degeneration in the native style. At the best, had that separation not taken place, more work might have been produced of the quality of the fourth-century heads from Arsos and Potamia. The female head from the former place (Pl. X)[1] is likely to become the most popular production of a Cypriote chisel that has yet come to light. This remarkable head presents a surprising contrast between the rather blank expressionless front view and the interesting individuality of the profile. The technique is also well above the usual level for Cyprus, and the whole conception has the charm of the freshness which is lost in the academic copies of fourth-century sculpture with which it has the good fortune to be compared. But this head is unique in quality among the products of Cypriote sculptors. As to the "Apollo" head from Potamia,[2] it is necessary to observe that the enthusiasm which this head excited at the time of its discovery in 1933 can only have been due to the deplorably low level of the rest of the fourth-century sculptures with which it was contrasted. In its weakness, which is that of a good-looking and rather attractive youth who lacks character, and may in bad company become vicious, it is a singularly accurate reflection of the Cyprus of its time.

It has been suggested[3] that it was the very policy of Euagoras, with his exaltation of Greek culture, that was responsible for the decline in the fourth century. It made the Cypriotes think that they were not Cypriotes but Greeks; they thus lost their national consciousness and aimed at an imitation of Greek art instead of cultivating their own. "The belief of the Cypriotes that they were Greeks was the cause of the downfall of their culture." As we have seen, however, the seeds of this decay were sown at a very early stage, and the native soil was favourable to their development.

In one, though a minor, branch of plastic art, and that is the coins, we can see very clearly the result which was produced for a time by the

---

[1] *S.C.E.* III, Pls. CXCIV, CXCV; Casson, Pl. I and p. 199.

[2] *I.L.N.* 23 Dec. 1933; Cyprus Museum, *Annual Report*, 1933, frontispiece; Casson, Pl. XV, 1, and p. 195, n. 4, where it is said, surprisingly, to be inspired by such work as the imported marble head mentioned below (p. 225), which is at least a century earlier.

[3] Gjerstad, *loc. cit.* p. 280.

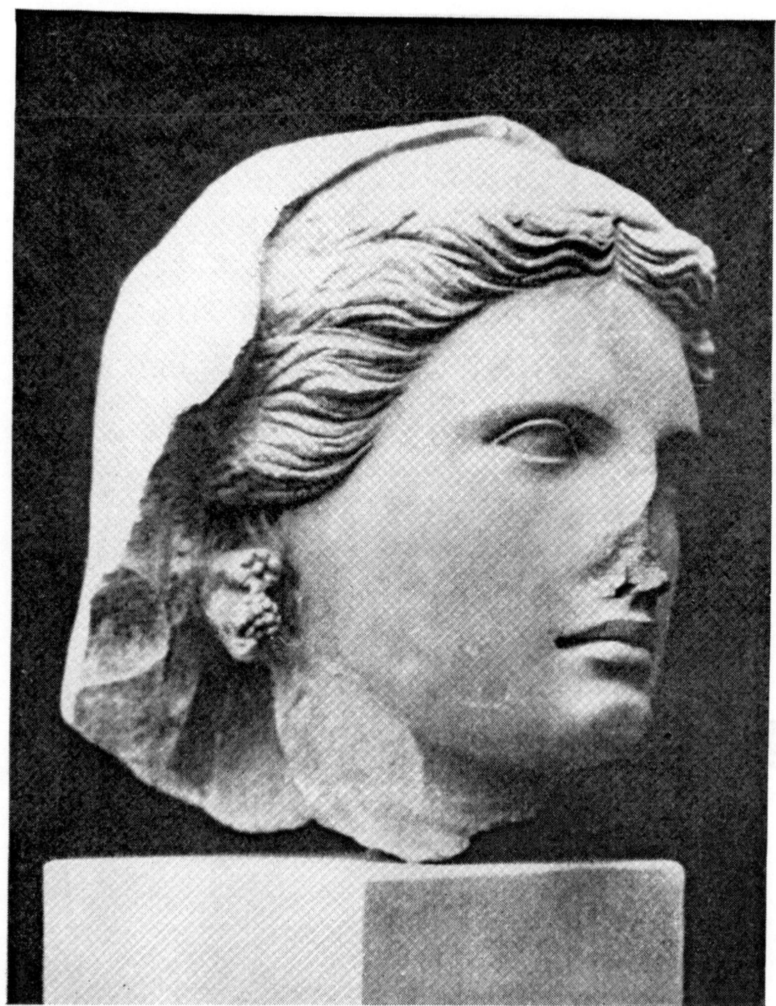

Cyprus Museum *Phot. Seymer*

HEAD FROM ARSOS

admiration of an influential ruler for all that was Greek. The coinage of Euagoras I stands out from the rest of the Cypriote series by reason of its excellence; the bearded head of Heracles (Pl. V 3a),[1] for instance, is well up to the average of the coinage of Greek cities of the same period. We know that it was the practice for die-engravers to receive commissions to work for cities or rulers other than their own—as a Syracusan engraver made dies for Opuntian Locris, and perhaps an Arcadian of Stymphalus for Chersonesus in Crete. Possibly then Euagoras employed a Greek engraver for the dies of his more important coins.[2] But the effect was not lasting, and the coinage of his successors no longer rises to the same level. A contemporary coin of Paphos,[3] so far as it is possible to judge of it in its ill-preserved condition, must have shown the same high quality; the figure of Aphrodite-Nemesis on the reverse is still magnificent (Pl. V 1). The distinctness with which this coin stands out in the Cypriote series makes it unlikely that it was the work of a native die-engraver.

There is, however, a record that Cyprus produced one artist who made a name for himself, the bronze-worker Styppax. True, that his fame is probably due chiefly to the legend which identified him with that slave of Pericles who was miraculously cured, after a fall from a building on the Acropolis, by a herb which Athena revealed in a dream to his master. He was the artist of the "Splanchnoptes"—a figure of a slave roasting the entrails of a sacrificed victim and blowing the fire with puffed-out cheeks.[4] Whether he was identical with the Styppax who made the starting-barrier in the hippodrome at Olympia is doubtful.[5]

In metal-craft it would be surprising if the land which produced bronze in such plenty was responsible for nothing original. An attempt has been made to credit Cyprus with the invention of the fibula or

---

[1] B.M.C. *Cyprus*, Pl. XI, 17; Spyridakis, *Euagoras I*, nos. 1, 3, 7.

[2] Such, possibly, was not only the Heracles head already mentioned, but also the seated youthful Heracles (Spyridakis, no. 8); it is unfortunately too much damaged to allow of an estimate of its quality; but the smaller denominations appear to be by a less accomplished hand.

[3] B.M.C. *Cyprus*, Pl. VIII, 7.

[4] Pliny, *N.H.* XXXIV, 81; XXII, 44; cp. Plut. *Pericl.* 13. References to modern literature in *R.E.* IV A, 454 (Lippold).

[5] He is mentioned in a brief list of famous engineers in a papyrus of the second century B.C. This does not suggest that he was an artist, though it does not prove the contrary. See H. Diels, *Antike Technik*,[3] 1924, p. 30, n. 1.

safety-pin,[1] which came into use in Greece, in substitution for the plain pin; but it more probably came from the north towards the end of the Mycenaean period, and reached Cyprus with other elements of Mycenaean culture, although, once there, it followed its own line of development.[2] But there is a group of bronze tripods and other allied stands, covering the period from the Late Mycenaean to the Geometric, which seems to be specially associated with Cyprus.[3] The origin of the bowls of mixo-oriental style, which have been mentioned in a previous chapter (p. 101), is uncertain; but in any case, even if, as some think, the credit for these productions may be given to Cypriote craftsmen, yet what has been said of Roman decorative art, that it never succeeded in escaping from Bond Street, may be applied to them.

The craft of the terracotta figure enjoyed a remarkable development in Cyprus. The comparative ease of modelling in clay, and the cheapness with which numerous copies of a model could be produced by pressing clay into a mould made from it, rendered it possible to meet without too much labour the immense demand for votive and funerary figures. These sometimes attained a colossal size, and the skill with which they were fired does no little credit to the Cypriote craftsman. The need for large figures in this material seems to have disappeared with the development of sculpture in stone; but the magnitude of the demand, before that came about, may be gauged by the crowd of figures which were dedicated at a mere rural sanctuary such as Ayia Irini (Pl. III). Incidentally, the painted decoration of Cypriote terracotta figures provides almost the only surviving indication—helped out by certain of the vases—of another art, for which Cyprus was once famous, the art of weaving. The ornamentation of the tunic worn by a colossal figure from Salamis, now preserved only in fragments, is an example.[4]

---

[1] Thompson, *Liverpool Annals*, v, 1913, pp. 10–12.

[2] Blinkenberg, "Fibules grecques et orientales" (*K. Danske Vid. Selsk., Hist.-fil. Medd.* XIII, 1, 1926), pp. 230 ff.

[3] W. Lamb, *Greek and Roman Bronzes*, 1929, pp. 32–5.

[4] According to Athenaeus (II, 48 b) the greatest names in the art of weaving were Akesas and his son Helicon of Salamis in Cyprus. A dedication at Delphi bore the couplet: τεῦξ' Ἑλικὼν Ἀκεσᾶ Σαλαμίνιος ᾧ ἐνὶ χερσὶ/πότνια θεσπεσίην Παλλὰς ἔπνευσε χάριν. Their date is not known; see Leonard in *R.E.* VIII, 1912, 8 f. For Akesas and Helicon and patterns on the terracottas of Cypriote monuments such as the large terracottas from Salamis (*B.M. Terr.* nos. A 107–19) in connexion with textiles, see E. Kunze, *Kretische Bronzereliefs*, 1931, p. 96, and especially E. Buschor, *Beiträge zur Gesch. d. gr. Textilkunst* (München Diss. 1932, pp. 47–50). As Prof. Wace points out

British Museum

a

b

TERRACOTTAS FROM LAPITHOS AND LARNAKA

But it was in making the small terracottas that the Cypriote village craftsman really enjoyed himself, as a child enjoys playing with his modelling clay, and with very much the same result—a technique which may be rudimentary, but nevertheless frequently gives expression to a lively and perhaps not always intentionally humorous fancy. This can be seen well illustrated in most collections, but as good an example as any is the group in the British Museum of votive figures from a cave near Lapithos [1]—figures of goddesses or women carrying infants, holding votive offerings, or playing musical instruments (Pl. XI *a*), crudely modelled, some in high relief against a flat background, others in the round with columnar or bar-like bodies, and picked out with bright colours, red, purple, green, yellow and black—a gay company.

In the period of Hellenic influence, the productions of the terracotta craftsman naturally became less quaint, and, as naturally, execution was not as a rule adequate to conception. An example is a somewhat impressive grave-statue of a seated woman, 0·755 m. high, in the Berlin Antiquarium, from a fourth-century tomb at Marium.[2] The head seems to have been from a mould, but the figure was modelled freehand. The claim, which has been made for it, to be the work of an Attic artist seems to be preposterous; it is rather an illustration of the inability of the native Cypriote to preserve the inspiration of his model, in this case doubtless a figure of Pheidian style. If it was made for the fourth-century tomb in which it was found, it indicates a time-lag which is in itself significant.

An important series of statuettes from a shrine of Artemis Paralia at Larnaka [3] includes some which have been claimed as Greek work and as early as the fifth century. Here again the claim seems unwarranted, and the best of the statuettes, a throned figure of the Cyprian Aphrodite (Pl. XI *b*), can hardly be earlier than the second quarter of the fourth century. There was, it is known, at Peiraeus, towards the end of the

---

to me, it is a mistake to speak of this decoration generally as "embroidery", the art being in most cases that of weaving.

[1] *B.M. Terr.* nos. A 127–46.

[2] Hermann, *op. cit.* pp. 40 f. and Taf. 1. It is ascribed to the late fifth century; but other figures found with it are of the fourth century.

[3] *B.M. Terr.* nos. A 261–395. The figure discussed in the text is A 261; reproduced in C. A. Hutton, *Greek Terracotta Statuettes*, fig. 13, and elsewhere. It has been supposed that the moulds for these figures were made in Athens and exported for use by craftsmen at Citium. That would be spoiling the original artist's market. But I doubt whether these figures are actually of Attic workmanship.

fourth century, and probably earlier, an important community of Citian traders, who in 333/2 were allowed to found a temple of their Aphrodite.[1] It may safely be conjectured that the cultus-figure was of the type represented by this Larnaka statuette, even if no closer connexion can be established.

Cypriote pottery is a subject of bewildering complexity, of which even the most competent specialist would be puzzled to give a brief summary. For the most part more curious than beautiful, it shows at two periods developments which are not paralleled elsewhere. The first is in the Bronze Age, when the potters break out into the most fantastic and, it would seem, unpractical constructions, such as have been described in an earlier chapter (pp. 56 f. and Pl. II *a*). The second is in the seventh century, when a pictorial style succeeds the Geometric. Here again a light-hearted rejection of all the conventions of ordinary ceramic decoration often surprises us. The results—as in the vases decorated with a single object, such as a bird (Pl. XII) or a ship—however infantile the technique, are nearly always lively and amusing, and sometimes show some feeling for colour. It has been remarked that the influence of this pottery, painted in matt red and black, in a tradition which goes back a very long way in the Near East, but is almost unknown in the Aegean, was felt in Crete, where it affected a local and short-lived fashion.[2] This pottery offers a pleasant relief from the dreary series of the more usual wares, which is all that the Cypriote could produce so long as he was subject to the discipline of his craft. These vases and those of the Bronze Age mentioned above (and, we may add, the quaint series of jugs, ranging from the end of the sixth century down to Hellenistic or Roman times, in which a small female figure holding a jug is modelled seated on the front of the shoulder of the vessel)[3] illustrate, like the early terracottas, the Cypriote character at play. When it tries to rise to seriousness, it is apt to be only dull.

The history of Styppax shows that Cypriote artists of talent, like Cypriote philosophers, were attracted from their native island to Greece, where there was more scope for them; although it might have been expected that the rulers of the Cypriote cities, whose wealth was so great and whose interest in art and literature, in some cases at least, must have been lively—witness the relations of Euagoras and Nicocles with Isocrates—might have given employment to native talent. Some evi-

---

[1] Above, ch. VII, p. 152.

[2] Payne in *B.S.A.* XXIX, pp. 281 f.

[3] Myres, *H.C.C.* nos. 936 ff.; Casson, pp. 204–5. The liquid issues from the small jug held by the figure.

Metropolitan Museum, New York

SEVENTH-CENTURY VASE

dence of that sort of interest, in respect of sculpture, is forthcoming; but it took the form of the importation of good work from abroad.

A very elegant archaic torso of a nude youth in the British Museum,[1] which was found at Marium, and dates from the late sixth century, is generally accepted as of Ionic Greek origin, whether "Island-Ionic", "Samian" or "East-Ionic". Another piece of Greek origin, the head of a youth, from an unknown site, is in the Nicosia Museum; but this is of later date, may be of the second quarter of the fifth century.[2]

But the finest of all works of sculpture of which the provenance is claimed for Cyprus is the well-known bronze head of Apollo at Chatsworth. This noble head, which is of Greek work, although its school is difficult to determine, dates from about 460 to 450. It is said, on good authority, to have been found at Salamis.[3]

Better known than any of the pieces already mentioned, except the last, is the pretty statuette of Artemis at Vienna,[4] which was found at Larnaka, whither it must have been imported in ancient times, and probably not long after it was made. A work of Praxitelean style, it has even been suggested, though without much conviction, that it may have been made as a parergon by the master himself, perhaps when he was working at Cos or Cnidus.

---

[1] Pryce, *B.M. Sc.*, I, i, p. 155, B. 325, Pl. XXXIV; Homan-Wedeking in *Ath. Mitt.* LX–LXI, 1935–6, p. 211.

[2] Markides in *J.H.S.* XXXIII, 1913, p. 48, Pl. I (Peloponnesian?); F. W. Goethert in *Arch. Anz.* 1934, col. 98 (Greek-Ionic); Westholm, *Temples of Soli*, p. 187 (compared with pediment sculptures of Olympia). I omit here the fragment of a large *kore* in the Cyprus Museum, which, according to Westholm, *loc. cit.* n. 11, appears to be not archaic but archaistic, and the relief from Mersinaki (early fourth century) because it does not seem to be pure Attic (*ibid.* n. 12).

[3] Furtwängler, *Intermezzi*, 1896, pp. 3 ff. Burlington Fine Arts Club, *Exh. of Greek Art*, 1904, no. 8. A. J. B. Wace in *J.H.S.* LVIII, 1938, pp. 90–5. Furtwängler referred it to Pythagoras of Rhegium; Mrs Strong left its school undetermined. As to the place from which it came, Mr Francis Thompson, Librarian and Keeper of the Collections at Chatsworth, kindly communicates the following entry from a volume in which the sixth Duke of Devonshire arranged documents relating to his purchases: "Note of 7 objects of antiquity bought by His Grace the Duke of Devonshire at Smyrna. March 1839. No. 1. A large Bronze head of Apollo found amongst the ruins of Salamis in Cyprus." The note is signed "H. P. Borrell". Borrell was a prominent merchant of Smyrna, who dealt in antiquities, and had the best reputation. But of course he may not have had first-hand information on this point.

[4] *Jahrb. d. kunsthist. Sammlungen des A. H. Kaiserhauses*, V, Pls. 1, 2; *K.B.H.* Taf. CCIII, 5; Furtwängler, *Masterpieces of Greek Sculpture*, 1895, fig. 141 (who makes the suggestion mentioned in the text); W. Klein, *Praxiteles*, 1898, p. 317; Beazley and Ashmole, *Greek Sculpture and Painting*, 1932, fig. 125 (second half of the fourth century).

CHAPTER XI

THE ROMAN PROVINCE[1]

When taken over by the Romans, Cyprus seems to have been associated with Cilicia,[2] which had been a Roman Province since 103 B.C. The first Roman to govern Cilicia after 58 B.C. has not up till now been identified.[3] Whoever he was, he was followed by P. Cornelius Lentulus Spinther (the consul of 57 B.C. and the man to whom Cicero owed his return from exile), who held the province from 56 to July 53 B.C.[4] His

---

[1] Marquardt, *Römische Staatsverwaltung*, I,[2] 1881, pp. 390 ff.; Schiller in *Handb. der Altertumswiss.* IV,[2] 2, 1893, pp. 185 f.; D. Vaglieri in Ruggiero, *Diz. Epigr.* s.v. *Cyprus*, 1910; Zannetos, Ἱστορία τῆς νήσου Κύπρου (1910), ch. vii; V. Chapot, "Les Romains et Cypre", in *Mélanges Cagnat*, 1912, pp. 59–83; Oberhummer, art. *Kypros* in *R.E.* XII, 1924, pp. 105 f. A slight sketch in A. H. M. Jones, *Cities of the Eastern Roman Provinces*, 1937, pp. 371–5. The few pages in Sakellarios may be ignored. Chapot's study has been invaluable in the compilation of this chapter, which carries the history down, approximately, to the separation of the Eastern and Western Empires in 395. It has had the advantage of the criticism of Prof. J. G. C. Anderson, who kindly read it in draft.

[2] Strabo, XIV, 6. 6, pp. 684–5, says that when the Romans took it, it became στρατηγικὴ ἐπαρχία καθ' αὑτήν, i.e. a separate praetorian province, as it was in his day. But there is no doubt that Cicero, when he became governor of Cilicia, was also governor of Cyprus, and it is probable that the same arrangement prevailed under his predecessors P. Lentulus and Appius Claudius. Cassius Dio (LIII, 12. 7, 8) mentions Cyprus and Cilicia and Phoenicia and Egypt as being in 27 B.C. Imperial Provinces; afterwards, Cyprus was handed back to the people (i.e. was made a public or proconsular (so-called "senatorial") province). He adds that he names these provinces in that way because each had in his time (the third century) its own governor, whereas anciently they had been combined two, or even three, under one.

[3] When Lentulus took over Cilicia in 56, he had the customary formal meeting with T. Ampius Balbus (Cicero, *ad fam.* III, 7. 5 (244 T. and P.), where *Lentulus Ampio* should be read for *Lentulus Appio*; Drumann-Groebe, *Gesch. Roms*,[2] II, p. 462, n. 8). It was accordingly supposed, on the ground of this passage of Cicero, and *ad fam.* I, 3 (97 T. and P.), that Ampius was proconsul of Cilicia; but as a matter of fact Asia was his province (Waddington, *Fastes*, pp. 59–60). When Lentulus went out to govern Cilicia, that province was enlarged by attaching to it part of what had belonged to the praetorian province of Asia: to wit, the three assize-districts (*dioeceses*, *conventus*) of Laodicea or Cibyra, Apamea and Synnada; this is the reason why Lentulus had to take over formally from Ampius. The arrangement was continued under the governorship of Appius Pulcher and Cicero, as is proved by Cicero's Letters.

[4] Cicero, *ad fam.* I, 7. 4 (114 T. and P.); Drumann-Groebe, *Gesch. Roms*,[2] II, pp. 462 f.

successor Appius Claudius Pulcher, the consul of 54 B.C., took it over in July of the next year, and held it until 51 B.C. Cicero (much against his will) was named as his successor early in that year,[1] and left Rome for the province in May. Arriving in August, he remained until 3 August of next year, having handed over the province to the quaestor C. Coelius on 30 July.[2]

Cicero's predecessors had regarded their provincial governorships as opportunities for personal gain, and had clung to them as long as possible; Cicero had every intention to deal honestly by the provincials, but was determined not to remain for more than a year. To Cyprus he despatched, for a few days only, as prefect with power to administer justice, Q. Volusius, whom he held to be an honourable and trustworthy man, in order that the few Roman citizens who were on business in the island should not be able to say that they could not have justice done them; for it was not lawful to summon the Cypriotes themselves to a court outside Cyprus.[3] Cicero found that his predecessors had exacted from the wealthy cities large sums of money as compensation for not having soldiers billeted on them in the winter; the Cypriotes, for instance, paid 200 Attic talents in this sort of blackmail. From this island, he says, not a single penny shall be exacted; nor will he allow any honours to be decreed to him, such as statues, shrines, *quadrigae*; verbal thanks alone will he accept. This was a great contrast to the confessed behaviour of Cicero's predecessors, under whom the plunderers who had descended upon the island like locusts had been actively encouraged. Cicero describes at length the methods of two of them, M. Scaptius and P. Matinius, friends and agents of M. Brutus.[4]

---

[1] Drumann-Groebe, *op. cit.* II, pp. 165 f. Appius Claudius, according to Cicero, was a bad administrator, favouring the tax-farmers and people like Scaptius (of whom, later). He complained that Cicero would not allow the public funds to bear the cost of provincial deputies going to Rome to bear witness in his favour; Cicero held that they should pay their own expenses: *ad fam.* III, 8. 2–5 (222 T. and P.).

[2] Drumann-Groebe, *op. cit.* VI, pp. 94–154.

[3] Cicero, *ad Att.* V, 21. 6 (250 T. and P.). Yet they came to Tarsus later for the case of Scaptius.

[4] Cicero, *ad Att.* V, 21 (250 T. and P.), 10–13; VI, 1 (252 T. and P.), 5–7; 2 (256 T. and P.), 7; 3 (264 T. and P.), 5. See Engel, *Kypros*, I, pp. 449–53; Liebenam, *Städteverwaltung*, 1900, pp. 337 f.; Drumann-Groebe, *Gesch. Roms*,[2] IV, p. 25; Tyrrell and Purser, *Corr. of Cicero*,[2] III, pp. 337–44; Gelzer in *R.E.* X, 977–80; G. Walter, *Brutus*, Paris, 1938, pp. 33 ff.

Brutus, it will be remembered, had been sent on by Cato to superintend the handling by Canidius of the property of the deposed king of Cyprus. He and Cato did not waste the opportunity which their visit gave them of establishing useful business-relations. Returning to Rome in 56, Brutus obtained for Salamis a considerable loan at 48 per cent.[1] There was some difficulty in effecting this, because the Gabinian Law[2] forbade provincials to raise loans in the capital. Brutus, however, was able by his influence to secure a *senatus consultum* exempting both the lenders and the Salaminians from any penalties under this law. After the money was advanced by Scaptius and Matinius, it occurred to them that the *senatus consultum* was of no avail, because another provision of the same Gabinian Law forbade judgment in favour of plaintiffs on a bond of this nature, in which more than 12 per cent interest was charged. The difficulty was got over by another *senatus consultum*: this bond should have the same validity in law as any others. All was thus well. Brutus himself, as he eventually admitted to Cicero, stood as security behind the ostensible lenders, Scaptius and company, for a large sum; they in their turn pledged to him their rights in the Salamis loan, so that, if it was not paid, he would be the loser. In order that Scaptius should be in a position to enforce payment Brutus obtained for him from the proconsul Appius Claudius the post of *praefectus* in the island, and he was thus in command of some troops of horse.[3] They were very useful to him, and when he insisted on payment and the city delayed, he imprisoned the Senate in the Senate House for some days, so that five of the Senators starved to death. He did not however obtain pay-

---

[1] This may seem exorbitant, but is paralleled at the time, e.g. Ditt. *Syll.*3 748, l. 37, and explained by the risky conditions of the period (Gelzer, *loc. cit.*). Six years afterwards the Salaminians estimated their indebtedness at 106 talents (reckoning 12 per cent compound interest), Scaptius at a little less than 200 (at 48 per cent). But it seems impossible from the details given by Cicero to arrive at the amount of the original loan.—As to the rate of interest, it may be noted that at the present day, by the Usury Law of 1919, the legal rate of interest must not exceed 12 per cent; so it was in the eighteenth century (Mariti, *Viaggi*, 1769, I, p. 297). This provision "is very easy of evasion and is indeed very often evaded" (Oakden, *Report on the Financial and Economic Resources of Cyprus*, 1935, p. 111).

[2] Whether the well-known law of 67 B.C. or the later Lex Gabinia-Calpurnia of the consulate of Gabinius, 58 B.C., is uncertain.

[3] Engel takes Cicero, *ad Att.* V, 21. 10 and VI, 2. 8 (250, 256 T. and P.), to mean tha Scaptius was made prefect of Salamis; Gelzer, that he was prefect of the auxiliary cavalry (*praefectus equitum*) in the island. The latter seems more probable.

ment, for when Cicero arrived in the province the matter was still outstanding; by 50 B.C., when he dealt with it, the debt had increased, according to Scaptius, to all but 200 talents; but Salamis admitted only 106 talents.

As soon as Cicero reached Ephesus, in July 51 B.C., representatives of Cyprus had met him and begged him to remove their persecutor. He at once gave orders for the withdrawal of the troops. But, when Scaptius demanded that he should be maintained in his office, he was told that, while the proconsul, out of consideration for Brutus, would see that he received his money, he would not be made prefect, since Cicero had decided not to give that office to anyone engaged in commerce in his province and least of all to Scaptius. Also 12 per cent interest would be permitted, and not 48 per cent; such was the rule that he had laid down in his edict on taking the province; and that edict would override any bond, whether supported by a *senatus consultum* or not. Brutus, to whom Scaptius complained, was indignant that Cicero should treat him (Brutus) so; and even Atticus thought Cicero was unreasonable. Could he not allow Scaptius a mere fifty[1] troopers? To which Cicero replied that fifty troopers could do no little harm among such gentle folk as the Cypriotes. Spartacus had begun his insurrection with a smaller troop.

The case came before the proconsul at Tarsus. Scaptius said that he was willing to accept 200 talents; the defendants that they were willing to pay 106; indeed, in a sense the money would be coming out of Cicero's own pocket, since he, unlike his predecessors, had not demanded from them presents, amounting to more than the debt to Scaptius. But 48 per cent stood in the bond, and Scaptius was able to put under Cicero's nose the *senatus consultum* of the year 56 B.C. which ordered whoever should be governor of Cilicia to decide in accordance with the terms of that bond. But, as a matter of fact, it did not authorize the exaction of an illegal rate of interest, and Scaptius expressed himself as ready to accept the sum due to him according to the legal calculation. The Salaminians produced the 106 talents, whereupon Scaptius, changing his mind, requested Cicero to allow the matter to stand over. He had seen the money, and hoped for more. Cicero weakly consented, although he recognized the shamelessness of the proposal, nor would he allow the debtor city to pay the money into a temple treasury (which would mean

---

[1] Chapot, p. 71, by a slip, says 500.

that no further interest would be charged). And so the matter rested for the decision of the next governor, whom doubtless Scaptius hoped to find more amenable.

The affair of Scaptius is a fitting pendant to the story of the taking of Cyprus by the Romans, and Plutarch missed an opportunity when he failed to make use of Cicero's deference to Brutus in his essay on *Shamefacedness*.

Cicero, even after he left his province, retained his interest in Cyprus. In 47 B.C. he wrote to C. Sextilius Rufus, who went in that year as first quaestor[1] to the island, warmly commending to him all the Cypriotes, especially the Paphians; and suggesting that he would do well to set an example to his successor, instituting reforms in accordance with the law of P. Lentulus and the decisions of Cicero himself.

From 47 B.C. until the death of Cleopatra Cyprus, as we have seen, returned to Ptolemaic rule. When in 27 B.C. the provinces came to be divided between Emperor and Senate, it was at first imperial—perhaps in combination with Cilicia. In 22 B.C. it was returned to the Senate,[2] to be governed henceforward by an ex-praetor with the title of proconsul, on whose staff were a legatus and a quaestor.[3]

With the reorganization of the Empire begun by Diocletian and carried further by Constantine the Great, the province of Cyprus fell into the first of the twelve great dioceses, that of the *Oriens*, commanded originally by the *praefectus praetorio Orientis*, then by the *vicarius Orientis*, and finally, from about 331, by the *comes Orientis*. Between 365 and 386, the Libyan and Egyptian provinces were separated off as a Diocese of Egypt. Cyprus remained in the Orient Diocese, which included Arabia, Mesopotamia, Palestine, Phoenicia, Syria, Cilicia and Isauria.[4] The provincial governor was a *consularis*, *vir clarissimus*. These con-

[1] Cicero, *ad fam.* XIII, 48 (929 T. and P.). From *primus in eam insulam quaestor veneris* we understand that hitherto Cyprus had had no quaestor of its own, but was under the quaestor of Cilicia-Cyprus. See Syme in *Buckler Anatolian Stud.* p. 324.

[2] Cassius Dio, LIV, 4. 1; Strabo, XVII, 3. 25, p. 840.

[3] The list of proconsuls and other officials is still very defective. The known proconsuls, legati and quaestors are enumerated in the Note at the end of this chapter.

[4] The authorities are the Veronese list *c.* 297, the *Notitia Dignitatum c.* 400, the list of Polemius Silvius *c.* 440 (all these in Seeck's edition of the *Notitia*), and Hierocles, *Synecdemus* (ed. Burckhardt, 1893, p. 36). The last may have been working *c.* 535 on a register drawn up under Theodosius II; see Jones, *op. cit.* p. 503. All conveniently set out in Bury's *Gibbon*, II, pp. 550 ff. and by Kornemann, art. *Dioecesis* in *R.E.* V, 1903, 727 ff. For Constantine's grouping see also Zosimus, II, c. 33 (pp. 98–9 Bonn).

sulares were appointed by the governor of the diocese, or by the Emperor on his recommendation.[1]

From the geographer Ptolemy we know that in the middle of the second century Cyprus was divided into four districts, those of Salamis, Paphos, Amathus (including Mt Olympus) and Lapethus. This arrangement very possibly went back as early as Augustus or earlier.[2] In any case it is curious that so important a city as Citium should have yielded place to Amathus.

Which of the places mentioned as existing in Cyprus in the period with which we are concerned had legal rank as cities, it is not possible to say with certainty, since none of the authorities before the time of Justinian can be assumed to recognize the distinction, and even later we may suspect that such a writer as Hierocles was not using information up to date. The most important places were: Paphos, at first the capital and a double community, including both Old and New Paphos; Salamis (afterwards Constantia), which gradually superseded Paphos; Amathus, Arsinoe, Chytri, Carpasia, Kerynia, Citium, Curium, Lapethus, Soli, Tamassus and Tremithus.[3]

---

[1] For Cyprus cp. Theod. Balsamon in Can. VIII Conc. Ephes. (Migne, *P.G.* 137, col. 365): πρὸ τοῦ ἀποξενωθῆναι τὴν βασιλείαν τῶν Ῥωμαίων ἐκ τῆς μεγάλης Ἀντιοχείας, δοὺξ ἐν αὐτῇ παρὰ τοῦ βασιλέως ἐπέμπετο, καὶ οὗτος στρατηγὸν εἰς Κύπρον ἀπέστελλεν, ὡς ὑποκειμένην τῇ Ἀντιοχείᾳ. The separation of Cyprus and other provinces from the administration of the Count of the Orient, however, took place, as we shall see, before the loss of Antioch. Sathas, Μεσ. Βιβλ. II, p. ιγ′. Constantine Porphyrog. *de Thematibus*, I, 15, shows that the fifteenth Theme was still supposed to be governed by a consularis in his time (although as a matter of fact Cyprus was not then in Byzantine hands). After the third century, "consularis" no longer implied that the person had actually been a consul, but was equivalent to provincial governor—such doubtless was Calocaerus who revolted under Constantine. The records of proconsular governors fail us early in the third century. Hereafter the names of governors can only be picked out here and there from sources not always historical. For example, Sabinus, who is said to have been governor during the persecution under Licinius (as to which the exceedingly unsatisfactory evidence is given by Hackett, *Orth. Ch. of Cyprus*, pp. 313, 325, 386, 420, 427; Sathas would put him in the seventh century!); Theodorus, at the time of the Council of Ephesus in 431 (Mansi, *Concilia*, IV, col. 1467); and so on.

[2] Ptol. V, 13 (14), 5; Engel, *Kypros*, I, p. 458. A. H. M. Jones, *Cities of the Eastern Roman Provinces*, p. 371, thinks it goes back to Ptolemaic times.

[3] Strabo omits Kerynia, and mentions several places (such as Aphrodisium, Arsinoe near Paphos) of quite minor rank because they were of importance to the sailor coasting round the island. Pliny's list seems to be peculiarly unauthoritative and disordered. He counts New and Old Paphos as two communities. He omits Lapethus, but adds

Paphos had been increasing in importance under the Ptolemies—perhaps because, now that there were no longer any local rulers, its fame as a religious centre gave it superior dignity, but perhaps also because of the silting-up of the harbour of Salamis, which was only slowly superseded by that of Arsinoe-Ammochostus. It seems, as we have said, to have taken definitely first place during the Roman period.[1] Its honorific titles, "Augusta Claudia Flavia, sacred metropolis of the cities throughout Cyprus", are enough to indicate its pre-eminence. This it retained until in the fourth century it yielded place to Salamis-Constantia. In 15 B.C. a severe earthquake laid it in ruins. Augustus came to the rescue with a gift of money, and decreed that the city should bear the name Augusta.[2] The title appears in inscriptions immediately or soon after that year.[3]

Epidaurum (of which no one else in antiquity makes mention, although Est. de Lusignan (*Chorogr.* fo. 17), followed by Kyprianos (p. 47), finds it in Pytharia in the Troödos district), and Golgi, which was or had been in existence (at Athienou, see p. 67, n. 4) but was probably of small importance in the first century. He mentions as dead places Marium, Cinyria (unidentified) and Idalium. His Corinaeum is perhaps Kerynia; but see ch. XII, p. 270, n. 6. As to Arsinoe, its place in all the early lists (except Pliny) is between Paphos and Soli, so that it is evidently the Arsinoe which superseded Marium at Polis tis Chrysochou (see below, ch. XII, p. 263, n. 1). The Arsinoe near Salamis is supposed to have had the see transferred to it after the destruction of Salamis by the Arabs, but later lists—though they may be copying from earlier—still speak of the see of Constantia or even Salamis. Tamassus and Tremithus are mentioned as early as Ptolemy as "cities" in the interior. The latter evidently became important as a junction on the road-system, which accounts for its appearance in the Tabula Peutingeriana (below, p. 237). If Stephanus of Byzantium can be taken as evidence for the time of Justinian, it was still only a village. But it had long been a see—Spyridon was bishop in 325, when Socrates (*H.E.* I, c. 12) speaks of it as a city. It is omitted by Hierocles but given by George of Cyprus; was it then, as Jones suggests (p. 374), raised to the rank of city before the time of George of Cyprus? There is, it may be remarked in passing, no evidence that Tremithus must have been originally a "village" of Citium, for there is no evidence that the power of that city extended so far.

[1] See above, ch. ix, p. 186, for the importance of Paphos under the Ptolemies. Cicero, writing to the quaestor Sextilius Rufus in 47 B.C., as we have seen (above, p. 230), specially recommended Paphos to his attention.

[2] Cassius Dio, LIV, 23. 7. Georgius Monachus (ed. de Boor, I, p. 294) confuses Paphos with Salamis and Cyprus with Syria in this connexion.

[3] *I.G.R.R.* III, 939=*O.G.I.S.* 581: base of a statue in honour of Marcia, wife of Paullus Fabius Maximus, erected by the senate and people of Augusta Paphos. The couple doubtless visited Paphos some time after 15 B.C.; probably before 11 B.C., since the consulship of Paullus is not mentioned; nor is his proconsulship of Asia, which dated probably in 9 B.C. (Waddington, *Fastes*, n. 59). There is really no evidence (*pace*

Cyprus Museum

HEAD OF BRONZE STATUE OF SEPTIMIUS SEVERUS

The island again received special consideration in A.D. 22.[1] The assumption of the right of asylum by the Greek cities of the provinces had become a scandal, and an enquiry before the Senate was ordered. The two temples of Aphrodite at Paphos and Amathus, and that of Zeus at Salamis, established their right before this tribunal. On a visit which Titus paid to Paphos[2] on his way to Syria in A.D. 69, after admiring the wealth of the sanctuary, he consulted the goddess, first as to his further journey by sea, which the oracle replied would be favourable. He then, in ambiguous phrases, enquired about his future prospects; the omens were generally favourable, and in a private interview with Sostratus, the priest, he received the assurance of his great destiny. It was doubtless in return for this excellent reception that Paphos was given the title of Flavia, although the inscriptions which record it are not earlier than the time of Severus.

The inscriptions bear witness to many other dedications to members of the Imperial family from the time of Augustus to that of Septimius Severus,[3] in whose reign the relations between the island and the Imperial family seem to have been close. The coins illustrate the temple of Paphos in a particularly elaborate way (Pl. V 8); and it may be noted that the most impressive Roman portrait found in Cyprus is the bronze statue of Septimius Severus, in the Museum at Nicosia (Pl. XIII).[4]

The *Koinon* of Cyprus, in the Roman period, first appears on the coins under Claudius, but was probably functioning from the beginning, in continuation of the system which had prevailed under the Ptolemies.[5] One of its chief functions would be the imperial cult, to

Dessau, *P.I.R.*[1] II, p. 49; see *R.E.* VI, 1781) that he was ever proconsul of Cyprus. Other inscriptions with the title Σεβαστή borne by Paphos: (*a*) *C.I.G.* 2629=*I.G.R.R.* III, 939; (*b*) *J.H.S.* IX, 1888, p. 227, no. 6=*I.G.R.R.* III, 941 (A.D. 15); (*c*) *J.H.S. vol. cit.* pp. 227–8, no. 7=*I.G.R.R.* III, 942 (Tiberius)=L.B.W. no. 2792; (*d*) *J.H.S. vol. cit.* p. 251, no. 107=*I.G.R.R.* III, 944 (Domitian); (*e*) Oberhummer, *Sbr. Bay. Akad.* 1888, p. 324, n. 13=*I.G.R.R.* III, 963. Later, by the time of Sept. Severus, the city had acquired the title Σεβαστὴ Κλαυδία Φλαουία Πάφος, ἡ ἱερὰ μητρόπολις τῶν κατὰ Κύπρον πόλεων: (*a*) L.B.W. no. 2785=*I.G.R.R.* III, 937; (*b*) *J.H.S.* IX, 1888, p. 252, no. 111=*I.G.R.R.* III, 947=*B.C.H.* LI, 1927, pp. 140–1=*S.E.G.* VI, 811; (*c*) *B.C.H. vol. cit.* pp. 139–43, no. 3=*S.E.G.* VI, 810.

[1] Tacitus, *Ann.* III, 62–3.

[2] Tacitus, *Hist.* II, 2–4; Suetonius, *Titus*, 5.

[3] Chapot, p. 77, n. 4.

[4] *Arch. Anz.* 1934, cols. 99, 101–2.

[5] A dedication by the Koinon in honour of Apollonia daughter of Craterus and her husband Patrocles son of Patrocles, founders of the Tychaion and high-priests for life

which there are scanty references in the inscriptions.[1] Another would be the control of the bronze coinage.

The Romans appear to have issued no coinage in the province until the time of Augustus.[2] From thence onwards to Caracalla, and perhaps to Elagabalus,[3] there is a fairly important series of issues. The only governors whose names they mention are A. Plautius (under Augustus) and Cominius Proculus (under Claudius, 43/44). On the coins of Claudius the *Koinon* of the Cyprians makes its appearance, and henceforward all the ordinary bronze[4] issues seem to be issued by the authority of this body, just as on the imperial Roman coinage the Senate had control of the coinage in the less precious metal. During the last three years of Vespasian, however, there was an extensive issue of silver by the Roman government. This series is the continuation of one which had been begun seven years before at Antioch on the Orontes; for some reason, perhaps as a special favour from Vespasian and Titus, the mint was transferred to Cyprus. The coins are dated by what is called "the new sacred year", with the numerals 8, 9 and 10, corresponding to 76/7, 77/8 and 78/9. It is not improbable that the transfer of the mint to Cyprus was connected with the measures taken to relieve the island

---

of Tyche at Paphos (*O.G.I.S.* 585), calls that city merely metropolis; but we can hardly infer from this that it is earlier than the time when Paphos received the title Augusta.

[1] Chapot, p. 78; *I.G.R.R.* III, 961: Ceionia Callisto Attica, wife of a high-priest of the Augusti; *ibid.* 994 (*O.G.I.S.* 582): Salamis honours Hyllus son of Hyllus, who had acted as gymnasiarch at his own expense in year 33 (of Augustus, i.e. A.D. 4) and as high-priest in Cyprus of Divus Augustus Caesar. (The rule against calling Augustus θεός during his lifetime was scarcely observed by the Greeks, as Dittenberger observes *ad loc.*) Where the office of high-priest or high-priestess is mentioned without qualification, it is to be assumed that it refers to the imperial cult: thus at Paphos, *I.G.R.R.* III, 948, 949(?), 950 (but the lady Claudia Appharion here is high-priestess of the temples of Demeter throughout the island), 951, 963 (?); Salamis, 995. We have also the high-priest and high-priestess of Tyche at Paphos (962).

[2] For the coinage of the province see B.M.C. *Cyprus*, pp. cxix–cxxxiv. It is unnecessary to repeat here the references to the older literature of the subject.

[3] According to Bosch, quoted by Westholm, *Temples of Soli*, p. 135, certain bronze coins of Elagabalus with ΔΕ (for δημαρχικῆς ἐξουσίας) in a wreath on the reverse, but no mint-mark (B.M.C. *Galatia, etc.* p. 205, nos. 447–50), were issued not, as hitherto supposed, from Antioch but in Cyprus. Otherwise the coinage stops with Caracalla.

[4] An extensive issue of bronze of two denominations, with the heads of Antoninus Pius and Marcus Aurelius Caesar, bears no indication that it was made in Cyprus, but, since specimens always come from the island, it was certainly minted there, for some special purpose unknown to us.

after the disastrous earthquake, which is generally dated to 77/8, but may have taken place a year earlier.[1]

The most interesting type of the coinage of this period, the Aphrodite temple at Paphos, has already been described in detail (Chapter IV, pp. 74 f. and Pl. V 8). A standing figure of Zeus, holding a libation-saucer in his right hand, and resting his left, on the wrist of which his eagle perches, on a short sceptre, is the only other type of importance. It probably reproduces the statue of the Zeus of Salamis. But it was doubtless issued, like all the other coins of the province, from the capital Paphos.

The institution of the province of Cyprus did not carry with it the inauguration of a provincial era, the various dates which have been associated with some such era being regnal years of the Emperors.[2] But the new calendar which was introduced at Paphos under Augustus illustrates the thorough way in which the new regime was officially recognized.[3] At some time between 21 and 12 B.C.,[4] possibly in 15 B.C., when Paphos received special favour from the Emperor after the earthquake, a calendar was introduced in which the names of the months all referred to Rome, and more particularly to the Julian family and its history. Aphrodite opens the year, not merely as the Paphian goddess, but as ancestress of the Julian family. But by the year 2 B.C. it was found desirable to revise the calendar. In that year Julia disgraced her name; Agrippa, Octavia and Drusus were dead; Tiberius had gone into exile. And so we find a new calendar instituted, in which the references are much more definitely to Augustus himself. The month of Aphrodite still opens the year, but the opening date is changed to 23 September, the birthday of Augustus.[5] The names of the offices held by him take the

---

1 The chroniclers may have put the earthquake in 77/8 in order to synchronize with the pestilence at Rome; they were evidently not quite certain of the date.

2 Dittenberger, *O.G.I.S.* 582, n. 2. A local era, dating from 182/3, has been noted at Paphos. Seyrig in *B.C.H.* LI, 1927, p. 140.

3 Kubitschek in *Oesterr. Jahresh.* VIII, 1905, pp. 111–16; A. von Domaszewski in *Archiv f. Religionswiss.* XII, 1909, pp. 335–7; Chapot, p. 75; Ginzel in *R.E.* XII, 1924, 58.

4 The month Agrippaios points to a date between 21, when Agrippa married Julia, and 12, when he died. The names of the months in this first calendar are Aphrodisios (May), Anchisaios, Romaios, Aineadaios, Kapetolios, Sebastos, Agrippaios, Libaios, Oktabios, Iulaios, Neronaios, Drusaios. Kapitolios must correspond to September, in which fell the chief festival of Jupiter, the *ludi Romani*; this shows that Aphrodisios was May.

5 The months are Aphrodisios, Apogonikos, Aineios, Iulos (Iulios?), Kaisarios,

place of the names of vanished members of the family. Rome takes the last place. The calendar expresses strikingly the lonely eminence on which Augustus now stood as the head of the Empire.

While this calendar was introduced, and used in Paphos and the western part of the island and even elsewhere, Salamis retained the Egyptian calendar with which it had become familiar under the Ptolemies, at least so far as the Egyptian names of the months were concerned; but the year began on 4 September, and the order of names was changed. The fact that the new Roman calendar was introduced in Paphos, while Salamis went on in the old way, reflects the change by which the former city had become the capital of the province. The confusion caused by this difference of calendars must often have been extremely troublesome; and it is not surprising to find Porphyrius, late in the third century, when he speaks of the date of a festival at Salamis, using the Paphian calendar.[1]

Of the road-system[2] which the Romans developed in Cyprus, as in all their provinces, we know only what is told us by a few milestones and by the Peutinger Map, a thirteenth-century copy of a map which dates from the time of the Empire (second to fourth century).[3] From this it is clear that a circular road ran round the island, keeping generally near the coast, except where it avoided the Acamas promontory and where it turned inwards over the Kerynia range to Chytri and thence to Salamis. Milestones recently discovered[4] show that in the west it

---

Sebastos, Autokratorikos, Demarchexusios, Plethypatos, Archiereus, Hestios, Romaios. Under later emperors the month Sebastos might be qualified by the emperor's name; thus an inscription of Old Paphos (*I.G.R.R.* III, 941) is dated on the first day Τιβεριείου Σεβαστοῦ.

[1] Above, p. 64, n. 5.

[2] See K. Miller, *Itineraria Romana*, 1916, pp. 827 ff. and, most recently, Gisinger in *R.E.* XIX, 1938, 1405 ff.

[3] Reproduced in *O.C.* p. 403. See also *O.K.* 106.

[4] Mr Mitford has kindly allowed me to use his draft of a forthcoming article on seven Roman milestones. They include three dating from the proconsulate of Audius Bassus; the cutting of the four inscriptions from which his proconsulate is known dates from between 28 Aug. and 10 Dec. 198. (I) Cyprus Museum, in two portions, both from places about 3 miles W. of Soli. Original inscription, a bilingual of Audius Bassus (198). This was partly deleted, and over it were cut at least two others, one between 9 Sept. 337 and April 340, and another perhaps 355–360. Distance III m.p. (II) About ½ mile S.W. of summit of Vouni. Year 2 of Macrinus and Diadumenianus, P. Cl. Attalus procos. Distance IV m.p. from Soli. (III) From Chrysochou, now in Ktima Museum. Between 25 Dec. 333 and 22 May 337. Distance III m.p. Traces of an

did not run across from Paphos to Soli on the line of the modern road which goes north from Stroumbi, but took the branch nearer the coast through Kathikas and Terra. From Citium a cross-road is marked passing through Tremithus and Tamassus to Soli.[1] The distances from Soli to Tamassus (XXIX) and from Tamassus to Tremithus (XXIIII) offer no difficulty, but that between Tremithus and Citium is given as XXIIII, which is about double the possible distance, and may be a mistake for XIIII. Tremithus was connected with Salamis direct, for the distance (XVIII) is marked although the line is not indicated. There is also a distance (XXIX) marked which may refer to a road between Amathus and Tamassus. This road must have turned considerably to the east to avoid the high ground; the distance as the crow flies is only about twenty-three English miles. We must regard the whole system as including a central road running the whole length of the central plain from Salamis to Soli, with side roads entering from the south, at Tremithus from Citium, at Tamassus from Amathus. There may have been one connecting Tamassus with Ledrae, but the latter place, afterwards to become the capital, was of small importance in Roman times.

Another road from Salamis served the Karpass, for at Ayios Theodoros has been found a milestone of the year A.D. 80 marking XVIII m.p. from Salamis.[2]

---

earlier inscription in Greek. (IV) At Terra, above Polis. Same as no. III, but distance VI m.p. (reckoned from Polis). (V) At Pano Arodhes, found about ¼ mile S.E. of the village. Audius Bassus procos. (Greek only). Same date as original inscription of no. I. Distance XV m.p. (reckoned from New Paphos). (VI) At Khapotami, E. of Kouklia (Old Paphos). Bilingual of Audius Bassus, same date as nos. I and V. Distance XIII m.p. (VII) At Mazotos, about 11 miles S.W. of Larnaka, said to have been found to the south of the village. Date probably between 8 Nov. 324 and 25 Dec. 333. Mileage lost. Mitford discusses the four other Cypriote milestones hitherto published, and shows that L.B.W. 2806 marks XV m.p. from Paphos, and L.B.W. 2807 VII m.p. from Curium. He traces the divergence of the modern road from the Roman, especially on the way N. from Paphos, as described in the text, and between Citium and Amathus, where it kept near the coast, whereas the modern road goes farther inland; there is also a short stretch from the Khapotami river to Pissouri, where the Roman road goes inland, the modern hugs the coast. Generally, so far as the evidence goes, the Turkish circular road followed the line of the Roman.

[1] Chapot, p. 83, makes the curious remark that this cross-road is the only road worthy of the name that has been maintained by the British Government. There is no modern road that follows such a line; and there are now some 870 miles of excellent roads (of which 640 miles are asphalted) which have been made and kept up since the occupation.

[2] *B.C.H.* III, p. 171; *Eph. Epigr.* V, 1884, p. 23, no. 32; *C.I.L.* III, 6732.

Milestones have also been found on the southern stretch of the coast-road; one of the year 198 between Pissouri and Kouklia; another, two hours from Curium towards Paphos, of Aurelian (271–275), renewed by Diocletian and Maximian (292–305) and Jovian (364), and others not yet published. Others come from the neighbourhood of Soli and Bellapais.[1]

The mines of Cyprus, which had been the property of the Cypriote kings and of their successors the Ptolemies, fell naturally to the Roman State.[2] In 12 B.C. Augustus allowed Herod the Great to take over a half of the output of the copper mines at Soli against a payment of a round sum of 300 talents.[3]

Some details concerning the mines of Cyprus are given by Galen, who visited the island about the middle of the second century, and describes a mine about 30 stades ($5\frac{1}{2}$ km.) from Soli, where the official in charge (*epitropos* of the Emperor) allowed him to visit the workings and take away specimens.[4] Among the miners in the fourth century were a number of Christians who in 310 had been transferred to the island from the mines in Palestine.[5] How far the mines continued to be

[1] *C.I.L.* III, 218, 219 (*I.G.R.R.* III, 967, 968). Two from the neighbourhood of Limniti (near Soli) are illegible. That between Bellapais and A. Epiktitos (Hogarth, *Devia Cypria*, p. 112; *C.I.L.* III, 12111) marks 35 m.p. from Salamis. The road must have wound considerably in crossing the Kerynia range, and perhaps, instead of descending sharply from the pass to Kerynia, as now, turned east to Bellapais; unless, indeed, as Mitford suggests, it crossed the range farther east at the low pass north of Leukoniko, and then went along the coast past A. Amvrosios and A. Epiktitos. But then it would have missed Chytri. On these stones, see K. Miller, *Itineraria Romana*, pp. 827 ff. (why he corrects Hogarth's 35 m.p. to 45 m.p. I do not know).

[2] Oberhummer's idea (*O.C.* p. 179) that the control of the mines was directly a function of the governor may be correct, but the inscription on which he bases it, according to which the ἀντιστράτηγος τῆς νήσου is ἐπὶ τῶν μετάλλων, is of Ptolemaic date (*O.G.I.S.* 165, and above, p. 175, n. 7).

[3] Josephus, *Ant. Iud.* XVI, 4, 5 (129). The way he puts the transaction is that Augustus and Herod made each other presents of half the produce of the mines and the sum of 300 talents, and that then Herod was given the ἐπιμέλεια of this half. Otto, *Herodes*, col. 93, points out that it is incorrect to say (as does Marquardt, *Röm. Staatsverw.* II,[2] p. 261, n. 1) that the whole of the mines were farmed out against half the produce.

[4] *De antidotis* (*Opera*, ed. Kühn, XIV, p. 7); *O.C.* p. 179; Chapot, p. 81; *S.C.E.* III, pp. 639 ff.

[5] Eusebius, *de martyr. Palest.* 13 (Schwartz, II, ii, p. 947; Migne, *P.G.* 20, col. 1513). According to the *Martyrologium Romanum*, 19 Kal. Jan., St Spyridon, bishop of Tremithus, had been condemned to the mines, presumably in Cyprus, under the Emperor Galerius (305–11). See below, p. 248.

worked in the Byzantine period is uncertain, but there are indications that they were not entirely neglected.[1]

But scanty light is thrown by the inscriptions[2] on the life of the cities. It has been observed as a singular fact,[3] which numismatists have not attempted to explain, that there was no municipal coinage; what coinage appeared was issued by the Koinon (or exceptionally, as we have seen, by the government) but not by the cities, and the types illustrate the cults of Paphos and Salamis, without referring to or, it may be presumed, exciting the jealousy of the other cities. Similarly the founders of the Tychaion at Paphos were honoured by the whole Koinon for their services and good will to the province and to their *patris*, i.e. Paphos.[4] This lack of rivalry—it can hardly be called strength of national sentiment—was, it is suggested, due to the long years of subjection to the Ptolemies, during which the inhabitants yielded obedience—willingly enough, it would seem—to rulers not of their own race. But the cause lay deeper than that. Cyprus, unlike many of the regions that were to become provinces of the Roman Empire, had hardly ever known anything like a democratic constitution; the people of the cities had almost without exception been the subjects of kings, and those kings ruled over single cities, not over a country including many cities in which individuality might have had a chance of development.

The cities had, of course, their municipal institutions,[5] and at Salamis, for instance, there was a council (*boule*), a popular assembly (*demos*), and a council of elders (*gerousia*). These bodies are usually known from inscriptions which record dedications in their name, but we have seen the Senate (presumably the *boule*) of Salamis playing an unhappy part in the quarrel with Scaptius (p. 228). Sometimes action is recorded as taken by the city (*polis*) generally, as at Salamis, Paphos, Citium and

---

[1] *O.C.* p. 180. Add Hudud al-'Ālam, *Regions of the World*, tr. V. Minorsky, Oxford, 1937, p. 59 (above, p. 10, n. 2). This work was compiled in A.D. 982/3. The view quoted in *S.C.E. loc. cit.*, that the mines certainly ceased to be worked between 364 and 700, and probably as early as 400, cannot accordingly be maintained.

[2] The details collected by Chapot, pp. 78 f.

[3] Chapot, p. 80.

[4] *O.G.I.S.* 585. Cp. *I.G.R.R.* III, 993: the Koinon honours Empylus of Salamis, but the only service mentioned is his acting as gymnasiarch at his own cost, and this was the concern of Salamis only.

[5] The evidence of the inscriptions in *I.G.R.R.* has been analysed by Chapot (pp. 78 ff.), who may be consulted for the references. The evidence is naturally very patchy, and further excavations may modify it considerably.

Curium; otherwise by the *boule* (Salamis, Citium), by *boule* and *demos* jointly (Salamis, Paphos, Lapethus), by *demos* alone (Salamis, Paphos), by the *gerousia* (Salamis).[1] At Soli, and doubtless elsewhere, the *boule* was chosen by a censor.[2] The Roman men of business in the larger cities may have had an organization of their own, though outside the municipal constitution; at Paphos, for instance, and at Salamis they combined to make dedications.[3] The municipal office of strategos survived into Roman times.[4] Public education was in the hands of the gymnasiarchs, who are mentioned at Paphos, Salamis, Citium and Lapethus, and frequently undertook the office as a liturgy at their own cost.[5] Most details are forthcoming from Lapethus,[6] in the reign of Tiberius, where Adrastus son of Adrastus built the temple and set up the statue of the Emperor in the gymnasium, appointing himself and his descendants gymnasiarch and priest of the gods of the gymnasium (Hermes and Heracles) in conjunction with his son Adrastus, who also chose himself to be gymnasiarch of the boys, all at their own cost. An ephebarch is mentioned in the same inscription, as also in one from Chytri; doubtless all the places with gymnasia had these officers, who, subordinate to the gymnasiarch, had special charge of the *epheboi* in the gymnasia. At Soli there was a public library (*bibliophylakion*).

Another special public service was rendered by citizens who went at their own expense on missions to the Emperor or elsewhere, on behalf of the island, like Heracleides son of Hermodamas of Citium, or Iulius Rufus of Paphos and Cleagenes son of Cleagenes of Salamis.[7]

Passing over other municipal officers of less importance, or about

---

1 *C.I.G.* 2639: [ἡ] κατὰ Σαλαμῖνα γερουσία. The *gerousia*, although its functions are obscure, was not a mere club; see Liebenam, *Städteverwaltung*, pp. 565 f.

2 *I.G.R.R.* III, 933. This man, Apollonius, was in charge of the public library and was also priest of Cybele, here called Pammateira. For Cybele at Soli as Aphrodite Oreia see Westholm, *Temples of Soli*, p. 149.

3 *C.I.L.* III, 12101 and 6051. This organization, as J. G. C. Anderson observes, would doubtless be a *conventus C.R....consistentium*, as elsewhere; cf. *C.I.L.* X, 3847, a dedication by [*C.R. in provi*]*ncia Cypro*, according to Mommsen's restoration.

4 Mitford in *Mnemosyne*, 1938, p. 110, n. 4, citing *B.M. Inscr.* 975 (Amathus).

5 The chief expense seems to have been the provision of oil, as in Graeco-Roman cities generally: Ramsay, *Cities and Bishoprics*, pp. 443 f.; Liebenam, *Städteverwaltung*, p. 375; Ditt. *O.G.I.S.* 479, n. 9.

6 *I.G.R.R.* III, 933; *O.G.I.S.* 583.

7 The latter two saw to the erection of a statue to Hadrian at Athens (*I.G.* III, 478 = *I.G.*[2] III, 3296).

whom we have for the most part but obscure information,[1] we note certain details of the functions of officials despatched from Rome. Thus a *logistes*, or *curator civitatis*, sent out to look after the finances, is recorded at Citium in the reign of Septimius Severus, and at Paphos under Caracalla.[2] The post of governor or inspector of the harbours (*limenarcha*) seems also to have been filled by an officer appointed from Rome.[3]

The general peace of the island under Roman rule was two or three times disturbed; indeed the Jewish insurrection of 115/6 was perhaps as grave a disaster as Cyprus ever suffered. There must have been a considerable Jewish population in cities like Salamis ever since Ptolemaic times.[4] Towards the end of the reign of Trajan, about 115/6, a wide-

---

[1] Chapot, p. 79: ἄρξας τῆς πόλεως at Citium; [οἱ ταμί?]αι ἄρξαντες at Soli. Ἄρχειν is probably a general term for or equivalent to στρατηγεῖν; cp. Ramsay, *Cities and Bishoprics*, pp. 368, 441, etc. At Salamis (*C.I.G.* 2639) the gerousia honoured a man who had been *agoranomos*, *dekaprotos*, and *pronoëtes*, and fulfilled other liturgies.

[2] C. Iulius Helianus Polybianus, *B.C.H.* LI, 1927, pp. 139–41.

[3] "Apollonius limenarcha Cypri", *C.I.L.* VI, 1440 (before Nero). The office is mentioned in the *Digest*, 11, 4, 4; 50, 4, 18, 10. He was doubtless in control of harbour-dues. For Egypt, see N. Y. Clauson in *Aegyptus*, IX, 1926. D. Stertinius Eision, twice limenarch in the little Boeotian port of Creusis (*I.G.* VII, 1826), can hardly have been an imperial official.

[4] Under Ptolemy I there seems to have been a considerable exodus from Palestine of Jews who settled in many places in the eastern Mediterranean, and Cyprus must have had its share of such settlers. Jewish communities in the island may have been charged with the duty of sending to Jerusalem the wine of Cyprus which was used in the sacrifices in the Temple (Neubauer, *Géog. du Talmud*, p. 369, quoted *O.C.* p. 23). According to I Macc. XV, 23, Cyprus was one of the many lands to which were sent copies of the letter which the Roman consul in 139/8 wrote to Ptolemy Euergetes II (Physcon), urging that the Jewish settlers should be well treated. The long list of kings and cities to which it was sent is not convincing; but there is no reason to doubt that there were many Jews in Cyprus at the time. (On the whole question of the authenticity of the letter and its relation to the *senatus consultum* in Josephus, *Ant. Iud.* XIV, 145, see A. Momigliano, *Prime linee di storia della tradizione Maccabaica*, 1931, pp. 151 ff. On the possibility of Κύπρος being a corrupt reading, Otto-Bengtson, p. 116, n. 4.) At the time of Hyrcanus, the Jews living in Egypt and Cyprus were in a flourishing state (Josephus, *Ant. Iud.* XIII, 284). Two at least of the generals who commanded the troops of Cleopatra III about this time (above, p. 202) were Jews. Later, as we have seen, Herod the Great had extensive interests in the island (p. 238), though whether a dedication at Paphos (*I.G.R.R.* III, 938) refers to him, or to another member of his family, or to Herodes Atticus, it is not possible to say. At the time of the mission of Philo Judaeus to Rome in the reign of Caligula (*Leg. ad Gaium*, 282), the most important islands, Euboea, Cyprus, Crete, were full of Jewish colonies. It was to the Jews in

spread insurrection of the Jews broke out in Cyrene, Egypt and Cyprus.[1] Expecting it to spread to Mesopotamia, Trajan entrusted to his terrible general Lusius Quietus the task of preventing it, which he did by wholesale massacre. Lusius was then sent to Palestine, which can hardly have been unaffected by the general unrest, and here again he carried out a ruthless pacification. Whether he went to Cyprus, we do not know.[2] In that island the Jews, led by one Artemion, are said to have perpetrated unspeakable outrages, following the example which had been set to them in Cyrene and Egypt. It is said that the dead in Cyprus numbered 240,000, and that Salamis was utterly destroyed and the non-Jewish population exterminated. The figure has been questioned, considering the present population of the island, which is roughly 350,000.[3] But Salamis was a very great city, and it has been calculated that the ancient aqueduct would serve some 120,000 inhabitants; so that double that number for the slain throughout the island is not incredible. We

---

Cyprus that the first Christians, who fled thither after the first persecution following on the death of Stephen, preached; and Paul and Barnabas, when they landed at Salamis in A.D. 45, preached there in the synagogues of the Jews. Barnabas himself was descended from Jews who had left Palestine to settle in Cyprus (Acts iv. 36), and it is said to have been a Jewish mob, instigated by fellow-Jews from Syria, that murdered him at Salamis. Finally, it may be mentioned that it was a Cypriote-Jewish magus called Simon whom the procurator Felix employed as his agent to seduce Drusilla, the wife of Azizus, king of Emesa (Josephus, *Ant. Iud.* XX, 142).

[1] Appian, Fr. in *F.H.G.* v, i, p. lxv; Cassius Dio, LXVIII, 32, and Xiphilinus; Euseb. *Hist. Eccl.* IV, 2; *Chron.* ed. Schoene, II, p. 164 (Helm, p. 196); Orosius, VII, 12. 8; Elias of Nisibin, *Chron.* (tr. Delaporte), p. 56 (Olymp. 223. 3, i.e. A.D. 115/6); Schürer, *Gesch. d. Iüdischen Volkes*,[4] I, pp. 662 ff.; Groag, art. *Lusius* (*Quietus*) in *R.E.* XIII, 1927, 1881–6. The chronology is much disputed; I have followed R. P. Longden, *J.R.S.* XXI, 1913, pp. 7–8, who comes to the conclusion that the revolt broke out in winter 115/6 or spring 116, and was crushed before midsummer. Cassius Dio mentions the revolt after the siege of Hatra (April 117).

[2] Among the troops despatched to deal with the revolt was a detachment of Legio VII Claudia p.f., commanded by a tribune of the legion, C. Valerius Rufus (*missus cum vexillo ab imp... Traiano... Cyprum in expeditionem*, Dessau, *Inscr. Lat. Sel.* 9491). The presence in the island of a mixed infantry and cavalry detachment, the *cohors* VII *Breucorum civium Romanorum equitata*, normally stationed in Pannonia, is proved by an inscription from Knodhara (about four miles west of Leukoniko); *C.I.L.* III, p. 41, no. 215; Cichorius in *R.E.* IV, 260.

[3] Chapot, p. 76. He underestimates the present population (see *Hdb.* 1930, pp. 41–2 and the Census Report, 1931, which estimates it at 347, 959; the Annual Report for 1937 estimates it for that year at 370,935). He suggests that Cassius Dio's figure covers both Egypt and Cyprus, but the text (καὶ ἐκεῖ) will not bear this interpretation.

have no indication of how many of the dead were themselves Jews, killed in the suppression of the revolt.

As a result of this outbreak, no Jew was allowed to set foot in the island, and even those who were driven there by adverse winds were put to death. Such prohibitions, however, are apt to be relaxed after a time, and there is some probability that before long Jewish communities grew up again in the island.[1]

Peace does not seem to have been threatened again until the year 269. After the failure of the Gothic invaders in Moesia, a portion of their fleet sailed raiding through the Aegean, and attacking Greece, the Cyclades, Crete, Rhodes and at last Cyprus. Here, however, little damage seems to have been done, and the expedition, ravaged by disease, eventually came to grief altogether.[2]

The Cypriote fleet had, as we have seen, played a considerable part in the wars of the pre-Roman period. It was still serviceable, though on a more modest scale, when Licinius, in 324, collecting ships from the eastern Mediterranean for the final struggle with Constantine, obtained a contingent from the island.[3] But only one contingent out of the whole fleet of 350 was smaller, Egypt and Phoenicia contributing eighty each,

---

[1] Chapot, p. 77, n. 2, cites from S. Menardos, in Ἀθηνᾶ, XXII, 1910, pp. 417–25, an inscription from Athienou, which mentions a priest named Joses son of Synesius and not only seems to imply the existence of a synagogue, but records its restoration, showing that it had existed for some time before. This inscription is shown by its lettering to be not earlier than the second century after Christ. A votive inscription (εὐχὴ Ῥαββὶ Ἀττικοῦ) in the Orthodox Archbishop's Palace at Nicosia, probably from Larnaka tis Lapithou (L.B.W. no. 2776; Th. Reinach in *Rev. Ét. Juives*, XLVIII, 1904, pp. 191–6) seems to belong to the third century. A Jew Isaac was converted by St Epiphanius (*Vita Epiph.* (ed. Dind.), I, p. 52. 47). Krauss in *Jewish Enc.* s.v. *Cyprus* argues, from the statement that the Jews in Cyprus were asked by the Jews in Tyre to join in a conspiracy against the Greeks in 610, that they must have been numerous; but this appears to depend only on Eutychius, and to be of small significance, if true (Reinach, *loc. cit.*). The number of Jews in Tyre was 4000 not 40,000. Menardos (p. 424) doubts the accuracy of Dio's statement that Jews were utterly banished from Cyprus, and also thinks that in the number of the dead thousands may have been changed into tens of thousands.

[2] Schiller, *Gesch. Röm. Kais.* I, 1883, p. 847. Trebell. Pollio, *Vita Claudii*, XII, I: "fuerunt per ea tempora et apud Cretam Scythae, et Cyprum vastare tentarunt: sed ubique morbo exercitu laborante, superati sunt." Zosimus (I, c. 46) mentions Rhodes and Crete, but not Cyprus. Cp. Zonaras, XII, 26, p. 605 and Syncellus, I, p. 720, Bonn.

[3] Zosimus, II, c. 22. On the date, see *Rhein. Mus.* LXII, 1907, pp. 493 and 517.

the Ionians and the "Dorians in Asia" sixty, Libya fifty, Bithynia and Cyprus thirty each, and Caria twenty. A great part of this fleet was lost in a storm after an unsuccessful engagement in the Hellespont with Crispus, son of Constantine, in the last months of 324.

During the reign of Constantine the Great, an attempt was made by one Calocaerus to establish himself as master of the island.[1] He had been sent there as governor by the Emperor, and legend associates him with the establishment of the regiment of cats at Akrotiri (C. Gata) to deal with the plague of serpents, which had multiplied during the great drought.[2] It would seem likely that Calocaerus was sent to take measures for the restoration of the island after the earthquake of 332/3. The Emperor despatched his nephew Delmatius to deal with the rebel, who was carried off to Tarsus and either crucified or burnt alive.

It is probably because Cyprus was comparatively happy, being without a history, under Roman government,[3] that we hear more of natural disasters during this period than before or after it; above all, seismic convulsions.[4] A prophecy in one of the earliest portions of the Sibylline Oracles, of which the authorship is attributed to a Jew of the Ptolemaic age, is supposed to refer to an earthquake some time before 180 B.C.,[5] perhaps that which shook Thera and Rhodes in 197. No other is mentioned until we come to Roman times, when a series of shocks is recorded, beginning with the memorable one of 15 B.C., when, as we

---

[1] Aurel. Victor, *de Caes.* 41, 11: "repente Calocerus magister pecoris camelorum Cyprum insulam specie regni demens capessiverat. Quo excruciato, ut fas erat, servili aut latronum more, etc." Oberhummer (*O.C.* pp. 392 f.), following Sakellarios (I, p. 392), holds that Calocaerus had been captain of the camel corps before he was sent to Cyprus, and that there were no camels in the island at this time. (But the camel was known there as early as the Bronze Age, see Gjerstad, *S.P.C.* p. 75—a tomb of Early Cypriote II at Katydhata.) His revolt was in the year after the earthquake of 332 (Hieron. *Chron.* a. Abr. 2350; Theophanes a. M. 5825 and the Arian historian in Bidez's ed. of Philostorgius, p. 207; Cedrenus, I, p. 519, Bonn: 29th year of Constantine).

[2] Hackett, *History of the Orthodox Church in Cyprus*, p. 359. For serpent-killing cats see Enlart, II, p. 462, n. 2 and compare Tschiffely, *Southern Cross to Pole Star*, 1933, p. 276 (Panama).

[3] The outburst of Sakellarios (I, p. 390) against the Roman treatment of the island is completely without justification, except so far as concerns the first few years of the regime.

[4] Oberhummer, *O.C.* pp. 137–46, gives the records known to him, down to modern times; others added by Sykutris, Κυπρ. Χρον. I, 1923, p. 345, and Indianos, Κυπρ. Σπ. II, pp. 137 ff.

[5] *Orac. Sib.* III, 457.

have seen, Augustus came to the rescue.[1] A very serious disaster followed in A.D. 76 or 77, when three or more cities were destroyed.[2] Two of these, if the allusions in the Sibylline Oracles[3] may be trusted, were Salamis and Paphos; a third may have been Citium.[4] In 332, and again ten years later, Salamis was badly hit; on the latter occasion it is said that what did not disappear under a tidal wave was levelled to the foundations.[5] Allowing for natural exaggerations, there cannot have been much of Salamis left standing after this, and the Emperor, relieving the survivors of taxation for four years, rebuilt it—on a much smaller scale —as Constantia, although the old name and the new seem to have been used indifferently for some time. Paphos was so badly knocked about by the earthquakes of the fourth century that it was not for some time rebuilt, for St Jerome says of St Hilarion that he went to Paphos, "that city so celebrated by the poets, which, destroyed by frequent earthquakes, has now only its ruins to show what once it was".[6] Nevertheless, we may be sure that, had Paphos not been stony ground for the

---

[1] The date 15 B.C. is from Cassius Dio, XXIII, 24, 7. The Armenian version of Eusebius dates it to 18 B.C.; St Jerome to 17 B.C. It is possible that the shocks went on for some years; *O.C.* p. 138 quotes passages from Seneca citing Paphos as frequently ruined by earthquakes. The earthquake of 15 B.C. may have been the last and worst of a series.

[2] Euseb. *Chron. Arm.* (8th year of Vespasian); St Jerome (9th year of Vesp.); Orosius, VII, 9. 11 (do.). Elias of Nisibin, *Chron.* (tr. Delaporte), p. 54 (Olymp. 213. 3, i.e. A.D. 75/6). Other references in *O.C.* pp. 138–9. See also p. 235, n. 1. The description of a volcanic eruption quoted by Gaudry (*Géologie de l'Île de Chypre*, p. 235) from Marianus Scotus is due to a confusion with the eruption of Vesuvius.

[3] *Orac. Sib.* IV, 128–9, 143–5. In IV, 142 Κύπρον may be an error for some other name, perhaps Κύρρον, for the line refers to the din of battle, and seems to be connected with the sacking of Antioch. The date of this book, according to Friedlieb, is about A.D. 80. In V, 450–3 Salamis and Paphos are also mentioned, as well as a tidal wave and a plague of locusts (*O.C.* pp. 335–6). The date of this book is thought to be early in the reign of Hadrian (though others put it under Commodus), but this and other prophecies about Tyre and Phoenicia may be taken from older oracles. VII, 5 also prophesies a destructive tidal wave in Cyprus.

[4] Oberhummer, *Sbr. Bay. Akad.* 1888, pp. 309 f., on the strength of a dedication to the Emperor Nerva as "founder"; but this is not earlier than 96/7, nearly twenty years after the earthquake.

[5] Malalas (XII, p. 313, Bonn), who dates the disaster and the foundation of Constantia to the reign of Constantius Chlorus, should have said Constantius II (337–361): *O.C.* p. 140. Elias of Nisibin (*Chron.* tr. Delaporte, p. 65) gives Ol. 278. 2 (A.D. 334/5) as the date of the earthquake which others put two years earlier.

[6] Hieron. *Vita S. Hilar.* 42 (Migne, *P.L.* 23, col. 50); cp. Seeck, *Untergang d. ant. Welt*, I, p. 347.

seeds of the new religion, it too would have been rebuilt like Salamis. And it became a bishopric at an early date, so that it must have recovered from its ruin.

From now onwards until the twelfth century the records of earthquakes fail us, for the enumeration by St Neophytus[1] is taken from the *Synaxaria* and does not directly concern Cyprus, until he comes to his own time, and is able to describe his own experiences.

Another visitation of nature was a terrible drought and famine, at some time in the first half of the fourth century.[2] It was supposed to have lasted thirty-six years, with the result that the island was depopulated, and not to have come to an end until St Helena (who, after the invention of the Cross, had come to Cyprus with the crosses of the two thieves and parts of the foot-piece of the cross of Christ) had founded the churches on Stavrovouni and at Tokhni.[3] This famine must have coincided with that which afflicted a large district of the eastern provinces, as recorded in 324, although the report of grain-riots in Cyprus rests on a doubtful reading.[4]

---

[1] *Oratio de terrae motibus*, ed. Delehaye, *Anal. Bolland.* xxvi, 1907, pp. 207–12 and p. 288. Since he gets his information from the Synaxaria, he is unable as a rule to name the year of the earthquake, but gives the day of the month. Most of the shocks he mentions can be identified from his source with shocks felt at Constantinople. Doubtless some of them affected Cyprus.

[2] If it were certain (*O.C.* pp. 214 and 437–8) that the biography of St Spyridon by Symeon Metaphrastes (tenth century) were a revision of the biography by Leontius bishop of Neapolis (Lemesos), whose date was 590–668, the record would be as early as that time. But as to the life by Leontius, see Delehaye in *Anal. Boll.* xxvi, 1907, pp. 239 f. For the drought and famine as described in the life by Metaphrastes, see Migne, *P.G.* 116, cols. 420 f. This story was again embroidered in the fifteenth century by Leontius Machaeras (ed. Dawkins, pp. 2 f. and 8). This last version dates the drought in the thirty-six years preceding the baptism of Constantine. Other late accounts give its duration as seventeen or even only seven years (*O.C.* pp. 214 f.).

[3] For variant versions see Hackett, pp. 433 ff. and Dawkins's notes on Machaeras. One of the consequences of the drought was the plague of serpents, to deal with which the monastery at C. Gata, with its serpent-hunting cats, was said to have been founded. See above, p. 244.

[4] In Theophanes (a.M. 5824, p. 29 de Boor), where the vulgate is Κύπρου, de Boor (followed by Bidez) prefers Κύρου (for Cyrrhus), which seems plausible, although the expression is awkward. The starving villagers assembled in mobs "on the land of the Antiochenes and τῆς Κύ(π)ρου", and raided the grain-stores. One would expect to read not Κύρου but Κυρηστῶν. The Emperor came to the relief of the sufferers, using the Church organization for distribution.

Cyprus first learned of the Gospel of Christ after the death of Stephen.[1] Those who were scattered abroad in the persecution that followed Stephen's stoning to death travelled as far as Phoenicia and Cyprus and Antioch; but they spoke of the Gospel only to the Jews. However, converts who went from Cyprus and Cyrene to Antioch seem to have preached to the Greeks also.[2] It was from Antioch that in 45 Paul and Barnabas, attended by John Mark, were sent out on a mission;[3] from Seleucia they crossed to Salamis, the native city of Barnabas, and preached in the Jewish synagogues there. Travelling through the whole island to Paphos, they had the famous encounter with the proconsul Sergius Paulus,[4] who desired to hear their preaching, and, it is said, was converted by the miracle which Paul performed, striking blind for a season the Jewish magus Elymas or Bar-Jesus. So resounding a success as the conversion of the Roman governor must have greatly increased the number of converts, though the Jews as a whole continued to be bitterly hostile. A second visit to Cyprus was paid by Barnabas after the quarrel with Paul.[5] Barnabas again took John Mark with him. Of the details to be read in the apocryphal *Acts* of St Barnabas, composed by a Cypriote of the fifth century, writing shortly after the invention of the tomb of St Barnabas at Salamis, but posing as John Mark, we need only mention here that the Saint was martyred by the Jews at

---

[1] Acts xi. 19, 20. For the history of the Church in Cyprus see especially the invaluable *History of the Orthodox Church in Cyprus*, by J. Hackett, 1901. The list of Orthodox archbishops is full of difficulties; see N. Cappuyns, "Le Synodicon de Chypre au XIIe siècle", in *Byzantion*, x, 1935, pp. 489 ff. For a critical account of the various saints, H. Delehaye, "Saints de Chypre", in *Anal. Boll.* XXVI, 1907, pp. 161–297.

[2] In Acts xi. 20 instead of Ἕλληνας some read Ἑλληνιστάς, i.e. Jews born out of Judaea and using Greek manners and language. But the antithesis between Jews and non-Jews is thus lost. Of Mnason the "early disciple" (xxi. 16) we do not know whether he was Jew or Greek.

[3] Acts xiii. 3–13. From iv. 36 we learn that "Joseph, who by the apostles was surnamed Barnabas" was "a Levite, a man of Cyprus by race".

[4] It is plausibly suggested that the Apostle adopted the name of Paul from the man who had treated him in so friendly a manner. Dessau in *Hermes*, XLV, 1910, pp. 361 ff. There is a well-known legend that Paul was scourged at Paphos; L. Philippou (in Κυπρ. Χρον. IV, 1926, pp. 187 ff.) gives his reasons for allowing the story the benefit of the doubt.

[5] Acts xv. 39. It may be mentioned in passing that the Greek Church attributes the evangelization of Britain to St Aristobulus, a brother of St Barnabas, and one of the seventy; his day is 31 Oct., but the Bollandists deal with him under 15 March (pp. 368–70). See L. Philippou in Πάφος, III, 1938, pp. 281–4.

Salamis, and that John Mark buried him with the copy of the Gospel of St Matthew which he had always carried with him. The invention of this tomb by Anthemius, archbishop of Constantia, in the reign of Zeno (474–91) was to be of great consequence for the history of the Church in Cyprus, as we shall see.

Of other persons mentioned in the legends connected with St Barnabas, perhaps the most important are St Heracleides, who is said to have been converted by Paul and Barnabas, and afterwards ordained bishop of Tamassus by Barnabas and John Mark, and St Auxibius, who according to his *Acts* went to Cyprus shortly after the death of Barnabas, was baptised and ordained bishop by John Mark, and sent to Soli, where he reigned fifty years. But of the historical truth, if any, underlying these legends, we know nothing.

St Spyridon, however, bishop of Tremithus, is an historical personage, having been present at the Council of Nicaea in 325,[1] and at that of Sardica in 343/4. He had been one of the confessors whom Galerius Maximianus, after putting out his right eye and ham-stringing him in the left leg, had condemned to the mines.[2] After his death, his body was removed to Constantinople at the time of the Moslem invasions (perhaps in 688), and eventually, in 1453, was carried to its present resting-place at Corfù, where he is the patron saint of the island.[3]

Historical, too, is St Hilarion, a contemporary of Constantine the Great. His life was written by St Jerome. He certainly spent the end of his days in Cyprus, probably in the neighbourhood of Paphos; but the tradition connecting him with the romantic mountain above Kerynia is late and probably baseless.[4] His body was stolen and carried off to Palestine soon after his death.

Finally, among the historical early saints of Cyprus is St Epiphanius, archbishop of Salamis-Constantia. Born about 310–320 in Palestine, he was elected to the see of Constantia in 368, and reigned there for thirty-six years. He died at a great age in 403. He played a great and not altogether dignified rôle in the religious disputes of his time, showing

---

1 Though not among the signatories, he is known to have been there from Metaphrastes, *Vita*, cc. 12–15 (*P.G.* 116, cols. 429–36) and Socrates, *Hist. Eccl.* I, c. 8. The latter calls him "Spyridon from Cyprus" and "bishop of one of the cities of Cyprus called Trimithous"; cp. Sozomenus, *Hist. Eccl.* I, 11.

2 Above, p. 238, n. 5.

3 Joh. Georg Herzog zu Sachsen, *Der hl. Spyridon, seine Verehrung u. Ikonographie*, Leipzig-Berlin, 1913.

4 Delehaye, *op. cit.* pp. 241–2; below, p. 271.

bitter hostility to the memory of Origen, and taking an active part in the persecution of Chrysostom. He has been characterized as combining the most extensive erudition with real mediocrity of intelligence and the most obstinate bias; but that is surely nothing unusual. In 401,[1] at the request of Theophilus, bishop of Alexandria, he summoned to Constantia a Council of all the Cypriote bishops, who at his instigation condemned the writings of Origen.[2] The widespread Marcionist Gnostic heresy also caused him anxiety,[3] and it would appear that its supporters were at one time strong enough to reduce the city to a state of siege.[4] On his death in May 403, on his way back from Constantinople, whither he had carried the decision of the Council of Constantia, it was proposed to bury him in the basilica of Constantia. His adversaries made a riot, but did not succeed in preventing his burial there.[5] On the other hand, his body seems to have been transferred later to Famagusta and to have lain in the little church on the south side of St George of the Greeks until it was carried off to Constantinople by Leo VI in the ninth century.

The legend of the visit of St Helena to Cyprus after her invention of the True Cross, and the foundation of the churches in Stavrovouni and at Tokhni, have already been mentioned. It is not possible now to estimate what basis of truth this legend possesses.[6]

Some time, probably, in the fourth century, Constantia definitely displaced Paphos as the metropolis of the island. In spite of the part which Paphos seems to have played in the earliest days of Christianity, when

---

[1] This is the date usually accepted, but F. Ludwig, *Der hl. Joh. Chrysostomus*, 1883, p. 73, because Epiphanius departed immediately afterwards to Constantinople, prefers the end of 402 or even after Easter 403. See, for the attack on Origen, St Jerome's Letters nos. 86–92. On the career and character of Epiphanius, see Hackett, p. 12; W. Bright, *Age of the Fathers*, 1903, esp. I, p. 542, II, pp. 62–5; Duchesne, *Early Hist. of the Chr. Ch.* II, pp. 466–8; III, pp. 30, 60; Palanque in Fliche and Martin, *Hist. de l'Église*, III, 1936, pp. 452 f., and Labriolle, in the same, IV, 1937, p. 33.

[2] Mansi, *Concil.* III, cols. 1019 f.

[3] *Panarion haer.* 42. 1, 2.

[4] Letter of St John Chrysostom (no. 221, Migne, *P.G.* 52, col. 733): τοῦ Σαλαμῖνος ἕνεκεν χωρίου τοῦ κατὰ τὴν Κύπρον κειμένου, τοῦ ὑπὸ τῆς αἱρέσεως τῶν Μαρκιωνιστῶν πολιορκουμένου. The untrustworthy biographer of Epiphanius, Polybius of Rhinocorura (ed. Dind. I, p. 66), gives a list of heresies in Cyprus, and says that the Saint obtained from Theodosius I an order expelling all their followers from the island.

[5] Hackett, p. 406. Jeffery suggests that the tomb in the north aisle may be that in which he was laid ("Basilica of Constantia", in *Ant. Journ.* 1928, p. 346, n. 2).

[6] See S. Menardos in Λαογραφία, II, 1910, pp. 266–98.

it was visited by Paul and Barnabas, it is reasonable to suppose that, as the centre of the chief pagan cult, it would be unfertile ground for the propagation of the new religion, although it is curious that we hear so little of conflicts between the two faiths such as enlivened the history of Alexandria and Gaza.[1] However this may be, Constantia was by the fifth century the acknowledged *metropolis*,[2] and its bishop, whatever may have been his precise title, the head of the Church in the island.

The organization of the Church in Cyprus during these early days of Christianity is quite unknown. The legends of the appointment of bishops by the Apostles are unhistorical. That there were at least three Cypriote sees represented at the Council of Nicaea in 325, by Cyrillus of Paphos, Gelasius of Salamis,[3] and Spyridon of Tremithus, we know. Since Cyrillus signed before Gelasius, Paphos may still have been superior to Salamis.[4]

At the Council of Sardica (343–4) the following bishops of Cyprus signed the letter of the Council:[5] Auxibius, Photius, Gerasius, Aphrodisius, Eirenicus, Nounechius, Athanasius, Macedonius, Triphyllius, Spyridon, Norbanus, Sosicrates. The names of their sees are un-

---

[1] The life of St Tychon of Amathus (Delehaye, *op. cit.* pp. 229 ff.) illustrates the conflict there; the Saint converted the priestess of Artemis, and broke in pieces the idol of Aphrodite which the Greeks were carrying in procession. (Cp. the Life in Latyšev, *Menol. Anon. Byz.* II, p. 66.) Cp. too the story of Mnason, the friend of St Paul, at Tamassus (Hackett, p. 379). The transition from paganism to Christianity is well illustrated at Curium, where the recent American excavations have revealed a house with a remarkably interesting inscribed mosaic dating from the early fourth century and illustrating the transition from paganism to Christianity. Written in elegiacs, in archaizing style recalling Homeric diction, it describes how the house now rests on the support of Christ, and how a new protector has arisen for Curium, taking the place of Phoebus Apollo: *Bull. of University Mus. of Pennsylvania*, VII, 2, April 1938, pp. 6 f.

[2] E.g. Sozomenus, writing under Theodosius II the history of the Church from 324 to 421, describes Epiphanius as being elected τῆς μητροπόλεως τῆς νήσου ἐπισκοπεῖν (VI, 32. 2). The Count of the Orient, in writing to the consular Theodorus in 431, speaks of the church of Constantia as metropolis, and the archbishop Olympius in 449 calls himself bishop of the metropolis of Cyprus. Other references in *R.E.* IV, 953. The idea that the title metropolis was conferred after the discovery of the tomb of Barnabas is clearly wrong. Sathas, Μεσ. Βιβλ. II, p. κη′.

[3] Only these two are mentioned in the lists (Gelzer, *Patrum Nicaenorum Nomina*, index; C. H. Turner, *Eccl. Occ. Mon. Iur. Ant.* I, i, pp. 80, 100). But see above, p. 248, n. 1.

[4] Mas Latrie, *H.* I, p. 75.

[5] Mansi, *Concil.* III, col. 69.

fortunately not given; but there can be little doubt that Triphyllius was the bishop of Ledrae, and Spyridon that of Tremithus.

The only other Council falling within the limits of this chapter is that of Constantinople in 381.[1] Cyprus was represented there by the bishops Julius of Paphos, Theopompus of Tremithus, Tychon of Tamassus and Mnemonius (Mnemius) of Citium. The Council lists therefore indicate the existence by the end of the fourth century of the sees of Salamis-Constantia, Paphos, Citium, Ledrae, Tamassus and Tremithus, and six others (since twelve bishops signed the letter of the Council of Sardica). The remaining six must be sought among Amathus, Arsinoe, Chytri, Carpasia, Curium, Lapethus and Soli; possibly also Kerynia and Neapolis. And another document shows that by 400 there must have been fifteen sees in Cyprus, for that is the number of Cypriote bishops addressed in a synodical letter by Theophilus, Patriarch of Alexandria.[2] He does not, unfortunately, give their sees, but their names were Epiphanius (the archbishop), Marcianus, Agapetus, Boethius, Helpidius, Eutasius, Norbanus, Macedonius, Ariston, Zeno, Asiaticus, Heraclidas, another Zeno, Kyriacus, and Ap(h)roditus.

Besides city bishops there were, in the time of Sozomenus,[3] writing in the first half of the fifth century, bishops of villages, and such minor sees may have existed in the fourth century. One of these, it has been suggested, may have been Ledrae; but although (in another context)[4] Sozomenus mentions its bishop Triphyllius, who, as we have seen, was at Sardica in 344, he does not say that Ledrae was a village; and one may doubt whether a village bishop would be summoned to a Council in his own right, although he might go as someone else's representative, like the deacon Dionysius who represented a bishop at Chalcedon in 451.

* * * * * *

Of the once extensive Roman buildings erected in Cyprus, especially in the cities of Salamis and Paphos, little indication remains except in foundations and fallen columns. The most important construction was

---

[1] Mansi, *Concil.* III, col. 570. The absence of the signature of Epiphanius is explained by Hackett (p. 12) on the supposition that he left early, as he was present at Rome in the next year.

[2] St Jerome, *Epist.* no. 92.

[3] *H.E.* VII, 19. Repeated by Georgius Monachus (ed. de Boor, I, p. 375). (Cyprus shared this peculiarity with the Arabians, and the Novatians and Montanists of Phrygia.)

[4] *H.E.* I, 11.

probably the immense limestone forum of Salamis,[1] which belongs to the early years of the Roman province, and covered, with its surrounding shops, an area of at least three and a half acres, with an open space of some 750 by 180 ft. within. The columns, of the Corinthian order, about 27 ft. high, were built with drums (not, as in the later Roman style, of monoliths), and the capitals were made in two pieces, each 2 ft. thick, with a horizontal joint. On a platform at the south end stood a temple dedicated to the Olympian Zeus.[2]

What has been identified as a second forum[3] remains as a collection of granite monolithic shafts. A third "forum" was cleared by the same excavations in 1890; it consists of a marble colonnade about 30 ft. high, attributed to the third or possibly second century, which was in the fourth century or later adapted as one side of a square enclosure, of which the other three sides were on a smaller scale, about 20 ft. high.[4]

The only Roman theatre which has been excavated in Cyprus is that of Soli, which the Swedish expedition cleared in 1930.[5] It appears to be

---

[1] G. Jeffery, *The Ruins of Salamis*, Cyprus, 1926, pp. 8 f., based on the report of the excavator, H. A. Tubbs, in *J.H.S.* XII, 1890; Gunnis, *Hist. Cyprus*, p. 420.

[2] This dedication is proved by inscriptions. One of these is in honour of Livia Augusta. (*I.G.R.R.* III, 984. Since she is not called Iulia, the inscription dates from before the death of Augustus, A.D. 14.) Another is a dedication by the Koinon of the province in honour of Empylus son of Empylus son of Charias who had served as gymnasiarch at his own expense. (*I.G.R.R.* III, 993. Dated "in the 9th year", probably of Augustus, therefore 18 B.C. rather than according to an era of the province beginning in 22 B.C. See above, p. 235.) Two agoranomoi, Pasicrates (?) son of Empylus. and Iason son of Carpion, record in a third inscription that they constructed all kinds of buildings (probably, if the restoration is correct, the colonnades) in the forum. L.B.W. no. 2758 after Sakellarios, I, p. 178, no. 11. By Jeffery, p. 19, this inscription is confused with the preceding, which is dated in the year nine, and interpreted as in honour of "Pasicrates and his father Empylus, architects of the Forum"! Finally, the traces of a Latin inscription made out from the holes of the pins used to affix the bronze letters on a marble frieze, have been read as recording the restoration of the forum of Salamis, which had fallen into ruin, by a *legatus Augusti pro praetore*; from this it has been inferred that the building took place before 22 B.C., after which the governor's title would be *proconsule* (*J.H.S.* XII, 1890, pp. 80 and 180).

[3] Jeffery, *op. cit.* pp. 12, 13.

[4] Jeffery, *op. cit.* pp. 13 f. A considerable amount of statuary of inferior quality was found, and removed to the Museum at Nicosia. Jeffery, p. 23, n. 1, says that the figure of Sarapis or Hades (*J.H.S.* XII, 1890, p. 126) was sent to the British Museum, but that is not so. None of this sculpture seems to be included in the Cyprus Museum Catalogue.

[5] *S.C.E.* III, pp. 548–82. There were great quantities of Roman architectural remains

Roman from the beginning, and to belong to the end of the second or beginning of the third century.

The great city of Salamis must always have had a water-supply, but the date of the first building of the aqueduct which brought water all the way from Kythrea is unknown, and the first records belong to Byzantine times.

Other architectural remains of Roman date in Cyprus hardly call for mention here, except the monolithic granite columns at New Paphos. Of those at the Church of Chrysopolitissa some still stand impressively upright, though whether in their original position or not seems to be uncertain. The field of the Forty Columns (Saranta Kolonnes) is the site of what must have been a great building of Roman date, erected perhaps over an earlier one; some twenty monolithic granite columns remain on the site.[1]

The most interesting remains of Roman sculpture to be found in Cyprus, after the bronze statue of Septimius Severus already mentioned, are the marble sarcophagi: one in the cloister of Bellapais, which was placed above another plain one and converted by the monks into a lavabo,[2] and one which used to stand outside the cathedral at Famagusta, but was removed in 1880, to serve as a tomb for the first English Commissioner of Famagusta, and placed in a small enclosure at Varosha. Both sarcophagi are of good Roman workmanship of the second century.

The Early Christian remains are represented by two classes of monuments:[3] the cemeteries and the churches. The Christians made use of the private tombs cut in the rock by their predecessors, and also constructed rock-cut or built tombs and martyria of their own.[4] The most impressive monument of the time, however, was the great basilica of Constantia.[5] It has been but imperfectly excavated, and the narthex and

---

at Soli as late as the eighteenth century; the site, like others in Cyprus, was plundered wholesale for building-stone for Egypt. Gunnis, p. 257.

[1] Hogarth, *Devia Cypria*, p. 5; Gunnis, p. 143.

[2] See Goethert in *Arch. Anz.* 1934, cols. 81–2 (above, p. 219, n. 2).

[3] See Γ. Α. Σωτηρίου, Τὰ παλαιοχριστιανικὰ καὶ Βυζαντινὰ Μνημεῖα τῆς Κύπρου (*Praktika* of the Academy of Athens, VI, 1931, pp. 477 ff.); and his large work Τὰ Βυζαντινὰ Μνημεῖα τῆς Κύπρου, I, Athens 1935 (cited henceforward as *Byz. Mn.*).

[4] See *Byz. Mn.* I, figs. 1, 2 and Pls. I–VII; and the article on the ancient Christian cemeteries of Cyprus in Κυπρ. Γράμματα, II, 1936, pp. 309–11.

[5] G. Jeffery, *Antiquaries Journal*, VIII, 1928, pp. 344–9; *Byz. Mn.* fig. 3 and Pls. VIII, IX. The figures in the text are those of Sotiriou; Jeffery gives 184 ft. length and 148 ft. breadth.

atrium are still underground. The main church is 70 m. long and 49 m. broad; with narthex and atrium its length must have been over 120 m. It was of the Hellenistic type, and had five aisles, with a single apse projecting from the east wall at the end of the central nave. The stone columns were built of drums from the first-century forum and provided with new capitals. It was destroyed by fire, probably when Constantia was sacked by the Arabs in the seventh century.[1] Popularly known as the Basilica of St Epiphanius, it is probable that it is the church which he is said to have built.

NOTE

PROCONSULS, LEGATES AND QUAESTORS IN CYPRUS

1. P. Cornelius Lentulus Spinther. 56–53 B.C. See above, p. 226.

2. Ap. Claudius Pulcher. July 53–July 51 B.C. See above, p. 227.

3. M. Tullius Cicero. July 51–July 50 B.C. See above, p. 227.

4. L. Coelius Tarfinus (Garifinus? Tamphilus?). End of the Republic? *J.H.S.* IX, 1888, p. 243, no. 68 = *I.G.R.R.* III, 953; *P.I.R.*[2] II, p. 298, no. 1249.

5. M. Ofilius (Uphilius). Procos. of Cilicia between 58 and 47 B.C. or of Cyprus after 22 B.C. *B.C.H.* LI, p. 143, no. 4; *R.E.* XVII, 2041, no. 6.

6. P. Paquius Scaeva. Under Augustus. *C.I.L.* IX, 2845; *P.I.R.*[1] III, p. 12, no. 93. After being praetor aerarii, proconsule prov. Cyprum optinuit, and later procos. iterum extra sortem auctoritate Aug. Caesaris et S.C. missus ad componendum statum in reliquum provinciae Cypri.

7. A. Plautius. Under Augustus, Coins: B.M.C. *Cyprus*, pp. cxix, 73, nos. 2–4; *P.I.R.*[1] III, p. 44, no. 343.

8. [V]arius Rufus. Under Augustus. *J.H.S.* IX, 1888, p. 240, no. 49 = *I.G.R.R.* III, 952; *P.I.R.*[1] III, p. 386, no. 193; or [L. T]arius Rufus, who was cos. suffectus 15 B.C. *P.I.R.*[1] III, p. 295, no. 14.

9. L. Axius Naso. Nov. A.D. 29. *L.B.W.* no. 2773 = *I.G.R.R.* III, 933 = *O.G.I.S.* 583; *P.I.R.*[2] I, p. 343, no. 1691. His legatus: M. Etrilius Lupercus. *P.I.R.*[1] II, p. 41, no. 74. His quaestor: C. Flavius Figulus. *P.I.R.*[1] II, p. 68, no. 181.

10. C. Ummidius Durmius Quadratus. Under Tiberius. (*a*) *C.I.G.* 2637; *L.B.W.* no. 2801; Oberhummer, *Sbr. Bay. Akad.* 1888, p. 336, no. 17 =

[1] See below, Note at end of Chapter XII.

I.G.R.R. III, 950. (*b*) *J.H.S.* IX, 1888, p. 237, no. 41 = *I.G.R.R.* III, 951. (*c*) *C.I.L.* X, 5182; Hogarth, *Devia Cypria*, p. 117; *P.I.R.*[1] III, p. 468, no. 600.

11. T. Cominius Proculus. Between 25 Jan. A.D. 43 and 25 Jan. A.D. 44. Coins: B.M.C. *Cyprus*, pp. cxxi, 76, no. 16. Inscr.: *B.C.H.* LI, p. 153, no. 11 = *S.E.G.* VI, 834; *P.I.R.*[2] II, p. 302, no. 1270.

12. L. Sergius Paulus, about A.D. 46–48. *Act. Apost.* xiii. 7. Possibly also *I.G.R.R.* III, 930; *P.I.R.*[1] III, p. 221, no. 376; *R.E.* II A, 1717.

13. Q. Iulius Cordus. A.D. 51? *C.I.G.* 2631, 2632 = *I.G.R.R.* III, 978, 971; *P.I.R.*[1] II, p. 188, no. 186; *R.E.* X, 570.

14. L. Annius Bassus. A.D. 52 or more probably 66 (12th year of Claudius or Nero). *C.I.G.* 2632 = *I.G.R.R.* III, 971; *P.I.R.*[2] I, p. 108, no. 637.

15. L. Vilius Mar[on]ius? First cent. A.D. Inscription of New Paphos. Hogarth, *Devia Cypria*, p. 9.

16. Q. Coelius Honoratus. End of first century. *L.B.W.* no. 2814; *I.G.R.R.* III, 970; *P.I.R.*[2] II, p. 297, no. 1244.

17. L. Bruttius Maximus. Titus, year 2. Inscription at A. Tychon, communicated by Mitford.

18. [Tele?]sinus. *J.H.S.* IX, 1888, p. 251; Hogarth, *Devia Cypria*, p. 117; *R.E.* VIII, 2469, no. 9. (These place him under Tiberius.) *P.I.R.*[1] II, p. 148, no. 149 (under Domitian).

19. ?.... Flaccus. Under Trajan or Hadrian. *C.I.G.* 2638 = *I.G.R.R.* III, 991; *R.E.* VI, 2434, no. 7; *P.I.R.*[1] I, p. 277, no. 209. The restoration which makes him proconsul of Cyprus is conjectural.

20. Ti. Claudius Iuncus. Under Hadrian? *L.B.W.* no. 2726 = *I.G.R.R.* III, 979 = *O.G.I.S.* 584; *P.I.R.*[2] II, p. 210, no. 904. To be distinguished from Aemilius Iuncus, who was cos. suffectus in 127.

21. Audius Bassus, A.D. 198. *L.B.W.* no. 2806 = *C.I.L.* III, 218 = *I.G.R.R.* III, 967; *P.I.R.*[2] I, p. 275, no. 1376. See above, p. 237, note.

22. Sex. Clodius ....nianus. Beginning of third century. *L.B.W* no. 2728 = *I.G.R.R.* III, 977; *P.I.R.*[2] II, p. 274, no. 1155.

23. Iulius Fronto Tlepolemus. A.D. 210/11. *B.C.H.* LI, 1927, pp. 139–43, no. 3 = *S.E.G.* VI, 810.

24. T. Caesernius Statius Quinctianus. Under Caracalla, between 211 and 217. *J.H.S.* IX, 1888, p. 252, no. 111 = *I.G.R.R.* III, 947; *B.C.H.* LI, 1927, pp. 140–41; *S.E.G.* VI, 811; *P.I.R.*[2] II, p. 35, no. 180.

25. P. Claudius Attalus. Under Macrinus and Elagabalus, 218. Cassius Dio, LXXIX, 3. 5; 4. 3. *P.I.R.*[2] II, p. 172, no. 795. Milestone, year 2 of Macrinus Augustus and Diadumenian Caesar. See p. 236, n. 4.

26. L. Gabo Arunculeius P. Acilius Severus. Procos. designatus prov. Cypri. Date unascertained. Inscription of Brescia. *C.I.L.* V, 4332, cp. 4333.

27. Ti. Claudius Flavianus Titianus Q. Vilius Proculus L. Marcius Celer M. Calpurnius Longus, quaestor pro pr. prov. Cypri, procos. prov. Cypri. Date unascertained. Kalinka in *Eranos Vindob.* 1893, p. 90, n. 2; *P.I.R.*[1] I, p. 372, no. 696.

28. D. Plautius Felix Iulianus. Date unascertained. *J.H.S.* IX, 1888, p. 248, no. 97; p. 249, no. 104; p. 253, no. 114 = *I.G.R.R.* III, 954–56; *P.I.R.*[1] III, p. 45, no. 352.

For the known *legati*, see Marquardt, *op. cit.* p. 391, n. 5; Liebenam, *Legaten*, pp. 133–35; Vaglieri, *op. cit.* They are:

M. Etrilius Lupercus in A.D. 29. See above, no. 9.

T. Lartienus Sabinus, 43/44. *S.E.G.* VI, 834.

L. Iulius L. f. Fab. Marinus Caecilius Simplex, *c.* 90.

M. Calpurnius M. f. Rufus, towards end of first century. *C.I.L.* III, 6072.

Ti. Flavius Philinus. *R.E.* XII, 2608, no. 145.

The following quaestors are recorded (see Vaglieri *loc. cit.*):

C. Sextilius Rufus, 47 B.C. See above, p. 320, n. 1.

C. Flavius Figulus in 29. See above, no. 9.

L. Servenius L. f. Aem. Cornutus before 72. *R.E.* II A, 1758.

P. Baebius P. f. Ofentina Italicus. *P.I.R.*[2] I, p. 346, no. 17.

L. Flavius L. f. Septimius Aper Octavianus. *R.E.* VI, 2616, no. 177.

Q. Marcius Faustinianus. *C.I.L.* XIV, 2931.

CHAPTER XII

BYZANTIUM AND ISLAM[1]

At the end of the fourth century, the province of Cyprus, as we have seen, was included in the Diocese of the Orient, under the Comes Orientis. This Diocese itself was grouped with four others—Thrace, Asiana, Pontus and Egypt—in the Prefecture of the Orient, under a Praetorian Prefect, on whose recommendation the provincial governor was appointed by the Emperor. The references to the history of Cyprus during the period with which this chapter is concerned are merely incidental to the history of the Empire as a whole, and throw very little light on any details of organization, civil or military, peculiar to the island. Like the rest of the provinces, it must have been bled by the Byzantine treasury, except when the power of extortion was transferred to the hands of the Arab invaders; and the unhappiness of the population under the imperial oppression made it the more willing to accept a change of masters.

We have but little information of the amount of the revenue, and that little is late. Thus it is said by some of the Oriental chroniclers that Muawiya, when he invaded Cyprus in the middle of the seventh century, laid on the island a perpetual tribute of 7000 or 7200 pieces of gold, and that it was equivalent to the tribute exacted at the time by the Greek Emperors. The sum seems ridiculously small, seeing that under the last Comneni the Emperor drew from it 700 pounds of gold a year,[2] or 50,400 besants. Richard I, however, in 1191, sold the island outright for 100,000 gold besants.

---

[1] In this chapter I have been able to profit by the great bibliographical resources of Prof. Norman H. Baynes, who has made a number of most fruitful suggestions. On the Oriental sources I have had much valuable advice from Dr Fulton, Mr J. Walker, and Mr E. W. Brooks.

[2] Arnold of Lubeck, *Chronica Slav.*, *M.G.H. Scr.* XXI, p. 178, quoted by Andreades, "Le montant du budget de l'Empire byz.", in *Rev. Ét. Gr.* 1921, pp. 36 f., where it is shown that the alteration of 700 to 7000 is unjustifiable. 700 lbs. was 50,400 besants or 756,000 francs, equivalent to some 3,750,000 francs of the nineteenth century or £150,000 sterling; and this did not include costs of administration.

During the first centuries of the Byzantine rule, the navy was allowed to sink to a low degree of efficiency. This must have favoured the neglect of Cyprus, so remote from the centre of the Empire;[1] but indeed the whole of the eastern basin of the Mediterranean must have been an easy prey to pirates. Thus the Isaurians, who from 404 to 407 ravaged the southern and eastern provinces of Asia Minor, Syria and Phoenicia, also included Cyprus in their depredations.[2]

In the reform of the provincial organization by Justinian in 535, the Count of the Orient ceased to exercise jurisdiction over the diocese as a whole, although his title, rank and salary were unaffected. He was henceforth civil governor of Syria and Cyrrhestica. Cyprus was so far removed from his control.[3] About the same time, however, from the "Lex ut Bonus",[4] naming Bonus "quaestor of the army", we learn of a new arrangement, by which five provinces, to wit Scythia, Moesia, Caria, all the islands of the Cyclades and the whole of Cyprus, were grouped together under his command as *quaestor Iustinianus exercitus*. It has been suggested that the object of this strange grouping was not merely to diminish the power of the Prefect of the East, but to place the financial expenses of administering the Danubian lands, exhausted by invasions, on provinces which were exceptionally rich. But if we remember the course taken by the fleets of raiding Goths, there is something to be said for supposing that the grouping represented a naval strategic line.[5] However, since the head of this wide-flung administration resided in the north, it was speedily discovered, and pointed out to the Emperor, that great inconvenience was caused to those who had to travel all the way from Caria or Rhodes or Cyprus, perhaps in stormy

---

[1] It was regarded as a suitable place of banishment for undesirables, such as the eunuch Eutropius, minister of Arcadius, in 399.

[2] Philostorgius (ed. Bidez), XI, 8, p. 139.

[3] *Nov.* VIII, cap. V. In the Notitia annexed to this Novella, Cyprus ranks equally with the other consular administrations of Palestina Prima and Secunda, Phoenicia, Syria Secunda, Theodorias, Osrhoene, Cilicia, Pamphylia, etc., as is shown by the amounts of the contributions due by the judge (governor) of the province: Sathas, Μεσ. Βιβλ. II, p. ιγʹ.

[4] *Nov.* XLI (536), cp. L (537); Joh. Lydus, *de magistr.* II, 29: προάγει τοίνυν ἔπαρχον ἐπόπτην τῶν Σκυθικῶν δυνάμεων, ἀφορίσας αὐτῷ ἐπαρχίας τρεῖς τὰς πασῶν ἐγγὺς εὐπορωτάτας, Κεραστίδα τὴν καθ' ἡμᾶς Κύπρον, κ.τ.λ. As frequently, the MSS. have Μυσία for *Moesia*.

[5] Bury, *Hist. Lat. Rom. Emp.* II, 1923, pp. 340–1; Chapot, "Les Romains et Cypre" in *Mélanges Cagnat*, p. 83; E. Stein, *Studien zur Gesch. des byz. Reiches*, 1919, pp. 165 f.

weather, to a region rendered unsafe by barbarian incursions, in order to have their causes tried by the governor. The Emperor therefore decided that cases from the island provinces should be dealt with in Constantinople by the quaestor in question, if he happened to be present in the capital, sitting with the quaestor of the Palace; but if he was in the north, then by a deputy. The journey from Cyprus to Constantinople in the winter season must still have been a cause of grievance.

How long this arrangement lasted we do not know. In any case it must have broken down when the Moslem invasions began. Then, from a military point of view, the Cibyrrhaeote[1] Theme became very important, and the defence of Cyprus, when possible at all, was the business of the commander of that Theme.

Under Justinian the principle of keeping separate the military and civil powers in the administration of the Empire began to break down, and by the seventh century the traces of the organization under military commands or "Themes", as they came to be called, are visible.[2] Normally these themes were commanded by *strategoi*—the equivalent of the *magistri militum* of the sixth century. Now Cyprus from the seventh to the tenth century was for long periods at the mercy of Moslem invaders, and could not be reckoned as definitely part of the Byzantine Empire. Constantine Porphyrogenitus has accordingly been criticized for including Cyprus in his list of Themes.[3] But he explains that Basil the Macedonian (867–886) established it as such, although he kept it for only seven years. Constantine VII himself never had possession of the island, which was finally recovered for the Empire by Nicephorus Phocas in 965. It has been observed that the seals of Cypriote officials preserve no record of a strategos,[4] such as we should expect to find in a Theme.

The military governors sent to the island under the Empire are

---

[1] From Little Cibyra (perhaps near Karaburun on the Pamphylian coast), to be distinguished from Great Cibyra in Phrygia. The Cibyrrhaeote Theme covered a considerable area of Ionia and Caria as well as Pamphylia, Pisidia and some of Cilicia. The district was not formally constituted as a Theme until the latter part of the eighth century (Bury's *Gibbon*, VI, p. 533, n. 3). The other two marine Themes were those of Samos and the Aegean.

[2] On this subject see Bury's *Gibbon*, VI, App. 3, pp. 532–5.

[3] Bury, *loc. cit.*; Const. Porph. *de Thematibus*, I: ιε′ θέμα τὸ καλούμενον ἐπαρχία Κύπρου...ὑπὸ κονσιλιάριον τούτεστι βουλευτήν...ὁ δὲ...Βασίλειος εἰς θέματος τάξιν ταύτην κατέστησε. His list was compiled about 934, from older sources chiefly.

[4] Schlumberger in *Arch. de l'Orient latin*, II, 1884, p. 438. See below, p. 260, n. 1.

generally called dukes, but from the eleventh century the title of *katapan* is also found for the Imperial legate, who governed the island with full sovereign powers—a "second lord".[1]

The institution of a military garrison, or at least a coast-guard, for the island, to protect it from invaders, was traced by Cypriote tradition to the time of Constantine,[2] who at the request of the inhabitants was said to have sent a captain to govern them and soldiers to protect them from the corsairs. But there can be little doubt that the establishment of this coast-guard on an effective scale dates from a later time than Constantine, and was necessitated by the menace of Islam. These *stratiotai* were paid out of a tax called the *stratia*, levied on the number of hearths. In the fifteenth and sixteenth centuries *estradiote* was the general name for such mercenaries, or Arnauts, for the most part of Albanian origin; and

---

[1] M.L. *H.* III, p. 812. He quotes the significant phrase from the life of St Lietbert, bishop of Cambrai (mid-eleventh century): "princeps illius insulae, quem Katapan, hoc est secundum dominum, vocant (*M.G.H. Scr.* VII, 1846, p. 536, n. 22=*Vita Lietberti*, c. 41). Schlumberger, *Sigillographie de l'Empire byz.* 1884, pp. 304–5, publishes some very rare seals of Byzantine officials in Cyprus, viz. (1) from the eighth or end of the seventh century, Joannes consul (*hypatos*) and procurator (*dioiketes*, more especially the chief revenue official, whose place was taken in the twelfth century by the *praktor*); (2) from the eleventh century, Michael, *vestis* (officer of the imperial wardrobe), judge and *katapan*; from the twelfth century: (3) Michael, *magister* (master of the imperial household) and *katapan*; (4) Elpidios Vrachamios, *kuropalates* (marshal of the Palace) and *dux*; (5) Leon, *a secretis* and judge; and (6) Leon, *commerciarius* of Cyprus and Attalia (collector of duties on commerce with the mainland). In addition to these, among the officers mentioned on seals in Cypriote collections (Cyprus Museum and Wing-Comm. Hubbard, who has since presented his collection to the British Museum) I noted the following: Sergios ὕπατος; Ioannes ἀπὸ ὑπάτων; Sergios ἔπαρχος; ἀπὸ ἐπάρχων Them..., Ioannes Lagi..., Leontios, Stephanos; στρατηλάτης: Theodoros, Dorotheos; Theodoros παλατῖνος; a πρακτήρ, and a τρακτευτής, both probably revenue officials of some kind (see Ensslin in *R.E.* VI A, 1871, for the latter); also a βεστίτωρ (see *vestis* above). All these seals seemed to me to be early, although, according to Dölger, *Beitr. z. Gesch. d. Byz. Finanzverwaltung*, 1927, pp. 71 ff., it was not until the twelfth century that the place of the *dioiketes* was taken by the *praktor* (of which πρακτήρ is doubtless an alternative form). On the honorary ὕπατοι, ἀπὸ ὑπάτων, see Bury, *Imp. Administrative System in the Ninth Century*, 1911, pp. 25 f.; on the ἔπαρχοι, ἀπὸ ἐπάρχων and στρατηλάται, pp. 23 f. For παλατῖνος, cp. Schlumberger, p. 561.

[2] Machaeras, § 9; Fl. Bustron (1560), ed. R. de Mas Latrie, pp. 45–6; Attar (*c.* 1540) in M.L. *H.* III, p. 520 and Sagredo (1562), *ibid.* p. 540; also Dawkins's notes on Machaeras, II, pp. 47–8. Est. de Lusignan (*Chorogr.* fo. 29), followed by Kyprianos (p. 98), attributes the organization to Calocaerus, who, he says, brought Albanians to the island for the purpose.

certainly there was a coast-guard of Albanians in Cyprus under Venetian rule;[1] but the Albanian origin of the earliest *stratiotai* is out of the question.[2]

The cities of Cyprus under the Byzantine Empire, enumerated by the various authorities, secular or ecclesiastical, number from thirteen to fifteen, and are for the most part the same as we have found in the

---

[1] M.L. *H.* I, 85, III, 238, with references. The Albanians formed a race apart, until they disappeared in the sixteenth century (Sathas in *Arch. de l'Orient latin*, II, 1884, *Doc.* p. 411).

[2] There is confusion, as Sathas (Μεσ. Βιβλ. II, p. νϛ' note) and others point out, of these original stratiotai with the Albanian mercenaries introduced by the Venetians. There was a tradition that in the Tyllyria, in the mountains above Chrysochou and Leuka, there was a colony from Telos near Rhodes introduced by Constantine with the duty of guarding the coast between the Gulfs of Pendaia (Morphou) and Chrysochou (Kyprianos, p. 41; M.L. *H.* I, p. 85, who however mistakes Telos for Delos). According to Sathas the establishment of the stratiotai in Cyprus was due to Tiberius III Apsimarus, who, before his seizure of the throne in 698, had been admiral of the Cibyrrhaeotes, and thus in close touch with Cyprus. It is also conjectured (Sathas, II, p. νϛ') that the stratiotai were recruited from the Mardaites or ἀπελάται of the Taurus, who were under the command of a *katapan* in Attalia on the Pamphylian coast. Sathas finds reasons for this conjecture in three facts: (*a*) the so-called apelatic poems are more plentifully preserved in Cyprus than elsewhere; (*b*) Mamas, the apelatic patron saint, came, according to legend, from Taurus to Cyprus; (*c*) the Mardaites in Attalia and the stratiotai in Cyprus were organized together against the Saracens. (It must, however, be observed that the exploits celebrated in the "akritic" poems are now generally considered to be not earlier than the tenth century, and the epic of Digenes Akritas is of the twelfth. Nor can the Mardaites have been *apelatai*, who used a different kind of weapons. See below, p. 287, n. 1.)—The original settlement of the Mardaites from Lebanon in the Cibyrrhaeote Theme had been the work of Justinian II (Theophanes, I, p. 557 Bonn, p. 363 de Boor; Nicephorus Patr. (ed. de Boor), p. 36). Sathas prefers Tiberius Apsimarus. It seems most probable that they first came to Taurus in the time of Justinian, although they may have been organized as a military force by Tiberius.—The Lusignans abolished the stratiotai, but retained the stratia. On this tax, see especially Dawkins on Machaeras, II, pp. 46–8. According to Machaeras the tax seems to have amounted to three hyperpers (gold besants), or six aspers (white besants) for each village-hearth, while the town-dwellers were quit for one hyperper. But there is some reason to believe that the tax (which was also called the hearth-tax or καπνικόν) was, in the original text from which Machaeras derives, stated as one *nomisma*, not three *nomismata*. Machaeras says four Cypriote hyperpers make one ducat. Now a little before his time, in 1374, the hyperper was half a ducat. Thus six Cypriote hyperpers or three Byzantine hyperpers would make 1½ ducats or about 15 francs. Since before the eleventh century this was about the value of the nomisma, Andreades (*Byz. Ztschr.* XXVIII, p. 322) suggests that in the original authority the amount stood at not three nomismata but one nomisma.—Dawkins further observes that the stratia is distinct from the tax (called the τρίτον) on the crops, paid by the villagers or *paroikoi*.

Roman province.[1] The list of Hierocles,[2] compiled about 535, but probably not up to date, gives us: Constantia metropolis, Tamassus, Citium, Amathus, Curium, Paphos, Arsinoe, Soli, Lapethos (Lapithos), Kirboia, Chytri, Carpasia, Kerynia (Kyrenia); later manuscripts intrude, by contamination from the Notitiae, Tremithus and Leukousia. George of Cyprus,[3] writing in the time of Phocas (602–610), gives the same places, omitting Kirboia and Leukousia. Constantine Porphyrogenitus, writing about 934, in place of Kirboia has "Kermia[4] or Leukosia"; he also includes Tremithus, and adds *Nemeuos*, a manuscript corruption of Nemesos (Neapolis). Constantine's list, however, is not based on contemporary information.[5]

We may assume that all the important cities of Cyprus had bishoprics,[6] so that the definitive list is: Salamis-Constantia, Citium, Curium, Tamassus, Paphos, Neapolis (Nemesos), Amathus, Arsinoe (Marium),

---

[1] See above, ch. XI, p. 231.

[2] Ed. Burckhardt, 1893, p. 36. A. H. M. Jones, *Cities of the Eastern Roman Empire*, p. 503, thinks that Hierocles, though he may have lived under Justinian, probably worked on a register drawn up under Theodosius II.

[3] Ed. Gelzer, 1890, p. 56. As to the date, however, see A. H. M. Jones, *op. cit.* p. 504, who thinks that he worked on the same list as Hierocles.

[4] The ed. princ. has Kerbeia.

[5] Of these places, Kirboia is not identified. (See the references in *R.E.* XII, 99.) It is evidently the same as the Kerbeia of the variant reading in Constantine (preceding note), who, as we have seen, equates it with the many-named Leukosia. On the other hand, the reading Kermia has been connected with the Keramaia mentioned by Theophanes (ed. de Boor, p. 424). Mas Latrie, however (M.L. *H.* I, p. 88 note), thinks Κεραμαία is a corruption of Κερατέων, which he would place between Citium and Amathus, "où se trouve le pays des Caroubes et le cap Caroubier". This is very unlikely. Sathas (Μεσ. Βιβλ. II, p. νθ′ note) points out that the Latin translation of the *Hist. Miscella* has *in portu Ciramea*, which supports the text of Theophanes so far as Κεραμαία is concerned; also that a city Κερατaία does not exist in Cyprus. He thinks that the Arabs, seeing that the Cibyrrhaeotes were guarding Cyprus well, made an attack not on the island, but on their chief harbour in the gulf of Ceramus in Caria, and that the Cibyrrhaeotes caught them there. The text of Theophanes should therefore read ἐν τῷ λιμένι των (τῶν Κιβυραιωτῶν δηλαδὴ) Κεραμαίᾳ. But the Ceramic gulf itself was much too large for its mouth to be blocked by the fleet of the Cibyrrhaeotes; and Ceramus itself does not seem to have had a harbour of any size. Est. de Lusignan (*Chorogr.* 1573, fo. 13 v°, *Descr.* fo. 28) believed there was an ancient town *Cormia* at the casale of Kormakiti, and D'Anville (*Mém. Acad. Inscr.* XXXII, 1768, p. 539) suggested this was the *Kermia* of Constantine; he is followed by Engel (I, pp. 77–8). *Kirboia* was, however, more probably in the interior.

[6] See Hackett, ch. VI.

Lapithos, Carpasia, Chytri, Tremithus, Soli, Kerynia, and Ledrae or Leukosia. Theodosias or Theodosiana was a temporary name (at the time of the Council of Chalcedon and later) of Neapolis.[1]

Some of these cities sank to insignificance before the end of Byzantine rule; others rose to greater importance. It will be convenient to consider them here individually, in so far as they concern the period now under consideration.

The future capital, Leukosia (Nicosia), took the place of the very ancient Ledrae,[2] although it was perhaps not on the same site. Whether

---

[1] That this Arsinoe is not Famagusta, as supposed by so many writers, but Polis tis Chrysochou, seems clear. It is enough to note that in all the earlier lists it is mentioned between Paphos and Soli. When the number of the Greek bishoprics was reduced by the Lusignans, the second Latin bishop was called bishop of Paphos (Old and New) and of Arsinoe, and the Greek bishop of those two cities was called bishop of Arsinoe and of the Greeks of Paphos; see Fl. Bustron (ed. R. de Mas Latrie), p. 53. Cp. M.L. *H.* I, p. 381; III, p. 329, n. 2. The identification with Arsos (Limassol district) has nothing to be said for it.—That Theodosiana or Theodosias (Oberhummer, *O.K.* p. 101) is Neapolis is proved by the *Life of Spyridon* by Theodorus, bishop of Paphos (ed. Papageorgios, Athens, 1901), c. 23, pp. 95 f.; cp. *Jahrbb. für prot. Theol.* XIII, p. 224: Ἰωάννου...γενομένου ἐπ. Θεοδοσιάδος, ἤτοι Νέας πόλεως τῆς Κυπρίων ἐπαρχίας. Gelzer (*Leontios' v. Neap. Leben des h. Iohannes des Barmh.* 1893, p. x note) thinks this John must have been the predecessor of Leontius, but Est. de Lusignan says that that was Tychicus (*Descr.* fo. 60, cp. Le Quien, *Or. Chr.* II, 1062). As to Leukosia, it is to be observed that Nilus Doxopatres, who compiled a list of bishoprics in 1143 (in Parthey's *Hierocles*, p. 285), omits it, as well as Nemesos. Yet Leukosia had by then long become a place of importance, as appears, for instance, by the part it played in the affair of Rhapsomates in 1092 (see below).

The lists of Cypriote bishops present or represented at Chalcedon offer some apparent inconsistencies (cp. E. Schwartz, "Über die Bischofslisten der Synoden von Chalkedon, Nicaea u. K'pel", in *Abh. Bay. Akad.*, Phil.-hist. Abt., N.F., Hft. 13, 1937, p. 54). The metropolitan of Constantia, Olympius, was represented by Epiphanius. Schwartz seems inclined to assume that this is the Epiphanius, bishop of Soli, who is mentioned in another list as himself represented by Soter, bishop of Theodosiana. It seems better to accept the identification of him (from the list Mansi, VII, col. 119) as bishop of Perga in Pamphylia; for other lists confirm the presence of that metropolitan at Chalcedon (cp. Schwartz, *Acta Concil. Oec.* II, ii, pars 2, 1936, p. 74 [166]). As to Didymus of Lapithos, who represented his metropolitan at the last session of the council, he was himself, at previous sessions, represented by Epaphroditus of Tamassus. It is possible that he did not arrive in time for the earlier sessions. Of the other bishops at this Council, Heliodorus of Amathus and Proëchius of Arsinoe were also represented by Soter of Theodosiana, and Photinus of Chytri by a deacon, Dionysius.

[2] Oberhummer, *Ztschr. der Ges. f. Erdkunde*, XXV, 1890, pp. 207–13; *Ledroi* in *R.E.* XII, 1924, 1125 f. I discuss the changes in the name of the capital in *Journ. Warburg Inst.* II, pt. 4.

Ledrae is represented by the table-hill of Leondari Vouno, 6 km. south-east of Nicosia, on which the remains go back to Mycenaean times, is not certain, though probable. But that there was an early settlement on the site of the present Nicosia seems clear from the tombs in the neighbourhood which are as old as the Bronze Age.[1] We have seen that *Lidir* is mentioned in the Assyrian lists of the seventh century B.C. (p. 107), and that there was a bishop of Ledrae, Triphyllius, in the fourth century of our era.[2] By this time indications of the name Leukosia begin to appear in the form *Leucothea* or *Leuteon*.[3] If Ledrae was on another site, this indicates that the see, while retaining its ancient name for a time, was being transferred to Leukosia. Yet another name, difficult to explain, may have been borne by the city, if any reliance is to be placed on Sozomenus's description of Triphyllius as "bishop of the holy church of *Kallinikesis* or *Leucontheon*".[4] As already observed, *Leukousia* is also found in Hierocles, but not in the original manuscripts (p. 262);[5] and

---

[1] Gunnis, p. 26.

[2] Above, p. 251; Council of Sardica, 343/4 (Mansi, III, 69–70); Sozomenus, *H.E.* I, 11 (Migne, *P.G.* 67, cols. 889–90) (about 370); St Jerome, *de vir. ill.* 92: T., Cypri Ledrensis sive Leucotheon episcopus; in the Greek version, Λήδρου ἤτοι Λευτεῶνος ἐπ.; Niceph. Call. VIII, 42 in Migne, *P.G.* 146, col. 165: T., ἐκεῖνον τὸν Λεδρῶν ἐπ.

[3] The story that the name was changed from Ledron to Leucoton or Leukosia by Leukos son of Ptolemy Soter (Est. de Lusignan, *Chorogr.* fo. 14 v°, *Descr.* fo. 30 v°) may be dismissed as a mere fancy.

[4] *Vita S. Triphylii, Acta SS.* 13 Iun. c. 3, p. 176: ψήφῳ θείᾳ, τῆς Καλλινεικησσέων μὲν πρίν, νῦν δὲ Λευκωσίας προχειρίζεται μητροπόλεως; and Theodorus (bishop of Paphos), *Vita S. Spyridonis* (in Lambecius, Comm. *de Bibl. Caesar.* VIII, 1679, p. 311; cp. the edition by Papageorgios, Athens, 1901, p. 84, c. 17 and p. 93, c. 21): T., ἐπίσκοπος τῆς Καλλινικησέων πόλεως ἤτοι Λευκῶν θεῶν ἁγίας τοῦ θεοῦ ἐκκλησίας. Cp. Wesseling on Hierocles, *Corp. Scr. Hist. Byz.* V, 3, p. 513. The name is still found in the thirteenth century, for Gregory of Cyprus (born about 1240), in his autobiography (Migne, *P.G.* 142, 21; La Meere, *La trad. manuscr. de la corresp. de Grég. de Chypre* (Inst. Belge de Rome), 1937, pp. 176–7), says that as a boy he εἰς τὴν Καλλινικησέων πλέονος παιδεύσεως ἕνεκεν πέμπεται. But this use is perhaps archaistic. For the name Λευκούπολις, used by St Neophytus, see *Anal. Boll.* XXVI, 1907, p. 213. In a list of metropoleis and bishoprics which he found mentioned (in an ancient digest of ecclesiastical law), Kyprianos (p. 391) gives ὁ Φωτολαμποῦς ἢ Λευκοσίας. Now Machaeras (§ 30) has in his list of famous prelates Τριφυλλίου τοῦ Φωτολάμπους, ἐπισκόπου Λευκωσίας. It looks as if Kyprianos mistook a complimentary name of Triphyllius ("brilliant"), or his father's name, for the name of his diocese.

[5] Sakellarios (I, p. 209), joining the two names, Τριμηθούντων Λευκουσία, produces the theory that it was subordinate to Tremithus. But then Tremithus should also have been mentioned independently. As regards the quantity of the second syllable there

again in the description of the fifteenth Theme by Constantine Porphyrogenitus (p. 262), where it is given as an alternative name for *Kermia*. By that time the name must have been well established, and it has no more rivals until we reach the Frankish period. We shall see that the city was of some importance as a centre of administration by the end of the eleventh century, for Rhapsomates seems to have had his headquarters there in 1092, and it was thither that after his capture the Duke's army returned (p. 298). John Comnenus also, it would seem, was governing thence at the time of the invasion by Renaud de Châtillon in the middle of the twelfth century (p. 307). That the Byzantines had built a castle there appears from the record that it was destroyed at the time of the revolt against the Templars in 1192. And indeed, it is probable that the place was walled at an early date, perhaps as early as the fourth century.[1]

Amathus had been so important under the Roman rule that, as we know from Ptolemy, it gave its name to one of the four divisions of Cyprus, taking precedence of the once important city of Citium. Later, "in the time of the Dukes" (p. 282, n. 1), it was a metropolis and their place of residence; we know that St John Eleëmon's father, the Duke Epiphanius, lived there in the latter half of the sixth century.

By that time, however, another place in the neighbourhood, the "new city" of Nemesos,[2] now Limassol, had begun to attain importance; its roadstead was better than that of Amathus.[3] In the fifth century,

---

seems to be no certainty; Λευκουσία tended to disappear (although it is found, for instance, in George Bustron), but the MSS. of Machaeras seem to use both Λευκοσία (Sathas, II, p. 68) and Λευκωσία (Dawkins, § 30). Therefore the assertion of Menardos (Τοπωνυμικόν, p. 352) that Λευκωσία is an invention of the nineteenth century seems to be unfounded. Both forms are still in use, to judge by the imprints of books published in the last few years.

[1] Est. de Lusignan (*Chorogr.* fo. 16 v°; cp. *Descr.* fo. 31) says that when the old walls were pulled down, in order to build the new ones, copper coins of Constantine the Great and Helena were found in quantities in many places, from which he dates the construction of the walls to the time of Constantine. There is no reason to doubt the identification of the coins, and the argument seems to be archaeologically sound.

[2] S. Menardos, Τοπωνυμικόν ('Αθηνᾶ, 18), pp. 324 f. Est. de Lusignan, *Chorogr.* fo. 8 v° (followed by Kyprianos, p. 23), speaks loosely in saying that the new city was founded by the first Lusignans. I discuss the changes in the name of Nemesos-Limassol in *Journ. Warburg Inst.* II, pt. 4.

[3] Amathus, however, did not therefore lose its bishopric, which lasted until the twelfth century, and was revived for a time after the Turkish conquest. To the early bishops (Hackett, pp. 317 f.) add Theodorus (Delehaye, "Une vie inédite de Saint-Jean-l'Aumônier", in *Anal. Boll.* XLV, 1927, p. 23), contemporary with St John Eleëmon.

at the time of the Council of Chalcedon (451), it had the name of Theodosias or Theodosiana, and sent a bishop to the Council.[1] Its most famous bishop, however, was Leontius (590–668), the biographer of St John Eleëmon.[2]

Of Citium[3] little need be said here. Bishops are recorded in 381 (Mnemius or Mnemonius), some time in the seventh century (Theodorus), in 680 (Tychon), in 787 (Theodorus). It fell gradually into decay, and its name was transferred from the site at Larnaka to a village farther south.

Paphos[4]—and by this we mean Nea Paphos, which was the administrative capital of Cyprus under the Romans—was, as we have seen, so badly shaken by earthquakes that it never recovered and has been allowed to remain in ruins, even to the present day. It appears that it did not retain even second place among the bishoprics, for in none of the lists down to the time of the Frankish occupation is it mentioned anywhere earlier than fifth or sixth. Little is heard of it during the Byzantine period;[5] there is a long gap in the list of bishops after Sapricius (who was at the Council of Ephesus, 431) until we reach the time of St Neophytus (p. 309 n.). A body of Varangians was stationed there in the first half of the twelfth century.[6] That a Byzantine fortress stood there in 1159 we know from St Neophytus, who was imprisoned in it for a night and a day;[7] and in 1191, according to one chronicler, it was one of the strongholds that surrendered to Richard.[8]

---

[1] Above, p. 263, n. 1.

[2] Below, p. 326. The history of St Auxibius (*Acta SS.* 19 Feb. p. 128) says that Tychicus was ordained bishop of Neapolis; this would seem to take the name Neapolis back to the time of the introduction of Christianity; but the history in its present form is not earlier than the fourth century.

[3] The best account of Citium in the Christian era is in Oberhummer's art. *Kition* in *R.E.* XI, 1921, 543.

[4] Hackett, pp. 314 f.; Jeffery, *Hist. Mon.* pp. 399 ff.; L. Philippou, *Tourists' Guide to Paphos*, 1936.

[5] The underground church of Ayia Solomoni was formed out of an ancient tomb, and has remains of proto-Byzantine painting. Sotiriou, *Byz. Mn.* Pl. 7b.

[6] Mentioned by the Abbot Nicolas of Thingeyrar, who returned from his travels in 1154 (*Antiquités Russes d'après les monuments hist. des Islandais*, Soc. roy. des Antiquaires du Nord, Copenhagen, II, 1852, p. 408—the reference is due to Prof. Dawkins).

[7] *Typ. Diath.* c. IV: πρὸς τὸ φρούριον ἀφικνοῦμαι τῆς Πάφου·...φοραθεὶς δὲ τοῖς φρουροῖς τοῦ νεοσταύθμου καὶ ὡς φυγὰς ἁλωθείς, ἐβλήθην εἰς φυλακὴν νυχθήμερον ἕν.

[8] Hoveden, ed. Stubbs, III, p. 111. In later references to the fortifications it is usually impossible to say whether the harbour defences or some others on land are meant; but

Kerynia was destined to play a great part in Cypriote history in Frankish times, though before then little is recorded of it.[1] It was an episcopal see from early Christian times, and the rock-cut cemeteries at Chrysocava and A. Mavra on the outskirts of the town are among the most important in Cyprus.[2] But the only bishop whose name is known is Theodotus, who is said to have suffered martyrdom under Licinius (314–324). Embodied in the thickness of the wall of Kerynia Castle is a little Byzantine chapel, cruciform in plan, with a dome (rebuilt) supported originally on four columns (of which three and fragments of the fourth remain), bearing Corinthian capitals of earlier date.[3] At the end of the eleventh century the town was already fortified, even if it had no castle, for it had to be taken by assault by John Ducas when he went to quell the revolt of Rhapsomates (p. 298). We do not hear of it again for a hundred years, when the usurper Isaac sent his wife and daughter to take refuge in the castle, which had to surrender to Guy de Lusignan. The fortress was thus already playing the part which fell to it with regularity later, the part, that is, of a strong place in which the rulers stored their treasures or to which they fled when they could not defend the capital.

Lapithos[4] (anciently Lāpēthos or Lāpāthos) has been since the Middle Ages the name of the large village some 2 km. up the hill[5] to the south-west of the ancient city, the site of which, on the shore, is known as Lambousa, and has been used as a quarry by the new village as well as

---

the latter are, at least in part, indicated by the citadel and forts built by James I about 1391 (Amadi, p. 495; Fl. Bustron, p. 352: "la citadella e le fortezze di Baffo"). The ruined castle on the hill is mentioned by Mariti in 1769 (*Viaggi*, I, p. 196).

[1] Oberhummer, *Keryneia* in *R.E.* XI, 1921, 344–7, gives a good sketch of its history. The form of the name *Kyrenia*, which is found since Christian times, and is now generally used, is thought to have been altered, under the influence of *Kyrene*, from the earlier *Keryneia*. Many Greek writers more properly use the latter. *Keraunia* (Ptolemy) is probably a learned corruption. There is some evidence for an early form with *Kor-*, although *Koroneia* in Steph. Byz. is surely a corruption inspired by the name of the Boeotian city.

[2] Sotiriou, *Byz. Mn.* Pls. 1b–4.

[3] Enlart, II, p. 574; Gunnis, p. 126; Sotiriou, *op. cit.* Pl. 23a.

[4] Est. de Lusignan, *Chorogr.* fo. 13 v°; Kyprianos, p. 39; Sakellarios, I, pp. 140–4; Hackett, p. 319; Jeffery, *Hist. Mon.* pp. 319–21; Oberhummer, *Lapethos* in *R.E.* XII, 1924, 763–6; Gunnis, pp. 313–18. Distinguish the present village of Lapathos, between Gypsos and Trikomo.

[5] This transference, as in the case of Rhizokarpaso, was probably due to the desire to escape piratical raids.

by the adjacent Karavas. The magnificent perennial spring of Kephalovryso makes Lapithos and Karavas among the most flourishing and attractive places in the island. The pottery industry still active at Lapithos appears to be of ancient origin. Bishops of Lapithos are mentioned in 451 (Didymus) and 655 (Eusebius), as well as Eulalius, of uncertain date.[1] We shall see that it was sacked by the Arabs in 653 (p. 285). The treasures of silver plate of sixth-century date found at Lambousa and Karavas are an indication of its importance at that time.[2] The remains of the lighthouse, an artificial fish-pond, and other constructions seem to be of Byzantine origin. The famous monastery of Achiropietos contains remains of early date; the main church, cruciform with a dome, has a domed narthex, and an apse which may be of early Christian times; a Frankish exonarthex has been added.[3] The beautiful little church of St Eulalius[4] is of Frankish date (fifteenth century ?), but was erected over a much earlier building, of which portions of a tessellated floor, probably not later than the seventh century, remain.[5] The strange rock-cut chapel of St Eulambius seems to have some claim to early Christian origin.

Carpasia,[6] the chief place in the peninsula of the Karpass, was the port on the north coast, among the ruins of which now stands the church

---

[1] The Cyprus Museum has two specimens of the early Byzantine seal inscribed Λαπιθου εκκλησιας.

[2] The first treasure (in the British Museum): Dalton, *Archaeologia*, LVII, 1900, pp. 159 ff.; B.M.C. *Early Christian and Byzantine Antiquities*, 1905, pp. 86–90; *Byz. Ztschr.* XV, 1906, pp. 615–17; *Byz. Art and Archaeology*, 1911, pp. 572–6; *East Christian Art*, 1925, p. 328 ("it is possible that the treasure was produced in Cyprus itself"; but in *Byz. Ztschr. loc. cit.* he preferred Syria or Egypt). The second treasure (partly in the Nicosia Museum, partly in the Pierpont Morgan Collection): Dalton, *Archaeologia*, LX, 1906, pp. 1–24; *Burlington Magazine*, X, 1907, pp. 355 ff.; and his two other books, *loc. cit.* Although one find-spot was given as near the monastery of Achiropietos, and the other as Karavas, it is probable, as Dalton says, that there was only one treasure.

[3] Sotiriou, *Byz. Mn.* fig. 15 and Pls. 25, 26. I do not understand Jeffery (p. 319) when he says that the church has "two domes over the transepts"; the only domes are over the crossing of the main church and the central bay of the inner narthex. There are no transepts, but Mr Megaw points out that seen from north and south the gable-ends of the bays containing the domes are reminiscent of transepts in a western church.

[4] Sotiriou, *op. cit.* fig. 42 and Pl. 47. [5] *Report of Dept. of Ant.* 1935 (1936), p. 4.

[6] Est. de Lusignan, *Chorogr.* fo. 12 v°; Kyprianos, p. 36; Hogarth, *Devia Cypria*, pp. 53 ff.; Sakellarios, I, pp. 157–60; Hackett, p. 320; Oberhummer, *Karpasia* in *R.E.* X, 1919, 1996–9; *Report of Dept. of Ant.* 1935 (1936), pp. 14–16. For the history from the fourteenth century, see Mas Latrie, "Les Comtes du Carpas", in *Bibl. de l'École des Chartes*, XLI, 1880, pp. 375–92.

of A. Philon, a fourteenth-century building covering one of Byzantine date. The recent excavations have revealed the plan of what was probably a baptistery building attached to the original church, perhaps as early as the fifth century. The only Greek bishop whose date is known was Philon, who was ordained by Epiphanius, about 382. The ancient town was ruined, perhaps in the days of the piratical raids of the Saracens, and the population settled farther inland at Rhizokarpaso.

Of Soli[1] practically nothing is known in the Byzantine period, except the names of a few of its bishops.[2]

Arsinoe (Polis tis Chrysochou), a bishopric from early Christian times,[3] is hardly mentioned afterwards until the reorganization of 1222.

Curium,[4] although it was a bishopric from an early date (its bishop Theodotus is said to have suffered under Licinius) fell into obscurity, its place being taken by Episkopi (so named, perhaps, as the residence of its bishops).[5]

The name of Chytri, which became by metathesis Kythri (and was inevitably confused with Cythera), is represented by the modern Kythrea,[6] the flourishing township on the Nicosia-Famagusta road; but the ruin-field of the Greek and Roman city seems to be on the hill above the church of St Demetrianus about 1 km. east of the upper quarters of Kythrea.[7] This site cannot have enjoyed much of the benefits of the finest spring in Cyprus, which now feeds the modern town,[8] and from

---

[1] Hackett, pp. 323 ff.; Oberhummer, *Soloi* in *R.E.* III A, 1927, 938–41; A. Westholm, *The Temples of Soli*, Stockholm, 1936, pp. 20 f.

[2] To the list add John, of whom there is a seal in the Cyprus Museum (sixth–seventh century?) inscribed Ιωαννου επισκοπου Σολων.

[3] On the common confusion with Ammochostus, see Delehaye, *Anal. Boll.* XXVI, 1907, p. 286; Oberhummer, *Marion* in *R.E.* XIV, 1930, 1803, and above, p. 263, n. 1. For the bishops, Hackett, pp. 318–19. Ariston and Nicon (perhaps the same as Nicolaus) were predecessors of Arcadius, for whose life by Neophytus see Delehaye, as above, pp. 197–207. In the British Museum, from the collection of Wing-Commander Hubbard, Kerynia, is a seal inscribed Αγιας Εκκλησιας Αρσηνοης (sixth–seventh century?).

[4] Hackett, pp. 312 f.; Oberhummer, *Kurion* in *R.E.* XI, 1922, 2211.

[5] Menardos, Τοπωνυμικόν, p. 379.

[6] Modern Cypriote *Kyrká*; Frankish forms *Chirga*, *La Quithrie*, *La Queterie*, *Quercherie*: Dawkins on Machaeras, II, § 32, n. 6.

[7] Sakellarios, I, 1890, pp. 202 ff.; Oberhummer, *Chytroi* in *R.E.* III, 1899, 2530–32; Hackett, p. 321; Jeffery, *Hist. Mon.* pp. 269 ff.; Gunnis, pp. 308 f. Palekythro, 4 km. south of Kythrea, had a Byzantine church, but in spite of its name does not seem to represent ancient Chytri.

[8] Fl. Bustron, p. 29 (more than fifty water-mills). *O.C.* p. 227. An ordinance of

which water was carried by a Byzantine aqueduct all the way to Salamis. In the time of Epiphanius the seat of the bishop (Pappus) was a "wretched city". It was sacked by the Arabs in the time of the bishop St Demetrianus (about 885–912).[1]

Tamassus[2] disappears from history with the Frankish occupation, its last bishop being that Nilus who founded the monastery of Machaera.[3]

Tremithus or Tremithoussia,[4] famous as the home and see of St Spyridon (p. 248), and for that reason more than any other frequently mentioned by ecclesiastical writers, is said to have been the scene of the defeat of Isaac Comnenus in 1191, though the tradition that the place was afterwards destroyed by Richard[5] is probably quite baseless.

These cities must have been grouped in larger administrative districts, which superseded the four great districts into which the island had been divided in Roman times. We are told by a late authority[6] that "after Constantine the Great" the island was divided into fourteen eparchies or circuits, and their names are given as Paphos, Avdimou, Chrysochou, Kilani, Episkopi, Nemesos, Mazotos, Halikai (i.e., Citium-Larnaka), the Mesaria, Leukosia including Tremithus, Ammochostus, Carpasia, Kerynia and Pendayia or the Soli district. Of the old cities, Arsinoe-Marium is here represented by Chrysochou, Curium has given place to Episkopi, Amathus to Nemesos, Tamassus and Chytri, like Tremithus,

---

1413 dealt with the ownership and division of rights in the use of the stream, a matter of much importance at the present day. M.L. *H.* II, p. 504. The spring head, as at Lapithos, is called Kephalovryso.

[1] Grégoire in *Byz. Ztschr.* XVI, 1907, pp. 204 ff.

[2] Oberhummer, *Tamassos* in *R.E.* IV A, 2095–8.

[3] Below, p. 310; Hackett, pp. 313–14. Menardos, Ἡ ἐν Κύπρῳ ἱ. Μονὴ τῆς Παναγίας τοῦ Μαχαιρᾶ, pp. 7 f., argues that the see of Tamassus ranked, for a time, as next to the archbishopric; Nilus calls himself πρωτόθρονος, and Hierocles, Leontius Machaeras, Florio Bustron and Kyprianos all mention it immediately after the archbishopric. This seniority is to be connected with the tradition that St Barnabas founded there the first Christian community in Cyprus, consecrating Heraclides as its first bishop. But Paphos was certainly second to Nicosia among the Latin sees in 1211 (W. von Oldenburg).

[4] Kyprianos, p. 43; Sakellarios, I, 1890, pp. 190 f.; Hackett, 1901, pp. 322–3.

[5] Est. de Lusignan, *Chorogr.* fo. 14 v°, *Descr.* fo. 30; Kyprianos, p. 42. As Mas Latrie says (M.L. *H.* I, p. 10), the ancient ruins were mistaken for destruction wrought by the English.

[6] Kyprianos, p. 267. Κουρίνεον, which he gives as an alternative to Kilani, is presumably taken from Est. de Lusignan, *Chorogr.* fo. 6 and 17 (cp. *Descr.* fo. 34), who perhaps got it from Pliny (Corinaeum).

come under Leukosia, Lapithos goes with Kerynia. Avdimou (Evdhimou in modern maps), Kilani, Mazotos and the Mesaria were mainly agricultural districts; the first two are still important wine-growing regions, though the best commanderia is grown not there but in the Larnaka district.

All the three points in the northern range which were to be of military significance during the Frankish period, St Hilarion (Didymus), Buffavento and Kantara, were fortified in Byzantine times. As to St Hilarion,[1] the tradition that it was the last resting-place of the famous ascetic is firmly rooted,[2] although it was already pointed out by Machaeras (followed by Florio Bustron) that the Hilarion buried there was not the elder, but a younger or later saint.[3] There is in the castle an octagonal chapel, with three apses, with a small oratory adjoining, of Byzantine date, and something in the way of a fortress must have existed before 1191, although the military constructions which have survived appear to be all of Frankish origin. It is extremely unlikely that an eminence of such strategic importance should have remained unfortified until the beginning of the thirteenth century, and in fact we know that there was a castle of Didymus which fell into the hands of Guy de Lusignan at the same time as Kerynia.[4]

Buffavento,[5] generally known by this Italian form of the name Bufevent given to it by the Franks, was called the "Castle of the Lion"

---

[1] Mas Latrie, *Arch. des missions scientifiques*, I, 1850, pp. 508–11; G. Rey, *Étude sur les Monuments de l'arch. mil. des Croisés*, 1871, pp. 239–48; Enlart, II, 1899, pp. 578–96; Jeffery, *Hist. Mon.* pp. 263–68; Sotiriou, *Byz. Mn.* fig. 13, Pls. 23 b and 58 a.

[2] Hackett, pp. 407–11; cp. Dawkins on Machaeras, § 32. 5, II, p. 59. Above, p. 248.

[3] Oberhummer (*Ztschr. d. Ges. f. Erdk.* XXVII, pp. 435 f.) finds the description in the *Life of St Hilarion* apt for the rugged and inaccessible nature of the mountain near Kerynia. On the other hand, the distance, twelve miles, from the sea, and the well-watered gardens and orchards are not very appropriate. Delehaye (*Anal. Boll.* XXVI, 1907, pp. 241–2) thinks that the name of Hilarion I became artificially attached to the place (which might well happen if the less famous Hilarion II was buried there); and in time it came to be believed, in defiance of St Jerome, that the body and not merely the spirit of Hilarion I was still there. The popular tradition is defended, not very convincingly, by S. Loïzidou in Κυπρ. Σπουδαί II, pp. 48–54.

[4] *Itin. Reg. Ric.* ed. Stubbs, II, c. 39: "Rex Guido tria interim obsedit castella; scil. Cherines et Didimus et Bufevent, quorum duo priora cito adeptus est.... Rex Guido... duxit exercitum ad aliud castellum Didimus nuncupatum, situ firmissimum, in nulla expugnabile."

[5] Bufevent, Buffavent, Buffavento, is certainly formed under the influence, though it is not a translation, of Koutzoventi, above which monastery it stands; Lusignan says

by the Greeks. It was already a stronghold in 1191, but was taken by Richard after Kerynia and St Hilarion had fallen to Guy de Lusignan. The existing remains, except possibly the foundations, are of Lusignan date.

Kantara[1] (Pl. XV) was also in existence as a fortress before 1191, when it surrendered to Richard.

The earliest monastic foundations in Cyprus went back, according to tradition, to the fourth century. The most important of these was the monastery of the Holy Cross on Stavrovouni, ascribed, like the church at Tokhni, to St Helena (p. 246).[2] Of pre-Gothic work at Tokhni there remains but a portion of an apse.[3] The church and monastery on Stavrovouni have been so often rebuilt that the pre-Frankish portions

---

it was so called because of its windy situation. For the Greek name Λιόντας or Ἰλιόντας, see Dawkins on Machaeras, § 258. On the fortress, see Mas Latrie, *Arch. des miss. scient.* I, 1850, pp. 512–14; Rey, *Étude*, pp. 249–52; Enlart, II, pp. 596–605; Jeffery, *Hist. Mon.* pp. 274–5. It is the most inaccessible of the three fortresses, indeed of all places, in Cyprus; the difficulties of the ascent and descent are emphasized by Florio Bustron (p. 24), van Bruyn (*Exc. Cypr.* p. 237) and later writers (latest by Mrs Chapman, *Across Cyprus*, pp. 238–42). Cp. Dawkins on Machaeras, § 611, II, p. 202. Another name for the fortress is the Queen's Castle; its origin is obscure (see Enlart, II, p. 596 and n. 1). One would connect it with the legend of the foundation of the monastery of A. Chrysostomos at Koutzoventi, but that the same or a similar name seems to be used for all three castles; see Menardos in Δελτίον τῆς ἱστορ. κ. ἐθν. Ἑταιρίας VI, 1901, p. 130; Ross, *Journey to Cyprus*, tr. Cobham, p. 58; Jeffery, *Hist. Mon.* pp. 245–6; information from Prof. Dawkins (for Kantara, see his note on Machaeras, § 419, 6).

[1] The name is commonly connected with the Arabic *kantara*, which means "bridge". Enlart points out that this meaning is inapplicable. But Oberhummer (*Ztschr. d. Ges. f. Erdk.* XXVII, 1892, pp. 452 f.) gives also the sense of "high place", and for the survival of an Arabic name in the neighbourhood points to Komi Kebir. (The word Komi, by the way, is possibly a Greek corruption of the Arabic Kom, "mound". On the other hand, it has been suggested that the Turks added *Kebir* to distinguish this Κώμη from smaller ones: Menardos, Τοπωνυμικόν, p. 347. Its inhabitants are known as Κωμῆται *par excellence*. On this view, the name is not an Arabic survival.) Note that the French always prefix the article (la Candare or Candaire), which recalls the Spanish *Alcantara*; although the use of the article by the French in such place-names is apparently arbitrary (Mas Latrie, *l'Île de Chypre*, p. 164). On the remains (curiously ignored by Rey), which are better preserved than those of the other two castles, see Mas Latrie, *Arch. des miss. scient.* I, 1850, p. 514; Enlart, II, pp. 648–54; Jeffery, *Hist. Mon.* pp. 245–7. Hogarth (*Devia Cypria*, p. 101) describes it as commanding the finest view in Cyprus, an opinion which few will dispute.

[2] On the legends connected with the history of these foundations see Hackett, pp. 433–54; Gunnis, pp. 439–41, 428–32.

[3] Enlart, II, p. 446.

are almost completely disguised.[1] The relic of the Cross is mentioned as early as 1106–7 by the Russian Abbot Daniel.[2] At that time the foundations must still have belonged to the Basilian Order which was originally established there.

By tradition almost contemporary with the foundations of Stavrovouni and Tokhni was that of St Nicolas of the Cats at Akrotiri, on the Salt Lake of Limassol; for its foundation is connected by legend with Calocaerus in the time of Constantine the Great (p. 244).[3] The monastery belonged to the Basilian Order.

Coming down to times when legend seems to have more support in history, we note that the eleventh and twelfth centuries must have shown a vigorous growth of monastic foundations—Kykko, Machaera, Koutzoventi, the Enkleistra, Chrysorrhogiatissa, Achiropietos are all evidence therefor.[4] As early as the twelfth century also, there was evidently a beginning of activity in the building and decoration of churches such as the Panayia tis Asinou (p. 323).[5]

The most significant episode in the history of Cyprus in the early Byzantine age was undoubtedly the struggle for the autocephaly of its Church.[6] Independently of its importance in the eyes of the ecclesi-

[1] Enlart, in *Revue de l'Orient latin*, IV, 1896, pp. 625 ff. The same, *L'art gothique*, II, p. 420. There seems to have been a small three-aisled Byzantine church, with three apses forming a trefoil at the eastern end; the most eastern bay has a groined vault flanked by two side apses, the eastern one having disappeared. The two next bays have cupolas on cylindrical drums; if the eastern bay also had a cupola, the church would have resembled Yeroskipos; but possibly it never had more than the two cupolas. The next bay, the original narthex, has no cupola; a new narthex was added, probably after the earthquake of 1492.

[2] *Pal. Pilgr. Text Soc.* 1888, p. 8.

[3] Enlart, II, pp. 460–6; Hackett, pp. 358–60; Jeffery, *Hist. Mon.* pp. 371–3; Gunnis, pp. 155–9.

[4] See below, pp. 308 ff., and generally Hackett, ch. VII, pp. 329–69.

[5] The interesting monastic church of Panayia tou Arakou near Lagoudhera was in existence by 1193, for the dedicatory inscription says it was painted in that year; but the existing paintings are later (A. Steel, in *I.L.N.* 6 Feb. 1937, pp. 214 f.).

[6] The admirably reasoned and fully documented discussion of this subject in Hackett's *Hist. of the Orthodox Church of Cyprus*, 1901, pp. 13–33, makes it superfluous to give chapter and verse for all the statements which follow. The most important details are of course in the discussion of the question at the Council of Ephesus (Mansi, *Conc.* IV, cols. 1465–9), resulting in the decision known as the Eighth Canon. No apology seems necessary for omitting reference to the repetitions of the story which, adding, so far as I have been able to ascertain, nothing new, swell out the flood of controversial literature on the current archiepiscopal question.

astical historian, it has value as an indication that the Cypriote Church, in defending its rights, could show a determination which seems to have been completely lacking to the people in the face of physical force.

How early the Patriarchs of Antioch began to claim the right of consecrating the metropolitan of Cyprus, we do not know. The claim seems to have been based chiefly on the fact that Cyprus, as one of the provinces of the Diocese of the Orient, was subordinate to Antioch, the seat of the governor of the Diocese. A Canon, alleged to have been adopted by the Council of Nicaea in 325, assumes that the Patriarch of Antioch has the right of appointing the archbishop of Cyprus, but may allow the suffragans of the island to elect their archbishop if by reason of winter weather communication is rendered impossible. But there is little doubt that this Canon, like the rest of the Arabic Canons of the Council, is a forgery, the object of which is fairly patent.

During the reign of Pope Innocent I (402–417), Alexander, the then Patriarch of Antioch, wrote to the Pope claiming that his predecessors had formerly exercised the right, but that the Cypriotes, contrary to the Nicene Canons, had taken it on themselves to ordain their own bishops. The Pope, accepting the statement of the Patriarch, ordered the Cypriotes to return to their obedience.[1] Whether they replied and confuted Alexander, we do not know, but they continued to exercise their independence. The commentators generally hold that Innocent's order was conditional on the statement of Alexander being correct.

The struggle came to a head at the Council of Ephesus in 431.[2] At that Council it was stated that two of the metropolitans, Troïlus and Theodorus, had already been ill-treated, the latter actually struck, when in Antioch, because they declined to admit the supremacy of the Patriarch.

In 431 Theodorus, the archbishop of Constantia, died. The Patriarch of Antioch at the time was John, who seized the opportunity to press his claims. He induced Flavius Dionysius, the Count of the Orient, to send orders to the Consular of Cyprus (who was also called Theodorus) to prevent, by force if necessary, the election of a new archbishop, until the question had been submitted to the General Council, which had been summoned to meet at Ephesus at Whitsuntide to consider the

[1] Innoc. *Epist.* 24. 3 in Galland, *Bibl. Vet. Patr.* VIII, 1772, p. 584; Migne, *P.L.* 20, col. 549; Jaffé, *Reg. Pont. Rom.* I, p. 47, no. 310; Hackett, pp. 13 f.

[2] Mansi, *Conc.* IV, cols. 1465 ff.; Hackett, pp. 16 ff. (with references to earlier writers); W. Bright, *Age of the Fathers*, 1903, II, pp. 331 f.

charge of heresy against Nestorius, Patriarch of Constantinople. The Count wrote to Theodorus on 21 May, giving orders that, if the election had already taken place when his letter arrived, the newly elected archbishop was to attend the Council, with his suffragans. The letter was carried by two military officers and a deacon of Antioch, empowered to enforce the order. They had also a letter to the Chapter of Constantia to the same effect. Heavy penalties were threatened in case of disobedience by the Consular or the Chapter. The Cypriote suffragans, in spite of these fulminations, proceeded to elect a new archbishop, Rheginus; but they obeyed the order in so far that he and four others departed at once for Ephesus. One of these, Sapricius of Paphos, died early in the course of the sessions, so that the defence of the Cypriote cause was left to Zeno of Curium, Evagrius of Soli, and the Protopapas Caesarius.

John's behaviour in the unseemly squabble which developed over the Nestorian question was probably not worse than that of his opponents, but it must have rendered the latter only too ready to sympathize with the Cypriote cause. In the seventh session, Rheginus presented a memorial, recounting the violence which had been done to his predecessors, asserting that the Count would not have interfered but for the instigation of John, protesting against this attempt to make illegal innovations, contrary to the decisions of the Council of Nicaea,[1] and appealing for the recognition of the independence of the Church of Cyprus. The Council carefully considered all the correspondence and documents, and questioned Zeno and Evagrius. These witnesses assured them that from the earliest apostolic age the local Cypriote synod had always appointed the archbishop; no bishop of Antioch or of any other place outside Cyprus had consecrated a bishop in Constantia or any other see in Cyprus, nor had the right of consecration which the Cypriotes exercised been in virtue of any concession from outside. Three archbishops, Epiphanius, Sabinus and Troïlus, as to whom Zeno was specially questioned, he showed to be no exceptions to this rule.

The Council finally came to the resolution embodied in what is known as the Eighth Canon of Ephesus. This resolution affirmed that if, as the Cypriotes asserted, it was not in accordance with ancient custom for the bishop of Antioch to hold consecrations in Cyprus, then

[1] The Sixth Canon of the Council of Nicaea confirmed the rights of "the Churches of Antioch and the other eparchies", and by the latter phrase must be understood all the other provinces, including Cyprus. See Beveridge in Hackett, p. 31.

the presidents of the holy Churches in Cyprus should have the unfettered right of making the consecrations of the bishops themselves, according to the Canons of the holy fathers and ancient custom. It will be observed that the decision is conditional; it does not actually endorse the assertions of the Cypriote bishops.

But, if the Council would not commit itself, it was evidently in itself satisfied, and the decision seems to have been accepted by John himself. That he had no real ground for disputing the Cypriote claim may be gathered from the fact that in a letter to the Patriarch Proclus of Constantinople he omitted Cyprus in a list which he gave of the provinces of the Eastern Diocese which were under Antioch.[1]

The position of the church of Cyprus, as independent of Antioch, appears to be reflected in the lists of bishops present, or signing, at various Councils of the fourth and fifth centuries. These lists are so arranged that the various provinces are grouped under the dioceses; so that Cyprus ought to come under the Diocese of the Orient. But already, at Nicaea, in 325, Cyprus, with Isauria, stands outside that Diocese; and so too at Constantinople in 381. At Chalcedon in 451 Cyprus is taken out and placed by itself at the end, after the Asian Diocese.[2]

Nevertheless the anomalous position of Cyprus, as it must have appeared, rankled in the minds of the Antiochene clergy, and some forty-five years later, in the reign of the Emperor Zeno, the dispute was revived by the Patriarch Peter the Fuller. Peter was a protégé of Zeno, by whose help he had succeeded in ousting Martyrius from the Patriarchate and taking his place (about 469). He was almost immediately expelled, but was reinstated for a short time about 476/7, and again towards the end of his life about 484/5. He died three or four years later.[3] His attack on Cyprus, since it was made during the reign of Zeno (474–491), must have dated from his third tenure of the see; for the date 478, to which it is assigned by one chronicler,[4] is in a year when Peter was not in the seat at Antioch, and a date in the reign of Anastasius

---

[1] Chr. Lupus (Wolff), *Opera*, VII (1726), p. 356; Hackett, pp. 21–2.

[2] E. Schwartz, "Über die Bischofslisten der Synoden von Chalkedon, Nicaea u. K'pel", in *Abh. Bay. Akad.*, Phil.-hist. Abt. N.F., Hft. 13, 1937, pp. 14, 84.

[3] In A.D. 488 according to Victor Tonnenensis (Mommsen, *Chr. Min.* II, p. 191): according to Theophanes in A.M. 5983, seventeenth year of Zeno=491 (de Boor, p. 135).

[4] Cedrenus (ed. Bonn), I, pp. 618–19.

(491–518), given by another, is too late.[1] We may therefore accept 488, the date given by Victor of Tunis.

Peter adopted a new line of attack, to meet with an even more crushing defeat than John. He claimed that Cyprus had been converted to Christianity from Antioch (which was true), and that, since Antioch was an apostolic foundation, Cyprus should be subject to it. The argument is obscure, in view of the firm tradition of the visit to Cyprus of the Apostles Paul and Barnabas. However, it seems to have carried weight and, supported by the Emperor, would probably have succeeded, but for the exceedingly opportune intervention of the Apostle Barnabas himself. Warned by him in what Gibbon would describe as a "seasonable vision", the archbishop Anthemius went in solemn procession to a place which the vision had indicated, dug under a tree, and opened a cave, in which he found in a coffin the remains of the Saint. On his breast lay, where Mark had placed it, the copy of Matthew's Gospel, written by Barnabas himself, which had always accompanied him on his journeys. The vision had also told Anthemius to appeal, with this new evidence, to the Emperor, which he accordingly did, proceeding to Constantinople with the relics. On the Emperor's order, the dispute was referred to a Synod summoned by the Patriarch of Constantinople. The claim that Antioch was the first see of St Peter, and therefore superior to Cyprus, was instantly refuted by the proof, now forthcoming, that Cyprus was just as much an apostolic foundation. The attack collapsed.

In addition to securing its autocephaly,[2] the see of Constantia received further extraordinary privileges: to this day the Archbishops sign with

---

[1] Niceph. Call. *H.E.* XVI, c. 37 (Migne, *P.G.* 147, col. 200).

[2] Theodorus Lector (sixth century) in the Excerpts alleged to have been made by Nicephorus Callisti (Migne, *P.G.* 86 (i), col. 184); [Leo Grammat.] p. 117 (Bonn); Theodos. Meliten. p. 82 (ed. Tafel); Joel, p. 43 (Bonn); Georgius Monachus, II, p. 619 (de Boor). Severus, Patriarch of Antioch, says in a letter (Assemani, *Bibl. Or.* II, pp. 81 f.) that, when in Constantinople in the time of the Patriarch Macedonius (495–511), he saw the magnificently written copy of the Gospel of St Matthew which was said to have been found in the time of Zeno in a city of Cyprus, with the body of St Barnabas. According to the first form of the legend, the saint's body had been burnt; the more useful version must have soon been established, though the definitive shape given to the legend may be due to the history of the saint's travels and of the invention of his relics written by the monk Alexander, guardian of the church built over the tomb. See Duchesne in *Mélanges G.B. de Rossi*, 1892, pp. 45–9; and cp. the *Itinera et Passio SS. Bartholomaei et Barnabae* in Latyšev, *Menol. Anon. Byz. saec.* X, II, 1912, pp. 34–40.

red ink (a distinction which none but the Emperor enjoyed), wear a purple cloak at Church festivals, and carry an imperial sceptre instead of a pastoral staff. These privileges, expressing recognition of temporal authority, seem somewhat excessive, and have had frequent repercussions down to the present day. Anthemius paid for them by presenting the copy of the Gospel to the Emperor. Zeno placed it in the Chapel of St Stephen in the Palace, where it was read every Good Friday. The remaining relics Anthemius brought back to Cyprus, where they were placed beside the altar in the church which he built on the place where the body was discovered. A monastery and hospice were also erected beside the church.[1]

That the chrism used in episcopal consecrations continued to be obtained from Antioch must not be regarded as a sign of dependence on that see. The consecration of the chrism being reserved to Patriarchs, the Cypriote metropolitans, who had not that rank, obtained it from the nearest possible source. This they continued to do as late as 1860, when the practice ceased, owing to troubles in Syria; after 1864 it was obtained from Constantinople.[2]

Thus the Church of Cyprus became finally in reality independent. In the statement of Cedrenus and others[3] that, after the defeat of Antioch in the time of Zeno, Cyprus was made subject to "Constantinople", it is to be assumed that this last word is an error for "Constantia".

The independence of the Church of Cyprus was again confirmed some

---

[1] The cave where the body of St Barnabas was discovered is about 100 metres from the church. At the church itself excavations at the east end have revealed the original bema, with remains of the marble floor, and, to the south of it, those of a chapel, with the tomb in which the relics were placed when brought back from Constantinople; the tomb is covered by a slab pierced with a circular hole, the *mensa martyris*. (Sotiriou, *Byz. Mn.* Pl. 17 and Κυπρ. Σπουδαί, I, 1937, pp. 182 f.)

[2] Hackett, pp. 31–2, correcting Mas Latrie, *H.* I, p. 81.

[3] Cedrenus, I, p. 619 (Bonn). The subjection to Constantinople is asserted by Theodos. Meliten. and Leo Grammat., but not by Theodorus Lector or Joel: Hackett, pp. 26–7. In this connexion, mention may be made of the account by John of Ephesus (ed. E. W. Brooks in Graffin-Nau, *Patr. Orient.* XIX, p. 154) of how James Burd'ana, who was made bishop of Edessa by Theodora in 542, had authority over all Asia Minor, and the islands of Cyprus, Rhodes, etc., as far as Constantinople. The personal influence of this champion of Monophysitism gave him the leadership of that sect, especially as the Monophysite patriarchate of Antioch was in abeyance, and Anthimus, the last Monophysite patriarch of Constantinople, had been deposed in 536. (Note from Mr Brooks; cp. Diehl et Marçais, *Le monde oriental de* 395 *à* 1081, p. 108.) Henceforward the Monophysites were called, after him, *Jacobites*.

two hundred years later, at the Quini-Sext or Trullan Council at Constantinople in 692.[1] At that time the Cypriotes and their Church were, as we shall see, exiles at Nova Justinianopolis, on the Hellespont. It was natural that on this transplantation it should be considered necessary to confirm the rights which had been accorded by the Council of Ephesus to the Metropolitan. Therefore the Thirty-ninth Trullan Canon says that the privileges granted at the Council of Ephesus shall be continued, so that Nova Justinianopolis shall have the right of Constantia, and the bishop established therein shall preside over the whole of the Hellespontine province, and be elected by his own bishops according to ancient custom.[2]

This confirmation has been quite unjustifiably taken to imply that the question had not been actually settled two hundred years before.[3] It was, as said above, merely considered necessary to restate the facts, in view of the transference of the Metropolitan and his flock to a new home. Since there he might naturally have come under the jurisdiction of Constantinople, his complete independence required reassertion.

Apart from these disputes concerning the Church, Cyprus, it would seem, enjoyed a peaceful existence during the fifth and sixth centuries. The struggles of the Empire with the Persians did not directly affect it, although the danger from that quarter came as near as Antioch, which was destroyed by Chosroes in 540. This was however but a passing menace, and Antioch was soon rebuilt by Justinian, though on a smaller scale, and renamed Theüpolis. Whether any of the disastrous earthquakes from which that unfortunate city suffered in the period with which we are concerned was felt in Cyprus, we are not authoritatively told, but it is unlikely that the island should have escaped altogether.[4] If good authorities do not mention such disasters in Cyprus, likewise

---

[1] For the date 692 rather than 691 see Bury, *Hist. Lat. Rom. Emp.* II, 1889, p. 327 n.

[2] Mansi, *Conc.* XI, col. 961; Hackett, pp. 37–8. John was to have the same privileges in the Hellespontine city as he had enjoyed in Constantia; the correct reading is τὸ δίκαιον ἔχειν τῆς Κωνσταντιέων πόλεως, not Κωνσταντινουπόλεως. See Georg. Philippou, Εἰδήσεις ἱστορ. περὶ τῆς ἐκκλ. τῆς Κύπρου, Athens, 1875, pp. 32 f., note.

[3] Sathas' opinion (II, pp. λ' f.) is dealt with by Georgios Philippou, *op. cit.* pp. 22 ff., note, quoted by Hackett, pp. 28 f.

[4] Kyprianos (p. 105) says many buildings were ruined in Cyprus in the reign of Justinian. Shocks are recorded at Antioch in 458, 525, 526, 528, 532, 553, 557, 561 (Capelle in *R.E.* Supp. IV, 356).

are they silent about the great bubonic plague which devastated the world from Persia to Italy in 542/3.[1] Since it started in Egypt and spread to Palestine and Syria and thence to Asia Minor, it is certain that it must have visited Cyprus.

On the architectural activity of Justinian in the island, the only actual record is of the building of the poor-house of St Conon and the restoration of his aqueduct in Cyprus.[2] It is generally assumed, but on insufficient grounds, that this was the aqueduct from Chytri to Salamis of which remains still exist.[3] A series of inscriptions shows that work was done on this Salamis aqueduct, probably in the last ten years of the sixth century and the beginning of the seventh, by the Archbishops Plutarchus and Arcadius I, and by the Emperor Heraclius in 618 or 633.[4]

A worthless tradition[5] ascribed to Justinian I the foundation of Ayia Sophia in Leukosia, but of such early work there is no trace. To his time or a little later have been assigned the now ruined churches of Aphendrika and Sykada near Rhizokarpaso, but this dating has not met with general acceptance.[6]

One important benefit was conferred on the island, in or soon after the time of Justinian, by the introduction of the silk-worm. The production of an inferior kind of silk from a wild silk-worm had long been known in Greek lands, but endeavours to procure the secret of the silk-

---

[1] Bury, *Hist. Lat. Rom. Emp.* II, 1923, pp. 62 f.

[2] Procop. *de aed.* 5, 9: τὸ πτωχεῖον τοῦ ἁγίου Κόνωνος. τὸν ἀγωγὸν αὐτοῦ ἀνενέωσεν ἐν Κύπρῳ.

[3] Since the skull of St Conon was preserved at Paphos (Kyprianos, p. 360), may not his "aqueduct" be the irrigation system of which the remains at Paphos have been described (*O.C.* pp. 222, 233)? St Conon, martyr, contemporary of the Apostles (see Delehaye, *Anal. Boll.* XXVI, 1907, p. 261), gave his name to a place in the Acamas, where there are Byzantine ruins (Gunnis, *Hist. Cyprus*, p. 382; L. Philippou, Ἀκαμαντὶς καὶ Μάριον, Paphos, 1938, p. 6). I take it this St Conon is different from St Conon the Gardener, who seems to be connected with Isauria (see *Synax. Eccl. Cpl.*, *Acta SS.* 68, cols. 514, 996).

[4] *C.I.G.* 8658, 8663; Oberhummer in *Sbr. Bay. Akad.*, Phil.-hist. Class. 1888, pp. 341 ff.; Sakellarios, I, pp. 179 f., nos. 24–7.

[5] Kyprianos, p. 104. Sathas (Μεσ. Βιβλ. II, pp. κη′ ff.) has demolished it, and its accompanying story of the Cypriote origin of Theodora (Philotheos ap. Kypr. p. 379); he also notes the absurd tradition mentioned by Constantine Porph. (*de adm. imp.* 47) that Justinian II was a Cypriote, though he was well known to be the legitimate son of Constantine Pogonatus.

[6] See below, p. 322 and n. 2.

worm proper from China had been in vain, until about 552[1] two monks who had lived in the Far East undertook to smuggle eggs of the worm through to the West. They brought the eggs concealed in a hollow cane. The worm was at once naturalized in Syria, but whether at the same time or later in Cyprus is not known. The industry became, but is no longer, one of the most important in the island.[2]

Towards the end of the reign of Justin II (who died in 578) or more probably soon afterwards,[3] the already very composite population of the island received an admixture of a large number of captives, who had been taken in Arzanene in Great Armenia by Maurice, afterwards the Emperor Maurice Tiberius, in his campaign against Chosroes.[4]

The only governor of Cyprus recorded in the sixth century is Epiphanius, the father of St John the Almoner. The saint was born at Amathus while his father was in office. He became patriarch of Alexandria about 610/11. When the Persians under Chosroes took the city in 616, he went back to Cyprus. One of his biographers relates that he intervened to make the peace between the people of Constantia and a general ("strategos"), called Aspagourius, who was refused admission to the city. Both sides were about to engage in battle, when John inter-

---

[1] Procopius (*Bell. Goth.* IV, 17); Theophanes Byz. *F.H.G.* IV, p. 270 (who says it was a Persian who demonstrated the culture to Justinian); Bury, *Hist. Lat. Rom. Emp.* II, 1923, p. 332.

[2] *Hdb.* pp. 174–5; *Ann. Rep. of Dept. of Agriculture* for 1936, pp. 15, 47 f. It naturally suffers increasingly from the competition of artificial silk.

[3] The capture of the prisoners is attributed by Theophylact Simocatta (III, 15. 15, p. 143 de Boor) to Maurice. But Tiberius II does not seem to have put Maurice in the high command against the Parthians until after the death of Justin, so that he could hardly have received so large a number of prisoners before 578. Bury (*Hist. Lat. Rom. Emp.* II, 1889, p. 104 note) inclines to that year.

[4] Theophylact Simocatta, III, 15. 15: the number of prisoners was ἐνενήκοντα πρὸς ταῖς δέκα χιλιάσι; of these a third were allotted to Maurice. He reported the capture to the Emperor, by whose orders the prisoners were distributed throughout the villages of Cyprus. John of Ephesus, *Eccl. Hist.* (trans. E. W. Brooks, *Corp. Scr. Chr. Or.* 1935, pp. 236, 257), and Agathias, IV, 29 (p. 272, ed. Bonn), do not give any figures. The figure 10,090 is certainly curious; but, assuming the text to be correct, it is clear that Sathas and others have completely misunderstood Theophylact, when they say that some 30,000 prisoners were captured by Maurice and distributed through Cyprus; presumably they ignore πρὸς ταῖς δέκα and take the total number as 90,000 and Maurice's share as 30,000. It is not clear from Theophylact whether all the 10,090 were settled in Cyprus, or only Maurice's third of that number. Most of the captives were probably, as Bury says, Christian Armenians.

vened and pacified them. The context of this story, and the name of the governor, might suggest that he was sent by the Persians; but an expedition across the sea on their part would be unprecedented, and we must assume that Aspagourius was the representative of Byzantium.[1]

It was not until after the close of the reign of Heraclius (610–641) that Cyprus saw the beginning of the Saracen invasions, which were to rob the Empire, at frequent intervals for some three and a third centuries, of the possession of the island. Meanwhile, we have slight indications that it was not neglected by that Emperor.[2] One, the record of work on the aqueduct of Salamis, has already been mentioned. Another is the fact that a mint was established and coins were struck, doubtless at the capital.[3] The issue, which however lasted only two or three years, from about

---

[1] *Menolog.* of Basil Porphyrog. ap. Gelzer, *Leontios von Neapolis' Leben des h. Iohannes d. Barmherz.* 1893, p. 115; cp. Moschus and Sophronius, *ibid.* p. 108. Delehaye, "Une vie inédite de Saint-Jean-l'Aumonier", in *Anal. Boll.* XLV, Brussels, 1927 (a Venice MS. in which Leontius and Sophronius are combined, and of which the life by Metaphrastes is a transposition). Neophytus Rhodinus, Περὶ ἡρώων, Rome, 1659, p. 85 (reprinted in Κυπριακὰ Χρονικά, III, 1925, p. 25), says that Epiphanius was duke of Cyprus, not, as Sathas takes it (II, p. κβ', n. 1), that he was in office under Heraclius, but that the Alexandrians asked Heraclius to make John patriarch of Alexandria. That was in 610/11. Lusignan (*Chorogr.* fo. 9) followed by Kyprianos (p. 24) says that in the time of the Dukes Amathus flourished and had the honour of being a Metropolis and their seat. This would explain why John was born there. He also died and was buried there (Delehaye, as above, p. 25); in the statement of Eutychius of Alexandria as to the place of his burial (quoted by O.C. p. 43 from the Latin transl. by Pococke), for *Astnta* we must without any reasonable doubt read *Amtnṭa*, i.e. Amathunta.—The Aspagourius episode at Constantia is puzzling. The wording of the passage (Delehaye, *op. cit.* p. 25) suggests that he was a military officer, not an ordinary governor, sent on an expedition against Constantia: στρατηγὸς ἐπὶ Κωνσταντίαν τὴν κατὰ Κύπρον σταλεὶς καὶ μὴ δεχθεὶς παρὰ τῶν τῆς πόλεως, εἰς πόλεμον ὡπλίσθη, κ.τ.λ. But if he was sent *against* Constantia, he cannot have expected to be peacefully received by the authorities of the city. Possibly therefore we must not press the wording. Was he leading an expedition, sent by the Byzantine government, to Alexandria, and had he stopped on the way? (N.H.B.)

[2] In this connexion, misinterpretation of an inscription (*C.I.G.* 8662; Sathas, II, p. κβ', n. 1) has led to the assumption that there was a "Count of Cyprus" named Flavius Thomas, who restored the work at one of the gates in Attalia; he was really Count and Consular of Pamphylia (Grégoire, *Rec. d. inscr. chrét. d'Asie Mineure*, no. 309).

[3] Copper folles of forty nummia, marked ΚΥΠΡ, bearing dates (so far as they can be read with certainty) 17 and 18, i.e. 626/7 and 627/8, possibly also 15. These coins continued in circulation, as is shown by countermarks, into the reign of Constans II (641–668): Wroth, *B.M.C. Imp. Byz.* pp. 222–3.

624/5 to 627/8, bore the figures of the Emperor between his young son Heraclius Constantine and his second wife Martina. It is an unimportant coinage, of copper only (though in this it is not inferior to the issues of other mints of the East, for under Heraclius gold and silver issues were confined to Constantinople, Carthage and Ravenna). It must have played but a modest part in the vast coinage which this Emperor, like Justinian I, found necessary to finance his campaigns.

The Emperor seems also, some time shortly before 626, to have made the Church of Cyprus the subject of a theological experiment.[1] For in that year, Cyrus, bishop of Phasis, writing to Sergius, Patriarch of Constantinople, says that when he met Heraclius in Lazica (in Colchis) he read the decree which the Emperor had issued to Arcadius, archbishop of Cyprus, setting forth the orthodox doctrine, but insisting on the single energy of Christ—the beginning of Monotheletism. It is suggested that "perhaps the success of this attempt at unity on a small scale within the limits of the island encouraged him to apply afterwards the same balm to the wounds of the entire Empire".[2]

It was in 632 (if we could believe a Greek writer—the Eastern historians know nothing about the matter) that the Arab invaders first showed themselves in Cyprus, under Abu-Bekr, the father-in-law of the Prophet.[3] We have no details of such a raid, except a doubtful tradition that it was Abu-Bekr's daughter who died in Cyprus and whose tomb is at Hala Sultan Tekke near Larnaka; and the probability is that it never took place.

---

[1] Hefele, *Hist. of the Councils*, v, p. 12; Bury, *Hist. Lat. Rom. Emp.* II, 1889, pp. 250f.

[2] Bury, *loc. cit.*, where it is pointed out that there were many Armenians settled in Cyprus (above, p. 281, n. 4) and Heraclius, who at the time was specially concerned with Armenia, may have thought of making a political weapon of Monotheletism to reconcile the Monophysite Church of Armenia with the Orthodox Greek religion. How far the experiment of Heraclius in Cyprus was a success, we do not know. Later, in 643, the archbishop of Cyprus, Sergius, supported Pope Theodore when he denounced the *Ekthesis* of Heraclius (Baronius, *Ann.* VIII, p. 407; E. W. Brooks in *C.M.H.* II, p. 400).

[3] Const. Porph. *de Them.* I, p. 40 (ed. Bonn). The improbability of the invasion by Abu-Bekr has been shown by L. Philippou, in Κυπρ. Χρον. III, 1925, pp. 164–8. Constantius, Archbishop of Sinai (about 1766), Κυπριὰς χαρίεσσα, in the Περιγραφὴ τῆς... Μονῆς... τοῦ Κύκκου, Ven. 1819, p. 138, quoted by Sathas, II, p. κβ', n. 2 (Eng. trans. in Cobham, *Exc. Cypr.* p. 314), says that this tomb of the niece of the prophet is at Larnaka, and is much revered by the Turks, who regard it as the tomb of the mother of Muhammad. (A more generally accepted tradition makes it the tomb of a relation of the Prophet who was accidentally killed during the invasion of 649; see above, ch. II, p. 21 and below, p. 329.) This is the only foundation for the assumption of

Under Constans II (641–668),[1] however, the Arab attack developed in full force. In 647 (648, 649 ?) Muawiya, emir of Syria, persuaded the Caliph Othman (a previous request to Omar had been refused) to allow him (provided he used only volunteers) to undertake an expedition, which was the first[2] maritime enterprise of the Arabs on a grand scale. He sailed from Acre accompanied by his wife Fakhita and by Ubada ibn as-Samit and his wife Umm-Haram, the daughter of Milhan, and a relation of the Prophet. His fleet numbered 1700; it was commanded by Abdallah ibn Kais, and included a contingent supplied by the governor of Egypt, Abdallah ibn Sa'd ibn Abi Sahr. Summoned to surrender and pay tribute, the Cypriotes, trusting in their walls, refused. Muawiya at first hesitated to land, but was persuaded by the Alexandrians to do so. He laid siege to Constantia, which was full of people, and where all the treasures of the island were stored, took it and destroyed it, massacring the inhabitants, living in the bishop's palace, and profaning (perhaps by using it as a mosque) the great basilica of Epiphanius. So he passed over the whole island, taking possession, and laying it under tribute. The booty was shared between the Egyptians and the Syrians. The annual tribute paid to the Greeks was 7200 gold pieces; Muawiya exacted an equal sum, though apparently he raised no objection to the continuation of the payment to the Greek treasury; presumably he considered it to be no business of his if the Cypriotes could be induced to pay twice over. But if this detail is correct, it shows that the Caliph made no claim to be the sole ruler of Cyprus, just as we shall see that some thirty years later the two rival powers agreed to draw equal sums in revenue from the island.

It was during this invasion, according to the most generally accepted tradition, that the "Righteous Woman", Umm-Haram, fell from her mount and was killed, and was buried in Hala Sultan Tekke.

Muawiya retired from the island on hearing that the imperial chamberlain Cacorhizus was approaching with a large force.

Sathas that Abu-Bekr took Larnaka. Mistranslation of the words of Theophanes concerning Ἀβουβάχαρος, οὗ καὶ τῆς θυγατρὸς ἐν αὐτῇ τάφος φαίνεται, has produced in some modern writers the statement that Abu-Bekr, as well as his daughter, died in Cyprus.

[1] For the doubtful theory that this Emperor issued coins from a mint at Constantia, see Wroth, *B.M.C. Imp. Byz.* I, p. 267, n. 2.

[2] Baladhuri says this was the first time the Moslems sailed in the Mediterranean; like all the other Eastern historians he does not know of any expedition by Abu-Bekr.

Under the terms imposed on the Cypriotes, they were to keep the Moslems informed of any projected attack from the side of the Greeks, to allow their island to be used as a half-way house for attacking the enemy, and to refrain from giving the enemy any support. However, in the year 33 (653/4), on the ground that the Cypriotes had lent ships to the Greeks for an expedition—or because the Greeks had sent troops to Cyprus—Muawiya despatched a second force of 500 ships under Abu 'l-Awar. It would appear that either before or upon his arrival many of the inhabitants fled to the hills, and took refuge in caves. From these they were dragged out "like eggs from an abandoned nest". Others, who had not been able to flee across the sea, took refuge in the city of Lapithos. Abu 'l-Awar spent some forty days in Constantia, destroying all the people "head by head"—so that it would seem that some still survived from the previous destruction. When he had plundered the whole island, he invested Lapithos, after offering terms of peace which were refused. His engines battered the walls, and eventually the inhabitants capitulated, obtaining from Abu 'l-Awar a promise that though he would take all their gold and silver and riches, he would do no harm to their persons. They were allowed to go to Greek lands or stay in the island. So with all the gold and silver from this city he returned to Syria. But an Arab garrison of 12,000 men was left behind in a city specially built for them. Mosques were also erected.[1] The terms of the tribute exacted on the former occasion were confirmed. Evidently a stable and permanent occupation was intended.

The terms remained in force until the Caliph Abd-al-Malik (685–705) added 1000 dinars to the annual tribute. Omar II (717–720) cancelled the addition; it was restored by Hisham (724–743); and finally the Abbasid Mansur (754–775), refusing to oppress the Cypriotes any longer, returned to the conditions imposed by Muawiya.[2]

Although we are not told that the basilica of Constantia was actually destroyed, it can hardly have escaped the general ruin. It is from this

---

[1] Est. de Lusignan, *Descr.* fo. 31 v°, says that there was once in Leukosia a mosque built at the time of the Saracen invasions, during the reign of Charlemagne. The seventh century seems to offer more suitable conditions for such a foundation than the less stable period to which Lusignan's tradition assigned it.

[2] The account of the two invasions given in the text does not pretend to be more than a patchwork made up of what seem to be the most probable elements in the discordant accounts of the western and eastern historians. These accounts are discussed in the Note at the end of this chapter.

time that tradition dates the transfer of the see of Constantia to Arsinoe Ammochostus (Famagusta). There it remained until the Latins transferred the primacy to Nicosia and to their own communion, when the Orthodox archbishop was sent away to the remote Rhizokarpaso.[1]

The garrison established in the island was withdrawn by the Caliph Yazid (680–683); according to one report he was bribed to remove it. Accounts differ on the question whether the city and the mosques which had been built for the troops were destroyed by Yazid himself or by the Cypriotes.[2]

From 653 on, for about a generation, we hear nothing of Cyprus.[3] It is probable that the island, having been twice plundered within a few years, offered little prospect of further booty, and the tribute seems to have been collected by the Arab, if not by the Greek, authorities.

However, in 688 or 689,[4] Cyprus was included with Armenia and Iberia in the terms of a treaty between Abd-al-Malik and Justinian II. Muawiya's failure before Constantinople in 677 had induced him, in 678, to make peace with Constantine IV on terms humiliating to the Arabs. This peace was renewed in 685 by Abd-al-Malik, and again in 688 or 689 with Justinian II. In this final form of the treaty[5] the Caliph engaged himself to pay 1000 nomismata and one horse and one slave for every day of the year.[6] This was a heavier tribute than had been

---

[1] For the later history of the see, cp. Hackett, pp. 318–9.

[2] Baladhuri, trans. Ḥitti, p. 237. Tabari (cited by Wellhausen, *Gött. Nachr.* 1901, p. 428). It hardly follows from the terms of the peace of 688/9, as Wellhausen, pp. 428–9, argues, that Yazid cannot have given up all claim to Cyprus, and that the Arabs must up till then have drawn, or claimed to draw, all the revenue therefrom.

[3] At the sixth General Council at Constantinople in 680, which finally condemned the Monothelete heresy, there were present from Cyprus Tychon of Citium, Stratonicus of Soli and Theodorus of Tremithus, the last also representing Epiphanius the archbishop of Constantia: Mansi, *Conc.* XI, cols. 640, 645 and 673.

[4] Theophanes, in the first year of Justinian II (685/6), A.M. 6178 (I, p. 555, ed. Bonn; p. 363, de Boor). A.M. 6178 is A.D. 687 according to Brooks (*Byz. Ztschr.* VIII, pp. 82 ff.). But Bury, following Weil, shows ground for the later date 688, since the Arab sources, which place the peace in the same year as the revolt of Said, as does Theophanes, date that revolt not earlier than 688 (*Hist. Lat. Rom. Emp.* II, 1889, p. 320 note). Cedrenus (I, p. 771 Bonn), first year of Justinian; Const. Porph. *de adm. imp.* c. 22, p. 103 Bonn; Zonaras, XIV, 22; Michael the Syrian, ed. Chabot, II, fasc. iii, p. 469.

[5] Paul. Diac. *Hist. Misc.* (Migne *P.L.* 95, col. 1058: A.D. 678).

[6] In the treaty of 678 the tribute had been 3000 lbs. of gold, fifty captives and fifty horses a year; in 685, one pound of gold, one slave and one horse for every day of the year. 1000 nomismata would be nearly 14 lbs. of gold, so that the annual payment in

exacted in 685; on the other hand, the treaty provided for the division between the two powers of the revenues of Armenia, Iberia and Cyprus. (As we have seen, such a division, in regard to Cyprus, seems to have been already in operation for some time.) Also—and this was fraught with great detriment to the Byzantine Empire—Justinian undertook to transplant from Lebanon the Mardaites, rude mountaineers who had served as a "brazen wall" of the Empire against the Saracens. Twelve thousand of them were transplanted to the Taurus, as we have seen.[1]

The astute Abd-al-Malik was greatly the gainer by this arrangement, as Justinian soon realized. In 692[2] the Emperor took as an excuse for breaking the peace the fact that the Caliph sent the tribute in the form of a Saracen coinage,[3] bearing inscriptions from the Koran, and not, like the nomismata in which payments had hitherto been made, the portrait

---

the new treaty would be over 5000 lbs. of gold. According to Abu'l-Mahasin (Weil, *Gesch. der Chal.* I, p. 396 note) the 1000 dinars were payable per week (not per day) on every assembly day (Friday); so too Tabari (*J.H.S.* XVIII, p. 189) and Baladhuri (*ibid.* p. 203).

[1] Above, p. 261, n. 2. Sathas (II, p. νγ') asserts that some were settled in Epirus, where their descendants survive as Mirdites. But this connexion, like those suggested with the Mardi, Maronites or Maniatae, is improbable. K. Amiantos, in Ἑλληνικά, V, 1932, pp. 130–6, prefers the derivation from an Arabic word meaning rebel (مرد), which was suggested by Assemani, *Bibl. Or.* I, p. 502 note, and approved by Reiske, note on Const. Porph. (ed. Bonn), II, p. 775. The story of the manner of their transference by Leontius in Le Beau, *Hist. du Bas-Emp.* (ed. Saint-Martin), XII, pp. 7 f., is based on doubtful authority. On the Mardaites in Syria, see Lammens in *Encycl. of Islam*, s.v.

[2] The Trullan Council, which confirmed the rights of the new see of Nova Justinianopolis, met at the end of 691 and beginning of 692 (cp. Bury, *op. cit.* II, p. 327 note). Theophanes (p. 365 de Boor) dates the breaking of the peace in A.M. 6183.

[3] The quarrel about the Saracen coinage is the subject of much confusion in both ancient and modern writers. The best accounts are in H. Sauvaire ("Matériaux pour servir à l'hist. de la numism. et de la métrol. musulmanes", in *Journal Asiatique*, Paris, 1882, pp. 27 ff.) and S. Lane-Poole, *Coins and Medals*, 1894, pp. 164 f., quoted in Bury's *Gibbon*, VI, p. 531. Note that Makrizi, in his treatise on the coinage (quoted by Lavoix, *Catal. des Monn. Musulm.* I, p. xiv), says that Muawiya had already struck coins with texts from the Koran, with the type of the Caliph girt with a sword. (See the text in L. A. Mayer's edition of the *Shudhûr al-'Uqûd*, Alexandria, 1933, p. 4; transl. by Tychsen, 1797, p. 81 and S. de Sacy, 1797, p. 15). There actually exist coins with the standing Caliph and, on the reverse, the cross deformed so as to be unrecognizable as the Christian emblem, and texts from the Koran. Abd-al-Malik introduced a new coinage with inscriptions only, and no figures. Note also that the "paper" exported from Egypt for Greek use, about which the trouble first arose, was papyrus, and bore a written protocol, not of course a water-mark.

of the Emperor and the cross—the latter a type especially offensive to Mohammedans. The Caliph protested that there was no reason to dissolve the peace, since the right weight of gold had been delivered and the Romans had suffered no hurt.[1]

But Justinian—with what the historian describes as irrational obstinacy—insisted, with the result that Asia Minor was invaded and he was heavily defeated near Caesarea, at Sebastopolis in Pontus, the greater part of his Slav auxiliaries deserting to the enemy.[2] Though he must have lost nearly the whole of Asia Minor, he retained his hold on the south coast of the Propontis; and there, near Cyzicus, he put into effect the curious plan of settling a large number of the inhabitants of Cyprus. The revenues of the island, as we have seen, were by the terms of the peace shared equally between the Emperor and the Caliph; Justinian decided that he would transplant the whole of the population, evidently with the view of depriving the Caliph of his tributaries. The chronicler Michael the Great describes his action as "pillaging" Cyprus; Abulfaraj says that he removed from Cyprus as captives the Arabs who were there. The majority of the victims of this forced migration were, however, the Christian Greeks. How many reached their destination on the Hellespont we do not know; but a large number were drowned by a storm that caught the transports, or died of disease. Many of those who survived drifted back to Cyprus.[3]

Nova Justinianopolis was the name which the Emperor gave to the settlement at or near Cyzicus. John, the archbishop of Cyprus, changed his title to archbishop of Nova Justinianopolis.[4] The Trullan Council,

---

[1] Theophanes, sixth year of Justinian, A.M. 6183 (Bonn, pp. 558–9; de Boor, p. 365, with the correct reading μηδεμιᾶς ζημίας); probably A.D. 691.

[2] The place where the battle took place was Sebastopolis Karana, south of Zela, in Pontus Galaticus and not far from Caesarea: Grégoire, in *Byz. Ztschr.* 1910, p. 259, correcting Brooks, *Byz. Ztschr.* 1909, pp. 154–6. Abulfaraj, trans. Bruns and Kirsch, I, p. 118 (*O.C.* p. 37) and Michael the Great (ed. Chabot, as above, p. 470) both say that the Slavs who deserted were settled at Antioch and Cyrrhus (Gouris). There is no ground for reading Cyprus here.

[3] Theophanes says "the remainder", which would imply that none reached the Hellespont, which was not the case. When the time came to restore the emigrants to Cyprus (see below) they had to be collected not only from Cyzicus, but from the Cibyrrhaeote and Thracesian Themes.

[4] Const. Porph. *de adm. imp.* cc. 47, 48. See Sathas, II, pp. λβ′ f. on the many confusions with Secunda Justiniana and Nova Justiniana made by earlier writers. But see below, p. 290, n. 2.

as we have seen (691/2), confirmed for the new see the rights which had been accorded to the archbishop of Cyprus in 431. The whole province of the Hellespont was placed under it, Cyzicus being especially indicated as subject to the archbishop of Justinianopolis, who, when necessary, was to ordain its bishop.

These privileges lapsed when Cyprus was recovered, and the Hellespont returned to the see of Constantinople.[1]

The life of this futile experiment appears to have been about seven years, after which, in 698, the Emperor decided to resettle the island, the population of which had been seriously depleted for that period.[2] The Emperor at this time—if the now generally accepted chronology is right—was not Justinian II, who had been in exile since 695, but Tiberius III Apsimarus. Tiberius, the former vice-admiral (*drungarius*) of the Cibyrrhaeotes, was naturally interested in the conditions of southern Asia Minor and Cyprus. He sent to the Caliph three noble Cypriotes, called *Phangoumes*,[3] accompanied by an imperial official of high standing and intelligence, asking that the Cypriotes who were in Syria should be returned to their home. The Caliph despatched throughout Syria a number of Saracen high officials, who collected all the Cypriotes and transported them to Cyprus. Similarly an imperial official collected all the Cypriotes in Romania, in Cyzicus and in the Cibyrrhaeote and Thracesian Themes, and sent them back to repopulate the island.

This resettlement must have required a considerable reorganization of the administration of the island, and it is a plausible suggestion that the establishment there of the *stratiotai*, to protect it against Moslem raids, was the work of Tiberius. This was part of the system in which the Cibyrrhaeote navy, the Mardaites centred in Attalia (who, mountaineers in origin though they were, seem to have taken to the sea and formed

---

[1] See Hackett, pp. 39 f., for the dispute about the duration of the privilege.

[2] So Const. Porph. *de adm. imp.* c. 47: "the island being taken by the Saracens and remaining uninhabited for seven years"—a loose statement. Constantine attributes the restoration of the Cypriotes to Justinian II, which Sathas (II, p. λγ′) has shown to be impossible. There seems to be nothing in favour of the alternative date in the reign of Constantine V proposed by Sakellarios (I, p. 397).

[3] Τοὺς λεγομένους Φαγγουμεῖς, apparently a general name for the leading families. Cp. M.L. *H.* I, p. 118. Constantine says they went to the Caliph at Baghdad, but that city did not yet exist at this time: Saint-Martin in Le Beau, *Hist. du Bas-Emp.* XII, p. 18.

an efficient naval force), and the garrison of Cyprus were organized together as a defence against Islam.[1]

On his return to Cyprus with his people, the archbishop again took the title of archbishop of Constantia or of Cyprus. But he and his successors continued also to sign as "archbishop of Nova Justiniana (more correctly Justinianopolis) and all Cyprus"; not that that is the name of the see in Cyprus, but merely to commemorate the fact that the archbishops once sat in the Hellespontine city of that name.[2]

Thus, for some two and a half centuries longer, Cyprus seems to have remained in a curiously indefinite position between the rival powers; never effectively controlled by either, and contributing in the form of taxation only so much as either could exact. It is probable that but for the efficiency of the Greek fleet, under the admirals of the Cibyrrhaeotes, the Arabs might have achieved an actual occupation, as they did in Crete. In any case Cyprus must have been always a kind of spring-board for either power making an attack on the other; as indeed an Arab writer of the tenth century says:[3] "When the Government has decreed an expedition, the governors of Egypt and Syria receive orders to make the necessary preparations. The place for the meeting of the fleet is Cyprus. The governor of the Syrian frontiers has the command in chief. The costs of a maritime expedition of this kind come to some 100,000 dinars."

Land raids into Asia Minor seem in these times to have taken place regularly, two or three times a year. Sea raids must have been less frequent, but when they occurred Cyprus was more likely than not to be the first objective. In the summer of 726, for instance, while Maslama invaded Cappadocia, Muawiya son of Hisham sailed against Cyprus.[4]

---

[1] See above, p. 261, n. 2. On the Mardaites as sailors, see Amiantos in Ἑλληνικά, v, 1932, p. 133.

[2] Kyprianos (p. 108) cites the signature at the sixth oecumenical Council at Constantinople in 680 when Theodorus, bishop of Tremithus, represents Epiphanius, archbishop of Constantia in Cyprus οὐχὶ ἔτι τότε νέας Ἰουστινιανῆς. Obviously this is a subsequent gloss, of little authority, and does not occur in the list of signatories (Mansi, *Conc.* XI, cols. 640, 645 and 673). The statement of Kyprianos (p. 30) that Ammochostus was restored by Justinian II in 683 and called Nova Justiniana is quite baseless. The archiepiscopal see in Cyprus was never called Nova Justiniana (or Justinianopolis), which was the name of the Hellespontine city. See Georg. Philippou, Εἰδήσεις ἱστ. pp. 32 f. note.

[3] Abulfaraj Kodama ibn Jafar (about 928, †948) quoted by *O.C.* p. 41 from de Goeje, *Bibl. geog. arab.* VI, pp. 195 f.

[4] Theophanes, a.M. 6218 (p. 404 de Boor), says merely that Muawiya invaded

In 743 Cyprus is again mentioned when the caliph Walid II appears to have raided it and carried off the inhabitants to Syria.[1]

The resulting insecurity may have interfered with the use of Cyprus as a place of call by pilgrims to the Holy Land, but could not entirely prevent it. The adventurous Englishman Willibald, for instance, having passed the winter of 722–3 in Lycia, called at Cyprus on his way to Syria, staying three weeks at Paphos, and also at Constantia. The island is significantly described as being "betwixt Greeks and Saracens".[2]

After a lapse of two centuries the terrible bubonic plague again broke out in the sixth year of Constantine V (747),[3] starting in Sicily and Calabria, and spreading like a fire to Greece and the islands. Here again we are not told specifically that Cyprus suffered. But the Arabs, while the whole Empire was distracted by this visitation, chose the moment for sending out from Alexandria an expedition against the island.[4] The fleet was said to number a thousand dromonds. The Emperor had timely warning, however, and the Cibyrrhaeote admiral was ordered to proceed to meet the enemy. Putting in at a port in Cyprus he found the Arab fleet already there, and took it completely by surprise, blocking the harbour mouth, and destroying all but three of the thousand dromonds which had set out from Alexandria.[5] It was a century before an Egyptian fleet was again effective.

Romania, but from Tabari and Elias of Nisibin he appears to have taken Cyprus on the way. Wellhausen in *Göttinger Nachrichten*, 1901, p. 443.

[1] Theophanes, a.M. 6234 (ed. de Boor, p. 417): Οὐαλὶδ τοὺς Κυπρίους μετῴκισεν εἰς Συρίαν. This, however, is the editor's insertion from the Latin version of Anastasius (II, p. 271: "Uhalid Cyprios in Syriam transtulit"). But it is confirmed by Biladhuri (tr. Ḥitti, pp. 238, 241), who says that Walid the son of Yazid expelled many Cypriotes to Syria because he suspected them; they were returned to their home by his son Yazid III (744). Also by Tabari (Wellhausen, *op. cit.* p. 445).

[2] Tobler and Molinier, *Itin. Hierosol.* I, p. 288.

[3] Theophanes, a.M. 6238 (p. 422 de Boor). He regards it as a judgement on the Emperor Constantine V Copronymus for his iconoclasm. Cedrenus (II, pp. 7f. Bonn) repeats Theophanes.

[4] Theophanes (p. 424 de Boor) and Cedrenus, II, p. 9 (the success of the Greeks is, however, not credited to the iconoclastic policy of the Emperor). Nicephorus Patr. (p. 64 de Boor, p. 72 Bonn); Paul. Diac. *Hist. Misc.* I, lib. XXII (Migne, *P.L.* 95, col. 1095); Caetani, *Chron.* p. 1620, under 127 A.H. (744/5). Paul. Diac. gives the strength of the fleet as thirty dromonds only.

[5] On the question of Ceramaea, the harbour where the action took place, see above, p. 262, n. 5. On the disappearance of the Egyptian fleet until it was rebuilt after 853, see Brooks in *Byz. Ztschr.* XXII, p. 383.

Whatever sort of control the Greeks continued to maintain, it was sufficient (though probably little more) to enable the Emperor to use Cyprus as a place of exile for undesirable persons. That, of course, means little; for it was only necessary to transport such offenders thither and leave them to the tender mercies of the Arabs. Thus in 770[1] the general Lachanodracon, carrying out his master's policy of persecution, collected at Ephesus all the monks and nuns from the Thracesian Theme, and told them that if they wished to obey the Emperor they must put on a white dress and marry at once; otherwise they would be blinded and sent to Cyprus; and this was done to many. This and similar measures stirred Constantine to effusive praise of Lachanodracon, as a man after his own heart, who carried out all his wishes. Cyprus, like other places of the Empire, must have received many immigrants flying from the iconoclastic persecution.[2] It is interesting to note that Paul, Patriarch of Constantinople, who instigated Eirene to summon the Second Council of Nicaea against the Iconoclasts in 787, was a native of Salamis.[3]

Meanwhile the raids went monotonously on. In 773 it is recorded that the Moslem fleet raided Cyprus and carried off the governor. This may have been connected with the adventure of Thumama ibn Wakkas (Banakas) in Cilicia which is mentioned in the year 772.[4]

Two more attacks on Cyprus were delivered during the caliphate of Harun ar-Rashid (786–809). Of the first, in 790,[5] we have no details except of a battle which took place in the gulf of Attalia. The Empress Eirene, having had warning of the expedition, despatched the whole

---

[1] Theophanes, a.M. 6262, thirtieth year of Constantine (p. 688 Bonn, p. 445 de Boor). Sathas, II, p. νθ′, regards this as proving Greek control of Cyprus; it proves only the power to transport criminals to a distant place and drop them there.

[2] Vasiliev, *Hist. of Byz. Emp.* I, 1928, p. 321.

[3] *Vita S. Tarasii* (ed. Latyšev), *Menologii Anon. Byz. Saec. x quae supersunt*, I, 1911, p. 132; Hackett, p. 380.

[4] E. W. Brooks in *C.M.H.* IV, p. 123. Theophanes (p. 446 de Boor), a.M. 6264 (=773): ἐκρατήθη ὁ Κούρικος Σέργιος ἔξωθεν Συκῆς, καὶ ὁ Λαχέρφαβος (v.l. Λαχέρβαφος) [Σέργιος] εἰς Κύπρον ἐκ προσώπου ὢν τῶν ἐκεισε (ἐκ προσώπου = viceroy). Banakas is the name of Theophanes for Thumama ibn Wakkas (p. 451 de Boor, A.M. 6269: Θουμάμας ὁ τοῦ Βάκα). Mr Brooks tells me he regards the sea raid on Syce and Cyprus and the exploit of Thumama, though mentioned in different years by Theophanes, as probably part of the same campaign. A. Lombard (*Constantin V*, p. 38) dates the latter in 770.

[5] Theophanes, a.M. 6282 (pp. 720 f. Bonn, p. 465 de Boor). Theophilus is described as ῥωμαλέος ἀνὴρ καὶ ἱκανώτατος.

imperial fleet, which on rounding the Chelidonian promontory met the Arabs, who had moved out from Cyprus and lay becalmed in the Gulf. They prepared for battle, but one of the Greek commanders, Theophilus, the strategos of the Cibyrrhaeote contingent, with more valour than discretion, advanced too rashly to the attack, and was captured and carried off to the Caliph. He was offered his life if he would apostatize, but refused and was put to the sword. The Greeks honoured him as a martyr (30 January).[1]

The second attack under Harun ar-Rashid took place in 806.[2] He had invaded Asia Minor, capturing many strong places, and the Emperor Nicephorus I had been compelled to make peace, the terms of which, besides the payment of a heavy tribute, included the undertaking not to rebuild the fallen fortresses. This undertaking Nicephorus immediately broke, and the Caliph retaliated by despatching a fleet to Cyprus under Humaid the son of Matuk or Mayuf, the wali of the Syrian coast. The invaders laid waste the island, burning and destroying the churches, and took away with them many captives (according to one account as many as 16,000, including the "bishop of Cyprus"). The captives were sold by the judge Abu 'l Bakhtara; the bishop fetched 2000 dinars.

Nevertheless Cyprus, whoever was its nominal sovereign, was in these days still considered a more desirable place for Christians to live in than Syria and Palestine. In 813[3] there was a great exodus from those

---

[1] Nicodemus, *Synaxaristes*, II, p. 91, ed. of 1819, quoted by Sathas, II, p. ξ', n. 1. His capture, according to this authority, was due to betrayal by his two fellow-strategoi. Hackett, p. 432, is presumably wrong in saying that he died in Cyprus.

[2] Theophanes, a.M. 6298 (p. 749 Bonn, p. 482 de Boor); El-Makin, tr. Erpenius, 1625, p. 152. The leader of the expedition seems to have been Humaid (cp. Theophanes, a.M. 6300), as we learn from Ibn Wadih and Tabari (E. W. Brooks in *Eng. Hist. Rev.* 1900, p. 745). His father's name was apparently Matuk (Hajji Khalifa, *Chronology*, O.C. p. 79). In the printed text of 1733 it is Ma'yūḳ, perhaps a mistake for Ma'tūḳ; a Turkish MS. in the British Museum has 'Abūḳ, which is impossible, and a Persian one Ya'ḳūb. (Information from Mr Fulton and Mr Sainsbury.) Brooks makes it Ma'yuf. On the other hand, there seems to have been another raid in the same year, led by Matuk or Mayuf son of Yahia, who, according to Tabari (Brooks, *loc. cit.*), because the people of Cyprus had broken the treaty, raided it and carried the people captive. This raid is mentioned by Abulfeda (*Ann. Mosl.*, tr. Reiske and Adler, II, p. 91; *O.C.* p. 56: "Maatuc filius Jahiae"; Ma'tūḳ ibn Yaḥya).

[3] Theophanes, a.M. 6305 (pp. 778 f. Bonn, p. 499 de Boor); year 2 of Michael I Rhangabe. It is to be doubted whether the migration from Syria described by Machaeras (§ 31, Dawkins and his note) belongs to this time and not to that of the loss of Jerusalem in 1187.

countries of religious and lay folk, flying from the immeasurable persecution by the Arabs. Those who did not suffer martyrdom escaped to Cyprus; of the refugees, some made their way to Constantinople, where they were kindly entreated by the Emperor Michael and the Patriarch Nicephorus, who also sent a talent of gold to Cyprus for the relief of those who stayed in the island.

Basil I the Macedonian (867–886), if we may believe the not impartial account of his grandson, Constantine Porphyrogenitus,[1] really effected a definite, though shortlived, settlement of the affairs of Cyprus, establishing it as a Theme, and sending thither his general Alexius the Armenian, who governed it for seven years. It fell again, however, into the hands of the Arabs, who, says Constantine, levy tribute on it as before. The same writer, however, is witness to the fact that in the time of his own father, Leo the Wise, it was in Greek hands; for in 902, at the time of the campaign of Himerius against the Saracens in Crete, it was governed by the protospatharius Leo, son of Symbatices. This governor, with the katapan of the Mardaites of Attalia, was charged with the task of preventing communications between Crete and Syria, and maintaining an intelligence service in the Gulf of Tarsus and in the ports of the Syrian coast, as far as Tripolis and Laodicea.[2]

Himerius, it would appear, in the course of these operations, committed in Cyprus actions which the Saracens regarded as a breach of the long-standing treaty. He took some Saracens and put them to death, instead of saving them, as the terms of the treaty required, from the Cypriotes. It was this action which provoked the revenge of Dimyana, to be mentioned below. A year or two later, in 904, it was possible for the Arabs on their return voyage from the successful siege of Thessalonica to land at Paphos, and bathe in the local waters without molestation.[3] Later, in the year 299 (911/2), on the ground that the Cypriotes had broken the old agreement by which they were to remain neutral and pay the tribute half to the Greeks and half to the Arabs, Dimyana, commander of the fleet which was operating in the Mediterranean, seized the island and held it for four months, burning and plundering, taking captives and seizing many places which he fortified.[4]

---

[1] Const. Porph. *de Themat.* p. 40 (Bonn).

[2] Const. Porph. *de Cerim.* pp. 657 and 660 (Bonn); Sathas, II, p. ξβ′.

[3] They were carrying Joannes Cameniata and his fellow-prisoners to Tripolis in Barbary: Joannes Cam. *de excidio Thessalonicensi*, c. 77 (ed. Bonn, p. 596).

[4] Masudi († 956 or 957), *Golden Meadows* (tr. Barbier de Meynard and Pavet de Cour-

The final liberation of Cyprus from the Saracens was not effected until the reign of Nicephorus II Phocas. In 960 Nicephorus had been sent by Romanus II against the Saracen stronghold in Crete, and had taken Candia after a famous siege of nine months. As soon as he had been proclaimed Emperor, in 963, he turned his attention to the East, attacking Cilicia, which by August 965 was in his hands. The Egyptian fleet was defeated off the coast of Asia Minor, and the conquest of Cyprus followed. Unfortunately we have no details of what happened there, except that the recovery of the island was the work of the patricius Nicetas Chalcutzes.[1] From this time onwards the Saracens ceased almost entirely to trouble the island, and what difficulties the Byzantine government encountered henceforth were due, with one exception, to internal revolts, or to incursions by Christian instead of Arab raiders.

It is worth while asking why Cyprus passed out of the field of war between the Greeks and Arabs. Some hint of an answer may be found, first, in the condition of the Empire of the Caliphs in the tenth century. That Empire began to fall to pieces as early as the middle of the eighth century, with the rise of the Omayyads in Spain. The whole of the North African region had become independent by 800; Syria and Egypt finally ceased to recognize the Abbasid Caliphs in 934. These lands from

---

teille, VIII, p. 282), quoted by *O.C.* p. 45. The same raid seems to be described in the *Life* of St Demetrianus, bishop of Chytri (*c.* 885–912), written probably before 965, and published by H. Grégoire, *Byz. Ztschr.* XVI, 1907, p. 232. Chytri was one of the places sacked. The translators of Masudi give the name of the general as Dimnana, but the correct form (as in Tabari and Ibn al-Athir) is Dimyana. "Dimyana the slave of Yazman" is first mentioned by Tabari as governor of Tarsus in A.H. 283. In 291 he was in Baghdad, whence he was sent in 292 to prevent a raid on Egypt. In 299 he accompanied Rustum ibn Bardawa on a spring or summer raid from the district of Tarsus, and besieged the castle of Malik the Armenian. Ibn al-Athir, VIII, 57, says that in 301 died "Dimyana, commander of the marches and of the Mediterranean sea". (Information from Mr Fulton.) This Dimyana is the Damianus of St Nicolas Mysticus, Patriarch of Constantinople, who, writing (before his banishment in 907) to the Saracen emir of Crete, says that the calamity which has befallen the Cypriotes was the work of this man, a renegade who became emir of Tyre and was recently dead. The patriarch exhorts the emir of Crete not to punish the Cypriotes because of the offence of Himerius. (*Epist.* I, Migne, *P.G.* 111, cols. 29–34.) The death of Damianus, emir of Tyre, from sickness during an expedition, which he undertook against the Greeks with a fleet and a large force, is also recorded by Cedrenus (II, p. 284 Bonn), but in the year, apparently, of the battle of Acheloüs (917).

[1] Cedrenus, II, p. 363 Bonn; Zonaras, XVI, c. 25, p. 80 Dind.

969 were under the Fatimid Caliphs, but their hold on Syria was shaken from time to time by the rise of minor dynasties, such as the Mirdasids in Aleppo (1023–1079). They also lost their Western provinces; and although they continued, until ended by Saladin in 1171, to be the most powerful and prosperous of the Muhammadan dynasties, it may well be that what energy among these diverse states was not used in defending themselves against each other, was directed towards commerce rather than war with the Greeks. (Occasional hostilities, it may be observed, did not in ancient times interfere, as they do now, with commercial and cultural relations between opposing powers.) It was different with the other great Empire which arose in the eleventh century, that of the Seljuks, who ruled the whole of western Asia, to the frontiers of the Greeks in Asia Minor and of the Fatimids in Syria. But the Seljuks of Rum, in Asia Minor, do not seem to have been inclined to maritime adventure. And thus Cyprus seems to have escaped further trouble. Perhaps it was not worth troubling, having been bled white by this time. At the end of the eleventh century we enter on the era of the Crusades; and Cyprus becomes the forward station, so far as maritime expeditions are concerned, for the efforts of Christendom against Islam. From the end of the twelfth century it was to enter upon a new phase under Latin rule, which may not in some respects have been an improvement on the Greek, but at least meant that it had not to suffer again, until the fifteenth century, at the hands of the Mohammedans.

In 1042/3 a revolt broke out, led by the governor of the island, Theophilus Eroticus,[1] who before his appointment to the governorship had been in command in Serbia. There in 1040 he had failed to stem the rising by which Stephen Bogislav gained independence for his people. In spite of this failure Michael IV appointed him to Cyprus. When, after Michael's death, and the brief reign and fall of Michael V Calaphates, the power seemed to have returned into the hands of the Empress Zoe, the ambitious governor thought his own opportunity had come. He was able to inflame the minds of the Cypriotes against the protospatharius Theophylactus, who held the office of judge and collector of public taxes,[2] accusing him of extortion—a charge which, in view of the record of Byzantine administration, must have found ready belief, whether it were true or not. His intention of doing away with this official however

[1] Cedrenus, II, p. 549; Glycas, p. 594; Zonaras, XVII, c. 22 (IV, p. 162 Dind.); Sathas, II, p. ξγ′.

[2] Δικαστὴς καὶ πράκτωρ τῶν δημοσίων φόρων.

was defeated without trouble by Constantine IX (Monomachus), who had mounted the throne as the elderly Zoe's third husband. Constantine despatched the naval commander Constantine Chage, who speedily reduced the rebels to order and conveyed Theophilus to the capital. There he was treated with unusual mildness, being merely dressed in woman's clothes, exhibited in the Hippodrome at the races, deprived of his possessions and allowed to go free. If he had been suspected of aiming at the Imperial throne, his fate would probably have been harder.

It was but natural that the governor of Cyprus should on occasion act on behalf of the Emperor in his relations with the Moslem rulers of Palestine. Thus, when the Christians living in Jerusalem were forced to rebuild a fourth part of the fortifications of the city, the Emperor sent the governor of the island to deal with the matter on the spot. The rebuilding was completed in 1063, and the Christians obtained a charter granting them the right to occupy a fourth part of the city.[1]

But the Byzantine governor of Cyprus, thanks to the Greek schism, was not always helpful to Christian pilgrims from the West. Thus, when St Lietbert, archbishop of Cambrai, landed in the island on his way to Jerusalem in 1055, the katapan detained him for several days, on the pretext, supposed to be false, of saving him from the hands of the infidels.[2]

We have fortunately a detailed account, from the pen of Anna Comnena, of another insurrection which blazed up in Cyprus some fifty years after that of Eroticus, in 1092.[3] This was altogether a more serious affair, being concerted between two chiefs, Caryces in Crete and Rhapsomates in Cyprus; these men may even have been in touch with the emir of Smyrna, Tzachas, who was ravaging the islands, and had seized Clazomenae, Lesbos, Chios and other places. The Emperor Alexius Comnenus despatched against the emir his brother-in-law, the Caesar John Ducas, whom he created Lord High Admiral (Grand Duke). Ducas recovered the lost places and put an end to the revolt first in Crete and then in Cyprus. As soon as the Cretans heard of his arrival at Carpathos they rose and slaughtered Caryces, and handed over their island to Ducas, who, leaving a sufficient garrison, sailed for

[1] Will. Tyr. lib. IX, c. 18. Cp. L. Dressaire, *Jérusalem à travers les siècles*, Paris, 1931, p. 112.

[2] See above, p. 260, n. 1.

[3] Anna Comnena, *Alexias*, pp. 430–3 (Bonn), IX, 2 (Reifferscheid). Glycas, p. 620 (Bonn), confuses Crete and Cyprus. Zonaras, XVIII, c. 22 (IV, p. 239 Dind.); Sathas, II, pp. ϛδ′ ff.

Cyprus and landing at Kerynia took it by assault. On hearing of the arrival of Ducas, Rhapsomates moved out of Leukosia and fortified a position in the hills above Kerynia. He tried to avoid battle, although he was not unprepared as were the imperial forces, which might have then been attacked with some chance of success. Either because he was entirely without military experience—it was said that he had only a few days before handled sword and spear for the first time, and could hardly sit a horse—or because he was terrified by the suddenness of the approach of Ducas, he was unable to make up his mind. Meanwhile Manuel Butumites, who commanded the army of Ducas, gained over some of the rebel's followers and enlisted them in his own ranks. Finally Rhapsomates sought an engagement, advancing slowly down the slopes of the range; but, when the two armies were nearly in touch, some hundred of his men broke away at a gallop, as though to attack Ducas, but with their spears reversed, and joined the enemy. At sight of their desertion Rhapsomates immediately took to flight and rode for Nemesos (Limassol), hoping to reach it and find a ship to carry him to Syria. Butumites, however, despatched by Ducas in pursuit, pressed him so hard that, disappointed in his hope of reaching the coast, he turned to the other side into the hills and fled to the Church of the Holy Cross (Stavrovouni), where he was caught by his pursuer; he was granted his life and carried to the Grand Duke. All the army then returned to Leukosia, from which the whole island was again reduced to order as far as the circumstances allowed. On receiving the report of Ducas, the Emperor took measures for the future security of the island. Calliparius, a man distinguished for his just but unassuming character, was designated as judge and assessor of taxes.[1] The military command was en-

[1] Κρίτης καὶ ἐξισωτής, *peraequator*, an officer who assessed the distribution of taxes (see Dölger, *Beitr. z. Gesch. d. Byz. Finanzverwaltung*, 1927, p. 79). Here we may take it that he was in charge of the revenue department as a whole. Modern writers make several statements about the episode which seem to require verification. Sathas describes Rhapsomates (like Caryces) as διοικητής and Mas Latrie (*H.* I, p. 89) calls him Duke, but the position which he held is not stated by any of the authorities. Sathas adds that the Emperor made Butumites *dioiketes* of the island ("or 'duke of Cyprus' as Anna Comnena says") in place of Calliparius; but Anna says nothing of the kind, while she does definitely say that the Emperor gave the civil administrative offices mentioned above to Calliparius, and the command of the garrison to Philocales. If Butumites remained for a time as Duke, Calliparius and Philocales would have been subordinate to him. Sathas (and Sakellarios, who so often slavishly follows him) says that Alexius slew the rebels in Crete and Cyprus. But Anna definitely says that it was

trusted to Philocales Eumathius as stratopedarch, and he was provided with warships and cavalry. We hear nothing more of Rhapsomates and his fellow-rebels after Butumites handed them over to Ducas.

It is commonly supposed that Butumites remained in command in Cyprus; and the legend of Kykko, which will be mentioned later, assumes this. But it is more probable that he returned to Constantinople.[1] When we next hear of him, he is with the Emperor in Asia Minor, where he was made Duke of Nicaea after its capture in June 1097. That he was in the island after the affair with the Pisan fleet in 1099 (see below) we know, for the Greek generals who met there sent him to negotiate with Bohemund I, Prince of Antioch. He returned unsuccessful to Cyprus, and the Greek fleet sailed for Constantinople.[2] The Emperor, to protect Cyprus from an expected attack by Bohemund, caused Corycus and Seleucia on the Cilician coast to be fortified. We next hear of Butumites in Cilicia in 1103, where he established a series of fortresses in the district of Marash, and then returned to Constantinople.[3] While in Cilicia he had with him certain favourites of the Emperor, especially Bardas and the chief cup-bearer Michael, who interfered with his plans. He obtained orders from the Emperor to send them to Cyprus, where they made themselves equally troublesome to the Duke Constantine Euphorbenus (Catacalo),[4] and were accordingly fetched back to the captial. It seems clear that Butumites was only occasionally in Cyprus after 1092.

Philocales was a man of remarkable qualities, if we may trust Anna Comnena, who describes him[5] as of noble birth, most enterprising and excelling most of his class in prudence, free of mind and hand, faithful to God and his friends, extraordinarily well-disposed to his masters. She

---

the Cretans themselves who killed Caryces and handed over the island to Ducas, and tells us nothing about the Cypriote rebels being put to death. Sakellarios (p. 404) assumes that Philocales, having been transferred from Cyprus, was sent back there. There is no certainty that his tenure of the command was interrupted (but see below, n. 4).

[1] So Anna Comnena says, IX, 2 *ad fin.*

[2] *Ead.* XI, 10 (Bonn, II, p. 119).

[3] *Ead.* XI, 9 *ad fin.*

[4] On Constantine Euphorbenus Catacalo see Mrs Buckler in *Archaeologia*, LXXXIII, 1934, p. 347. She thinks he was Duke of Cyprus between two tenures of Philocales. His son may have been the *magistros* Nicephorus who built the church of Asinou (below, p. 323).

[5] Anna Comn. *Alex.* XIV, 1 (Bonn, II, p. 249). Contrast her description of the unwarlike Rhapsomates, who, being a rebel, had no countervailing merits.

finds compensation for his lack of military training (he did not know how to draw a bow or use a shield to protect himself) in his skill in contriving ambuscades and defeating the enemy by all kinds of stratagems. But Anna is no impartial witness, and a different picture is drawn by Archbishop Nicolaus Mouzalon, who describes the monstrous cruelties of the administration in his time, and by an obvious allusion attacks him as an apt pupil in vice of a vicious master, i.e. the Emperor.[1] This man remained in command of the military and naval forces of Cyprus, and in that capacity was concerned also with operations on the Syrian coast. Thus he is mentioned as commanding the Greek garrison of Laodicea in Syria in 1099.[2] Raymond de St Gilles, Count of Toulouse, who had recently occupied that port as well as Maraccae (the fortress of Margat or Markab) and Balanea (Banyas), had on the instructions of the Emperor handed over Laodicea to Andronicus Tzintziluces, and the other two places to the troops of Philocales, then Duke of Cyprus.[3] In the summer of that year Bohemund attacked Laodicea, and was assisted by the remains of a Pisan fleet, which had been despatched by Daimbert, archbishop of Pisa, and, according to the Greek account,[4] had been rather severely handled by the Greeks off the Lycian coast. The remaining vessels went marauding among the islands and descended on Cyprus. At one point, they sent some of their men inland to forage. Philocales however was not far off, and came down in force to the shore. Those who had remained with the ships cast loose in a panic and sailed for Laodicea. The remainder, returning to the shore and finding themselves deserted, threw themselves into the sea.

Raymond remained until his death a firm ally of the Emperor. When he sat down to besiege Tripolis in 1102, he appealed to Alexius for help. By the Emperor's orders the Duke of Cyprus sent ships with masons

---

[1] Εὐμαθὴς εἰς κακίαν, ὀξὺς μαθητὴς τοῦ κακοῦ διδασκάλου. Mouzalon, Παραίτησις (ed. Doanidou), Ἑλληνικά, VII, 1934, p. 112, v. 41; Dölger, *Byz. Ztschr.* XXXV, 1935, p. 8. Philocales is also described as an unscrupulous governor in an unpublished life of St Cyril Phileotes: V. Laurent in Ἑλληνικά, IV, 1931, p. 332, who publishes a seal which may be either of him or of the later person of the same name, who was Prefect of the City at the end of the twelfth century.

[2] Caffaro, *Liberatio Orientis* (*M.G.H. Scr.* XVIII, p. 45); Muralt. *Chr. Byz.* p. 87. Caffaro speaks of him as *Archantus* (governor?) *unus qui tenebat insulam Cypri et Filocarius vocabatur*, and adds (*Greci*) XX *salandrios et milites et clientes multos ibi tenebant.*

[3] Anna Comn. *Alex.* XI, 7 (Bonn, II, p. 105). On the date, which is uncertain, see F. Chalandon, *Essai sur le règne d'Alexis I Comnène*, pp. 208 ff.

[4] Anna Comn. *Alex.* XI, 10 (Bonn, II, p. 118).

and all that was necessary to build the fortress of Mont Pèlerin over against Tripolis.[1]

Raymond, however, died in this same fortress on 28 Feb. 1105. Of the two claimants to his succession, his natural son Bertrand and his nephew William II Jourdain, Comte de Cerdagne, the Emperor endeavoured to gain over the latter, ordering the Duke of Cyprus (but whether this was Catacalo or Philocales is not known) to send Nicetas Chalintzes to him with a large sum of money and obtain from him the same oath of allegiance as his father had rendered. With what result, we are not told.[2]

In 1109–10 the Emperor, in an endeavour to restore to prosperity the coast districts of western Asia Minor which had been reduced to ruin in recent years, became involved in a war with Hassan, emir of Cappadocia. Philocales, at his own request, had been entrusted with the task and appointed to the command of the forces based on Attalia. To effect his purpose, he had to expel the Turks who still occupied the interior, and this brought the emir Hassan on the scene with a large army. Philocales, however, completely defeated the enemy in sections, employing some of those stratagems for which Anna praises him.[3]

Since the retirement of Bohemund in 1104[4] the Emperor had had to deal with Tancred, who in 1112 rejected with contumely the demand that he should give up Antioch. At this time Philocales was still (or once more[5]) Duke of Cyprus; and he was ordered to supply Butumites with ships and money, with which to gain over Baldwin, king of Jerusalem, and the other Franks. The ambassadors, having collected the money and ships from Cyprus, first, by the Emperor's instructions, visited Tripolis and found Bertrand favourable to their cause. They deposited the money

---

[1] Anna Comn. *Alex.* XI, 7 (Bonn, II, pp. 106f.). W. B. Stevenson, *The Crusaders in the East*, 1907, p. 54. On the other hand, the Duke seems not to have been very ready to help Tzintziluces when besieged by Tancred in Laodicea (Anna Comn. *Alex.* XI, 7 *ad fin*).

[2] Anna Comn. *Alex.* XI, 8 *ad fin*. Chalandon, p. 238, assumes that the Duke was Philocales.

[3] Anna Comn. *Alex.* XIV, 1.

[4] Bohemund left Antioch to Tancred in 1104. The date of his death is uncertain; it was in 1109 according to Anna Comnena and William of Tyre; but Röhricht (p. 67), Chalandon (p. 249, n. 6) and Grousset (I, p. 419) prefer 1111, the date given by others. The story of the embassy is told by Anna Comn. *Alex.* XIV, 2.

[5] Philocales is the governor attacked for his cruel administration by Archbishop Mouzalon, who occupied the see from about 1107 to 1110. See pp. 300, 303.

in the bishop's palace at Tripolis, and went on what turned out to be a fruitless errand to Baldwin. On their return, they found Bertrand dead, and having with some difficulty recovered the money from his son and the bishop, by threatening to cut off supplies from Cyprus, they took it back to Philocales.

We hear no more of Philocales in connexion with Cyprus. But the career of this distinguished man was not over, for from seals of his,[1] of which no less than four have survived, we know that he attained to the offices of *magister*, Grand Duke (i.e. Lord High Admiral) and *praetor* of the combined themes of Hellas and Peloponnese.

Too many Byzantine officials, we cannot doubt, lacked such merits as, on the balance of the evidence, may be credited to Philocales, notably loyalty to his Emperor. A contemporary writer describes the various ways in which corrupt commanders ruin the fleet, and goes on to say that, under pretence of protecting the coasts and islands, they levy from the Cyclades and both mainlands, and equally from Crete and Cyprus, wheat, barley, pulse, cheese, wine, meat, oil, coins and anything else the islands possess.[2]

The legend of the most famous and wealthy monastery in Cyprus, that of Kykko in the Marathasa district, connects its foundation with Butumites. The story may be read in many places,[3] and centres on the

---

[1] Schlumberger, *Sigillographie de l'Emp. Byz.* pp. 188 ff. He wrongly says that Philocales is given the title of *magister* by Anna Comnena. He cites from *Pandora* (no. 454, Athens, 15 Feb. 1869—not 1861—p. 437, no. 87) a document at Patmos dated 1192 in which, he says, Philocales bears the three titles mentioned in the text; but if I understand the description aright, it is doubtful whether these titles occur in the document, and in any case 1192 seems to be the date of the true copy, not of the original; Philocales must have been long dead by then. Or is this the other Philocales (above, p. 300, n. 1)?

[2] Λόγος νουθετητικὸς πρὸς βασιλέα, in B. Wassiliewsky and V. Jernstedt's ed. of Cecaumeni *Strategicon* (St Petersburg, 1896), p. 102. The work is found in the same MS. and generally attributed to the same author as the *Strategicon*, and was perhaps addressed, Wassiliewsky thinks, to Alexius I. (Information from Mrs Buckler.)

[3] Machaeras (ed. Dawkins), § 37; Strambaldi (ed. R. de Mas Latrie), p. 16 (Hackett, p. 332 note); the Περιγραφὴ τῆς...Μονῆς...τοῦ Κύκκου, Ven. 1751, pp. 25 ff., quoted at length in Hackett, pp. 332 ff.; M.L. *H.* I, p. 92; Gunnis, pp. 302 ff. The original MS. of the *Perigraphe* was burnt in a fire in 1365. Hackett and Gunnis also give various other legends connected with the icon of the Virgin, attributed to St Luke, which is said to have been brought from Constantinople by the founder, the monk Esaias. Esaias had cured Butumites of sciatica or some other disease and, having also cured the daughter of the Emperor Alexius of the same complaint, had extracted from him the

icon of the Virgin attributed to St Luke, which is said to have survived the numerous perils of raids and fires which have endangered it.

An attack on Laodicea by a fleet from Cyprus in 1097 may have been inspired by the knowledge that the Crusaders were passing through Asia Minor on their way to Antioch. Or it may have been a mere raid, the counterpart of the raids from the Syrian coast from which Cyprus had so long suffered. On 19 Aug. 1097,[1] a flotilla of twenty-two ships coming from Cyprus entered the port of Laodicea, carried off all the merchandise in the place and sailed away.

The historians on whom we depend for our knowledge of the events described in the preceding pages throw no light on the internal condition of Cyprus during this period. But chance has preserved a remarkable poem by Nicolaus Mouzalon, archbishop of Cyprus from about 1107 to 1110, written after his resignation of the see.[2] It testifies abundantly to the sufferings of the Cypriotes under the Byzantine officials. The quarrel between the secular and ecclesiastical powers was of course perennial, and the archbishop may have been prejudiced, and have exaggerated his shadows. But, all allowances made, enough remains to show the condition of the Cypriotes to have been miserable in the extreme (vv. 885–910): their food was such as the Baptist ate, they went naked to the day, sheltered only in caves; the fruits of their labours were taken from them; those who could not pay the taxes were hung up, and dogs hung up beside them and pricked on to tear their flesh. If one who was wanted by the officials escaped, his neighbour was held responsible and punished in his stead.[3] The clergy were equally oppressed (vv. 652 ff.); bishops were hanged and tortured to death, deacons sent to the galleys, relics stolen and sacred vessels used for profane purposes; all such offences were condoned by the secular authorities. There were also black sheep among the clergy, who acted as tools of the government officials, and were encouraged and protected in their

---

holy icon, which was taken to Cyprus, a church and monastery being founded with funds given by the Emperor, and endowed with three villages by Butumites. This land was seized by the Latins when they occupied Cyprus.

[1] Kamal ed-Din, "Chronicle of Aleppo", in *Rec. Cr. Or.* III, 1884, p. 578; *O.C.* p. 51.

[2] Sophia I. Doanidou, Ἡ παραίτησις Νικολάου τοῦ Μουζάλωνος, in Ἑλληνικά, VII, 1934, pp. 109–50. See Maas and Dölger in *Byz. Ztschr.* XXXV, 1935, pp. 2–14; also the review by L. Philippou in Κυπρ. Γράμματα, I, 1935, pp. 274 ff. A contemporary encomium on Mouzalon, delivered when he was Patriarch of Constantinople (1147–51), is edited by Hero Korbete, Ἑλληνικά, VII, 1934, pp. 301–22.

[3] On the system of mutual surety (ἀλληλεγγύως, v. 912): Dölger, *loc. cit.* p. 14.

criminal courses. Thus, says the archbishop (vv. 267 ff.), he saw this lovely island, like the king's daughter all glorious within, this blessed island no island of the blessed, this Elysian field the home of a wretched people, girt round by the streams of the sea, but oppressed within by unescapable misfortunes; its inhabitants more miserable than Tantalus,[1] reaping but eating not (oh vain labour!), gathering grapes but drinking not (oh bitter toil!).

Besides Eumathius Philocales, who, as already remarked (p. 300), is identified by an obvious allusion as the governor responsible for this reign of oppression, another offender is mentioned by Mouzalon in a similarly allusive way;[2] it would seem that he was the head of the financial administration, the dioiketes. These officials were too much for Mouzalon, whose attempts to obtain redress were rudely rebuffed. He gave up the struggle and resigned the see, retiring to a monastery, from which however he emerged to hold the Patriarchate of Constantinople for a few years (1147–51).

So far as external politics were concerned, the first half of the twelfth century seems for the most part to have passed peacefully. Pilgrim traffic went on as usual. Among those who visited the island was Erik the Good of Denmark, who, on his way to the Holy Land, died of fever at Paphos on 10 July 1103. He was buried at the Cathedral, near the present church of Chrysopolitissa.[3] Relations with the Moslems were not altogether unfriendly; jealousy of the Latins doubtless affected the attitude of the Emperor. When Baldwin captured Beirut on 13 May 1110, the Moslem emir fled by night to Cyprus, and the inhabitants of the city conveyed secretly to the same island what they could save of their precious possessions.[4] The Doge of Venice, Domenico Michiel, on his expedition against the Moslems, put in at Cyprus in 1123, but, although he was at war with the Emperor, it is not recorded whether he did any damage.[5]

---

[1] Ταλάντεροι μένουσι καὶ τοῦ Ταντάλου, v. 275. A bad pun which I fortunately cannot reproduce.

[2] 'Ο δ' εὐσεβής, φεῦ, τὸν Σατὰν σεβῶν μόνον, v. 48: Dölger, *op. cit.* p. 9. It may be conjectured that his name was Eusebius, or the like.

[3] Langebek, *Scr. Rer. Dan.* I, p. 174; III, p. 430, n. *a*; Nicolas of Thingeyrar (as above, p. 266, n. 6); Riant, *Expéd. et Pèler. des Scand. en Terre Sainte au temps des Croisades*, Paris, 1865, pp. 161 f.; L. Philippou, *Paphos Guide*, 1936, pp. 12 f.

[4] Röhricht, *Gesch. des Kön. Jer.* p. 83; W. B. Stevenson, *The Crusaders in the East*, Cambridge, 1907, p. 59.

[5] William of Tyre, lib. XII, c. 22; Romanin, *Storia doc. di Venezia*, II, 1854, p. 38; Chalandon, *Jean II Comnène*, etc. 1912, p. 157.

Cyprus Monuments Committee *Phot. C. J. P. Cave*

WALL PAINTING AT A. CHRYSOSTOMOS

Relations with Christians in Syria remained close. There is some evidence for the influx of Maronites into the island at this time, in the appointment by Maronite Patriarchs of two monks, in 1121 and 1141 respectively, to be abbots of the monastery of St John Chrysostom at Koutzoventi.[1] To that monastery was to come, about 1152, St Neophytus, who was afterwards to settle at the Enkleistra near Paphos (p. 309).

In 1136/7 the whole population of a place called Tell Hamdun in Little Armenia was removed to Cyprus by John II Comnenus, when he conquered it from its Armenian ruler.[2]

In 1142, we are told, the same Emperor conceived a plan which, if it had come to anything, might have had far-reaching effect in face of the rapidly approaching threat of the Latins to Cyprus. He proposed, it appears, to create, in favour of his son Manuel, a hereditary principality including Attalia, Antioch and Cyprus. Instead of detaching so important a region from the Empire, this may have really meant reconstituting the ancient duchy of Antioch, and placing his son Manuel in command.[3] But we hear no more of this plan.

---

[1] This must be meant by *Cuzapanta*, as Assemani (*Bibl. or. Clem.-Vat.* I, p. 307) renders the name (*Kuzaband* in the original) which has puzzled Oberhummer (*O.C.* p. 39). Assemani's Latin rendering of the second passage is partly unintelligible, and the original text is very difficult. I owe to Prof. A. S. Tritton the following rendering: "When it was the date 1452 (Greek) in the month of Tammuz the blessed on the 10th day, there came into the presence of me, Peter Patriarch of the Maronites, sitting on the throne of Antioch, in the name of Jacob, from the town of Ramat in the diocese of Batrun, the son the monk Daniel of the monks of the convent of Kaftun. And I had given him authority from God and my insignificance that he should be head and manager of the convent of St John Kuzaband in the island of Cyprus the guarded by God." On Koutzoventi (Koutsovendis) monastery, see Hackett, pp. 356 f., and Gunnis, pp. 293 ff.: on the interesting remains of the Byzantine Katholikon, Sotiriou, *Byz. Mn.* figs. 33–4 and Pls. 29, 30, 77. The painting of the Epitaphios on the outer wall, one of the few of first-rate quality in Cyprus (Pl. XV), is probably as early as the twelfth century.

[2] Ibn al-Athir (*Rec. Cr. Or.* I, p. 424); Ibn al-Qalānisī (H. A. R. Gibb, *The Damascus Chronicle of the Crusades*, 1932, p. 241). Gibb attributes this transplantation to Manuel, but the Emperor at the time was John II Comnenus (Caloioannes), and "Kiyālyānī" of the text is evidently meant for the latter name. This authority says that the place belonged to Ibn Haitham.

[3] So Chalandon (*Jean II Comnène*, etc. 1912, pp. 184 f.), on Cinnamus, I, 10, p. 23. The plan would have constituted a state combining Cilicia, Upper Syria and Cyprus, the significance of which is explained by Iorga, *Brève Histoire de la Petite Armènie*, 1930, p. 30.

The growing penetration of Cyprus by the western powers is illustrated in 1148 by the grant made by Manuel Comnenus to the Venetians, extending to them in Crete and Cyprus the same commercial privileges which they enjoyed in other parts of the Empire. This grant, so full of consequences for the future, fell at the moment when Manuel was seeking the alliance of the Venetians, with a view to recovering Corfù from the Normans. Like all such concessions, it was due to the straits in which the Empire was involved.[1]

The next tribulation which came upon Cyprus was, in the first instance, due to the rise at the end of the eleventh century of a new power in southern Asia Minor: the state of Armeno-Cilicia, which grew up as the kingdom of Greater Armenia, waned and was finally extinguished by the Turks. It was the Prince Thoros II (1145–68) who finally made Armeno-Cilicia independent of the Empire. Against him, the Emperor Manuel enlisted the services, first of Masud I, Sultan of Rum, with ill success, and then, about 1155, of Renaud de Châtillon, a French adventurer who had in 1153 married Constance, Princess of Antioch. As some atonement for having ousted the suitor whom the Emperor had favoured, Renaud consented to attack Thoros. A battle of which the issue is obscure took place at Alexandretta, but soon afterwards Renaud made peace with the enemy, it is said because Manuel had failed to keep a promise to pay him a large subsidy.[2] Renaud decided to compensate himself, and, either of his own motion or at the instigation of Thoros, an expedition in which both were concerned was launched against Cyprus.[3] Thoros probably did no more than supply a contingent, though some authorities imply that he actually accompanied the expedition.

---

[1] The chrysobull is dated Oct. 6656, ind. XI, i.e. 1148; Tafel and Thomas, *Urkunden zur ält. Handels- und Staatsgesch. der Rep. Venedig*, I, pp. 114–24; Heyd, *Hist. du Commerce du Levant*, tr. Raynaud, I, p. 359; Chalandon, *Jean II Comnène*, etc. p. 321; Aimilianos in Κυπρ. Σπουδαί, I, 1937, p. 12. M.L. *H.* II, p. 4 and n. 2, shows that there were Latin merchants resident at Lemesos in 1191, and cites Matteo Camera (*Ist...di Amalfi*, p. 206) for evidence of Amalfitan merchants in Cyprus as early as 1168. But Camera gives no date and, as Heyd observes (*op. cit.* I, p. 360), no authority, although his statement is likely to be true.

[2] William of Tyre, XVIII, 10 (*Rec. Cr. Occ.* I, p. 835; Migne, *P.L.* 201, cols. 719–20). The untrustworthy Armenian version of Michael the Syrian (*Rec. Cr. Arm.* I, p. 350) says that Renaud's motives were two: first that the Greeks ill-treated the Franks in Cyprus, second that they encouraged the Turks to kill the Armenians. This is not in the Syriac version.

[3] William of Tyre, *loc. cit.*; Cinnamus, IV, 17, pp. 178 f. (Bonn); Gregory the Priest,

The actual course of events is obscure, though all the authorities save one (and that one, oddly enough, is the Greek Cinnamus) lay stress on the fearful outrages that were perpetrated by the invaders, who treated the Greeks "as if they were infidel Musulmans". The Duke of Cyprus at the time was John Comnenus, son of the sebastocrator Andronicus, and thus nephew of the Emperor Manuel. With him was Michael Branas. Warning of the impending attack had come, probably from friendly Latins in Antioch; and the Duke and his lieutenant had collected such an army as they could scrape together. It would seem that John's headquarters were at Leukosia, and Branas was sent to the coast to repel the invasion. According to Cinnamus, he handled Renaud severely at the landing but pursued him too impetuously towards Leukosia; and both Branas and the Duke, who came out to assist him, were taken prisoners. Other writers say that the Greeks were taken by surprise and that there was no defence, or that, even though they were warned, they collapsed at once. The invaders ranged through the island, burning towns and churches, mutilating the inhabitants, both lay and clergy, by cutting off their hands and feet, noses and ears. What plunder in gold, silver and valuable vestments Renaud could carry away he took with him; the inhabitants were driven down to the shore and set free after they had agreed a huge indemnity, the price of their lives and their cattle; and hostages were taken from the principal clergy and lay people and held until the ransom was paid.

The news excited the helpless rage of the Emperor, and the indignation of contemporaries. In the words of William of Tyre it was a piacular crime. It might have been intelligible if it had been a case of Christian against Musulman. But this was the age of the Crusades, and of the Latin kingdoms in the Holy Land; and it has been observed[1] that the intelligent Latins in those parts saw that their interests were ill-served by antagonizing the Greeks, and could not condone Renaud's act of piracy. The Cypriotes sent a message of bitter complaint to the Em-

---

Rec. Cr. Arm. I, p. 187 (*O.C.* p. 33); Michael the Syrian (ed. Chabot), III, fasc. iii, p. 315; Abulfaraj (Bar-Hebraeus), tr. Bruns and Kirsch, I, p. 355 (*O.C.* p. 38); Sempad, *Chron.* (*Rec. Cr. Arm.* I, p. 621; *O.C.* p. 86); John Dardel, *Chronicle of Armenia* (*Rec. Cr. Arm.* II, p. 7). The authorities differ about the date; 1155 or 1156 seems most probable. See Chalandon, *Jean II Comnène*, etc., pp. 437 f. Also G. Schlumberger (*Renaud de Châtillon*, pp. 68–79), who believes that Thoros did not accompany Renaud, but made an expedition of his own soon after. F. Tournebize, *Hist. pol. et rel. d'Arménie*, I [1900], pp. 178–9.

[1] Chalandon, *op. cit.* p. 439.

peror; and when Manuel was at Mamistra in 1159, Renaud appeared before him in garments of humiliation and grovelled on the ground, offering up his sword and praying for pardon in a manner that raised the gorge of the Franks who were present.[1]

All too soon after Renaud had removed himself from the scene, the Egyptian fleet, which had left Cyprus alone so long, showed itself again. In the year 1158, we are told, there were various expeditions by sea and land, which brought back many prisoners, among them "the brother of the Count, governor of the island of Cyprus". Es-Salih, the vizir of Egypt, received him with honour and sent him back to the Emperor of Constantinople. Thanks to these raids, all hands were full of booty.[2]

Among the dismal annals of this time, it affords some relief to note an event of some moment in the religious history of Cyprus which took place in 1159.[3] On St John Baptist's day (24 June) of that year, St Neophytus, a native of Leukara near Amathus, then a young man of twenty-five, who had begun his novitiate seven years before at A. Chrysostomos, found a cave in a lonely spot in the hills above Paphos which suited his desire for solitude. Such retirement, however, is seldom

---

[1] William of Tyre, lib. XVIII, c. 23 (*Rec. Cr. Occ.* I, pp. 859 ff.).

[2] Ibn Muyassar, *Rec. Cr. Or.* III, p. 473 (A.H. 553); *O.C.* p. 53. The writer speaks of the "king" of Cyprus, but must mean the Duke.

[3] L. Petit in *Echos d'Orient*, II, pp. 257–68 and 372; Delehaye in *Anal. Boll.* XXVI, 1907, pp. 274–6; I. Ch. Chatzeïoannes, Ἱστορία καὶ ἔργα Νεοφύτου, Alexandria, 1914. Corrections and additions by L. Philippou, in Κυπρ. Χρον. III, 1925, pp. 264 ff. Hackett, pp. 348–54. For the Ritual Ordinance (Τυπικὴ Διάταξις), see E. H. Freshfield and F. E. Warren in *Archaeologia*, XLVII, 1883, and Chatzeïoannes. A list of the known *Diataxeis* is given by W. Nissen, *Die Diataxis des Mich. Attaleiates von* 1077, Jena, 1894, and that of Neophytus described (from the imperfect text then available), pp. 13–15. He thinks Neophytus may be identical with the εὐλαβέστατος ἱερομόναχος κύριος Νεόφυτος mentioned in the *Typikon* of Nilus, founder of Machaera (see below). The "Misfortunes of Cyprus" in Sathas, Μεσ. Βιβλ. II, pp. 1–4; Chatzeïoannes, pp. 232–4; Rolls Series, vol. 38 (1864); *Rec. Cr. Grecs*, I, pp. 559–63; Cobham, *Exc. Cypr.* pp. 9 ff. K. Dyovouniotes, in Ἐπετηρὶς τῆς Ἑταιρείας Βυζ. Σπουδῶν, Athens, XIII, 1937, pp. 40–9, describes two other works, Ἡ πεντηκοντακέφαλος βίβλος and an interpretation of the *Song of Songs*. The former, in c. 31, describes a barbarian raid on a place called Cholestrio near Dikomo, and a subsequent battle between the Emperor Manuel and the Musulmans. (Was this the disaster of Myriokephalon in 1176?) Of the upper enkleistra, to which the saint retired in 1199 (*Theosemia*, p. 139 of Chatzeïoannes), hardly anything remains. For the decoration of the existing one, see below, p. 324; and for the cave where, according to tradition, but not on the evidence of Neophytus himself, he lived before going to the Enkleistra, at Souskiou near Kouklia, see Sotiriou, *Byz. Mn.* fig. 46 and Pl. 74 b.

permitted for long to men with a reputation for sanctity. This was the origin of the monastery of New Sion, generally known as the Enkleistra *par excellence*. After its construction, which was more or less complete by 1183, he made himself a cell higher up the cliff, accessible only by a ladder. Thither he retired in 1199, descending on Sundays to teach his disciples. In his cell he composed a Rule for his disciples, a first version in 1167, a second in 1189, a third in 1209.[1] The Rule limited the number of the monks to eighteen, and excluded women and female animals from the monastery. The community later (1631) acquired the privileges of a *stauropegion*, that is to say, became free from local control and subject only to the Patriarch.

A striking letter of the Saint, bitterly complaining of the treatment of his island by Isaac Comnenus and Richard Lion Heart, and meting out condemnation about equally to both, was probably written about 1196.[2]

---

[1] Sathas (II, p. ρκγ′, n. 1) cites Kyprianos (p. 350) as evidence for the Rule having being composed in 1190; but all that Kyprianos says is that Neophytus lived about 1190, "as we learn from his *diatheke*". Neophytus himself says that his Rule was first composed eight years after he began to live in the Enkleistra, i.e. in 1167. He goes on to say that "when he who controlled the course of my life (ὁ τῆς ζωῆς χορηγός) extended the duration of it, and five and fifty years had already passed away, and there was need of another diatheke...." This cannot mean fifty-five years after the first diatheke, for that would bring the date to 1222, whereas the copy is dated 1214. It must mean either that he was fifty-five years old, which would make the date 1189, or that it was fifty-five years since his seclusion in 1159, which would make it 1214. Now this second version was confirmed by the bishop of Paphos, Basil Cinnamus, on 6 Jan., Ind. VIII, which may correspond to 6 Jan. 1190. We may therefore accept 1189 as the date of the second version.

The MS. from which Warren and Freshfield edited the Rule was copied in Cyprus in 1214, Neophytus being then still alive. W. and F. date the confirmation by Cinnamus 1205 (an eighth indiction fell Sept. 1204–Sept. 1205), but a date fifteen years earlier fits, as we have seen, with the fifty-fifth year of Neophytus. The references to the English conquest, which induce W. and F. to date the confirmation later than 1191, may have been inserted in a later revision of the Rule. That was presumably the one for which a second confirmation was given by Bacchus, bishop of Paphos, in May, Ind. XII, which would then be 1209. We therefore date the various versions of the Rule to 1167, 1189 and 1209. There seems to be no evidence for one in 1214, which is only the date of the making of a copy.—As to the church of the monastery, Paschalides shows that it was probably founded about 1261 (in Διαλέξεις περὶ τῶν κορυφαίων Κυπρίων φιλοσόφων καὶ πεζογράφων, 1937, p. 47). For the *stauropegia*, *ibid.* pp. 47–8.

[2] Soon after, according to Sathas, II, p. ρκγ′; not until 1195 or 1196 according to Mas Latrie, *H.* I, p. 125; in 1203 according to Warren, *loc. cit.* The writer speaks of Cyprus having suffered for twelve years, and mentions, in this connexion, the usurpation of

It has been somewhat rashly conjectured that the Saint afterwards became archbishop of Cyprus. A letter written in 1223 by the Patriarch of Constantinople, Germanus,[1] mentions the expulsion from his throne of the most blessed archbishop of the Cypriotes, the lord Neophytus; if he was the founder of the Enkleistra, he must have been then in his ninetieth year. Rather than submit to the authority of the Latin archbishop, Neophytus went into exile.

Another famous monastery, that of Chrysorrhogiatissa, according to a tradition which may be based on fact, and is recorded on one of its icons, was founded in 1152 in the reign of Manuel Comnenus.[2]

The monastery of Machaeras[3] also dates from the twelfth century. Its site was first occupied by a hermit Neophytus, with a disciple Ignatius, who, when his master died, was joined by another ascetic, Procopius. These two, desiring to build a monastery, obtained from the Emperor Manuel Comnenus (1143–1180) funds, a grant of land, and exemption from the jurisdiction of the bishop of the diocese. The real founder of the monastery was, however, Nilus, who came thither in 1172, after the death of Procopius, and eventually succeeded Ignatius. Nilus obtained from the then bishop of Tamassus, Nicetas Hagiostephanites, the confirmation of the independence of the monastery as a *stauropegion*. Further privileges, it is said, were obtained from Isaac Angelus (1185–1195) and Alexius III (1195–1203).[4] This history is given by Nilus himself, in his *Typike Diataxis*, which dates from 1209. Nilus himself

---

Isaac (1185) and the capture of Jerusalem by Saladin (1187). This seems to indicate 1196 as the date.

[1] Sathas, II, p. 7. That the Saint was promoted to some ecclesiastical dignity is suggested, says Sathas, by his being described in the heading of the letter (Marciana DLXXV Greci) as πρότερον μοναχὸς καὶ Ἔγκλειστος. But the correct reading of the abbreviation (which Mr Ralegh Radford has kindly verified) is not πρότερον but πρεσβυτέρου.

[2] Λ. Φιλίππου, Ἡ ἱερὰ μονὴ Χρυσορρογιατίσσης, Paphos, 1935, pp. 12 ff.

[3] S. Menardos, Ἡ ἐν Κύπρῳ ἱερὰ μονὴ τῆς Παναγίας τοῦ Μαχαιρᾶ, Peiraeus, 1929; Hackett, pp. 346 f. W. Nissen, *Die Diataxis des Mich. Attaleiates von* 1077, Jena, 1894, pp. 15–16, describes the *Typikon* of Nilus, and suggests identifying the first settler Neophytus with the man who was elected Patriarch of Constantinople in 1153, but was deposed after six months before actually taking office. On the origin of the name of the place, perhaps from a kind of darnel (μασhαιρᾶς) which flourishes there, see Charalampous, in Κυπρ. Χρον. x, 1934, p. 310.

[4] Menardos, *op. cit.* p. 7, points out that, since, at the time of the later privileges granted to Machaera, Cyprus was in the hands of the usurper Isaac and then of Richard and the Franks, they can only have been issued to refugees in Constantinople, and had

eventually became bishop of Tamassus, a see which at that time seems to have ranked next to Constantia.

Returning to our annals, we note that St Neophytus himself records a serious earthquake as taking place soon after his settling at Enkleistra. It ruined fifteen churches in the province of Paphos alone, including that of the B. V. Limeniotissa in the fortress of Paphos.[1]

In 1160 the Emperor Manuel lost his first wife, Bertha of Sulzbach (Eirene), whom he had married in 1146. For a second wife he negotiated first with Raymond III of Antioch, Count of Tripolis, for the hand of his sister Melissenda.[2] But, after allowing the negotiations to drag on for more than a year, he suddenly in July 1161 changed his mind and married Marie, daughter of Constance, Princess of Antioch. This marriage concerns the history of Cyprus, because we learn incidentally first that the Duke of Cyprus at the time was Alexius Ducas (not Alexius Comnenus the eldest son of Nicephorus Bryennius); secondly that after the breaking off by Manuel of the negotiations with Raymond, the Count, following the bad example recently set by Renaud de Châtillon, took his revenge on Cyprus. He placed the ships, which had been prepared to carry his sister to Constantinople, in the hands of pirates, commissioning them to raid indiscriminately all the lands of the Emperor, ravaging, burning and slaying without regard to sex, rank or religion; an order which they executed in Cyprus and elsewhere.[3]

Manuel's ill-success against the Turks, culminating in his defeat in 1164 at Harim in Syria, led to an attempt to reorganize the defence of Cilicia. He chose his instrument badly, in his cousin Andronicus the son of Isaac Comnenus, afterwards the Emperor Andronicus I. In 1166 he made this brilliant but fickle adventurer Duke of Cilicia—a post he had

---

value as raising the monastery to the rank of an imperial foundation and a bulwark against foreign domination.

[1] *Orat. de terr. mot.* (ed. Delehaye, *Anal. Boll.* XXVI, 1907, p. 211). There had been a severe earthquake over the greater part of Syria and the Orient in Aug. 1157 according to Yusuf ibn Taghribirdī (Nodjoum ez-Zahireh), *Rec. Cr. Or.* III, pp. 508 f. Cyprus may have felt it; but this was before Neophytus went to Enkleistra.

[2] On the history of this affair see Horna in *Byz. Ztschr.* XIII, 1904, pp. 315 ff.

[3] William of Tyre, lib. XVIII, c. 33, *Rec. Cr. Occ.* I, p. 878 (does not specifically mention Cyprus); Const. Manasses, *Hodoiporikon* (ed. Horna), *Byz. Ztschr.* XIII, 1904, p. 343, bk. IV, vv. 56 ff.; p. 336, bk. II, v. 58: Alexius Ducas (Δουκόβλαστος) as κυριαρχῶν Κυπρίων. This was not Alexius, daughter's son of the Emperor Alexius, who was sent to Antioch to settle the marriage with Mary; he is described by Cinnamus (v, 4, p. 210 Bonn) as μέγας δούξ, i.e. Lord High Admiral, not as Duke of Cyprus.

previously filled, when he was badly defeated by Thoros II. The point that concerns this history is that, for the purposes of the organization, the Emperor added the revenues of Cyprus to those of Cilicia.[1] Andronicus took the revenues, but speedily deserted his post (1167), and Cyprus, once more, saw no return for all that had been extorted from her.

We have now reached the last episode in the history of Cyprus as a province of the Byzantine Empire. Isaac Ducas Comnenus[2] was a grandson of the sebastocrator Isaac, one of whose daughters probably married a Ducas. His great-uncle, the Emperor Manuel, had made him governor of Cilicia. Captured by the Armenians, he was thrown into prison, from which he was sold for a price to the Templars, about the time when Andronicus seized the imperial power. There was no love lost between him and Andronicus, who, however, allowed himself to be

---

[1] Cinnamus, VI, 1, p. 250 Bonn. Cp. Nicetas, *de Man.* IV, p. 180 Bonn. On the romantic adventures of Andronicus read Gibbon (Bury's ed., V, pp. 232 ff.).

[2] The chief authority for the revolt in Cyprus is Nicetas Choniates, *Is. Ang.* I, 5, p. 483. Cp. Neophytus, *de calam. Cypri* (Sathas, II, p. 3; Cobham, *Exc. Cypr.* pp. 10f.).
The following simplified table may make it easier to understand the relationships of the Comneni mentioned in this narrative.

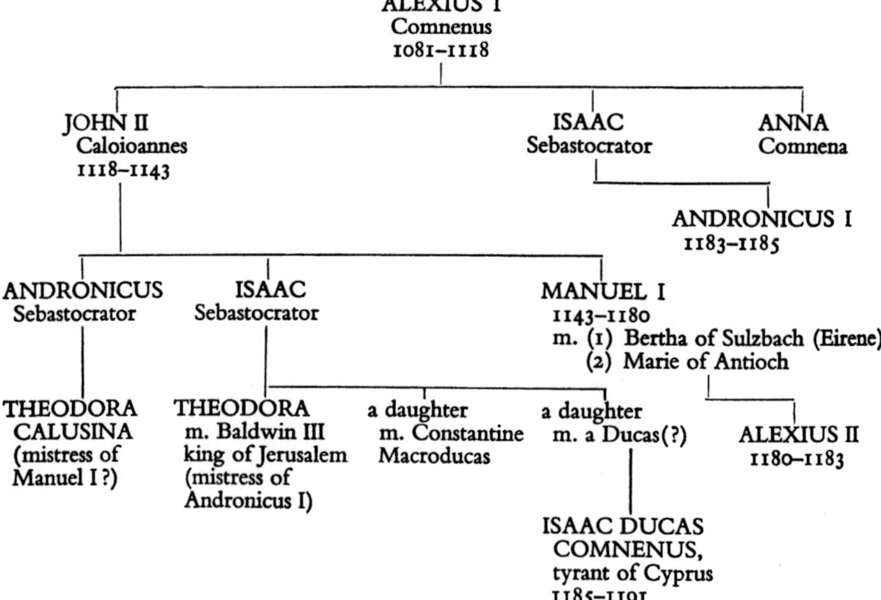

persuaded by Theodora Comnena to take pity on her nephew, buy him back from the Templars, and permit him to return, on the personal security of two distinguished men, Constantine Macroducas and Andronicus Ducas. Isaac used the money which was sent him to collect a force in Isauria, and cross to Cyprus. There he presented to the authorities forged letters of appointment as governor of the island. No sooner was he accepted as duke, or katapan, than he threw off the mask, and showed himself, if we may believe our authorities, a more brutal oppressor than Andronicus himself, or any of the Emperors, had been. No tyrant who had ever vexed the unfortunate Cypriotes was loaded with more bitter abuse than Isaac earned at the hands of those who describe his career.[1] But we must read these descriptions with reserve.

[1] Nicetas Chon. and Neoph. *locc. citt.* He is accused of wanton murder, κοίταις ἀθεμίτοις, ravishing of virgins, robbing the wealthy of all their possessions and reducing them to beggary and starvation. Nicetas describes his foaming paroxysms of rage, and how he cut off with an axe one of the feet of Basilius Rentacenus, his old tutor, who had been taken prisoner. Michael the Syrian (ed. Chabot, III, fasc. iii, p. 402) says that he compelled the Greek bishops to institute a "Patriarch" in opposition to the Patriarch of Constantinople; this Patriarch crowned him Emperor, and remained in office until Richard's conquest; he died in Cyprus. The account of Isaac's earlier career given in the text is from Nicetas. Very different is the version of the English chroniclers, the author of the *Gesta Regis Henrici II*, etc. commonly attributed to Benedict of Peterborough, and Hoveden. The former (ed. Stubbs, I, pp. 254 f.) says that Isaac, a comely man and a good soldier, flying from Andronicus I, collected an army and attacked the Sultan of Iconium. Captured by Ruben of the Mountain, he was offered to the Sultan, who refused him. Ruben then sent him to the Prince of Antioch, Bohemund III (the author calls him Raimund). The prince demanded a ransom of 60,000 besants. Isaac appealed for help to the rich men of Cyprus, who sent him half the sum, which he paid over; for the other half he left his son and daughter as security. (Incidentally it may be remarked that, if it was possible to raise 30,000 besants, there must have been no lack of wealth in the island, although it was doubtless concentrated in the hands of the ruling class.) Isaac was accepted in Cyprus as prince, on the ground of his relationship to Manuel. When the prince of Antioch asked for the remainder of the ransom, Isaac refused to give it to his messengers, but handed it to the Templars, who were robbed of it by pirates. Isaac maintained that this was a plot of the prince of Antioch, and refused to pay again; Isaac's hostages were consequently kept in custody for two years until the capture of Jerusalem, when they were released. Meanwhile Isaac, refusing obedience to the Emperor, or to pay him the usual annual revenue of Cyprus, assumed the imperial diadem and called himself Holy Emperor of Cyprus. (Cp. Hoveden, ed. Stubbs, II, pp. 203–4.) The author of the *Gesta* (pp. 261 f.) has also a passage on Isaac's crimes; he killed his wife and his only son, the latter because he confessed to liking the Latins; he caused gold and silver statues of himself to be made and set up in the churches, on the walls

It is fair to say that if he was a usurper, he does not compare unfavourably with Andronicus I either in his right to the throne, in his method of seizing it, or in his conduct as a ruler.

Andronicus, when this revolt was reported to him, fell beside himself with rage, and revenged himself on Isaac's sureties, Constantine Macroducas and Andronicus Dùcas, who were stoned and then, still breathing, impaled. It was said that he feared to be attacked in his capital by the rebel, for sorcerers had prophesied that one Isaac should dethrone him.[1] This was one of his last acts, for in September 1185, on the approach of the Normans, his subjects revolted, proclaimed Isaac II Angelus Emperor, and murdered the hated tyrant with every refinement of cruelty.

The new Emperor, after a vain attempt to buy off the rebel, despatched against him a fleet of seventy long ships, under the veteran admiral John Contostephanus; his second cousin Alexius Comnenus was in command of the troops which they carried (1186). Since Alexius had been blinded some time before by Andronicus, it is not surprising that he was an inefficient commander.

Isaac in Cyprus had timely notice of the expedition, and enlisted the support of the Sicilian admiral Margarito, who was in the neighbourhood. He himself attacked and captured those who had landed, while Margarito seized their ships which had been left empty, and handed them over. Isaac put some of the prisoners to the sword (including his old tutor Basil Rentacenus), and kept others in his service; the trierarchs he gave to Margarito as his share, while the crews were allowed to return home. This detail shows that he did not consistently behave with the inhumanity with which he is generally credited. Margarito carried the officers off to Sicily.

After this, Isaac was left in undisturbed possession of the island, until fate overtook him in the person of Richard Lion Heart.[2] It was, how-

---

of which he had his achievements painted; on Good Friday, in the chief cathedral church, he sat before the altar, in the place of the Cross, and caused the people to worship and offer sacrifice to him; he and his household ate flesh on that day, and he ordered all others to do the same. Many other examples of his hybristic behaviour are given, but, as Iorga points out (*France de Chypre*, pp. 13 f.), they were largely in accordance with Byzantine practice, which the English chronicler naturally would not understand; so that he considers that the fate which befell the tyrant was a divine judgement.

[1] Nic. Chon. *Andr. Comn.* II, 9, p. 442 (Bonn). Cp. *Constantinopolis Expugnata*, vv. 51 ff. (*Rec. Cr. Grecs*, I, p. 649).

[2] Numismatists have been tempted to assign coins to Isaac. Sabatier, *Monnaies*

ever, probably just before or at the same time as Richard's arrival that the defencelessness of the island was illustrated by a raid, made by some Frankish renegades. These, having got hold of some ships, went on a marauding expedition at the expense of the Christians. Landing somewhere in Cyprus on a feast-day, they joined the inhabitants in their celebrations in a church by the sea. They then took all the congregation prisoners and carried them off to Laodicea: twenty-seven women and much booty, each of the adventurers obtaining 4000 pieces of silver as his share.[1]

The fall of Isaac,[2] bringing with it the end of all hope of recovery of Cyprus for the Byzantine Empire, was a side-issue, which developed

---

byzantines, II, p. 227, Pl. 58. 9, attributes to him a bronze *nomisma* inscribed Ἰσαάκιος Δεσπό(της) ὁ Δούκας, with a figure of St Theodore on the reverse. Wroth (*B.M.C. Imp. Byz.* II, p. 597) accepts this attribution as probable. A seal with the inscription Κ[ύριε] βοηθεῖ τῷ σῷ δούλῳ Ἰσαακίῳ Δεσπότῃ τῷ Κομνηνῷ is given to him by Schlumberger (*Sigillographie byz.* p. 425); this also has the type of St Theodore. The difference in nomenclature (Ducas on the one, Comnenus on the other) is curious; but there is some probability on other grounds that his father was a Ducas (Ducange, *Familiae Byzantinae*, p. 185). Wroth rejects, in favour of Isaac Angelus, the attribution to the tyrant of Cyprus of a variety of other *nomismata*, billon or bronze, inscribed merely Ἰσαάκιος Δεσπότης, like the coins which are generally accepted as belonging to the Emperor Isaac. The attribution is due to Lambros (in Sathas, Μεσ. Βιβλ. II, pp. 561 ff.), who bases it on the ground that all the specimens he knows were found in Cyprus, and that they differ perceptibly in style from those of the Emperor. Wroth sees no such difference, and asks whether they are found in Cyprus exclusively. There seems to be no recent evidence to decide the point.

[1] Beha ed-din ibn Shaddad, in *Rec. Cr. Or.* III, p. 213. He says he learned (presumably at Aleppo) by a letter from Antioch about the result of this raid, on 12 rabia second 587, i.e. 9 May 1191. The raiders must then have returned shortly before that day, so that their raid probably just preceded or coincided with Richard's arrival.

[2] Modern accounts in M.L. *H.* I, pp. 2 ff.; A. Cartellieri, *Philipp II August*, II, 1906, pp. 187–94; Zannetos, Ἱστορία, 1910, I, pp. 577 ff. (who misreads the *Itin. Reg. Ric.* and makes Richard conquer the island on his way back from Palestine); K. Norgate, *Richard the Lion Heart*, 1924, pp. 140 ff.; G. Jeffery, *Cyprus under an English King*, 1926 (who assumes that modern Limassol did not then exist, and transfers events to Amathus); N. Iorga, *France de Chypre*, 1931, pp. 16–19. Cartellieri, p. 187, gives a full list of the authorities; I note here only the more important. Of the Greek authorities, (1) Nicetas Choniates, *Is. Ang.* II, 8, p. 547 (Bonn) is very brief; but note that he says that Richard made a present of the island to Guy, and that this error is not confined, as Mas Latrie implies, to English chroniclers (M.L. *H.* I, p. 37, n. 3 and II, p. 21). (2) St Neophytus gives a fuller account in his *de cal. Cypr.* (above, p. 308, n. 3). The western writers: (3) Richard himself, in a despatch to his Justiciar, 6 Aug. 1191 (in Stubbs, *Chron. and Mem. of the Reign of Richard I*, vol. II, Rolls Ser. 38, 1865,

into a major operation, of the Third Crusade, which had been inspired by Saladin's capture of Jerusalem, on 2 Oct. 1187. Its king, Guy de Lusignan, who was afterwards to found the Lusignan dynasty in Cyprus, had been captured, with his brother Aimery, Constable of the kingdom, at Hattin on the preceding 3 April; Acre fell five days later. Guy was released next year in exchange for Ascalon. By the end of 1188, the Christians held, of places of any moment in Syria, only Tyre, Antioch and Tripolis.

Richard Lion Heart of England and Philip Augustus of France, having started on the Crusade, were held up by contrary winds at Messina, and decided to spend the winter of 1190 there. Richard was betrothed to Alice, the French king's sister; but relations between the two rulers, already strained, were not improved by this enforced idleness. Eventually an agreement was patched up,[1] and Berengaria, daughter of the King of Navarre, took the place of Alice as the future queen of England. She was brought to Messina by Richard's mother, Eleanor of Aquitaine; the ceremony of betrothal took place, and on 10 April Richard's fleet sailed, carrying (but not in his own ship) his sister Joanna of Sicily and his bride Berengaria. They met heavy weather, and were separated. The three ships which carried the ladies and their

---

p. 347), reports briefly that he, the usurper Isaac having attempted by armed force to exclude him from the port, and ill-treated many of his men who had been wrecked, robbing them and imprisoning them so that they should starve to death, attacked Isaac and quickly defeated and captured him and his only daughter, and conquered all the island. (4) Ambroise, *Estoire de la Guerre Sainte* (ed. Gaston, Paris, 1897). Written about 1195 or 1196 by a partisan of Richard and Guy; held by the editor to be the original poem of which the work next to be mentioned is a free translation into Latin prose, but rather derived from a common original; cp. J. G. Edwards in *Hist. Essays in hon. of J. Tait*, 1933, pp. 59–77. Vv. 1346–2126 describe the Cyprus episode, corresponding to cc. 28–41 of the *Itinerarium.* (5) *Itinerarium regis Ricardi* (formerly attributed to Geoffrey de Vinsauf; by Stubbs to Richard, Canon of Holy Trinity, London), ed. Stubbs in Rolls Ser. 1864, pp. 177–204. (6) Ernoul, *Chronique* (ed. L. de Mas Latrie), 1871, pp. 270–3. (7) Cont. of William of Tyre, so-called *Eracles*, in *Rec. Cr. Occ.* II, pp. 159–70; a superior version in M.L. *H.* II, pp. 1 ff., and another, with many variations, *ibid.* III, pp. 591 ff. (8) [Benedict of Peterborough], *Gesta Regis Henrici II*, etc., ed. Stubbs, Rolls Ser. 1867, II, pp. 162–8. (9) Roger of Hoveden, *Chronica*, ed. Stubbs, Rolls Ser. 1870, III, pp. 105–11. (10) William of Newbury, *Hist. Rer. Angl.* (ed. H. Hamilton), 1856, II, pp. 59 f. (11) Richard of Devizes, *Chron.* (ed. Howlett), 1886, pp. 423–6.

[1] Rigordus, *de gestis Phil. Aug.*, in Bouquet, *Recueil des hist. des Gaules*, XVII, p. 32; Rymer, *Foedera*, 1816, I, p. 54; Cartellieri, pp. 164 ff.

escort parted from the rest and eventually found their way to Lemesos. Two (but fortunately not that with the ladies) were wrecked off this port. Among the bodies which came ashore was that of the vice-chancellor of England, Roger Malcael or Malchiel, wearing round his neck the king's seal, which Richard afterwards redeemed from the peasant who found it.

Isaac had little love for the Latins, so little indeed that he is said to have murdered his only son for liking them. He was also in league with Saladin[1] and had done his best to hamper the attempts of the Franks in Syria to obtain supplies from Cyprus, imposing heavy dues and then prohibiting them altogether. He had given orders that none of the Crusaders should be allowed to touch at any port of the island.[2] Warned of the expected arrival of the fleet at Lemesos, he had brought troops to prevent the crews from landing. Such as escaped alive from the wrecks he treated brutally, robbing them of all they had,[3] demanding hostages, and refusing them shelter within the town. Some of the English, however, led by Roger de Harcourt and William du Bois Normand, cut their way through and reached the ship with the two ladies, which lay off the shore. Isaac attempted, with the offer of food and presents, to entice Joanna and Berengaria on land, in order to hold them to ransom; but they were better advised; Joanna excused herself on the ground that she could not land without her brother's permission, and asked only for leave to take in fresh water. This Isaac refused, and, in order to prevent a forcible landing, fortified the beach with hulks of ships and stones and fittings from the houses in the town. He then prepared his ships to seize the coveted prey, but it put out to sea. At this point Richard's ship arrived from Rhodes (having narrowly escaped destruction in the Gulf of Adalia), followed by the remainder of his fleet (6 May 1191).

On what followed the authorities are even more than usually discordant. According to one group—the English—it was only after severe fighting, in which the king distinguished himself, in keeping with his reputation, by feats of valour, that the English were able to land.

---

[1] Ambroise, v. 1389; *Itin. Reg. Ric.* I, p. 183.

[2] Guillaume le Breton, *Philippis*, in Bouquet, *Rec. des hist. des Gaules*, XVII, p. 164, lib. IV, vv. 200–4.

[3] To say, as Iorga does (*F.d.C.* p. 9, n. 2), that Isaac was exercising the usual royal prerogative of wreck, is to interpret the chronicler in a sense which is not borne out by the passage cited.

According to the other writers the landing was unopposed; it is true that the Greeks guarding the shore refused permission to the crews to land for water and provisions, but when Isaac saw that the king's forces were actually landing and approaching Lemesos, while Richard with his ships moved along the coast, he evacuated the town and retired with all his troops to Kilani, in the hills to the north. Richard was indeed welcomed by the resident Latin merchants, who came to him on board his ship, and informed him of Isaac's flight and of the readiness of those who were left behind to accept him as their lord. He gave orders to his men to camp outside the walls, and do no harm to the people. It must be admitted that this less romantic account is the more likely to be near the truth, especially as it agrees with the statement of Neophytus, who was no friend to either party, that when the English came, all the people came to him, and the Emperor, seeing himself deserted, submitted.[1]

On the third day after landing, Richard sent to Isaac at Kilani, inviting him to a conference, to which, on receiving a safe-conduct, he agreed. He came down to Kolossi, and thence proceeded to meet the king. At the interview, Richard begged Isaac to withdraw his opposition to the Crusade, and invited him to join it. Isaac agreed to everything except personal service; he dared not leave the island, since the Emperor of Constantinople disputed his right to it, and the people would revolt in his absence. But he offered to send a body of two hundred men, to allow provisions to be purchased without payment of dues, and to leave his daughter in the king's hands as hostage.[2]

Nevertheless, he had approached Richard only to gain information of his power and intentions, and that same night he fled back to Kolossi, from whence he sent an insulting message, demanding that the king should quit the island without delay.

Richard, indignant, landed his horses, which till then had remained in the ships, attacked Isaac's camp and captured it, returning with im-

---

[1] See the discussion of the discrepant versions by M.L. *H.* II, pp. 19 f.

[2] Another less likely version (see the *Gesta*, p. 165) makes Isaac offer terms, including compensation in 20,000 marks of gold for the plundering of the ship-wrecked English, and promise to accompany the king to Palestine with 100 knights, 400 light horse and 500 foot, to hand over his daughter and his Empire, and surrender his castles as a pledge; these conditions having been accepted, Isaac did homage to Richard. Ambroise, v. 1788 (*Itin. Reg. Ric.* c. 37, p. 198) makes the indemnity 3500 marks of silver. No satisfactory explanation of the discrepancy suggests itself, and in the circumstances it seems unprofitable to estimate the equivalents in modern money.

mense booty, including the imperial standard, which was afterwards dedicated at St Edmundsbury, on the tomb of the martyr.[1]

At Lemesos, Richard was joined by a number of lords from Syria, with a hundred and sixty knights,[2] of the party opposed to Conrad of Montferrat. The most important was Guy de Lusignan, who came to seek support for his claim to the crown of Jerusalem. With him were his brother Geoffrey, Richard's man in virtue of his possessions in Poitou; Humfry of Toron, Guy's brother-in-law; Bohemund III, Prince of Antioch; Raymond III of Tripolis, his son; and Leo, brother of Ruben of the Mountain,[3] King of Armeno-Cilicia. Guy and some at least of the others swore fealty to Richard.

On 12 May Richard celebrated his marriage with Berengaria, in the Chapel of St George at Lemesos, and she was crowned queen of England (but not of Cyprus) by John Fitz Luke, bishop of Evreux.[4]

Meanwhile, Isaac had retreated in the direction of Leukosia, and sent his wife and daughter on to safety, as he thought, in the castle of Kerynia. (His wife was a daughter of Thoros II of Armenia.) Richard now sent his army along the coast as far as Kiti (Larnaka), in order to avoid penetrating the hilly country, and thence to Famagusta. From Kiti he might easily have marched north into the Mesarea to find Isaac, but it seems that he sailed on to Famagusta, and his army took the same direction. They found the place undefended. There Richard stayed three days. Envoys who reached him from Philip, urging him to make haste to Acre, were told that not for anything would he leave Cyprus until he had dealt with Isaac, and secured for the Crusaders so important a source of supply. Then he marched towards Leukosia; at Tremithoussia the two hosts met. According to one version the engagement was fierce, and was only decided when Isaac, having penetrated into the thick of the fray, and actually struck Richard a mighty blow with his mace, was overwhelmed and taken prisoner.

A less romantic and more acceptable narrative may be reconstructed from other sources. It discounts this last episode, making of the en-

---

[1] Hoveden, III, p. 108; *Gesta Regis Henrici II*, etc., p. 164; Dugdale, *Monasticon*, 1846, III, pp. 104–5.

[2] Beha ed-din ibn Shaddad, in *Rec. Cr. Or.* III, p. 214.

[3] At this time, Leo II had already (in 1185) succeeded his brother Ruben III. According to the *Gesta* these lords were all present at the interview when Isaac swore fealty to Richard.

[4] M.L. *H.* II, p. 5, n. 5.

counter a mere skirmish (Isaac employing poisoned arrows). He escaped to Kantara, or took refuge in the Karpass, near C. St Andreas. The three strongholds of Kerynia, Didymus (St Hilarion) and Buffavento were still in his possession. Richard, having occupied Leukosia, fell sick. Guy besieged Kerynia, which surrendered; Isaac's wife and daughter thus fell into Richard's hands. In dismay, Isaac gave orders to St Hilarion to yield. Richard was about to attack Buffavento, when Isaac finally made complete surrender (end of May), bargaining only that he should not be put in irons. This condition was accepted and, the tale goes, fetters of gold and silver were provided.[1]

The booty which Richard seized in Cyprus was great.[2] The people, who accepted their new master as a welcome change from the tyrannous Greek, yielded up half of all their possessions; Richard in return confirmed to them by charter the laws and institutions which had been granted to them by Manuel Comnenus.[3] Frankish garrisons took the place of Greek. Richard de Camville and Robert de Turnham were appointed justiciars and sheriffs to administer the island, with orders to send supplies thence to the Crusaders in Syria. Isaac was given in charge

---

[1] A variant account in the *Gesta* is that Richard sent Guy in pursuit of Isaac, while he himself with some of his ships sailed in one direction, sending the rest under Robert de Turnham right round the island, capturing all the castles round the coast; Guy achieved no success. The battle of Tremithoussia is not mentioned, but Isaac is said to have given himself up after the surrender of Kerynia and Buffavento. The *Gesta* also has the romantic picture of Isaac's daughter coming out of the castle of Kerynia, falling on her knees, and throwing herself on Richard's mercy (p. 167). The Cont. of William of Tyre (*Rec. Cr. Occ.* II, pp. 167–8; M.L. *H.* II, p. 6) makes Richard go direct from Kiti to Tremithoussia; at any rate, he does not mention Famagusta. Roger of Hoveden (ed. Stubbs, III, p. 111) adds Paphos (*castellum quod dicitur Baffes*) to the fortresses which surrendered. The story of the silver (or gold) fetters is repeated by all the authorities who mention the material, except Neophytus, who says that they were of iron. M.L. *H.* II, p. 7, note.

[2] See especially Ambroise, vv. 1669 ff., 2069 ff., and *Itin. Reg. Ric.* pp. 194, 203 f. for the spoils: arms, silks, furniture, gold and silver plate, the emperor's pavilion and bed, wines, horses, mules, cattle and even poultry. Philip Augustus afterwards claimed half the treasure, on the strength of the agreement to share all the proceeds of conquest which was made at Vézelay and renewed at Messina on 8 Oct. 1190 (Cartellieri, pp. 110, 140, 209). The terms of the treaty made at Messina in March 1191 included nothing on this point.

[3] As a curiosity, note that the Cypriote magnates are said to have been made by Richard to shave off their beards in sign of the change of the dominion of the island: "tanquam in signum commutationis alterius dominii", *Itin. Reg. Ric.* p. 201. We shall find this western distaste for the long beards of the Greeks causing trouble again.

Cyprus Monuments Committee *Phot. C. J. P. Cave*

KANTARA CASTLE

to Ralph Fitz Godfrey and then, on Ralph's death, to the Hospitallers, who took him to Margat near Tripolis, where he remained in prison, probably until after Richard left Syria. He seems to have died in 1195, but was heard of again before then. His wife and daughter were placed in the care of the two queens. The girl was to have a curious career.[1]

Richard's conquest of Cyprus must not be regarded as a mere episode in his crusade. Saladin had all but destroyed the Latins in the Holy Land. The situation was at once relieved; the provisioning of the crusading forces became possible, and it was on Cyprus that their operations for another century were based.[2]

The arts of Cyprus in the period covered by this chapter have lately attracted considerable attention, and been discussed and illustrated in expensive publications. The interest of the architecture and wall-paintings is great, but their picturesque setting and romantic associations have made it difficult even for scholars to maintain in judging them the standards which they would apply in lands farther west. Cyprus has that peculiar fascinating power of blunting the critical faculty.

Botched construction and re-construction, earthquake and the hand of time have seen to it that there are but few remains of the Byzantine churches of Cyprus which can give us any idea of their once imposing character.[3] The mother of them all, the basilica of Salamis, has already

---

[1] Ernoul (p. 273) says that Richard took Isaac's wife and daughter both to Syria; cp. *Eracles*, p. 169, where we are told (wrongly) that they were imprisoned in the same place as Isaac, that (p. 200) Richard took them both with him when he left Palestine (this is correct), and that Isaac was already dead then. But from Nicetas, p. 611, it appears that the report of his death was false. He was released, probably about 1195, and put forward a claim to the Empire, intriguing with the Turks; but he died, perhaps of poison, in the same year (cp. Hoveden, III, p. 306). For the whole question of the history of Isaac, his wife and daughter after their capture, see the discussion in *Rec. Cr. Grecs*, II, pp. 489 f. La Monte (*Feudal Monarchy*, p. 221, n. 1) by a slip makes Ernoul say that the Templars had charge of Isaac, but in the passage in question Ernoul is speaking of the island, not of Isaac.

[2] Cp. R. Grousset, *Hist. des Croisades*, III, p. 49.

[3] The student of the subject should refer to Sotiriou's sketch Τὰ Παλαιοχριστ. κ. Βυζ. Μνημεῖα τῆς Κύπρου (*Prakt. Acad. Ath.*), 1931, and his large work, *Byz. Mn.* I, 1935; also, for St Barnabas, his article in Κυπρ. Σπουδαί, I, 1937, pp. 175–87. See also Megaw's review of the second publication in *J.H.S.* LVI, 1936, pp. 269 f. The whole of what I have said above has been considerably modified and expanded in accordance with the observations of Mr Megaw, who kindly looked through it.

been described in an earlier chapter (pp. 253 f.). The subsequent development of church-architecture down to the tenth century is so obscure and opinions vary so widely[1] that not even a summary can be attempted here. It seems improbable that any important buildings can have been put up during the periods of the Arab raids, that is, from the middle of the eighth century to 965. Churches, for instance, like those at Aphendrika, which have been attributed on the one hand to the sixth or seventh century, on the other to the 'Romanesque', would not have been built at a time when the population of places like Ayios Philon and Lambousa was moving inland to escape the raiders. Whether the earlier or the later date is to be preferred must be left to the specialists.[2] The most peculiar type of Cypriote church is that represented by Peristerona and Yeroskipou, which are on a basilica plan, but have the side aisles separated from the nave not, as in the Greek basilica, by columns, but by walls pierced with arches, and have five domes, arranged as they might be on a cruciform church, although the plan is not cruciform. That is to say, it is a local adaptation of the domical system of roofing, which was disseminated through the expanded Empire of the Basilian dynasty, to a type of building for which the basilica was the only local precedent. This type, again, is hardly likely to have developed during the three-centuries struggle with Islam. On the other hand, it is reasonable to suppose that there was a revival of the arts in the island after its recovery by Byzantium in 965.

The rarity of examples of the true style of Byzantine construction, in brick, shows once more how remote the island was from the centre of

---

[1] Thus, while Sotiriou deals with the three-domed type, represented by St Lazarus at Larnaka and St Barnabas near Salamis (which has lost its eastern dome), as early, Megaw regards it as a late development, showing the influence of Gothic architecture. An article in Κυπρ. Χρον. IX, 1933, pp. 314–17, maintains the view that St Lazarus was originally a church with five domes.

[2] On this problem I may quote Mr Megaw (28 Dec. 1938): "I am not at all satisfied that on the existing evidence the vaulted basilicas of the Aphendrika type can be dated before the Byzantine reconquest. Perhaps they were the first churches built after 965 before the local builders became aware of the domical style which had been developed in the 'home' provinces. Certainly they do not belong to the Early Christian period (before the Arab raids), as the wood-roofed basilica with colonnades was then in vogue, to judge by the Salamis basilica and capitals of this period throughout the island." The Aphendrika churches are discussed by Enlart (I, pp. 396 ff.), as Romanesque, and by Sotiriou (Τὰ Παλαιοχριστ. κ. Βυȝ. Μνημεῖα, p. 8 and *Byz. Mn.* I, figs. 4, 5 and Pls. 10–13) as sixth–seventh century.

influence. The church of St Hilarion and that formerly at Koutzoventi which was pulled down in 1900 are the most important examples.[1]

From the same reason which prevents our assuming activity in building during the period of Arab raids, it seems to follow that the three remaining mosaics—the finest of which is that of the Virgin between SS. Gabriel and Michael in the apse of the church at Kiti[2]—are more likely to belong to the tenth or eleventh than to the ninth century. Of the wall-paintings[3] for which Cyprus is famous nothing of importance is preserved earlier than the twelfth century. The Epitaphios at A. Chrysostomos (Pl. XIV), which may be of the middle of the twelfth century, has already been mentioned (p. 305, n. 1). The date 1106 is, on the evidence of an inscription, assigned to certain of the paintings in the church of Asinou.[4] Nineteen of the original paintings of this date survive, and do not appear to have been repainted. They are fifty years older than the paintings of Nerez in Macedonia, with which the Epitaphios of A. Chrysostomos has been compared. The dignified painting of SS. Constantine and Helena, in half-figure, above the three full lengths of St Theodosius the Cenobiarch, St Arsenius and St Ephraim Syrus, may be taken as representative of the style; but a higher level was to be reached in the middle of the next century in the Virgin and Archangels in the vault of the church. Of little artistic quality, though of great interest owing to their association, are the paintings due

---

[1] For St Hilarion, see above, p. 271. For the church within the monastery of Koutzoventi, which was pulled down in 1900, see the plan reproduced by Jeffery in *Proc. Soc. Ant.* 1915–16, p. 15. It had a large dome on squinches.

[2] Smirnov's date of fifth or sixth century for the Kiti mosaic is, I believe, no longer accepted by anybody. The mosaic is illustrated by Sotiriou, *Byz. Mn.* Pl. 61. Enlart, *L'art gothique*, II, p. 440, dates it to the eleventh or twelfth; that of Kanakaria (Sotiriou, *loc. cit.*) to the twelfth or thirteenth. Mr Megaw writes: the mosaic "in the Kanakaria church, which is the less sophisticated, is perhaps the earlier, and the product of an austere provincial school, whereas the Kiti mosaic recalls the more naturalistic, neo-classical style favoured by the capital.... Sotiriou's plan of the former church suggests that originally it conformed to the Aphendrika type." He adds that at Kiti the apse is of earlier date than the rest of the church, so that the mosaic need not be so late as might be supposed from the general style of the church; but that composition and style of figure-drawing are definitely against a date before 965.

[3] Generally called frescoes, but it is doubtful whether any of them are in *buon fresco*, i.e. painted while the plaster was damp. For illustrations, see Sotiriou, *Byz. Mn.* Pls. 62 ff.

[4] See in *Archaeologia*, LXXXIII, 1934, pp. 327–50, the paper by the Bishop of Gibraltar, Major Seymer and Mr and Mrs Buckler.

partly at least to the hand of St Neophytus himself in the Enkleistra.[1] These were finished about 1183. In one of them, horribly defaced by modern graffiti, we have the portrait of Neophytus, kneeling at the feet of Christ, who is enthroned between the Virgin and the Baptist;[2] in another, on the west wall of the middle chamber, is the figure of Neophytus between two angels, painted by himself.

The portable icon, judging by the number of examples with which Cypriote churches are littered, though not (except in Nicosia) by their condition, must have played a considerable part in Cypriote religious life. Its interest is not in its quality, but in its illustration of the legends and iconography and history of costume. It is, of course, impossible to obtain any information as to the real nature of the allegedly oldest icons. The most famous is that of Kykko, which professes to go back to the hand of St Luke, and may be the one which was given to the founder of the monastery by the Emperor in the eleventh century; it is covered up with metal ornament and jealously guarded from expert examination.[3] Others apparently of early Byzantine style are in such a state that reproduction is a mockery. Otherwise, the only icon of any importance pretending to an origin earlier than 1200 is the Virgin and Child of the Phaneromeni in Nicosia, and that has been hopelessly repainted.[4]

---

[1] See above, pp. 308 f. In the inscription on the corner-vaulting in the first chamber we are told that the building and painting were done by St Neophytus in year 6704 of Adam (by the Constantinople reckoning = A.D. 1195/6), and the painting and other decorations partly restored by the monk Neophytus in the year 911 (the 6000 numeral being omitted, this is A.D. 1402/3): ἐλαξεύθη οἰκοδομίθη κὲ ἱστωριογραφίθη... ἐν τὸ ϛψδ' ἔτι τοῦ 'Αδάμ, ἐν δὲ τὸ ͵ια' ἔτι ἀνεκενίσθη κ.τ.λ. On the other hand, the *Diataxis* (c. 5) says that the work was completed (ἱστορήθη τελείως ἡ 'Εγκλείστρα καὶ ὁ πλησίον αὐτῆς κρημνὸς λαξευθείς) in the twenty-fourth year after Neophytus settled there, i.e. 1183/4. Mr Buckler, observing that Chatzeïoannes misreads the first date as 6701 and the second as 7011, suggests that the date in the *Diataxis*, in spite of the use of τελείως, may, with the inaccurate vagueness usual in Byzantine writers, refer to the beginning of the painting.

[2] Sotiriou, *op. cit.* Pl. 73 a.

[3] Sotiriou, *op. cit.* Pl. 116.

[4] "It may be hazarded that it was first painted in the eleventh or twelfth century, that it was restored and added to in the fourteenth, and that after that date it underwent various repaintings which affected the Virgin's face more than any other part": D. Talbot Rice, *The Icons of Cyprus*, 1937, no. 27, Pl. XVIII. This finely illustrated work provides the first systematic collection of material for a critical study of the subject. A few specimens are illustrated by Sotiriou, *op. cit.* Pls. 116–30. The authorities of the Phaneromeni have made a most praiseworthy attempt to rescue the more important examples of the art, and those from churches in Nicosia are now safe and admirably exhibited.

Little can be said at this stage, for lack of material, on the subject of Byzantine literature in Cyprus. Nicolaus Mouzalon, whose poem on the condition of Cyprus in his time has been described above, was not a Cypriote (he came of a known Byzantine family); but he identified himself so closely with his flock that he may perhaps be mentioned here. His idea of Greek style may be gauged by the story that he threw a Life of St Paraskeve of Callicrateia, which had been written in the vernacular, into the fire, and ordered a deacon to write a new one in good Greek. The poem on his resignation does not conflict with this evidence; but the burning indignation which inspires it atones for any artificiality of diction.[1]

The narrative balladry known as the "akritic" poetry was so called because it celebrated the exploits of the Akritai, corresponding to the old Roman *milites limitanei*, who defended the Byzantine frontiers against Islam, as well as against the freebooters of the provinces.[2] But it originated outside Cyprus, in Cappadocia and Pontus, probably in the tenth century, and was not imported thence into the island until a later date, during the twelfth century at the earliest. These ballads were sung by travelling minstrels, who have been compared to the *jongleurs* of France. The Cypriote *poietarides* took over the akritic ballads from Asia Minor and recast them in their own idiom. In other Greek lands, except in Crete, this class of professional ballad-singers has disappeared; in Cyprus it has survived to the present day. No great poet arose anywhere to combine the traditions on which the ballads are based into a real work of art, for the long Byzantine epic of Digenes Akritas has been rightly described as a pedantic work of no poetic value.[3]

Only two Cypriote prose-writers of the Byzantine age call for men-

---

[1] Krumbacher, *Gesch. d. byz. Lit.*[2] 1897, pp. 212 and 791.

[2] Krumbacher, *ibid.* p. 832, explains ἀπελάται as meaning in the first place cattle-reivers, and then generally freebooters; it was the exploits of the Akritai against these and Islam that formed the matter of the akritic poetry.

[3] There is hardly any trace of specifically Cypriote church-poetry, though St Epiphanius is said to have written hymns and St Neophytus also wrote verses. See L. Philippou in Διαλέξεις περὶ τῆς Κυπριακῆς ποιήσεως, Paphos, 1938, pp. 44–53. For a summary of the history of Cypriote popular poetry see L. Philippou, Τὰ Ἑλληνικὰ Γράμματα ἐν Κύπρῳ, Leukosia, 1930, II, pp. 3–21, with references to the literature. Cp. also K. Chatzeïoannou in Διαλέξεις (as above), pp. 27–31. Add, for the Digenes question, Ch. Diehl and G. Marçais, *Le monde oriental de* 395 *à* 1081, 1936, pp. 515–16 (references to earlier literature). Krumbacher and these authorities do not deal with the origin of the Cypriote ballads.

tion. Leontius, bishop of Neapolis (about 590–668),[1] was a remarkable author of popular biographies, of which two (lives of St John the Almsgiver and of the Monk Symeon) have survived in the original, and a third, that of St Spyridon, perhaps in a revision by Metaphrastes (tenth century). Based on contemporary sources, both written and oral, and to a large extent on personal knowledge, his works give a lively picture of the Christian society of the time, and are examples of its popular reading, affording a welcome relief from the arid theological controversies which fill so much Byzantine literature. Another vivid personality, in the twelfth century, is the monk Neophytus, the founder of the Enkleistra.[2] Because of its historical interest, his best-known work is the letter concerning the calamities of Cyprus, to which reference has already been made (p. 309). His style, like that of most literary efforts of the time, may be deplorable, but it cannot disguise the passionate resentment of the writer against the oppressors, whether the tyrant Isaac or his conqueror the accursed Englishman, "who horribly despoiled the land and then sailed away to Jerusalem, where he achieved nothing against his fellow criminal Saladin, but only sold the island to the Latins for 200,000 pounds of gold". The other important work of Neophytus was his *Typike Diataxis* or Ritual Ordinance, which, while laying down the rules for the community, also gives the only trustworthy (albeit still obscure) information which we have about his life and the early history of the foundation. He wrote at least fifteen other works, a Commentary on St Basil's *Homilies on the Six Days' Work*, a tract called *Theosemia*, and a number of sermons, including that on earthquakes to which reference has already been made, and others which have not been preserved.

NOTE

The First Moslem Invasions of Cyprus (see p. 284)

The earliest of the western authorities on this subject is Paul the Deacon (end of eighth century) in *Hist. Miscella* (Migne, *P.L.* 95, 1049), who says that, in the seventh year of Constans, Muawiya, invading Cyprus with 1700 ships, took Constantia and all the island and exterminated it, but retired on hearing that Cacorhizus was advancing against him. Theophanes (writing 811–15)

---

[1] H. Gelzer, "Ein griechischer Volkschriftsteller des 7. Jahr.", in *Hist. Ztschr.* LXI (N.F. XXV), 1889, pp. 1–38; the same, *Leontios von Neapolis' Leben des heil. Iohannes des Barmherzigen*, 1893; O.C. p. 438; Delehaye in *Anal. Boll.* XXVI, 1907, pp. 239 f.

[2] See above, pp. 308 f.

also gives the date in the seventh year of Constans = A.D. 647/8 (I, p. 525 Bonn, pp. 343 f. de Boor). But his date A.M. 6140 is equivalent to A.D. 649 (E. W. Brooks, *Byz. Ztschr.* VIII, pp. 82 ff.). After ravaging the island, Muawiya retired because he heard of the approach of the chamberlain Cacorhizus with a large force. The year after his attack on Cyprus, Muawiya took Aradus, which capitulated on the condition that the inhabitants should be allowed to settle where they pleased. The suggestion of Sathas (II, p. κδ′, n. 1) that they settled in Cyprus, because there is a place there called Aradhippou (near Larnaka), is hardly worth mentioning. (Why not also Aradhiou on the Nicosia-Limassol road?) Constantine Porphyr. (*de adm. imp.* 20) merely says that Muawiya ravaged Cyprus. The earliest of the eastern authorities is Pseudo-Dionysius of Telmahre (original MS. finished A.D. 775), who gives no details but the date 960 of the Greeks = 648/9, in which year he also dates the capture of Aradus (ed. Chabot, 1895, p. 7). Next comes Baladhuri († 892), who gives alternative dates, A.H. 28 (i.e. A.D. 648/9) or 29 (649/50) for the first invasion, and 33 (653/4) or even 35 (655/6) for the second (*Origins of the Islamic State*, tr. Ḥitti, pp. 235 ff.). But his story of what happened is very different from most others. According to him, Othman, in giving permission, made the condition that Muawiya should be accompanied by his wife, Fakhita; accordingly she went with him. The "archon" of the Greeks, when the Arabs first arrived, offered terms, which were agreed on the tribute stated in the text (an equal sum to be paid, if they liked, to the Greeks) and observation of neutrality, as described above. Thus the Moslems treated the Cypriotes very well, and it was only when the pledge of neutrality was broken that, in the year 33 or 35, the island was again seriously invaded, Constantia captured by force, the inhabitants slaughtered, many prisoners taken, and a garrison established. He does not mention Abu 'l-Awar, and attributes this second expedition, like the first, to Muawiya himself. Arabs and Greeks each doubtless laid the blame for the barbarous treatment of the Cypriotes on the other side; the weight of evidence seems, however, to be in favour of the version given in the text. To return to the authorities: one of Baladhuri's sources gives the names of a number of those who took part in the expedition; one puts the tribute at 7200 gold pieces, another at 7000, and so does Tabari (839–923), who also mentions the treaty; but whereas Baladhuri says that the Cypriotes were to remain neutral, he makes it bind them to assist the Arabs (*Chronicle*, tr. Zotenberg, III, pp. 562 f.). Tabari also says that an Egyptian fleet under Ibn Abi Sarh conveyed Muawiya's forces from Acre (Wellhausen, *Göttinger Nachrichten*, Phil.-hist. Kl., 1901, p. 418). Eutychius, Patriarch of Alexandria, 934–950 (Pococke's Latin tr. of his *Annals* in Migne, *P.G.* 111, col. 1112), says nothing of any ravaging of the island; he dates the treaty in year 28 (648/9) and puts the tribute at 7200 gold pieces (the same to the Greek Emperor). This sum, as more precise, is more likely to be correct than 7000. Elias of Nisibin (early eleventh century) dates the invasion A.H. 28, and also gives the amount of the tribute as 7200 dinars, "the same as that paid to the Romans" (*Chron.* tr. Delaporte, p. 85). Michael the Great or the Syrian (1126–99) (ed. J.-B. Chabot, t. II, fasc. iii, 1904, pp. 441 f.) does not mention any tribute, but adds that Muawiya gave much of the booty to the Egyptian troops, whom he sent back to their country. An anonymous Syrian chronicle, published by Chabot (*Corpus Scr. Chr. Orient.*, *Scr. Syr.* sér. III, t. XV, pp. 268 ff., 271 f.), to which Mr C. Moss called my attention, generally follows Michael, but has some details of interest. It was completed about 1203/4. It describes the fleet of 1700 ships, with the contingent from Alexandria. Muawiya at first hoped for peaceful terms, but the Cypriotes made no offer. So, persuaded by the Alexandrians, he landed, and the Arabs scattered over the whole island, destroying, enslaving and slaying without pity. Constanti[n]a is described as wealthy, with a population of all nations, and fine buildings. Muawiya committed all kinds of wickedness, including "making priests for the temple of the Athlete" (using the church of Epiphanius as a mosque ?). These ills are attributed by the writer, following Michael, to the wrath of God at the falling away of the Christian priests from the doctrine of Epiphanius. The captives and treasure were divided into two portions, and lots were cast, and the Alexandrians drew the first. The invaders remained as long as they pleased and then took the captives, some to Alexandria and some to Syria. There is no mention of the imposition of a tribute. The account of the second invasion describes the dragging of the refugees out of the caves and the siege of *Lapathos*; Abu 'l-Awar gave the inhabitants leave to go to Greek territory or remain in Cyprus. He stayed in Constanti[n]a forty days. From Ibn al-Athir (1160–1233; quoted by Dulaurier, *Journ. Asiat.* sér. IV, t. XIII, p. 361, whence O.C. p. 49; I owe further details to Mr J. Walker) we learn the names of some of the Companions of Muhammad who accompanied the expedition, corresponding in part with those given by Baladhuri. He states that Abdallah ibn-Kais remained in command, and made fifty raids by land and sea, but, landing at a Greek port, was attacked by the inhabitants and killed. This must have happened after the Cyprus campaign was over. The author of a Treatise on War against the Infidels (quoted, but not dated, by Dulaurier, *loc. cit.*) also mentions Umm-Haram and her husband, who, he says, was sent to Cyprus by Muawiya. This statement, implying that Muawiya did not go himself, contradicts all other authorities. (Unless he means that they were on the second expedition.) El-Makin (1205–73), in his *Hist. Sarac.* (tr. Erpenius, 1625, p. 37), giving the date 27 = 647/8, speaks of a tribute exacted over two years.

The date according to Abulfaraj or Bar-Hebraeus (*Chron. Syr.* ed. Bedjan, 1890; ed. and tr. Bruns and Kirsch, 1789, I, p. 110; *O.C.* p. 37) was 960 a. Gr. = 649. Abulfeda (1273–1331), in his "Moslem Annals" (tr. Reiske and Adler, I, 1789, p. 263; *O.C.* p. 56), implies that Muawiya's fleet was partly his own, partly one from Egypt under or sent by the governor, Abdallah ibn Sa'd; he also mentions the exaction of a tribute of 7000 pieces of gold. We need not follow the authorities later (for Dhahabi, 1274–1347, date 33 = 653/4, and Firuzabadi, 1329–1414, who has 48 = 668/9, see *O.C.* p. 43), except to quote Suyuti (1445–1505), *Hist. of the Caliphs*, tr. H. S. Jarrett, 1881, pp. 159 f., who under year 27 (647/8) mentions Ubada ibn as-Samit and his wife Umm-Haram, daughter of Milhan, a woman of the Helpers, her fall from her mule and burial in Cyprus. On Umm-Haram and Hala Sultan Tekke, see above, p. 21. I do not understand why Caetani (*Chronogr.* A.H. 28, p. 309, no. 16) calls Umm-Haram the wife of Muawiya.

The account in the modern Turkish writer, Sureyya Beg, *Fitrat-ul-Islam*, Istambul, 1909, pp. 36 f., is confused and in some details inaccurate.

As to the place specially mentioned as captured in the second expedition, the name in the Oxford MS. Huntingdon, no. 52, the basis of all editions of Abulfaraj, is *Pāthōs*. Bedjan, in his edition of the Chronicles (Paris, 1890), suggested the emendation *Lapāthōs*. Bar-Hebraeus derives from Michael, in whom also the reading is *Pāthōs*. Chabot, however (p. 442, n. 5), accepts Lapāthōs, which is confirmed by the reading of the anonymous Syrian Chronicle. The only difficulty in the way of accepting it is that the form *Lapathos* is found only in Strabo and the *Stadiasmus Maris Magni*, and in the time with which we are concerned the Greeks probably called it Lápethos or Lápithos. *Epatha* (var. *Pathos*) is found as one of the cities of Cyprus visited by the Russian pilgrim deacon Zosimus in 1421 (*O.C.* p. 70), where Paphos is almost certainly meant. At the same time *Labathos* is apparently found in a late Turkish source (Hajji Khalifa, †1658, *O.C.* p. 76).

For the name of the leader of the second expedition the form Ἀβουλαούρ found in some MSS. of Theophanes (p. 345 de Boor) seems to be more correct than the Ἀβουλαβάρ adopted by the Bonn edition, or Ἀβουλαθάρ which de Boor prefers, following Anastasius.

A monument which may be connected with the earlier of the two invasions is the epitaph of an Arab (Urwa, son of Thabit), who died in Cyprus in the month of Ramadan, A.H. 29 (May 650). See Combe, Sauvaget et Wiet, *Répertoire chron. d'épigraphie arabe*, I, 1931, pp. 5 f., and cp. *Arch. de l'Orient latin*, I, p. 590.

ADDENDA

P. 42. Alashiya is mentioned as early as the middle of the nineteenth century B.C., as appears from references to copper from that region in tablets of the time of Hammurabi of Babylon; see Dossin in *Syria* XX, 1939, p. 111.

P. 52, l. 2. Pottery with incised inscriptions discovered in 1939 in an excavation four miles from Nicosia shows that the Cypriote syllabary continued to be used as late as the first century B.C.

P. 101. The colossus from Amathus. In Δράγμα *M. P. Nilsson... dedicatum* (Lund, 1939), pp. 514–28, A. Westholm gives good reasons for assigning this figure to a Roman date.

P. 214, note. To the literature on the arts in Cyprus, add now C. Watzinger, 'Kypros', in W. Otto's *Handbuch der Archäologie*, I, Pt. 3, 1939, pp. 824–48.

P. 305, n. 1. The village of Koutzoventi was formerly Maronite; the church in question was allowed to fall into ruins when the Maronites disappeared from the village. Mrs Bardswell in *Eastern Churches Quarterly*, III, p. 307.

INDEX

The following abbreviations are frequently used:

A.	Ayios, Ayia
abp	Archbishop (always of Cyprus)
Ath.	Athenian
bp	Bishop
Byz.	Byzantine
C.	Cyprus
Cpl	Constantinople
Emp.	Emperor
k.	King
Mt	Mount
Ptol.	Ptolemy, Ptolemaic
R.	River
s.	Son

The accentuation of modern place-names is generally indicated.

A

C (*see also* K)

F

T

CAMBRIDGE: PRINTED BY WALTER LEWIS, M.A., AT THE UNIVERSITY PRESS

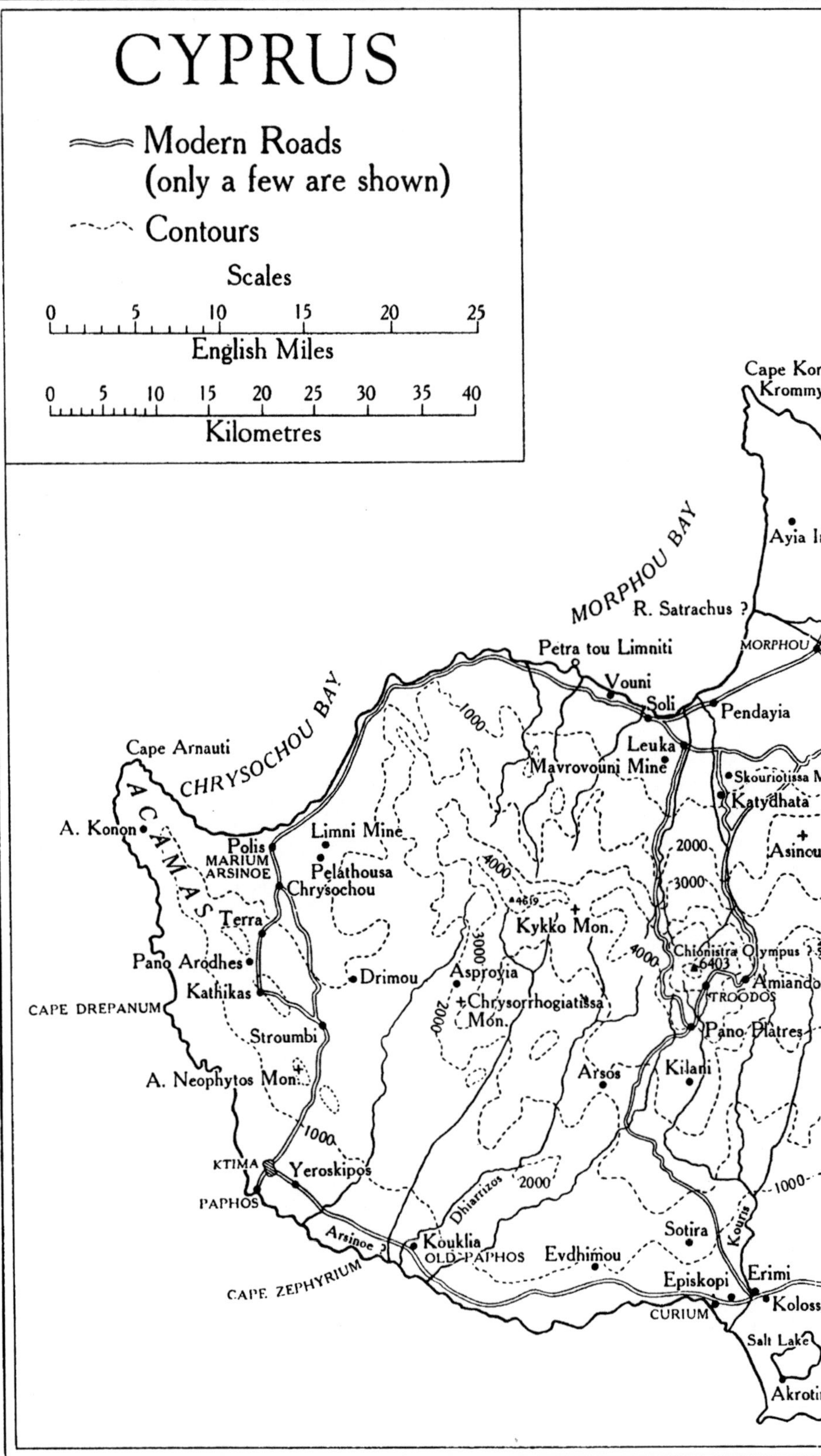

CYPRUS
Modern Roads
(only a few are shown)
Contours
Scales
0
5
10
15
20
25
English Miles
0
5
10
15
20
25
30
35
40
Kilometres
Cape Kor
Krommy
Ayia Ir
MORPHOU BAY
R. Satrachus ?
MORPHOU
Petra tou Limniti
Vouni
Soli
Pendayia
Leuka
Mavrovouni Mine
Skouriotissa M
Katydhata
Asinou
CHRYSOCHOU BAY
Cape Arnauti
ACAMAS
A. Konon
Polis
MARIUM
ARSINOE
Limni Mine
Pelathousa
Chrysochou
Terra
Pano Arodhes
Kathikas
CAPE DREPANUM
Stroumbi
A. Neophytos Mon.
Drimou
Asproyia
Chrysorrhogiatissa Mon.
Kykko Mon.
4619
Chionistra Olympus
6403
Amiandos
TROODOS
Pano Platres
Arsos
Kilani
1000
2000
3000
4000
KTIMA
PAPHOS
Yeroskipos
Dhiarrizos
Arsinoe ?
Kouklia
OLD PAPHOS
CAPE ZEPHYRIUM
Evdhimou
Sotira
Kouris
Episkopi
CURIUM
Erimi
Kolossi
Salt Lake
Akrotiri

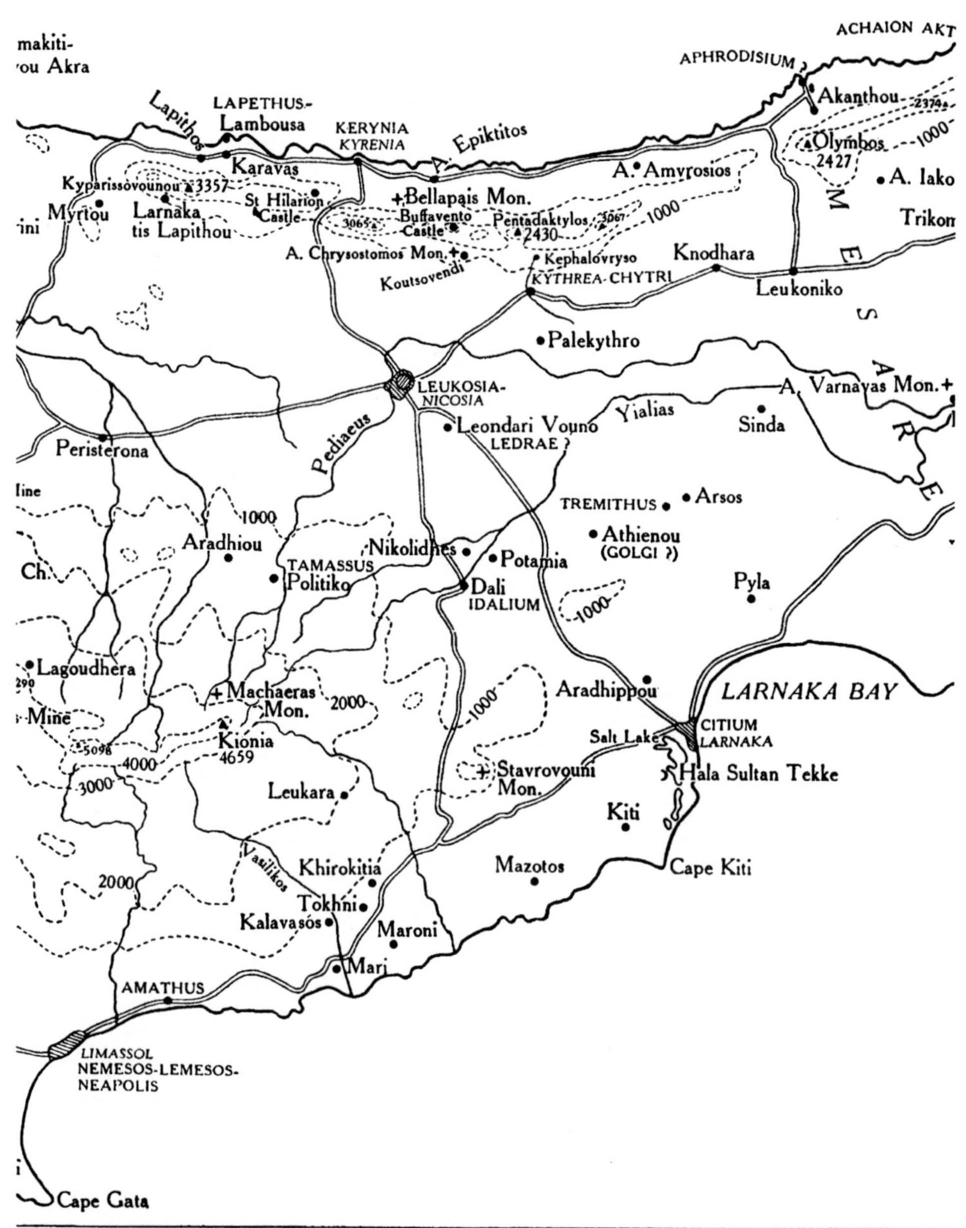

ACHAION AKT
APHRODISIUM ?
Akanthou
2374
1000
Olymbos
2427
A. Iako
Trikom
makiti-
ou Akra
Lapithos
LAPETHUS-
Lambousa
KERYNIA
KYRENIA
Epiktitos
Karavas
A. Amvrosios
Kyparissovounou 3357
St Hilarion
Castle
Bellapais Mon.
Myrtou
Larnaka
tis Lapithou
Buffavento
Castle
3065
Pentadaktylos
3067
1000
2430
A. Chrysostomos Mon.
Koutsovendi
Kephalovryso
KYTHREA-CHYTRI
Knodhara
Leukoniko
M
E
S
A
R
E
Palekythro
LEUKOSIA-
NICOSIA
A. Varnavas Mon.
Yialias
Sinda
Leondari Vouno
LEDRAE ?
Pediaeus
Peristerona
TREMITHUS
Arsos
1000
Athienou
(GOLGI ?)
Aradhiou
Nikolidhes
Potamia
TAMASSUS
Politiko
Dali
IDALIUM
1000
Pyla
Ch.
Lagoudhera
Machaeras
Mon.
2000
1000
Aradhippou
LARNAKA BAY
Mine
Kionia
4659
5098
4000
3000
Salt Lake
CITIUM
LARNAKA
Stavrovouni
Mon.
Hala Sultan Tekke
Leukara
Kiti
Vasilikos
Khirokitia
Mazotos
Cape Kiti
2000
Tokhni
Kalavasós
Maroni
Mari
AMATHUS
LIMASSOL
NEMESOS-LEMESOS-
NEAPOLIS
Cape Gata

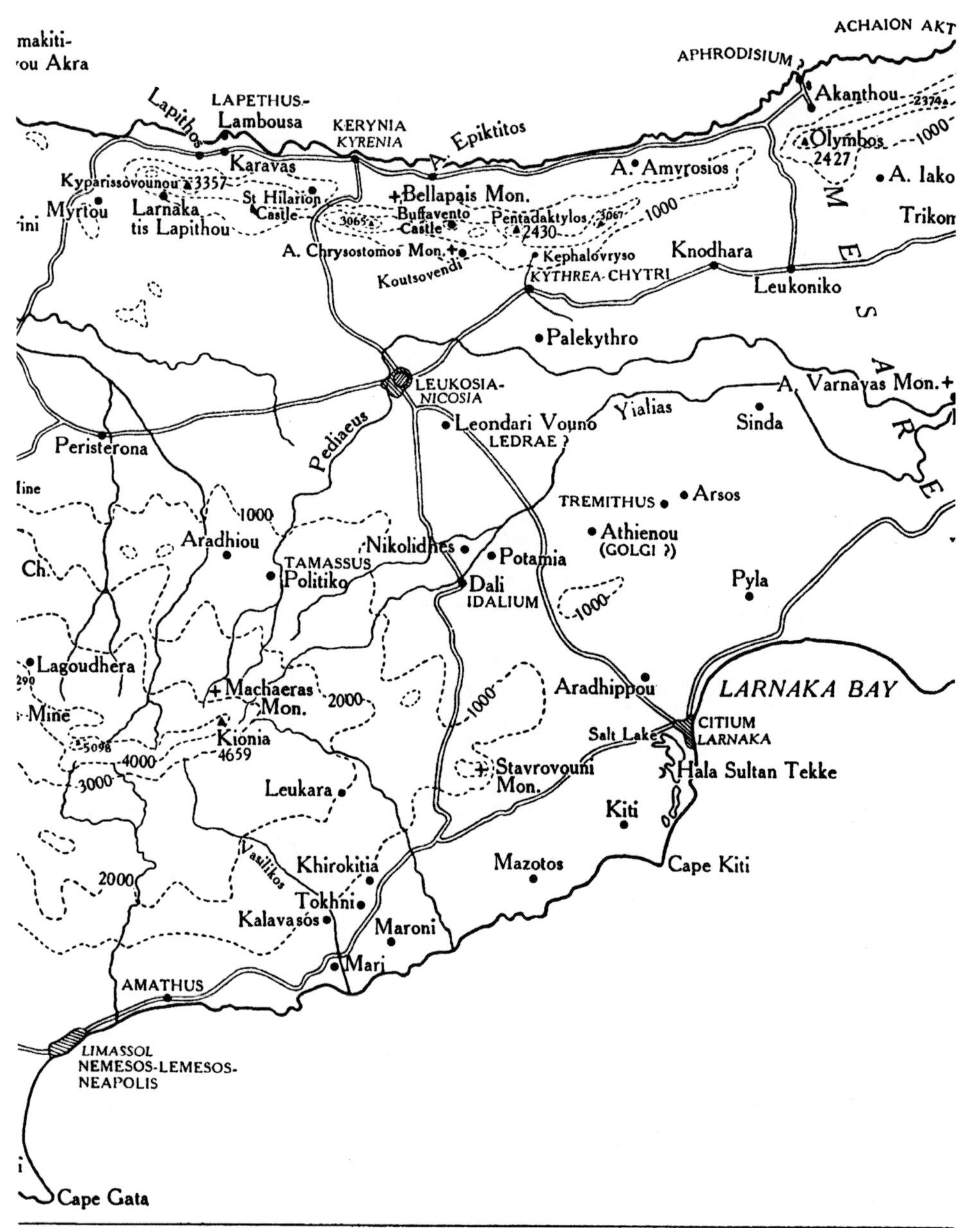

ACHAION AKT
APHRODISIUM ?
Akanthou
2374
1000
Olymbos
2427
A. Iako
Trikom
MESAREA
makiti-
ou Akra
Lapithos
LAPETHUS-
Lambousa
KERYNIA
KYRENIA
A. Epiktitos
Karavas
A. Amvrosios
Kyparissovounou 3357
St Hilarion Castle
Bellapais Mon.
Myrtou
Larnaka tis Lapithou
3065
Buffavento Castle
Pentadaktylos
3067
2430
1000
A. Chrysostomos Mon.
Kephalovryso
Knodhara
Koutsovendi
KYTHREA-CHYTRI
Leukoniko
Palekythro
LEUKOSIA-
NICOSIA
A. Varnavas Mon.
Yialias
Sinda
Leondari Vouno
LEDRAE ?
Peristerona
Pediaeus
TREMITHUS
Arsos
1000
Athienou
(GOLGI ?)
Aradhiou
Nikolidhes
Potamia
TAMASSUS
Politiko
Dali
IDALIUM
Pyla
1000
Lagoudhera
Machaeras Mon.
2000
1000
Aradhippou
LARNAKA BAY
Mine
CITIUM
LARNAKA
Salt Lake
5098
Kionia
4659
4000
3000
Stavrovouni Mon.
Hala Sultan Tekke
Leukara
Kiti
Vasilikos
Khirokitia
Mazotos
Cape Kiti
2000
Tokhni
Kalavasós
Maroni
Mari
AMATHUS
LIMASSOL
NEMESOS-LEMESOS-
NEAPOLIS
Cape Gata

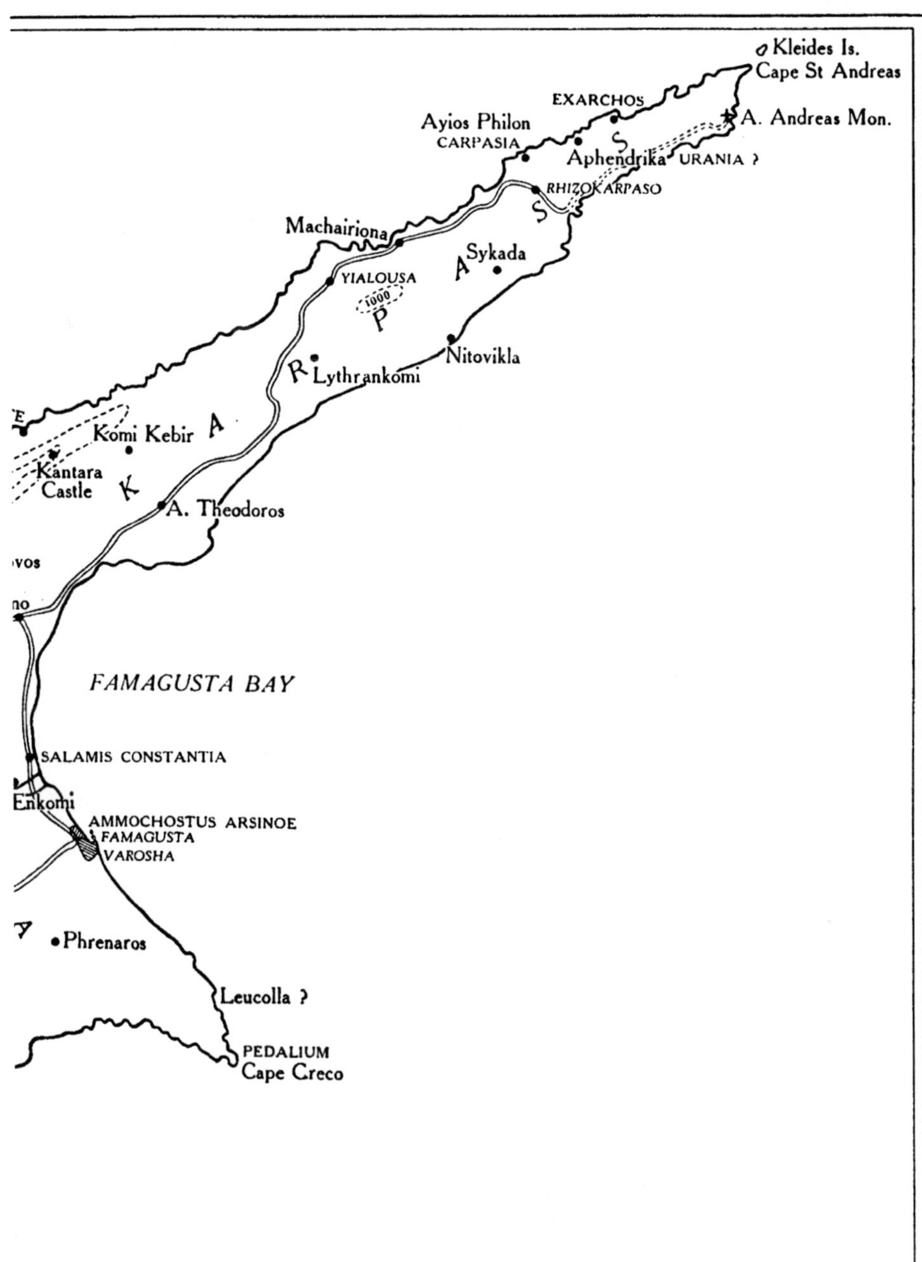

Kleides Is.
Cape St Andreas
EXARCHOS
Ayios Philon
CARPASIA
A. Andreas Mon.
Aphendrika
URANIA ?
RHIZOKARPASO
Machairiona
Sykada
YIALOUSA
1000
K A R P A S S
Nitovikla
Lythrankomi
Komi Kebir
Kantara
Castle
A. Theodoros
FAMAGUSTA BAY
SALAMIS CONSTANTIA
Enkomi
AMMOCHOSTUS ARSINOE
FAMAGUSTA
VAROSHA
Phrenaros
Leucolla ?
PEDALIUM
Cape Greco

Breinigsville, PA USA
03 January 2011
252595BV00003B/22/P

9 781108 020626